Manifest
Destiny's
Underworld

ROBERT E. MAY

Manifest Destiny's Underworld

Filibustering in Antebellum America

The University of North Carolina Press

Chapel Hill and London

This book was published with the assistance of the
William Rand Kenan Jr. Fund of the University of
North Carolina Press.

Designed by April Leidig-Higgins
Set in Ehrhardt by Copperline Book Services, Inc.
Manufactured in the United States of America

The paper in this book meets the guidelines for perma-
nence and durability of the Committee on Production
Guidelines for Book Longevity of the Council on Library Resources.

Library of Congress Cataloging-in-Publication Data
May, Robert E. Manifest destiny's underworld: filibustering in antebellum America / Robert E. May.
p. cm. Includes bibliographical references and index.
ISBN 0-8078-2703-7 (cloth: alk. paper)
1. United States—Territorial expansion—History—
19th century. 2. Filibusters—America—History—
19th century. 3. United States—Foreign relations—
1815–1861. 4. United States—Military relations.
5. Political culture—United States—History—19th
century. 6. Popular culture—United States—
History—19th century. I. Title.
E415.7 .M25 2002   973.5—dc21   2001059831

cloth   06 05 04 03 02   5 4 3 2 1

To my colleagues,
present and past,
in the Purdue University
Department of History

CONTENTS

ILLUSTRATIONS AND MAPS

IT WAS A STRANGE DUEL by tall tale. In *Harper's New Monthly Magazine* for August 1855, the writer and illustrator David Hunter Strother, using his familiar pseudonym "Porte Crayon," recalled the time he swapped yarns with the free-spirited teamster Tim Longbow in a western Virginia barroom. Longbow claimed to have sailed from San Francisco, gone six weeks aboard ship without any food but biscuits and a caught whale, swum across the entire Central American isthmus, and hiked all the way from Panama to New Orleans, before asking Crayon to identify the "singularest thing" he had ever seen in his own travels. Crayon countered with the North Pole, and predicted that it would soon belong to the United States. After all, people were "getting up some filibustering parties to get hold of it as soon as possible, for the purpose of extending to its benighted inhabitants the blessings of American freedom during the winter, lights and firewood included." Longbow was convinced, shouting "Hurra for liberty!" and promising to help out by providing booze and food.

What did Crayon mean by his seemingly bizarre retort about filibustering in the Arctic? Strother's readers would have instantly realized that Crayon was lampooning his countrymen for their insatiable desire to absorb foreign domains into the United States. No one at the time was talking seriously about taking over the uninhabitable North Pole, but many Americans were very vocal in their demands that their nation expand elsewhere. Nor would readers have required explanations as to what filibustering had to do with America's territorial ambitions.

The term "filibuster" carried a far different connotation before the Civil War than it does today. During that period, the word generally referred to American adventurers who raised or participated in private military forces that either invaded or planned to invade foreign countries with which the United States was formally at peace.

Although these expeditions violated the U.S. Neutrality Act of 1818 (which prohibited such private warfare) as well as U.S. treaties and international law, thousands of Americans either joined such groups as recruits or provided them with material support as part of a movement that crossed American ethnic, regional, and class lines. The sons of some of the South's wealthiest planters joined indigent northern city dwellers in filibuster armies. Politicians, newspapermen, lawyers, doctors, authors, overseers, immigrants, and young apprentices all filibustered. Occasionally, college students even abandoned their courses to enlist. Not a month passed when a filibuster expedition was neither in progress nor in some stage of preparation.

The most famous filibuster was William Walker, the so-called "gray-eyed man of destiny." This native Tennessean not only conquered and actually ruled Nicaragua for a while, but he had ambitions of making all of Central America into a personal empire. However, U.S. filibusters also attacked Canada, Mexico, Ecuador, Honduras, and Cuba. In fact, America's adventurers were dreaded throughout the Western Hemisphere, and as far away as the Hawaiian Kingdom. The British government even feared a filibuster landing in Ireland.

The expeditions captured the attention of American newspaper and illustrated journal editors, and sometimes attracted heavy press coverage for days or weeks at a time. The phenomenon infiltrated American theater, music, advertising, and literature. It also touched the lives of countless ordinary and famous Americans alike who never actually joined filibustering parties. There is room, in recounting filibustering, for the African American leader Frederick Douglass, the railroad and shipping magnate Cornelius Vanderbilt, many of the prominent authors of the day (including Nathaniel Hawthorne, Ralph Waldo Emerson, and Henry Wadsworth Longfellow), "Boss" Tweed of New York, and the future Confederate spy Rose Greenhow. Some of mid-nineteenth-century America's best remembered army officers, including Robert E. Lee, Winfield Scott, George B. McClellan, and P. G. T. Beauregard either exerted themselves to prevent expeditions, or contemplated joining them. Even Abner Doubleday, reputedly the founder of baseball, turns up in documents about filibustering.

Often damned at home and abroad as pirates, the filibusters were also worshipped as heroes by masses of people. In some ways, they epitomized the romantic spirit of an age which produced the slogan "manifest destiny" to connote the supposed, providential mission of the United States to take over the continent. Meanwhile, the U.S. government's legal and military branches made ineffectual efforts to prevent the expeditions, having little more success against them than do modern federal officials against the international drug trade and undocumented aliens.

Filibusters played a surprisingly significant role in the sectional controversy that triggered the Civil War. Most of the prominent leaders of both North and South, including Henry Clay, Stephen Douglas, Daniel Webster, John C. Calhoun, Jefferson Davis, Sam Houston, and all the presidents from Polk to Lincoln confronted filibustering's political, legal, or diplomatic implications. Houston actually considered leading his own expedition into Mexico, all the while protesting that he did not believe in filibustering!

Ironically, the filibusters' invasions of foreign domains helped to subvert the very process of territorial expansion that they were presumably advancing. They also jeopardized U.S. commercial penetration of the tropics, caused crises with European and Latin countries that threatened to erupt in war, and bequeathed a legacy of anti-Americanism in Mexico and Central America that lingers into the modern era.

Not surprisingly, given their salience, *Harper's Weekly* on May 23, 1857, prophesied that the filibusters would one day "occupy a conspicuous page in history." But this was not to be. Gradually the filibusters slipped from this nation's historical memory, perhaps, in part, because they were immediately overshadowed as mid-nineteenth-century historical players by Civil War soldiers. For whatever reason, relatively few Americans today have ever heard of Walker and his ilk.

This book intends not only to call the filibusters into this country's historical memory, but also to reveal them in a new light. Though historians have written many biographies of filibusters and accounts of particular expeditions, they have rarely treated the broader issues raised by these episodes.

In the mid-twentieth century, historians such as Rollin G. Osterweis (*Romanticism and Nationalism in the Old South*, 1949) and John Hope Franklin (*The Militant South*, 1956) viewed the invasions as the work of romantic southern imperialists, consumed by myths of themselves as knightly, Cavalier warriors, to expand their labor system into other countries and salvage their political power within the Union by increasing the number of slave states. More recently, scholars have looked at filibustering quite differently. Richard Slotkin, for instance, has related popular images of William Walker to American frontier mythology in a chapter of *The Fatal Environment* (1985), pointing out that American expansionists perceived the filibuster as a Caribbean variant of the hardy western pioneer. Walker and his soldiers displaced benighted Latin American peoples in the cause of progress much as settlers dispossessed Indian tribes. Janice E. Thomson's treatment of filibustering as one of several varieties of non-state international violence in a chapter of *Mercenaries, Pirates, and Sovereigns* (1994) provides a rare glimpse of filibustering's place in the overall course of modern world history.

Such studies, however, are more suggestive than authoritative. Only a handful of historians have written book-length works about pre–Civil War filibustering, notably Joe A. Stout Jr.'s *The Liberators* (1973), Charles H. Brown's

Agents of Manifest Destiny (1980), and Tom Chaffin's *Fatal Glory* (1996). Stout and Chaffin, however, confine their scope to attacks upon single countries—Mexico and Cuba respectively—and Brown emphasizes narrative over analysis. All these works make major contributions to knowledge. Chaffin's book, for instance, convincingly discredits the stereotype that only Southerners filibustered. But none of them provides a satisfying overview of the entire filibustering movement. As a result, the adventurers, though extremely important in their own time, have yet to find their niche in America's remembered history. James M. McPherson's *Battle Cry of Freedom* (1988) is one of the very few major synthetic treatments of mid-nineteenth-century U.S. history that attempts to integrate filibustering into the broader American story in a meaningful way.

The following pages attempt the first fully analytical study of the mid-nineteenth-century filibustering movement. I try to address, in a systematic way, questions about U.S. filibustering rather than about particular filibusters and specific expeditions.

The first three chapters provide an overview of American filibustering before the Civil War. Chapter 1 asks when and why Americans began filibustering and using the term. It not only traces filibustering back virtually to the nation's earliest history, but also explains the development of federal antifilibustering legislation and treats the U.S. government's conflicted response to the initial expeditions. Chapter 2 covers the particular outbreak of U.S. filibustering after the Mexican War, paying attention not only to the period's actual invasions, but also to the many aborted escapades of the day. The chapter tries to provide a capsule history of these plots, as well as a sense of how many Americans got caught up in the movement. Chapter 3 investigates filibustering's place in American popular culture and attempts to position it within a global context. Did only Americans filibuster? If not, was there anything that distinguished U.S. filibustering from similar impulses elsewhere?

The next four chapters probe the expeditions themselves. This section of the book begins by considering, in chapter 4, why Americans decided to organize and enlist in these ventures. What could possibly have driven them to participate in such dangerous and illegal affairs? Chapter 5 explores the inability of U.S. authorities to stop the expeditions. Were federal authorities simply inept? Were they in collusion with the adventurers? Or should we attribute their failure to other causes? Chapter 6 considers the matter of filibuster finance, transport, and supply. How did filibusters ever muster the resources to invade foreign lands? This section of the book winds up with a discussion, in chapter 7, of what it was like to actually participate in these affairs.

Chapters 8 and 9 concern filibustering's consequences. The former addresses filibustering's impact upon U.S. foreign policy, and suggests that the expeditions not only seriously disrupted U.S. relations with foreign nations but also interfered with American business interests abroad, nearly drove the nation into war, and possibly retarded America's territorial expansion. Chapter 9 argues that the expeditions significantly exacerbated the breakdown in North-South relations that led to the Civil War. This third section of the book concludes with an explanation of filibustering's history beyond Fort Sumter and reflections upon the legacy that America's brazen antebellum adventurers left behind them.

Finally, a word about my definition of filibustering. At the beginning of this preface, I defined filibusters as members of private military expeditions who invaded the domain of countries at peace with the United States. I would emphasize here the importance of the adjective private, and argue that expeditions proceeding with either the explicit or implicit permission of their governments (such as the Bay of Pigs invasion of Cuba, with its CIA collaborators, during the Kennedy presidency) fail the test of privacy. Further, revolutions by Americans already living in foreign domains do not qualify, unless they also involve Americans invading the revolting areas as members of military parties. Filibusters had to involve expeditions.

I draw attention to these matters because historians tend to use the term filibustering loosely, applying it, for instance, to such affairs as the West Florida uprising of 1810, Andrew Jackson's invasion with some three thousand men of Spanish Florida in 1818, and John C. Frémont's uninvited intrusion with fifteen men into Mexico's Alta California in 1845. The West Florida rebellion involved U.S. settlers already in the Spanish province, instigated by U.S. government agents, capturing Baton Rouge, creating a short-lived independent republic, and inviting U.S. annexation. Jackson when he entered Florida and Frémont when he entered Mexican California were both commanding federal forces and acting as commissioned officers of the U.S. Army. Furthermore, it is possible that their aggressions had implicit, and possibly explicit, consent from Washington. Jackson, who may have been dissembling, claimed prior presidential authorization for his invasion by means of a message transmitted through a third party.

I hope to contribute to a revival of interest in a fascinating group of people who captured the imaginations or hatreds of multitudes of their own coun-

trymen, and who significantly affected American relations with foreign countries, as well as how Northerners and Southerners felt about their Union.
Studying the filibusters, I believe, is one way to better understand our national character, if there is such a thing. At the least, it helps to illuminate our
country's past.

THIS BOOK IS dedicated to my colleagues in Purdue University's Department
of History, in appreciation for all the collegiality, encouragement, and assistance that I have received from them over the course of more than three
decades at the institution. I cannot imagine a more positive working environment than the one that I have been so fortunate to experience at historic University Hall on the Purdue campus. I am especially grateful to the many colleagues who have critiqued chapters of this book or otherwise provided advice
about it, most especially Janet Afary, Charles R. Cutter, Ariel E. de la Fuente,
Raymond E. Dumett, James R. Farr, Elliott J. Gorn, Sally A. Hastings,
Charles Ingrao, Gordon Mork, Michael A. Morrison, Donald L. Parman,
Nicholas K. Rauh, Randy W. Roberts, Michael G. Smith, Whitney Walton,
Harold D. Woodman, and Melinda S. Zook. My debt is especially deep to
Chuck Cutter, who has repeatedly and patiently assisted me respecting mat-
ters of Mexican and Central American culture and history, and provided me
with a number of valuable bibliographic tips. Any remaining errors of fact, in-
terpretation, or omission are solely my responsibility.

Likewise, I have benefited greatly from the support of Purdue administra-
tors. Both of my recent department heads, John J. Contreni and Gordon R.
Mork, have assisted my work in countless ways. The Dean's Office of the
School of Liberal Arts has supported my research with a Faculty Incentive
Grant, and my writing with a semester's relief from teaching responsibilities
as a fellow in the Center for Humanistic Studies. The University's generous
sabbatical leave program, moreover, provided me with an additional two se-
mesters off from teaching over the course of the approximately fifteen years
that I have devoted to this project.

The Beinecke Rare Book and Manuscript Library at Yale University further helped this project along by awarding me the Frederick W. Beinecke Fel-
lowship in Western Americana. This support was invaluable in terms of allowing me to explore a number of key documents about filibustering,
especially in relation to California history, that I might otherwise never have
considered.

Many scholars, archivists, and librarians, likewise, deserve much greater thanks than a few words here can provide. My good friend (and lately fellow Hoosier) Professor Antonio Rafael de la Cova, truly today's expert when it comes to Cuban filibustering, especially merits notice; Tony most generously supplied me with copies of a number of rare documents that have greatly facilitated my research. Likewise another longtime friend, Lynda Lasswell Crist, without any prompting on my part, sent me material about filibusters that she came across as editor of *The Papers of Jefferson Davis*. Howard Jones, whose friendship, encouragement, and insight I have treasured for nearly as long as I have been in the historical profession, gave a very close reading to my chapter on U.S. diplomatic history, and provided many suggestions that have, I feel, greatly improved this work.

I am also very appreciative of the many helpful suggestions provided by the University of North Carolina Press's readers, as well as by David Perry, the Press's very perceptive editor-in-chief. Joan Cashin, Tom Chaffin, Edward M. Coffman, Stanley Engerman, William Skelton, and Peter C. Stewart, as well as the young adult fantasy author (and close student of history) Lloyd Alexander, have shared research leads, documents and reflections with me that have also been tremendously helpful. Two former undergraduate students in my courses, George Avery and Mark Jaeger, alerted me to documents about filibusters that they uncovered in the course of their own research on Arkansas and Indiana, respectively, during the Civil War era. Another former student from my undergraduate courses, Chris Courtney, volunteered as my research assistant during the spring of 1994. Ernest Ravinet of the Hoosier Blue and Gray Civil War Round Table at Cambridge City, Indiana, helped with some technical matters respecting filibuster weaponry.

Far too many archivists and librarians have assisted my research for a complete listing here. But several have gone so far out of their way to help that I would be remiss in not mentioning them individually. I would especially like to thank Don E. Carleton, Center for American History, University of Texas; Evelyn M. Cherpak, Naval Historical Collection, Naval War College; Martha Clevenger, Missouri Historical Society; Marielos Hernandez-Lehmann, Latin American Library, Tulane University; George Miles, Beinecke Rare Book and Manuscript Library, and Margit Kaye, Sterling Library, Yale University; Martha Mitchell, Brown University Archives; William C. Parsons, Music Division, Library of Congress; Barbara Rust, National Archives—Southwest Region; George Schroeter, Mobile Public Library; John D. Stinson and Debra Randorf, New-York Historical Society; and John White, Southern Historical Collection, University of North Carolina. I also owe much to the staff at Purdue's HSSE Library. Reference librarian David Hovde, history librarian Lawrence J. Mykytiuk, government publications coordinator Bert T. Chapman, and the team in the Interlibrary Loan office have especially put themselves out on my behalf.

Further, I owe an incalculable debt to the clerical staff of Purdue's Department of History, most recently its administrative assistant Peggy C. Quirk and secretary Mary Wanger. Peggy and Mary have fielded my many requests for computer and other advice and assistance with incredible patience.

Finally there is Jill, my passionately intellectual wife and fellow Purdue professor, whose scholarly interests spill well beyond her defined field of children's and adolescent literature, and have included a lot of research in history. Jill's red flags compelled me to rewrite, rework, and, I am convinced, improve many of the pages that follow. For some thirty-five years, ever since we met in graduate school, Jill's love and support have energized my obsession with antebellum American history. *Manifest Destiny's Underworld*, in ways that defy description, is hers as much as mine.

Manifest Destiny's Underworld

CHAPTER ONE

Narciso López's Predecessors

Around the Moro's grim *façade*
The soul of Lopez wanders
And Crittenden—a glorious shade!
Beside him walks and ponders.
O, God of Peace! that such as these,
Like dogs, should be garotted—
Choked out of life by Spanish beasts,
Fierce, bloody and besotted.
—*Democratic Review*, December 1854

WERE ONE TO TRACE American filibustering to the date that the term came first into use, then it started either in 1850 or in 1851. Still fumbling as late as 1849 for the right label to pin on private military expeditions, U.S. citizens employed a variety of phrases including "Aaron Burr scheme" and "buffalo hunt," none of which gained lasting currency.[1] The Venezuelan native Narciso López's attempts to overthrow Spanish rule of Cuba in May 1850 and again in August 1851, however, jolted Americans into refining their terminology.

In both instances, López landed on the island with hundreds of men whom he had recruited in the United States. Spanish troops repulsed his 1850 expeditionary force shortly after its arrival on the steamer *Creole* at Cárdenas on Cuba's northern coast. López's army occupied the Cárdenas railroad station and captured the town's military garrison, but absorbed over fifty casualties in one day of fighting. Forced to reembark and flee to the United States when Spanish reinforcements precluded his intended advance toward Matanzas (and, ultimately, Havana) and threatened to trap him, López was lucky to escape alive. The *Creole* reached Key West, Florida, barely ahead of a pursuing Spanish warship.

López would not be so fortunate the next year, after his forces came on shore at a tiny coastal village about sixty miles west of Havana. Within three weeks, Spanish troops crushed the invaders, killing many of them in battle, capturing survivors, and then executing some of the prisoners. Colonel William Crittenden, the nephew of U.S. attorney general John J. Crittenden of Kentucky, and fifty of his men were shot by a firing squad on August 17. On September 1, Spanish officials had López garroted on a plaza of the Punta— a small fort on the western shore of Havana's well-protected harbor entrance,

roughly opposite one of the island's best-known landmarks, a larger fortifi-
cation known to Americans as Morro Castle.

According to reports reaching American newspapers, huge audiences of onlookers cheered during the executions of the invaders. Some accounts described spectators as mutilating the bodies of Crittenden and his men after
their deaths. One State Department informant in Havana even claimed that
the Crittenden party's executioners had shot to maim rather than kill, and that
the knife-wielding mob had taken the responsibility of finishing the men off.[2]

Although these expeditions occurred during a national crisis over slavery
in California and other issues that threatened to destroy the Union, Americans
found their attention drawn to López's daring endeavors. In rapt, often horri-
fied fascination, Americans waited impatiently for reliable accounts of his
fate. In one of his several diary entries about the invaders, for instance, the
New York lawyer George Templeton Strong remarked, "No certain news yet
about Lopez and his gang." Similarly, on the very day that López was executed,
U.S. Senator Sam Houston of Texas expressed frustration that no news had
arrived from Cuba, telling a correspondent that he feared disaster. Even Senator Henry Clay, then at the middle of efforts to find a legislative solution to
save the Union, could hardly overlook the Cuban business. His son, serving as
U.S. chargé d'affaires in Portugal at the time of López's first foray, alerted
him that "news of the Cuba invasion" was causing a "sensation" in Lisbon.
By that time, Clay had already implored the Senate not to be "diverted" from
the "grave" California question by the Cuban matter.

Once reliable information actually arrived, Americans became so transfixed
by the story in Cuba that they sometimes relegated to secondary importance
the sectional crisis and the "Compromise of 1850" that temporarily resolved
the difficulty. "The Cuban invasion is now the only staple of home news," an
observer in New Orleans maintained shortly after the failure of López's 1850
attempt. "How the recent Cuban Excitement has overlaid all other subjects,"
observed another Southerner during the López frenzy. Clay, meanwhile, worried that disunionists would use Cuban affairs to obscure their own intentions.[3]

Few Americans kept closer watch on the filibusters than did U.S. government officials, as the invasions seriously endangered U.S. relations with Spain
and other European powers. Ralph Waldo Emerson observed in his journal
that telegrams from Savannah were reaching President Millard Fillmore
"every hour" with "news of the Cuban invaders." Fillmore's second annual
message to Congress, submitted in December 1851, gave approximately twice
as much attention to the Cuban invasions as to the North-South crisis over
slavery.[4]

Painting by Charles Jarvis
of U.S. Senator Henry Clay
around the time of the
López expeditions. (From
McClure's Magazine 9
[Sept. 1897]: 946)

In seeking a term that would characterize not only López's expeditions but
also other invasion plots, Americans fastened on filibuster—a modification of
the French word *flibustier* and the Spanish *filibustero*, which were themselves
derivatives of an old Dutch term for freebooter. Thus, when hearing about
López's execution, Strong exclaimed, "If this little band of militant philan-
thropists and self-consecrated missionaries of Republican scum has been ex-
terminated, it will be long before filibusterism recovers from the shock." Anticipating the same fate for adventurers invading Mexico, the correspondent
of a New Orleans newspaper in Rio Grande City, Texas, observed that such
"filibusters" might want to give confession to a priest at Mexican army headquarters on the border.[5]

The term *filibustering* entered circulation so suddenly that in September
1851 a religious journal in Boston actually took note of its advent, cautioning
to no effect that this "vulgarism" might become accepted language if the

press kept utilizing it. But rather than discard the word, commentators started exploring its etymological links to possible sources such as Cape Finisterre in northwestern Spain, *flibot* (Spanish for a light boat), and other conceivable forerunners. Soon the term became so salient in everyday American speech and text that *Harper's New Monthly Magazine* could pronounce that filibustering was destined to "occupy an important place in our vocabulary."[6]

DATING U.S. filibustering from the coining of the word, however, would be misleading, since filibustering expeditions occurred during the earliest years of the Republic. In fact, the first federal impeachment trial in U.S. history hinged on William Blount's filibustering plot during John Adams's administration. In July 1797, Blount, one of Tennessee's first two U.S. senators, drew an impeachment charge by the U.S. House of Representatives after the administration received correspondence indicating that he was planning to invade territory beyond U.S. boundaries. Though unable to refute the evidence, Blount (and his counsels) contended that Senate members were not impeachable civil officers, and he escaped conviction when the Senate passed a resolution that it lacked authority over his case.[7]

Most of the early Republic's pioneering filibusters including Blount chose as their destinations neighboring Spanish colonies in North America—especially New Spain's provinces of East and West Florida, Texas, and Louisiana.[8] However, in 1806 Francisco de Miranda targeted Spanish holdings further south. That year, he led some two hundred recruits on an expedition from New York port to his native Venezuela. Some adventurers, moreover, looked northward to British Canada. The Vermonter Ira Allen turned up in Paris in 1796, seeking arms and the collaboration of French expeditionary troops for an invasion that would liberate Canada and convert it into an independent democratic republic called United Columbia. Allen's New Englanders would march northward from Missisquoi Bay on Lake Champlain while French forces attacked Quebec by an invasion up the St. Lawrence River. Allen's plot collapsed after a British warship intercepted his shipment of 15,000 muskets and 21 cannon back across the Atlantic. Still, he spent years trying to revive his filibuster, and submitted revised plans to unreceptive French officials as late as December 1799.[9]

Little mystery attaches to the filibusters' concentration on Spain's North American provinces. Nearby Americans held long-standing grievances against Spanish officials. Spain's authorities closed the lower Mississippi River Valley to U.S. trade between 1784 and 1788, and they imposed tariffs on American imports and exports through New Orleans between 1788 and 1795. After the

United States and Spain signed the Treaty of San Lorenzo ("Pinckney's Treaty") of 1795, the governor of West Florida required nearly prohibitive 12 percent duties from Americans shipping goods via the Mobile River. Borderlands Americans also resented Spain's failure to resolve disputed land claims in the area, and they accused Spanish authorities of instigating Indian attacks against them. Most important, Spain's North American holdings, particularly the Floridas, seemed to lack enough troops and loyal subjects to repel American invasions.

Spanish habitations in turn-of-the-century East Florida barely extended beyond a corridor of land in the northeastern corner of today's state of Florida. Pensacola, the capital of West Florida, represented the only sizable Spanish settlement on the peninsula's Gulf side. Although both provinces, and Louisiana, fell under the administrative authority of the captains general of Cuba, they never received sufficient garrisons to deter filibustering. Spanish troops in all East Florida at the time of one American filibuster totaled a mere 408 men. Nowhere in North America did Spanish officials maintain a regular schedule of border patrols.[10]

Conditions became especially ripe for filibusters after revolution broke out throughout Spain's colonial empire in the Americas. Between 1810 and 1824, rebellions overthrew Spanish authority everywhere in the Western Hemisphere except for Cuba and Puerto Rico. The revolts occurred after the invasion of Spain in 1808 by the armies of Napoleon Bonaparte—an invasion that brought years of turmoil to Spain and distracted Spanish authorities from colonial affairs across the Atlantic. Capitalizing on this opportunity, U.S. filibusters converged on Spanish domains, frequently as affiliates of Latin American revolutionaries. The U.S. army officer Augustus W. Magee, for example, in 1812 led the vanguard of the Mexican insurgent José Bernardo Maximiliano Gutiérrez de Lara's Republican Army of the North across the Sabine River into Texas. Americans who filibustered with the Scotsman Gregor McGregor and "Commodore" Luis-Michel Aury to Amelia Island in East Florida in 1817 likewise joined leaders who claimed revolutionary credentials.[11]

Some early U.S. filibusters hoped to annex liberated colonies to their own country. James Long's unsuccessful 1819 expedition to Texas, organized primarily in Mississippi and Louisiana, grew out of southwestern irritation at news of the recently negotiated Adams-Onís Treaty between the United States and Spain, which, though it acquired Florida, surrendered American claims to Texas. George Mathews, one of the most elderly filibusters in U.S. history, similarly had expansionist intentions.[12]

Mathews's escapade began as a collaboration with President James Madison on the eve of the War of 1812. Worried that Spain, allied with Great Britain against Napoleon in Europe, might cede its remaining holdings in Florida to Great Britain, a far stronger military power, the president asked Congress to authorize a temporary U.S. occupation of any part of Florida designated for such a transfer. Congress in January 1811 granted Madison's request. Later that month Mathews, a former governor of Georgia then seventy-two years of age, received an appointment from the Department of State as one of two commissioners empowered to investigate conditions in East Florida: the commissioners could negotiate East Florida's annexation to the United States should the Spanish provincial governor be receptive; they could occupy the province, with the assistance of U.S. ground and naval forces, if they found that Spain was ceding it to Britain.

Mathews discovered no willingness on the part of Spanish officials to treat for Florida's cession to the United States; nor did he uncover evidence of a pending cession to Britain. But rather than give up his mission, Mathews converted it into a filibuster. Commanding a mixed force of borderland Georgians, Americans residing in Florida, and even a few of Florida's Spaniards, Mathews and his filibusters, in a campaign beginning in March 1812, captured Fernandina on Amelia Island, took other settlements in northern East Florida, and besieged the capital of St. Augustine. Meanwhile, Mathews established a puppet government for East Florida whose sole purpose was to cede itself—that is, the entire province of East Florida—to Mathews as an agent of the U.S. government. What had been effected by arms, in other words, could be presented to world opinion as peaceful annexation: a willing people (the inhabitants of the new "Republic of Florida"), according to a draft treaty that Mathews forwarded to the Department of State on March 21, voluntarily chose to cast their lot as a territory in the American Union![13]

As with later expeditions, volunteers in these first U.S. filibusters did not necessarily follow the same sirens as their commanders. Recruiters realized that it took promises of land, good pay, pensions, political appointments, and other rewards to convince men to serve in such dangerous affairs. Then, too, some filibusters hoped to strike it rich from privateering or smuggling operations connected to their expeditions. The adventurers who in 1816–17 captured Galveston and Fernandina, previously centers of privateering, smuggling, and even piracy, continued such endeavors after their takeovers—all in the name, supposedly, of the Latin American revolutions.[14]

WHATEVER THEIR intentions, U.S. filibusters engaged in criminal behavior. Private military expeditions in peacetime naturally risk retaliatory attacks by invaded countries. Responding to the danger that filibusters might draw nations into unnecessary wars, theorists of international law, long before the American Revolution, established the principle that sovereign states must stop persons from using their jurisdictions to mount expeditions against the territory of countries with which their own nations are at peace.

America's founding fathers (many of them lawyers by profession) had versed themselves in the Swiss author Emmerich de Vattel's *The Law of Nations* (1758) as well as the tracts of Hugo Grotius and other codifiers of international law, and had followed its precepts about private military invasions. Although no supranational organization then existed to rule on or enforce international law, it made sense for early American leaders to outlaw filibustering, not only because of their intentions to found a country based on law, but also because they were sensitive to their new nation's relatively limited military power. Article 1, Section 8, of the Constitution empowered Congress to penalize "offences against the Law of Nations." Under this mandate, the nation's lawmakers responded with "neutrality" enactments in 1794, 1797, 1800, 1807, 1817, 1818, and 1838 to repress filibustering expeditions and other infringements of international law.[15]

The Neutrality Law of 1818, which superseded all previous legislation, became the bane of American filibusters. Its Article 6 provided for the imprisonment to a maximum of three years and fines of as much as three thousand dollars (a far more considerable sum then than today) for persons who, within U.S. jurisdiction, began or aided "any military expedition or enterprise . . . against the territory or dominions of any foreign prince or state, or of any colony, district, or people, with whom the United States are at peace."[16]

Despite this legislation, it would be a mistake to assume that American leaders, many of them avid territorial expansionists, shared an unwavering commitment to eradicate private expeditions. To be sure, one can cite instances aplenty when federal officials intervened against filibusters. Most early U.S. presidents issued proclamations against filibustering activities. Cabinet members summoned governors, district attorneys, marshals, and military officers to interdict pending expeditions, and even tipped off Spanish officials about filibuster movements so that defensive military preparations might be made in targeted colonies. From time to time, federal authorities prosecuted filibusters for violating the neutrality laws. Yet there were occasions when federal authorities found it convenient to overlook, or even assist, filibuster plots in the expectation that they might eventuate in U.S. territorial growth.[17]

No filibuster of the early Republic benefited more from federal complicity than did East Florida's intrepid invader George Mathews. His Patriots capitalized on the cooperation of U.S. army and naval officers even though those very officers were unsure whether the Madison administration expected them to provide Mathews with direct military support. Fernandina might never have surrendered to Mathews's forces had not the gunboats of Commodore Hugh Campbell of the U.S. Navy aimed their artillery at the town. Subsequently, U.S. army troops occupied Picolata, a Spanish settlement on the St. John's River, on Mathews's behalf, and participated, along with U.S. naval forces, in the filibusters' siege of St. Augustine—even fighting a bloodless engagement against its defenders.

Though in April 1812 the Madison administration disavowed the invaders on the rationale that Mathews had violated his instructions, U.S. troops persisted in East Florida as late as the spring of 1813. For some time, a U.S. marine captain governed Fernandina, imposing taxes, establishing closing times for grog shops, and making other administrative decisions, all under the fiction that Mathews had the authority to accept the cession by the Patriots of East Florida to the United States. Further, between November 1812 and February 1813, the Madison administration mobilized regular, volunteer, and militia troops on the Georgia-Florida frontier, in the expectation of following up Mathews's initiative with a full-scale campaign to conquer all of Spanish Florida. The cancellation of this plan because of congressional opposition, and the final disintegration of Mathews's movement in 1814, should not obscure the considerable aid previously rendered the filibusters by the U.S. government.[18]

Besides, just a few years later, the U.S. government capitalized on Luis-Michel Aury's filibuster to get permanent possession of Amelia Island. On the pretext that Aury's privateering risked dragging the United States into disputes with foreign countries, the Monroe administration in 1817 directed U.S. army and naval officers to seize the island. Federal forces held possession from their late December takeover (which the filibusters only resisted verbally) until 1821, when the island became part of the American domain by virtue of ratification of the Adams-Onís Treaty. Ironically, Spanish leaders might have approved Florida's transfer earlier, had they not been irritated by apparently unfounded reports that the Monroe administration had sponsored James Long's filibuster into Texas two years earlier.[19]

WITH LATIN AMERICAN independence assured by the mid-1820s, U.S. filibustering entered a period of dormancy, only to revive in the mid-1830s when new revolutionary stirrings erupted in adjacent lands. The Texas Revolution

of 1835 began as an uprising against Mexican rule by Anglos and some Te-
janos already living in Mexico's state of Texas-Coahuila. However, so many
private American military companies hastened to Texas, once word of the uprising arrived in the United States, that the Texas Revolution became transformed into the most successful filibuster in American history. More than
three of every four soldiers in Texan rebel armies from January to March
1836 crossed the border after October 1835. A second wave of American expeditionists, including the Mississippi militia officer and recent governor
John A. Quitman, set out for Texas starting in April 1836 in reaction to news
that Mexican commanders had executed rebels who surrendered at the
Alamo and Goliad, instead of treating them as prisoners of war.

After chairing a meeting in his hometown of Natchez that passed resolutions to avenge the Alamo, Quitman declared that he would lead men to Texas
within days, and that persons wishing to go should show up at the appointed
time with a mount, a shoulder arm, and pistols. Quitman and some seventeen
followers left Natchez on April 5 amid considerable fanfare and crossed the
Sabine River into Texas on April 9. By April 12, the little party was deploying
at Nacogdoches, which Quitman heard was in danger of attack from a 3,000-
man force of Mexicans and allied Indians. "Each of my Natchez boys swears
he is good for ten Mexicans," Quitman noted proudly in his journal that day.
"If I must die early, let me die with these brave fellows and for such a cause."
It simply is hard to imagine the Texans winning and then maintaining their
independence without the assistance of such volunteer companies from the
United States.[20]

President Andrew Jackson went through the motions of trying to stop the
filibusters. He announced in his December 1835 message to Congress that he
opposed the expeditionists, and he had cabinet members put U.S. district attorneys and army officers on alert to halt the exodus of volunteers. However,
federal border authorities, probably because they favored the rebels, perhaps
because they were overwhelmed by the sheer number of lawbreakers, allowed
the crossings to proceed virtually unmolested, and Jackson never intervened
to reverse these lapses. Quitman, who skirted around one U.S. army garrison
on his way west rather than test the government's will, nonetheless assumed
that government authorities were on the filibusters' side. "There is no necessity for 'bearding the lion in his den,' and incurring risk of detention," he
mused, "though I doubt not the officers sympathize with us." By his leniency,
Old Hickory set a precedent of presidential impotence against filibustering
that would be remembered. "[P]erhaps the President did not mean any more
than Genl Jackson did by his Proclamation against the volunteers in Texas," a

filibuster suggested almost twenty years later, as his associates went ahead with planning an invasion of Cuba despite Franklin Pierce's recent proclamation against illegal expeditions.[21]

Filibusters likewise played a conspicuous role in the Patriot uprisings that broke out in the provinces of Lower and Upper Canada (today, Quebec and Ontario) during 1837, though with noticeably less success. Americans started filibustering into the Canadas when the revolutionaries, after military setbacks, fled to Rochester, Buffalo, Cleveland, Detroit, Burlington, and other points across the U.S. boundary. Enticed into joining the Patriots by promises of Canadian land, silver dollars, and other rewards, hundreds (and eventually several thousands) of borderlands residents, many of them insecure, young laborers dependent on seasonal employment, went off fighting for Canadian freedom.

In December 1837 Rensselaer Van Rensselaer of Albany, New York, the son of a general in the War of 1812, led twenty-four men across the Niagara River to Navy Island, near the Canadian shore, as a vanguard for the intended return to Canada of William Lyon Mackenzie and other refugee revolutionaries on American soil. Hoping to rally Canadians before their arrival, the filibusters raised the flag for a provisional government of Upper Canada, and Mackenzie released a proclamation dated Navy Island, December 13, promising Canadians religious freedom, political democracy, and economic progress while offering American and Canadian volunteers alike three hundred acres of land. By the day after Christmas, 523 adventurers had gathered on the island.[22]

The filibusters received a tactical setback but a recruiting boost when on December 29 loyalist Canadians, commanded by a British militia officer, seized the *Caroline*—an American steamboat taking supplies and recruits to Navy Island. After capturing the vessel near Fort Schlosser on the U.S. side of the river, the raiding party set it on fire, towed it to mid-river, and abandoned it just above Niagara Falls. Borderland Americans rallied to the filibuster cause after news circulated that the vessel had been attacked while at anchor in U.S. territory and that an American had been killed during the capture. False reports that the raiders had left the *Caroline* by the falls with helpless Americans stranded on board further inflamed the situation. Mackenzie's force on Navy Island grew to about eight hundred men, causing concern in Washington.

Determined to keep the peace with Britain, a far more powerful nation than Mexico, President Martin Van Buren not only issued a proclamation against the invaders on January 5, 1838, but also had his cabinet members instruct customs officials, district attorneys, and marshals to take preventive action. Further, the president wisely sent one of the U.S. Army's ranking generals and shrewdest strategists, the War of 1812 hero Winfield Scott, to pacify the border. Scott, an insufferable egotist, nonetheless had already demonstrated considerable tact in dealing with potentially explosive domestic problems. In 1841 he would become commanding general of the entire army.[23]

Federal intervention proved decisive. U.S. authorities interrupted Mackenzie's timing by taking him briefly into custody on January 4, 1838. Scott's threat to confiscate vessels in the filibusters' service dampened the willingness of nearby shipowners to hire out vessels for the Navy Island operation. As a result, the filibusters ran short on supplies. Once frigid weather set in, they gave up, withdrawing from the island on January 14. Meanwhile, to the west, Van Rensselaer's second-in-command Thomas Jefferson Sutherland failed in a planned filibuster from Detroit against Toronto. His men disbanded after their ship ran aground in the Detroit River and they came under attack by Canadian militia.[24]

Rather than desist, however, the Patriots and allied Americans regrouped and unleashed coordinated attacks against the whole U.S.-Canadian border from Vermont to Michigan. On February 22, 1838, Van Rensselaer and several hundred men occupied Hickory Island in Canadian territory, preparatory to an intended assault on Kingston (at the junction of the St. Lawrence River with Lake Ontario). This invasion failed when most of the volunteers, learning of approaching Canadian militia, backed out of continuing the campaign. On February 24, some one hundred fifty adventurers crossed the iced-over Detroit River to take Fighting Island, holding it for about two days before being driven back by gunfire from the Canadian shore. On February 28, five to six hundred filibusters commanded by the Canadian physician Robert Nelson crossed Vermont's northwestern border armed with cannons on sleighs and muskets looted from the Vermont state arsenal at Elizabethtown, and established a short-lived Independent Republic of Lower Canada. Intimidated by advancing British forces, the filibusters recrossed the boundary and surrendered on March 1 to U.S. army Colonel John E. Wool. That same day and the next, filibusters around Detroit attempted unsuccessfully to take Pelée Island in Lake Erie.[25]

Repeated failures caused the movement to go underground. Over the next several months, to avoid detection by either U.S. or British authorities, American Patriot sympathizers formed secret societies to plan future operations: the Canadian Refugee Relief Association; the Frères Chasseurs, or Brother Hunters; and the Sons of Liberty. Two similar groups were founded in 1839. Eventually these organizations merged into what became known as Patriot Hunters or Hunters' Lodges.

Invasions soon resumed. On May 29, 1838, members of the Canadian

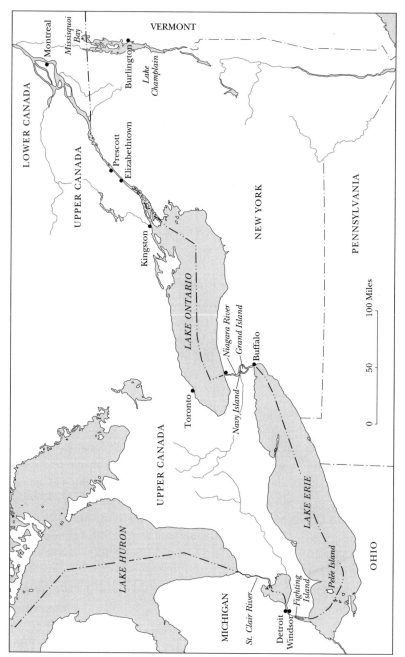

MAP 1. The U.S.–Canadian Filibustering Frontier, 1837–1838

Refugee Relief Association, dressed as Indians, avenged the *Caroline* by burning the Canadian vessel *Sir Robert Peel* while she was at Wells Island on Lake
Ontario. In June several hundred filibusters crossed the Niagara River. They
established an encampment on the Canadian side, destroyed property, and
suffered four men killed before surrendering to British regulars and Canadian
militia. The Sons of Liberty planned a summertime attack on the Michigan
state arsenal preparatory to a campaign against Windsor, but aborted that operation because authorities at the arsenal were under alert.[26]

Pre–Civil War filibustering to Canada climaxed that fall. In early November filibusters connected with Nelson's "Republic of Lower Canada" were
prevented from a boundary crossing by U.S. army patrols and the seizure of
their chartered sloop by U.S. customs officials. However, on November 11,
four hundred filibusters began their campaign to take Prescott and nearby
Fort Wellington on the Canadian side of the St. Lawrence River. Although
part of the force was diverted to recruit reinforcements, 150 or so invaders
took possession of a windmill and other buildings below Prescott on November 12, raised their flag, and captured an American steamship and an American ferryboat. They received 110 reinforcements before seizure of their vessels by a U.S. marshal aided by federal troops cut off help from the American
side. The filibusters, consequently, had little chance of victory in their "Battle of the Windmill"—an affair that ended with 20 Patriots dead, 157 taken
prisoner, and the rest in flight.

Undaunted by this disaster, the former Ohio militia brigadier general Lu-
cius Bierce commanded 135 Hunters in a December 3–4 crossing of the Detroit River for an attack on Windsor. These invaders burned barracks, a couple of houses and a steamer, killed a few defenders, and issued the obligatory
proclamation calling for a Canadian uprising, before being routed by Canadian militia. Twenty-one invaders died in battle; other Hunters were taken
prisoner or died from exposure as they fled the battle site.

Filibuster reinforcements poured into Detroit. However the movement,
now plagued by the presence of 2,000 U.S. regulars on the frontier and other
preventive measures by the Van Buren administration and state authorities,
had played out. Cross-border raids and filibuster plotting continued in
1839–41. Many Hunters hoped to provoke an Anglo-American war as a
means of freeing the Canadas. But in 1842, northward filibustering suffered
a crippling blow when the United States signed the Webster-Ashburton
Treaty with Britain, resolving most border difficulties.[27]

Meanwhile, few filibusters departed southward from U.S. territory in the
early 1840s, though transplanted Americans participated in the Texas Re-

public's disastrous "Mier expedition" into northern Mexico in 1842 and some Americans got captured and executed in a foray from New Orleans to the Mexican state of Yucatán in 1844. Certainly no filibuster army materialized to answer the call of a Mississippi paper for "thousands of bold and adventurous spirits from 'the States'" to conquer Mexico City's treasures on behalf of the "Anglo-Saxon race."[28]

PARADOXICALLY, the Mexican War that erupted in the spring of 1846 both inhibited filibustering and guaranteed its revival. Now, on the one hand, adventurous Americans could satiate their filibustering inclinations by joining their country's largely-volunteer army. Why participate in an illegal military venture, when one might invade foreign domains with the government's blessing? On the other hand, the war's end in 1848 created a pool of latent filibusters — conquering soldiers accustomed to military campaigning who dreaded being mustered out of the service (if they were volunteers) or being posted to routine peacetime assignments (if they were regulars).

In the months between the U.S. Army's entry into Mexico City in September 1847 and the end of the war, some U.S. soldiers considered enlisting in an expedition to Yucatán, which had seceded from Mexico in 1846 and maintained neutrality during the fighting. Simultaneously, Cuba's Havana Club (Club de la Habana), made up mainly of Creole merchants, planters, and professionals who favored the annexation of their island to the United States,[29] took steps to enlist restless American war veterans in a rebellion to overthrow Spanish rule.

Trying to repress a bloody insurrection by Mayan Indians that erupted in 1847, Yucatán's ruling elite unsuccessfully solicited the United States to assume a military protectorate over their state, and also offered $8 a month and 320 acres of land to American volunteers willing to soldier against the Indians. By the late spring of 1848, word was racing through U.S. forces occupying Mexico's capital of this opportunity for continued military service. "There are officers in the city of Mexico trying to raise companies to go to Yucatan," observed one of Pennsylvania's volunteers on May 27. That same day, an American occupation newspaper instructed soldiers how they might sign up.[30]

At virtually the same time, the U.S. consul in Havana, Robert B. Campbell, informed the State Department of Cuban rebels' hopes that "a few of the volunteer regiments now in Mexico" might "obtain their discharge" and join a revolution against Spanish rule that they hoped to initiate in the immediate future. Campbell's information was accurate. That May, the Havana Club

Contemporary lithograph depicting the entrance of General Winfield Scott and American troops into Mexico City on September 14, 1847, after their conquest of the city. (Courtesy of the Library of Congress)

sent an agent and interpreter to Mexico in the hope of persuading U.S. General William J. Worth, one of the heroes of the American conquest of Mexico City, to lead this filibuster. To accommodate the arrival of these auxiliaries, moreover, Narciso López, a former Spanish army officer and functionary, postponed his own separately planned uprising for Cuban independence from June 24 until mid-July.[31]

Possibly the Yucatán and Cuban plots had linkages to each other, with the peninsula intended as a way station to the island. Campbell, who was privy to many of the Cuban rebels' plans, notified Commodore Matthew C. Perry, commanding U.S. naval forces in the region, that the plotters expected the Americans to arrive via Yucatán.[32]

Though much remains in doubt about what occurred when the Cuban agents caught up with Worth in Mexico, the general reportedly gave tentative approval to the filibuster, promising, as one of the high-ranking Cuban rebels put it, to accept the call "contingent upon his resignation of his rank in the [U.S.] army." Possibly, Worth even took preliminary steps to involve his fellow army officer Robert E. Lee in the plot. Lee had won considerable notice for his engineering feats during the Mexico City campaign. In a letter alluding rather obliquely to both Cuba and Yucatán, the army lieutenant Henry J. Hunt alerted Colonel James Duncan, "Genl. W. bids me to say to you . . . that he has some rich developments to make in which the pious Capt. Lee figures conspicuously."[33]

Whatever the case may have been, both the Yucatán and Cuban schemes ran into resistance from Washington. President James K. Polk, who in June 1848 authorized the American minister in Spain to try to purchase Cuba, could ill afford to tolerate filibustering, which would naturally alienate the very Spanish officials who had to be persuaded to sell their colony. Tipped off not only by Campbell, but also by the New York newspaperman John L. O'Sullivan (whose sister was married to a wealthy Cuban opposed to Spanish rule) and by some Cubans who turned up for a White House interview facilitated in part by Senator Jefferson Davis of Mississippi, Polk had his cabinet take preventive measures. Secretary of War William L. Marcy gave an "awful" blow to "go-ahead" soldiers, as one reporter phrased it, by cautioning U.S. occupation commanders in Mexico to be on their alert against filibustering and by stipulating that troop transports returning to the United States avoid Cuban ports. Secretary of State James Buchanan cautioned Campbell against even giving the impression of collaboration with Cuban insurgents, and passed on to Spanish officials what the administration had gleaned about the intended uprising. Buchanan's intimations failed to grease Spain's cession of Cuba; but they did help Spanish authorities in July preempt López's uprising by jailing a number of the alleged conspirators.[34]

Yet Polk's policies only delayed what in retrospect seems to have been filibustering's inevitable revival. Even before the last remnants of the U.S. army withdrew from Mexico in August 1848, adventurers in southern Texas were conspiring with Mexican revolutionaries to carve out of northern Mexico an independent Republic of the Sierra Madre (also known as the Republic of the Rio Grande). Helen Chapman, married to a U.S. Army assistant quartermaster who was engaged in transferring army supplies from occupied Matamoros to the U.S. side of the Rio Grande, informed her mother that the plotters intended to include Tamaulipas, Nuevo León, and Coahuila in their new polity. Their organization was so "extensive" that she expected to hear of "the Texas story all over again." Disturbed by press reports about the plot, Polk and Buchanan again used their influence against filibustering, realizing, as Buchanan put it, that any expedition would make an immediate mockery of the American pledge in its peace treaty with Mexico to respect the boundary dividing the two nations.[35]

Meanwhile, Buchanan fended off complaints from the Venezuelan government about rumored expeditions being mounted against Venezuela from U.S. soil. He also received an apology from Viscount Palmerston, the British foreign secretary, for the arrest and detention of Americans traveling in Ireland.

It had turned out, Palmerston explained, that they had been wrongly suspected of filibustering to overthrow British rule there. In September, Campbell reported that new plots were already being hatched in Havana for an
"armed invasion" by American citizens.[36]

By the fall of 1848, it seemed that borderland revolutionaries had called off
the Sierra Madre movement. According to a press report from Galveston,
some adventurers led by Lorenzo A. Besançon, who had captained the Louisiana Mounted Volunteers during the war, arrived prematurely at Corpus
Christi only to be sent home. Relieved by the apparent evaporation of the
threat, Buchanan took credit for stopping the expedition, and instructed the
U.S. minister to Mexico to cultivate the goodwill of Mexican leaders by
stressing to them the administration's successful antifilibustering efforts.[37]

However, at the very time that the Sierra Madre scheme was put on hold,
discharged U.S. soldiers were finally making their way to Yucatán. On October 29, a New Orleans newspaper reported that eighty Americans were already serving in Yucatán's armed forces, and that David G. Wilds (a former
U.S. Army lieutenant) had arrived in the Crescent City on a recruiting mission for Yucatán's government. In November, George W. White, who had
been an infantry captain of Louisiana Volunteers during the Mexican War,
posted placards in New Orleans for "fighting men" willing to join Yucatán's
military. "Colonel" White raised his quota so quickly that he embarked for
the peninsula before the end of the month. In December his regiment of just
under 1,000 volunteers, including Lorenzo A. Besançon as lieutenant colonel
and second-in-command, went into action. Although hundreds of the volunteers arrived back at New Orleans in March and April after the regiment disbanded, Besançon and a battalion of Americans remained in service well into
the spring.[38]

One might argue that Colonel White's volunteers were mercenaries rather
than filibusters, since they served at the invitation of Yucatán's ruling authorities. But because Besançon had prepared to filibuster across the Rio Grande
before his arrival in Yucatán, and because White officered an intended invasion of Cuba in 1849, immediately after his return to the United States from
Yucatán, this would seem to be splitting hairs. It is easy to imagine White, Besançon, and company trying to convert their intervention in Yucatán into an
attempt at conquest, had the opportunity to do so presented itself. Yucatán's
leaders seem to have suspected as much. A number of White's subordinate
officers complained to a reporter after their return that Yucatecan authorities
had always kept their "regiment divided, and the different battalions sepa-
rated by long marches," for fear the Americans would take over the country.[39]

Clearly, numbers of American veterans of the Mexican War had contracted a filibustering spirit. Soon they and like-minded young Americans and recent immigrants would be invading lands throughout the Gulf-Caribbean region, and intimidating peoples as far away as Hawaii. Symptomatic of things to come, the aborted plots and Yucatán intervention of 1848 heralded America's coming filibustering epidemic.

CHAPTER TWO

Harry Maury's America

Success to Maury and his men,
  They'll safely cross the water;
Three cheers for Southern enterprise,
  Hurrah for Gen. Walker
—*Mobile Mercury* (quoted in *Tuskegee Republican*, December 30, 1858)

HARRY MAURY WAS only slightly inconvenienced. True, the Mobile lawyer and merchant captain had raised men for General Quitman's filibuster to Cuba, only to be notified, in late March 1855, that Quitman had canceled the expedition. Maury would have the unwelcome task of telling his recruits to return to their jobs and homes. But overcoming his "personal disappointment," Maury expressed confidence that Quitman's chivalrous nature would eventually induce him to reassemble the expedition. Something would surely be done by the famed general, Maury assumed, for Cuba's "helpless women and children" suffering under Spain's autocratic rule. Besides, Maury had other filibusters to choose from should Quitman really call it quits. "Please keep me advised of your address," he asked one of Quitman's collaborators, adding, "if I do go on any other expedition I will let you know at once."[1]

Had Maury joined an alternative filibustering expedition, it likely would have been the scheme of the Texas entrepreneur Henry L. Kinney to "colonize" part of Central America. Kinney's project was well known in Quitman's circle. Two months earlier, Quitman had received a letter of regret from a follower who reported that he had just signed on as a staff surgeon in "Colonel" Kinney's movement, as well as a missive from Mike Walsh, a lame-duck congressman from New York, announcing that he might seek one of Kinney's commissions. Late in February 1855, a New Orleans newspaper announced that Maury had opened a recruiting office for Kinney in Mobile.[2]

But there were other filibusters reportedly in the works. U.S. Senator Jeremiah Clemens of Maury's own state of Alabama, for instance, was rumored to be organizing an operation to Ecuador. Supposedly Clemens had contracted to raise 2,100 men and provide 6 vessels to assist an effort by the former Ecuadorian president Juan José Flores to regain control over the country. In return, Flores would provide Clemens—a former Mexican War colonel—and his followers with land grants, as well as the right to market guano deposits on Ecuador's Galápagos Islands.[3]

Throughout the year, moreover, Americans plotted attacks against their southern neighbor. In January, for instance, while serving on the commission to survey the new U.S.-Mexican boundary necessitated by the recent Gadsden Treaty, the U.S. Army major and topographical engineer William H. Emory posted a letter from El Paso intimating that even though he despised "filibusterism," he was conspiring with influential people across the border who favored the annexation of Chihuahua to the United States. A Vermonter running a private school in San Antonio notified his mother on July 1, "A 'filibuster' expedition is in progress from this vicinity against Mexico. . . . Some of my acquaintances have gone." Almost certainly, this New Englander's friends had become involved in plans of the Texas Ranger William R. Henry for a border crossing. Just seventeen days later, Henry broadcast a call for volunteers in a San Antonio newspaper. In October, Henry's band would join another group of Texans and cross the border for a short-lived invasion.[4]

Maury would more likely have heard of Ecuadorian and Mexican plots than about what William Walker was up to in distant California. Walker, who already had filibustered two years earlier into Mexican Baja California, was planning an expedition to Nicaragua. He had to slow the pace of his preparations, though, after taking a wound to his foot in a duel.[5]

Had Maury been privy to official diplomatic correspondence, moreover, he might have wondered whether there were still other options. On March 12, the U.S. commissioner to Hawaii (then also known as the Sandwich Islands) alerted the Department of State that he anticipated an American filibuster against Honolulu. Later in the year, U.S. Secretary of State William L. Marcy complained about the British government's decision to dispatch a large fleet to the western Atlantic on the basis of rumors that Americans had organized a filibuster to Ireland.[6]

That Maury might have been able to choose from so lengthy a filibustering menu is less curious than one might suspect. Throughout the period between the end of the Mexican War and the beginning of the Civil War (1848–61) it was common for two or more U.S. filibustering expeditions to be in some stage of preparation or in actual progress. As an English observer put it regarding America's most notorious filibuster, William Walker was merely a "straw upon the wind," since there were hundreds of men ready to fill his shoes if he faltered. Harry Maury's America, it would seem, had become a filibustering nation.[7]

IT TOOK A foreigner to unleash American filibustering in the aftermath of the Mexican War. Not only did Narciso López command the first significant il-

MAP 2. The Texan Filibustering Frontier, 1850s

legal invasions from American soil since the Canadian rebellions of the 1830s, but his landings in Cuba helped to spawn further expeditions by providing orientation and field training for many officers and enlistees in later filibustering bands.

Swarthy, dark-eyed, and mustached, López arrived in the United States on

July 23, 1848, when he debarked from an American vessel at Bristol, Rhode Island, having barely escaped arrest in Cuba during Spain's crackdown that month on revolutionary activity. Over the following year, López organized a military expedition from American soil to free Cuba from Spain's rule. Although many of his activities during this period remain unknown, it is clear that he made New York (and to a lesser extent Washington) the nerve center of a conspiracy that soon reached all the way to the Gulf Coast. In New York, López drew on the assistance of the Cuban Council (Consejo de Organización y Gobierno Cubano; headed by John L. O'Sullivan's brother-in-law, Cristóbal Madan), an organization of exiles from the island and an offshoot of the Havana Club.

Since López did not speak English, he also leaned heavily on Ambrosio José Gonzales, a Cuban educator and member of the Havana Club who had attended an academy in New York City during his youth and was fluent in the language. Gonzales arrived in the United States shortly after López, sailing from Havana to New Orleans on assignment from the Havana Club to follow up on its attempt (mentioned in chapter 1) to get the U.S. Army general William Worth in the revolutionaries' fold and put him in touch with López. Sometime after arriving, Gonzales joined López's staff in the principal subordinate role of adjutant general, and rendered invaluable service as López's frequent traveling companion and liaison with potential American supporters.[8]

By mid-summer of 1849, López and his cohorts, with financial assistance from the Havana Club, had acquired vessels and made elaborate arrangements for their filibuster. George W. White, recently returned from Yucatán, recruited and commanded a minimum of 450 men, and possibly as many as 600, who had been raised in New Orleans and its vicinity for the invasion. On July 31, White's band landed at tiny Round Island, López's assigned rendezvous in the Gulf of Mexico near Pascagoula, Mississippi. Had everything gone according to plan, White's force would have eventually combined with hundreds of additional troops before invading Cuba's southern coast. Gonzales later asserted that López intended a two-pronged expedition of approximately 1,200 men that would leave New York and Round Island.[9]

Throughout late August and into September, newspapers reported that López's agents were holding meetings and raising recruits at eastern urban centers such as New York, Baltimore, and Washington.[10] A Philadelphia newspaper afterward broke the story of a young man who had told the editors about being recruited with other Philadelphians, and of how they had gone to New York City where the filibusters had quartered them at a hotel and then boarded them on a steamer in preparation for departure. In early 1850, a Louisville sheet published a public letter from a former U.S. Army officer, Edgar Basil Gaither, asserting that he had raised 500 Kentuckians for the enterprise.[11]

Before López's scheduled departure, Rose Greenhow, the future Confederate spy, tried to rally support for the venture. On August 29, 1849, after taking breakfast with "the main spring or mover in the matter," Greenhow penned a letter from Washington to Senator John C. Calhoun of South Carolina, a former secretary of state, briefing him about the filibusters' pending embarkation: "Now I must tell you of the progress of the Cuba affair. . . . The expedition will sail on Saturday, that is to say a steamer with a thousand men from New York or some point North, with one part of the forces, and a steamer of a thousand ton with 12 or 15 hundred more, from New Orleans simultaneously." Greenhow's note reinforced John L. O'Sullivan's attempt of five days earlier to flatter Calhoun into collaboration. The famous Carolinian should become a "tower of strength" to the filibusters, O'Sullivan had implored, by writing fifty letters to key contacts who might "act with the requisite energy, promptitude, head and heart, in this matter." Calhoun, however, remained uninvolved.[12]

Even had Calhoun immediately thrown his influence behind López's movement, it would have come too late. At the very moment when Greenhow was soliciting him, U.S. naval officers were blockading Round Island. Just the day before, Commander Victor M. Randolph had proclaimed to the "vagrants" on the island that they were mercenaries and lawbreakers, and warned them not only that he would prevent their boarding oceangoing steamers, but that starting the next day he would cut off their shipments of provisions from the mainland. About a week later, federal authorities in New York seized vessels intended for the expedition. Although Randolph eventually curtailed his attempt to starve out the Round Island filibusters, most of them had tired of waiting by mid-September and accepted the Navy's free transportation back to the mainland, though a handful hung on for another month. A few of the men, rather than return to the mainland, enlisted as ordinary seamen on one of the blockading vessels.[13]

Rather than capitulate, however, López renewed planning a filibuster. But now he encountered resistance within the Cuban exile community in New York. In the wake of the Round Island debacle, members of the council concluded that he had been impulsive, and that more advance planning ought to go into any future attempt. As a result, throughout the late fall of 1849 and over the winter, council members bickered with López over the timing of the next attempt and the disposition of arms and other resources recovered from the canceled invasion.[14]

Had Madan and his council cohorts felt more comfortable about the domestic political situation in the United States, they might have cooperated more energetically with López. But by early 1850, Madan was increasingly conflicted over whether it was a good time even to attempt revolutionizing his homeland, given the current disputes dividing the American people over slavery and its expansion. Heated debate had broken out in Congress, as well as in the nation's press and in state legislatures, not only over whether California and other parts of the recent Mexican Cession should be allowed to have slavery, but also about such explosive issues as the slave trade in the District of Columbia, Texas's boundary with New Mexico, and southern demands for a stronger fugitive slave law. From the moment that it convened on December 3, 1849, the first session of America's 31st Congress found itself consumed with sectional issues.

Strongly proslavery, neither the council nor the Havana Club wished to liberate Cuba unless it would afterward be annexed to the United States with its labor system intact. But how could the Cubans be certain that this would happen at a time when northern "freesoilers" in and out of Congress were demanding that slavery be prohibited from every inch of America's newest territory in the southwest? As Madan put it, America's "domestic disagreement" made it "inexpedient and criminal" to begin "any thing of a revolutionary nature without seeing clearly the sure safe arrival at annexation." Madan worried that Cuba risked a slave insurrection should revolutionary currents be unleashed without "the frank and determined aid of the respectable classes of the South." From the council's perspective, Southerners were too distracted to provide such assistance for the time being. López's decision to forge ahead with planning for an immediate expedition, therefore, amounted to putting "personal and ambitious considerations" above Cuba's welfare.[15]

Frustrated by the council's inaction, Gonzales and other members of López's faction announced in the American press in December that they were organizing their own junta in Washington, which they called the Junta for the Promotion of Cuban Political Interests (Junta Promovedora de los Intereses Politicos de Cuba), and provided a post office box for people wishing to contact López by mail.[16] Moreover, to enhance their movement's appeal to potential American volunteers and financial contributors, they made renewed efforts to identify a prominent American military figure who might be willing to head their invasion force or serve as second-in-command.

The search for an American leader, by this time, had become something of a quest among the Cuban exiles. General Worth had expressed continued interest in the command, which reportedly included an offer to him of $3 million, during his negotiations with Gonzales. He even sent an agent to Havana to flesh out the details. However, the general apparently never made a firm commitment, and the filibusters considered other prospects after the War Department in late 1848 assigned Worth the command of Military Departments nos. 8 and 9 in far-off Texas and New Mexico. In retrospect, it was just as well for the filibusters that Worth faded from the picture, since he died the following May.[17]

Between Worth's exit and the end of the Round Island fiasco in September 1849, the Cubans and their American associates made overtures to several other possible candidates. For instance, at some point between April and July of 1849 López and Gonzales apparently attempted, without success, to persuade Jefferson Davis and Robert E. Lee, two more Mexican War heroes, to assume the role intended for Worth. Then, as the men assembled at their Round Island rendezvous, the filibusters briefly placed their hopes on Senator Thomas J. Rusk of Texas, a onetime brigadier general in the Republic of Texas's army. On September 13, John L. O'Sullivan expressed delight that Rusk had offered "to raise 500 of your gallant Texans and lead them yourself" in a liberating army. Rusk should travel to New Orleans, O'Sullivan suggested, where at the rank of major general he could "take the position of head of the whole American part of the movement second only to the General commander-in-chief" (meaning López), and earn himself a lump sum payment of $100,000 at the end of the campaign.[18]

Now in early 1850, as López finalized his plans for another attempt to invade Cuba, he turned, with more success, to yet one more American military hero—John Anthony Quitman, who had just become governor of Mississippi. Muscular, more than six feet tall, mustached, and bearded, Quitman gained national fame during the Mexican War for his gallant leadership in the fighting at Monterrey in 1846 and in the storming of Mexico City in 1847. Beginning the war as a brigadier general of volunteers, Quitman received a promotion to the rank of major general in the regular army during the American advance on the Mexican capital. By the time he was mustered out of the service at the end of the war, Quitman had proven his bravery and demonstrated superior leadership abilities. Widely hailed not merely for his military abilities but also for the compassion that he displayed for common soldiers in his command, Quitman would surely attract recruits and money if he would only agree to serve.[19]

In February, López and Gonzales left the East Coast and traveled westward and southward via the Ohio and Mississippi rivers, making contact with various sympathizers and potential recruiters and donors at Louisville and other points as they traveled, and intending to offer Quitman the command once they arrived in Mississippi. Meanwhile, the Cuban Council tried to preempt them. In January, Madan had asked the profilibustering Pennsylvanian George Cadwalader, another general from the war, whom he would recommend to supersede López in the command. Cadwalader, who had a close personal relationship with Quitman, apparently recommended him, because in a letter dated February 24 the Council formally offered Quitman the command and promised to "lavish" on him Cuba's wealth if he would raise a four-thousand-man expedition. The "impetuous" López "would certainly" cooperate in a subordinate capacity, were someone as influential as Quitman calling the shots.[20]

López and Gonzales showed up in Jackson, Mississippi's capital, on March 17, by which time the governor was already mulling over the council's proposition. Tempted by the thought of becoming "the Liberator of a beautiful & rich island in the Gulf" and trading his administrative duties for the excitement of military campaigning, Quitman queried Mansfield Lovell, one of his former aides-de-camp in the Mexican War, as to whether he would serve as prime minister or secretary of war in the government that the filibusters would establish in Cuba. Then, in a meeting at the Executive Mansion on the 17th, López and Gonzales tendered their own offer, making the governor "general-in-chief" of the entire operation, with López as second-in-command, and promising that Quitman and any soldiers whom he raised would be "liberally and fairly remunerated for their military services." According to this proposal, López would lead an initial invading force to the island in the near future, raise his flag for an independent Cuba, and send Quitman proof that the island's inhabitants were rallying to the cause. Then Quitman would rush to Cuba (presumably with an auxiliary force) and take over the combined revolutionary army, leaving López in charge of civil affairs on the island until its annexation to the United States.[21]

Citing his official gubernatorial duties, Quitman the next day halfheartedly declined the command, making it clear that his instincts were to sign on and that he might be free to do so in the immediate future. Quitman's response left the door open so far that his participation in the plot was sought by a number of Americans associated with López such as O'Sullivan, Laurent J. Sigur (editor of the *New Orleans Delta*), and John Henderson (a lawyer, former U.S. senator, and onetime colleague of Quitman's in the Mississippi legislature).

Though no definitive evidence survives, everything points to Quitman's caving in to the pressure soon after his meeting with López and Gonzales, and agreeing to command a secondary landing in Cuba provided that a genuine rebellion for independence erupted on the island after López's initial attacks

John Anthony Quitman, a few years after he became involved in Cuba filibustering. This engraving was made sometime during Quitman's service in Congress from 1855 to 1858. (Courtesy of the John Anthony Quitman Papers, Louisiana and Lower Mississippi Valley Collections, LSU Libraries, Louisiana State University, Baton Rouge)

on Spanish forces. At the very least, Quitman became implicated at some level in the plot, for in April 1850 he traveled to New Orleans, around the time that the first contingent of López's troops sailed, in response to Gonzales's urgent appeal that the filibusters depended on his "aid in getting us out." Moreover, in mid-May, while the expedition was in progress, Henderson alerted Quitman that a "squad" of 300–600 men was being mustered in anticipation of Quitman's embarkation.[22]

Quitman may even have turned over Mississippi state arms to the filibuster organizers. Well after the expedition, he responded to rumors about the arms by conceding that a transfer had occurred, but asserting that it had been made "by some means unknown to him." He also seems to have solicited a U.S. naval officer to spy on Spanish defenses in Cuba. On May 26, Lieutenant Henry J. Hartstene, visiting Havana aboard a mail steamer, sent Quitman a detailed report about gun emplacements, movements of Spanish troops, and other particulars that would assist "the enterprize if carried out soon."[23]

Quitman, however, remained stateside, as the encouraging news that he was apparently awaiting never came. López's army, consisting mostly of American recruits but including European immigrants to the United States and a handful of Cuban exiles,[24] successfully got away from its rendezvous in and around

New Orleans. But it lost almost 10 percent of its manpower even before arriving on Cuba's coast. Worse, little went right during the actual invasion.

Rather than sail directly from the mouth of the Mississippi River to Cuba as a flagrantly hostile squadron and risk attracting U.S. naval attention and likely interdiction, López had his vessels *Georgiana, Susan Loud,* and *Creole* sail separately for the island of Mujeres off Mexico's Yucatán peninsula, with the intention of attacking Cuba only after the vessels all appeared at the rendezvous. But when the *Georgiana* sailed off course and encountered unfavorable winds, the filibusters had to alter their advance base to Contoy, a sandy cay twelve miles from Mujeres (see map 4). Thirteen men abandoned the expedition at Mujeres, after López sent them there as part of a detachment to obtain fresh water. Additionally, López permitted thirty-nine men to quit the army at Contoy, just before he boarded the rest of his forces on the *Creole* for his invasion of Cuba. Instead of attacking Spanish troops in Cuba with 570 soldiers, López wound up commanding only about 520.[25]

Beginning at about 2:30 A.M. on the morning of May 19, 1850, López and his army effected an uncontested landing at Cárdenas. Then, after some confusion in locating military targets to attack, the invaders skirmished against enemy forces at the town's plaza and demonstrated the kind of audacious bravery that filibusters would characteristically display throughout their military campaigns, by making a frontal assault on Spanish defenders at the building that housed the local governmental offices. By early morning, the filibusters not only captured Cárdenas's jail, city hall, and customs house, but also took into custody the town's garrison and government officials. A handful of surrendered Spanish soldiers even joined their cause.

López's projected liberation of Cuba, however, turned into a military debacle within hours. Gonzales and several regimental officers suffered wounds in the fighting, and a few of the other filibusters had already met their deaths. More importantly, Spain's lieutenant governor at the port, a nephew of Cuba's captain general, managed to get out word about the attack before surrendering, as well as issue orders that workers cut the railroad westward out of town to Matanzas. This diminished the filibusters' prospects of making a rapid advance toward Havana, farther west, even as it became evident that the local population was far less enthusiastic about López's cause than anticipated. The filibusters behaved fairly respectably during their brief tenure as occupiers, paying shopkeepers for food and the prodigious quantities of alcohol that they consumed that day. However, most residents fled town or shunned them, and there was no sign that the Cuban people were rallying.

Upon learning around mid-afternoon of the approach of some 2,000 Spanish troops, López discreetly began reembarking his force. But before he could get all his men on board the *Creole*, Spanish cavalry and infantry arriving on the scene attacked his lone regiment still on shore, causing the filibusters another thirty-four casualties. López completed his embarkation so precipitately that he left several followers behind. Yet he remained in danger. The *Creole* grounded on the way out of the harbor, breaking free only after the filibusters threw tons of ammunition and other items overboard, and ninety men allowed themselves to be temporarily removed by rowboats to a nearby island. Then the Spanish steam warship *Pizarro* spotted the *Creole*, and literally chased the filibusters all the way to Key West.[26]

Lucky to be alive but refusing to accept defeat, López subsequently began planning a second landing in Cuba, despite efforts by federal authorities (discussed in a chapter 5) to prosecute him and many of his key associates for their patent violation of the Neutrality Act. From June 21, 1850, until March 7, 1851, López and fifteen conspirators were under indictment. Yet, by early April 1851, a year after the launching of the Cárdenas affair, the resourceful filibusters were ready to sail again.

According to a spy who infiltrated the movement, López this time hoped to invade Cuba with 4,000–5,000 men: the *Cleopatra* and another steam vessel or two would carry a few hundred men recruited in New York City and Philadelphia to a rendezvous in the South, where the filibusters would join a larger force and additional transports before initiating the actual expedition. In order to mislead federal authorities in New York, the *Cleopatra*, without the filibusters on board, would seek clearance to Baltimore from port authorities. Then, separate parties would board a smaller steamer at New York and a sloop at South Amboy, New Jersey, that would convey them to nearby Sandy Hook—a peninsula in New Jersey that separates New York City's lower bay from the Atlantic Ocean (see map 3). From this point they would transfer to the *Cleopatra* for their oceangoing escapade.[27]

Should we trust this spy's figures? Ambrosio Gonzales claimed in a March 1851 letter to Mirabeau Buonaparte Lamar, a former president of the Republic of Texas, that he had already succeeded in arranging for 1,000 men to join the expedition, and that another 1,800 men in the "Southwest" had committed to the cause. Since Gonzales made this boast in a letter soliciting support from Lamar, we might suspect him of exaggerating his recruiting accomplishment to gain the assistance of a well-connected public figure. However, given López's successes at recruiting along the Gulf coast for his other expeditions, it would be dangerous to dismiss Gonzales's claim as a fabrication. Reports reaching the U.S. district attorney in Mobile of up to 150 "strangers of irregular life" congregating at Pascagoula lend partial credibility to Gonzales's intimations.[28]

We can be certain that the filibusters again intended to raise several hundred men for a New York contingent. In an undated letter posted about this time, one of López's recruiters reminded O'Sullivan that the "General" had sent both of them to New York under "the strictest instructions . . . to bring together four hundred men." Moreover, they apparently came close to achieving this goal. Under the heading "THE CUBAN INVADERS IN NEW JERSEY," the *Newark Daily Advertiser* published an April 6 report from its Perth Amboy correspondent about the arrival at South Amboy of some fifty men ready to act "the emigrant." Later in the month, the *New York Mirror* observed that the number of filibusters at South Amboy had grown to between one and two hundred men, and that they were "awaiting the arrival of others."[29]

In all, López's agents in the spring of 1851 appear to have raised upwards of 1,000 men for an expedition that came close to sailing. On April 10, the editor of the *Savannah Republican* telegraphed President Millard Fillmore that Georgia's railroads had become "crowded with an army of adventurers destined for Cuba." A force of sixty-three men, which set out prematurely from Rome, Georgia, on the 9th, had to return once it became apparent that the expedition was unprepared to sail. Soon afterward, López's volunteers in far greater numbers were reported on the move throughout Georgia and northern Florida. By late April, some 600 expeditionists had collected in and near Jacksonville, most of them congregating at a sawmill a few miles down the St. Johns River, waiting for the arrival of the *Cleopatra*.

However, once news reached the South that federal officials in New York had detained the *Cleopatra* and arrested O'Sullivan and several other New York conspirators, the filibuster leaders had to postpone the invasion to a later date. "Every arrival of the cars," noted a Griffin, Georgia, newspaper on May 22, "brings back to their homes some of the youngsters who were duped into the idea of taking Cuba by storm."[30]

Two months later, with fewer troops than attacked Cárdenas, López got off his second expedition to Cuba. As had been the case the year before, things began going wrong even before his feet touched Cuban soil.

López was residing at the home of Laurent Sigur in New Orleans, with many of his preparations unfinished, when in late July intimations started reaching him and the city's newspapers that resistance to Spanish rule had suddenly erupted in Cuba. López's supporters in the city held rallies for recruits and funds on behalf of his cause at Lafayette Square on July 23 and the courtyard at Bank's Arcade on July 26. Then, on July 28, the New Orleans press announced definitively that a major insurrection against Spanish rule had broken out in the vicinity of Puerto Príncipe (later Camagüey) in central Cuba on July 4, that the leader of the revolt had chosen that date—with its obvious significance for Americans—for a declaration of independence, and that the rebels had routed Spanish troops. The Crescent City erupted in an outpouring of pro-Cuba fervor. One of the expedition's officers later recalled how a "blaze of sympathising excitement about Cuba" broke out, and how placards appeared on walls calling people to public meetings. "Cuba, Cuba, Cuba was the topic of the newspapers, the Exchange, the street corners, and the barrooms." Throwing caution to the wind, López decided that it would be safer to leave at once and capitalize on the rebellion in progress than to prolong his preparations and risk the rebels' defeat before he arrived.

So over the next few days, López and his associates intensified their recruiting efforts, preparing to leave as soon as the ship that they had acquired, the steamship *Pampero*, was in good enough repair to sail. One young man in New Orleans who succumbed to the excitement explained to his brother in a letter dated July 31 how he had enlisted just minutes earlier, after being drawn to the wharf by the firing of cannon. Once there he had learned that "Most of the Towns" in Cuba's interior had already revolted, that "several thousand patriots" were in the field, and that the rebels had repulsed Spanish troops in battle "with considerable loss."

López boarded many such enthusiasts on the *Pampero* in the early morning hours of August 3, and put to sea a couple of days later with between 400 and 450 men in all, a much smaller force than the thousands of men he had wanted. In his rush, he not only left behind hundreds of volunteers who arrived in New Orleans only about a week after the *Pampero* departed, but also Gonzales, who was far away at Fauquier White Sulphur Springs in western Virginia recovering from a serious ailment, most likely a malarial attack.

Making matters worse, López had to improvise strategy as he went. He planned to pick up reinforcements and artillery at Jacksonville in northern Florida, before actually sailing for Cuba. But as the *Pampero* approached Key West on its way to Jacksonville, López learned that it lacked sufficient coal to include the detour. On August 10, while pondering what to do as his vessel lay at anchor at Key West, López heard from visitors to his ship that the revolution in Cuba had spread to thirteen towns and that it was now widening westward. More encouraged than ever, López and his officers determined to strike immediately, assuming that they could send the *Pampero* back for the men and supplies at Jacksonville once they were safely ashore in Cuba. Presumably Florida's U.S. senator and Key West resident (and future Confederate naval secretary) Stephen Mallory contributed to the filibusters' confidence, when, during his visit to the vessel, he put a hair ring on López's finger for good fortune.[31]

Even as Mallory made this profilibustering gesture, however, López was doomed. His filibuster hinged on the mirage of Cuban masses rallying to his standard. Yet reports reaching the American press of uprisings in the island were grossly exaggerated, and Spanish authorities entirely quashed the token uprising that was occurring a month before López even arrived off Cuba's coast. Making matters worse, López failed to achieve surprise. Cuban officials spotted the *Pampero* on August 11, when because of a navigational error it appeared off Havana harbor, which was not López's intended destination.

On August 12, as López and his men effected their landing near the small village of Morrillo on Bahía Honda bay sixty miles west of Havana, Spanish forces were already marching against them from Havana by land, and encircling them by railroad and by sea. Wrongly assuming that he would be able to link up with insurrectionary forces east of Havana, that his revolutionary proclamations would rally the Cuban people, and that the *Pampero* would accomplish its round trip for reinforcements, López violated a cardinal rule of warfare—that commanders should be wary of dividing their forces in the face of a superior enemy. López pressed inland toward Cuba's mountainous interior terrain with almost three quarters of his men, leaving the remainder under Colonel William Crittenden to safeguard his supplies until carts and oxen were acquired to bring them away from the coast. López did confiscate carts and oxen after arriving at the nearby village of Las Pozas, but on learning of Spanish forces in the area sent word to Crittenden to abandon the supplies and close up with him. It was too late. Spanish forces put both López's and Crittenden's detachments under attack on the 13th, and although the filibusters were able to repulse both assaults and inflict more casualties on the Spaniards than they themselves suffered, Crittenden made the mistake of chasing after his attackers with about eighty men. When the Spanish reattacked, Crittenden's party found itself entirely cut off from the main filibuster body, though some forty men whom Crittenden had left with the supplies did subsequently unite with López at Las Pozas.

Over the next two weeks, Spanish forces crushed the invasion. Authorities on the Spanish war vessel *Habanero* picked up Crittenden and fifty men still with him off the coast, after they commandeered four launches back near their landing site on August 14, in a futile attempt to repeat the prior year's flight to Key West. López held out longer than most of his men, but he was forced to surrender on August 28, and was executed a few days later.[32]

THOUGH NEWS OF the deaths of López and many of his cohorts including Crittenden shocked many Americans, it hardly curtailed interest in Cuban filibustering in the United States. The very month after López's execution, enthusiasts in the southern Louisiana town of Lafayette formed the quasi-filibustering Order of the Lone Star, an organization made up initially, according to its leader Dr. John V. Wren, of persons who had been unacquainted with López but who were "sympathetically favorable to his expedition." Their name drew on the precedents of the West Florida and Texas revolutions, and their constitution's preamble proclaimed a mission of extending "the area of liberty."[33]

The Order spread rapidly in the Gulf South, with affiliated "divisions" materializing as far away as New York City. Undoubtedly the group's rituals helped to attract some of its members. So, we may assume, did its social events, such as the "LONE STAR Fancy and Dress Ball" in Lafayette, announced by the *New Orleans Daily Delta* on December 27, 1851. The Mississippi native and New Orleans lawyer Henry Hughes, who applied for admission in October 1852 (a couple of years before he emerged as one of the South's leading proslavery polemicists) and recorded his initiation in his diary, had ambitious designs for the group. Hughes hoped that the Order would expedite his "life-aim" of creating a "Universal Republic."[34]

How close the Lone Stars came to launching an expedition remains murky. In May 1852, Spain's consul in New York claimed that Dr. Wren was in the city, that he was enlisting men in collaboration with O'Sullivan, Armstrong Irvine Lewis (who had captained both the *Creole* and the *Pampero* in López's invasions of Cuba), and another collaborator, and that the men were being sent to rendezvous at Mobile and New Orleans for a Cuba expedition. That September, Spain's minister complained to the State Department that in some American cities the filibusters were not only engaging in flagrant recruiting with press support, but they were even publicly announcing their schedule for military drills and target practices. Still, the Lone Stars deferred action, perhaps in expectation that Franklin Pierce, the Democratic nominee for president in that year's election, would acquire Cuba from Spain once he was installed in office. In January 1853, the *Democratic Review* opined that the Order should refrain from attacking Cuba, not because there was anything improper about American citizens "going with arms in our hands to any country" in the "service of liberty," but rather because private expeditions generally failed.[35]

Even then, Cuban filibustering persisted. In October 1852, Cuban exiles formed a new junta in New York City.[36] In April 1853, its agents called on

John Quitman in Natchez, in order to renew and this time formalize his commitment to lead a liberating invasion of their island. During a visit to New York in August, Quitman contracted with the Cubans to serve as "civil and military chief" of an uprising to overthrow Spanish rule in their homeland. The Cubans gave Quitman "absolute control and disposal of all the funds . . . now in the hands of the revolutionary party, as well as those which may hereafter be received," and authorized him to issue bonds, grant commissions, charter vessels and otherwise act in the junta's name. For his part, Quitman agreed to surrender power and create an independent government on the island shortly after he defeated the Spanish military forces.[37]

Quitman seems to have absorbed, rather than superseded, the Order of the Lone Star. Adventurous persons in the Order, as they became aware of Quitman's intentions, melded into the general's ranks. Writing in reference "to the Lone Star Expedition," one Mississippian confided to Quitman that as "a member of that Division of Jackson No. 12. 3rd degree standing" he hoped to be included in the endeavor. Other Lone Star enthusiasts found their way into Quitman's support network. The Pennsylvania attorney John Cadwalader (George Cadwalader's brother) intimated his intention "to send a subscription to the Lone Star association for the redemption of that island." Pierre Sauvé, a planter from St. Charles Parish, Louisiana, who had attended the Lone Star ball at Lafayette in 1851, helped to organize the financing for Quitman's proposed invasion.[38]

Believing that López's movement had failed primarily because of its leader's impulsiveness, Quitman insisted in his correspondence with the junta and other collaborators that he would only sail for Cuba after assembling sufficient manpower (as well as matériel and funding) to guarantee success. Quitman considered an army of three to four thousand men optimal. Anything less would be suicidal.[39]

Although Quitman informed a prospective officer in February 1855 that he had not yet achieved his manpower goal, he had well-placed persons assisting his recruiting, and he likely did not fall short by much. In June 1854, an editor in Kosciusko, Mississippi, offered to raise a band of fifty to one hundred men for Quitman because he had learned that very day that Quitman was "on the point of leaving New Orleans for Cuba." Various collaborators announced recruiting accomplishments in missives to Quitman, sometimes even identifying their enlistees by name. One agent, John Allen, claimed in a public letter to have raised fifteen hundred men in Kentucky alone.[40]

All the while, participants were regularly dropping out of the conspiracy even as new recruits signed up. Because of funding and legal difficulties, Quitman delayed his scheduled departure for month after month, in the process driving men out of his ranks. Consider the aspirant who informed Quitman in the spring of 1854 that he wanted to filibuster. When almost a year passed without any news from the "chief," this volunteer "trammelled" himself in matrimony. Then, merely days after his wedding, he learned to his immense frustration that Quitman wanted his services after all! The U.S. naval lieutenant Robert W. Shufeldt offers another example: while the plot was in progress, he resigned from the service to become a merchant ship captain for the New York and Alabama Steamship Company. Fearing that rumors of his involvement with Quitman might cause him problems with Spanish authorities in Cuba during the biweekly voyages to Havana that he would be making in his new capacity, Shufeldt quit the expedition, and pleaded that Quitman's associates repress all word of his prior collaboration.[41]

Eventually, Quitman decided anyway that the odds had shifted against a successful invasion, and he canceled the operation. Not only did federal authorities seize one of his ships, but Spanish authorities in Cuba discovered and repressed in time an insurrection scheduled for February 12, 1855, executing the leader Ramón Pintó as well as others of the plotters. President Pierce and Secretary of State William L. Marcy, moreover, refused to relax their enforcement of the Neutrality Laws and, in a personal interview with Quitman, shared information that they had received about a Spanish defensive buildup in Cuba. On April 29, Quitman tendered the junta his formal resignation as filibuster commander.[42]

Apparently the Order of the Lone Star survived Quitman's resignation, at least in some locales. On July 3, the *Galveston Weekly News* announced that the "Island City Division Order of the Lone Star" would participate in the next day's Independence Day celebration. Several months later Isaiah Rynders, a Tammany Hall rabble-rouser and U.S. deputy surveyor for the port of New York, made a public point of his membership. He stormed into the office of the *New-York Times* to lambaste its editor for insinuating that his belonging to a "division of the Lone Star Order" proved that he supported filibustering.[43] But Quitman's divorce from the junta effectually ended American filibustering against Cuba, at least until after the Civil War.

ON SEPTEMBER 22, 1851, a Texas newspaper reported the fate of two companies of Narciso López's recruits, stranded at Mustang Island when the filibuster set out for Cuba the previous month without waiting for all his troops. Half the men on the island, off Texas's coast near Corpus Christi, had returned to their homes or dispersed to other points; but the remainder had constituted themselves into a new company, elected officers, acquired horses, and intended to "march in a few days for the seat of war—the Northern States of Mexico."[44]

These filibusters surely intended joining the "buffalo hunt" then in progress to carve out a new republic from Mexico's northern reaches. Any effort to calculate the number of Americans engaged in filibustering after the Mexican War certainly needs to take into account such expeditions into Mexico, though none of these filibustering parties were as large as the groups that accompanied López to Cuba, or that Quitman was counting on for his expedition.

Earlier that month near Guerrero in the northeastern Mexican state of Tamaulipas, the Tejano borderlands leader José María Jesús Carbajal (sometimes spelled Carabajal or Carvajal), a longtime figure in the Sierra Madre movement, had issued a proclamation rekindling the cause of norteno separatism.[45] Carbajal's pronouncement demanded not only the withdrawal of government troops from Mexico's northern states, but also a grace period of five years for certain American goods to cross the Rio Grande duty free. When Francisco Avalos, commanding Mexican forces on the northern frontier, sent troops to arrest Carbajal, he fled across the Rio Grande to Texan soil. At Brownsville, a town on the river near the Gulf of Mexico, he procured arms and other supplies from merchants who stood to gain trading advantages with Mexico if his tariff policies were adopted. Then he gathered an invading party at Rio Grande City, a sleepy village about ninety miles upriver from Brownsville on the American side, and recrossed the border with a band of followers to initiate what became a series of filibusters to revolutionize northern Mexico.[46]

Carbajal had little difficulty relating to and recruiting Anglos for his scheme, given his personal history, relatively light complexion, and fluency in English. He had attended a Protestant academy at Bethany in western Virginia (today in West Virginia) for four years during his younger days, and he had played an active role in the Texan revolution. A U.S. army officer on the border noted that he "has completely ingratiated himself with the people along the frontier. . . . He is . . . fair for a Mexican . . . speaks good English & was educated in the United States." Hundreds of Anglos participated in his border crossings and campaigns.[47]

On September 20, 1851, commanding some seventy Americans and one hundred Mexicans, Carbajal initiated the so-called Merchants War by capturing the village of Camargo, across the border from Rio Grande City on the San Juan River, a few miles from its confluence with the Rio Grande (see map

2). For the rest of the month and into October, Carbajal used Camargo as his base, as he waited for reinforcements from the United States, especially promised help from the well-known Texas Ranger captain John S. "Rip" Ford. This Mexican War veteran, former Republic of Texas legislator, and sometime lawyer, doctor, and newspaperman had agreed to join the insurrection once his Ranger company was mustered out of federal service on September 23. Ford arrived along with twenty-nine other Rangers in Carbajal's camp about October 1 and received a commission as a colonel of American volunteers in the insurgent army.[48]

On October 9 the combined forces evacuated Camargo to move against Matamoros, a city above the mouth of the Rio Grande roughly opposite Brownsville, Texas. More Anglo filibusters from the United States joined Carbajal during the campaign, so that he commanded an army of approximately four hundred men, including a company of volunteers from Brownsville, by the time he arrived at Matamoros. Some of the men from the Brownsville unit recrossed the river each night to sleep in their own homes.

During the afternoon of the 20th, Carbajal's advance took a fort on the northwestern outskirts of the city, to the horror of a U.S. newspaper correspondent across the Rio Grande who confessed humiliation at the thought that his fellow countrymen were attacking "the unoffending inhabitants of a neighboring republic" under the phony pretense of bringing them freedom. Moreover, the filibusters could not even behave with dignity, he lamented. Rather, the Americans took to "yelling," "whooping," and randomly firing their guns like "wild savages" once they had gained possession of the enemy works.[49]

Unfortunately for the attackers, General Avalos's command of regulars and local defense forces had prepared for them by erecting barricades to protect the city, fortifying rooftops with sandbags, and stocking supplies. Carbajal's three six-pound cannon lacked the power to dislodge the defenders, and although his army continued to receive reinforcements from the Texas side, including as many as twenty-seven deserters from the U.S. army post opposite Camargo at Ringgold Barracks, it was not enough. Carbajal's soldiers attempted several assaults on Avalos's positions in the city between October 22 and 26, but they were repulsed each time, and in one of the attacks Rip Ford suffered a head wound that caused him to give up his command and seek treatment in Brownsville. Another casualty during the action was the resident U.S. consul at Matamoros, J. F. Waddell, who took his wound on the 24th when joining an effort to put out a fire that the filibusters had set in a large building near his office. In a dispatch to the State Department, Waddell condemned the filibusters for committing acts of "atrocious barbarity" during their futile efforts to crack the Mexican defenses.

Carbajal kept Matamoros under siege into early November, when on the 8th his army began a retreat, with Mexican forces in pursuit. Ford, who by this time felt sufficiently recovered from his wound to rejoin his companions, took a steamer across the river and caught up with Carbajal at Reynosa, fifty miles upriver from Matamoros on the Mexican side; but Carbajal sent him back to the American side to drum up recruits in Texas's interior. However, time was running out on the invaders. Carbajal's force safely reached Camargo on November 16, and near the end of the month attacked some two hundred Mexican soldiers at Cerralvo, driving them into a stone house and pinning them down for two days, in an attempt to capture artillery there. But the defenders, though losing horses, gear, ammunition, and wagons to the filibusters, managed to salvage their artillery. Carbajal had to give up the siege and flee back across the Rio Grande with the approach of Mexican reinforcements.[50]

Twice more, Carbajal's filibusters invaded northern Mexico from Texan soil. But General Avalos undercut Carbajal's appeal along the border with reductions in duties on American goods, and neither incursion had the staying power of the 1851 campaign. In the first instance, Carbajal crossed the river below Rio Grande City on February 20, 1852, and marched on Camargo with a force of 244 men, including about 60 Anglos, but ran into heavy Mexican resistance the next day. Although the filibusters this time had a twelve-pound gun with them and were able to repulse several Mexican charges by firing double loads of canister, they reportedly took scores of casualties and suffered large numbers of desertions once night set in, causing Carbajal and his twenty-two remaining companions to seek safety across the river.

In the second case, Carbajal authorized a raid against Reynosa by about eighty filibusters under "Major" A. Howell Norton, who had lost his right arm in 1851 at Matamoros. Norton's band entered Reynosa on the morning of March 26, 1853, and demanded that the inhabitants pay him a large sum of money for Carbajal's cause. When it became evident that the money would not be forthcoming, he took the alcalde and another inhabitant hostage and demanded $4,000 in ransom, before settling for $2,000 and fleeing back across the river. For some time after the raid, rumor had it that Carbajal was mounting yet another filibuster. But the next invasion of Mexico would occur far to the west of Carbajal's scene of operations.[51]

JUST AS filibustering can be traced to the first years of the United States, so it should be linked to the opening moments of California's statehood. By the time that the López, Quitman, and Carbajal conspiracies had run their course, Anglos in America's newest state had taken up filibustering with considerable gusto, and made California into one of the nation's hubs of filibustering intrigue.

In early May 1851, California's quartermaster general Joseph Morehead, under suspicion at the time for embezzling proceeds from the unauthorized sale of state arms, boarded the barque *Josephine* at San Diego with forty-five followers for a seaborne expedition to Mazatlán in the state of Sinaloa on Mexico's Pacific coast. Morehead's band seems to have been one component of a planned infiltration by land and water of Sonora—Mexico's northwesternmost state, just north of Sinaloa on the Gulf of California. However, the group never made it past Mazatlán as an organized force. After vigilant Mexican authorities there boarded the *Josephine* in a search for weapons, the filibusters prudently assumed the role of miners looking for employment, and refrained from any kind of hostile activity that would risk their being taken into custody. Likewise, Mexican officials kept a close watch on groups of men apparently connected with Morehead who arrived during the summer by sea at La Paz, the territorial capital of Baja California (on the Gulf of California near the southern tip of the peninsula), and by land in Sonora itself (see map 5). The band in Sonora grew to sixty-seven men by the time Mexican officials expelled it in November. The suspected filibusters at La Paz dispersed into historical anonymity.[52]

Several months later, Alexander Bell, a historically obscure figure who according to his nephew had once captained a steamboat on Alabama's Tombigbee River and been a spy during the Mexican War, got together some forty adventurers in and around San Francisco and sailed with them for South America's Pacific coast, as part of a multinational filibuster against Ecuador. Agents of Juan José Flores, a native Venezuelan who had served as president of Ecuador for much of the 1830s and early 1840s but was now in exile in Peru, had enlisted Bell in the scheme, involving upwards of seven hundred men from a variety of countries, to assist in a campaign to restore Flores to power in Ecuador. Bell's American band united with Flores's forces in the spring of 1852, but the invading coalition was unable to rally native support and took many casualties in raids on villages near Guayaquil. By summer, Flores's army was disintegrating from desertions, with Captain Bell surfacing in Panama. There he posted a letter dated August 2 that got published in a California newspaper, relating that he had got in "plenty of fighting" and complaining that Flores's army was "not worth a d——n," yet predicting that he would one day fight with Flores again. Flores escaped overland to Peru and continued to plot new expeditions for several more years, but there is no evidence that other American military parties sailed in his support.[53]

About a year after Flores's campaign concluded, William Walker left California state with his first filibustering comrades. Thirty years old and usually taciturn among strangers, Walker was a former part-owner and co-editor of the *New Orleans Daily Crescent*. He impressed many of his contemporaries as a most unlikely candidate for the rigors and macho camaraderie of filibuster campaigns, standing only five feet six inches tall and weighing about 115 pounds; besides, his smooth, freckled face lacked the whiskers and rough features of so many of the day's military adventurers. One reporter even dismissed his "tone of voice" as "monotonous." Still, this apparently uncharismatic man found ways to convince others to follow him in incredibly dangerous ventures. On October 16, 1853, Walker and forty-five adventurers departed from San Francisco harbor aboard the schooner *Caroline*, apparently bound for the Sonoran coast, with hopes of conquering the state and gaining control of its mineral wealth. However, interference from U.S. authorities had stripped Walker of much of his manpower just before departure. Realizing that for the time being he lacked sufficient soldiers to take Sonora, Walker changed his immediate target to lightly populated Baja California, hoping to establish a base there pending reinforcements.

Walker's invaders committed their first hostile act on November 3, by seizing La Paz and taking captive its governor. During their occupation, which only lasted a few days, Walker proclaimed the establishment of an independent "Republic of Lower California," raised a flag with two stars (for both Baja California and Sonora), issued two decrees, and took his second gubernatorial hostage when the incumbent's replacement arrived on the scene. Walker declared himself president, and announced a cabinet and preliminary policy decisions (*e.g.*, that his state would be based on free trade and Louisiana's legal code).

Reembarking his men on the *Caroline* on the sixth, Walker left La Paz with his force intact, taking no casualties but inflicting several in a last-minute skirmish when some of the inhabitants fired on a party of his men who were gathering wood. Walker's band stopped briefly at Cape San Lucas at the tip of the peninsula, and then proceeded northward up the Baja peninsula's Pacific coast, putting in at Ensenada, less than one hundred miles south of San Diego, on November 29. Ensenada had the advantage of being much closer than La Paz to expected reinforcements from California as well as to land routes into

William Walker.
(Courtesy of the National
Portrait Gallery, Smithso-
nian Institution)

Sonora, and Walker designated it his new republic's capital. He also sent his secretary of state Frederick Emory to San Diego with a formal address to the American people, in which Walker justified his aggression with claims that Mexico's government had failed completely in its governance of Lower California. Upon reaching San Diego on December 2, Emory announced that the filibusters had achieved a telling military triumph at La Paz. Over the next several days, California's coastal press duly released Walker's propaganda and news of the filibusters' supposed victory in battle, triggering a temporary boom in recruitment activity in San Francisco.

Over time, Walker's prospects boiled down to whether enough reinforcements would arrive from California to compensate for the enmity that his invasion was arousing around Ensenada. Walker sent out details to raid neighboring ranches for horses, saddles, cattle, and provisions. As a result, Mexican landowners and bandits in the area organized irregular forces to resist the occupation. These improvised bands not only killed and wounded several filibusters in skirmishes, but also for over a week starting on December 5 kept

the invaders under siege at Ensenada. Although the filibusters drove their an-
tagonists off with a surprise charge on the night of the 14th, they suffered
from supply deficiencies and desertions in the days afterward. Further, during the siege Walker lost both his hostages and his vessel when the Mexican
governors persuaded the *Caroline*'s mate to sail away and return to La Paz
rather than risk awaiting the outcome of the standoff.

Finally, on December 28, a party of approximately 150 reinforcements arrived from San Francisco aboard the barque *Anita*, accompanied by Henry P.
Watkins, their recruiter and Walker's onetime partner in a Marysville, California, law practice. A month later, 125 more reinforcements, enlisted by
Walker's quartermaster-general Oliver T. Baird, reportedly boarded the
steamship *Goliah* at San Francisco bound for San Diego, apparently planning
to make their way from there into Lower California by land. About fifty of
them did arrive at Ensenada, but Walker still lacked sufficient force to mount
a credible threat against Sonora.

Despite these setbacks, Walker made the best of a deteriorating situation
and issued a proclamation on January 18, 1854, creating his intended Republic of Sonora, with Lower California and Sonora as its constituent states.
Meanwhile Watkins, who returned to California, tried to raise more troops. In
February, Walker transferred his army to the inland town of San Vicente.
Then on March 20, he took some one hundred men, driving about the same
number of cattle before them, on a northeasterly march across steep terrain
toward Sonora, over two hundred miles away, in a desperate bid to make his
two-state republic a reality. On April 4, the filibusters swam and took rafts
across the Colorado River (several miles above where it empties into the head
of the Gulf of California) into Sonora, but were unable to get their cattle
across with them. Walker proceeded only a short distance into Sonora before
deciding, after disaffection erupted in his ranks, to retrace his route to San Vicente. Encountering Mexican irregulars upon reaching his former headquarters, and suffering from more desertions, Walker finally conceded the hope-
lessness of his situation, and in mid-April fled with what was left of his band
for the United States. He reached his homeland in May, after engaging in several skirmishes with his enemies, who avoided a pitched battle with the filibusters but harassed them all the way to the border.[54]

DISREGARDING Walker's failure, gringo adventurers continued to plan and
wage filibuster campaigns below the border throughout the mid- and late
1850s. On October 1, 1855, for example, the Texas Ranger captain James

Hughes Callahan led 111 men, including William R. Henry's volunteers, across a rain-swollen Rio Grande near Eagle Pass in an expedition authorized by his state's governor for the purpose of pursuing and attacking Indians who had been raiding Texas settlements and using Mexican soil as a safe haven. Callahan's invaders plundered and burned the town of Piedras Negras before recrossing the river on October 6.[55]

Less than two years later, a boyhood acquaintance of William Walker's commanded his own invasion of Mexico. A one-time attorney from Vicksburg, Mississippi, who sang in a Whig party glee club celebrating Henry Clay's 1844 presidential candidacy, Henry Alexander Crabb moved to California in 1849 after losing a political race earlier in the year. Eventually establishing his residence in Stockton, Crabb served his locality as city attorney, and became active in California state politics and filibuster affairs, having the gall to ask a U.S. army general in San Francisco as early as 1853 for a passport so that he could invade Sonora. When Walker went on trial in San Francisco the next year for his attack on Mexico, Crabb was summoned to court as a witness to testify about his knowledge of the plot. With dark, deeply recessed eyes, a bushy brow, a beard, and a full face, Crabb looked the part of a filibuster far more than did Walker, whom he had known when they were both youths in Nashville.[56]

In March 1857 Crabb and sixty-eight members of his "Arizona Colonization Company" invaded Sonora, taking a land route from Los Angeles. Two smaller parties of adventurers who were connected to Crabb's plot also entered the Mexican state in what must be judged the most thoroughly crushed of the many unsuccessful filibusters of the day. Only one member of Crabb's party survived the expedition. The rest either died in battle or were executed by Mexican firing squads.

Given William Henry's background, it is not especially surprising that in February 1859 he confided to his state's governor Hardin Runnels that he was recruiting one hundred men for a border crossing. More remarkably, in early 1860 Sam Houston, Runnels's successor, gave thought to personally conducting a filibuster. During his gubernatorial campaign the previous year, Houston had proclaimed, "I am no friend of filibustering." Yet the governor now considered leading a thrust into Mexico in response to hysteria in southern Texas over the recent raids of the Tejano social bandit Juan Cortina, who had been operating on both sides of the border since briefly occupying Brownsville the previous September and freeing prisoners from the city's jail. In February 1860 Houston notified U.S. Secretary of War John B. Floyd that though he hesitated doing anything that might "raise even a question as to the

Henry Crabb. (Courtesy of
the Arizona Historical Society, Southern Arizona Division, Tucson)

propriety of his action," he would recruit ten thousand volunteers for an invasion of Mexico unless the U.S. government sealed the border against Mexican threats. Houston might not have been bluffing. As his filibustering intentions became public knowledge, adventurers implored the governor to find a
spot in his ranks for companies that they intended to raise for the invasion. In
deference to countermeasures against Cortina by the U.S. army, however,
Houston announced that he would refrain at least for the time being from a
border crossing.[57]

Although Houston deferred his attack, George Bickley's Knights of the
Golden Circle mustered near the Mexican border on a couple of occasions
over the following months. A Virginian by birth who earlier in the decade had
been a member of the faculty of the Eclectic Medical Institute in Cincinnati,
Bickley had attempted all sorts of pursuits before organizing his Knights in
1859 and becoming their "president general." He had written books and journal articles, edited several periodicals, attempted land speculations, and apparently even practiced phrenology. Given to lying about his own background
(he claimed a medical education in England), Bickley seems to have created
the Knights on the rebound from personal disappointments, quite possibly as
a scheme to recoup his fortunes by collecting membership fees. Before becoming a filibuster, Bickley had alienated his second wife (his first wife had
died in 1850 after a two-year marriage) by trying to appropriate her property,

been fired as the editor of a Cincinnati weekly magazine, and failed to make good on his debts. At any rate, Bickley boasted in April 1860 that the Knights had forty thousand members, of whom sixteen thousand were enrolled in the organization's "army."

Given Bickley's historical reputation as a charlatan, we can assume that he grossly exaggerated. Still, enough evidence survives of men joining this secret society that we should be wary of dismissing it as inconsequential. A Montgomery, Alabama, paper in February 1860 observed "[l]arge numbers" of Knights "passing through this city every day en route for Mexico." That March, a reporter in Baltimore claimed that four thousand young men in that city had joined the Knights and begun drills for their invasion of Mexico. A Texas Ranger, James Pike, remembered in his memoirs that a Knights recruiter had turned up at an encampment in the spring of 1860 and managed to seduce "nearly all the rangers" into his organization, claiming misleadingly that Governor Houston had agreed to command their invasion. In May 1860 a U.S. army lieutenant complained to his father that the Texas border town of Brownsville had become "overrun with the K.G.C.," that he had talked with many of the members, and that they intended to "fillibuster in Mexico." By mid-summer, recruits in far-off Southampton County, Virginia, were joining the Knights. A Memphis newspaper in October reported that two thousand Knights had assembled on the Rio Grande, ready to "pour" across the border.[58]

Some of the most anxious Knights apparently crossed the border on their own hook. Major Samuel P. Heintzelman, then conducting the U.S. Army's operations against Cortina, noted in April 1860 that "K.G.Cs" had "straggled into Matamoros" and were "behaving badly." But Bickley never ordered his troops to launch their invasion. That summer, Heintzelman heard that some of the Bickley's Knights had taken up horse theft as their newest avocation.[59]

DESPITE ALL THESE plots and expeditions against Mexico, U.S. filibustering's center of gravity shifted southward to Central America in the mid- and late 1850s. Both Henry L. Kinney and William Walker took expeditions to Central America in 1855. By conquering Nicaragua, Walker would become the preeminent filibuster in U.S. history.

Described by one of his boosters as a large-framed man over six feet tall, with a face made ruddy and weathered by exposure to the elements, Kinney was a native Pennsylvanian who had spent some years in Illinois before drifting to Texas in 1838. Soon emerging as one of the Republic's most talked-about public figures, Kinney served in its congress and at the 1845 Texas

Constitutional Convention before going off to the Mexican War as a division quartermaster of the Texas Volunteers in General Zachary Taylor's invading forces. He resumed his political career after peace was achieved, holding a seat in several sessions of the Texas state legislature. Known as one of the founders of Corpus Christi, Kinney engaged in a maze of business enterprises and land speculations during his time in Illinois, where he served as Daniel Webster's land agent for a while, before engaging in a range of trading, ranching, newspaper, and speculative schemes in Texas. His filibuster simply diverted his entrepreneurial instincts in new directions. That he was trying to recoup his fortunes after several business disappointments, and that his marriage had failed several years earlier, only makes his Central American gamble more understandable.

In association with a consortium of investors from the mid-Atlantic States, Kinney laid a legal foundation for his filibuster by claiming title to 22,500,000 acres in Mosquitia—Great Britain's protectorate on the Caribbean coast of today's Nicaragua and Honduras (see map 4). Publicly, Kinney insisted that his Central American Land and Mining Company (also called the Nicaraguan Land and Mining Company) had no intention of invading anything, but instead would send peaceful settlers to its holdings, where they would settle on plots ranging from 160 to 640 acres. However, British authorities had repudiated the original land grants on which Kinney based his claims. Kinney, who had won notoriety in the Mexican War for his daring missions as a scout and messenger, instructed his colonists to arm themselves and enlisted them for a year at pay scales pegged to those of the U.S. Army. The whole scheme, as perceptive observers realized, smacked of an invasion. One newspaper quipped that Kinney had surrounded himself with "young filibusters, who are desirous of taking part in any cause where more fighting than work is to be done." Kinney planned an expedition of hundreds of men, but because of federal interference was lucky to get off from New York harbor aboard the schooner *Emma* on June 6 with a mere eighteen accomplices.[60]

Once in Central America, Kinney only received a handful of reinforcements. Correspondence from Kinney's expedition following its arrival in July 1855 at the port of Greytown (formerly San Juan del Norte) within Britain's Mosquito Protectorate reveals that twenty-two men reinforced Kinney by August 16, and that a few additional filibusters arrived later that month. Though Kinney manipulated his own selection as "Civil and Military Governor of the City and Territory of San Juan del Norte" by what one scholar has called a "rump convention" of his followers and "renegades," and although he remained there until July 1857, he never gained a significant number of additional adherents. Rather, he suffered defections to his rival Walker, who gained control over most of Nicaragua by the end of the year. When Kinney returned to Greytown in April 1858 in a hopeless attempt to reestablish himself, he did so in command of what must have been the era's smallest expedition—six men![61]

Shortly after midnight on May 4, 1855, about a month before Kinney's departure for Central America, fifty-six men left San Francisco with Walker on the brig *Vesta*, bound for Nicaragua's Pacific coast, across the isthmus from Kinney's projected Mosquito colony. Walker not only commanded more manpower from the beginning than Kinney did, but he had the advantage of a better contract for filibustering. At the time, Nicaragua was in the throes of civil war. A crony of Walker's had reached an agreement with Nicaraguan Liberals, or Democrats, by which Walker would bring "colonists" to help the Liberals against their Conservative, or Legitimist, enemies, in return for a large land grant.[62]

Walker and his "Immortals" (as they were later called) arrived on Nicaraguan soil at Realejo on June 16. The next day, Walker and two cohorts mounted horses and proceeded to the Liberal headquarters at León, a city in sight of some of Nicaragua's beautiful volcanoes, where his waiting allies commissioned him as a colonel and incorporated into the Liberal army his band, which they dubbed La Falange Americana (the American Phalanx).[63]

Walker's troops met defeat in their first battle, an attack on July 29 on Conservative forces holding the interior town of Rivas, a key point near the Transit Road from Lake Nicaragua to the Pacific. From the beginning, Walker had the strategic sense to realize that reinforcements and supplies from the United States could reach him if he maintained control over the combined river, lake, and overland route by which travelers and goods commonly crossed Nicaragua's narrow domain between the Caribbean Sea and the Pacific, of which the Transit Road was a part. Naturally, he selected military objectives such as Rivas with this goal in mind. In the fighting, the filibusters took fewer casualties than their enemies but nonetheless suffered six fatalities (including two high-ranking officers) and twelve men wounded, and had to abandon their assault.

Walker's fortunes rebounded quickly, however. His Phalanx, with the help of some 175 Nicaraguan Democratic troops under the native Indian colonel José María Valle, thoroughly repulsed a conservative attack on their positions at Virgin Bay on September 3, absorbing no fatalities and causing the Legitimist attackers about sixty casualties. On October 13 Walker's troops took the enemy capital of Granada; and days later Walker executed the secretary of foreign affairs in the Legitimist régime, who had been taken into custody, after news arrived that Legitimist forces had fired on American civilians crossing Nicaragua, killing some of them. The seizure of Granada and Walker's threats of more executions induced the Conservative general Ponciano Corral to agree to a treaty ending the hostilities and creating a fourteen-month provisional, coalition government, with the elderly former Legitimist customs official Patricio Rivas serving as president. The agreement not only disbanded most of the Conservative forces but also allowed Walker to retain power for himself as commander-in-chief of the republic's army.

Early in November, Walker got a break that allowed him to eliminate his most important rival. Valle turned over to him intercepted letters that Corral, who had taken the position of minister of war in the coalition, sent out calling on other Central American states to invade Nicaragua. This gave Walker justification to have Corral executed for treason, which he did despite his court-martial's recommendation that the guilty prisoner be shown mercy, and despite, as Walker's memoir put it, the "sobs and anguish and tears" of Corral's daughters and the many other women of Granada who visited him the night before the scheduled execution in a futile effort to persuade him to change his mind.

The following June, Walker took the final step in his rise to power, by issuing a proclamation renouncing as traitors his puppet ruler Rivas (who had turned anti-filibuster) and Nicaragua's current minister of war, and calling for new elections. In tainted balloting on July 10, 1856, Walker defeated his closest rival for the presidency by what was reported in the filibusters' organ *El Nicaragüense* as a margin of 11,488 votes. Two days later, Walker swore an oath of office as president in a ceremony held at Granada's plaza.[64]

The filibuster régime lasted until the spring of 1857, when Walker was defeated by a coalition of the other Central American states and his Nicaraguan enemies (including many alienated Liberals), with assistance from Britain's government as well as the American steamboat magnate Cornelius Vanderbilt. The latter's investments in transit operations to, from, and across Nicaragua had been damaged by Walker's policies, and he had good cause to seek revenge against the filibusters. Sadly, during the waning days of his tenure, Walker made one of his most ruthless and detested decisions. Forced in December 1856 for military reasons to have his troops evacuate Granada, the Legitimists' former capital and a city dating back to its founding by the Spanish in the sixteenth century, Walker ordered the place burned. Finally, on May 1, Walker surrendered to a U.S. naval officer serving as an intermediary between the filibusters and their enemies, with the understanding that he and his men would be evacuated to the United States.[65]

Since reinforcements kept arriving in Nicaragua on various vessels from the United States almost until the surrender, Walker's invasion became, over time, the most numerically significant filibuster of the period. On June 1, 1857, shortly after returning to New York after Walker's defeat, the European soldier of fortune and military historian Charles Frederick Henningsen claimed that exactly 2,518 men joined Walker's cause during his tenure in Nicaragua. Commissioned a brigadier general and given command of Walker's artillery after arriving at Granada in October 1856 with ordnance stores and arms from New York, Henningsen deserves consideration as a credible source, especially since his estimate is roughly confirmed by other data. Walker's muster rolls show that he enrolled more than nine hundred men by July 1, 1856, and U.S. newspapers and other sources indicate the embarkation of hundreds of recruits for Nicaragua after that date. Moreover, a traveler arriving in San Francisco from Central America in October estimated the filibuster army at sixteen hundred men, a figure that obviously took no account of soldiers who had died in Walker's service, much less those who had deserted or been granted honorable discharge.[66]

Of course, in calculating the number of Americans who filibustered to Central America before the Civil War, one considers not only those men who served during Kinney's and Walker's initial invasions, but also the many adventurers who joined Walker's later aggressions. Spiritually still the filibuster after his return to U.S. soil, Walker seems to have been consumed by only one thought from the moment that he arrived in New Orleans on May 27, 1857—how best to recapture power in Nicaragua. Addressing a crowd on Canal Street, Walker announced, "duty calls upon me to return." Immediately he plunged into the minutiae of arranging another expedition, informing the former U.S. assistant secretary of state A. Dudley Mann that "enough" had been "done in New York" to allow him "a speedy return to Central America." He even had the gall to alert U.S. Secretary of State Lewis Cass that as "the rightful and lawful chief executive" of Nicaragua, he would be returning with his "companions" to that country.[67]

Walker's single-mindedness led not only to his second filibuster to Nicaragua that fall, but to three subsequent ones to Central America, the last of which cost him his life. Despite invoking the charms of "quiet and domestic life" in one letter,[68] Walker proceeded so methodically from one scheme to the next that his expeditions merge almost seamlessly in the historical record.

Walker's initial encore began on November 14, 1857, when the Mobile and Nicaragua Steamship Company's vessel *Fashion* slipped out of Mobile harbor with Walker and his associates aboard, and ended after Walker's arrival in Central America later that month. On December 8, U.S. Commodore Hiram

Paulding compelled Walker and most of the expeditionists to surrender after they had established an encampment on the Central American coast near Greytown; moreover, between December 23 and 25, the U.S. naval captain Joshua R. Sands, commanding the U.S. steam frigate *Susquehanna*, rounded up an additional forty-five invaders, commanded by the filibuster colonel Frank P. Anderson, who had been landed separately by the *Fashion* south of Greytown. Anderson's group managed to capture a fort held by Costa Rica up the San Juan River before being taken into custody.

According to the American commercial agent at Greytown, Walker arrived in the vicinity with "about two hundred men." This figure correlates roughly with a note in the journal of one of Walker's officers that "195 all told" had traveled with him from New Orleans to Mobile before the expedition, as well as several documents indicating that Walker's force totaled 186 men.[69]

Walker commenced planning his next Nicaraguan filibuster immediately after the breakup of the *Fashion* expedition. Walker arrived back in the United States on December 26, 1857, still claiming to be Nicaragua's lawful president. Damning the Navy's interference, he announced his intention to persist in a public letter dated January 4, 1858, to President James Buchanan, a piece of propaganda designed to subject Buchanan to so much public pressure that he would relent in his enforcement of the Neutrality Law. Five days later, Walker intimated to his former naval commander Callender Fayssoux his hope that they could " leave again for Nicaragua."

In December 1858, Walker got off a party of expeditionists from Mobile aboard the schooner *Susan*, this time under the command of Colonel Anderson, who was given the responsibility of establishing a foothold in Central America before Walker's arrival with a shipload of reinforcements. A correspondent for the *New York Herald* listed by name ninety-seven filibusters on board, not including the ship's captain. After the *Susan* grounded on a coral reef in the Bay of Honduras, ending the expedition, its captain reported to the vessel's owners that there had been 112 "hands" on ship, making clear that every passenger was a filibuster, since the crew had deserted before the vessel left Mobile.[70]

Determined to "yet get back to our country—ours by every right legal and moral," the indefatigable filibuster devoted most of 1859 to plotting yet another expedition. Walker sought men and funding in New York, around New Orleans and Mobile, and in San Francisco; he also sent agents to the Isthmus of Tehuantepec in southern Mexico under assignment to establish an advance base there for his return to Nicaragua. After encountering difficulty raising funds in California, where he sojourned for part of the spring, Walker con-

centrated on his eastern and southern operations. However, Walker post-
poned the expedition that fall because of intervention by federal authorities.
Not only did U.S. customs officials keep Walker's reputed vessel in New York
under close watch; they also denied clearance to Walker's troop transport, the
Philadelphia, at New Orleans. This prevented the vessel from descending the
Mississippi River and picking up Walker's recruits, who had taken a tugboat
downriver to the Southwest Pass (one of the Mississippi's outlets into the
Gulf of Mexico) in anticipation of boarding Walker's ship at that point. A
federal marshal, accompanied by U.S. army troops, gave the expedition its
final blow on October 7, 1859, by taking the gathered filibusters, whom he
numbered at "about seventy-five," into custody.[71]

Walker's finale unfolded over the spring and summer of 1860. Initially,
Walker intended to send his recruits, ten to twenty men at a time, to Aspinwall on the Caribbean coast of New Granada (now Colón, Panama), and to
use that port as a staging base. However, Walker shifted his sights northward
to Roatán, the largest island in Britain's colony of the Bay Islands off Honduras's Caribbean coast. During the spring, Walker's men, traveling in small
parties, made their way to Roatán. Walker then joined them on June 16.[72]

After British officials landed troops and artillery on Roatán, Walker evacuated the island rather than risk that the authorities might seize his munitions
or make arrests. For a while, the expeditionists sailed around the Bay of Honduras, putting in at Cozumel Island off the Yucatán peninsula and other points
as they awaited the arrival of further reinforcements, munitions, and provisions. Finally, on August 5, they went into action, capturing Trujillo on the
Honduran mainland, which they held for two weeks. Walker and his men fled
Trujillo by land, however, after the British warship *Icarus*, commanded by
Norvell Salmon, arrived on the scene, and Salmon demanded their surrender.
Pursued eastwardly along Honduras's Caribbean coast by both the *Icarus* and
Honduran forces, Walker surrendered to Salmon on September 3, expecting
to be treated, along with his men, as British prisoners of war. Instead, Salmon
turned them over to the Hondurans. Honduran authorities had Walker exe-
cuted by firing squad on September 12.[73]

How many men were foolish enough to join Walker's mission impossible?
Salmon's report to his superior officer noted the surrender of seventy-three
filibusters in all. However, Walker lost expeditionists during the campaign
from desertions, battle wounds, and other causes. Salmon discovered, for instance, that Walker had left three wounded filibusters behind when he abandoned Trujillo, as well as three other followers. Our best guide to Walker's
1860 expedition, a ledger maintained by Callender Fayssoux, indicates that

five schooners, making eleven voyages in all, carried 147 men from American soil who intended to participate in Walker's campaign. Fifty of these adventurers either failed to link up with Walker before his capture or embarked just before news of his execution arrived in the United States.[74]

AS FOR THE TOTAL number of antebellum Americans who took part in filibusters, that depends on one's definition. If filibustering includes only those adventurers who actually invaded foreign countries, then it was a marginal phenomenon. Perhaps as few as five thousand persons, including unnaturalized immigrants and foreigners temporarily in the United States, filibustered from American territory during the entire period between the Mexican and Civil wars, and a significant proportion of these were repeat offenders who participated in more than one expedition. Given the more than thirty-one million people enumerated in the 1860 U.S. Census, such figures seem inconsequential.

But such calculations understate filibustering's manpower. For one thing, we err by excluding American men who conspired to invade foreign soil as members of private military parties but whose expeditions never arrived at their intended destinations. Consider the case of the future U.S. senator Matthew S. Quay of Pennsylvania. After studying law, teaching school, and publishing a newspaper, the young Quay likely became a filibuster in late 1852, then shortly afterward backed out of whatever scheme he had joined. In December 1852 one of Quay's correspondents noted that he was not surprised by the contents of Quay's recent letter from New Orleans, given one of their earlier conversations that caused him to infer that Quay was "on a fillibustering expedition." In February 1853 Quay received a letter from a cousin announcing her relief that he had abandoned "that Cuban expedition."[75] Quay never actually invaded a foreign country. But he apparently signed on with a filibustering group.

Thousands of additional Americans would have filibustered had it not been for developments beyond their control, including federal efforts to enforce the Neutrality Act. The Round Island adventurers of 1849, John Quitman's volunteers for Cuba, and George Bickley's Mexico-bound Knights, for instance, were every bit as dedicated to filibustering as the men who died in López's ranks in Cuba. They just never quite got abroad. Henry Kinney intended to take many more men than eighteen to Central America. The owner of the *United States*, a 1,500-ton steamer that Kinney originally intended should carry his expedition before it was placed under surveillance by U.S.

authorities in New York, testified in an affidavit that the vessel had been "fitted up with accommodations for five hundred passengers." Likewise, Walker could easily have commanded more soldiers than he did during his 1855–57 tenure in Nicaragua had it not been for federal intervention and inefficient recruiting operations. On one occasion, for example, the U.S. district attorney in New York caused forty suspects to be ejected from the steamer *Northern Light* before its sailing for Central America.[76]

According to various reports, had Commodore Paulding not broken up Walker's November 1857 expedition, General Henningsen, commanding hundreds of reinforcements, would have made a second landing in Nicaragua. Even after news of Paulding's intervention reached the United States, additional adventurers prepared to rush to Nicaragua. Some hoped to reinforce Colonel Anderson's party; others wanted a role in the next filibuster. "I would like to join Genl. Walker . . . and from my popular bearing upon the surrounding country, think I could carry with me a company of from 60 to 100 fighting men," announced one North Carolinian on January 18. In May 1858 Walker claimed privately that seven hundred men had already committed to his next expedition.[77]

Should we expunge from filibustering's record the enlistees who deserted from expeditions before they left U.S. territory, others left behind by their expeditions, and still others who were waiting in the wings when expeditions returned? In October 1855 Henry McCulloch, a legislator and veteran of the Texas Rangers, had twenty-three men ready to reinforce James H. Callahan's filibustering party, when he learned that Callahan had returned from Mexico to U.S. soil. In October 1856 one of Walker's recruiters in New Orleans reported that "a large number" of recruits had arrived in New Orleans from beyond Louisiana's state lines, but that they had returned to their homes because of a lack of funds to support them while awaiting passage. In 1857 a group of Nicaragua-bound filibusters changed their minds and jumped ship when their vessel, the steamship *Sierra Nevada*, put in at Manzanillo harbor, Mexico, during their passage from San Francisco to Nicaragua. Henry Crabb left several sick soldiers at the border when he moved into Sonora. Before news of his death reached California, moreover, a company of Stanislaus County men, headed by a former sheriff, moved out intending to join his expedition. All such men were filibusters.[78]

I would also contend that one did not even have to join a military unit to be a filibuster, since U.S. law treated all persons involved in pre-expedition planning as criminals. One federal judge, John McLean, made this point most explicit in a charge to the grand jury of a U.S. district court. McLean argued

that the "offence is committed by any overt act which shall be a commencement of the expedition, though it should not be prosecuted. . . . 'To provide
the means' is within the statute. To constitute this offence the individual need
not engage personally in the expedition. If he furnish the munitions of war,
provisions, transportation, clothing, or any other necessaries to men engaged
in the expedition, he is guilty, for he provides the means to carry on the expedition." McLean's expansive definition requires us to open filibustering's
ranks to organizers, recruiters, suppliers, and financial backers. Any individual complicit in an expedition becomes a filibuster.[79]

But do McLean's standards incriminate those who were merely active sympathizers? Was Governor Runnels of Texas a filibuster for overseeing a meeting at Houston in January 1857 to arrange collections for Walker's cause in
Nicaragua? What about persons who allowed adventurers to store weapons on
their property? Do we include partisans who shielded filibusters from arrest,
such as the son of the former South Carolina governor James Hamilton and
the several Georgians who allowed Gonzales to hide out on their plantations
in the weeks following the breakup of the April 1851 Cuba conspiracy? Clearly, McLean's definition greatly enlarges the pool of filibusters. The question
becomes when to bar admittance.[80]

Finally, we may not even know about, much less have statistics for, all the
filibuster plots of the pre–Civil War period. We should dismiss as an outright
fabrication a rumor, reported to the Department of State by one of its agents
in 1849, that an expedition of as many as 10,000 men might be setting out for
Japan. We probably should also assume that scattered reports in 1858 and
1859 about the Sons of Malta, a new fraternal order, misrepresented the organization as having designs on Cuba, though resolutions passed in October
1860 by the Cairo, Illinois, chapter deploring William Walker's death hint that
some of the Sons indeed had profilibustering sympathies. Most likely, too,
"General" N. S. Reneau was a filibustering pretender.[81]

Reneau, a Tennessee native who had served as a private in the Mexican
War, notified President James Buchanan on January 6, 1859, of his readiness
to invade Cuba. In 1854 Buchanan, then American minister to England, had
joined several other U.S. diplomats in drafting the notorious "Ostend Manifesto," in which they proposed that the United States seize Cuba if Spain refused to sell it. In December 1858, moreover, just a month before Reneau's
letter, Buchanan had suggested a negotiating strategy to acquire Cuba in his
annual message to Congress.[82] Undoubtedly expecting a sympathetic response from a man whose 1856 presidential campaign had revolved in part
around the likelihood of his acquiring Cuba, Reneau proposed to command
an expedition of 5,000 men in support of a pending revolution for independ-

ence that he claimed would be led by the island's Spanish ruler, Captain-General José de la Concha. But he would only do this if Buchanan would support him with five warships or $100,000 in federal funds. The money would let him charter vessels to convey an army to the island.

Reneau enclosed in his letter a copy of an October 25, 1858, message that he had supposedly sent to the captain-general, insinuating not only prior collusion with Concha but also, amazingly, that Reneau had already consulted with Buchanan about the scheme. If we are to believe Reneau, the president had promised U.S. military protection of a liberated Cuba, once the rebels formally declared their independence and requested annexation to the United States. In October 1859 Reneau contacted Buchanan again, this time claiming that he had seven to eight thousand men ready to embark for Cuba, that he needed $10,000 in secret service funds, and that Buchanan's secretary of the interior had promised that there would be no governmental interference with his scheme![83]

Although a correspondent for the *New York Herald* noted that Reneau had been observed strutting around Memphis wearing a sash, epaulettes, and long sword and was apparently "deranged," a number of newspapers in the United States took Reneau seriously enough to take his conspiracy at face value. A paper in Natchez, Mississippi, for instance, noted Reneau's arrival at Vicksburg in May 1859 for a "Cuban Convention" that he had called. A writer for a Memphis sheet the next October affirmed that Reneau had assembled hundreds of "brave, bold, and daring fellows" to "Americanize" Cuba in December. Still Reneau never did launch his invasion, and we must assume that the *Herald* got it right. During the Civil War, Buchanan would remember Reneau as a "monomaniac" who had afforded the president's cabinet "much amusement" with his demands.[84]

But we had better reserve judgment as to whether any Americans participated in schemes that targeted Peru. In the winter of 1857–58 Peruvian leaders became convinced that exiles were in the process of organizing an expedition of several hundred "Yankees" out of New York, with the intention of "defrauding" their country.[85] Additionally, some U.S. filibusters may have had their eyes on Canada, Haiti, Hawaii, and Ireland. Stephen B. Oates, in his biography of John Brown, notes that Brown and his men acquired the cutlasses that they used to kill proslavery settlers at Pottawatomie in the Kansas Territory in 1856 from "an Ohio filibustering society called the Grand Eagles, whose members had indulged in fantasies of attacking and conquering Canada." Given the extent of filibustering to Canada in the 1830s and late 1860s, it would be surprising if at least some Americans did not engage in Canadian filibustering plots between the Mexican and Civil wars.[86]

Very possibly John T. Pickett, who had invaded Cuba with López in 1850, struck a filibustering deal involving a thrust against Haiti with the Hungarian revolutionary Louis Kossuth during his tour of the United States in 1851–52.. Pickett would raise men for an expedition to conquer Haiti that Kossuth would organize in collaboration with the authorities of the Dominican Republic; afterward the combined forces would sail from Haiti to liberate Hungary. The Dominican Republic, a former Spanish colony, and Haiti, a black republic and former French colony, shared the Caribbean island of Hispaniola (or Saint Domingue) near Cuba, but had experienced hostile relations for much of their histories as independent countries. Earlier in the century, Haiti had even conquered the Dominican Republic and then ruled it for years. Thus there was a rationale for the supposed plot.

In December 1851 Theodore O'Hara, who had been a fellow officer of Pickett's in López's ranks, sent Pickett a letter in the hope that it would arrive before he sailed. O'Hara observed, "from the official statements claimed in the President's message things in the Island wear not a very favorable aspect for our enterprise." Very possibly, O'Hara referred to a passage in President Millard Fillmore's annual message to Congress (Dec. 2, 1851) stating that peace had been achieved "between the contending parties in the island of St. Domingo." Obviously, peace between the Dominican Republic and Haiti would have precluded the former's cooperation in an invasion of the latter, lessening the chances of a successful filibuster. Less than a year later, Pickett arrived anyway in the Dominican Republic, around the same time that the journal *Our Times* claimed that U.S. citizens in a "Dominican Encampment of the Brotherhood of the Union" were planning a filibuster to Haiti. However, Pickett got nowhere in his negotiations with Dominican leaders, and his plot, whatever it was, collapsed.[87]

By that time, Hawaii had gone through a filibustering scare of its own. In November 1851 Hawaiian officials suspected thirty-two or thirty-three American passengers arriving at Honolulu aboard the vessel *Game Cock*, some of them former California vigilantes, of entertaining filibustering intentions against their independent kingdom. It is by no means certain that the suspected passengers truly intended a takeover; if they did, they may have been preempted from attacking by defensive preparations previously initiated by the Hawaiian government. The next spring, however, just before sailing back to California, one of the passengers who had sailed on the *Game Cock* boasted that he would soon be returning to conquer the islands as part of a 4,000-man filibustering army already being assembled. The scaremonger did indeed return. But he traveled alone, and announced upon arriving that he intended to found a banking establishment. Nothing ever came of his threat.[88]

John T. Pickett. (Courtesy
of the Filson Club Historical Society, Louisville, Ky.)

The historical record remains just as clouded about U.S. filibustering
across the Atlantic as it is about expeditions crossing the Pacific. In January
1856 federal authorities in Ohio issued warrants against twenty naturalized
Irish natives for organizing an expedition to liberate Ireland from British rule,
and arrested thirteen of the suspects, but never proved their case. Whether a
filibustering plot was really in progress remains a mystery.[89]

AND WHAT OF Harry Maury? As it turns out, he became one of filibustering's
repeat offenders. He never made it to Cuba with John Quitman or even to the
Mosquito Coast with Henry Kinney, but he did emerge as a mainstay in
William Walker's Central American escapades in the late 1850s.

It was Maury who captained the *Susan* in the December 1858 expedition
from Mobile, an experience that despite its failure only whetted his appetite
for further filibustering. In July 1859, at a time when Walker was counting on
him to raise men for his next Nicaraguan expedition, Maury became so im-

patient to filibuster again that he studied army tactics in preparation, apparently, for joining an invasion of Mexico by land should Walker put things off for too long: "During the next month I shall either go to sea or to Mexico, provided the General has no use for me. I consider myself amphibious, as I have been studying military tactics. . . . The General speaks to me of ultimate success, but not of immediate action. Whenever he does go, I follow." The general, however, had "use" for Maury after all. In fact, Maury suffered arrest as one of the leaders in Walker's fall 1859 fiasco. A year later, after learning of Walker's execution in Honduras, Maury gave fleeting thought to leading one hundred men on a mission to avenge the death of a man whom he once had described as inspiring him with more "respect & warm attachment" than did any other person.[90] Maury, by 1860, had become an American filibustering addict.

CHAPTER THREE

America's Second Sin

Border ruffians, fillibusters,
Will be swept by strong nor'westers;
Bully Brooks and all such cattle
Fall lifeless by this ballot battle.
—"John Fremont's Coming"
  (quoted in Thomas Drew, comp.,
  The Campaign of 1856)

INSIDE THE smoking room of a ship bound for Europe in August 1856, an English traveler debated with an American passenger concerning which of their respective homelands was better. As might be expected from the citizen of a country that had abolished slavery, the Englishman substantiated his claim of Britain's moral superiority by emphasizing human bondage in the United States. "Every sixth child in America," he complained, "is born into Slavery." However, the Englishman also charged Americans with another national sin. God, he predicted ominously, would not only "punish" their country for slavery, but also for its filibustering expeditions.[1]

Were this Englishman's opinions unusual, they would hardly merit our attention. But many foreign observers of the American scene in the 1850s, such as the Costa Rican official in Washington who pronounced filibustering America's "social cancer," implicated the United States in a similar manner. Furthermore, such critics rarely made the effort to differentiate Americans who opposed filibustering from those who supported it. Parisian journalists, for instance, according to an overseas correspondent of an American newspaper, identified "all American citizens" with the López expeditions to Cuba. Making matters worse, foreign observers occasionally implied that filibustering was uniquely American. Americans, one British diplomat reported to his government, gravitated into filibustering because of their unusual practicality as a people as well as their "reckless daring and disregard of consequences utterly unknown to any other country or age." Other peoples, he seemed to be saying, did not do such things.[2]

Although American commentators found it difficult to deny the addiction of some of their countrymen to filibustering, they were less willing to concede that such behavior was peculiar to the United States, much less unprecedented. This was especially true of filibuster defense lawyers, who were eager to incriminate others in the deeds of their clients. Henry Stuart Foote, for instance, a former U.S. senator and Mississippi governor, pleaded during one trial that the phenomenon had been "customary among all nations" over the course of history. In a separate case, another attorney argued that William Walker's invasion of Lower California and Sonora followed the "practice" of "every nation in the world."[3]

Any American, however, might take nationalistic umbrage at the charge that only their nation filibustered. Rather than allow his English antagonist an uncontested victory, our smoking-room debater retorted that England's "pedigree" came from the filibuster William the Conqueror, that England had filibustered in Ireland, and that its East India Company had filibustered "all over the world." In a similar incident, Pennsylvania's antislavery congressman Galusha Grow became agitated during an audience with the Empress of France during his trip to Paris in 1855. When she complained about U.S. designs on Cuba, he responded that "every country" had its "adventurers" who committed "unlawful acts," and that the United States should not be judged by them.[4]

U.S. Secretary of State Daniel Webster became so incensed at British and French censures of American filibustering that he considered drafting a state paper defending America's record of repressing illegal expeditions as compared to that of the European powers. Webster solicited historical evidence for his case from the U.S. minister to France William C. Rives. Rives responded that British and French filibusters had invaded Portugal, and that filibusters had been supported by the British in South America and Sicily, by the French in Spain, Belgium, and Baden, and by the Prussians against Denmark.[5]

American polemicists maintained that filibustering represented an old, indeed ancient, practice that had been engaged in by their "Anglo-Saxon forefathers" and diverse other peoples over the course of human history. Had not Attila the Hun, Alaric the Goth, and Robert Guiscard (the eleventh-century Norman invader of southern Italy) all filibustered? Why should anyone be shocked at William Walker's excesses, when Holland, Portugal, Spain, France, and England had sustained similar enterprises for the last four hundred years? Certainly Sir Francis Drake and Sir Walter Raleigh filibustered, not to mention Spain's colonizers of the New World. In 1858 theaters in New York and Washington advertised performances of "Columbus El Filibustero," a burlesque whose title certainly insinuated the joint culpability of Europeans in filibustering's history.[6]

In addition to identifying precedents for U.S. filibustering, American commentators insisted that filibustering was still going on in other countries and identified specific peoples who they believed were just then engaging in the practice. A California newspaper, for instance, ascribed the Crimean War to Czar Nicholas I's "filibustering annexationing expedition" against Turkey. Other newspapers argued that Europeans were filibustering in Central America, such as the British colonizers who had taken over the Bay Islands off the Honduran coast and the French canal promoter Felix Belly, who secured transit concessions from Nicaragua. The *New-York Daily Times* considered the Englishman James Brooke a filibuster for his conquests in Borneo. America's minister to Great Britain, George Mifflin Dallas, alluded to what the "filibustero Garibaldi" was doing in Italy. One newspaper correspondent saw filibustering as cropping up virtually everywhere: the English were doing it in Persia; the Russians in northern China; the French on North Africa's Moorish coast; and the Spanish in San Domingo.[7]

Above all, Americans normalized their countrymen's aggressions by fastening on the doings of British adventurers in India over the past century. "[W]hisper to him the word 'India,'" advised the contemporary Virginia historian Hugh Blair Grigsby, after learning about what he assumed was an attack on U.S. filibustering in a private letter that the English writer Thomas B. Macaulay had sent to one of Grigsby's correspondents. Similarly, a New York paper identified Robert Clive—the eighteenth-century British conqueror in India—as a filibuster, a Philadelphia sheet bore the headline "BRITISH FILIBUSTERING AND ANNEXATION IN EAST INDIA," and the North Carolinian Thomas L. Clingman cited the British East India Company's "fillibustering operations" in one well-publicized congressional speech. How could the English call the López expeditions piracy, wondered one Southerner, "forgetting their own beautiful career in India"? Not surprisingly, when Indian natives rose up in the anti-colonial Sepoy Rebellion of 1857, George Mifflin Dallas had no doubt that Hindus had taken on "English fillibusters."[8]

Not only did American apologists find comfort in British precedents in India, but they frequently argued that the doings of English adventurers in the subcontinent dwarfed in scope anything that their American counterparts had attempted in the Western Hemisphere. The British, as the *Philadelphia Public Ledger* put it, were "engaged in a species of filibustering and conquest in India which exceeds the wildest dreams of manifest destiny in this country." Similarly, Secretary of State William L. Marcy deflected British protests of U.S. recognition of William Walker's régime in Nicaragua by noting Britain's recent absorption of the Indian kingdom of Oudh—a region "ten times as large" as Nicaragua. American commentators, moreover, sometimes argued that U.S. filibusters had at least pretenses to legitimacy, because they generally invaded foreign domains after being invited to do so by rebels within them—something that could not be said for British conquerors in India.[9]

But were American rebuttals accurate? Did filibustering really have a global history stretching backward into the distant past? Perhaps Americans misconstrued what occurred in other places and eras in order to validate their own bizarre behavior. After all, a number of historians have defined filibustering as a "uniquely American phenomenon."[10]

SURELY AMERICAN apologists got things wrong regarding the British record in India. Robert Clive and other British conquerors carried out their aggressions as officers of the East India Company, a concern chartered by the Queen of England in 1600. Rather than repudiate or rebuke the company for its military campaigns, the British government supported the company with troops, and, in the India Act of 1784, imposed a Board of Control, appointed by the Crown, to supervise the East India Company's directors in London. After the Sepoy Mutiny, Queen Victoria, by means of a proclamation issued in India on November 1, 1858, supplanted the company's ruling governor general with a viceroy responsible to the monarchy. Clearly, the East India Company's conquests fail our definition of filibustering expeditions: they were hardly the doings of private adventurers acting without their government's consent.[11]

American apologists also jumbled their facts respecting Christopher Columbus, who could never have undertaken his trans-Atlantic crossing in 1492 without the support of the Spanish monarchs, Isabella of Castile and Ferdinand of Aragon. The queen and king underwrote most of Columbus's costs, supplied him with two of his ships, conferred on him a royal title ("Admiral of the Ocean Sea"), and formally contracted with him concerning his rights to minerals, spices, and other items in lands that he discovered or conquered in their names. Likewise, it was absurd to accuse Russia's czar of filibustering in the Crimea: the czar hardly qualified as a private adventurer.[12]

Americans may even have erred by including James Brooke (1803–68) in their assortment of international filibusters. This soldier of fortune, who managed to gain control of a large chunk of Borneo, seems to fit the filibuster mold. But did he really filibuster?

After resigning his commission in the East India Company's Bengal Army, Brooke expended his inheritance on a 142-ton vessel and sailed with a crew of nineteen men from London for the Far East in December 1838. In August of the next year, he appeared in the province of Sarawak in northwestern Borneo—part of the domains of one of Borneo's rulers, the Sultan of Brunei. Brooke entertained vague designs of extending British influence in Borneo at the expense of the Dutch. But he did not proceed there surreptitiously (his voyage had the blessing of the British governor of Singapore), nor did he truly invade Borneo. Rather, some time after his initial arrival, Brooke began to serve the province's constituted authorities in a military capacity and assisted them in putting down insurrections. In return for these services, Brooke in September 1841 was named rajah and governor of Sarawak by Prince Muda Hasim—the sultan's designated successor. Brooke subsequently established a dynasty that ruled Sarawak for a century and gradually extended its boundaries.[13]

We surely can credit Brooke, who inspired Rudyard Kipling's story "The Man Who Would Be King," with an American kind of filibustering spirit. At least he so impressed Laurence Oliphant, a fellow product of the British empire. During a visit to the United States in late 1856, Oliphant, the son of the chief justice for Britain's colony of Ceylon, received a free ticket to Nicaragua from Pierre Soulé, former U.S. senator and minister to Spain, who hoped that Oliphant could be won over to Walker's cause and that he would then influence British policy on behalf of the filibusters. Oliphant made the journey that winter, in company with some of Walker's recruits. On returning to England, he informed curious inquirers that the famous American filibuster struck him as "the same sort of fellow as Sir J. Brooke."[14] Whether Brooke actually filibustered, however, is another matter.

Yet for all such instances of mistaken identity, U.S. apologists were fundamentally right: other peoples than Americans filibustered, and they would continue to do so long after William Walker's death.[15] Some of these non-American filibusters, to be sure, used U.S. soil as a staging ground for their escapades, and thus, in a way, were part of America's filibustering story. The French adventurer Count Gaston de Raousset-Boulbon, for instance, in 1852–53 and again in 1854 led hundreds of Frenchmen resident in California on expeditions into Mexican Sonora. In the spring of 1859, the Cuban exile José Elías Hernández launched an unsuccessful expedition, apparently consisting only of fellow refugees, from New York City to liberate his homeland.[16] However, many non-American expeditions left sovereignties other than the United States.

One example is the Greek native and Russian general Alexander Ypsilantis (1792–1828), who in 1821 filibustered to liberate Greek and Balkan peoples from Ottoman rule. Ypsilantis, while organizing his campaign in Bessarabia, implied that he had Czar Alexander I's endorsement and promise of assistance. However, his crossing into the Danubian principality of Moldavia qualifies as a filibuster, since Alexander never made good on Ypsilantis's claim that troop reinforcements would be forthcoming from Russia, and since the Russian foreign ministry immediately disavowed Ypsilantis's invasion in an official dispatch. Certainly the liberator's fate matched that of many U.S. filibusters. After his defeat in battle with Ottoman troops, Ypsilantis fled to Transylvania, where he was put under arrest and then incarcerated by Austrian authorities.[17]

Less than two decades after Ypsilantis's failure, South America produced one of the nineteenth century's premier filibusters: Juan José Flores, Ecuador's first president, who served several terms before fleeing in 1845 during an insurrection against his rule. Traveling to Europe, Flores promised high pay, land, and livestock to 2,000 men recruited in Spain, Ireland, France, and the Canary Islands for an expedition to reconquer Ecuador and, apparently, install a European prince as its monarch. Flores benefited at first from complicity by the Spanish government and tolerance from the British government. However, leaks of information and consequent unfavorable publicity helped bring down the Spanish government, and caused British officials in late 1846 to seize Flores's ships and press charges against the expedition's leaders for violating the Foreign Enlistments Act (Britain's version of the U.S. Neutrality Laws). Flores had to abort his scheme, but he continued his filibustering intrigues for about a decade. In 1852 Flores used Peru as a base for an unsuccessful invasion of Ecuador involving six vessels and hundreds of men.[18]

William Walker's Sardinian contemporary Giuseppe Maria Garibaldi best conforms to the model of a nineteenth-century, non-American filibuster, even though he waged some of his campaigns for Italian unification in the name of King Victor Emanuel II of Sardinia (and later of Italy) and held various commissions in the Sardinian army. Garibaldi's invasion of Sicily in May 1860 occurred after his removal as commander of Sardinia's army of Central Italy, and thus constituted filibustering, as did his dispatching of some sixty volunteers from the Sicilian expedition on a diversionary invasion of the Papal States. Although some documents suggest that the Sardinian prime minister Camillo Benso di Cavour and Victor Emanuel privately encouraged Garibaldi's irregular campaigns at various times, the fact is that Cavour reacted to Garibaldi's Sicilian expedition by ordering his arrest. The hundred or so Garibaldini who in May 1862 mounted an expedition to the Austrian province of Tyrol likewise filibustered. In 1862 Garibaldi was wounded and captured during a filibuster to Rome, undertaken in defiance of a proclamation by Victor Emanuel, now king of Italy. Twice in 1867, Garibaldi suffered

arrests for involvement in unauthorized expeditions. No wonder that the perennial U.S. filibuster Chatham Roberdeau Wheat, a veteran of private campaigns in Cuba, Mexico, and Nicaragua, departed for Europe in September
1860, the month that William Walker died, to join Garibaldi. As King Leo-
pold I of Belgium explained to Queen Victoria, Garibaldi and Walker were
two of a kind.[19]

Later in the century, the activist daughter of a Japanese samurai joined fellow adventurers in Nagasaki for an intended expedition to Korea, and British
filibusters helped lay the groundwork for the Boer War. Japanese authorities
crushed the 1885 "Ōsaka Incident" before Fukuda Hideko and her associates
could get off, partly, according to Fukuda, because her male comrades daw-
dled too long with geishas at brothels. But in December 1895, Leander Starr
Jameson, the doctor of Cecil Rhodes, prime minister of Britain's Cape Colony
in Africa, commanded five hundred men in an invasion of the Boer republic
of the Transvaal. After their defeat in battle by Paul Kruger's Boer forces,
Jameson and other captured filibusters were turned over to British authorities
for punishment. In a sentence handed down in London, Jameson received a
fifteen-month incarceration for his illegal expedition and his followers were
given shorter terms. Needless to say, the incident strained relations between
British colonists and Boers in southern Africa.[20]

Americans, therefore, never monopolized filibustering's ranks. Foreign critics erred when they insinuated that such expeditions only originated in the
United States. American apologists sometimes applied the term filibustering
too casually in their haste to implicate others in the practice, but they could
muster evidence for their case.

BUT SHOULD THE matter of comparative filibustering be put to rest without
addressing matters of degree? The consistency by which Americans engaged
in filibustering, the vigor with which they did it, and the extent to which filibustering infiltrated American popular culture may be the crux of the matter, rather than the shared culpability of different nations. So common were
reports of expeditions in pre–Civil War America that some observers jumped
to the conclusion that filibustering represented, as a Connecticut paper put it,
"a new trait" in the "national character." Along similar lines, a cynic suggested in *Harper's Weekly* that filibustering had become "one of the most ami-
able virtues of our beloved fellow-countrymen," and a U.S. army lieutenant
complained about a "filibustering spirit that has run wild in this country."[21]

If indeed an idiosyncratic "filibustering spirit" distinguished the pre–Civil

War United States from other countries, it was to no small degree unleashed by the American press, and became most apparent while expeditions were actually afoot and in their immediate aftermath. Such an instance occurred in the last days of August and the first days of September 1851, during Narciso López's final expedition to Cuba, especially after news arrived in the United States that fifty of the invaders had been executed by Spanish authorities in Cuba and later that the entire expedition had been crushed and López executed.

American newspaper editors, regardless of their political persuasions and whether or not they supported filibustering, ran with this sensational story. The four-page *Washington Daily National Intelligencer* on August 25 totally surrendered to Cuban news: all six columns on page 2 dealt entirely with López's expeditions, and page 3 included eight short articles on the filibusters (the newspaper's only other pages were exclusively devoted to advertisements). Readers of the *Richmond* (Ind.) *Palladium* of September 3, to give another example, encountered only slightly more modest coverage: eight different articles and reprinted editorials on the expedition appeared in that day's issue under the heading "CUBAN WAR." Many papers gave the story sustained attention for weeks.[22]

Aroused by this media overkill, protesters throughout the country convened "indignation" meetings to denounce what many people deemed Spanish butchery, and in some instances to consider raising volunteers to avenge the dead invaders. President Millard Fillmore, who strongly opposed filibustering, believed that the agitation (which included attacks on Spanish property in the United States) was infecting every large American city. Fillmore complained bitterly about the ability of "a mercenary and prostituted press," abetted by "designing" telegraph operators, to incite such support for an illegal cause.[23]

A reporter in Pittsburgh considered the city's protest meeting the largest popular gathering in its history. In Philadelphia, where an estimated 15,000 people turned out for a similar affair, an observer exclaimed that people had gone "mad" over the incident. In New York, according to an out-of-town reporter, the "massacre" dominated conversation "at the table, in the reading-room . . . and in the counting-house." At Savannah, demonstrators raised the filibusters' Cuban revolutionary flag on the cupola of the Exchange, fired off artillery, exploded firecrackers, and illuminated the city with candles in honor of López and his fallen comrades.[24]

Similar events occurred between December 1857 and February 1858, after news arrived that William Walker had invaded Nicaragua for the second time, and then that the U.S. naval commodore Hiram Paulding had broken up the expedition by surrounding Walker's encampment on Nicaragua's coast and forcing the filibusters to return to the United States. For some time, Paulding's arrest of Walker reigned as the nation's number one news story, as editors debated the legality and propriety of Paulding's intercession. Not only did daily papers throughout the country run articles about the incident, but so did weeklies such as *Frank Leslie's Illustrated Newspaper* and even some religious publications. As late as February 9, Josiah Gorgas, commanding the U.S. arsenal at Augusta, Maine, judged the affair one of the three most reported subjects in the press.[25]

Given the lack of public opinion polling in those days, there is no way to accurately measure the extent to which the incident concerned ordinary American people. Surely the *Louisville Daily Courier* exaggerated by claiming that Walker had become the "theme of conversation" not only among men and women but even among children. Still, the matter surfaced frequently enough in the private correspondence of politicians to substantiate the primary point made by the *Courier*: that few living men then occupied "the public mind" as much as Walker. Several state legislatures and both houses of Congress debated resolutions about Paulding's intervention. A traveler passing through the nation's capital at the time explained that "Filibusterism in Central America" had joined Kansas affairs as one of the two "exciting" issues before Congress, an impression confirmed by many other observers in Washington. The correspondent of the *New-York Christian Inquirer* went so far as to claim that the Walker and Paulding matter had thrown "completely into the shade" the Kansas and Mormon questions that had previously been the hot topics before Congress.[26]

But one should not make so much of what might be termed filibuster "crises" as to obscure the sustained attention that filibustering received from American journalists before the Civil War. Throughout these years, American newspapers provided intensive coverage of filibustering escapades, both arousing and feeding off public interest in the adventurers. Thus, shortly after the steamer *Goliah* arrived in San Francisco in December 1853 with accounts of William Walker's invasion of Mexico, newsboys took to the streets crying "Herald! the Extra Herald!—with full particulars of the revolution!" Several days afterward, the San Francisco sheet drew its readers' attention to the availability of a "neat map" of Walker's "NEW REPUBLIC," as part of its continuing coverage. The St. Louis merchant who complained in a June 1854 business letter that his papers, regardless of their place of publication, seemed filled with "Gas" about filibustering might have expressed the same kind of frustration during many other months in the 1850s.[27]

Newspapers and magazines covered virtually all the expeditions and plots, but they especially competed to satiate public curiosity about America's most notorious filibuster, publishing innumerable accounts of William Walker's doings (often introduced by capitalized, large-font headlines ending in exclamation points), as well as his likenesses and biographical sketches. Thus *Harper's Weekly* ran a feature in May 1857 about "THE NICARAGUAN LEADERS," offering portraits and biographies of Walker and several of his fellow officers whose identities were already "familiar to every one." The next month, a California paper noted the appearance of the *San Francisco Pictorial Magazine*, which in its first number had "a likeness of Gen. Walker" as well as several illustrations of Nicaragua's San Juan River. In the first half of 1856 alone the *Springfield* (Mass.) *Daily Republican* printed a sequence of pieces and editorials about Walker's regime in Nicaragua under such headings as "Progress of the Filibusters," "The Filibusters in Nicaragua," "The Filibusters getting into Difficulty," and "Filibuster Matters." And in the following summer, the front pages of the *Columbus* (Ohio) *Gazette*, the *Fayette* (Miss.) *Watch Tower*, and other papers contained accounts of Walker's inauguration as president of Nicaragua and the text of his inaugural address. It should be little wonder that during Walker's sojourn in New York City after his expulsion from Central America, autograph seekers besought him "at every turn" seeking his signature. America's mass media had converted Walker into one of the day's most salient public personalities.[28]

During Walker's tenure in Central America, several papers assigned correspondents to accompany the expeditionists, or later arranged for correspondents to report from filibuster domains. One journalist explained to his sheet that "a number of reporters of the different papers in New Orleans" had accompanied him aboard ship to Nicaragua, and that since arriving he had observed a correspondent of the *New York Tribune* thrown from a mule when riding near Masaya. During his final foray, Walker left behind at Trujillo, Honduras, a correspondent from the *New York Herald* who had thus far accompanied his expedition.

Those papers with their own correspondents on the scene naturally boasted about their superior coverage; thus the *New Orleans Daily Picayune* proudly highlighted letters from "'C. C.,' our intelligent and very reliable correspondent" in Walker's domain. Few such correspondents, however, would pass as objective journalists in the modern sense: many were themselves filibuster soldiers or had other kinds of vested interests in the expeditions. "W. S. T." of the *New York Evening Post*, who sent letter after letter from Henry L. Kinney's expedition to Central America, was none other than the *Post* staff member William Sidney Thayer—who served as secretary in Kinney's government. Michael Flood Nagle left for Nicaragua in September 1856 both to join Walker's army and as a correspondent for the immigrant paper *Meagher's Irish News*.[29]

Part of filibustering's "gas" in the press consisted of second-rate poetry, occasionally in the form of verses within the New Year's addresses to subscribers (sometimes called "carrier's" addresses) that were a feature in some papers at the time. The Carrier's Address for 1855 in the *Texas State Gazette* (Austin) claimed that thousands of filibuster volunteers would have invaded Cuba during the previous year, had it not been for President Franklin Pierce's invoking the Neutrality Law against them:

> Ten thousand soldiers in a moment rise,
> To drive the harlot [Spain] from her Cuban prize;
> But the high law which we ourselves had made,
> Reluctant stopped them and the act forbade;
> They pause in their sorrow for a better day,
> And curb their hearts to suffer and obey.

More didactically, a Louisville sheet, after Walker's first expulsion from Central America, chided the hypocrisy of Americans who would have embraced Walker had he conquered Nicaragua, but who had shunned his cause once he became a loser:

> We play the part of the Roman populace—
>   Applauding only where success attends
>   The effort of our heroes, or our friends—
> We crown with bays the winner of the race,
> And on the vanquished turn an *icy face*!
>   Though his, indeed, may be the nobler soul
>   Who struggles on, yet reaches not the goal.
> Should Walker win the realm and wear the crown.
> The welkin world would ring with his renown—
> Though his might only be the pride of place—
>   But with a spirit nothing seems to daunt—
>   Comforting calumny, desertion want,
>   A pestilent climate, and the terrible taunt
> *Of brothers*! we consign him to disgrace![30]

Newspapers notified readers about upcoming events that concerned filibustering, as when a San Francisco sheet in October 1855 specified that the next meeting of the city's lyceum would argue "Whether or not Walker's invasion of Nicaragua is justifiable." More importantly, the press provided a means for filibusters to communicate directly with the public through "cards" (generally paragraph-long statements that today we might label press releases) and other announcements —a most invaluable service in a pre-electronic age. Thus the *New York Evening Post* in May 1855 published Henry L. Kinney's card along with instructions on how readers might sign up for Kinney's enterprise. The next year, the *Cincinnati Daily Enquirer* announced the schedule for lectures about Nicaraguan affairs by Parker H. French, Walker's former appointee as minister to the United States. Many newspapers, in fact, printed material that in one way or another assisted Walker's cause, such as this notification in the *Vicksburg Daily Whig*:

> For Nicaragua!
> A COMPANY OF EMIGRANTS will leave
> Vicksburg, between now and the first of June,
> FOR NICARAGUA. All those wishing
> to join said Company will apply to R. J. McGinty.

Subscribers to the *New Orleans Daily Creole* discovered where they might purchase 6-percent bonds or land scrip in support of Walker's movement.[31]

Not only did the filibusters utilize the press, but the adventurers were manipulated by the press in turn. Merchants capitalized on the filibusters' notoriety as a way of drawing the public's attention to their advertisements. The owners of Yerby's dry goods store in Washington spotlighted their merchandise by comparing the customers rushing to buy their summer stock at low prices to the speed of López filibusters fleeing Cuba. Similarly, Eshelby's in Cincinnati suggested that Cuban expeditionists had undoubtedly purchased their boots and shoes from their store. A saloon in San Francisco in February 1854 promoted its room and board arrangements by alluding to William Walker's apparent conquest of Sonora. A merchant in Tampa, Florida, in 1856 suggested that while people were celebrating Walker's success in Nicaragua, they should stick with the muslins, calico, ginghams, and groceries that they were accustomed to buying at W. G. Ferris & Son. More imaginatively, a pill company in New York the next year claimed that Walker would have permanently conquered Nicaragua, had his men only protected themselves from tropical diseases by taking Brandreth's pills![32]

Such advertisements attest to filibustering's niche in the urban popular culture of antebellum America, as do the titles of several pre–Civil War U.S. theatrical productions. In 1850 the Chesnut Street theater in Philadelphia staged the "Invasion of Cuba," about Narciso López's recent campaign. Dan Rice's

Amphitheatre in New Orleans, four years later, ran a local playwright's burlesque, "Those 15,000 Fillibusters! Or, The Fairy Light Guard," mocking the
former Mexican War general John A. Quitman for deferring his filibuster to
Cuba until additional funding was secured: the playbill listed its chief character as "General * * *, Commander-in-Chief of the 15,000 provided they
raise the *Dimes*." In the summer of 1856, actors at Purdy's National Theatre
in New York performed the three-act "Nicaragua, or, Gen. Walker's Victories," and the San Francisco Minstrel Company reportedly amused onlookers
with "Nicaraguan State Secrets." After Walker's expulsion from Nicaragua
the next year, theaters in Sacramento and San Francisco ran the "Siege of
Granada" about a climactic moment in Walker's failing tenure in Central
America. This play featured the New York actor C. E. Bingham—who had
been literally on scene during the event depicted in the play, after traveling to
Nicaragua in a quest for a land grant from the filibuster chief. In December
1858, a theater in Mobile, Alabama, offered "Where's Our Susan," a farce
about how Walker's ship *Susan* had recently evaded port authorities and put
out to sea. The very next month, the St. Charles Theatre in New Orleans
staged "The Filibuster, or Adventures in Cuba."[33]

On occasion, theaters transcended their role of representing the filibustering experience and themselves became a part of it. During the López excitement of August and September 1851, one theater in New Orleans dedicated a
performance to "the benefit of the Cuban cause," presumably an indication
that its managers intended to apply ticket revenues to help additional filibusters set out for Cuba. When William Walker turned up in New York City
in June 1857 after his first expulsion from Nicaragua, he received an invitation by the Bowery Theatre's managers to attend their establishment. As
Walker and some of his aides entered to the screams of a cheering throng and
advanced to the front box that had been draped with American flags and reserved for them, the orchestra struck up "Hail Columbia" and "The Star
Spangled Banner" in his honor. Responding to shouts from the crowd for a
speech, Walker rose and told the audience that his movement served the glory
of the American people. Walker apparently thought his appearance beneficial.
A few days later, he announced his intentions to attend productions at other
New York theaters.[34]

Similarly, American authors responded to filibustering as both insiders and
observers. Nathaniel Hawthorne hobnobbed with John L. O'Sullivan just
after O'Sullivan's arrest, as Hawthorne's wife noted, for Cuban filibustering.
A few years later, Hawthorne applauded President Franklin Pierce's official
recognition of Walker's regime in Nicaragua. The famous urban fiction au-

"Those 15,000 Fillibusters!" Ad for a burlesque at Dan Rice's Ampitheatre, New Orleans. (Courtesy of the Southern Filibusters Collection, Louisiana and Lower Mississippi Valley Collections, LSU Libraries, Louisiana State University, Baton Rouge)

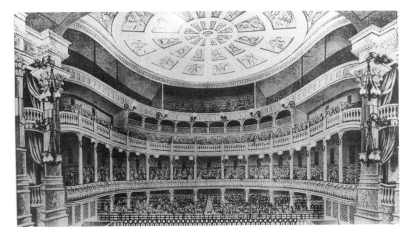

Interior of St. Charles Theatre in New Orleans, 1855. Three years later this theater became the setting for a play about Cuba filibustering. (Courtesy of the Special Collections, Tulane University Library, New Orleans, La.)

thor and magazine editor Ned Buntline (alias for Edward Z. C. Judson) not only gave a public oration about Cuba filibusters and apparently raised funds on their behalf, but he also produced a tale of deceit about them. In *The Mysteries and Miseries of New Orleans*, a woman avenges her husband's killing of her seducer by causing the defeat of Narciso López's final expedition. After learning that her husband has been acquitted by a jury and become an advance agent for López's landing, Buntline's avenger tips off Cuba's captain general, forges a letter that causes the filibusters to land in a locale where they can be quickly crushed, and arranges a separate, private execution for her husband so that she can personally explain her revenge in excruciating detail as he succumbs to the garrote. At least one prominent author gained his filibustering knowledge more intimately. Charles W. Webber, a novelist and short story writer whose work was sometimes compared by contemporaries to that of Herman Melville, died at Rivas, Nicaragua, fighting in Walker's army.[35]

During these same years, publishers, newspapers, and booksellers throughout the United States heralded the appearance of books and pamphlets about filibustering. DeWitt and Davenport used bold lettering to notify readers of the *New-York Daily Tribune* that *The Life of Gen. Narcisso Lopez*, "by a Flibustiero," would be "READY ON WEDNESDAY MORNING." The *Daily Alta California* (San Francisco), on another occasion, announced receiving from a publisher a history of the French count Gaston de Raousset-Boulbon's foray to Sonora. The paper predicted that this "interesting" work would provide a valuable reference tool for future time, when Raousset's "sad tale" would be "told around the winter firesides." A Philadelphia paper described *The Destiny of Nicaragua*, by one of William Walker's officers, as "a most entertaining Pamphlet," and noted that it was "everywhere for sale." Although a review in the *Washington Constitution* of Walker's memoirs *The War in Nicaragua* (1860) called the work inferior to Julius Caesar's "Commentaries," it nonetheless conceded that the filibuster's "long expected volume" held enough interest for people to seek it eagerly at Franck Taylor's bookstore.[36]

Filibustering intruded on popular culture in other ways. Artists and photographers produced portraits of filibustering celebrities, such as the famous daguerreotyper Mathew B. Brady, who persuaded William Walker to sit for a photograph. Songwriters composed tunes about filibustering, such as "The Filibuster Polka," a three-page piece of sheet music published in 1852 by a Baltimore music dealer. Presumably some pianists played "Nicarauga [*sic*] National Song," a piece published in Louisville that celebrated Kentucky's "legion" fighting for Walker's "glorious cause." In 1856 promoters of John C. Frémont, the Republican Party's presidential candidate, peddled two campaign songs to the tune of "Old Dan Tucker" that integrated antifilibustering themes. The last verse of "John Fremont's Coming" promised that Frémont would sweep all filibusters aside once he was in office. The sixth verse of "Get out of the way, old Buchanan" maintained that the Democratic candidate, James Buchanan, was undeserving of votes, because he would support William Walker's cause in Nicaragua.[37]

Antebellum Americans sometimes held memorial masses and torchlight processions for deceased expeditionists. On the first two anniversaries of the deaths of Henry Crabb and his companions in Sonora, for instance, residents of San Francisco held requiems "for the repose of their souls." St. Patrick's Cathedral in New York City provided the setting for a Mass in remembrance of Narciso López, and filibustering enthusiasts in New Orleans commemorated the anniversary of his death with a two-hour torchlight procession as well as oratory in Lafayette Square. According to one press account, masses of people crowded the streets and ladies filled overlooking windows and balconies, as the New Orleans procession passed by.[38]

More frequently, Americans participated in balls, serenades, parades, rallies, and welcoming ceremonies in honor of filibusters. In December 1856, toward the end of Walker's tenure in Nicaragua, a crowd of New Yorkers passed beneath a transparency inscribed "ENLARGE THE BOUNDS OF FREEDOM" to enter a rally to raise money for his cause. Months later, at the very time that newsmen were engaged in an interview with the defeated filibuster in a New York hotel room,

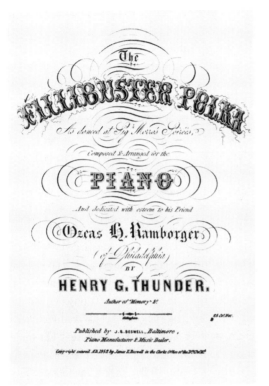

"The Fillibuster Polka."
(Courtesy of the Music Division, Library of Congress)

a fine military band was heard in Broadway, and we noticed that he instantly became restless, and after a moment's hesitation, he went to the window to learn the cause. Fortunately for the good fame of the citizen soldiery of our country, the ever to be honored National Guard was in solid columns, making the hard pavements echo with their manly tread. The morning was stormy, and the rain was descending in torrents, but these veterans among our local military moved with undaunted front, and coming opposite the hotel, the regiment halted, formed a line, and came to a rest. "I wish, General," said one of the gentlemen present, "that this regiment was going with you back to Nicaragua." The "model filibuster" smiled significantly at the suggestion.

Walker arrived at Mobile harbor in January 1858, after his failed second expedition to Nicaragua, to a cannon salute in his honor. Not only did an "immense concourse" assemble to watch his coming ashore, but later in the day an even larger crowd gathered before his hotel, demanding that the filibuster address them with cries of "Walker! Walker!" That summer, Walker's supporters in Atlanta spent days barbecuing pigs, sheep, goats, and cattle in preparation for a feast to celebrate Walker's visit to that town.[39]

Such displays naturally disgusted antifilibustering Americans, who condemned them as virtual endorsements of outlawry. "While I write," U.S. Representative John Letcher of Virginia complained from Washington in 1858, "the music is heard in compliment to the Fillibuster Walker, who is staying at this House. I look upon him as no better than a Pirate." But it was difficult to suppress demonstrations by filibuster enthusiasts in a nation that permitted freedom of speech and assembly. A newspaper in Stockton, California, noted in January 1854 that a "terrible fracas" erupted when local police tried to break up the meeting of a "secret Filibustering Society" at a saloon.[40]

Americans even swarmed onto docks to cheer filibusters in the very act of setting out on their illegal expeditions. One of Narciso López's officers recalled in a post-mortem about the 1850 expedition that a large crowd had given López's Kentucky volunteers three cheers as their boat left its pier near New Orleans. This scene played out over and over again in subsequent years. "Great numbers of citizens crowded the landing," a reporter observed about an 1856 filibuster exodus, before noting how the onlookers waved handkerchiefs and hats as the adventurers' steamer faded into the distance. "The multitude . . . were on the *qui vive* for the fillibusters," the *New-York Times* noted in 1859, "and long before the Northern Light left her dock at the foot of Warren-street, there was a large crowd collected, anxious to witness the departure of these illustrious individuals. . . ." One gets the sense, from this reporter's comments about onlookers being "curious to see the fillibusters," that more persons than merely the adventurers' accomplices participated in these rituals. Apparently, filibustering represented a warped form of spectator sport for America's urban population.[41]

From similarly voyeuristic impulses, Americans jammed into federal courtrooms when filibusters went on trial. Correspondents covering their cases constantly resorted to phrases such as "throngs," "packed," "densely crowded," "large concourse of citizens," and "numerous crowd of spectators" to describe the many onlookers who turned up to get a glimpse of the filibusters and find out whether they were going to jail.[42]

Filibustering even made its appearance in American higher academic life, as is evidenced in the minutes and other files of antebellum collegiate debating societies. Thus John Washington Graham's senior oration before the Dialectic Society of the University of North Carolina in 1856 touched on such matters as the contribution of the "Minnie Rifle" to William Walker's conquest of Nicaragua, and how Nicaragua would prosper commercially once

Walker solidified his hold on the country. Debating societies at institutions as diverse as Western Reserve College in Ohio and Brown University, as well as the University of North Carolina, addressed such questions as: "Should the U.S. interfere with the Walker expedition in Central America?"; "Is President Taylor justified in taking measures to prevent the invasion of Cuba by our citizens?"; "Was the execution of the fifty Americans at Havana justifiable[?]"; "Would the U. States have been justifiable in assisting the Filibusters of Nicaragua?"; "Should we or should we not condemn the course of Gen. Wm. Walker in Central America. . . ?"; and "Were the Hondurans justifiable in killing Genl. Walker?"[43]

Occasionally, filibustering affected collegiate life more directly. Whether filibusters attempted to recruit at American colleges remains unclear, but it is evident that some American students kept up on the adventurers and fantasized about joining them. Henry Wadsworth Longfellow in 1853 encountered some "youths" from a nearby Kentucky institution whom he described as bright but nonetheless "inclined to filibustering in Cuba." In 1857 a student at the University of Missouri ruminated about going to the "Walker State" in time for a rumored invasion of Cuba from Nicaragua, but worried that his frail constitution would not withstand the rigors of a military campaign.[44]

Most college students of such inclinations managed to keep their impulses in check. A few, however, capitulated. "I simply gave up to the spirit of the times," recalled Asbury Harpending in his published reminiscences. Harpending claimed that he "ran away from college to join an aggregation of young gentlemen but little older than myself, who enlisted under the banner of General Walker, the filibuster," but never made it out of the country because his party was intercepted and forced to disperse. On September 9, 1851, at the time of López's final expedition, Charles C. Jones Jr., attending Princeton, mentioned a student who that very morning had left for Mississippi, showing a "disposition to join in the Cuban expedition." Three years later, John Quitman received letters from students at VMI and the University of Mississippi with aspirations of being included in any upcoming movement on Cuba.[45]

Perhaps the most telling testimony to filibustering's infiltration of antebellum American culture is its impact on language. Americans exposed filibustering's hold on their subconscious thoughts when they corrupted the term into a catchall for any kind of American territorial expansion, and when they applied it to behavior that had nothing to do with foreign countries. There was a rough logic to some of these mutations, as when the *Springfield* (Mass.) *Republican* alluded to "Missouri Filibusters in Kanzas" [*sic*] and when the

New-York Tribune denounced the "Kansas filibusters" of the Alabamian Jefferson Buford: Southerners hoping to make Kansas into a slave state after the Kansas-Nebraska Act of 1854 did invade the territory as members of armed companies. At other times, such usages had nothing to do with either foreign domains or military invasions.[46]

Often, however, Americans seized on the term *filibustering* to connote whatever type of political behavior they deemed aggressive and offensive, paving the way for later usage of the word as legislative obstructionism. The *Harrisburg* (Pa.) *Morning Herald*, an American Party newspaper, repeatedly used the term to damn local Whig politicos who insisted on nominating their own candidate for office rather than joining the Americans in common battle against the Democrats. The famed Texas Ranger and U.S. marshal Ben McCulloch called southern secessionists "ultra Filabusturs" [*sic*]. The Northern abolitionist Henry W. Bellows stigmatized proslavery southern editors as "moral fillibusters." When Mayor Fernando Wood of New York led a state delegation to the Democratic national nominating convention of 1860 that was denied recognition, the *New-York Times* mocked his "fillibustering expedition to Charleston."[47]

But one need not restrict filibustering to political behavior. Commercial activity abroad also merited consideration as filibustering. Secretary of State Daniel Webster believed, for instance, that U.S. fishermen who illegally penetrated Canadian territorial waters engaged in filibustering, and a Boston weekly described a railroad conductor who set sail for Chile to establish a stagecoach line there as entering into "HONEST FILLIBUSTERISM." However, any kind of human activity might qualify, as when "filibustering Yankees" swallowed their turkey meat. But need the activity even be human? Was not a bald eagle daring enough to attack a drake "A FEATHERED FILLIBUSTER"?[48]

IN THE END, we must concede that America's foreign critics were correct: the United States, in the years following the Mexican War, deserved its reputation of being, as one British diplomat put it, a land of "Fillibustero-ism." The vast majority of Americans neither filibustered themselves nor even supported filibustering. Yet filibustering appears to have penetrated daily life in the United States more persistently than anywhere else in the world. Anyone in America, even a slave, might be drawn into filibustering's orbit. After escaping bondage, William Craft recalled the time that he had heard a slave trader address "a great Filibustering meeting." Many Americans, moreover, had their own passing encounters with the adventurers. Engaging a fellow traveler in casual conversation, a passenger on a Mississippi River steamboat in 1854, for instance, discovered that his new acquaintance had already been on one filibuster to Cuba, and was at that very moment on his way to participate in another.[49]

Masses of pre–Civil War Americans found themselves engrossed with the filibusters, if only in awe of their brashness and daring, and followed press accounts of the expeditions much like modern Americans who follow developing news stories on television. The former Kansas territorial legislator Henry Miles Moore, for instance, wrote in his diary after "news" arrived of Walker's execution, "Thus ends the life of this great Filibuster This Grey eyed man of destiny as he has been so often called." Revealingly, even persons opposed to filibustering sometimes demonstrated a vulnerability to its allure. Merely days after denouncing people who filibustered, an editor in Little Rock, Arkansas, in a sudden turnaround, noted that an upriver acquaintance had just dropped by while on his way to invade Cuba, and toasted: "We glory in his spunk, and wish him success in his undertakings." More shockingly, Frederick Douglass, a man with every reason to hate William Walker for having reestablished slavery in Nicaragua during his tenure there, nonetheless on the eve of the Civil War could not resist using him as a model. Should the southern states dissolve the Union, Douglass predicted, "men could be found at least as brave as Walker, and more skillful than any other filibuster, who would venture into those States and raise [among the slaves] the standard of liberty."[50]

Pre–Civil War Americans, it would appear, itched often at what the *New-York Times* called their country's "great fillibustering flea."[51] The trick is not deciding what mid-nineteenth-century country produced the most filibustering, but rather, what drove Americans to do it.

CHAPTER FOUR

John Goddard's Lesson

O Cuba is the land for me,
I'm bound to make some money there!
And set the Cubans free—!
—Chorus to Filibustering song, 1850
(quoted in [J. C. Davis], *History of the Late Expedition to Cuba*

WASHINGTON'S police chief wasted little time before beginning his filibustering education. On June 11, 1850, John H. Goddard left the nation's capital on secret assignment from the Interior (or "Home") Department: he was to proceed to the Deep South, and there assist U.S. district attorneys who were trying to collect evidence to prosecute participants in Narciso López's invasion of Cuba the previous month.

On arriving in Charleston on the 13th, Goddard immediately joined an excursion up the Ashley River, and before the day ended he met a steamboat captain who admitted providing some of the filibusters with free transportation to Charleston after their return from Cuba. Over the next few weeks, Goddard made contact with a number of participants in the landing at Cárdenas. Apparently, neither the captain nor the invaders suspected Goddard's identity. All spoke candidly about their attitudes regarding filibustering as well as their recent experiences.

The captain, who claimed to have commanded a vessel in Mexican waters during the recent war, unequivocally endorsed the filibusters' cause. In fact, he was prepared "at any time to take a hand and use his boat to transport the men" should they try to invade Cuba again. The invaders, who seemed youthful to Goddard, identified their occupations before enlisting with López, and indicated that they expected to be involved as well in his next attempt on the island. One had been a Cincinnati theater's "property man," another was a barber, two were blacksmiths, and one was a steamboat engineer on the western rivers. Several were mechanics. Although some of the filibusters professed patriotic reasons for their behavior, virtually all of them, once plied with alcohol, confessed more mercenary priorities. They had been attracted primarily, it turned out, to López's offer of $7 monthly salaries, bonuses, and positions in the liberation government. Still, the men believed that their undertaking had been respectable. After all, the heroic Mexican War general

John A. Quitman and other "first men" in the country were sustaining the cause.[1]

Goddard's interviews, with all their socioeconomic undertones, point us to an intriguing puzzle. What drove American men to join filibustering expeditions? Did a shared ideology of some kind inspire them? Or was Goddard right when he disparaged these adventurers as merely "persons of desperate habbits [sic] and reckless dispositions, whose entire aim seemed to be plunder or gain of money"?

IN AUGUST 1849 a correspondent for the *New-York Daily Tribune* observed that filibustering represented "one of the fruits of the last war," and predicted that hundreds of "young bloods" who fought in Mexico would soon become expeditionists. To no small degree, what followed fulfilled his prophecy.[2] When the Ashley River steamboat captain and returnees from Cárdenas brought up the Mexican War and General Quitman in their discussions with Goddard, they unintentionally gave testimony to the war's connection with what might be called the filibustering decision.

Narciso López, for example, depended on America's new pool of military veterans for his invasions of Cuba. John S. Slocum, a former U.S. army captain and López recruiter who had himself served in Mexico, promised his fellow wartime captain Albert Tracy in June 1849 that "almost all the officers who are going are officers who were with us in Mexico"; and the next year's invasion proved Slocum correct. Theodore O'Hara, who commanded López's Kentucky Regiment, had served in Mexico as an assistant quartermaster of the Kentucky volunteers with the rank of captain, and achieved the brevet rank of major for his role in the fighting at Contreras and Churubusco. His fellow Kentuckian Chatham Roberdeau Wheat, the colonel of López's Louisiana Regiment, had captained a company of Tennessee mounted volunteers in Winfield Scott's Mexico City campaign. Several lesser-ranking officers serving under O'Hara and Wheat, such as Major Thomas T. Hawkins and Captain William Hardy, had also done duty in Mexico. William H. Bell, a lieutenant colonel in the filibuster army, had lost an arm in the fighting at Buena Vista.[3]

Later expeditions likewise returned Mexican War soldiers to military duty. The filibuster commanders Joseph Morehead, John A. Quitman, and Henry L. Kinney had themselves served in Mexico. William Walker's Nicaraguan army employed as brigadiers Collier C. Hornsby, who had been a captain during the war in the 12th U.S. Infantry, and Birkett D. Fry, a lieutenant in the U.S. Voltigeurs during the campaigns in Mexico. In the winter of 1856–57

Ward B. Burnett, the colonel who commanded the 1st New York Volunteers in General Scott's Mexico City campaign, played a key role in Walker's New York City operation. We should not be surprised, therefore, that when in December 1856 the steamer *Tennessee* left New York with reinforcements for Walker's régime, a report in the *Times* noted that its passengers included two officers who had "participated in the Mexican war." The *Pittsburg Post*, at the time of Walker's second invasion of Nicaragua, pointed out that Walker's latest officer corps included Colonel Thomas Henry of Albany, New York, who had "served as sergant [*sic*] at the battle of Cerro Gordo," and Lieutenant Colonel G. T. Tucker, a Vermonter who had served as a captain in Mexico and been "honorably mentioned" in wartime dispatches.[4]

Filibustering's attractiveness to veterans can be explained in part by the difficulties that some returning soldiers experienced finding employment and otherwise readjusting to civilian life. F. C. M. Boggess, who enlisted in López's first attack on Cuba, later recalled how attractive filibustering had seemed to "thousands of discharged soldiers" who at that time were "at a loss for something to do to earn a living." Certainly this seems to have been the case with Albert Tracy, who had achieved the rank of regular army captain in Mexico, where he gained some attention for his painting ability. After being mustered out of the service in August 1848, Tracy became an artist. Unable to sell a sufficient number of his paintings to live comfortably, Tracy seriously considered joining Narciso López's first filibuster force at Round Island.[5]

Moreover, filibustering offered veterans a means of perpetuating treasured wartime associations and the male camaraderie of camp life and the battleground. A member of the 1850 Cuba invading force observed aboard ship that some of the men passed their leisure moments recounting their experiences in Mexico. Later, John Quitman's Cuba filibuster plot had the trappings of a Mexican War reunion. Quitman had not only held high rank in the war, but also inspired intense devotion during the campaigns among both his officers and his enlisted men. As a New Yorker put it when casting his fate with Quitman, friends of Quitman well remembered how he had "shared alike with the humblest privates in the ranks, the perils and privations of the late War with Mexico."[6]

As noted in chapter 2, when Quitman first considered filibustering in 1850 he instinctively contacted one of his aides-de-camp in the Mexican War, Mansfield Lovell, and asked him to join the enterprise in an important capacity. No sooner did word get out through the press and the veterans' grapevine that Quitman might head an invasion of Cuba than a member of South Carolina's Palmetto regiment, which had served under Quitman during the advance on Mexico City, asked for a role in the new campaign, noting that he had enjoyed the fortune of being with Quitman where he had "obtained so much honour."[7]

Once Quitman formally became the Cuban Junta's commanding general in 1853, he brought Lovell, still an officer in the regular U.S. Army, and additional Mexican War comrades into the fold. Another wartime aide, C. C. Danley, editor of the *Arkansas Gazette and Democrat*, provided recruiting help and promised to promote the cause in his paper. Gustavus W. Smith, an engineering officer who had played a prominent role in the fighting at Mexico City, became one of Quitman's closest advisers. Smith and Lovell, classmates at West Point, had continued their association in Mexico; Lovell in his wartime diary mentions their downing toddies together. Both men resigned their U.S. Army commissions on the same day, December 18, 1854, to filibuster with Quitman. Cadmus M. Wilcox, yet another member of Quitman's Mexican War staff, took a seventy-day leave from the U.S. Army in May 1854, intending to go to Cuba as a visitor and reconnoiter it in preparation for Quitman's attack, in which he expected to take part.[8]

Yet filibustering represented far more than a by-product of the Mexican War. Many filibusters had never served in the conflict. More important, the expeditionists had much in common besides service below the border.

Narciso López's officer corps and support network, for instance, was top-heavy not only with war veterans but also with Freemasons. Masonic rituals emphasized the international brotherhood of man and the obligation to help peoples in distress, especially the victims of despotism and tyranny. Such values, as well as Masonry's traditional tinge of anti-Catholicism, conveniently allowed for filibustering expeditions to free the peoples of Central America and the Caribbean from autocratic governments and Catholic institutions.

López, Ambrosio Gonzales, Wheat, and Hawkins were all members of the order, and the invaders' flag incorporated Masonic symbolism—most obviously an equilateral triangle superimposed upon the flag's left side. Shortly before his scheduled execution by Spanish authorities, one captured filibuster even sent his friend a farewell letter enclosing his father's Masonic medal.[9]

John Quitman was particularly well connected within Masonic circles, having served as a multi-term grand master of Mississippi's state lodge. In May 1851 a Mason in Augusta, Georgia, encouraged Quitman regarding the planned Cuba expedition, citing the "fraternal regard with which as 'Brethren of the Mystic tie' we regard each other." One C. G. F. Bell, who identified himself as a Master Mason, that same year incorporated Masonic symbolism in a letter encouraging Quitman to accept the filibuster command.[10]

Freemasonry also threaded its way through the period's other filibustering movements. According to the wife of a U.S. army officer stationed on the Mexican border, José Carbajal had joined the Masons. If this was the case, it may help to explain the involvement in Carbajal's cause of such men as Hugh McLeod. A Master Mason and former Texas Republic congressman from Galveston, McLeod belonged to four lodges over a twenty-five-year period. Later McLeod promoted William Walker's Nicaraguan cause in addresses at Masonic lodges. Though Walker was not a Mason, many of his officers were. Walker, in fact, remembered in his autobiographical *The War in Nicaragua* that on one occasion when he could not understand a message from his enemies on a "small slip of paper containing some cabalistic signs," he turned for help to two of his officers, both Masons. One of them, who held "high standing in the mystic order," confirmed the symbols' Masonic character and helped Walker to interpret the message. One of Walker's Masonic officers was George R. Davidson. After Captain Davidson died in Walker's service, a companion observed in a letter back to California that Davidson had been buried by "brothers Wheeler, the American Minister, Rust of Forrest City Lodge of your State, Hornsby, Alpha Lodge, La., Mason, and myself."[11]

Sensitive observers recognized the impossibility of tracing filibustering to any single source. In July 1852, when he was trying to enforce the Neutrality Law in Texas, Persifor F. Smith, a U.S. army departmental commander, identified multiple reasons for the invasions in an official report. According to the general, profilibustering propaganda in the press played a part. So did the desire of Texans for revenge against Mexicans for past grievances, the plans of slaveowners to use invasions as excuses to repossess fugitive slaves in Mexico, and the restlessness of Texas Rangers whose units had been mustered out of state service. Smith also contended that smugglers, knowing that any disorder would abet their illegal violations of customs regulations, had a hand in the schemes, and that local residents rendered aid to the filibusters, hoping that the invasions would compel the federal government to station troops in the vicinity as a preventive measure. Military spending to sustain such troops would pump money into the local economy.[12]

Of course, Smith's report also fails as a definitive explanation of filibustering. Several of the general's observations apply only to expeditions along the Texan border, and are not very helpful regarding expeditions that left other parts of the country. Smith alerts us to filibustering's multiple causes; but he invites us to seek further answers.

PART OF THE explanation has as much to do with the vulnerability of attacked areas as with the Americans who did the invading. As had been the case earlier in the century, turmoil in Hispanic domains to the south especially drew the attention of American expeditionists. Mexico, for example, experienced nearly continuous political instability, national indebtedness, and domestic strife after achieving independence from Spain in 1821. In 1822 the revolutionary leader Agustín de Iturbide had himself crowned emperor, only to be overthrown less than a year later and executed in 1824. In 1827 Mexico's vice-president attempted to oust Mexico's president in a military coup. The next year, armed resistance over a disputed election caused a change in national leadership. In 1831 Mexican authorities executed a former president. From May 1833 to August 1855, Mexico experienced an incredible thirty-six presidential changes. The "Ayutla Revolution" of 1854–55, led by Juan Álvarez, an elderly caudillo (or regional boss) from Guerrero who had played an important role in Mexico's independence struggle, and Ignacio Comonfort, a sometime militiaman and onetime customs collector in Acapulco, brought to an end the last of Antonio López de Santa Anna's several tenures as president. After Álvarez served briefly as interim president, Comonfort succeeded him and then gained election as president under Mexico's new constitution of 1857, only to be overthrown in January 1858. Subsequently, Mexico endured three years of civil strife that historians have dubbed the War of the Reform (Guerra de la Reforma).[13]

Likewise Nicaragua (which did not emerge as a fully independent state until 1838) during roughly the same period plunged into what E. Bradford Burns describes as "a long period of anarchy." Not only did the Nicaraguan people suffer greatly from civil war and banditry, but their country's gold and silver mines declined greatly in productivity, their government fell deeply in debt, and their capital changed locales more often than that of any other Latin American country. Meanwhile Nicaragua's chief executives assumed and exited office approximately once per year.[14]

Spain's colony of Cuba superficially enjoyed more stability than did Mexico or Nicaragua. However, Spain's administration of the island was plagued by corruption, and Spanish officials imposed excessive taxation, crippling mercantile regulations, and increasing political repression on the Cuban people. Reacting defensively to the loss of most of their empire in the Western Hemisphere, Spanish leaders eliminated Cuban legislative assemblies in 1825, and in 1837 terminated the colony's right to send delegates to their national congress, or Cortes. Spain's answer to demands in the 1830s by the island's *criollo* population (native-born Cubans of Spanish descent) for increased autonomy was to purge them from governmental positions and reserve assignments for Spanish-born *peninsulares*, as well as to tighten military surveillance and press censorship. Furthermore, Spanish officials announced programs, as we shall see later, that caused many Cuban planters to fear the eventual abolition of slavery. As a result, large numbers of Cubans favored independence from Spain, some of them hoping for eventual annexation to the United States. The island seethed with discontent.[15]

The Carbajal expeditions into Mexico illustrate the necessity of linking filibustering to the domestic situation within invaded countries. Texans who crossed the Rio Grande with Carbajal were not merely invaders; rather, they also joined an ongoing struggle between Mexicans that had been raging for decades and lay at the heart of Mexico's incessant civil strife.

Ever since independence, Mexican "Federalists"—generally liberal republicans who wanted to model their nation partially upon the United States federal system of shared powers between the government in Washington and its constituent states—had been contending against Mexico's Conservatives, who wanted to strengthen Mexico City's power over local politicos and sometimes promoted monarchical or dictatorial forms of rule. Mexico's constitution of 1824 established a decentralized system of government, under which most provinces became states with their own constitutions, legislatures, and sources of revenue. However, Santa Anna and the national congress between 1834 and 1836 transformed the government to the centralized model by converting states into dependent departments and replacing state legislatures with indirectly elected seven-member juntas.

This transformation not only helped to prompt the Texan Revolution, but it also triggered resistance by Carbajal and other Federalists throughout northern Mexico (and in other parts of the country). Armed Texans frequently participated in the resulting military campaigns of the borderlands Federalists, and ties between the Federalists and Americans persisted even after the outbreak of the Mexican War. In fact, Federalists made formal proposals to U.S. army generals before and during the conflict for cooperative efforts to establish an independent Rio Grande republic. Texans who filibustered with Carbajal in the 1850s, therefore, were replaying history as much as creating it.[16]

William Walker's expedition into Lower California and Sonora in 1853–54 similarly revolved around disorganization below the border. When Walker later went on trial for the expedition, he insisted that its primary purpose had been to provide the defenseless people of Sonora with protection against Indian attacks. He recounted that during a visit to Guaymas before his expedition he had unsuccessfully sought a contract from Mexican officials by which he would defend the people of Sonora from Apache "savages" in return for the right to land within the department for a colony. Walker asserted that he never would have initiated his expedition, had not the inhabitants of Guaymas pleaded with him to return anyway with a force of protective Americans.[17]

Walker's statement misrepresented his conquering intentions as philanthropy. Bonds that he issued before the expedition for an independent Republic of Sonora belie his claim. However, Walker indeed had visited Guaymas a few months before his expedition accompanied by Henry Watkins, hoping to procure a colonization grant; and his remarks show an awareness of Sonora's disorganized condition. Just as he insinuated, Mexico's central government, so deeply in debt that it could ill afford to maintain its borderlands military forces, had been unable to repress Apache (and Yaqui) Indian attacks in Sonora. Further, Mexican authorities had attempted to counter the Indian threat by establishing frontier military colonies. In these settlements, which stretched from Tamaulipas in the east all the way to the territory of Baja California in the west, soldiers fulfilled six-year terms of service against the Indians in return for salaries, tax relief, and promises of land allotments at the end of their obligations.[18]

Henry Crabb's expedition three years later was, if anything, even more attuned to Sonoran turmoil. Crabb had married the daughter of a prominent Sonoran who had moved to California and become a merchant in Los Angeles. Crabb's brother-in-law, J. M. Ainsa, maintained a store at Buena Vista in southern Arizona, just three miles above the Sonoran border. Before his invasion, Crabb had reached an agreement with Sonora's governor Ignacio Pesqueira, by which Crabb's "Arizona Colonization Company" would help Pesqueira repress the insurrectionary forces of the former Sonoran governor Manuel María Gandara, Pesqueira's longtime nemesis, in return for mining rights and land grants. However, Pesqueira consolidated his power by the time Crabb was ready to enter his state, and nullified the agreement.

Crabb may or may not have intended conquest rather than colonization when his expedition initially left California. But by the time Crabb's heavily armed party crossed into Mexico at Sonoyta in southern Arizona, he well knew that authorities across the border were treating him as an invader, and he pushed on anyway in filibustering style. In a letter to the prefect of Sonora's El Altar district dated March 26, 1857, Crabb denounced Sonora's authorities for "collecting a force to exterminate" him and his companions, noting that he had heard reports of Mexican plans to poison wells along his intended route. The point, again, is that Crabb's forces would never have entered Sonora in the first place had it not been for the beckoning disorder below the border.[19]

Certainly William Walker's intervention into Nicaragua hinged on civil strife within the country. After particularly bloody warfare erupted in 1854, one of the factions contending for power, the "Liberals," turned to American adventurers for extra manpower in their effort to overcome the "Legitimists." That December, Francisco Castellón, supreme director of the Liberals, contracted with Byron Cole, a California newspaper crony of Walker's who had traveled to Central America to promote a Honduran gold mining scheme, for an influx of three hundred "colonists" commanded by Walker (who had just returned to California from his Mexican fiasco). The filibusters would receive a combined land grant of 52,000 acres in return for their services. Had Nicaragua been united politically, it is extremely unlikely that Walker would ever have filibustered there.[20]

Virtually every filibuster plot against Cuba assumed that its oppressed population would rebel against occupying Spanish forces as soon as the expeditionists arrived. As Narciso López's confidant John L. O'Sullivan put it to the future presidential candidate Samuel J. Tilden while López was at sea bound for Cuba's coast in May 1850, the volunteers would surely succeed if they only evaded Spanish warships and made it to the island's coast, since then the "people would certainly rise." In April 1851 inaccurate newspaper reports of a popular uprising in Cuba caused some of López's followers in Georgia to set out prematurely for the filibusters' planned rendezvous. Similar false reports the following July led adventurous Americans to spontaneously enlist with López, and, as seen in chapter 2, they also induced López to launch his last invasion of Cuba precipitately.[21]

John Quitman, López's successor as leader of the Cuban conspiracy, operated from similar assumptions. Quitman announced, when soliciting money from one wealthy contact, that his army would be "aiding a revolutionary movement in Cuba." Quitman called off his expedition in 1855 in part because Spanish authorities in Cuba, who had been tipped off, made a series of preemptive arrests and took other steps to lessen the possibility of any mass rebellion in support of invaders.[22]

DWELLING ON Latin American political instability, however, would be like blaming victims for crimes of violence instead of their perpetrators. To fully understand America's criminal adventurers, it is necessary to further explore what motivated Americans to join in the invasions, however open to attack the violated countries may have been.

On the logic that sometimes the simplest answers are best, we might consider whether filibustering merely exemplified what Abraham Lincoln in his

1838 address to the Young Men's Lyceum of Springfield, Illinois, identified as an "increasing disregard for law" infecting the country. Lincoln's remark had been prompted by a rash of vigilante attacks and mob riots rather than filibustering. However, many filibusters did impress their contemporaries as being distinctly unsavory types. One federal official charged that such "desperate looking creatures" would "murder a man for ten dollars," and some commentators attributed filibustering to the very upsurge in lawlessness that had concerned Lincoln. Britain's chargé d'affaires in Washington even traced the expeditions, in words that have resonance today, to an American gun culture. So many Americans packed pistols, John S. Lumley concluded, that law-enforcement officers in the United States were afraid to arrest suspected filibusters. Lumley concluded that Americans obviously valued human life less than Europeans did.[23]

Expeditions departing from southern Texas and California's Pacific ports originated in areas that were notorious for armed, transient populaces and vigilante activity. As the Vermont native and schoolteacher George S. Denison observed from San Antonio in 1855, about a month before the Callahan expedition invaded Mexico, "Everybody carries pistols here when traveling, & many carry them always. On election day ninety-nine out of every hundred voters had pistols belted on them, & I saw some of them drawn." The very next year, San Francisco provided the setting for what the historian Richard Maxwell Brown identified as the "greatest American vigilante band" in the nation's history—San Francisco's vigilance committee of 1856. One California vigilante, only half in jest, claimed that his state owed William Walker a reward for drawing away so much of its criminal element![24]

Many filibusters displayed violent tendencies before seeking to take part in expeditions. In 1848, Henry Crabb killed the editor of the *Vicksburg Sentinel* during an altercation on a city street. In 1851 a filibuster applicant told John Quitman that although he had fled Mississippi rather than wait to "be demanded as a fugitive from another state, for the crime of killing a man," he deserved a slot in the upcoming Cuba expedition. If necessary, he could get worthwhile Mississippians to vouch for him. One of José Carbajal's conspirators suffered arrest in January 1852 on a murder charge from Colorado County, Texas, at the very time that he was standing trial in Galveston for filibustering against Mexico. In 1855 Thomas C. Hindman, a lawyer from Helena, Arkansas, and former Mississippi state representative, dared not fulfill his prior commitment to invade Cuba, for fear of jeopardizing bail that he had posted after his arrest for shooting a man in the hall of the Arkansas House of Representatives. A number of prominent filibusters, including William Walker, engaged in duels prior to their filibustering.[25]

Walker's filibustering expeditions to Nicaragua especially attracted aggressive types. Jennings Estelle, who served as a second lieutenant in William Walker's Nicaragua army, had stabbed a man in the streets of San Francisco before being hastened aboard a vessel bound for Nicaragua by an influential cousin. In August 1856 a San Franciscan who had attempted to rape a woman in the city reportedly escaped the musket of the intended victim's husband "by enlisting in the Army of Nicaragua and immediately leaving town with his fellows." George Tillman, older brother of the later famous U.S. Senator Benjamin Tillman, killed a man in a faro dispute in 1856 and fled to Walker's Nicaragua rather than face murder charges.[26]

Filibustering also ensnared men who had run afoul of the law in less violent ways. Parker French, who served for a while as the Walker Nicaraguan government's designated minister to the United States, for example, had previous notoriety as a thief and confidence man. No sooner did Walker's fall 1857 expeditionists arrive back in the United States at Norfolk, Virginia, after their failed invasion than authorities arrested one of his officers on an outstanding charge of grand larceny in Philadelphia.[27]

However, it would be risky to portray filibusters as collectively uncouth and criminal. When a Pennsylvanian in September 1854 offered John Quitman's expedition a company of sixty-one men, noting that its officers included an engineer, two attorneys, a printer, and a doctor, he explicitly attested to the respectability of his volunteers. William Walker held degrees from the University of Nashville and the University of Pennsylvania, had studied medicine in Paris, and had completed a European tour that lasted over a year before returning to the United States and turning to law, journalism, and filibustering. The college-educated Theodore O'Hara, something of a dandy in dress, had already written "The Bivouac of the Dead" by the time he turned filibuster:

> The muffled drum's sad roll has beat
> The soldier's last tattoo;
> No more on life's parade shall meet
> The brave and fallen few.
> On Fame's eternal camping ground
> Their silent tents are spread,
> And Glory guards with solemn round
> The bivouac of the dead.

Composed to commemorate a burial of Kentuckians who had died at the battle of Buena Vista during the Mexican War, this romantic dirge gained fame over the years. It would come to decorate the gateway to Arlington National

Cemetery as well as more Civil War monuments and cemeteries than any
verse of its kind.[28]

If we pin on Henry Crabb the stigma of accused killer, we likewise must
concede his stature as a former city attorney in Stockton, California, member
of both branches of California's legislature, and presidential elector. The filibuster leaders John Quitman and Henry Kinney exceeded Crabb in public
reputation. Quitman had served in Mississippi as a state representative and
senator, delegate to the state constitutional convention, chancellor, and governor long before he became a Mexican War hero, let alone a filibuster. In
1848 Quitman had placed second on the first ballot for the Democratic vice-
presidential nomination at the party's national nominating convention.[29]

So many other public figures became involved in filibustering, especially as
officers and organizers, that it is impossible to enumerate more than a few of
them here. Quitman's collaborators during his 1853–55 Cuban plot included
the governor of Alabama John A. Winston, the former attorney general and
secretary of state of the Republic of Texas (and briefly governor of the state of
Texas) James Pinckney Henderson, the Louisiana banker and railroad president Samuel Jarvis Peters, a former mayor of Jackson, Mississippi, and many
other officeholders, newspaper editors, and wealthy planters and businessmen. John S. Ford played a key role in the Carbajal movement at the same
time that he was serving in Texas's state senate. Thomas J. Rusk, a fellow
Texan, invested in Henry L. Kinney's bonds while serving in the U.S. Senate.
James Cooper of Pennsylvania, who completed his term in the Senate in
March 1855, was president of Kinney's front organization, the Central American Land and Mining Company. Edward J. C. Kewen, who took part in
William Walker's occupation of Nicaragua, had previously been elected attorney general by the California state legislature. Granville Oury captained a
party of twenty-four reinforcements for Henry Crabb's incursion into Sonora
shortly following his own election to the New Mexico territorial legislature.
William T. McCoun represented the San Joaquin district in California's senate before dying for Henry Crabb in Sonora.[30]

At least one filibuster officer sensed a conflict of interest between his official
duties and his adventuring abroad. William R. Henry, at the time he released
public letters in the fall of 1857 summoning Texans to join him in Walker's
second invasion of Nicaragua, was sheriff of Bexar county. Concerned that
the citizenry might be upset at his abandoning his post, he promised that he
would leave "for a few months only" and that he had appointed competent
deputies to carry out his duties in the interim.[31]

Additionally, numerous relations of eminent public figures filibustered,

Theodore O'Hara.
(Courtesy of the Filson
Club Historical Society,
Louisville, Ky.)

such as the sons of the former governors Samuel Bigger of Indiana and James Morehead of Kentucky, as well as John Marshall, the son of a former Kentucky congressman and a grandnephew of the former chief justice of the U.S. Supreme Court. Jefferson Davis's brother-in-law was arrested for filibustering to Mexico at the very time that Davis was serving as U.S. secretary of war.[32]

TO SAY THAT rising lawlessness inadequately explains filibustering, however, is not the same thing as to argue that societal change in America had no bearing on the expeditions. Rather, other transformations were occurring in the country that influenced why American males associated together in filibustering conspiracies. Several clues to the socioeconomic underpinnings of filibustering come from an anonymous War Department informant. In an undated letter, an "old soldier of 1814" shared with the Fillmore administration what he had learned during recent chats with urban youths from Philadelphia and New York who had joined filibuster units. Many of these "Boys," he reported, would have preferred to enter the U.S. Army or Navy, had they not been underage. Some were immigrants. But the greatest number were native-born Americans, many of them apprentices who had been "thrown adrift" (meaning that they had been dismissed) because of the financial failures of the mechanics who employed them.[33]

To a considerable degree, antebellum filibustering deserves remembrance as a phenomenon of America's urban environment. Most of the expeditions, with the exception of Texan crossings of the Rio Grande into Mexico, departed from cities such as New York, Mobile, New Orleans, and San Francisco and drew a large share of their enlisted manpower from those and other ports. In part, this can be explained by the availability of docks, shipping, and capital in these centers. But it also had a lot to do with the growth and changing nature of America's urban population, as well as the impact of the industrial and market revolutions on the urban workplace.

During the pre–Civil War period, America's urban population increased about three times as fast as the country's population as a whole. This was partly because many Americans moved from rural areas into cities: far more people migrated "eastward and cityward" than they did to the supposedly beckoning western frontier. But urban growth also reflected the arrival of vast numbers of foreign immigrants. In the late 1840s and the early 1850s, for instance, some 200,000–400,000 immigrants arrived annually just in New York. That city, by the mid-1850s, had more German-speaking people than all the municipalities in the world other than Berlin and Vienna. Similar trends occurred in other filibustering ports. According to 1850 census data, 54.3 percent of the population of the southern filibustering capital of New Orleans had been born abroad.[34]

Geographical mobility insulated young American males from parental restraints that might have otherwise inhibited them from engaging in expeditions. Some rather mature men filibustered, such as the fifty-one-year-old López follower Joel D. Hughes, who was married and had children. Mark B. Skerrett, a captain and then a colonel in William Walker's army, was described by a fellow soldier as having an "iron-gray" beard and hair, as well as "lines of middle age furrowing his face." But the typical filibuster, especially in the enlisted ranks, was youthful. As one federal judge observed, many of the filibusters were "mere boys." In 1851 a U.S. army captain complained that José Carbajal was harboring an army drummer boy who had deserted within his ranks. According to a participant in Henry L. Kinney's expedition to Central America, one of the most fearless members of the group was a fifteen-year-old named Daniel Webster, who "whistled and sang as if he was in his element" after Kinney's vessel grounded on a reef. A list giving the ages of eighty-four López filibusters indicates that fifty-five of them were under the age of twenty-five.[35]

Many youthful filibusters apparently masked their intentions from their mothers and fathers, assuming parental disapproval if they announced their plans in advance. In July 1851 one young man joined the López expedition while passing through New Orleans. He then wrote to his brother, "I do not wish you to let any of the folks know that I have gone to Cuba, until you hear of our landing, then you may let them know if you think proper." John Marshall, a functionary in William Walker's Nicaraguan government, waited well after arriving in the tropics before writing home that he assumed his father by then had learned from his brother of his "having emigrated" two months earlier from California to Nicaragua. In some cases, filibusters practiced outright deceit rather than risk parental rebuke or interference. Thus one of Walker's closest associates noted in February 1859 that Frank Anderson had traveled to Panama to make preparations for Walker's next invasion of Central America, but "wrote to his Father that he was going on business for the U.S. Government."[36]

In most cases, filibusters undoubtedly were right in assuming that their parents would disapprove of their intentions. F. L. Claiborne, a well-known planter and public figure from Adams County, Mississippi, offered his twenty-year-old son to the Quitman expedition in June 1854, but such support was rare. More representative of parental reactions was that of James C. Pickett, co-editor of the *Washington Globe*. In 1849, after press reports linked his son John to Cuban filibustering, the elder Pickett released a public letter disavowing any connection on his own part to the filibuster cause, saying that he would neither support nor pray for its success. The next year, a Cincinnati newspaper reported the presence in town of some "old farmers" from neighboring rural counties "on the hunt of sons who had slipped off from home quietly" to participate in the invasion of Cuba.[37]

America's urban milieu had even more to do with fostering the period's expeditions than geographical mobility did. Teeming port cities not only provided the anonymity that allowed young men from the country to discover filibustering opportunities without their parents' getting wind of their intentions, but they also provided filibustering organizers with a ready pool of unemployed urban males, native- and foreign-born alike, who were vulnerable to their offers. As one astute employee of a New Orleans counting house observed in a letter to his father in 1855:

This is a city in which I would dread being idle, as it is a kind of rendezvous for all reckless characters and men of desperate fortunes—whose acquaintance I should judge it would be hard to shun were a person out of Employment—for they are always looking up young men without prospects, for various filibustering and piratical expeditions. There are at present numbers of such men in town recruiting for Col Walker's forces in Nicaragua and they find but little difficulty in procuring young men for their purposes—for what are men to do who have nothing to employ them and no prospects of making their expenses.

Similarly, a New York newspaper reported the proceedings of a meeting of filibusters connected with Narciso López's Round Island plot in 1849, noting that the gatherers were "stout" youths "who are out of employment." No wonder. New York at that time had a surplus of youthful male laborers ripe for filibustering inducements. By 1850 approximately 57 percent of New York's total population consisted of males between the ages of sixteen and forty-five.[38]

Wisely, filibuster organizers set up almost all their recruiting offices in large cities, sometimes operating out of the hotel rooms and law offices of supporters, at other times renting temporary office space. In 1856 Walker's supporters in New Orleans maintained two offices, which led to a somewhat unseemly rivalry, as one of the recruiters complained that the other had better furnishings, and that the public should be spared from the "spectacle" of the filibusters competing for the same volunteers.[39]

Although terms varied from one expedition to the next, filibuster recruiters generally offered their enlisted men subsistence plus pay roughly comparable to or better than that of service in the U.S. Army, with the promise of bonuses should their expeditions be successful. Between the end of the Mexican War and the enactment of a pay raise by Congress in 1854, U.S. army privates made $7 per month, while corporals earned $9 and sergeants $13. The 1854 legislation increased the pay of each rank by $4. Congress also provided various enlistment, reenlistment, and longevity bonuses during this same period. For instance, according to the 1854 act, soldiers received an extra $2 per month if they were in their second enlistment. Officers, naturally, received considerably more pay. An army second lieutenant, before the pay raises of 1857, received an annual base pay of $300, with servant and subsistence allowances bringing his total up to approximately $1,000 a year.[40]

In contrast, Narciso López's recruiters offered most prospects either $7 or $8 a month (the amount varied by recruiter), as well as substantial bonuses. In 1849 López's agents offered $1,000 rewards after twelve months of service. In 1850 and 1851 López "guaranteed" bounties of $1,000 for privates serving a year, and as much as $4,000 and $5,000, or the same value in Cuban public lands, for officers.[41] John M. Jarnigan, secretary of war for William Walker's "government" in Lower California, announced in late 1853 that privates, corporals, and sergeants alike would make $4 per month for serving the filibuster republic. However, Walker upped his ante to $25–$30 a month, with a land bonus of 250 acres after six months' service during his 1855–57 tenure in Nicaragua. During his second Nicaraguan expedition, Walker demanded a full year of service for the same payoff.[42] Henry L. Kinney in 1854–55 promised recruits for his Mosquito Coast settlement $25 a month (or bonds of his government if the enlistee preferred), with land offers ranging from 320 to 640 acres. A Knights of the Golden Circle recruiter in 1860 promised enlistees $18 a month as well as land taken from wealthy Mexican estates.[43]

Naturally, filibuster recruiters promised prospective officers even more. Walker only offered colonels and lieutenant colonels in his 1853 Mexican invasion $10 a month, and majors $9. However, Hannibal Rakow, who signed up as an officer in López's aborted spring 1851 expedition, testified later in court that he was promised $240 a month as well as feed for his horses and a bonus of $5,000–$6,000 if the expedition was successful. John Brenizer, a surgeon in Walker's Nicaraguan army, informed his family back home that he was making $200 per month.[44]

Such financial inducements illuminate why immigrants, who generally were at the lowest end of the urban wage scale and often faced discrimination in hiring, demonstrated a willingness to filibuster. Various contemporary listings and rosters of filibusters confirm the liberal sprinkling of immigrants within filibuster ranks. A list of 137 captured participants in López's summer 1851 expedition, for instance, reveals that twenty-eight of them hailed originally from the European continent, ten from Ireland, and one from Malta. William Walker's Nicaraguan army register reveals the place of birth for 905 of his soldiers and indicates that 154 were born in Europe, with 9 from Canada, the East Indies, the West Indies, and Latin America. A register of twenty reinforcements for William Walker's 1860 expedition indicates that two of them had been born in England, three in Ireland, and one in Germany.[45]

Not all immigrant filibusters should be regarded merely as victims of America's urban labor market. Cuban exiles, for example, filibustered primarily to liberate their land from Spanish rule. This was true even of Domingo de Goicouria, who joined William Walker's forces in Nicaragua as a general in early 1856 but split with Walker later that year. Goicouria signed on after Walker contracted to help Goicouria liberate Cuba once Nicaragua was fully pacified. Some immigrants, particularly those serving in the filibuster officer corps, moreover, regarded the expeditions primarily as a means of salvaging frustrated military careers. Thus William Alfonse Sutter, the son of John

A. Sutter of California gold fame, led a company to William Walker's Nicaragua after being disappointed in his hopes of admittance to the U.S. Military Academy.[46]

Many immigrants-turned-filibuster were exiles from recent failed European revolutions who naturally gravitated into the expeditions as a means of perpetuating already established military careers. In 1848 uprisings against monarchical and authoritarian governments had erupted in France, what are now Germany, Italy, and Hungary, and many other parts of Europe; furthermore, revolutionary ferment had plagued Russian-ruled Poland and other Continental locales uninfected by genuine insurgencies, and new outbreaks of agitation against British colonial rule had occurred in Ireland. When, within eighteen months, virtually all the revolts with the exception of the French rebellion had ended in failure, many revolutionaries found their way to the United States, and in certain instances to filibuster ranks.

López and Walker especially welcomed the veterans' military expertise. One of López's recruits, for instance, testified that he had been promised by the filibusters "the same rank" he "held in the Baden Army." During his 1850 expedition, López issued red flannel shirts to his soldiers, in honor of the color adopted by European revolutionaries two years earlier. Furthermore, a number of filibuster officers and organizers simultaneously played a hand in European resistance movements. Theodore O'Hara invested in at least five of Louis Kossuth's 4-percent bonds, with the stipulation that payment of the principal would occur after Hungary established its independence from Austria. The Irish-born U.S. congressman and filibuster Mike Walsh in 1855 boarded an oceanic vessel carrying letters intended for Kossuth, Giuseppe Mazzini, and other European revolutionists.[47]

Some former European revolutionists had the sense to spurn filibustering opportunities. Charles Radziminski of Warsaw, who had served as a lieutenant in an uprising of Poles against Russia's czar in 1830, ultimately turned down what he described as a tempting offer to command the Cuban filibusters' cavalry in 1850.[48] Many others, however, took the bait. Thus Michael Nagle, described by a newspaper correspondent as an "Irish political exile," sailed for Walker's Nicaragua in September 1856. Walker's autobiography alludes to a captain in his service named Schwartz who had "served for some time as an artillery officer in Baden during the revolutionary troubles of 1848."[49]

Louis Schlesinger, an officer in Louis Kossuth's failed Hungarian rebellion against Austrian rule, became one of the most publicized of the revolutionary exiles who took up filibustering. Indicted for involvement in Narciso López's aborted spring 1851 conspiracy, Schlesinger (listed as Ludivig Schlezinger in one source) served on López's staff in the following summer's invasion of Cuba, was captured by Spanish authorities, and for a while was imprisoned at Ceuta in northern Africa. Subsequently Schlesinger, by asserting that his entire prior life had "been a military one," gained entry into John Quitman's Cuban conspiracy. Less than a year after Quitman called off the invasion, Schlesinger journeyed to Walker's Nicaragua, secured a colonel's commission, and commanded an unsuccessful offensive against hostile Costa Rican forces.[50]

Still, it appears that the great majority of European immigrants in filibuster ranks enlisted because of problems coping within America's urban economy. In April 1851 a writer for the *New-York Daily Tribune* claimed to have inside information that a group of Hungarians and Italians had signed on with López's plot "because they had no other means of saving themselves from starving." In fact, one of these immigrants had been so short of funds that he had been sleeping on the streets before enlisting. In December 1856 the New York correspondent of a St. Paul paper reported the holding of pro-Walker public meetings "in all the wards inhabited by foreigners," and implied that the only thing holding back some of these filibustering enthusiasts from going to Nicaragua was a lack of funds to cover their ship passage.[51]

Whether the prototypical urban filibuster was a disadvantaged immigrant, however, is another matter. Substantial numbers of skilled workers also attached themselves to filibuster units. Police Chief Goddard, as we have seen, discovered several mechanics, a term then in common use for skilled artisans, in the López expeditions. Repeatedly, filibuster leaders discussed enlisting urban mechanics. Congressman Mike Walsh of New York, recruiting for John Quitman, intimated in one letter that he had been told by Quitman's New York agents that "one or two hundred men who are good mechanics" might be secured there. James Cooper explained in a letter from Philadelphia on May 30, 1855, that sixteen men, all "intelligent mechanics," had attended that night's Henry L. Kinney meeting, wishing to leave at once. Kinney's expedition, according to one participant, consisted of "mostly young, unmarried men, mechanics and merchants, with a sprinkling of western frontiersmen."[52]

It was no coincidence that filibustering appealed to urban mechanics, as the nature of their workplace had changed greatly in recent decades. In the early years of the republic, mechanics generally operated small shops, often with the assistance of wage-earning "journeymen" as well as apprentices who learned the methods of their particular trade in return for their labor. Eventually journeymen and apprentices became independent mechanics in their own right. Frequently, master craftsmen and their workers not only worked closely together but also resided together. However, the growth of factory production and the emergence of a capitalist market in the early nineteenth century greatly undermined the respectability of skilled labor as well as employment conditions in the shops of mechanics. In a losing competition against factories, mechanics lowered wages, speeded up production, and hired as their assistants strangers rather than the acquaintances (and sons of acquaintances) whom they previously welcomed into their shops and homes. No longer bound by close social ties to their employers or confident of ever owning their own shops or being able to adequately support a family, urban workers increasingly lived independently in boardinghouses and often put off marriage.[53]

Urban mechanics and their employees fought back most obviously against their declining status and worsening labor conditions by means of strikes, trade associations, and political agitation. Especially during the late 1820s and early 1830s, they formed a number of workingmen's parties. But they also relieved their frustrations by taking part in a generally homosocial, often violent, and sometimes illegal sporting subculture that included boxing, gambling, cockfighting, membership in volunteer fire companies and gangs, raucous theater productions, and visits to brothels. Filibustering, which as we saw in chapter 3 had its own links to urban theaters, represented an exaggerated extension of this sporting subculture. Youths involved in this subculture were commonly referred to as "b'hoys," and it is revealing that in 1851 a reporter in the nation's capital used the term to describe participants in a filibuster rally. When eastern mechanics, their apprentices, and other urban youths joined expeditions and risked their lives in battle, they not only sought escape from economic hardships but also reclaimed their threatened masculinity.[54]

Out on the Pacific coast, filibustering recruiters largely filled their ranks with the human refuse of the great California gold rush of 1849. Young men especially in San Francisco but also elsewhere in the nation's newest state often experienced great difficulty finding employment, and those who did get jobs generally had trouble covering their expenses in a highly inflated economy.

The Morehead, Walker, and Crabb expeditions to Mexico, as well as Walker's initial expedition to Nicaragua, all originated in California and seem to have drawn young men who were experiencing financial hardships of one sort or another. Thus the filibuster officer Oliver T. Baird, who in January 1854 turned up in the interior on a recruiting drive for Walker, had reportedly been denied employment by a theater company just before accepting his filibuster assignment. Several months later Charles Rand, a San Francisco merchant, informed his family back east that thirty-three survivors of Walker's recent Republic of Sonora and Lower California had marched by his store, and cynically remarked that one of them had owed Rand's firm $149 before investing the amount "in Fillibuster stock."[55]

Failed miners especially found their way into California's filibuster ranks. Rand observed in February 1857 that six hundred recruits had left for Walker's Nicaragua "who were enlisted out of the thousands in the mines now doing nothing." One of them seems to have been David Deaderick III, who later explained in a magazine article that he had sought out one of Walker's agents in San Francisco that same winter after his gold digging had been treated "unkindly" by "Fortune." Sleeping in the streets of Oroville at night, Deaderick started thinking about Walker's Nicaragua after reading in the village paper about the likelihood of frost in the days ahead.[56]

Perhaps the most striking testimony comes from the autobiographical account of a Quaker from Pennsylvania, whom one would hardly expect to be attracted to such a violent pursuit as filibustering. But Charles Edward Pancoast, who sold away his mining tools in April 1852 and floundered around San Francisco looking for work, almost allowed himself to be seduced by Henry Watkins into Walker's invasion of Lower California and Sonora. While dining with Watkins (with whom he had been previously acquainted) after a chance encounter on a San Francisco street, Pancoast found himself intrigued by the sudden offer of a lieutenancy in Walker's army, with a chance of sharing the expedition's spoils and perhaps achieving a high office in the filibuster's government. "This was a rosy picture, and very alluring to a Young Man with no Employment and small means," he remembered, before also recalling how his "Quaker education" brought him back to his senses and led him to decline the proposal.[57]

ALTHOUGH filibustering related profoundly to urban America's social and economic transformations, many filibusters came from rural areas, as Henry Forno indicated in 1855 when he identified the majority of one company of sixty-eight men as stout and hardy "country men." Moreover, some expeditionists recruited in coastal ports were there only temporarily and actually lived in interior areas. Thus one of López's followers explained to John Goddard that he resided on an Arkansas plantation but enlisted during a trip to New Orleans to purchase clothing for the slaves.[58]

Nor did Americans have exclusively mercenary intent when they joined invading parties. Professional considerations, for example, better explain the motivations of most of the U.S. army officers who contemplated accepting commissions in filibuster armies.

After the Mexican War, the reduced regular service offered relatively few opportunities for promotion or battlefield experience, and the army's brief skirmishes against western Indians rarely achieved the scale necessary to attract newspaper coverage. Meanwhile filibuster exploits gained the public limelight. Naturally the expeditions intrigued officers bent on advancing their own careers and reputations.

Such circumstances in 1856 induced one West Point cadet, George Bayard, to harbor thoughts of applying for a captain's commission in William Walker's army after his graduation. The filibusters needed "scientific men," Bayard reasoned, telling his mother that in Nicaragua "to a young man of energy & talent 'there is no such word as fail.'" Besides, filibustering service would prove "more pleasant than Indian fighting in New Mexico," as well as offer the kind of legitimate military experience that would be useful should the United States again go to war with a foreign power.[59]

Similar thinking affected many other army officers, including a number of men who within a few years would be generals in the Confederate and Union armies. In 1856, for example, P. G. T. Beauregard became so restless at his posting as superintending engineer at the New Orleans customhouse that he considered resigning his army commission and joining Walker, to whom he went so far as to have references sent. The next year, Johnson Kelly Duncan, like Beauregard a future Confederate general, suggested to the future Union army commander George McClellan that they join Walker's second invasion of Nicaragua, warning that if they forfeited the opportunity they might wind up merely accumulating money "amidst the quiets of peace." In 1858 Duncan joined with Mansfield Lovell, yet another later Confederate general, in a plot against Mexico that involved coaxing John Quitman out of filibustering retirement and getting him to command a "legion" of U.S. adventurers. Although Bayard, Beauregard, and Duncan never completed their conversion into filibusters, other army officers made the gamble, such as Philip Thompson, the dragoon captain who joined Walker's staff after ruining his army career by showing up drunk at a court-martial.[60]

U.S. Army officers were by no means the only militarily inclined Americans who came to regard filibustering as a professional outlet. The expeditions also enticed members of volunteer fire and militia companies. In September 1852, for instance, the secretary of Mississippi Fire Company No. 2 in New Orleans summoned its entire membership to ceremonies commemorating their "late members" and other New Orleans firemen who had filibustered to Cuba the year before and been executed by a Spanish firing squad. The *Daily Alta California* in 1856 noted that two filibusters who recently lost their lives in Nicaragua had previously been members of both the city's Monumental Engine Company and its Marion Rifles. George Bolivar Hall, the son of a mayor of Brooklyn, New York, rose from private to lieutenant colonel in New York's militia before becoming involved with López, Quitman, and Walker.

Such young men apparently found the quasi-military functions of their fire and militia companies satisfying for a while, but then sought the greater challenge of engaging in battle as filibusters. A New Yorker explained when applying for a filibuster slot following what he described as fifteen years of service in the militia, "I should like to put in practice in Nicaragua the benefit of those years of study."[61]

Although one adventurer claimed that he joined an expedition to impress a young woman whom he was interested in, others filibustered to distance themselves from dysfunctional marriages or romantic disappointments. "Anna Buford & her spouse parted some time last fall finally & forever," remarked an acquaintance of the couple in January 1858, before noting that Anna's husband had been a "brute" and "all dog" and that he had announced his intention to go to Nicaragua. A colonel in one of the Cuba expeditions recorded in his journal how rejection by a love interest had brought a companion into the filibuster ranks: "My friend—from Kentucky, confidently told me on our way to the gulf, pointing to a fine ring upon his finger, that that should be sent to the bottom of the gulf, for it was given him by Miss—, and that they had quarreled and he had turned soldier." However, though U.S. Senator John Thompson implied in a speech that filibusters tended to be sexually deprived and much has been made by historians of William Walker's relationship with a deaf mute, apparently never consummated, it is uncertain whether filibusters were more prone to sexual dysfunction than males in the general population. More suggestive are documents indicating that filibusters tended to crave female adulation and liked to boast about it.[62]

Undoubtedly in a few cases, filibustering represented a desperate attempt at diversion from psychological problems that today might be diagnosed as depression. William H. Clowes informed a filibuster contact in January 1858 that he wanted to invade Central America with William Walker, yet improbably committed suicide less than a week later. An acquaintance of William McCoun implied that McCoun's enlistment in the Crabb expedition constituted a reaction to news from his wife back east that one of his small children had accidentally killed himself with a gun that he was playing with.[63]

Then, too, some men enlisted in filibusters to settle scores, to achieve revenge, or simply to protect their families. When recruiting for the Quitman expedition in 1854, John Allen of Kentucky called upon men "eager to avenge the death of Crittendon [*sic*]" and the other "brave men" who fell while serving in Cuba under López. In 1855, when raising fifty to sixty men for a crossing of the Rio Grande into Mexico, Henry McCulloch told Texas's governor how he resented any implication that he was out for spoils. McCulloch claimed that his sole purpose was to protect women and children living near the border from Indians using Mexican soil as a base for their raids. James Pike, who declined a chance to join the Knights of the Golden Circle, asserted that those of his fellow Texas Rangers who did sign up did so almost exclusively to "retaliate" for prior "Mexican depredations on the Rio Grande."[64]

But above all, we need to remember that many young men primarily filibustered to inject adventure into their lives, and, as one of John Quitman's principal organizers suggested in a letter seeking enlistments, "show their manhood." America's pre–Civil War filibusters came of age when romanticism was infusing the nation's culture. Romanticism, which celebrated individual virtue, human instinct and spontaneity, adventure, travel to exotic locales, and heroism, provided an intellectual climate conducive to American filibustering.[65]

As Robert W. Johannsen explains, many American youths at that time grew up reading the historical romances of Sir Walter Scott, which popularized concepts of medieval chivalry and knighthood, and they hoped to model themselves on Scott's heroic characters. Although Johannsen was concerned with the profound impact of romanticism upon the soldiers who fought in the Mexican War, as well as with how Americans on the home front perceived the conflict, his observations help to explain why filibusters sometimes gravitated to knightly imagery in their writings and attire, and why sympathizers frequently conceded their claims to chivalric stature.

We should not be surprised that Albert Tracy's mentor advised him against joining López's Round Island expedition in 1849 lest he be compared to Scott's mercenary character Dugald Dulgetty of Drumthwacket, and that several months later one of López's recruiters disclaimed identification with the very same literary figure. Similarly, William Walker tried to rally his Sonoran invaders by invoking their "chivalrous" desires to rescue "helpless" female inhabitants from rape by merciless Apaches. Allusions to gallantry, chivalry, and knighthood pepper contemporary descriptions of the filibusters' personalities and their expeditions. The anonymous author of a personal reminiscence of López's invasion of Cuba in 1850 called the invasion "the most extraordinary piece of Knight-errantry on record—at least since the days of . . . Don Quixote.'" William Stewart's 1857 reminiscences about his recent experiences in Nicaragua recalled a captain in the filibuster service who had worn a "dancing black plume" during the fighting. The aptly named Knights of the Golden Circle even adopted a costume, apparently never worn on campaign, resembling a medieval coat of mail.[66]

Compelling evidence suggests that many men took up filibustering for travel and adventure. In 1854 an applicant informed John Quitman that he wanted to visit Cuba, and filibustering was the way that he would "prefer going." In the next year the Mexican War veteran Robert Farquharson announced to Quitman his resignation as President Pierce's appointee as secretary of the Washington Territory, saying that he preferred the "life of adventure" promised by Quitman's upcoming expedition. In March 1857 a college student in Missouri pondered joining William Walker to escape from a "'dull' state." "I am half . . . in the notion to be off for Nicaragua," this youth explained to a friend. "The roar of the cannon, and the Sound of the musketry, I can hear every morning (most) And as they echo among our cliffs and dales, they seem to me, to have a sweeter sound than the merry notes of the College bell . . . or the christian rings of sabbath goings." The next fall, Frank Mc-Mullen of Texas tired of administering his late father's estate, turned it over to his mother, and sought excitement in William Walker's invasion of Nicaragua. James Pike considered joining the Knights of the Golden Circle "primarily" for the "prospect of adventure," but objected to a required oath and remained out of the order.[67]

The spur-of-the-moment nature of many filibuster enlistments further suggests the movement's romantic impulses, as volunteers fell under the sway of filibuster hype, and let their emotions rule their minds. A farmer's son from the Upper South, for instance, left the family place with the idea of seeing "the world," coincidentally arrived in New Orleans in the days before Narciso López's last invasion of Cuba, became thoroughly swept up in all the ferment, and signed on. He later recalled how cannon explosions enticed him from his hotel gallery to the streets, where he encountered newsboys hollering about a "great revolution" in Cuba. So he joined in the excitement, screamed until he was hoarse, "hooped things up all knight," attended every Cuba meeting that was announced, and virtually asked everyone whom he met how to enlist until a boardinghouse landlady put him in touch with a recruiter. Similarly, William Stewart remembered that California mountain towns "were literally illuminated with flaming posters" boosting William Walker's cause at the time that he joined a company bound for Nicaragua. In some instances, local women contributed to the excitement by giving banners that they had designed to departing companies.[68]

No wonder many recruits harbored stereotypically romantic visions of achieving, as a participant in López's 1850 expedition put it, "glory or the grave." Should their causes fail, they would at least die gloriously on the field of combat. In fact, some of William Walker's reinforcements in Nicaragua in late 1855 expressed disappointment upon discovering that their filibustering predecessors had already pacified the country. How would they ever have the opportunity to "participate in the perils" of battle?[69]

SO FAR, we have been contemplating why Americans filibustered. But we also need to recognize that many of the adventurers became repeat offenders, and consider the possibility that repeaters may have joined their later expeditions for different reasons than the ones that initially led them into the practice.

Given the paucity of biographical material about many of the adventurers, it is impossible to determine exactly how many of them filibustered more than once. However, Callender Fayssoux's ledger of reinforcements for William Walker's 1860 expedition alerts us to the frequency of the practice, by stipulating which men had previously served in Walker's Nicaraguan army in 1856 or participated in the Nicaragua-bound *Susan* expedition of 1858. Of the 145 adventurers listed in the 1860 expedition, 18, or more than 12 percent, were repeaters.[70]

That is a striking figure, given filibustering's perils. But Fayssoux's list did not account for participants in 1860 who had belonged either to Walker's fall 1857 invasion of Central America or his interrupted 1859 plot. Nor did it indicate whether any of the participants had filibustered for Walker in Mexico or in Nicaragua before 1856, or served any other filibuster commander. It did not even identify all the 1860 filibusters who had been in Walker's 1856 army. The 12 percent figure is in fact far too low for the 1860 expedition.

The 1860 expedition's Michael Burk and Philip Smith are probably the M. Burk on E. J. C. Kewen's list of the original Walker "Immortals" who invaded Nicaragua and Private Philip Smith on William V. Wells's list of Walker's forces at Granada, Nicaragua, in November 1856. T. Howard, T. H. Stewart, Noah J. Parsons, George L. Williams, James Cox, and James Dixon are almost certainly the Thomas Howard, Thomas Stewart, N. J. Parsons, George Williams, J. H. Cox, and James Dixon listed by New York newspapers in the summer of 1857 as returning to the United States from Walker's Nicaragua. Very possibly, too, Fayssoux's T. S. Johnson is the Thomas Johnson who was taken into custody by the Navy in December 1857 while participating in Walker's second invasion of Nicaragua. The H. Cook and William H. Kennon of the 1860 register match the Captain H. C. Cook and William Kennon of the November 1857 expedition; William White and John Ryan were probably the private William White and lieutenant of ordnance John Ryan reported in the *New York Herald* as participating in the *Susan* affair. Captain William Scott may have been the William W. Scott arrested by U.S. authorities for involvement in the aborted 1859 expedition. It is even possible that Fayssoux's James Butler of Louisiana was the J. F. Butler of New Orleans reported in the *New Orleans Daily Picayune* as a deserter from Walker's 1856 Nicaraguan army, and that Fayssoux's R. Harris was the Lieutenant R. A. Harris in Company K of the Louisiana Regiment of the 1850 López invasion of Cuba.[71]

Fayssoux's accounting of the 1860 reinforcements, therefore, presumably overlooked at least fourteen former Walker filibusters. If we add the fourteen to the eighteen that Fayssoux did identify, we come up with a minimum of thirty-two repeaters out of the total reinforcement manpower, or approximately 22 percent. Other expeditions, likewise, drew a significant portion of their manpower from those who had been involved in one or more prior filibustering plots.

No sooner did filibusters return to the United States than they began weighing the advantages and disadvantages of joining additional expeditions. Although many returnees arrived disillusioned and jaded, a surprising number of their peers immediately expressed an interest in trying their hand at the practice again. Thus one of López's 1850 adventurers intimated after escaping from Cuba to Key West, Florida, just ahead of a pursuing Spanish warship, "The most of us wish to return home; . . . Others wish to go back with Lopez, and even propose attacking and taking the Spanish man of war, now in the harbor." Similarly, a veteran of Juan José Flores's campaign in Ecuador confided to a fellow campaigner just days before his death in the fall of 1853 an "ardent wish that he might live long enough to 'strike one more blow for Flores.'"[72]

It was natural for returning filibusters to join successor schemes, given the efforts of filibuster leaders to keep their organizations intact as they initiated plans for future invasions. Walker informed Callender Fayssoux after his second return from Central America that he would travel to Mobile and New Orleans to determine whether they could "leave again" for Nicaragua, and stipulated that Fayssoux keep him posted as to the addresses of his former officers. Conversely, subordinate officers made it easy for their leaders to stay in touch. Thus one adventurer informed Fayssoux in August 1859 that he had joined Argentina's navy as a lieutenant, but would prefer navigating "in Uncle Billeyes servise" and hoped to be informed as to upcoming opportunities.[73]

All of Walker plots, not merely his last one in 1860, benefited from repeaters. Timothy Crocker, a second lieutenant and then a major in Walker's invasion of Lower California, became an Immortal less than two years later and was fatally shot during Walker's first battle in Nicaragua. George R. Davidson, a captain in Walker's foray into Mexico, later died of cholera while serving at the same rank in Nicaragua. Lieutenant Colonel Charles Gilman suffered an amputated leg from a wound that he took in Lower California, yet later joined Walker in Nicaragua. A correspondent aboard a steamer bound for Nicaragua in March 1856 described one of five filibuster recruits on board as "a young man who went with Col. Walker after Lower California and Sonora, a gunsmith by trade," who hoped to "make himself useful to the forces in Granada." Walker's November 1857 expedition included six of his original Immortals and an additional thirty or so men who had formerly served with him in Nicaragua. A year later, a New Orleans correspondent noticed that "the old heroes of the first and second [Nicaraguan] campaigns" were rallying to Walker's newest scheme. S. D. McChesney and Jules G. Dreux, recruiting reinforcements for Walker in New Orleans at the time that he died by firing squad in Honduras, had both been held for questioning by federal authorities in 1858 for involvement in the *Susan* expedition and earlier had served as captains in Walker's Nicaraguan army.[74]

The same applied to the López and Quitman conspiracies. Many adventurers participated in two or more of López's plots. Quitman, who inherited López's mantle, benefited naturally from an existing Cuban filibustering infrastructure. In February 1855 Major Thomas Hawkins and Colonel Theodore O'Hara of the 1850 López expedition raised troops for Quitman in Kentucky. López's veterans there and elsewhere naturally rushed to the standard. R. A. Harris, for instance, noting that he had already "served in a former expedition" to Cuba, "again" offered his services. Allison Nelson, who claimed to have been "laboring in the cause since López's first expedition," contributed funds, provided advice on recruiting methods, and expressed a "great desire" to go, if he could only find someone to care for his wife and three small children during his absence.[75]

More striking, however, are cases of filibuster crossovers—adventurers who joined expeditions unrelated to those of their prior affiliations. The filibuster fellow traveler Laurence Oliphant claimed that a majority of the 300 Walker reinforcements who joined him aboard a Nicaraguan-bound ship from New Orleans on December 31, 1856, "had been in one or other of the Lopez expeditions to Cuba," and that many of them exhibited sword and bullet wounds, as well as scars from manacles, dating from those affairs. Perhaps Oliphant exaggerated. But filibusters did shuttle around. Conceding this phenomenon, one of John Quitman's organizers observed in early 1855 that José Carbajal was mounting a new expedition against Mexico and would undoubtedly drain from Quitman's ranks "a number of those depended upon for Cuba."[76]

Rip Ford and Bob Wheat both participated in Carbajal's Rio Grande plots before connecting with Quitman's conspiracy.[77] Powhatan Jordan planned in December 1854 to accompany Quitman, but by January 1855 he had signed on as staff surgeon for Henry L. Kinney's expedition to Central America.[78] Months later, a correspondent in Mobile encountered a man intending to go out as a lieutenant to join Kinney's forces and noted that the adventurer was "one of those who served . . . in the López expedition."[79]

As late as March 1855, shortly before William Walker arrived in Central America, his younger brother Norvell was deeply involved in Quitman's Cuban plot. Yet before the year was out, Norvell would be serving in Nicaragua at the rank of first lieutenant. William C. Mason, a student at the Virginia Military Institute, sought a lieutenancy or higher in Quitman's enterprise in 1854; two years later he died of yellow fever while serving as a captain in Walker's army. "Colonel" John ("Jack") H. Allen of Kentucky participated in the López and Quitman Cuban conspiracies, suffered arrest by U.S. authorities as a key figure in Carbajal's movement, and, naturally, served in Walker's Nicaragua. Hugh McLeod followed a similar path, though he avoided arrest for his filibustering activities.[80] Theodore O'Hara, noted for his role in López's expedition, turned up in Callender Fayssoux's papers as one of the organizers of Walker's *Susan* expedition of December 1858. Fayssoux, who commanded William Walker's Navy in Nicaragua, who participated in the invasion of November 1857, and who helped organize that of 1860, had initially traveled to Nicaragua in 1856 bearing an introduction that cited his role in López's landing at Cárdenas, Cuba. Fayssoux's voucher might well have added that he had also participated in the Round Island plot of 1849 and the invasion of 1851![81]

Once adventurers became willing to take part in virtually any expedition rather than return to their prior occupations, they joined what the *New York Herald* rightly identified as the filibustering "profession." They no longer filibustered primarily for the purposes that initially attracted them but rather to perpetuate what had literally evolved into a career. How revealing it was for Samuel A. Lockridge, who was deeply involved in William Walker's movement as well as several plots embracing Mexico, to inform a U.S. Army officer in 1860 after determining that the Knights of the Golden Circle were a "humbug" and not worth his time that he barely knew what to do next since

"I have spent a great portion of my life filibustering." For Lockridge, and many of his peers, filibustering had become an end in itself.[82]

Careerists risked their lives, it would seem, primarily to reexperience the male camaraderie they had formerly achieved on filibuster ships, in filibuster camps, and on the march. Scholars of pre–Civil War American masculinity have observed that the market revolution of the early nineteenth century caused considerable insecurity among American males, as they grappled with an increasingly competitive workplace that valued personal achievement over inherited status. To compensate for their disorientation, men cemented intimate, indeed "romantic," relationships with others of their sex that were remarkably untroubled by homophobic inhibitions. Such findings appear to apply to the filibusters. They certainly illuminate why one filibuster in 1857 might claim "all the external traits and characteristics of romantic heroism" for the members of William Walker's officer corps, as well as assert the impossibility of finding men anywhere who could match the "personal beauty and physical power" of the "better class" of his companions in Nicaragua.[83]

When Roberdeau Wheat informed John Quitman in 1853 that he stood "prepared now as ever to follow you or to go wherever you may order," he attested to the depth of filibuster bonding. So too did the many adventurers who referred affectionately to their fellow soldiers as "the boys," their "brethren," and "comrades," and greeted each other with what E. J. C. Kewen described as "fond" embraces. The former captain under López who told John Goddard that he "would sooner rot in jail than testify against his comrades" exposed the sense of mutual obligation and loyalty that connected filibusters. So did the member of William Walker's army who celebrated the "utmost good feeling" that prevailed in his company, akin to that of "a band of brothers," in a letter to a friend back in the United States. Perhaps, though, William Stewart best exposed filibuster intimacy in his 1857 published reminiscence of Walker's recent defeat, when he recalled the "glorious fellows" who fought at his side. Stewart hoped to once again "have the satisfaction of tipping a glass of *agua[r]d[i]ente* with every mother's son of them."[84]

Between expeditions, filibusters and especially members of the officer corps perpetuated this sense of community. Assembling in various filibustering centers, the adventurers gathered to recount former exploits and map out their next expeditions. Thus a visitor to the St. Charles Hotel's bar in New Orleans described it as a place where men "pledged each other before parting, to join some adventurous expedition"; and the *New-York Daily Times* noted in 1857 a gathering of William Walker's agents and officers at the city's Pewter Mug, after which they called at the residence of Walker's former artillery commander, where, noted the *Times*, a number of other "prominent Filli-busters of this City" were already on hand. Veteran officers of José Carbajal's 1851 campaign in Mexico, on the other hand, assembled in May 1852 at a more rural setting—a massive state fair being held at Corpus Christi, Texas—so that they could plan another invasion.[85] Over time, America's filibusters developed so strong a sense of community that they deserve remembrance as a distinct, if often overlooked, antebellum American subculture.

ALTHOUGH AMERICANS satisfied disparate personal needs by filibustering, most expeditionists and their backers also shared a contributing ideology that influenced their decisions. Many Southerners who filibustered, for instance, did so at least in part as a means of expanding slavery or otherwise advantag-ing their "peculiar institution." As John Hope Franklin observed early in his career, it was "no mere accident" that the majority of "leading filibusters" hailed from the slave states. After all, Franklin argued in *The Militant South*, it was natural for a population prone to dueling and professing chivalric ideals to vent its "martial spirit" in the attempted conquest of new lands. Besides, white southerners hoped that by carving new slave states out of the tropics they might gain political power in Washington to fend off abolitionist assaults on slavery and open up opportunities for new plantations. Franklin pointedly noted that George Fitzhugh, possibly the Old South's most notorious pro-slavery ideologue, justified filibustering both in the abstract and southward in a piece entitled "Acquisition of Mexico—Filibustering" for the December 1858 issue of the New Orleans periodical *De Bow's Review*.[86]

Franklin was right that slavery cast a lengthy shadow over the expeditions. As we will see in chapter 9, which is devoted to the slavery question, not only did a number of filibustering commanders publicly as well as privately pro-mote their schemes as a means of strengthening the South's labor system, but lesser officers and ordinary enlistees sometimes gravitated to the expeditions because of their commitment to slavery. Still, filibustering represented other intellectual currents as well, not only for its many northern practitioners but also for a large number of those from the South.[87]

For one thing, people from all regions of the United States shared a wide-spread conviction, stimulated by the nation's military accomplishments and territorial acquisitions in the Mexican War, that as a "go-ahead" people they were capable of accomplishing almost anything that they set their minds to doing. Mid-nineteenth-century Americans, as Allan Nevins noted some time ago, were a people in a rush, a people who celebrated individual agency in effecting change. We might dispute Nevins's projecting particular character traits upon an entire people, yet his observations illuminate the audacity, confidence, and impatience that made at least some of the filibusters tick.[88]

More precisely, the filibusters, generally youthful as we have seen, sometimes saw themselves as exemplars of the contemporary intellectual and nationalistic movement known as "Young America," and its cousin "manifest destiny." Originating in New York literary and Democratic party circles in the 1830s, Young America drew inspiration from European revolutionary movements (such as Young Italy) and by the mid-1840s had gained a following throughout the country. Initially, Young Americans celebrated their nation's comparative youth, democratic institutions, emergent culture, and rapid progress as compared to Europe's older, supposedly declining, nations. But by 1852 the phrase had evolved into an ill-defined crusade identified with particular Democratic leaders, such as U.S. Senator Stephen A. Douglas of Illinois and the journalist and entrepreneur George N. Sanders of Kentucky, as well as with the causes of U.S. territorial growth, America's presumed mission to support European democratic revolutionary movements, and, sometimes, filibustering. The steamship magnate George Law of New York City exemplified these linkages: he cultivated ties with European revolutionaries, supported Douglas's presidential ambitions in 1852, promoted U.S. annexation of Cuba, and emerged as one of the filibusters' most important arms suppliers.[89]

The filibuster officer Theodore O'Hara exposed Young American sympathies when he confided to his fellow filibuster John T. Pickett, "[Your] enthusiasm in favor of Douglas & Young America accords entirely with my own views," explaining that he personally had been boosting Douglas for president even before getting to know George Sanders. Similarly, a member of William Walker's Nicaraguan army informed an American journal that Granada's streets were now "thronging with the representatives of 'Young America.'" When Walker's appointee as minister to the United States, Appleton Oaksmith, solicited enlistments by citing Nicaragua's appeal "to the representatives of 'Young America,'" he likewise connected to this movement. One group of Walker reinforcements out of New York even organized a "Young America Pioneer Club" aboard ship on their way to Central America.[90]

Naturally, such Young American filibusters championed their nation's "manifest destiny," as well as related precepts of white American racial superiority over Hispanic peoples. The New York newspaperman, Young America apostle, and later filibuster accomplice John L. O'Sullivan popularized "manifest destiny"—a term apparently coined by one of his writers (and later a filibuster promoter), Jane McManus Storm—in the mid-1840s to justify Amer-

ican territorial expansion. At that time, the U.S. government was considering
the annexation of the Republic of Texas as well as attempting to acquire all of
the Oregon Country (then an imprecisely defined area including not only the
present state but also land along the Pacific Coast all the way to Alaska) in a
dispute over ownership with Great Britain. O'Sullivan's slogan and supporting language suggested that God manifestly, or obviously, favored U.S. territorial claims throughout North America over those of competing powers because America's democratic political institutions were superior to the governing
systems of other countries. According to O'Sullivan, Americans would fulfill
their providential destiny by spreading "federative self government" and
"liberty" across the continent.[91]

Yet O'Sullivan did not depend on political criteria alone to justify U.S. territorial growth. Reflecting contemporary American romantic nationalism,
which equated democracy with Caucasians, the journalist and other expansionist ideologues also invoked an American "Anglo-Saxon foot" treading
upon adjacent areas, and predicted that progressive "Anglo-Saxon emigration" would bring ploughs, educational improvements, and other enhance-
ments such as mills and courts into neighboring domains. Some of the day's
extreme racialists, moreover, envisioned American Anglo-Saxons eventually
displacing (or outbreeding into extinction) inferior Hispanic peoples throughout the tropics, much as white Americans had already dispossessed Indians in
the Western United States.[92]

One cannot discount the influence of this ideology, widely disseminated by
America's expansionist politicians and press, upon the expeditionists. The
New Orleans Daily Creole, for instance, imagined "bold [American] pioneers"
imposing "Anglo-American institutions" upon the "feeble descendants of the
once haughty and powerful Spaniard" who inhabited Nicaragua at the time of
William Walker's intervention. Nicaragua's "Rip Van Winkles" would surely
benefit from the "Progress" that Walker was imposing upon them. Similarly,
the *San Francisco Daily Herald* all but instructed young men in the city to join
reinforcing parties for Walker's invasion of Mexico by promising that the people of Sonora craved the advent of "a race bold enough to drive out the
Apaches." Prospective volunteers might well have read in the very same number a letter from the *Herald*'s San Diego correspondent alleging that Mexican
visitors to California had become infatuated with American legal institutions
during their sojourns, and therefore would not stand in the way if U.S. adventurers took care of their Indian difficulties. A mere 500 "Fillibusters"
would be enough to strip Mexico of its "Golden Sierras" and the state of
Sonora.[93]

Certainly filibustering leaders, recruiters, and publicists coopted O'Sullivan's language, as E. J. C. Kewen made evident in a public letter from William Walker's Nicaragua to a San Francisco newspaper: "Call it 'manifest destiny,' . . . call it what you will . . . Nicaragua is free; . . . republican rule has been inaugurated." Similarly, William Wells, who promoted Walker's cause in an 1856 book, noted that the filibusters had demonstrated that the "term 'Manifest Destiny' is no longer a myth for paragraphists and enthusiasts"; and Patrick Henry's grandson William R. Henry summoned Texans bent upon "the extension of the area of freedom" to Central Americans to join the second Nicaraguan intervention of the "Man of Destiny." Henry's words invoked Walker's well-known sobriquet in the United States: "Gray-eyed man of destiny." The nickname married O'Sullivan's term to a folk belief current among Central Americans that a man with gray eyes would one day free them from oppressive Spanish rule.[94]

Many filibusters and prospective enlistees believed that the expeditions would endow less fortunate peoples with America's superior political institutions. P. G. T. Beauregard confided an interest in joining Walker's Nicaraguan cause, since Walker seemed bent on "the establishment of a Central American Republic, based on our own system." A filibuster private affiliated with the Carbajal movement, according to one onlooker, inspired the gathered citizenry of Rio Grande City, Texas, with talk of bringing "freedom, liberty, and other expressions peculiarly American" to Mexico's population. But filibusters bound for Cuba especially claimed an altruistic mission to extend freedom, since that island, unlike other invaded domains, remained under the auspices of a European monarchical power. As a member of López's 1851 invading party informed his brother, America's "liberty loving young men" had to "take a hand" in the island's affairs. Two years later, G. Bolivar Hall offered his services to John Quitman's expeditionary forces so that he could assist "the Cause of Republican Liberty." That same year, a Mississippi college student told Quitman that a "people strugling [sic] beneath oppression" merited assistance from American "republican institutions."[95]

Surely, some filibusters reasoned, they were no more criminals than were America's revolutionary fathers, who had fought for their own nation's freedom, or those sympathetic Europeans such as Lafayette who had crossed the Atlantic to join the cause. As one Kentuckian explained his affiliation with López to his family, "Start not, mother, at this announcement, you know the blood that my grandfather shed in the revolution hallowed the ground from which I have eaten bread." López inspired such notions by telling his filibusters to consider themselves George Washington's sons, as did the *Savannah Morning News* by categorizing the expeditionists as belonging to the

"Paul Jones school of free-booters," an allusion to the Revolutionary naval hero.[96]

Similarly, filibuster leaders and recruiters appropriated manifest destiny's racialist codes, by arguing that their expeditions would rescue invaded peoples from stagnation, reactionary Catholicism, and barbarism. Henry's appeal for recruits labeled Central Americans as "superstitious and ignorant." Rip Ford privately cited Mexico's "anarchy" as justification for filibusters seizing "another slice" of the country and claimed that the Mexican people had been "oppressed, ground down by taxation, debased by ignorance, and paralyzed by the influence of the priests." Henry L. Kinney urged that a former business contact invest in his Central American project because the isthmus, once "settled up by good American citizens," would become "one of the most productive and rich countries in the world." Parker French issued a card promoting William Walker's "heroic effort to spread Liberty and Civilization" in the same region. Walker's widely disseminated inaugural address as president of Nicaragua not only claimed that filibusters had "redeemed Nicaragua from anarchy and ruin" but promised that they would now educate the natives and bring about "modern civilization" in the country. Earlier, Walker had justified his incursion into Lower California in 1853–54 by claiming in a public letter that Mexico had failed the peninsula by neglecting to provide it with communication networks, and that it would remain "half savage and uncultivated" with its minerals unexploited unless Americans intervened. In a similar announcement, George Bickley of the Knights of the Golden Circle implored Christian "Anglo-Americans" to save and Americanize Mexico by first subduing the "barbarous brutes" plaguing the country, and then applying their agricultural and mining tools to its rich resources.[97]

Evidence abounds, moreover, that many Americans considered joining filibuster expeditions in part because they had already internalized a lack of respect for Hispanic peoples, and were naturally receptive to enlistment propaganda. Just before the last López expedition, an American visited Havana on his way east from California via the Panama crossing, and had what should have been a completely satisfying experience. He attended bullfights, cockfights, and Spanish military reviews in the city, and also toured local attractions such as Morro Castle—the magnificent fortress guarding the harbor. Yet, though infatuated with this "loveliest region town & country on gods earth," our visitor could only question the right of such "Transatlantic degenerate don sons of bitches as the inhabitants of old Spain" to continue their rule over the island. He would have to join the next "speculation" to Cuba, he decided, could he but learn how to gain a spot. Other prospective filibusters had similar thoughts. W. Grayson Mann, recently secretary to the American minister in Brazil, for example, urged William Walker in mid-1857 to change his focus from Nicaragua to Brazil, claiming that he would then join Walker to help prevent "the fairest portion of God's Creation rotting away in the hands of a decrepit race incapable of developing its resources."[98]

Sadly, the act of filibustering rarely corrected such prejudices. Instead, many invaders decided upon contact that Mexicans and Central Americans were indeed "greasers" and "mongrels," and sometimes expressed a desire to crush them characteristic of the era's most extreme racialist ideology. At best, the filibusters expressed patronizing attitudes unworthy of their own country's supposed dedication to the principle of self-government. Thus one of Walker's lieutenants, during a quarrel with a fellow officer, exclaimed that he filibustered to assist the "civilization" of an "unfortunate people" and that Nicaragua's resources would soon be exploited "through Anglo-Saxon agency." The attitude of the Texan adventurer Jack Everett, after Mexican recruits deserted José Carbajal's standard, says it all. The disgusted Everett could only conclude that his state's "miserable neighbors" lacked the capacity for self-government and needed a "good thrashing" before being furnished with a decent constitution.[99]

CHAPTER FIVE

Samuel Hay's Puzzlement

To Nicaragua Walker's Bo[u]nd
He scorns your mean frustration
Impartial Judges, Northern Spies,
And Buck's Administration
—Mobile Mercury (quoted in *Tuskegee
Republican*, December 30, 1858)

THE U.S. ATTORNEY for the District of Texas was thoroughly perplexed. Since being appointed to office by President Franklin Pierce soon after his inauguration in the spring of 1853, Samuel D. Hay had been trying to win convictions in the filibuster cases started by his predecessor, William Pitt Ballinger. But rather than provide him with the resources to do the job, the authorities in Washington appeared to be obstructing justice. What was going on?

During the January 1852 term of the U.S. district court in Brownsville, Ballinger had initiated a grand jury investigation of filibustering in his jurisdiction. The jurors on March 4 had indicted José Carbajal and eleven of his associates, who had been seized by U.S. Army dragoons three days earlier in the immediate aftermath of Carbajal's second filibuster into Mexico. Ballinger had then persuaded the presiding district court judge, John C. Watrous, to grant continuances until the next court term in Brownsville (with the defendants posting bond to secure their appearances), so that he could assemble witnesses and evidence. Because of Judge Watrous's absence, however, this session did not occur until June 1853, by which time Hay had replaced Ballinger. Another delay then ensued, because the eight defendants who appeared for their trials persuaded Judge Watrous to grant them a change of venue to Galveston.

Finally, in January 1854 at Galveston, Hay had the opportunity to try the eight filibusters, but it did not go well. The judge threw out the case against Carbajal on a technicality, after a defense plea that five of the grand jurors who had brought the indictment were not bona fide householders in the district. In the next case the trial jury rendered a not guilty verdict. After losing two more cases, Hay, reading the handwriting on the wall, had entered a *nolle prosequi* (dismissal of the charges) respecting the four other filibusters who had appeared for trial.[1]

What bothered Hay was less the outcome than a lack of support from his government. His predecessor had received authorization from Washington to hire two local attorneys in Brownsville to assist in the prosecutions, A. W. Arrington (for $1,000) and Franklin Cummings (for $500). Naturally, once the cases were transferred to Galveston hundreds of miles away, the lawyers faced additional expenses for travel, room, and board. So they asked for a doubling of their fees. Hay was appalled not only that Pierce's secretary of state, William L. Marcy, and the attorney general, Caleb Cushing, failed to answer his letters endorsing the request from Arrington and Cummings, but also that when Marcy finally telegraphed a response directly to Arrington, he denied the additional funding. The government's decision caused the Brownsville attorneys to withdraw from the case (with Arrington reportedly going on a "debauch" in his frustration) and more importantly left Hay without associate counsel for the January 1854 trials. Hay had eventually persuaded a Galveston attorney to assist him, warning that there was no guarantee of any reimbursement by Washington for his work.[2]

In light of the administration's unresponsiveness, Hay wondered whether he should continue prosecuting filibusters. Indictments remained outstanding against the four Carbajal associates who had failed to appear in Brownsville for their trials, as well as against three men who had taken part in a March 1853 violation of Mexican sovereignty. During the latter escapade, the invaders had allegedly captured and robbed a resident of Reynosa in the name of Carbajal.[3] Given Washington's attitude, Hay had to wonder whether it was foolish to pursue such cases.

Immediately after the Galveston debacle, Hay vented his discouragement. Seeing himself as a martyr to the cause of justice, he complained to his fellow Texan Sam Houston, then serving in the U.S. Senate, "If I get nothing beyond the paltry fees which the law allows for all the trouble and labor which these prosecutions devolved upon me . . . I shall still have the consolation as long as I live of remembering that I did my duty in them." Subsequently, Hay articulated his frustrations with Marcy and Cushing in a lengthy letter to Pierce's secretary of war Jefferson Davis, and indicated that he was desperate for a signal from the administration as to its true desires. "Now before going to Brownsville in June next," he implored, "will the Government give me no intimation as to its policy touching these important trials[?] Is it intended that I shall prosecute them vigorously. . . [?] If the Government should continue to fail to indicate its policy . . . it may become an embarrassing question to me how far under my oath of office I should be bound to prosecute." But Hay could hardly have been reassured by Davis's response: a curt one-sentence answer indicating merely that he had referred Hay's letter to Marcy and Cushing.[4]

Hay's frustration raises a disturbing question. Did the Pierce administration deliberately leave its district attorney foundering to assist the adventurers? And if Pierce supported filibustering, why could not other presidents do
so as well? Perhaps America's filibustering epidemic boils down to Washington's disinterest in enforcing the Neutrality Act. Certainly observers leveled
such charges at the time. The *New-York Daily Times* suggested that the Carbajal expeditions could never have occurred had not "the business" been "at
least winked at by the authorities." And the *Atlantic Monthly* believed that the
"very blind eyes and very slippery hands" of port officials trying to stop
William Walker resulted from "secret communication with Washington."
Some historians concur. One student of California's history announced authoritatively that from "the White House on down," U.S. authorities "rarely
discouraged filibustering." Samuel Hay's story provides a potentially critical
clue to Washington's ineptitude at upholding international law in the pre–
Civil War years.[5]

ELECTED PRESIDENT IN 1852 after López's disastrous final expedition against
Cuba, Franklin Pierce inspired renewed hope within the American filibuster
community. As a former Mexican War general, rumored member of the Order
of the Lone Star, and nominee of the expansionist Democratic Party, Pierce
attracted backing from many who wanted the U.S. government to more ag-
gressively pursue territorial gains than it had been doing under the usually
cautious Whig incumbent, Millard Fillmore. In May, the month of the Democratic nominating convention, the British traveler Laurence Oliphant, visiting Washington, was stunned by all the unfamiliar nomenclature, including
the term "filibuster," that he was constantly overhearing around town. Sensitive to the filibusters' faith in Pierce, the Whigs' organ, the *Washington National Intelligencer*, had suggested during Pierce's campaign against the Whig
candidate Winfield Scott that the public would be voting "yea or nay on the
question of Flibustierism" when it went to the polls.[6]

In the months following his election, Pierce gave indications that the filibusters had judged him correctly. His inaugural address included a strident
call for additional national expansion, and he included filibusters among his
early appointments. Pierce made John L. O'Sullivan his chargé d'affaires in
Lisbon, and then minister to Portugal. As U.S. consuls he named George N.
Sanders, whose *Democratic Review* had recently published O'Sullivan's article
arguing for more limited enforcement of the Neutrality Law, to London and
the former López filibuster John T. Pickett to Vera Cruz, Mexico. The president even turned over two cabinet positions concerned with enforcement of

President Franklin Pierce.
(Courtesy of the Library of
Congress)

the Neutrality Law to notorious expansionists with apparent links to the filibuster camp. In public addresses in 1852, Secretary of War Davis had likened
filibusters to Lafayette and other liberty-loving European heroes of the
American Revolution, and blasted Fillmore for treating them as pirates. Attorney General Caleb Cushing, during the Polk administration, had served as
an intermediary between Cuba filibusters and the president; in September
1853 Cushing drew attention for attending a banquet in memory of the fallen
López filibusters in Washington.[7]

Further incriminating evidence survives in the correspondence of the
Cuba filibustering leader John Quitman. About a year after Pierce assumed
office, Quitman received assurances from Senator Stephen Douglas of Illinois
and Congressman Philip Phillips of Alabama, conveyed to him by third parties, that the president had agreed to refrain from interfering with Cuba filibustering. But the adventurers were advised to be circumspect and not attract
publicity. Too much coverage of their preparations, Quitman was told, would
make it embarrassing for Pierce to remain inactive.[8]

Nor is this the entire case against Pierce. In February 1854 the president convinced the U.S. Senate to delete an antifilibustering clause from the pending Gadsden Purchase treaty. Under Pierce's prodding, the Senate eliminated wording that would have committed the United States to providing Mexico with armed assistance in the apprehension of "lawless adventurers" on the "high seas." During the winter of 1854–55, Pierce's organ, the *Washington Daily Union*, endorsed Henry L. Kinney's proposed expedition to Central America's Mosquito Coast—a stand consistent with the newspaper's earlier attacks on Presidents Taylor and Fillmore for firming up despotism in Cuba by excessive enforcement of the neutrality statutes. Meanwhile, Pierce's cabinet deferred intervention, despite complaints from Central American governments that Kinney's operation was a filibuster. Rumor had it that the president and other administration officials even had a vested interest in the scheme. But the most damning evidence against Pierce is the most obvious: in May 1856 the administration granted formal recognition to William Walker's régime in Nicaragua.[9]

Yet Pierce's administration did more to disrupt the expeditions than to further them, and the president certainly never came through on his supposed promises to the Cuba expeditionists. Assuming that Pierce really made the promises attributed to him, he apparently changed his mind by June 1854. That month, the U.S. attorney for the Southern District of Mississippi, Horatio J. Harris, intimated to one of Quitman's correspondents that he had received instructions about the president's determination to prevent any filibuster against Cuba. On June 17, moreover, U.S. Senator John Slidell of Louisiana informed James Buchanan, then U.S. minister in England, that Pierce had asked him to get word to the adventurers by telegraph that they should call off their expedition, since the president hoped to acquire Cuba through diplomatic means. Quitman continued his uphill battle to launch his expedition despite the discouragement from Washington and criminal proceedings against him in federal court (described later in this chapter), but he finally canceled the plot entirely after a meeting with Pierce at the White House the following March.[10]

Through all this, neither Attorney General Cushing nor Secretary of War Davis intervened on the filibusters' behalf. Cushing may never have been genuinely in their camp; Pierce's private secretary later recalled that Cushing exploded in anger whenever the filibusters came up in conversation. Davis was truly intrigued by filibustering; after leaving office, he announced publicly that he would "rejoice" if Walker's attempt to reconquer Nicaragua succeeded and if the country came to share America's "Representative liberty" and governmental stability. Yet Davis kept his filibustering instincts under control while serving as war secretary, and he was widely suspected in filibuster circles of having influenced the president's shift against Quitman, a longtime rival in Mississippi politics. In a speech after leaving the war office, Davis argued that Pierce would have dishonored the nation had he achieved expansion by fraudulent means.[11]

Not only did Pierce fail to come through for Quitman, but he did less for the period's other filibusters than may seem apparent. His recognition of Walker's régime in Nicaragua in May 1856 came after a half-year's procrastination. In October 1855 Marcy had specifically instructed the U.S. minister to Nicaragua, John H. Wheeler, to abstain from official dealings with Walker's government, on the rationale that it had achieved its status by force and did not represent the Nicaraguan people. Over the following months, the administration had ordered its port officials to prevent reinforcements for Walker from leaving their jurisdictions. Further, the administration threatened Walker's supposed minister to the United States with arrest, unless he left the country.[12]

More important, official recognition did not necessarily amount to approval. By the time that the Pierce administration established relations with Walker's government, the filibusters had consolidated their rule over much of Nicaragua under a native Nicaraguan president, and had sent a native Nicaraguan as their minister to the United States. Since Walker's government appeared to have de facto control over Nicaragua, and since U.S. policy had been to recognize governments with such authority, Pierce's shift made sense. Once Walker in July seized the Nicaraguan presidency for himself and chose an American as his new envoy to Washington, Marcy permanently broke relations with the filibuster government. In all, U.S. recognition lasted less than three months.[13]

During the second period of nonrecognition, furthermore, Pierce and his cabinet faced down rumors spread by some of Walker's operatives that Pierce's hostility to Walker's cause derived from involvement with Kinney's competing Central American project. In early 1857 the administration arrested some of Walker's operatives in New York City. At their examination in February before a U.S. commissioner, in order to discredit the government's case against them, the filibusters introduced documents purporting to show Pierce's links with Kinney. All that their evidence actually revealed, however, was that Pierce's private secretary Sidney Webster and the *Daily Union* editor A. O. P. Nicholson had connections with Kinney, and that a letter from Webster about Kinney matters had been sent in an envelope bearing Pierce's frank. Rather than be intimidated by the filibusters' charges against Pierce, Attorney General Cushing challenged them to produce genuine evidence that Pierce had any interest in Kinney's scheme, and told federal authorities to continue the case "without fear."[14]

In fact, as shown later in this chapter, the Pierce administration took strong action against Kinney's movement in the spring of 1855, damaging its prospects and almost crushing it entirely. Upset by the interference, one of Kinney's supporters had used a Biblical analogy in a public letter conveying the filibusters' disappointment at finding Pierce's supposedly sympathetic attorney general in the enemy's camp: "Cushing . . . is singularly opposed to Kinney. . . . Give me Saul among the prophets and Cushing among the antifilibusteros! They are equally in place."[15]

Had Pierce acceded to the Gadsden Treaty's antifilibustering clause, moreover, he would have endorsed a concept abhorrent to most Americans. The deleted provision stipulated that filibusters would be "punished by the government of that nation to which the vessel capturing them may belong, conformably to the laws of each nation." Since Mexican law did not guarantee jury trials to accused individuals, concurrence by the United States in the clause would have allowed American citizens to be imprisoned or even executed without benefit of a privilege enshrined in the U.S. Constitution's sixth amendment.[16]

RATHER THAN "wink" at filibustering, all of antebellum America's presidents took the plots seriously. They brought the problem before cabinet meetings, and they adopted measures to ward off rumored expeditions. Most obviously, by promulgating presidential proclamations, they made prevention a matter of urgent policy and public record. Their seven such decrees, issued over a combined twelve years in office, disproportionately amounted to nearly one quarter of all U.S. presidential neutrality proclamations for the entire period 1793–1914.[17]

Presidential neutrality proclamations condemned filibustering on legal, pragmatic, and moral grounds. In his denunciation of Cuba filibustering on May 31, 1854, Pierce not only explained that filibustering plots contravened the clauses and spirit of U.S. treaties with Spain, but also moralized that filibustering was "derogatory to the character" of the nation. Pierce reminded Americans that they would violate their "duties" and "obligations" as citizens and commit high misdemeanors if they joined such undertakings, and cautioned that federal authorities would "interpose" themselves to maintain the "honor" of the American flag and "prosecute with due energy" those persons who persisted in their involvement. He even called on private American citizens to assist federal officials in enforcing the Neutrality Act.

Other presidential proclamations sounded similar themes. Millard Fillmore informed Americans in April 1851 that "such expeditions can only be regarded as adventures for plunder and robbery" and that violators would "subject themselves" to "heavy penalties." The following fall, Fillmore announced that a pending expedition would "degrade the character of the United States in the opinion of the civilized world" and that "all well-disposed citizens" who cared about preserving their country's peace and laws should join U.S. civil and military officers in stopping the plot.[18]

Antebellum presidents used their annual messages and other communications to Congress as further opportunities for discrediting filibustering. Fillmore's first annual message (December 1850) hypothesized wishfully that the American people opposed "hostile military expeditions" against foreign powers at peace with their country, even though Americans sympathized with oppressed people anywhere who were struggling for their liberty. James Buchanan devoted a six-paragraph passage in his first annual message to an anti-filibustering diatribe and called on Congress to adopt legislation that would restrain American citizens from "committing such outrages" in the future. Buchanan not only suggested that filibustering tarnished the American "character" but equated it with robbery and murder and argued that it damaged U.S. commercial interests abroad.[19]

Skeptics might dismiss such pronouncements as hypocritical ploys to mollify angry foreign diplomats and domestic critics. Words come cheaply. Indeed, in 1849 one federal agent alerted the Department of State that filibusters in New York were laughing at President Zachary Taylor's denunciation on August 11 of expeditions against Cuba and Mexico. Two of John Quitman's correspondents claimed inside information after Pierce's May 1854 proclamation that it was intended for public consumption only, and that the president had no intention of energetically opposing the Cuba expedition.[20]

However, presidents sometimes expressed personal feelings about filibustering that conformed to their public stances. Zachary Taylor in one private letter explained that he "fully" agreed "with the views of the Cabinet in relation to the measures necessary to prevent any aggressions by our citizens upon any friendly power." More important, if presidential proclamations did little to dissuade hard-core filibusters, they surely caused second thoughts among those undecided about joining the filibuster ranks. In explaining to John Quitman in June 1854 why Robert Shufeldt had dropped out of the Cuba scheme, the Mobile operative Joseph W. Lesesne intimated that Shufeldt had become "unsettled" by Franklin Pierce's neutrality declaration.[21]

Besides, all these presidents mobilized the federal civil and military establishments against the adventurers. U.S. marshals and their deputies, sometimes with the cooperation of federal soldiers and customs officials, searched for evidence, served arrest warrants, and guarded filibusters while they were in federal custody. U.S. customs officials searched vessels in their ports and nearby for evidence of filibustering intent, denied clearance to suspicious ships, and deployed U.S. revenue cutters to interdict those filibustering ships attempting to leave the coast. The Army tried to stop filibusters from crossing the U.S.-Mexican frontier, while the Navy joined the Revenue Cutter Service in guarding the coastline and tried to stop the filibusters once they successfully escaped to sea. U.S. attorneys gathered evidence so that filibusters could be identified, arrested, and prosecuted. A miscellany of additional federal employees, including U.S. commissioners and temporary detective agents, similarly played a hand in the containment process.

Presidents and their cabinet officers pointedly and repeatedly reminded federal employees of their antifilibustering obligations, using dramatic phrases like "Look out" to drum their point home. In 1849 President Taylor's naval secretary wanted his "Home Squadron" commander to use "all proper means" to halt the Round Island plot. The next June, Secretary of State John M. Clayton urged the U.S. district attorney in New Orleans to arrest Narciso López. The president, he emphasized, "instructs me to enjoin it upon you as you value the faith and character of your country to spare no pains to execute the law. Do your whole duty." When President Fillmore issued an antifilibustering executive order to customs collectors in Key West, St. Augustine, Savannah, Charleston, Baltimore, and Philadelphia, as well as marshals at Galveston, New Orleans, and Mobile, he mandated that they "take all proper measures, and employ such part of the land and Naval Forces of the United States, or of the militia" as needed to stop expeditions. In September 1857 President Buchanan's secretary of state, Lewis Cass, issued a circular to U.S. attorneys, marshals, and collectors telling them that the president wanted the Neutrality Law enforced with "all legitimate means" at their command. Three months later, Cass urged the confiscation of a suspected filibuster ship and telegraphed the U.S. attorney in New Orleans, "Be vigilant in your endeavors to prevent illegal expeditions against Central America, and in prosecuting offenders."[22]

Despite Pierce's supposed support for the expeditions, his administration also incorporated strong language within its antifilibustering directives. Secretary of State Marcy encouraged the U.S. district attorney in New Orleans, E. Warren Moise, and his colleague at the customs house, Solomon Downs, to "omit nothing" in enforcing the Neutrality Act within their district. Even after the collapse of William Walker's invasion of Baja California and Sonora in the spring of 1854, the administration kept U.S. officials in San Francisco on high alert. Marcy stressed that Mexico needed to be convinced "of the scrupulous fidelity of this government to its duties and obligations towards her as a neighbour and a friend." In December 1855 Attorney General Cushing instructed U.S. attorneys in Boston and southern Ohio "not to fail" in bringing criminal action against persons involved in a rumored filibuster plot against Ireland. And so it went, in order after order.[23]

It requires a highly conspiratorial perspective to dismiss such directives as irrelevant. In order to believe that America's presidents really wanted the filibusters to succeed, one must assume either that they had a prearranged understanding with federal officials in port cities that such instructions were for public consumption only, or that presidents and cabinet officials sent supplementary instructions, which have since disappeared from the historical record, telling public officers to ignore orders to enforce the Neutrality Act. Such assumptions defy logic.

There is further proof that federal authorities meant business: presidents and their cabinets provided funds for supplementary legal counsel, so that U.S. district attorneys could successfully prosecute the expeditionists. In June 1850 the Department of State urged the U.S. attorney in New Orleans, Logan Hunton, to hire a "gentleman of the Bar" to assist him in a case pending against Narciso López; eventually the government paid the Louisiana lawyer, planter, and future Confederate secretary of state Judah P. Benjamin $5,000 for his services as Hunton's choice. Later in the year, the department urged Hunton's counterpart in New York, J. Prescott Hall, to spare no expenses in his investigations of filibustering. During the Buchanan administration, Attorney General Jeremiah S. Black, at the request of the president, solicited the Mobile attorney Robert H. Smith to join the government's team to prosecute filibusters in Alabama. Black described the "arrest and prevention of those criminal enterprises" as "so important" that the government should make "every possible effort to that end," mustering "the ablest professional talent" it could get.

Such efforts represented a determined effort to get filibusters behind bars, as a dismayed John L. O'Sullivan realized in 1851 when facing trial for collusion with López. Incensed at the government's hiring of the prominent Ogden Hoffman, he complained directly to Secretary of State Daniel Webster that it was unfair for his prosecutors to employ an attorney of such "known eloquence and ability." O'Sullivan whined about now facing such unfavorable odds that he would have to incur the "hardship" of hiring his own extra lawyer![24]

Throughout the pre–Civil War years, moreover, the government paid out money for detectives, secret agents, the testimony of witnesses, and all sorts of miscellaneous expenses to suppress the expeditions. In 1853, for instance, the secretary of the navy encouraged his commanders on the Pacific coast to charter a private mail steamer at government expense, if they lacked sufficient naval strength to repress "lawless expeditions." In 1857 Secretary of State Lewis Cass authorized the U.S. district attorney in New Orleans to rent a private steamer and put a marshal and posse on board, if necessary, to arrest filibusters before they left port. Sometimes federal resources were diverted from other missions to ward off expeditions. Secretary of State Marcy observed in 1855 that the government had deployed two thirds of the army's "whole available military force" on the Californian, New Mexican, and Texan borders with Mexico in an effort to stop filibustering, even though it meant leaving American settlers on the Indian frontier without protection against possible attack. In 1859, troubled by reports that 200 of William Walker's men were on the verge of slipping out of New York harbor on a new expedition, Secretary of the Treasury Howell Cobb retained a revenue cutter at the port that he had intended to send to the coast of Florida to enforce U.S. laws against the African slave trade.[25]

THE EVIDENCE THAT presidents and their cabinets upheld the Neutrality Act may be compelling, but it does call into question the vigor with which military and civil officers implemented presidential policy at the local level. Something must explain America's anemic antifilibustering record. And the record shows that the U.S. Navy was riddled with officers who at best felt ambivalent about implementing their orders to repress the filibusters. In 1854, for instance, naval officers keeping a watch on Walker's movements at Ensenada in Baja California landed and apparently fraternized with the filibusters during a visit to their encampment. Not only, according to a correspondent, did the officers have discussions "of the most friendly nature" with Walker, but they allowed themselves to be dined by the invaders. In 1858 the naval officer and ordnance expert John A. Dahlgren expressed considerable reluctance to interfere with Walker's Central American movement. Ordered to patrol against filibusters in Nicaraguan waters during the summer of 1858, Captain Dahlgren complained that the region's tropical climate would expose him and his crew to yellow fever, and so enervate his men that ordnance exercises would prove impossible. Why should the government, he wondered, prevent America's urban "scum" from going to such a wretched place? No happier when stationed on antifilibustering patrol in Mobile Bay months later, he protested, "If Walker is to be hunted up I would like to be relieved by some other officer."[26]

Surprisingly, the very commodore of the U.S. Home Squadron who crushed Walker's second invasion of Central America proved susceptible to filibustering's siren. Hiram Paulding, while on station in Nicaraguan waters during Walker's first intervention on the isthmus, observed that everyone who met Walker was "favourably impressed." Surely, Paulding decided, Central America's "unhappy race" of throat-cutters, before Walker's advent, had "foolishly wasted & thrown aside the bounteous gifts of providence" in "one of the fairest & best portions of the globe." Though proclaiming himself no "Fillibustero," Paulding nonetheless wanted America's "enterprising race" to "go to Nicaragua" and use their "stouter hearts & stronger hands" to tame what had become a "howling wilderness." His countrymen would surely inject into it the "beautiful system of government" of the United States, "the only plan that has ever yet been devised for the general harmony & good will of the human race."[27]

Another example is provided by the naval commander Charles H. Davis. In language notable for its sexual stereotypes, Davis reasoned to his superior officer in March 1857, after observing that Central American forces warring against Walker refused to exit their barricades even when they had sufficient troops to defeat him, that native peoples lacked the masculinity to cope with filibustering invaders:

> The truth is Commodore, if the Americans establish themselves here, it will be by the same law that the Turks govern the effete races of Asia Minor . . . a law of nature—When I passed immediately from the American Camp to that of the Allies, and observed the strong contrast between the serious count[en]ances, and the personal proportions of the men of Northern origin I had just left: and the mild unthoughtful faces (with large womanly eyes) and the full round forms of the guard drawn up to receive me . . . I discerned at once the secret of Walker[']s frequent successful resistance against such great odds.

People never should assume, Davis declared, that Central America's "effeminate" peoples had the same passion for independence as North Americans did.[28]

Some army officers fell into the same ethnocentric trap. Lieutenant Ambrose P. Hill, while on antifilibustering patrol on the Rio Grande during the Carbajal disturbances, complained that his own second lieutenant was a "terrible Filibuster" in his sympathies. Captain William Tecumseh Sherman confessed to his brother of so wanting America to annex Cuba that he "sometimes" found himself hoping that the filibusters would succeed. Several army officers resigned from the service to join John Quitman's intended expedition to Cuba, and Cadmus Wilcox, an instructor of tactics at the U.S. Military Academy, expressed an inclination "to turn Phillibuster at once." Wilcox even applied for a leave of seventy days so that he could reconnoiter the island for the upcoming invasion. P. G. T. Beauregard believed so strongly in Anglo-Saxon supremacy over mixed-race Latin Americans that, as indicated earlier, he came extremely close to sacrificing his U.S. army career for a commission from William Walker.[29]

Other enforcement arms of the government contained such filibustering fellow travelers as Isaiah Rynders, the deputy surveyor of customs in New York City who, it will be remembered, publicly admitted his affiliation with the Order of the Lone Star. In May 1856, less than a year before his swearing in as U.S. marshal, Rynders addressed a public meeting in the city, telling the crowd that William Walker deserved their assistance because the backwards peoples of Nicaragua needed an injection of American "vitality." Warming to his subject, Rynders enthused, "if to go among an unenlightened people to elevate them in the scale of moral and social excellence is to be a filibuster, then write me down as a filibuster." Later in the year, at another rally, Rynders endorsed Walker for establishing a government based on "free principles," while stating for the record that he would always put his public duties before his private sympathies.[30]

When a federal secret agent turned up in Mobile in December 1858 on an investigation of filibustering activity, he felt compelled to hide his identity from the port's U.S. marshal, so convinced was he that this official was "secretly" in the enemy camp. Apparently he had cause. Just days later, this very marshal facilitated the escape of Walker's *Susan* expedition. Though the district attorney had put in his trust arrest warrants against every man on the ship as well as a libel to have the *Susan* forfeited, the marshal delayed serving the papers for thirty-one hours.[31]

Given the prevalence of such attitudes, filibusters not surprisingly counted on sympathetic federal officials to look the other way during the preparatory stages of their expeditions. In February 1855 one of the Cuban movement's bond hawkers in Georgia reassured John Quitman that the customs collector at an embarkation point was a "Lone Star" who would be cooperative, and that the federal judge was sympathetic and "would not put himself out of the way to trouble" them. In 1860 one of William Walker's operatives managed to get "upon social terms" with the collector in New Orleans and predicted that the official would be lax in his enforcement of the Neutrality Act.

IT WOULD BE fanciful, however, to jump from the profilibustering tendencies of some military officers and filibuster officials to the presumption that covert support for expeditions characterized all of America's military and civil establishment. Rather than coddle filibusters, federal civil and military officials more typically disparaged them. Many army officers, for example, worried that the expeditions controverted their nation's honor. For reasons including the growth of careerism within the service and attacks on the army by politicians and newspapers, the service's officer corps had by this time developed what one scholar has defined as a "growing sense of nonpartisan subordination to the civilian authority of the nation-state"—or what we might label a professional ethic.[32] If the government proclaimed an antifilibustering mission for its military, then, by this logic, army officers had to do their duty, or they would tarnish their own profession.

West Pointers, who were educated at government expense, exposed to a curriculum that incorporated ethics and international law, and increasingly numerous within the officer corps, perhaps naturally professed such attitudes. John C. Pemberton, a graduate who not only joyfully applauded news that the Cuban filibusters had failed but also desired that Spanish authorities on the island "shoot or hang every man they can catch," certainly rejected the filibustering cause. So did the arsenal commander Peter V. Hagner, class of 1836, who less dramatically reasoned that filibusters caused their nation to "suffer discredit." Second Lieutenant Edward L. Hartz, an 1855 Academy graduate who was posted on the Rio Grande during the Knights of the Golden Circle plot against Mexico, believed it required by "reason and justice" that the federal government "should not only not recognize nor encourage but should to the extent of its power prevent all attempts to extend the 'Area of Freedom' in the way proposed." Even William Tecumseh Sherman, also an alumnus, came down soundly on the antifilibustering side in the end, realizing that the expeditions violated America's "Solemn treaties," and impaired the very annexation of Cuba that he had initially thought they might facilitate.[33]

But antifilibustering sentiments hardly demanded a West Point education. General John E. Wool, who had served in the officer corps since the War of 1812 but never attended the academy, exulted privately at news reports that the Costa Ricans had gained the upper hand over William Walker ("I hope it is true, for I am wholly and totally opposed to all Bucaniering [*sic*] expeditions"). Wool advised a fellow officer to resist his impulse to join the Henry Crabb expedition to Mexico on the basis that it was a "plundering expedition" that would never prevail.[34]

Army officers condemned filibustering for more than its patent illegality and immorality. Colonel Ethan Allen Hitchcock, commander of the army's Pacific Division in the early 1850s, worried that the revolutionizing of Cuba, which had slavery, might disrupt the Union, since filibuster organizers had been promising their followers large estates in the island. Inevitably an expedition premised on such assurances would bring up the dangerous "negro question" again. Captain Joseph H. La Motte, in contrast, observed that José Carbajal's attacks against Mexico had been "ruinous" for American business interests on the border. Other commanders resented the proportion of their time consumed by antifilibustering responsibilities. General Persifor F. Smith, administering the army's 8th Military Department out of San Antonio, became annoyed in the summer of 1852 when the Carbajal disturbances forced him to deploy five companies of mounted riflemen on the border in order to discourage Mexican forces from retaliating into Texas. Since his men and horses were not yet acclimated for service in "the hottest region on the continent," such patrols would monopolize his soldiers' time at the expense of constructing quarters for the coming winter. During the Knights of the Golden Circle plot in 1860, Lieutenant Colonel Robert E. Lee, then the army's ranking border commander, complained that he and his staff had many "filibustering reports & Mexican aggressions to scrutinize & discuss," making it hard to know which ones to take seriously.[35]

The Navy had its own officers who disparaged filibustering. During his mission against the Cuba filibusters in 1849, Commander Victor M. Randolph reassured the Navy Department of his determination to stop the "band of reckless adventurers." Stationed on the USS *Susquehanna* in Nicaraguan waters in 1856, Seth Phelps confided that aboard ship William Walker's soldiers had the reputation of being "'shoulder hitters,' 'strikers,' 'bouncers,' 'killers,' & the like, ready to commit outrage & plunder upon friend or foe." Phelps believed that Walker's following among Nicaraguan natives was limited to those who supported him out of fear, and he opposed recognition by the United States of the filibuster régime. In 1858, perturbed that his vessel had been transferred from European waters to antifilibustering duty in Central America, Phelps lamented Walker's surviving his second invasion: "society" would have been far better off had he met his death. That same year,

General Persifor F. Smith.
(Courtesy of the National
Archives, photo no. 111-SC-
98106)

Samuel Francis Du Pont told his wife how shocked he was that William
Walker, who had "violated openly the laws of his country & brought dishonor
on her flag & name," would be received at all by the Buchanan administration
when he arrived in Washington, much more be allowed to shake hands with
the secretary of state.[36]

Civil officials likewise expressed chagrin about filibustering, and pledged
their cooperation in carrying out Washington's antifilibustering directives.
The U.S. marshal at Galveston, Texas, reassured President Fillmore, "I am
politically and personally opposed to all these contemplated aggressions on
other powers." In 1852 the U.S. district attorney for South Carolina pronounced filibustering a form of piracy and promised "zeal" in repressing illegal activity in his district. When in early 1854 Attorney General Cushing required the U.S. district attorney for California, S. W. Inge, to "use the utmost
vigilance in the detection and prosecution" of filibusters, Inge replied that
Cushing's directives would be "strictly pursued." During William Walker's
second foray to Nicaragua, the port of Mobile's collector promised Secretary
of State Lewis Cass that he would "use all the means" at his command against
the expedition.[37]

Naturally, some federal officials dissembled, since they risked sacrificing their positions if they did not at least go through the motions of enforcing the Neutrality Act. Secretary of State Daniel Webster warned the U.S. collector in New Orleans in January 1851 that federal officers would be "held to a strict accountability" respecting their antifilibustering duties. In December 1858 U.S. Attorney General Jeremiah S. Black instructed his special counsel in Mobile to determine why the filibuster vessel *Susan* had successfully departed from port for Nicaragua, noting that if the counsel discovered the U.S. marshal to be "in default," he had best suggest a replacement.[38]

Indeed, there is evidence of hypocrisy in the case of Inge. He apparently played a profilibustering hand just before the departure from San Francisco in 1853 of William Walker's expedition to Lower California, after the Army's Colonel Hitchcock detached soldiers to seize Walker's intended vessel, the *Arrow*. Inge stalled before acting on Hitchcock's request that the vessel be libeled, and then before searching the ship for arms. This procrastination allowed the filibusters to transfer their military stores to an alternative vessel, on which they eventually sailed. Further, both Inge and the U.S. collector urged that Hitchcock return the *Arrow* to the filibusters rather than risk their overpowering his small posted guard and getting the vessel back anyway. Hitchcock disgustedly concluded that the two officials had been "corrupted" by the profilibustering U.S. senator from California William M. Gwin, with whom the collector had been observed engaged in conversation.[39]

In at least two cases, U.S. presidents removed officials whom they suspected of abetting the expeditions. Immediately after the last López filibuster, President Fillmore fired the collector in New Orleans, William Freret, within days of receiving evidence from Spain's minister that Freret had been unduly lethargic in responding to evidence of the expedition's impending departure. In December 1857 President Buchanan replaced Franklin H. Clack as U.S. attorney for the Eastern District of Louisiana, in anger that Clack had permitted Walker's being released from federal custody on just $2,000 bail before his second invasion of Nicaragua. Possibly the Pierce administration thought about dumping Inge. During an interview with a recently retired army officer, Secretary Marcy said that he would not be taken in by Inge's "tricks," and that the cabinet approved of General Hitchcock's seizure of the *Arrow*.[40]

BUT SHOULD A FEW cases taint the entire federal enforcement apparatus? More typically, federal officials made conscientious exertions to prevent filibustering operations within their jurisdictions. In his memoirs about service with the Second U.S. Dragoons, the former regimental officer Theophilus

Rodenbough described the army's efforts in 1851–52 to "disarm" José Carbajal's filibusters on the Mexican border as a "'neutrality campaign'" of six months' duration. That Rodenbough used this particular phrase and that he put it in quotation marks is significant. His words remind us that the army waged sustained efforts against filibustering, and they imply that others in the service also considered these efforts to be major operations.[41]

Rodenbough might well have been describing the exertions of officers such as William Prince and Ambrose P. Hill, both of whom served on the Rio Grande frontier in the fall and winter of 1851–52. Prince, a captain commanding the 1st Infantry Regiment at Ringgold Barracks, kept a diary in which he described breaking up gatherings of filibusters, guarding ferries, coordinating strategy with Mexican officers on the border, and encamping in frigid weather. Hill, then a lieutenant and later a Confederate general, conveyed the rhythms of military life in the field in his letters: "We are in the strong hold of the Filibusters—Carvajal being but some 40 miles from us with some 400 men. There is a store here, and ferry across the river. We have to prevent their crossing, should they attempt it. . . . When I left Florida, I had hoped I would not see a tent again for five years. Tis very cold here, and our men suffer terrible."[42]

What was true for the army also applied to the government's naval and civil officers, who waged their own "campaigns." In 1850, for instance, the U.S. attorney for Delaware decided to visit virtually every town and village in his district, to determine whether there was any truth to allegations that ninety to one hundred filibusters intended to board a schooner within his jurisdiction. The next year, the U.S. collector at San Francisco maintained "a constant watch" over the harbor. "Our boats," he reported, "are moving quietly around the shipping and I do not think they can escape us. Our guns are kept loaded with 32-lb. shot and matches kept burning from dark until daylight."[43]

In December 1857, reacting to rumors that filibusters were about to leave their vicinity aboard a vessel called the *Alnah*, federal authorities in New York port "ransacked the harbor" in an unsuccessful search. U.S. Marshal Rynders, despite his profilibustering tendencies, personally commandeered a steam tug to scour the bay. The *New-York Times* provided a wonderful account of Rynders's chasing down several vessels, including a barque that was being pulled to sea by a fast tug. Rynders, seeing a fair number of men on the barque's deck, presented "that clenched fist which has so often brought Tammany to a standstill" to the captain of the tug, and triumphantly forced him to pull the suspected barque back to port, leaving her at anchor within gunfire range of a U.S. revenue cutter. However, on searching the suspected vessel, Rynders discovered some female acquaintances of his in her cabin, but nothing "to show her a filibuster." Determining that the men on board were mostly railroad workers bound for Cuba, federal authorities in the port let the vessel go.[44]

Few federal officials campaigned more effectively against filibusters than did Isaiah D. Hart, the collector at Jacksonville, Florida, at the time of Narciso López's second invasion of Cuba in 1851. Upon learning on September 8 that the *Pampero* had returned to U.S. waters for reinforcements after dropping off the expedition on the Cuban coast, and that the vessel had crossed the bar of the St. Johns River and was passing upstream from Jacksonville, Hart began countermeasures within an hour, ordering the only revenue cutter then at his disposal to pursue the *Pampero* upriver, "search all creeks & Lakes" for her, and seize the vessel unless there was armed resistance (in which case the cutter's commander was ordered to remain nearby and keep the filibuster vessel under watch). He also appealed for assistance to the collector at St. Augustine, who then rushed fifty U.S. Army soldiers to Jacksonville. When Hart realized that he might need artillery to prevent the *Pampero* from escaping back downriver to the ocean, he "dispatched an express to St. Augustine" and procured two cannon. After Hart's revenue inspectors caught up with the *Pampero*, and, meeting no resistance, took possession and brought the vessel to the wharf at Jacksonville, the collector posted a "strong guard" on board to deter any attempt by the filibusters at repossession. In addition, Hart sent his inspectors back out in an attempt to recover filibuster arms and ammunition that had been unloaded from the *Pampero* before she was taken into federal custody, and he summoned to Jacksonville the U.S. attorney for the Northern District of Florida, George P. Call, so that legal process could be initiated for federal confiscation of the filibuster ship.[45]

Call complied with Hart's request, as well as with instructions from the State Department drawing his attention to the third section of the Neutrality Act, which authorized the forfeiture of privately armed vessels (including armaments and other equipment on board) fitted out for the purpose of serving a foreign "people" with whom the United States was at peace. In October, Call libeled the *Pampero* in admiralty proceedings before the federal court at St. Augustine, construing the "disloyal inhabitants" of Cuba as a foreign people embraced by the legislation. On December 11 the court decided for the government, ruling that the U.S. marshal for the district should sell the vessel at public auction before January 22, 1852.[46]

Repeatedly, federal authorities in New York obstructed the sailing of filibusters to Cuba. During López's 1849 plot, District Attorney Hall commandeered partially dressed sailors and marines from the navy yard and caused them to board the suspected vessel *Florida*, and board and seize the *Sea Gull* and the *New Orleans*. Eventually Hall released the ships, but only after ensuring that the filibusters' charters for the vessels had been canceled, and munitions removed from the *Sea Gull*. On April 23, 1851, federal authorities struck again. After chartering a private steamer, borrowing a revenue cutter, and talking New York's police chief into the loan of a police force for an unfruitful search in nearby waters for the suspected filibuster ship *Cleopatra*, U.S. marshal Henry F. Tallmadge on April 24 discovered the dilapidated, leaky ship at the North Moore Street pier, and detained it under the watch of a marine guard from the navy yard. On his third search of the vessel, Tallmadge turned up twenty-four kegs of gunpowder and other military matériel, providing more than enough justification for federal authorities to hold the vessel for more than a month. Finally on May 31, after the immediate threat of an expedition had passed, the government released the ship, but only after its owner, the filibuster John L. O'Sullivan, pledged that he would restrict her to coastal trading ventures. O'Sullivan, who had expended some $19,000 to make the *Cleopatra* seaworthy, then sold the vessel and sent the proceeds to López's operatives in New Orleans.

In January 1855 U.S. officials put one of the final nails into the Quitman conspiracy's coffin by seizing the steamer *Massachusetts* off the New Jersey coast and, after discovering on board thousands of flint-lock muskets, ammunition, harnesses, and provisions, initiating proceedings in admiralty against the vessel. By the time a federal judge on March 19 decided to dismiss the libel, Quitman had decided to resign his filibuster command.[47]

Federal authorities similarly interfered with filibuster vessels departing for other points, as when Colonel Hitchcock's seized the *Arrow* at San Francisco. In May 1855, in response to public notices that Henry L. Kinney's *United States* was about to sail from New York for the Mosquito Coast, President Pierce personally directed Captain Charles Boarman, commander of the U.S. Navy Yard at Brooklyn, to intercept the vessel should it attempt to leave port. Boarman deployed warships and a revenue cutter to blockade the *United States* in the East River. Federal authorities also seized the vessel that transported Walker's second expedition to Nicaragua, the *Fashion*, immediately after its return to Mobile in January 1858, and later in the year they took preventive action against vessels involved in Walker's next attempt. That November, the U.S. customs collector in Mobile, Thaddeus Sanford, under strong pressure from the Buchanan administration, denied clearance to the expedition's intended transport, the *Alice Tainter*. When the filibuster managers in response surrendered their charter of the ship (which was reloaded with cotton intended for Europe) and attempted to get their expedition off on Captain Maury's *Susan* by applying for a clearance to take provisions to Key West, Sanford yet again denied their request. In October 1859 the U.S. collector in New Orleans, Francis Hanson Hatch, helped to break up Walker's penultimate attempt against Central America by denying clearance to the steamer *Philadelphia*. He then searched the vessel, which led crew members to throw munitions into the sea so that they would not be caught with incriminating evidence. Later that month, federal authorities libeled the ship in the U.S. district court.[48]

Federal officers also repeatedly arrested filibusters, far more often than one might assume given all the speculation about their supposed profilibustering inclinations. True, the authorities generally brought to trial only the officers and organizers of the expeditions, often dismissing charges against mere recruits: filibuster privates and subalterns were regarded as "dupes" rather than the perpetrators of criminal behavior, the equivalent of today's drug users as compared to drug pushers.[49] Furthermore only a few prosecutions of leaders, for reasons to be addressed later, culminated in jail terms and fines. The fact remains, however, that federal officials usually executed the Neutrality Law in good faith.

The approach of the federal authorities is typified by their reaction after the rout of Narciso López's first invasion of Cuba in the spring of 1850 and the filibusters' arrival at Key West. The U.S. attorney for the Southern District of Florida, William R. Hackley, attempted to arrest all the expedition's officers in town at the rank of major or above, and took several of them into custody, as well as Armstrong Irvine Lewis, the master of the filibuster transport *Creole*. Although López and two other wanted officers fled before they could be served with warrants, federal authorities, urged on by telegraphs from Washington, pursued their cases in different cities over the following days and weeks.[50]

Federal tenacity resulted in López's arrest and a momentous filibuster court case. On June 21, after hearings before a U.S. commissioner, the grand jury for Judge Theodore H. McCaleb's U.S. District Court for Eastern Louisiana in New Orleans found true bills against sixteen filibuster soldiers and stateside conspirators, among them López, Ambrosio José Gonzales, John T. Pickett, Chatham Roberdeau Wheat, Theodore O'Hara, John L. O'Sullivan, John Henderson, Cotesworth Pinckney Smith, and John A. Quitman.

During the grand jury proceedings, Logan Hunton, the U.S. district attorney in New Orleans, called the bluff of a witness who threatened to implicate Secretary of State Clayton in the expedition if compelled to testify. The very threat, Hunton insisted, now made the witness's appearance "absolutely necessary." Subsequently, Hunton crowed that the witness could not substantiate his threat with "a solitary fact." Federal authorities, moreover, showed audacity in going after Smith and Quitman: at the time Smith was chief justice of Mississippi's highest state court (the High Court of Errors and Appeals) and Quitman was Mississippi's governor. Quitman gave considerable thought to resisting arrest, and while U.S. officials gingerly prodded him to be cooperative he stalled for months about surrendering.

The filibuster trials commenced on December 16 before the U.S. Circuit Court in New Orleans, Judge McCaleb presiding. In February 1851, with still no resolution to the first case called, that of John Henderson, Quitman finally resigned his governorship, and he then traveled down the Mississippi in the custody of a federal marshal to post bond and await his own trial.[51]

Federal authorities in New York City initiated additional legal actions against Cuba filibusters in the spring of 1851, breaking up an expedition before it even got off. In addition to seizing the *Cleopatra*, federal officials arrested six persons connected to the plot, including Armstrong Lewis, and, once again, John L. O'Sullivan (described by one columnist at the time of his arrest as "rather tall," clean-shaven, "contemplative," and "intellectual"-looking). On March 8, 1852, the trial of *U.S. v. John L. O'Sullivan, and others*, which would last nearly a month, commenced before Judge Andrew J. Judson in federal district court in New York City.[52]

Like O'Sullivan, John Quitman more than once faced possible jail time for Cuba filibustering activities. While presiding over the April 1854 term of the U.S. Circuit Court in New Orleans, Justice John Archibald Campbell of the U.S. Supreme Court charged a grand jury to investigate infractions of the Neutrality Act within their jurisdiction. Although the grand jurors called on six rumored filibuster conspirators, including Quitman, to testify, they made little headway, partly because Quitman and two other witnesses invoked the Fifth Amendment. On July 1 the jurors reported their inability to uncover clear evidence of a conspiracy. Unwilling to let things rest, Campbell compelled Quitman and his two recalcitrant associates to post $3,000 bond apiece as a guarantee of their compliance with the Neutrality Act for nine months.[53]

For all of President Pierce's supposed stake in Henry L. Kinney's plot, federal authorities in 1855 acted forcefully in court against Kinney's expedition. Secretary of State Marcy, the antifilibustering conscience in Pierce's cabinet according to a lot of contemporary speculation, in an exchange of correspondence in February questioned Kinney's claims of peaceful intent. Marcy sent Kinney a copy of a document in the government's possession, endorsed by

Kinney, indicating that the expedition was to be organized militarily with Kinney as "commander-in-chief," and warned that Washington would take remedial action if this was indeed the case. Beginning in late April, unsatisfied by Kinney's consequent promise that he would modify his company's structure to satisfy Marcy's complaint, the administration struck on several fronts.[54]

On April 25 Attorney General Cushing informed John McKeon, the U.S. district attorney for the Southern District of New York, that he had consulted with Pierce, and that the president wanted McKeon to begin legal action against both Kinney and his intended transport, the steamer *United States*. That same day, Marcy censured ties between Joseph W. Fabens, the U.S. commercial agent in Greytown, and Kinney. Fabens had returned to the United States from Central America and become secretary of Kinney's company. Marcy cautioned Fabens in a letter on April 25 that he had read reports of Fabens's involvement in the press, and that such behavior was highly improper for a U.S. official, given indications of Kinney's military intentions. Subsequently, Marcy summoned Fabens to Washington to grill him about the expedition.[55]

Matters came to a head quickly. After considering McKeon's evidence of Kinney's hostile intent, the grand jury for the U.S. District Court in New York found true bills against Kinney and Fabens. The U.S. marshal, on the evening of April 26, arrested Kinney at the Metropolitan Hotel; and on May 3 his counterpart in Washington took Fabens into custody, returning him to New York for trial. Several days later, Marcy removed Fabens from his position as commercial agent. When McKeon decided to postpone trying the case until the next court session (in order to gather witnesses) and Kinney, under bond, left New York for Philadelphia, federal officials took additional action to prevent any expedition from being launched before the district court reconvened. The U.S. attorney in Philadelphia persuaded a grand jury for his own district's U.S. court to indict Kinney, based on evidence that arrangements were in progress for a second vessel, carrying about 300 Philadelphians, to sail for Greytown along with the *United States*. A U.S. marshal then served the warrant on Kinney.[56]

Federal authorities also put William Walker, America's premier filibuster, on trial twice for his expeditions, arrested many of his cohorts, and took other legal steps to obstruct his plans. In February and March 1854, for instance, during Walker's invasion of Mexico, U.S. officials struck against those of his associates who had returned to California for supplies and reinforcements. On February 23 General John Wool (General Hitchcock's replacement in what was now called the Department of the Pacific) arrested one of the invasion's key figures, Henry P. Watkins. Subsequently, District Attorney Inge sought grand jury indictments of Watkins, Walker's quartermaster general Major Oliver T. Baird, and the filibuster army captain George R. Davidson. On March 1 the grand jury returned indictments against all three men, and the next day Watkins and Davidson were arraigned before Judge Ogden Hoffman, federal judge for the northern district of California (and son of the well-known New York attorney of the same name). Then, on March 8, the Navy's Commander Dornin seized in San Diego the secretary of state for Walker's bogus "Republic of California," Frederick Emory, who had also returned to California. Watkins's trial began later that month in San Francisco in Hoffman's district court.[57]

Additional prosecutions followed Walker's flight from Mexican soil. Upon arriving at the U.S. border near San Diego, Walker reached an agreement with the U.S. Army's major Justus McKinstry and captain Henry S. Burton, by which as "President of the Republic of Sonora" he surrendered himself and his remaining command on May 8. In return, McKinstry and Burton guaranteed the filibusters food, quarters, and steam conveyance from San Diego to San Francisco, where, it was agreed, Walker and his men would turn themselves in to General Wool. Walker obeyed the terms of his parole, and on May 26 District Attorney Inge submitted to the grand jury indictments of Walker and two other surrendered filibusters, Howard A. Snow, the naval secretary in Walker's Lower California régime, and John M. Jarnigan, the war secretary. That October, after several delays, Walker went on trial in the district court, Judge Isaac S. K. Ogier presiding.[58]

During the winter of 1855–56, about two months after Walker's power grab in Nicaragua, federal authorities cracked down on the filibuster's operation in New York City. On December 24–25 District Attorney McKeon prevented the *Northern Light* from embarking for Nicaragua, forced suspected filibusters to disembark, and retained custody of the vessel until officials of the Accessory Transit Company, which owned the *Northern Light*, provided $100,000 in security for release from libel proceedings. On January 15 McKeon obtained from the grand jury for the U.S. Circuit Court for the Southern District of New York indictments of twelve of the expedition's principal figures, and he reported the next day that he already had ten of the accused filibusters under arrest. McKeon also arrested five suspected filibusters aboard the *Star of the West*, also owned by the Accessory Transit Company, just before the vessel's sailing on January 9, and gathered evidence that filibusters intended to take the *Star* on her next scheduled sailing to Nicaragua in February. To avert McKeon's seizure of the ship, the company's president, Cornelius Van-

derbilt, promised that his vessels would henceforth refrain from carrying filibusters to Nicaragua. The following winter, McKeon arrested five more of
Walker's New York associates, including two of his principal recruiting
agents.[59]

Although federal authorities could not touch Walker himself while he remained within Nicaraguan territory, they certainly took action after he returned to the United States. In November 1857, as Walker was finalizing preparations for his second invasion of Nicaragua, federal authorities in New
Orleans arrested Walker and forced him to post bond to appear before the
U.S. Circuit Court in the city; and they also seized his intended transport,
then docked at the levee, and subjected it to a rigorous, but unfruitful, search.
Later in the month, after Walker got off anyway, federal authorities in Charleston took into custody Thomas J. Mackey, an alleged recruiter in South Carolina, and compelled Mackey's examination before the U.S. commissioner in
Charleston. The commissioner determined that there was sufficient evidence
to compel Mackey's appearance in district court at the January 1858 session.[60]

Further prosecutions occurred after the Navy's Commodore Paulding in
December broke up the expedition after its arrival in Central America and
compelled the filibusters' return to the United States. Complying with the
terms of his surrender to Paulding, Walker traveled back to the United States
on a commercial ship, leaving his officers and men to be transported in U.S.
naval vessels, and turned himself in to Rynders, the U.S. marshal, on his arrival in New York City on December 26. Rynders escorted Walker to Washington, arranging a meeting on December 29 with Secretary of State Lewis
Cass. Although Cass refused to arrest Walker on the spot, on the reasoning
that the State Department lacked the authority to do so, the administration
took action soon afterward to bring Walker to justice. On January 12, 1858,
Attorney General Jeremiah Black asked the U.S. district attorney in New Orleans, Thomas J. Semmes, to arrest Walker and bring him to trial if Walker
appeared anywhere in his district or within his "reach."[61]

When Walker turned up in Mobile, Semmes sent documents to A. J. Requier, his counterpart there, showing that Walker had violated the terms of his
bond in undertaking the expedition. Requier had Walker arrested on January
23 and brought before the U.S. district judge in Mobile, John Gayle, who earlier in the month had charged a grand jury to investigate violations of the
Neutrality Law in the district; but Gayle discharged Walker on a writ of habe-
as corpus, noting that as of yet the government had failed to secure a true bill
against Walker from a grand jury. After one failure to convince the grand jury
in New Orleans to find a true bill, Semmes might have let matters rest, had

not Walker, claiming to be Nicaragua's legal president and thus illegally apprehended by Paulding, demanded a public trial to clear his name. Finally, on February 3, Semmes succeeded in getting the grand jury to find true bills against Walker and his second-in-command Frank Anderson, as well as four of Anderson's subordinate officers, one of whom was subsequently discharged from arrest. Walker's case came to trial on May 31 before judges Campbell and McCaleb in the U.S. Circuit Court at New Orleans.[62]

Federal authorities also prosecuted filibusters in connection with Walker's later plots. Before the *Susan* expedition to Nicaragua in December 1858, Judge McCaleb in New Orleans instructed a grand jury to investigate violations of the Neutrality Act within the district court's jurisdiction, and federal authorities in the port arrested persons suspected of involvement in the plot, to compel their testimony before the jurors. Around the same time, in a session of the U.S. Circuit Court in Mobile, the port from which the expedition originated, Judge Campbell tried to intimidate the filibusters by charging his court's grand jury to investigate violations of the Neutrality Law in the district. Walker was compelled to testify before the jurors. Furthermore, as mentioned earlier, federal authorities in Mobile attempted unsuccessfully to arrest every man aboard the *Susan* just before she left Mobile Bay.

In October 1859, at the time of Walker's botched efforts to get off yet another expedition from New Orleans, U.S. Attorney General Jeremiah S. Black telegraphed the authorities in Mobile that they should use whatever means were "requisite" to arrest those who should have been taken into custody earlier in the year for the *Susan* escapade. A U.S. marshal subsequently arrested seventy-five filibusters involved in the new plot, and then hauled Harry Maury, who had been publicly recruiting for the expedition, as well as Frank Anderson, Callender Fayssoux, and William W. Scott (apparently a captain in the expedition), before a U.S. commissioner in New Orleans for examination. Meanwhile, Judge McCaleb issued yet one more antifilibustering charge to a federal grand jury in the Crescent City.[63]

Finally, federal authorities initiated a miscellany of additional legal actions against suspected filibusters. In September 1851 Justice John Catron of the U.S. Supreme Court, sitting as judge for a U.S. Circuit Court session in Nashville, charged a grand jury that if it wanted to avoid "national disgrace" and dishonor to the state of Tennessee, it had better discharge its duty on indictments against local filibusters submitted to it by the district attorney: just weeks earlier, he noted, filibuster operatives in the city had convened a sizable meeting at the courthouse, and had conducted parades under banners and to military tunes, in an effort to raise money and "young," "idle," and "thoughtless" men for Cuba filibustering. In the spring of 1854 General Wool arrested the French and Mexican consuls in San Francisco on suspicion of their involvement in the plot of Count Gaston de Raousset-Boulbon of France. The next year, a paper in Stockton, California, announced the arrest and detention for a day in San Diego by federal authorities of "the notorious 'Jimmy-from-Town'" and other men suspected of plotting a thrust into Lower California. In January 1856 federal authorities arrested thirteen naturalized Irish immigrants, all members of the Cincinnati branch of the Irish Emigrant Aid Association of Ohio and allegedly involved, since May 1, 1854, in plotting an expedition to overthrow English rule in Ireland. The next month, the case came before the U.S. Circuit Court for the Southern District of Ohio.[64]

DWELLING ON filibustering's federal fellow travelers, therefore, is counterproductive. We learn more by probing whether U.S. military officers and civil officials truly commanded sufficient resources to do their job. Part of the government's difficulty derived from a shortage of marshals to cover all of filibustering's hot spots. In the spring of 1851 adventurers bound for Cuba flagrantly stocked a storehouse in Jacksonville, Florida, with gun carriages, muskets, and other military equipment, knowing that they could get away with it since the town lacked a resident U.S. marshal. Later that year, during the return of the *Pampero* for reinforcements, the U.S. collector at St. Augustine pleaded for marshals with the State Department. Similarly, Colonel William Harney of the U.S. Army complained from Ringgold Barracks during the Carbajal disturbances that it was difficult to stop filibusters given "the absence of the proper civil functionaries" on the border. Harney noted that the town of Brownsville had the only U.S. marshal on the entire Rio Grande at the time.[65]

Since army officers hesitated to arrest filibusters except at the behest of U.S. district attorneys and marshals, such deficiencies were bound to compromise enforcement efforts. Section 8 of the Neutrality Act of 1818 authorized the president to use America's land and naval forces "for the purpose of preventing the carrying on of any such expedition," implying that army officers might make arrests. Still, military arrests smack of martial law, a state of affairs that did not exist in the country at that time, and one that ran counter to long-standing American traditions of subordinating the military to the civil power. Might they be subject to prosecution for false arrest, some officers wondered, it they apprehended suspected filibusters without prior authorization from U.S. district attorneys, courts, and marshals?

Few officers fretted more about this issue than did Colonel Harney, who on November 24, 1851, assumed authority on the Rio Grande frontier under assignment from General Persifor F. Smith, the army's departmental commander in Texas. On September 22 President Fillmore had ordered Smith to use land and naval forces, and the militia if necessary, to prevent filibustering, adding that in cases of doubt Smith should consult with the U.S. attorney for his district. Smith, in turn, had given Harney responsibility for preventing filibusters into Mexico, sending him a copy of the president's order.[66]

No sooner did Harney arrive on the scene than he ordered Captain Prince to take a company of mounted infantry from Ringgold Barracks to Roma and other points on the lower Rio Grande, and intercept filibusters at ferries or other likely crossing points into Mexico. However, Harney confided to fellow officers his uncertainty whether Fillmore's phrasing required the army to coordinate its antifilibustering measures with civil officials. Seeking advice, Harney asked W. B. Brashear, a lawyer and the deputy U.S. collector at Rio Grande City, to call at his headquarters at Ringgold Barracks; he also contacted District Attorney Ballinger in Galveston. After Brashear visited and asserted that the army indeed needed the approval of civil authorities before arresting filibusters, Harney restricted his antifilibustering patrols. He instructed subordinates to "use no more force than is authorized by law, and in no case to proceed to the extremity of shedding blood, except on the positive demand of the United States Marshal or his legal representative." Later, however, Ballinger informed Harney that Fillmore's orders to General Smith provided all the legitimacy that the army needed for aggressive intervention, since the president himself was a "Civil Authority."

By the time Ballinger's letter arrived at Harney's headquarters on February 1, the colonel had reached the same conclusion. The previous day, Harney had ordered Captain Gabriel R. Paul of the 7th Infantry to take forty mounted men and find the filibusters' camp or camps, seize their ammunition and arms, and order them to disperse, using force if necessary. Unfortunately, however, the suddenly energized Harney did not distribute copies of Fillmore's order to his junior officers, some of whom, including Captain Paul, were familiar with their commander's qualms and had their own misgivings about acting independently of civil authority. Paul refused to carry out Harney's instructions, on the grounds that doing so might constitute an illegal act. Harney then drafted another company commander of the 7th, Captain Robert Selden Garnett, for the task. But Garnett also declined, submitting a written protest that Harney's order was illegal since it lacked the "sanction, in due form, of the civil authorities."[67]

The issue of civil authorization permeated the resulting courts-martial in May of the recalcitrant captains. Paul claimed that he had been uninformed of Fillmore's orders to Smith. Both captains procured defense witnesses who testified that it had been the army's practice when arresting filibusters during the Canadian "Patriot" disturbances of the 1830s to have present U.S. marshals or their deputies. Garnett contended that had he killed filibusters when enforcing an illicit order, he might have been liable for prosecution in a Texas state court for manslaughter, and been hanged; further, he inserted into the trial record a written opinion from Judah Benjamin affirming that the president could authorize generals to act against filibusters "without the interposition of the Civil Authorities at hand," but also maintaining that no officer would be obliged to carry out Harney's commands "without being officially informed" of the president's instructions. Officers should not render "blind obedience" to orders. The courts-martial vindicated both captains, finding that there was no criminality involved in their disobedience since they were unaware of the president's letter to General Smith, and judging them innocent of showing disrespect to their commanding officer.[68]

These rulings, which implied that junior officers could resist their superiors' antifilibustering orders, reverberated through the service's high command. General Smith, though confirming the decisions, strongly dissented from the courts' logic, arguing that there was no clause in the Neutrality Act implying that army officers needed special presidential permission to enforce the law. Any officer refusing compliance with an antifilibustering order mistakenly assumed that he was "better informed of the law than he who issues the order." In Washington, Secretary of War Charles M. Conrad issued a rebuttal of the sentences to the entire army: junior officers should simply "act upon the reasonable presumption" that their superiors were authorized to conduct antifilibustering missions.[69]

In his cover letter conveying the trial documents to Washington, Smith recommended that Congress pass legislation to grant civil immunity to army officers arresting filibusters. But nothing was resolved, and during the Callahan filibuster crisis in 1855, Smith attempted to straddle the matter. Applying the logic that the army need only intervene in emergencies, Smith ruled that officers might arrest persons planning future invasions but should leave the apprehension of former filibusters to civil authorities.[70]

By that time, qualms about military arrests had played havoc in California. During William Walker's invasion of Mexico, Secretary of War Davis sharply chastised General Wool, after Wool informed Washington that federal civil authorities in San Francisco seemed uninterested in enforcing the Neutrality

General John Ellis Wool.
(Courtesy of the Library of
Congress)

Act, and that he had therefore taken the initiative to arrest Walker's collaborator Henry P. Watkins. Davis, with support from the *Washington Daily
Union*, Pierce's organ, countered that Wool might provoke a public backlash
against the army by such behavior, and that the administration's prior instructions never anticipated that the general would "originate arrests and
prosecutions for civil misdemeanors." Furious at the rebuke, Wool responded
that if Davis had not wanted him to initiate arrests, he should have told him so
earlier, and that had Davis so tied his hands, new invasions of Mexico would
have undoubtedly resulted.[71]

The dispute sapped Wool's enthusiasm for enforcing the Neutrality Act.
When in August 1854 the customs collector asked for his intervention against
a rumored expedition to Hawaii, Wool responded that his hands were tied
until the "civil authorities" formally requested his aid. In fact, William
Walker later made the unsubstantiated, but possibly true, charge that he was
able to procure Wool's blessing before launching his invasion of Nicaragua
in 1855.[72]

Not only did the U.S. government employ an insufficient number of marshals to cope with filibustering, but it also lacked the necessary soldiers. After the Mexican War army manpower fluctuated for several years between about 9,000 and 11,000 men, before legislation in 1855 set the service's authorized strength at 17,867 men and officers. Even though army manpower was dispersed rather than concentrated, these numbers fell far short of what was needed to cover the service's antifilibustering assignments.[73]

In May 1850 the army had no soldiers manning its barracks at Key West when the survivors of the first López expedition arrived there aboard the *Creole*. The federal district attorney for Florida's southern district subsequently reported that he had been compelled "from want of force" to allow filibusters of lower rank than major to go free, for fear that mass arrests would spur resistance. The next year, during the final López expedition, Collector Freret in New Orleans mentioned the army's manpower shortfall there as an impediment to his preventing reinforcements bound for Cuba from leaving the city and proceeding downriver to the Gulf of Mexico. Since the thirty-four-man garrison at New Orleans lacked the capability to forestall a filibuster exodus, the collector advised that the navy compensate by rushing armed steamers to the Balize (a strip of land immediately above the mouth of the Mississippi River), so that the government could intercept the filibusters before they entered the Gulf. In California Wool badgered Washington for extra soldiers, insisting that troop shortages crippled his efforts: how could he possibly stop filibustering, he wondered, when he only controlled "about 1,000 men, decreasing every day by discharges and desertion," in an assignment that included Utah, Washington, and Oregon as well as California?[74]

Army officers faced even greater challenges in Texas, where an insufficient soldiery patrolled the lengthy Rio Grande, a waterway sometimes so shallow that it hardly presented a barrier to invading Mexico. A correspondent observed in November 1851 during the Carbajal disturbances that there was "scarcely a bend in the river that cannot be forded with the exception of a few feet of swimming." The next February, Captain Prince argued that the army could hardly be expected to keep filibusters from penetrating a boundary that was merely "a river, fordable at almost any point & extending from the mouth of the Rio Grande . . . about 800 miles."[75]

After the Mexican War the army committed but 1,488 troops to the whole state, which amounted roughly to a mere 1 soldier per 180 square miles. Later, army manpower increased: by 1853 the War Department had 2,649 soldiers in Texas; in 1855, the figure had risen to 3,449 officers and men. But these numbers remained inadequate, especially since only a fraction of the army's personnel in Texas could be afforded for border patrols. Troops customarily had assignments elsewhere, especially the protection of roads, emigrants, and settlements in the northern and western parts of the state against attacks by Lipan Apaches, Comanches, and other Indian tribes. Captain Prince noted that the army at the time that he was writing had only 450 men within 100 miles of the Rio Grande.[76]

If anything, the navy and revenue cutter service faced even greater limitations in their efforts to patrol America's coasts against filibuster exits. Because of damages sustained during the Mexican War, the revenue cutter service (or revenue marine) controlled only eight active vessels in January 1849, though six other vessels were in construction. True, the navy, now maintaining between forty and fifty warships, had more than doubled its number of active warships since the 1820s. But because of the expansion of American overseas trade, the navy carried out an increasing number of commercial and diplomatic missions in distant parts of the globe, making many of its vessels unavailable when filibustering emergencies arose at home. Revealingly, President Fillmore confided to Secretary of State Webster on one occasion that the administration had "few vessels" to enforce the very antifilibustering circular that he had just issued to the navy's officers.[77]

Civil officials, naval officers, and authorities in Washington complained constantly that they lacked a sufficient number of cutters and warships to prevent filibustering departures, or if they did have vessels at their disposal, that they were in such poor repair, had such a great draft, or were so slow as to be virtually useless. During the Cuba plot of 1849, for example, Commander Victor M. Randolph struggled to maintain an adequate force on station off Round Island, even violating orders to return a paddle-wheel steamship to her base at Pensacola. At the time the Pampero returned from Cuba for reinforcements in 1851, the district attorney in Savannah reported that he was in the absurd position of having to watch the entire coast from Savannah to northern Florida with a single sailing cutter. She could never catch a steam filibuster ship, he insisted, amid the coastal district's "mud flats, sand bars and tortuous narrow passages and shallow creeks . . . inaccessible to any vessels but steamers of light draught." When Walker sailed for Mexico in 1853, the collector in San Francisco, noting that he lacked control over an effective revenue cutter, begged the commander of America's Pacific Squadron for help. Two years later, the Home Squadron's commander reported that he was left with only two slow-moving sail vessels for antifilibustering duty after sending off his steam warships on special Navy Department assignments in the Mediterranean and other places.[78]

Similar difficulties plagued federal authorities in New York at the time of Henry L. Kinney's expedition. After being alerted by Pierce to Kinney's pending departure, Commodore Boarman informed the Navy Department that he had only the paddle-wheel steamer *Vixen* available to carry out orders to intercept the expedition. As a result, Boarman hastened repairs on a surveying vessel, got a revenue cutter added temporarily to his command, and asked the army's commanding general, Winfield Scott, to make up the deficiency. Forts Schuyler and Hamilton were two natural choke points, and Boarman wanted Scott to have soldiers at both forts fire on the filibuster vessel if she evaded the navy and ran for the open sea: the unfinished Fort Schuyler stood at Throgs Neck, where the East River meets Long Island Sound; Fort Hamilton overlooked the Narrows, an outlet to Lower New York Bay and the ocean (see map 3). But Fort Schuyler still lacked artillery and garrison at the time of Boarman's request, and President Pierce withheld approval as to Fort Hamilton's guns, for fear that the soldiers might accidentally fire on the wrong vessel.[79]

Given these inadequacies, we should not be surprised that some filibusters brazenly defied federal officials, hoping to get their way through force or intimidation. In November 1851 one party of Carbajal's followers crossed the Rio Grande to Mexico in broad daylight and within sight of a U.S. customs collector, who called on them to desist in the name of the United States. When a small party of U.S. soldiers appeared on the river bank and backed up the collector by drawing their pistols, the filibusters from their boat aimed their own arms back at the party on shore, causing the collector to back down. The very next month, a group of filibusters in Texas simply ignored a direct order from a U.S. army officer that they should break up their encampment. In December 1855, after District Attorney McKeon seized the *Northern Light* at New York, William Walker's followers took hostage the marshals whom McKeon had left on board when he disembarked, and then they tried to escape from the harbor, only to be turned back by cannon fire from a U.S. revenue cutter. Even more revealing is an instance in 1859, when seventy-five filibusters (guarded by a mere two deputy marshals) escaped from the U.S. army barracks near New Orleans. Earlier, the U.S. marshal had conceded the filibusters' terms that they should surrender "to the civil power alone," even though some U.S. soldiers had been put at his disposal. The marshal later explained that had he not acceded, "a scene of violence and slaughter" would have ensued since "these men were generally armed to the teeth."[80]

Perhaps the most outrageous instance of filibuster audacity occurred in December 1858. After the U.S. collector for Mobile denied clearance to Wil-

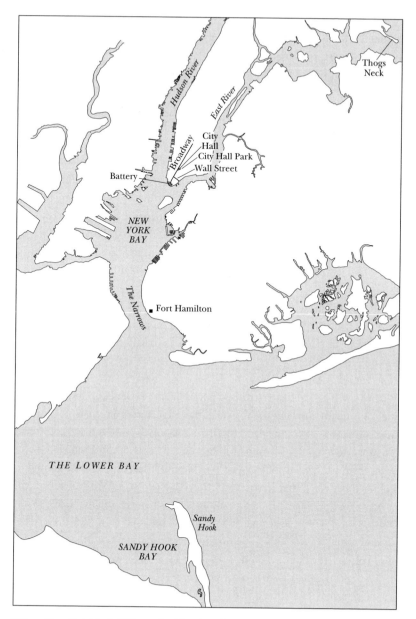

MAP 3. New York City's Filibustering Frontier, 1850s

liam Walker's intended vessel, the *Alice Tainter*, "friends" of the shipowner gathered and became, as the collector reported to Washington, "very violent, some of them proposing to tear down the custom-house." Subsequently, the filibusters launched their expedition anyway on Harry Maury's *Susan*. Captain J. J. Morrison, aboard the cutter *Robert McClelland*, intercepted the *Susan* after the vessel attempted to leave port surreptitiously, and discovered arms in the hold. But when Morrison ordered Maury to return to the bar of the Dog River and wait there until further instructions arrived from the collector, Maury denied wrongful intent and some of the filibusters on board grabbed their guns. In the hope of averting bloodshed, Morrison struck a deal that the filibusters should drop anchor where they were and, with a revenue lieutenant on board, await the collector's instructions, warning that he would sink the *Susan* should Maury run for open water. Nevertheless, that night, under the cover of fog, Maury made his escape, crossing the bar to Mobile Bay at about 4:20 A.M. Later, Maury transferred his captive revenue lieutenant to a commercial vessel bound for New Orleans and continued on his way to Central America.[81]

EMPHASIZING THE difficulties confronting U.S. civil and military officers, however, deprives the filibusters themselves of agency. Given filibuster secrecy and deviousness, it would have been difficult if not impossible for federal authorities to stop the expeditions, even if they had far more resources at their disposal. Not all filibusters, to be sure, were discreet. In 1857, for instance, one of William Walker's officers stupidly confided to a U.S. army officer on leave in New York that the next expedition would depart from New Orleans, and the officer passed the information on to the War Department. The Virginia agricultural reformer Edmund Ruffin was taken aback on another occasion when a Walker booster to whom he had just been introduced shared plans about an upcoming invasion, without even inquiring whether Ruffin favored enterprises of this sort.[82]

More characteristically, however, filibuster organizers obscured their preparations. Thus one of John Quitman's inner circle asked a close friend for a $250 loan to help him get by until his "great undertaking" was completed, and implored, "Please keep the intimations herein contained within your bosom and laugh at all stories of fillibustering expeditions to Cuba." Sometimes expedition organizers were so bent on preventing leaks that they did not even inform the recruits as to their destinations.[83]

Filibustering planners exercised particular caution in their correspondence. John L. O'Sullivan not only reassured John Quitman in 1850 that if he agreed to accept a filibuster command, financiers of the projected Cuban invasion would be kept in the dark about Quitman's identity until they swore a "pledge of secrecy"; he also stipulated that Quitman send his telegraphic response indirectly to O'Sullivan's father-in-law in New Orleans, so that prying operators could not piece together what was going on. To further mislead the operators, Quitman was told that he should not sign for the telegraph himself but rather find a friend to do so. William Walker, similarly concerned about careless disclosures, kept specifics to a minimum in his letters. Thus in October 1858 he obliquely asked Fayssoux to discover "the expense of hiring a suitable vessel for the objects Col. R. will mention to you." In August 1859 Walker informed Fayssoux that he was unwilling to tell him "on paper of the arrangements made" during his visit to New York City. Of course, euphemisms provided another way to hedge one's correspondence. One conspirator characterized his promised financial support for an expedition as a "subscription" to "the 'Great Charity.'"[84]

Occasionally, the filibusters resorted to cloak-and-dagger methods or disinformation campaigns to throw federal officials off their track. In 1851, according to a government informant, filibuster leaders in New York City bribed telegraph operators to leak federal messages concerning their operations, so that they could keep a step ahead of the law. In August 1858, hoping that his cohorts would "go on as quietly as possible" with their preparations, William Walker informed Callender Fayssoux that he was telling everyone in Mobile that his destination was Georgia when it was in fact New York City. Later in the year Walker instructed one of his operatives to purposely spread rumors that the Nicaraguan movement would originate in New Orleans, so that federal attention would be diverted from Mobile, the true base of operations. In 1859 Walker informed Fayssoux that he would sign "James Wilson" to a telegraph announcing that he had arrived in St. Louis on his trip back from California.

Walker even developed a secret code, in which Greek letters stood for persons (e.g. "Omicron" for the New York steamship magnate Marshall Owen Roberts) and his intended steamship the *Philadelphia*, and numbers for places (e.g. "First" for New Orleans). So in one letter he noted that "Sigma" could not have left New York City on the *Empire City*, and in another he requested that Fayssoux "call on Omega" and demand settlement of an outstanding draft, lest the owner of it expose "secrets important to Omega and Omicron." On one occasion, Walker reported more obscurely, that a "Telegraphic connection just concluded here shows that The electrick current from Beta to Gamma must in due course reach Delta & so to Omega & c."[85]

In some instances, filibusters hid armaments aboard their vessels. When the *Philadelphia* sailed from New York City for New Orleans in September 1859, the ship carried boxes of muskets, balls, and bayonets, all carefully stowed below other cargo. In cases where the filibusters lacked clearances for their ships, they often loaded, coaled, and boarded them, and sailed out of port in the wee hours of the night, in order to avoid detection.[86]

Federal officials found such furtiveness exasperating. E. Warren Moise, the Pierce administration's attorney in New Orleans, informed the Department of State in 1854 that persons who knew about the intended invasion of Cuba "of course avoid saying any thing to the public officers." This made any interference on his part problematic, even though he was fairly certain that the filibusters had established their headquarters within the city. Thomas J. Semmes, Moise's counterpart during Walker's plot against Nicaragua in 1858, lamented his inability "to obtain tangible proof of the complicity of anyone" in the anticipated filibuster, because the expeditionists had been using so much "caution and secrecy."[87]

Federal officials not only had to infiltrate covert operations but also had to counter the filibusters' pretense of remaining in technical compliance with the law. Filibustering leaders studied the Neutrality Law looking for potential loopholes, and often found them. William Walker, for instance, boasted to one confidant, "I know the Act of 1818 pretty thoroughly and do not intend to violate its provisions." Federal intervention, as a result, faltered in a morass of legal, jurisdictional, and procedural restrictions governing the circumstances under which arrests could be made. As a U.S. district attorney put it about a Cuba plot, "the leaders of the enterprise have had good legal advisers and have not rendered themselves amenable to our laws."[88]

Nothing caused U.S. officials more consternation than the challenge of differentiating filibusters from legitimate emigrants and travelers. Since the beginning of the American Republic, a nation founded by emigrants and the descendants of emigrants, U.S. leaders had defended the right of expatriation. As Thomas Jefferson explained in 1793, "Our citizens are entirely free to divest themselves of that character by emigration . . . and may then become the subjects of another power." By the filibustering era, this right had been asserted so often—especially before the War of 1812, when Americans insisted that British naval officers had no right to impress English seamen who had become naturalized Americans—that it was deeply ingrained in American political culture. Attorney General Jeremiah Black forcefully articulated the idea in an official ruling in 1859. He argued that the "natural right of every free person . . . to leave the country of his birth in good faith and for an honest purpose, the privilege of throwing off his natural allegiance and substituting another allegiance in its place—the general right, in one word, of expatriation, is incontestible."[89]

Capitalizing on this American tradition, filibusters regularly assumed the guise of legal emigrants in an attempt to gain immunity from arrest. During the Round Island plot of 1849, John L. O'Sullivan proposed that filibustering was done "legally," since "volunteers" could "go as emigrants, California adventurers via Cuba, passengers going to Cuba." Similarly Henry L. Kinney's associate Joseph W. Fabens insisted that Kinney's followers "organize under the style of the Central American Agricultural & Mining Co.—and the colonists must go out as the first settlers of California went with their tents mining tools &c."[90]

Most filibuster leaders, in fact, identified their escapades as attempts to travel to or through foreign domains on their way to California, or to establish invited settlements within foreign countries. The federal courts had qualified the right of emigration by stipulating that it had to be exercised lawfully and not to escape criminal liability.[91] But it was no easy matter, given the lengths to which the expeditionists went to play their emigrant roles, for federal officials to justify making preemptive arrests.

Since the Neutrality Act prohibited military expeditions, the filibusters repeatedly maintained that their enterprises were neither expeditions nor military. After President Pierce issued his proclamation against John Quitman's Cuba plot in 1854, for instance, one conspirator, John Henderson, retorted in a public letter that his cohorts had "no intention of infracting either the law or treaty." Similarly, in September 1857 William Walker reassured Secretary of State Cass that he and his companions would not violate the Neutrality Law during their upcoming return to Nicaragua, and he professed "scorn and indignation" at insinuations that they would do so. George Bickley, the head of the Knights of the Golden Circle, dared Cass to prove that he would violate the law if he made a treaty with a Mexican state governor to bring in "Emigrants."[92]

To strengthen their case, filibuster leaders frequently deferred blatant military preparations until they had passed beyond America's territorial limits. A participant in the López expedition in 1850 explained, "it was understood before we left home who were to be our officers, but no elections were held, appointments made, or commissions issued, until we were in the Gulf of Mexico, and far more than three leagues from land."[93] In 1854 Quitman bluntly informed applicants that he could not promise officerships, because these had to be delayed until his expedition was beyond U.S. territory. The following February, one of his conspirators made arrangements to send recruits to a plantation rendezvous "in the character of wood choppers." To the same end, William Walker postponed designating formal companies during his second invasion of Nicaragua until his vessel was out to sea. In 1859 a group of his men pretended to be fishermen, while they waited to board their transport.[94]

When performing this charade, filibuster officers did not distribute uniforms or arms until they passed beyond U.S. territorial limits. Federal investigators reported that the Round Island expeditionists lacked arms or munitions. The pseudonymous "O. D. D. O.," a participant in the 1850 López expedition to Cuba, recalled that it was not until his vessel was at sea a full ten days that an officer broke into several boxes and distributed shoulder arms, percussion caps, and ammunition. Naturally America's quintessential filibuster played the same game. William Stewart, who joined an expedition to Walker's Nicaragua in early 1857, recalled that the men were not provided with their muskets and ammunition until arriving at Greytown. In October 1858, before the *Susan* expedition, Walker informed the U.S. customs collector in Mobile that his followers would take nothing with them but agricultural and mechanical implements as well as household items.[95]

Members of seaborne expeditions often held normal passenger tickets, just like other travelers. In 1850 Narciso López's recruits carried steerage tickets provided by their officers as they boarded what were ostensibly commercial vessels to Chagres, the port on Central America's eastern coast to which their vessels were legally cleared. Once Walker established himself in Nicaragua in the fall of 1855, virtually all his subsequent recruits until his overthrow traveled to Central America aboard commercial vessels, many of them with tickets provided gratis by Walker's recruiting agents. In New York in early 1857 his agents even dangled a flag from an upper-story window overlooking Broadway that promised "Free Farms and Free Passage" to persons willing to travel to Nicaragua.[96]

Filibusters invading Mexico disguised their criminality in other ways. Rather than organize full-blown expeditions on the American side, they sometimes crossed the porous border individually or in small parties, and perfected their military organization once in Mexico. Such tactics put American civil officials and military officers on the spot since, as General Persifor Smith explained to the War Department, it was virtually impossible to otherwise distinguish the filibusters from the "ordinary" people residing in towns near the border. As one U.S. marshal instructed his deputy, federal authorities were obligated to stop anyone crossing the border if they discovered "anything like organization on the American side, munitions or warlike implements," but they had better not interfere with American citizens "passing into

Mexico, under peaceable appearances." President Fillmore alluded to the same difficulty when he observed that it was not yet clear from newspaper reports whether Texans in Mexico were "engaged in the fight . . . as an organized military body or individuals."[97]

The various subterfuges made it difficult for federal officials and military officers to justify the arrest of suspected filibusters. In 1849, for instance, a federal spy successfully infiltrated the Cuba filibusters' Round Island encampment, only to discover that the adventurers traveled to the base in small parties, did not drill, and eschewed uniforms (although they all wore forage caps). During the aftermath of the final López expedition, the U.S. district attorney in Mobile reported men leaving for New Orleans with the apparent intention of filibustering, noting that his hands were tied because they traveled in parties of just five or six men, "without arms, & without any apparent organization." At the time of Walker's régime in Nicaragua, District Attorney McKeon in New York asked Washington whether he could seize a vessel loaded with filibusters carrying tickets to San Francisco via Nicaragua. The tickets granted their holders the "privilege" of staying in Central America for up to thirty days. In December 1858 the U.S. district attorney in New Orleans cautioned Washington that there was little he could do if filibusters exited the city in twos and threes and then launched a new expedition to Nicaragua from a prearranged remote spot on the coast.[98]

An incident in 1858 illuminates how such constraints protected even notorious filibusters. That April, a U.S. army captain in Texas learned that William Walker's former artillery chief Charles Frederick Henningsen was in Laredo on his way to Monterrey. Yet the officer did nothing, despite having "little doubt" that Henningsen intended an expedition. Henningsen had yet to be spotted amid a body of armed men. Even an infamous filibuster could approach the Mexican border unmolested, so long as he avoided the trappings of a military movement.[99]

As for vessels, unless federal officials uncovered munitions aboard probable filibuster transports, they had difficulty justifying their seizure. "I have considered . . . the question whether I have the power under the act of 20th April 1818, to detain the vessel, although she may have no arms or munitions," the U.S. collector in Mobile informed the Treasury Department during the Round Island plot of 1849, noting that he could not find specific language in the legislation allowing him to interfere. However, he hoped that Washington might concede him "a constructive power" to justify a refusal of clearance, based on the necessity of enforcing America's treaty obligations.[100]

Matters became especially sticky regarding vessels bound for Nicaragua under William Walker's régime, which almost always carried passengers in transit across the Central American isthmus to and from California in addition to the filibusters aboard ship. How were federal officials to distinguish the criminals from the peaceful travelers? During the López plots, the Fillmore administration had assumed that its officials could guess the difference between "bona fide" travelers and filibusters. But this was easier with López's vessels, which were obviously troop transports, than with the commercial vessels bound for Nicaragua during Walker's tenure. As Secretary of State Marcy put it, international law respected the right of "unassociated individuals" to voluntarily leave for another country, even if they subsequently joined that nation's military establishment, and it was improper for any "liberal government to hold an inquisition" into their motives.[101]

Such distinctions came into play in December 1856, when U.S. District Attorney John McKeon in New York City mustered federal marshals and posted a revenue cutter to block the departure of the commercial steamer *Tennessee*, crowded with filibusters and other passengers bound for Nicaragua, before being presented with a copy of the colonization contract under which this particular body of Walker's "Emigrants" were supposedly to sail. Faced with superficial evidence that the travelers lacked military organization and that they intended to take up land grants and become farmers and mechanics rather than join Walker's army, a skeptical McKeon decided that he had better let the ship sail, barring any last-minute discovery of incriminating evidence.[102]

Making matters worse, federal officials had to operate in jurisdictions where public opinion frequently supported the expeditions. Commander Victor M. Randolph remarked in September 1849, when he was enforcing the U.S. Navy's blockade of Round Island, that it was customary in that "quarter of the world" for people to eulogize the filibusters as "chivalrous American citizens," while denouncing the Navy and him in particular for preventing heroes from fulfilling their destiny. An army officer's wife complained from Brownsville, Texas, that even the slightest military measures against the Carbajal adventurers caused local townspeople to "become hostile in feeling," making life highly uncomfortable for military personnel. One Texas judge even gave passports for filibusters to use when they invaded Mexico. When an army officer complained, the judge retorted that the Neutrality Act of 1818 did not apply to Texas, since it was adopted before Texas became a state.[103]

Federal officers involved in seizing suspected filibuster ships, or denying them clearance, risked mob reprisals. William Freret, the New Orleans customs collector fired by President Fillmore for presumed complicity with the

López filibusters, explained in one letter how stupid it would have been for him and a mere company of U.S. soldiers to try to apprehend a force of "desperate men" at the wharf. How could they have effected such arrests among a population "with the invaders heart and soul," he wondered, without sparking a "frightful massacre"? Since Freret took steps to have the navy and army intercept the filibusters once they left the friendly confines of New Orleans, and since he ordered the commander of a revenue cutter to fire on any suspected vessel downriver that refused to submit to a search, he might well have been sincere. The *New York Evening Post* reported in June 1855 that carpenters and other workingmen involved in fitting out the *United States* became furious at the navy's attempt to prevent the ship from sailing, and convened a public meeting at which various threats were uttered against the blockaders.[104]

Additionally, federal officials had to worry about civil lawsuits, should they persist in their efforts. Shipowners might claim that they had used their vessels in legitimate commercial pursuits rather than filibustering at the moment of seizure, and that they had suffered monetary losses while their ships were detained. Freret informed the Spanish consul during López's last expedition that he dreaded being sued for damages should he interfere with the *Pampero*. In December 1858 Collector Sanford alerted the Treasury Department from Mobile that after he had denied clearance to the *Susan* the owner of the vessel had immediately called on him and threatened to keep him "busy for a month to come, as he intended to demand clearances daily and bring a suit" for each refusal. Sanford wondered how long he could hold out against such harassment.[105]

These concerns were not entirely misplaced. In 1859 Robert H. Smith, a lawyer retained by the federal government, billed the government $500 for his services after successfully defending Sanford against a suit in the Alabama circuit court over Sanford's denial of clearance in November 1858 to the filibuster vessel *Alice Tainter*. Colonel Hitchcock entered a legal thicket after he had William Walker's brig the *Arrow* seized in San Francisco harbor on the night of September 30, 1853, before the ship's intended departure for Mexico. The day after the seizure Walker obtained a writ of replevin from a California court asking for repossession of the vessel. When Hitchcock rebuffed a sheriff's attempt to enforce the writ and instead persuaded District Attorney Inge to libel the *Arrow* for violating the Neutrality Law, the filibusters responded with a $30,000 suit for damages and had Hitchcock cited for contempt of court. Making matters worse, the filibusters got an expedition off anyway using another vessel. Eventually, without Hitchcock's permission and to his eventual disgust, Inge struck a deal by which the court dropped all charges against Hitchcock in return for the federal government's agreement to end its libel on the *Arrow*.[106]

If American army officers and civil officials worried about exceeding their authority within the United States, naval officers faced their own jurisdictional enigmas once the filibusters escaped to sea. According to international law, all states had the right to arrest their criminal citizens aboard vessels on the high seas. Naval officers wondered, however, whether this rule governed vessels carrying legal clearances from U.S. collectors of customs. Thus one squadron commander informed the secretary of the navy that he assumed he should detain seeming filibuster vessels encountered at sea with troops and munitions but with legal clearances; still, he wanted official authorization to do so. Another flag officer asked hypothetically what to do if he fell in with a cleared vessel on which known filibusters bore arms but were unorganized militarily. Should the collector's clearance govern the situation, he inquired, or would the presence of notorious filibusters aboard warrant his seizing the ship and sending her back to the United States?[107]

Even more perplexing was the matter of what should be done once the filibusters arrived in the territorial waters of another country. Departmental orders constantly exhorted naval officers to intervene against filibusters attempting to land abroad. In the spring of 1851, for instance, the secretary of the navy, William A. Graham, instructed the commander of the Home Squadron to "prevent" filibusters from "landing on the Coast of Cuba"; and later that year Graham ordered the commodore of the Pacific Squadron to "repair" to the Sandwich Islands if he discovered that an expedition was in progress and to use "all lawful means to arrest and prevent its landing there." At the time of William Walker's second expedition to Nicaragua, the Navy Department specifically instructed Commodore Hiram Paulding not to allow the landing of filibusters or their arms in Central America or Mexico.[108]

But how far could naval officers go, given international law's proscription against one state arresting its criminals within the territorial limits of another country? Did this yield to the obligation to prevent the international crime of filibustering? Unfortunately, until the late 1850s instructions from Washington offered little guidance on this vexing point. What, for instance, did Secretary of the Navy James C. Dobbin mean by his dispatch to Commander Thomas A. Dornin, patrolling off the coast of Mexico in the USS *Portsmouth* during William Walker's invasion? Dobbin admitted that he could not "instruct" Dornin "to invade Mexican territory with a view to making war upon Walker and his associates," but he also explained that Dornin should treat the filibusters as "lawless men inflicting grievous wrongs upon their Country's reputation." Further, Dobbin hoped that Dornin might terminate "this inexcusable invasion of a portion of Mexican Territory." No wonder, given such muddled instructions, that one naval officer in October 1857 confessed to worrying about finding himself "embarrassed when required to act in a foreign and neutral port," and asked Washington for clarification.[109]

These issues came to a head during William Walker's second invasion of Nicaragua, after his steamer in November 1857 landed about fifty men south of Greytown at the mouth of the Colorado River, before building up steam and speeding by the U.S. sloop-of-war *Saratoga* and depositing Walker's main force of about 150 followers at Punta Arenas, a spit of land opposite Greytown. After the landings the ineffective commander of the *Saratoga*, Frederick Chatard, sent two messages to his superior Hiram Paulding, commander of the Home Squadron, then on station at Aspinwall. Chatard admitted that he might have prevented Walker's landing had he been more vigilant as the *Fashion* approached Greytown, but he expressed doubt that he had the legal right to intervene now that the vessel had docked and Walker was on foreign soil. Confessing "mortification" at being outsmarted, Chatard suggested that Paulding bring his own more powerful vessel, the frigate *Wabash*, to Greytown, so that filibuster reinforcements might at least be prevented from landing. Paulding complied, arriving at Greytown harbor on December 6. But he demonstrated fewer inhibitions about the niceties of international law than Chatard had. Rather than allow Walker to continue his campaign, Paulding deployed sailors and marines ashore, trained artillery on the filibuster camp, and compelled the filibusters to surrender. Later that month, Captain Joshua R. Sands of the U.S. Navy took the party that had landed at the Colorado River into custody.[110]

Paulding's intercession prompted heated debate in the press, Congress, and legislative halls throughout the United States, with Walker and his supporters insisting that the commodore be censured for violating international law and that the navy atone for his error by conveying the filibusters back to Nicaragua. President Buchanan withstood the pressure to a point, noting in a special message to Congress on January 7, 1858, that Nicaragua had not complained about Paulding's transgression of its territory, which had relieved the state of "a dreaded invasion." Still, the president conceded that Paulding had "exceeded his instructions"; he returned to the filibusters the weapons and stores that Paulding had confiscated from them and took steps to ensure that naval commanders exercised greater restraint in the future. The secretary of the navy, Isaac Toucey, issued orders to Paulding's successor in command of the Home Squadron, James M. McIntosh, emphasizing that although McIntosh should prevent filibuster landings abroad, he had better pay close attention to Buchanan's strictures against Paulding for capturing filibusters on foreign soil. Similar orders went out to the commander of the Pacific Squadron. But some confusion persisted. In January 1859 the Pacific Squadron commander John C. Long inquired whether he could land forces to prevent filibustering invasions if asked to do so by authorities in the violated countries.[111]

Manpower limitations, deficiencies of resources, and legal constraints therefore hampered federal civil and military antifilibustering efforts during the antebellum years. Although these limitations by no means entirely explain the federal government's inability to fully uphold the Neutrality Law, they certainly merit recognition in any assessment of America's blemished enforcement record.

FINALLY, WE REACH the matter of deterrence. When prosecuting the Carbajal filibusters in Texas in 1852, District Attorney Ballinger expressed optimism that grand jury indictments might dampen the filibustering spirit by convincing people that the government was truly serious about prosecuting these crimes.[112] But it is doubtful whether federal prosecutors scored enough victories in court to dissuade Americans from participating in expeditions.

Even had federal prosecutions consistently led to convictions, it is unlikely that the government could have stifled filibustering. Organizers, expedition leaders, and enlisted men alike seem to have been cavalier about the risks of $3,000 fines and three-year jail terms. Not that $3,000 was an insignificant sum. Around the time of Narciso López's first filibuster, a mason working on the Erie Canal in New York State typically made a daily wage of about $1.50, and a sailor aboard a merchant ship out of San Francisco did worse, taking home about $30 a month. During William Walker's campaigns against Nicaragua, the average daily wage for skilled workmen in Philadelphia ran at about $1.25, except during the hard times of the "Panic of 1857," when they fell considerably lower. When Walker died in 1860, patrolmen in New Orleans made $45 a month, and machinists nationwide took home an average of $1.61 a day. For common laborers, making but $1.03 a day in 1860, a $3,000 fine could potentially wipe out about eight years in wages![113] Still, if filibusters worried about the financial penalties, they left scant evidence of their concern in their letters, interviews, court testimony, and reminiscences.

Not only were most filibusters relatively indifferent about the legal consequences of their behavior, but they also did not always allow arrests to stop them. On a number of occasions, filibusters free on bond while their trials were pending risked forfeiting their bonds rather than cancel their intended expeditions. The U.S. district attorney in New York, J. Prescott Hall, drew attention to the "inefficiency of all civil proceedings" against filibusters in August 1851, when he questioned in an official dispatch what good it had done to arrest Armstrong Lewis for involvement in the *Cleopatra* affair. After his indictment, Lewis "appeared, pleaded not guilty and gave bail in five thousand dollars for his appearance;" yet even as Hall wrote, the press was reporting that Lewis had captained the vessel *Pampero* in a new invasion of Cuba. Henry Kinney's surety in Philadelphia forfeited $5,000 after Kinney sailed for the Mosquito Coast while he was under bond to appear in court. Walker's surety in New Orleans lost $2,000 when Walker slipped out of the city for Mobile in November 1857 and then embarked on the *Fashion* for Nicaragua.[114]

Filibustering recidivism, however, surely had something to do with what happened when the adventurers did appear for trial. Unfortunately, the government compiled such a dismal prosecutorial record that few of the criminals had cause to worry about prison time or financial loss. Government attorneys lost virtually every filibustering case that they prosecuted. The government's signal success occurred in the trial of William Walker's associate Henry Watkins in Judge Hoffman's district court in San Francisco in 1854, when a jury on March 24 rendered a guilty verdict. Furthermore, after this trial and the imposition of a sentence by Judge Hoffman, Frederick Emory entered a guilty plea, saving the government the necessity of a trial in his case. Yet even in these instances, the court's message was mixed. Judge Hoffman limited his sentences in both cases to $1,500 fines, only half the maximum under the Neutrality Act; and District Attorney Inge entered a *nolle prosequi* in the case against the third Walker filibuster arrested in March, George R. Davidson, citing an inability to collect sufficient evidence to put him on trial. Making matters worse, Emory in June got excused from paying his fine on an affidavit of poverty.[115]

Virtually all other criminal actions against filibusters ended in hung juries or acquittals, if they even reached the trial stage. We have already noted District Attorney Hay's inability to secure convictions in several Carbajal filibuster cases in Texas. At the June 1854 session of the district court at Brownsville, Hay dropped charges against the four defendants still awaiting trial. The government's prosecution in 1850–51 of John Quitman and the fifteen other López collaborators collapsed in March 1851; after three separate juries failed to reach a verdict respecting John Henderson, a discouraged U.S. district attorney, Logan Hunton, decided that it would be fruitless to continue with any of the cases. Similarly, in New York City, juries divided in the *Cleopatra* actions against John L. O'Sullivan and Armstrong Irvine Lewis, leading the district attorney to terminate that prosecution. Perhaps most notably, William Walker won vindication in his first filibustering trial, and his liberty after a jury deadlocked in his second trial. Reportedly the San Francisco jurors who found him innocent of filibustering to Mexico needed only eight minutes to determine their verdict.[116]

In part, these results should be attributed to the impressive array of defense lawyers assisting accused filibusters, some of whom provided their services gratis. Ogden Hoffman, the same New York lawyer who outraged John L. O'Sullivan by representing the government in a filibuster case in 1851, agreed to serve as a defense attorney for both Henry L. Kinney and Joseph W. Fabens in 1855. Hoffman's associate counsel in both cases, John Van Buren, was the son of the former president Martin Van Buren and a former attorney general of the state of New York. Three years earlier, John Van Buren had served as a defense lawyer in O'Sullivan's filibuster trial. Sergeant S. Prentiss, a former Mississippi Whig congressman and one of the most gifted orators in the country, joined López's defense team in 1850. The former vice president George Mifflin Dallas defended Kinney in Philadelphia. William Walker's many attorneys included two former U.S. senators, Henry Stuart Foote of Mississippi and Pierre Soulé of Louisiana. Both before and after his single congressional term, moreover, the former New York City alderman and recorder Francis B. Cutting defended filibusters in court.[117]

In a few instances, federal judges rendered procedural decisions that helped the invaders to remain at large, the most egregious example occurring at Savannah in 1850 during the aftermath of López's first invasion of Cuba. That May, U.S. District Attorney Henry Williams had his efforts to prosecute López and his aide-de-camp José María Sánchez Iznaga foiled by an unfriendly procedural decision by Judge John C. Nicholl in U.S. district court. On Saturday the 25th, after the two filibusters had arrived in the city, Williams caused a federal marshal to arrest them and, at 10:30 P.M., bring them before Judge Nicholl for examination. When Williams requested that the case be postponed until Monday the 27th so that he might gather witnesses and evidence, Nicholl, taking note of López's desire to take a train to Mobile on Sunday, ruled that the case must proceed immediately. Not surprisingly, after a few hastily gathered witnesses gave useless testimony, at about midnight Nicholl determined that there was no evidence against the filibusters and that they should be discharged from custody.[118]

Judge Hoffman, so lenient in his sentencing of the convicted filibusters Watkins and Emory, even displayed sympathy for filibusters over the course of the proceedings. In his charge to the jury, Hoffman endorsed the motives of the expeditionists, registering his admiration for "the gallant ambition of the man who attempted to build up a flourishing colony on a territory now devastated by the savage." When levying the light sentence, Hoffman credited the "high character and otherwise unblemished reputations" of men who had mistakenly thought that they would answer "the call of humanity or the dictates of patriotism" by filibustering.[119]

But most federal judges demonstrated bias against filibustering if anything, especially in their charges to grand and trial juries, which resembled presidential neutrality proclamations. Samuel R. Betts, U.S. district judge for the Southern District of New York, emphasized when charging a grand jury in New York City in May 1850 that the filibusters' recent setback in Cuba by no means absolved either expeditionists or their backers. Rather, since the Neutrality Act branded "as a national offence" the very first "effort or proposal by individuals" to organize a filibuster, the jurors should help the United States maintain its "high character for justice and good faith toward others" within the international community. When instructing the grand jury in New Orleans about Quitman's conspiracy, Judge Campbell affirmed that so long as squads of men intended to filibuster, it mattered little if they armed themselves beyond U.S. territory: they remained "pirates" and lawbreakers, as did their underwriters. At William Walker's trial in San Francisco for invading Mexico, Judge Isaac S. K. Ogier sternly told jurors that they were "not the judges of the law" but rather that they had to "take the law from the Court," "put aside all considerations of philanthropy" during their deliberations (thus, as he also made clear, ignoring whatever benevolent motives might have inspired Walker), and stick to the narrow matter of whether Walker had violated the law. Judge McCaleb, in charging a grand jury to investigate Walker's aborted Nicaraguan plot in 1859, emphasized the need to prevent American citizens from plundering Nicaraguan homes, and told jurors that indictments would dissuade "deluded persons" from risking their lives in invasions. One circuit court judge reminded a trial jury that America's first neutrality act could be traced to George Washington, "the sanction of whose great name" ought to get the attention of "every right-hearted American citizen."[120]

The primary impediment to winning convictions in these cases was public opinion. According to the Sixth Amendment of the U.S. Constitution, criminal defendants must by tried in "the State and district wherein the crime shall have been committed." This clause guaranteed that nearly every filibustering trial occurred in a port city or Texas borderland town, where profilibustering sentiment ran rampant. Trials and examinations often occurred in an intimidating milieu, as supporters of the accused crammed into courtrooms, cheering on the defense. When Narciso López came forward to speak during his appearance before Judge Gayle in 1850, according to the *Savannah Daily Morning News*, the audience "broke forth in a burst of applause that was utterly beyond the power of the court and its officers to suppress, and which demonstrated in an unmistakable manner, the sentiment of our people toward the distinguished speaker." Outbursts of this kind, and the sight of filibusters entering court with large retinues of supporters, sometimes including local public officials, naturally influenced the course of filibuster trials.[121]

Profilibustering public opinion ensured that prosecutors would find it virtually impossible to impanel truly unbiased juries. How could such persons be found, for instance, in Brownsville, Texas, where a newspaper reporter discovered in October 1851 that the few citizens who were brave enough to speak out against filibustering "had their lives threatened"? Robert Smith, a special counsel for the United States, reported from Mobile in December 1858 that the "outlaws" were "beyond the reach of the courts," since public opinion had completely silenced persons in the city who opposed the expeditions.[122]

Of course the filibusters hardly required majority support in any of their trial venues. All they needed was enough persons in their camp to guarantee hung juries. Thus after the jury stalemated in the *Cleopatra* trials at New York, District Attorney Hall explained to the State Department that he had been "told by the foreman, that one of the Jury . . . refused to reason or converse upon the evidence of the charge—but took the ground resolutely, that he would not under any circumstances convict the accused!" In most cases, it was hardly so close. The district attorney prosecuting John Henderson in New Orleans reported to Washington that Henderson's third jury voted eleven to one for acquittal. The jurors chose to overlook evidence against the accused so incriminating that Henderson "was constrained, during the trial, to rise before the Court and Jury and admit his full and active participation in setting on foot the Expedition." Given this tendency of public opinion, it is hardly surprising that one U.S. attorney lobbied congressmen to repeal the law limiting venires to the cities and parishes where court sessions occurred.[123]

District Attorney Ballinger realized all too well the primary reason for the federal government's inability to stamp out filibustering. In a part of the country where "a large proportion" of the population either filibustered itself or sympathized "deeply" with such enterprises, it would be absurd to think that civil authorities could accomplish anything. All filibuster crimes were "bailable," he noted, and the filibusters could always count on "the State of public feeling . . . as rendering convictions on final trial, impossible."[124]

DURING THE antebellum period, the United States government compiled a tarnished record in repressing filibustering. Not only did one expedition after another set out from American ports and border regions, but the filibusters generally escaped punishment for their crimes, even when U.S. civil and military authorities took them into custody.

U.S. presidents and their cabinets did act repeatedly to repress the expeditions, however, and managed to reduce their frequency and manpower. Had federal efforts been completely ineffective, such filibustering collaborators as U.S. Senators John Slidell of Louisiana and Albert G. Brown of Mississippi would not have attempted, as they did, to get suspensions of the Neutrality Law enacted by Congress. As one of John Quitman's correspondents put it, the filibusters might muster "a few soldiers" for an invasion of Cuba under present circumstances, but could raise a "pretty good company" "if Senator Slidell's project prevails."[125]

Most likely, District Attorney Samuel Hay in Texas deserves remembrance for misjudging, rather than gauging, the mood in Washington. In July 1854, half a year after Hay registered his lack of confidence in the Pierce administration, Secretary of State Marcy expressed his own disappointment to Secretary of War Davis that the government's "civil authorities" on the Mexican border had been ineffective against "marauding expeditions." Marcy wanted the War Department to take up the slack by issuing orders that army officers on the frontier demonstrate "constant vigilance" against filibusters. That November, Davis commended the U.S. marshal Ben McCulloch of Texas, after learning that he had taken vigorous steps to counter a new filibuster against Mexico that reportedly was being organized in his district.[126]

Rather than intend to sabotage Hay's prosecution of José Carbajal, Marcy and Attorney General Cushing apparently jeopardized Hay's efforts inadvertently because of bureaucratic confusion. An exchange of correspondence between them in March 1854 hints that each believed Hay to have been acting under the authority of the other, and that therefore neither saw any urgency in answering Hay's inquiries. On March 8 Marcy forwarded to the attorney general Hay's request that his recent hire, the Galveston attorney Hugh McQueen, be compensated. Cushing the next day returned the account to Marcy, noting that it had been the State Department that had originally authorized the hiring of special counsel, and that therefore Cushing had "no authority in the matter, either to instruct the District Attorney, or to decide on the rights of Mr. McQueen." More revealingly, Cushing observed that the whole matter highlighted "the defective and anomalous condition of the law business of the government."[127]

Surely Cushing meant, at least in part, Congress's regular failure to appropriate money to enforce the Neutrality Act. Without funding from Congress, the attorney general and federal departments were reduced to covering extra expenses for enforcing the neutrality legislation out of operating funds, and they bickered repeatedly over where fiscal responsibility lay. On one occasion during the Pierce administration, the War, Treasury, and State Departments all contested responsibility for a charge of $1,200 that the Army had expended upon transporting thirty-four surrendered filibusters by private steamer, with the comptroller's office in the Treasury Department arguing that Treasury's judiciary fund was liable only if the prisoners were prosecuted in court. It took a special section in the Civil and Diplomatic Appropriations Act of March 1855 to resolve the impasse. Before leaving office, Marcy alerted James M. Mason, chairman of the U.S. Senate's Committee on Foreign Relations, that Congress's omission was "one of the principal causes" of the government's lack of success in stopping the expeditions.[128]

CHAPTER SIX

Francis Smith's Integrity

One day, while walking down Broadway,
What should I meet,
Coming up the street,
But a soldier gay,
In a grand array,
Who had been to Nicaragua;
He took me warmly by the hand,
And says, "old fellow," you're my man.
How would you like
A soldier's life,
On the plains of Nicaragua?
Then come with me down to the ship,
I'll quickly send you, on your trip,
Don't stop to think, for there's meat and
    drink
On the plains of Nicaragua.
—"I'm Off for Nicaragua!"
(quoted in *Frederick T. Shaw,
Dime American Comic Songster*)

THE "CUBAN FILIBUSTER" who turned up at the Virginia Military Institute in Lexington, Virginia, in the summer of 1851 obviously knew little about its superintendent. A graduate of the U.S. Military Academy at West Point and superintendent of VMI ever since its founding, Francis Henney Smith was a strict disciplinarian who demonstrated a strong devotion to his country and its statutes. In one address to his cadets, he affirmed that Virginia was "loyal to the National Constitution" and that his charges would "rally around her standard as one man" should ever the nation go to war.

Had the filibuster realized Smith's nature, perhaps he would not have dared solicit him for arms from the institute's arsenal, which he sought to facilitate the illegal invasion of Cuba being carried out by Narciso López's followers. As it was, he apparently received a frigid rebuff. Smith subsequently explained in a letter to the Department of the Navy that he not only turned the request down but also told the filibuster that he would welcome an opportunity to help the authorities arrest any persons "engaged in such an unlawful enterprize."[1] One can imagine the filibuster beating a rather hasty exit.

This encounter raises questions about how the pre–Civil War filibusters went about funding and supplying their expeditions. We investigated in chapter 4 the enticements that filibuster leaders employed to snare their recruits. But we have yet to learn the sources of the arms, supplies, and vessels that made their ventures possible. Francis Smith's account of VMI's hapless visitor makes one wonder if the filibuster leaders had their act together at all. Should we attribute the filibusters' high failure rate abroad to disorganization at home?

TO BEGIN WITH THE obvious, filibustering demands the invasion of a foreign country or dependency. One does not attempt such things casually. Though some of the expeditions of the pre–Civil War years had a haphazard quality to them, most were the products of considerable advance planning and mobilization. The challenges facing John Quitman, as he struggled between 1853 and 1855 to assemble an expedition against Cuba, are illustrative. According to the contract that he signed with revolutionary Cuban exiles on August 18, 1853, Quitman gained "absolute control and disposal" of all funds belonging to the Cubans' "Junta" as well as whatever money they collected in the future, in return for his services in liberating the island. Cuban sources subsequently donated some $80,000 to the cause, funneling the funds to Quitman through the president of the Junta, Gaspar Betancourt Cisneros. But Quitman discovered that this amount was insufficient, given the anticipated costs of arming, supplying, and transporting an army sufficient to overpower the defenders of Spain's treasured colony. By June 1854 Quitman's agents obtained 1,000 Sharps rifles and 1,500,000 cartridges for the expedition, but they still required some 3,000 knapsacks, 20 wagons, 1,000 Mississippi rifles, 1,500 percussion muskets, 7,000 pair of shoes, and other items for an invading force then anticipated at 3,000 men. Quitman indicated that it would take $200,000 to cover his outstanding needs.[2]

For the next half year Quitman and his agents strained to raise the desired funds. In July 1854 one of the expedition's organizers encountered a Charlestonian who asserted that if Quitman merely announced his intentions to depart for Cuba, so many men would turn out that federal authorities would be rendered "powerless" to prevent the expedition. "I told him," the agent reported to Quitman, that "men was not the thing desired twas money we wanted some $200,000." That September, one of Quitman's associates in Texas implored him to compel Cuban revolutionaries to "make up the $200,000." True, the Cubans had already contributed considerably to the project, "but then what is that additional sum, compared to the complete & permanent freedom of this Island?" The following January, as his expenses continued to mount, Quitman intimated to a contact in Georgia that if he did not raise $50,000 quickly, he stood to forfeit half a million dollars already invested. A month later, desperate to be off, Quitman sent instructions to New Orleans that virtually his entire account in the Louisiana State Bank, which he estimated at $18,995, should be invested in the expedition if necessary. Ultimately, these efforts came to naught, and Quitman canceled the operation.[3]

Filibusters like Quitman needed large sums not only to acquire stockpiles of weapons, tents, provisions, and other campaign necessities, but also to pay for their recruiting agents and offices, printing, uniforms, and other expenses. A newspaper correspondent in Jacksonville, Florida, observed in the spring of 1851, after noting that the Cuban filibusters there had deposited in a local storehouse large quantities of arms, gun carriages and other military equipment, as well as 300–400 bushels of oats, "I have never seen so many implements of war, except in an arsenal." Around the same time in New York, John L. O'Sullivan provisioned the intended filibuster transport *Cleopatra* with approximately 125 barrels of beans, beef, and bread, as well as sugar, tea, and other supplies including kegs of powder and blankets. William Walker, before his second expedition to Nicaragua, contracted to have 500 of his flintlock muskets converted to the percussion cap principle. The ship to be used in his aborted expedition of 1859 carried four barrels of lead, three cases of rifles, five kegs of gunpowder, two cases of cartridge boxes, and much more military paraphernalia.[4]

Of course, the amount of military stores stockpiled by filibuster organizers little mattered unless the expeditions had the means of arriving at their destinations. As we saw in the last chapter, American adventurers had relatively little difficulty crossing the usually shallow Rio Grande into Mexico. Expeditions against Cuba and the Central American states, however, depended on the availability of seaworthy vessels.

The purchase and leasing of troop transports drained the finances of seaborne operations, as Narciso López's organizers discovered when assembling his several attacks on Cuba. On August 24, 1849, the filibuster's agents spent $7,500 to charter the *New Orleans*, a 760-ton steamship that was one of several vessels acquired for that year's aborted plot, for a voyage of up to thirty days from New York to any port on the Gulf of Mexico or the Caribbean Sea. The lease stipulated that the ship be ready to sail as soon as she was loaded and cleared. The next April, the filibusters purchased outright for $16,000 from a concern in New Orleans the steamer *Creole*, which they employed immediately in López's landing at Cárdenas. Just before López's aborted expedition in the spring of 1851, John L. O'Sullivan bought the *Cleopatra* in New York for $13,600.[5]

Later expeditions repeated this pattern, with the exception of William Walker's last invasion of Central America. In 1854 John Quitman learned that three vessels were available in Mobile for his expedition, one by lease and two by purchase, but that the total cost would run him between $65,000 and $70,000. According to one of Quitman's conspirators, Domingo de Goicouria, treasurer of the Cuban Junta, eventually bought a steamship for the expedition (the *Massachusetts*) that was in such bad repair at the time as to require $45,000 of precious funds simply to get her seaworthy. In 1855 Henry L. Kinney leased the *United States* for $20,000 for his intended expedition to "colonize" Central America's Mosquito Coast. But Walker diverged from this pattern in 1860, when he leased and purchased several small vessels rather than large steamships to transport his men. Costs, as a result, were much lower. Thus Walker chartered one schooner for a month at $150.[6]

Not only did backers of seaborne expeditions have to pay out hefty sums for transport, but their costs invariably mounted sharply just before embarking. Ideally, recruits would have turned up at embarkation sites on the day of sailing. But organizers dared not cut things too closely, given the distances that many recruits had to travel from their homes to departure points. Ambrosio Gonzales informed John Quitman in April 1850 that the organizers of the pending Cuban expedition intended for the filibusters to arrive in New Orleans on the day of embarkation, but most filibuster leaders included some slack in their schedule. Thus the circular for William Walker's expedition in the fall of 1858 instructed participants to arrive at Mobile "three or four days previous to the day of departure." During the days before the sailing, filibuster leaders had to pick up their recruits' lodging and food expenses.[7]

Making matters worse, planners could never be certain of the exact day that their vessels would show up at the appointed points, or that they would appear in good repair. If the vessels arrived late, if they were seized or otherwise interfered with by the authorities, or if the expeditionists arrived at the point of departure too early, interim costs escalated. Sometimes delays also compelled the filibusters to pay additional charges to extend the charters of ships. The owner of Henry Kinney's leased vessel testified in May 1855 that Kinney was liable for a demurrage charge of $1,200 a day while the government occupied him with court appearances.[8]

OBVIOUSLY filibustering required considerable funding. Filibuster operatives covered their expenses in a variety of ways, in a few instances even drawing upon support from U.S. state governments. As we have seen in chapter 2, some arms belonging to the state of Mississippi ended up under the control of the López filibusters in 1850, possibly with the connivance of John Quitman, who was governor at the time. Similarly, the next year, Governor George W. Towns of Georgia provided help to López's circle. On April 12, 1851, Britain's consul in Savannah alerted Her Majesty's minister in Washington that arms from the Georgia state arsenal, "through the connivance of Governor Towns," had been sent to the Savannah railroad depot for the use of filibusters in transit to López's rendezvous. Although it is possible that the consul had picked up false rumors, Ambrosio Gonzales's letters to his fellow Cuban exile Cirilo Villaverde in February and to Mirabeau Lamar in March implicate the governor. According to Gonzales, Towns had supplied 400 shoulder arms, 2 cannons, and other war matériel. In 1855 James Callahan purchased supplies for his foray from Texas into Mexico on credit, with the understanding that the Texas legislature would reimburse the providers once the expedition was over.[9]

More commonly, filibuster organizers shifted some of their costs onto recruits, requiring that volunteers pay their own way to points of rendezvous or departure and that recruits supply their own shoulder arms and other campaigning necessities such as blankets. Narciso López, for example, specified in a cavalry captain's commission that volunteers for the company would have to bring their own arms, with the understanding that once the expedition arrived in Cuba the volunteers would be reimbursed. In November 1858 a newspaper correspondent noted that the townspeople of Port Gibson, Mississippi, had taken up a subscription to defray traveling expenses to Mobile as well as side arms for local volunteers intending to join William Walker's pending operation. One of Walker's agents in 1860 sought out recruits capable of paying all or most of their own ship passage to the Caribbean island of Roatán, the advance base for Walker's anticipated attack on the Central American mainland.[10]

Such demands on recruits covered only a small fraction of the costs of the expeditions. In most cases, filibuster organizers also had to make expenditures out of their own pockets and attract contributions from sympathizers, or their invasions would never be accomplished. In June 1851, for instance, the proprietor and editor of the *New Orleans Delta*, Laurent J. Sigur, sold off his interest in the paper in order to buy for the filibusters the steamer *Pampero*, which carried López to Cuba two months later on his final invasion. John S.

Ford personally equipped the former Texas Rangers who rode with him into José Carbajal's camp in the fall of 1851. The New York shipping magnate George Law offered 5,000 muskets to the Quitman plotters in 1854, and in 1856 he provided rifles for William Walker's Nicaraguan army.[11]

LAW WAS BY NO means the only shipping magnate who assisted Walker. Walker exploited the prior involvement of several American capitalists in Nicaragua, striking a deal by which shipowners from New York and San Francisco underwrote the costs of conveying his reinforcements. To understand Walker's arrangements with American shipping leaders, one has to go back to a deal cut by a U.S. diplomat with the government of Nicaragua several years before Walker even thought of invading Central America. At the height of the California Gold Rush in 1849, the U.S. chargé d'affaires in Guatemala, Ephraim George Squier, secured a contract with the Nicaraguan government on behalf of the American Atlantic and Pacific Ship Canal Company, a syndicate headed by the steamship magnate Cornelius Vanderbilt and Joseph L. White, a lawyer in New York and former congressman from Indiana. This arrangement gave Vanderbilt and White the right to construct a canal across Nicaragua and monopolistic privileges in operating a transit route across the country. In return for getting twelve years to build the canal and eighty-five-year privileges as to alternate means of transit (such as roads and rivers) , the company agreed to give Nicaragua $10,000 down, $10,000 a year while the canal was being constructed, and 10 percent of the annual net profits that the company made off any transit route that it established.

Vanderbilt never built his canal. But he did establish transit service across Nicaragua from Greytown on the Caribbean to San Juan del Sur on the Pacific (and back) that competed vigorously with American companies getting travelers to and from California via the Panamanian isthmus. Although the isthmus across Panama was narrower than that across Nicaragua, the Nicaraguan route used proportionately more navigable waterways and was 500 miles closer to the United States. In August 1853 one group of travelers made it from San Francisco to New York via Vanderbilt's Nicaragua route in a mere twenty-two days.

Typically, by mid-1853, California-bound travelers would ascend the San Juan River from Greytown to the first of several rapids, walk around them on a forest path, board a lighter-draft steamer, debark further upriver at the Castillo Rapids (by the ruined Spanish fortress Castillo Viejo), get around them on a portage railway, and then board yet another steamer for a short trip to the El Toro Rapids, where they again debarked. After walking by the rapids, passengers took a large lake steamer to Virgin Bay, on Lake Nicaragua's western shores, and then traveled the mere twelve miles remaining to the Pacific by mule or foot along a macadam road to San Juan del Sur. Company steamships from New York and San Francisco took passengers to and from the two termini of the transit, and travelers could check their luggage for their three-day trip across the isthmus and take advantages of vendors and hotels along the route. By early 1854 carriages made the land segment of the journey quicker and more comfortable.

Meanwhile, in 1851, Vanderbilt reached a revised accord with Nicaragua's government separating his canal and transit privileges, the latter going to a new concern called the Accessory Transit Company. By 1853, this company was raking in immense profits, partly because it used bookkeeping shenanigans to avoid paying the share of its profits due Nicaragua's government.[12]

After Walker in 1855 captured Granada and became commander in chief of Nicaragua's army under President Patricio Rivas's coalition government, he cut a deal to put this transit operation to his own advantage. In a complicated power shakeup, the steamship and ironworks magnate Charles Morgan had replaced Vanderbilt as president of the Transit Company and head of the New York end of the firm's business, and had established a close relationship with Cornelius K. Garrison, who ran the Pacific Coast operation from San Francisco (part of the time while mayor of San Francisco). However Vanderbilt, still a director, retained large amounts of Transit Company stock; and the company had outstanding liabilities. It had not paid its required $10,000 to the Nicaraguan government for 1855, nor the stipulated 10 percent of net profits since the inception of service.

Walker sided with Morgan and Garrison in a plot to squeeze out Vanderbilt entirely from the transit operation and strengthen his régime in the process. In October 1855 Charles J. Macdonald, representing Garrison, turned up in Granada and lent Walker $20,000 in specie, with the understanding that Walker would pay it back by crediting the amount against the annual payments due Nicaragua under the Transit Company's contract. Then, in December, Garrison's son arrived and in collusion with Macdonald and Walker's associates worked out the details of the coup against Vanderbilt. In return for Morgan's and Garrison's agreement to furnish Walker's reinforcements with transportation to Nicaragua (the passenger charges to be deducted from Nicaragua's claims against the company), Nicaragua would annul Vanderbilt's contract on the grounds that the company had failed to fulfill its financial obligations. In its stead, Walker's regime would give Gar-

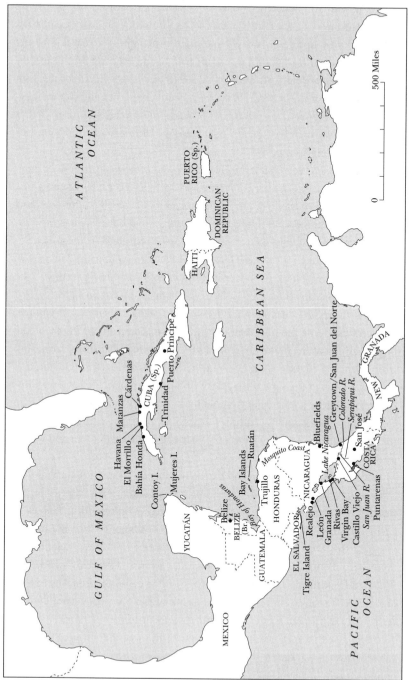

rison and Morgan a new charter for exclusive transit rights as well as all Accessory Transit Company property in the country. On February 18–19, 1856, President Rivas, under pressure from Walker, signed the necessary decrees of revocation and assignment (though he modified some of the provisions). Before the news circulated in the United States and Transit Company stock inevitably crashed, Morgan sold off his and Garrison's holdings—ironically at inflated prices because Vanderbilt had been buying up shares in a successful effort to regain the presidency and control of the concern.

Ultimately, Walker paid a heavy price for the cabal: an angry Vanderbilt would cooperate with Walker's Central American enemies and help to bring him down. But from the spring of 1856 until early 1857, the *Texas*, the *Tennessee*, the *Sierra Nevada*, and other steamers of a new Morgan and Garrison line carried American filibusters from New York, San Francisco, and New Orleans to Nicaragua's coasts, virtually free of cost to Walker. Moreover, in August 1856 Morgan and Garrison agreed to pay Nicaragua a peso for every ton of freight and passengers that it conveyed to or across the country.[13]

SHIPOWNERS IN the United States not only covered many of Walker's transportation costs during his tenure in Nicaragua but continued to help him after his expulsion from the region in the spring of 1857. During the aftermath of his return, Walker kept Macdonald within his inner planning circle,[14] and he dangled the promise of transit concessions before other shipping magnates in the United States to secure transports for his plots to reconquer Nicaragua. Unfortunately, his financial arrangements remain murky. Walker and his associates revealed few details in their letters, apparently for fear that federal authorities would discover their intentions and prevent their operations.[15]

Walker's invasion in the fall of 1857 depended primarily on sympathetic merchants in Mobile, Alabama, who developed a front organization to mask his filibustering intentions. That November, Julius Hessee & Co. announced in the *Mobile Daily Register* the creation of the Mobile and Nicaragua Steamship Company, which supposedly would run its steamship *Fashion* on a regular schedule to and from San Juan del Norte, with notice of her initial departure being released "in due time." When the vessel later that month carried Walker's party to Nicaragua, a manifest was submitted to federal port authorities stipulating a cargo of innocuous merchandise such as nails, tinware, blankets, sugar, and salt being shipped to Nicaragua by a local merchant, H. G. Humphries. During the expedition Humphries further legitimized the enterprise by announcing his intention to establish a firm, H. G. Humphries & Co.,

Commission Merchants and Factors, at San Juan del Norte. In February 1858, after Commodore Paulding broke up the expedition on the Nicaraguan coast, Alabama's legislature helped to pave the way for Walker's next foray. It chartered the Mobile and Nicaragua Steamship Company, which had as its principal shareholders Hessee, Humphries, and associates including Jones Withers (a former U.S. Army officer who had been deeply involved in Quitman's filibuster plot). The act of incorporation authorized the company to construct, buy, or charter vessels to call at and trade with any ports between Mobile and Greytown or other ports on the Caribbean Sea or the Gulf of Mexico.[16]

While continuing to collaborate with Hessee and Humphries, Walker also sought an understanding with H. G. Stebbins, president of the Atlantic and Pacific Ship Canal Company, and the company's vice president Joseph L. White. After Walker's expulsion from Nicaragua in the spring of 1857, Stebbins, White, and various other American shipping magnates (including Vanderbilt) began vying to secure the Nicaraguan transit concession, now presumably up for grabs, from Nicaragua's new régime. Stebbins and White initially won the competition, securing a transit agreement from Nicaragua's designated minister to the United States. Confident that great profits lay ahead, Stebbins in December 1857 even submitted a formal request to the State Department for the U.S. Navy to protect the vessels that his company was planning to send to Lake Nicaragua and the San Juan River from the "lawless" Walker, then in the midst of his second Central American invasion. However, Nicaragua's government subsequently revoked its minister's contract with Stebbins and White.

Capitalizing on the Nicaraguan government's change of policy, Walker contacted Stebbins and White after his return to the United States, using as an intermediary George H. Bowly, resident commission merchant at San Juan del Sur, Nicaragua, for the New York firm E. Bowly and Company. In July 1858 Bowly intimated to Walker from New York that he had been negotiating terms for a ninety-nine-year transit lease and that Stebbins's company had at its disposal the steamers *Hermann* and *Washington*. Despite considering Bowly's proposed concession overly generous, Walker ventured to New York City to finish the discussions in person. Returning to Mobile in October, Walker informed Callender Fayssoux, his most important collaborator, that he had made "very satisfactory arrangements" while in the North. Then he met with White in Washington in early November.[17]

Although the *New-York Times* reported that Walker had reached terms with Stebbins and White regarding their claims to the transit concession should his expedition succeed, it is uncertain whether Walker finalized a deal.

The *Times* noted concern among federal authorities that Walker had procured from Stebbins and White the vessel *Washington*, which the shippers announced would depart from New York on December 6 in an effort to test their transit claims in Nicaragua. But White denied that his ship was involved in filibustering; and Walker's allusion to making "very satisfactory" arrangements may have concerned acquiring weapons rather than transports, since he told Fayssoux in the same letter that he had seen "Mr. Law in reference to the arms in New Orleans" and that Law had turned the weapons over to him. Furthermore, Walker on October 19 asked Fayssoux to "ascertain" and "report" the expense of "hiring a suitable vessel" in New Orleans for "two weeks or upwards." When Walker's filibusters actually departed, they did so aboard H. G. Humphries's *Susan* out of Mobile, rather than the *Washington* out of New York. Later, Humphries and Julius Hessee provided much of the financing for Walker's attack on Honduras in 1860.[18]

Still, in August 1859, after the failure of the *Susan* expedition, Walker during another trip to New York did reach an arrangement with the United States Mail Steamship Company. Its officers agreed to divert to Walker's filibustering purposes the *Philadelphia*, a 1,238-ton paddle-wheel steamer, possibly in return for promises of future transit concessions. On September 19, 1859, loaded with boxes containing bayonets, muskets, and ammunition, the *Philadelphia* steamed out of New York City for Louisiana's Gulf coast with the intention of picking up William Walker's expeditionists. Only last-minute intervention by federal authorities prevented the vessel from conveying that year's Walker filibuster to Nicaragua.[19]

MOST CHARACTERISTICALLY of all, the filibusters financed their expeditions by resorting to standard capitalistic practices: issuing stock and bonds. The Cuban conspirators of 1850, for example, issued $2,000 bonds, signed by López, promising investors payment in five annual installments at 6 percent interest and guaranteed by Cuba's public lands and "the fiscal resources of the people and Government of Cuba." William Walker followed a similar course for his invasion of Mexico, signing $500 bonds, dated May 1, 1853, of what was termed an "Independence Loan" for his projected "Republic of Sonora." Each bond stipulated that the buyer would receive a square league of land "to be located on the public domain" of Walker's anticipated republic. Henry L. Kinney's Central American Colonization Company was initially capitalized at $5,625,000, based upon the issuance of 225,000 shares at $25 each, with 100 acres on the Mosquito Coast pledged for each share.[20]

Walker's Nicaraguan intervention began under the auspices of a Nicaraguan Colonization Company, capitalized at $100,000 with each share worth $1,000. During his tenure as president of Nicaragua, Walker authorized the marketing in New Orleans of a twenty-year $500,000 loan, at 6 percent interest payable annually at the Bank of Louisiana, with 1 million acres of his republic's land set aside as security to the bondholders. Walker's later plots also raised capital through bond sales. In July 1858 a newspaper reporter in Alabama described Walker's $500 bonds, which depicted a palm tree, five burning volcanoes, and a five-pointed star in the sky. The symbolism indicated Walker's intentions of uniting Central America's five republics under his rule.[21]

Filibuster organizers sometimes invested in their own bonds, a notorious case being that of former U.S. senator from Mississippi, John Henderson. According to Ambrosio Gonzales, Henderson virtually sank his life savings of $40,000 in López's expedition in the spring of 1850. In November 1850 Henderson pleaded with John Quitman to make a financial commitment to López's next expedition, lamenting his own inability to help the filibusters, since he had put up more than half the cash advanced for the previous expedition and was now greatly in debt. More commonly, filibuster organizers entrusted bonds to agents and sympathizers who attempted to market them to third parties, sometimes for commissions and traveling expenses. In May 1854 John Quitman's collaborator John S. Thrasher released to Juan M. Macías (a Cuban exile from Matanzas who had played a key role in López's movement) for sale in Savannah 439 bonds totaling $99,000, mostly in $150 and $300 denominations. William Walker informed Callender Fayssoux in February 1860 that he had just encountered Dr. William H. Rives of Montgomery, Alabama, who had offered to sell filibuster bonds there; Walker therefore instructed Fayssoux to turn over to Rives five $1,000 bonds and ten $500 bonds.[22]

Despite the illegality of their projects, the filibusters succeeded in unloading some of their stocks and bonds. In December 1854 one of John Quitman's many agents informed him that he had sold $3,033.33 in bonds, naming buyers and the amounts that they invested, and that he had accepted pledges for an additional $5,600 worth. Another of Quitman's backers wrote to an acquaintance in February 1855, "Don't you want some Cuban bonds. Trowbridge can give you all the information you want on the point. I am in $1,000, Trow $1,000, and I want you in 1,000. It is a good egg." Kinney sold 5,000 of his own shares in the Mosquito Coast project to Senator Thomas J. Rusk of Texas, at $5 a share. Walker's agents found buyers in New Orleans for about $43,000 worth of his 1856 twenty-year bonds. Occasionally, suppliers for the expeditions accepted bonds in lieu of monetary payments. Thus in 1856,

Walker's appointee as minister to the United States contracted with a gun manufacturer for 2,120 rifles, with partial payment in Nicaraguan bonds.[23]

The filibusters rarely sold as many bonds as they hoped and frequently lamented to each other how slowly their bonds were moving. So, for example, Samuel Walker alerted Quitman in May 1854 that "subscriptions do not come in so fast as we cd. wish," and Walker confessed during a fund-raising tour in the summer of 1858 that it was "uphill work" collecting funds. To help move his bonds, Quitman issued a mandate in the spring of 1854 requiring all recruits to pay $50 for the right to participate in his enterprise, with the understanding that enlistees would receive $150 worth of his Cuban bonds as soon as they paid the fee. Some recruits forked over the money. Others found Quitman's demand objectionable and backed away from participation.[24]

Invariably, filibusters sharply discounted their bonds to move them at all. Buyers were wary of speculating in expeditions that were not only illegal but also militarily risky and prone to cancellation, and would do so only under the most favorable terms. Thus Ambrosio Gonzales implored the former president of the Republic of Texas, Mirabeau Buonaparte Lamar, in March 1851 to induce the expedition's "friends" in Columbus, Georgia, to take its "Cuban Bonds," announcing that to raise the remaining $10,000 that López needed to purchase a second steamship for his next expedition, he would sell them at a bargain—a mere ten cents per dollar of the bonds' face value. In fact, Gonzales was offering the approximate going rate for filibuster bonds throughout the 1850s. In 1858 the New Orleans correspondent of a California newspaper noted that given the extent of approval in New Orleans for William Walker's movement, Nicaraguan bonds there had been "commanding 12½ cents on the dollar, and steady at that."[25]

Filibuster schemers, therefore, constantly found themselves reduced to scraping for cash. In mid-1859, when he was considering using the Isthmus of Tehuantepec in Mexico as a staging base for his next invasion of Nicaragua, Walker came up with $400 so that Bruno von Natzmer, a Prussian who had formerly served as colonel in his Nicaraguan army, could travel from San Francisco to the isthmus and make preparatory arrangements. However, Walker's hands were tied when Natzmer, after arriving at his destination, declared that he needed additional funds. "I could not send Col. N. any money for the simple reason that I had none to spare," Walker explained to Fayssoux. Walker was very grateful the next year when one of his men volunteered to pay his own passage to Roatán, the advance base for his final expedition. After Walker departed for the island, Fayssoux, coordinating operations back in New Orleans, lamented that Walker had already expended their available funds. Nothing remained for recruiting advertisements in the local newspapers, much less for the purchase of a printing press (though Fayssoux did raise the funds to buy 17,250 percussion caps).[26]

IN RETROSPECT, it is evident that America's filibusters rarely acquired the kind of funding that they needed to have even a remote chance of conquering and holding foreign domains. In the case of John Quitman's Cuba plot, financial deficiencies compelled cancellation of his expedition. In other cases, shortages weakened departing forces, increasing their vulnerability once they arrived at their destinations.

Still, the point is less that many filibusters operated on a shoestring than that they usually pushed on. A diarist in Los Angeles observed in March 1857 that only a few members of Henry Crabb's Sonoran invading force had dropped out of the expedition, although Crabb's "crowd" lacked the funds to buy horses. The filibusters had been promised mounts for their journey, but most of the adventurers nevertheless left the city "in good spirits" on foot, trusting that they would be able to buy horses or mules en route to Mexico.[27] Too many of America's filibusters, like Crabb's followers, persisted in their expeditions despite serious deficiencies in funding, supplies, and manpower. Such imprudence was a formula for disaster.

CHAPTER SEVEN

New York's Visitors

On the lakes the sun was setting, in a canopy
  of gold,
Making brilliant all the landscape, mountain,
  strand and ruins old;
Shimmering downward on the valley, and its
  wealth of fruits and leaves,
Where a thousand perfumed flowers with the
  forest inter-weaves;
Brightly gleamed the orange blossoms 'round
  the rent and siege-stained wall,
Over which our banner floating marked the
  city's recent fall—
While in the shade, beneath a cross, a dying
  comrade lay,
Midst a heap of reeking bodies, 'reft of life
  that bloody day.
  —*New York Sunday Courier*
  (quoted in *Philadelphia Saturday
  Evening Post*, April 12, 1856)

GROPING FOR language to describe William Walker's returning veterans, New York's newspapermen confessed frustration. "Such words as skeleton and scarecrow fall short of the reality," lamented the *Times*. "There is no power in pen to correctly describe their personal appearance," remarked the *Tribune*, which added that perhaps only a camera could do justice to the filibusters' pathetic appearance.[1]

Three times during the summer of 1857, survivors of William Walker's war in Nicaragua infested the city of New York. On June 30 the U.S. Navy's screw frigate *Wabash* dumped 120 men, 13 women, and 3 children from Walker's "republic" at the city's docks. On August 4 another screw frigate, the *Roanoke*, arrived at New York with 204 filibusters. On August 18 the *Tennessee*, a commercial side-wheel steamer owned by Charles Morgan & Sons that had once been engaged in bringing filibuster reinforcements to Nicaragua, disgorged 260 men who had deserted from Walker's army before its surrender.[2]

Rarely had New Yorkers seen such pitiful men as William Walker's defeated soldiers—particularly his rank-and-file.[3] Using language that could easily be applied to survivors of such later horrors as the Civil War's Andersonville prison and Nazi concentration camps, observers dwelled on the filibusters' sunken cheeks, yellowish skins, "feverish eyes," and emaciated limbs. Large numbers of the veterans suffered from debilitating wounds and diseases that they had contracted in the tropics. Others returned with stumps for the arms and legs that they had sacrificed for Walker's cause. Many of the filibusters debarking at the docks lacked hats, shirts, stockings, and shoes. The little clothing that the filibusters did wear was all in tatters.[4]

What should city authorities do about these destitute, near-starving, and stranded men? The city's financial resources were already strained to their limits by its own poor. Some of the filibusters returned from Nicaragua with a little money or had friends and relations in the city, and either left New York for their own homes or melded into city life. But the great majority were desperately in need of assistance.[5]

The city's superintendent of the Out-Door Poor Department, George Kellock Jr., committed the most seriously wounded and sickly of the soldiers to Bellevue Hospital, and admitted a few of the others to the city almshouse. But the governors of the almshouse decided that the great number of filibusters would have to fend for themselves. So Walker's soldiers drifted to City Hall Park, where they listlessly whiled away their days. One veteran, the *Times* reported, occupied himself by entertaining neighborhood "urchins" with a Costa Rican monkey that he had brought back to the United States. The few soldiers who sought jobs to support themselves apparently met with rebuffs. Sometimes the veterans ventured from the park into other public areas such as the Battery and the Merchant's Exchange. Most everywhere they turned up, the veterans related wartime adventures to curious passers-by, begging donations in return. A quarter bought enough cream cakes from a woman vendor in the park to temporarily satisfy the cravings of several filibusters. Larger donations allowed some of the men to hunt up meals at nearby saloons and begin saving money for travel to their own homes. Nighttime found some filibusters encamped on the steps of the Hall of Records; others slept on planks at the ward station houses of the city police.[6]

Eventually, New Yorkers rid themselves of the hapless returnees. Public figures such as Isaiah Rynders raised considerable sums at filibuster aid rallies. Boarders at the Astor House, near City Hall Park, helped out with contributions. Some Texans passing through the city took filibusters with relatives in Texas back home with them. An agent for a Hudson River steamboat company provided free passage upriver for other filibusters. Most important, the governors of the almshouse reconsidered their position, and funded the exodus of a number of the filibusters from the city. Better to pay out a little money now, the *Tribune* explained, than permit the filibusters later to become "charges upon the Alms-House Treasury."[7]

New York's travail with the welfare of filibustering had ended. But the story begs further reflection. Did filibustering expeditions always come to such sorry ends? If so, what went wrong? Such questions demand that we refocus our attention from filibusters to filibustering. It is one thing to identify participants in these invasions and explore their motivations. It is another matter entirely to comprehend what it was like to actually participate.

ALTHOUGH SOME expeditions started off in promising fashion, all of them ultimately failed, usually with dire consequences for the participants and their loved ones. Not once did manifest destiny's filibusters repeat the success of their predecessors in Texas. Rather, the New England religious journal which headlined the suffering of Walker's veterans in the summer of 1857 "The Wages of Sin" might well have been discussing almost any expedition of the pre–Civil War years.[8]

The wife of a U.S. Army officer discovered as much rather early in the period. Riding with some companions near the U.S.-Mexican border one evening during the Carbajal expeditions, Teresa Vielé came upon the corpse, wrapped in a Mexican pancho, of a man who had been wounded in the previous day's fighting and then died after being taken back into U.S. territory. Recalling, some years later, that she never found out the man's name, Vielé also remembered that a number of papers about "filibuster life" had been discovered on his body, as well as a plea for his return from a "lady-love" and a letter from his mother. The last, "written in a delicate, tremulous hand," begged her "dearest boy" to come home.[9]

Though just a vignette, Vielé's story in many ways sums up filibustering's futility and familial tragedy. Many other Americans besides this mother, for all of manifest destiny's hold on the public imagination, resisted having their male kin risk their lives on its behalf. In January 1856, for instance, a young woman of about eighteen turned up in the office of the mayor of New York, pleading unsuccessfully that the city's authorities intervene to stop her brother from departing for Walker's Nicaragua that day aboard the steamer *Star of the West*. Three months later, a woman in San Antonio would implore her son, "do not think of Nicaragua John, there is too much cutting and slashing there for a family man."[10] Unfortunately far too many young American males ignored such pleas. As a result, many of the mothers, fathers, brothers, sisters, and other relatives of filibusters had their worst fears confirmed.

That was surely the case for recipients of what might be remembered as the

Crittenden farewells. In the hours before they executed Colonel William Crittenden and his fifty companion filibusters on August 16, 1851, Spanish authorities in Havana allowed their captives to write final letters, some of which later appeared in the American press. Crittenden got off a couple of such missives, one of them to a friend, the other to his uncle, the U.S. attorney general. In these letters Crittenden recounted the circumstances of his capture, his disillusionment with filibustering, and his desire to "die like a man," as well as his last thoughts about family and acquaintances. Beseeching a friend to see to it that his mother learned of his fate, Crittenden lamented, "I am afraid that the news will break her heart." Revealingly, Crittenden's companions struck similar themes in their final thoughts. As one of them put it in his missive to an editor in Louisville, Kentucky, filibustering had shown itself to be "a great humbug."[11]

Among the striking consistencies running through antebellum America's filibustering story were how thoroughly the invaders were repulsed, and how macabre the experiences were that many of the adventurers endured. Most of America's filibusters sooner or later suffered horribly from deprivation, disease, and battle wounds. A large number of them, like Vielé's unknown soldier and Crittenden's fifty, perished. Over and over, glory proved elusive.

For some adventurers, the filibustering experience soured prematurely, as they exhausted their spending money during the seemingly interminable delays before expeditions departed. Richardson Hardy, editor and proprietor of the *Cincinnati Nonpareil* and a lieutenant in López's expedition of 1850, arrived in the New Orleans vicinity on April 11 after traveling down the Ohio and Mississippi Rivers with fellow adventurers from Ohio and Kentucky, only to be informed that he and his companions were ten to fifteen days early. When the expedition's paymaster allotted the early birds a living allowance of just $1.50 per week, Hardy later recalled, they grew resentful. The expedition's organizers temporarily quieted the unrest by covering the men's local hotel bills and moving them to cheaper quarters. But rebelliousness still simmered, especially after the recruits learned that high-ranking officers were lodging at the St. Charles and Verandah hotels in New Orleans, and charging to the expedition their juleps and their visits to theaters and masked balls. Finally a committee including Hardy persuaded a reluctant paymaster to meet the volunteers' monetary demands rather than risk having them quit. After a similar experience the next year, another of López's followers sent a public letter about the problem to a Louisville paper. This adventurer warned that any persons intending to filibuster had better "provide themselves plentifully with money," because they would undoubtedly discover in New Orleans that no arrangements had been made for them.[12]

In addition to enduring financial difficulties, some of the adventurers fell sick, and many of them vented their frustrations in heavy drinking, brawling, and even pillaging. Awaiting their conveyance to Cuba in 1849, restless members of the Round Island contingent killed cattle belonging to the keeper of the lighthouse and smashed the keeper's windows. Later, during the navy's blockade against provisions from the mainland, some of the men, rebelling against a diet that was reduced to rice and coffee, tried to plunder commissary stores set aside for the sick. This attempt sparked a fracas that left one filibuster stabbed to death and a second man wounded. Another volunteer died there of "brain fever" (most likely malaria). The diarist M. C. Taylor noted the next year that the "boys" had engaged in a row at an auction, and that one of the recruits had fallen ill and been hospitalized in New Orleans.[13]

Given these difficulties, recruits not surprisingly suffered from bouts of homesickness and harbored second thoughts about their decisions even before leaving American soil. One of Narciso López's volunteers, according to Taylor, became so distressed after arriving in New Orleans that, he blurted out, he might as well drown himself, since "he was 1500 miles from home and did not have a cent." In 1856 one of William Walker's agents reported from New Orleans that "a large number of young men" who had come to the city to filibuster had become "disheartened and returned to their homes."[14]

Other recruits tried to quit expeditions at sea. A San Francisco newspaper in December 1853 noted that two men sneaked aboard the steamer that had been towing their filibuster barque out to sea from San Francisco harbor, and returned to port in it. In early 1856 a contingent of New York City recruits for the Nicaraguan army, after being provided with free tickets to Central America, attempted to blend in with the commercial passengers aboard their ship as a way of escaping their military obligation. Appalled at the turn of events, their captain reported back to New York from the ship that only a skeleton group of nine men remained willing to serve under him in Walker's army. Later that year a number of Walker's recruits aboard the steamer *Tennessee* out of New York decided to back out of service and return home when their vessel had to put in to Norfolk harbor because of a broken shaft and transfer its passengers to another ship.[15]

Many seaborne adventurers suffered from motion sickness and survived harrowing experiences on the way to their destinations. While bringing reinforcements to Walker in Mexico, the *Anita* apparently came close to sinking. Heavy seas washed supplies overboard, and passengers became convinced that they would drown. As water seeped between the decks, some of the "frightened hombres," according to one of their officers, "were heard praying loudly." Henry Kinney's vessel, the *Emma*, lodged on a reef off the Caicos Islands in the British Bahamas, forcing the filibusters to abandon ship. Kinney managed to continue his escapade by salvaging his supplies and acquiring two small schooners locally; these enabled him to convey his forces across hazardous waters to Grand Turk Island, where they chartered a brig to carry them the rest of the way to their Central American destination. The members of William Walker's *Susan* escapade in 1858 were less successful, but possibly more lucky. They gave up their expedition and eventually returned to the United States after their vessel broke in two on a coral reef in the Bay of Honduras. But it was a close call. One of the filibuster officers was thrown into the sea during the incident and almost drowned; the entire force had to be evacuated from the vessel, a few men at a time, by canoes through heavy surf. Some of the filibusters were stuck on the wreck for nearly a week and went for thirty hours without food or water. In what seems to have been the worst naval filibustering disaster before the Civil War, fifteen to twenty Americans in the *Flores* expedition to Ecuador perished when their vessel exploded.[16]

Still, most participants commenced their adventures in buoyant spirits, hardly grasping the odds against them until arriving on foreign soil. In 1849 an officer at the Round Island encampment described his routine as virtually idyllic. Not only were the grounds the "finest" in the world, but the filibusters were enjoying a life of leisure. After reveille, all the officers had to do was drill their men. Afterward they passed their time fishing, playing marbles and cards, and catching crabs. In 1851 officers and men greeted Narciso López's boarding of the *Pampero* with "wild hurrahs," and days later, when the vessel weighed anchor for the Gulf of Mexico, the men waved their handkerchiefs and cheered again. An adventurer bound for Nicaragua exulted in a letter to a friend that he was "going filibustering now sure," after his steamer exited San Francisco harbor.[17]

As their expeditions neared their destinations, the great majority of filibusters, like so many of America's volunteers in the Mexican and Civil Wars, welcomed the prospect of combat, apparently unconcerned that many of their commanders were military amateurs. Richardson Hardy later recalled that all his comrades assumed their own invincibility in battle. Aboard Narciso López's Cuba-bound vessel the *Creole* in 1850, M. C. Taylor observed, "Today was spent in drilling the men in the manual of arms. They were extremely merry." Taylor also noted how "magnificent" it was "to hear the grand roaring of musketry and rifles" break out as the filibuster forces arrived at Cárdenas. "We are approaching Honduras," one of William Walker's followers reported to a New York paper, "and . . . all is activity on board. . . . Lead is being run into balls, and . . . we 'smell the battle' not 'afar off.'" Recruits on another of Walker's troop ships felt a thrill when guns and ammunition were made available as their vessel approached Greytown harbor, and they made an excited dash for the weapons.[18]

Such euphoria rarely survived for long, though filibusters sometimes won their initial skirmishes or battles on foreign soil and occasionally occupied towns and villages during the early stages of their campaigns. José Carbajal's forces captured Camargo and several other Mexican borderland communities after crossing the Rio Grande in 1851, and they then laid siege to Matamoros before being forced to recross the river. During a break in the filibusters' assault on Cerralvo in November, Major Jack R. Everett got off a letter to the United States, proclaiming exuberantly, "we have routed the enemy in every sense of the word. We have driven them through every house in the town to a large stone building. . . . To-day we expect to capture their whole force. . . . 'God and Liberty' is our cry, and will be untill the honor of Carvajal . . . shall wave o'er the ruins of prostrate despotism."[19]

William Walker's troops even experienced a relatively peaceful interlude during their invasion of Baja California in the fall and winter of 1853–54. During the several months that he occupied Ensenada, Walker boarded some of his men in local adobe homes, the rest in tents. In letters back to the United States from the town, the filibusters conveyed the impression that their lives were relatively comfortable, mentioning among other things the delights of drinking aguardiente and dining on venison, clams, chocolate, and other delicacies. Not only did the filibusters enjoy "good health," but many of them had become active in a regimental riding school. "It would do our friends at home good," one invader declared, "to see some of us . . . careening, hatless and with coat-tail flying," breaking in wild horses that they had gathered. Another discounted the danger of the enterprise, noting that conditions were "proverbially dull" and that the filibusters especially enjoyed relaxing with newspapers from home. Two of Walker's officers, however, enlivened matters by risking their lives in an affair of honor, each firing four shots and taking wounds before their seconds terminated the duel.[20]

Even more domestic images of filibuster life emerge from Henry Kinney's colony on Central America's coast, especially in William Sidney Thayer's letters to the *New York Evening Post*. Thayer recounts that after arriving at Greytown in July, Kinney's followers procured "respectable employment" in a "variety of occupations," and soon afterward attended a fandango to which he had been invited at a two-storied dwelling in town. There the expedition's "gallant Colonel" engaged the lady of the house in the first quadrille, inspiring his followers to seek their own dancing partners. Thayer noted, in an intriguing aside (given American racial mores), that the filibusters danced with women "of various shades" and that some of their partners were of black and brown complexions.[21]

Thayer reported in late August that three of Kinney's men had already completed a weeklong expedition into the interior and that they had "marked out haciendas for their future residence." Moreover, Kinney's weekly the *Central American*, which appeared on September 15 for the first time, celebrated the supposed virtues of filibuster life amid the "Hills of Zion." Here, the paper reported, peaceful colonists discovered a land where gold mines equaled those in California, whose fruits and plants were "more matured and in a greater variety" than in Florida, and where one could make three crops of corn in a single year. Advertisements, articles, and editorials convey the impression that schools, first-class restaurants, and other businesses are springing up, while mining companies race to exploit the gold. Kinney has himself established an experimental plantation to test the area's suitability for various vegetables and grasses.[22]

We should never overlook the boosterism attached to such effusive reports. Despite Jack Everett's optimism, Carbajal's invaders failed to capture a single enemy artillery piece at Cerralvo, even though seizing the guns was a primary objective of their assault. Most likely, Everett drafted his battle account to entice reinforcements from Texas. Certainly one of Walker's followers in Mexico exposed such ulterior motives. After noting in a message back to California how he and his companions had been enjoying "pretty good times" with "nothing much to do, and plenty to eat," this filibuster exclaimed, "Tell some of the other boys to come down, and we will have first rate times." Likewise, one should be wary of reports of economic miracles in Kinney's colony. According to one report, Kinney and his followers as late as April 1856 had less than ten acres of land being tilled. Kinney himself admitted in a letter that month that his colony had thus far had "a hard time of it."[23]

Filibustering invaders rarely sustained their few successes for more than a few days or weeks. Many campaigns became transformed almost immediately into survival stories. Narciso López's filibusters in 1851, for instance, defeated Spanish forces in several encounters during the first few days after they landed at the village of El Morrillo on Cuba's northern coast, west of Havana, in the early morning hours of August 12. Yet within two weeks, their invasion had been thoroughly crushed. Those men who had not already died in battle or ambush, been captured and executed, or surrendered to Spanish authorities were reduced to an ever-dwindling band of wandering, exhausted, rain-drenched, barely clothed, and famished fugitives hoping to link up with a force of reported anti-Spanish Cuban insurgents that did not exist. One eye-witness reported that the men appeared to be "shocked and wordless," and a survivor revealed in a letter after his capture that his band at one point had nothing to eat but a single horse for five days. López and his demoralized men tried desperately to keep one step ahead of numerically superior Spanish forces. But by August 29 virtually all the filibusters had been taken prisoner or died. López's execution on September 1 occurred a scant three weeks after his landing.[24]

Certainly Henry Crabb and his followers never had a chance. They began their suffering long before initiating their ragged march into the interior of the Mexican state of Sonora on March 27, 1857, having already survived a difficult crossing of desert terrain in southern California and what is today southernmost Arizona, just to reach the Mexican border village of Sonoyta. Crabb and his men not only had to regularly extricate wagons that became deeply stuck in sand, but they also ran so short of water that they had to divide their force of eighty-nine men in two. Crabb and sixty-eight men forged ahead to Sonoyta, leaving a twenty-man party under Freeman S. McKinney of San José to come up later. Once at Sonoyta, Crabb ran so low on provisions that he decided to move on Sonora prematurely, without waiting for McKinney's party.[25]

Just outside Caborca on April 1, not even a week after he left Sonoyta, Crabb and his party, greatly outnumbered, came under attack from Mexican troops. After returning fire, the filibusters found shelter in a large adobe house on the town plaza. The filibusters took a number of casualties, including several deaths, in an unsuccessful attempt that same day to rout the Mexicans from a church on the opposite side of the plaza, and then settled in at the house where they immediately came under siege and, eventually, artillery fire. The Mexicans forced Crabb's surrender on April 6 by firing flaming arrows into the building's roof of straw thatch. At sunrise the next day, the Mexicans executed Crabb and his entire force except for one underage soldier, and then cut off Crabb's head and preserved it in an earthen jar filled with vinegar. Not far away, Mexican troops also intercepted McKinney's followers, reduced to sixteen because of three sick men and a soldier caring for them who remained behind at Sonoyta, and executed them as well. Some days later, a small party of Mexicans crossed the border at Sonoyta, burst into the house just on the American side occupied by the four men whom McKinney had left behind, took them out of bed, and shot them, leaving their bodies to rot.[26]

Most members of Granville Oury's party of twenty-four reinforcements for Crabb, recruited in the Tucson area in March and early April, survived

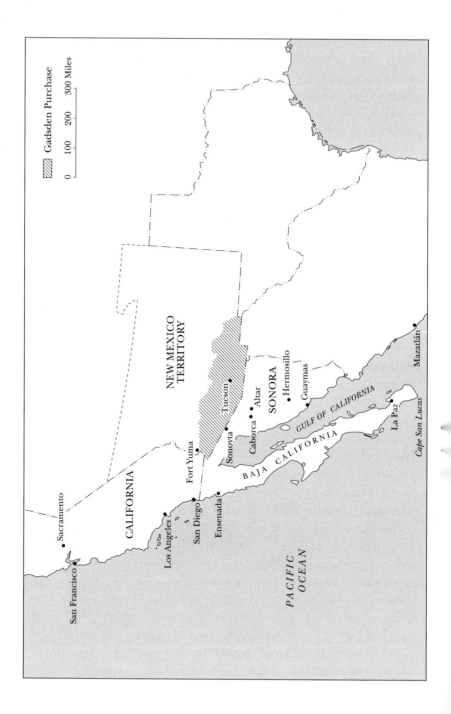

their phase of the campaign, but they endured considerable suffering before it ended. Oury's party had to fight through Mexican resistance (taking several casualties) to get within a few miles of Caborca, before determining that a large enemy force had Crabb under siege and that they could never break through. John C. Reid, a member of Oury's expedition, later remembered the retreat to the U.S. border as a horrific experience, during which the men suffered from relentless exposure to the sun and "almost unbearable thirst." Reid recalled how cactus thorns tore at his legs, how he wore out the soles of his shoes, and how each step became more painful than the last given the lacerations of his feet. At least Reid escaped the fate of one of his fellow filibusters, who had fled during a skirmish with Mexican forces earlier in the campaign, and upon whose exposed, lacerated body Reid stumbled while making his own way back to the U.S. border.[27]

Even less fatal filibustering campaigns, including William Walker's thrust into Baja California and Sonora, generally had their horrors and led to the deaths of a significant number of participants. At least twenty-five men, or more than 10 percent of his entire invading force, died or suffered wounds during Walker's Mexican campaign, including a small body of men whom Walker left at the town of San Vicente in Lower California during his attempt to invade Sonora. In March 1854 enemy forces massacred this party. Conditions during the later stages of Walker's operation grew so intolerable that scores of his troops deserted and fled to the U.S. border. A correspondent for a California paper described these survivors as arriving shoeless, hatless, and nearly starving at the army's Fort Yuma, where Major Samuel Peter Heintzelman humanely furnished them with army rations lest they perish. Walker himself survived the campaign, but barely. After being harassed for weeks by numerically superior Mexican irregulars, the "Colonel" and his thirty-three bedraggled, remaining companions, carrying little but their arms and moldy beef, managed to recross the U.S. boundary near San Diego, where, as noted in chapter 5, they surrendered on May 8 to U.S. army officers.[28]

WILLIAM WALKER's conquest of Nicaragua of course provides a glaring exception to the rule that filibustering invaders experienced abbreviated histories. But ultimately even America's most successful filibustering invaders paid dearly for their transgressions. Although Walker never achieved effective control over all of Nicaragua, he did consolidate his rule over part of it during 1855 and 1856, and held Rivas, Virgin Bay, and other points into 1857. As a result, his soldiers experienced the semblance, although illusory, of conquest

"Engagement between the American Filibusters and the Costa Ricans." (Reproduced from the *London Illustrated Times*, May 24, 1856; by permission of the British Library [shelfmark: London Illustrated Times])

and stability. This held true not only for much of late 1855, but especially be-tween late April 1856, after the withdrawal of invading Costa Rican forces, and mid-September, when a coalition of Central American countries began an ultimately successful military campaign to oust them.

Reports flowed from Nicaragua to the American press not only of Walker's military triumphs but also of his having established a functioning govern-ment. Thus "C." informed the *San Francisco Daily Herald* in late 1855 that the régime had "appropriated" the "Government House" on Granada's plaza for its "different offices." In October 1856 the *Baltimore Sun* reported on a dinner that Walker had thrown for the visiting dignitary Pierre Soulé, the for-mer U.S. minister to Spain, noting that the affair was attended by John Tabor, editor of *El Nicaragüense*, Charles Callahan of Walker's customs service, Ma-jor B. F. Crane, his acting postmaster general, and representatives of all his other "civil" departments, as well as by army officers and the U.S. minister to Nicaragua. As late as January 1857 B. G. Weir, one of Walker's officials, re-ported to a California paper from Rivas that he was "holding the Court here every day."[29]

Meanwhile, some of Walker's soldiers sent letters home boasting about the glories of filibustering, and travelers returned to the United States from Nicaragua with glowing stories of the good life there. Soon after Walker's capture of Granada in October 1855, John S. Brenizer, a surgeon-turned-solder in Walker's army, informed his family that he was in "good health and in fine spirits" and that his comrades believed he was becoming "as fat as a plum." Brenizer attributed his fortunate condition to Nicaragua's "Pudding like" climate, which was so mild that he had yet to wear either overcoat or woolen mittens. The next summer, Brenizer reported that he took daily siestas in a hammock and promised to have a daguerreotype taken and sent home. Then his folks could view his new mustache and goatee and see what a "live Fillabustar" looked like.[30]

A filibuster stationed at Masaya made Walker's Nicaragua into a gourmet's delight. This adventurer informed a stateside friend that the men were dining on tortillas, plantains, beef, chocolate, chicken, eggs, and "fruit of all kinds that could please the palate," and that they passed their time "drilling, messing, trying to learn Spanish with the Senoritas, horse-racing, mule-racing, cock-fighting," while occasionally taking time out for duels and baths. From Granada, another filibuster exulted that he was "contented" for the first time in his life. He was breakfasting on boiled eggs and stewed chicken, had his own "niggar cook," and planned to find a wife since there were four women for every man.[31]

Many of the adventurers were rapturous about the country itself, rendering Nicaragua's landscape in romantic imagery. One soldier, for instance, described the wonders of panoramic rivers and flowers in perpetual bloom, and gushed over the awe-inspiring nighttime belching of five volcanoes. Our Granada commentator discovered "the most luxuriant crops" rotting for need of harvesters; another soldier reported that the climate was "delightful" and his command healthy, and that one could buy such tropical fruits as oranges, pineapples, and limes for very little money. B. G. Weir pronounced Nicaragua "the finest country on earth" in a letter to a California paper. Weir assumed that the filibusters would ultimately "overrun all Central America," given the size of their army, their ample supply of ammunition, and their superiority in heavy guns.[32]

During his tenure, Walker initiated what he envisioned as the Americanization of Nicaragua, and ultimately all of Central America. Soon after his coalition government took power, Walker offered 250 acres of Nicaraguan public land for free to any Americans emigrating to the country; claimants had to settle on and make improvements to a tract provided by his director of colonization Joseph W. Fabens, the recent U.S. commercial agent in Greytown and a defector from Henry Kinney's organization. An extra 100 acres would be provided to anyone bringing a family into the country. That November, Walker entreated the chancellor of the University of Nashville, a former college friend, to persuade someone "skilled in geology and botany" to migrate to Nicaragua. Walker claimed in his letter that the country offered great opportunities to naturalists and promised that his government would look after any scientifically inclined Americans who came down.[33]

Later, Walker took more drastic steps to displace native Nicaraguans and replace them with Americans. Two days after his inauguration Walker decreed that all public documents written in English would have equal legitimacy with those in Spanish, paving the way for the drafting of English-language deeds that would give Americans the upper hand in land litigation. A couple of days later, he issued another decree announcing the appropriation and sale of estates belonging to persons who had opposed his regime since the creation of the Rivas coalition government in October 1855. A further ruling provided that all persons must register their lands within half a year, a system that discriminated against natives who were unfamiliar with American registration procedures.[34]

Immediately, word filtered back to the United States of Walker's land bonanza. James T. Coleman, a lieutenant in Walker's light infantry battalion, alerted his family on July 17, 1856, that "superb cocoa plantations" had already been confiscated for sale at auction and that Californians on hand were "chuckling to themselves at the splendid opportunity for speculation." His relations should tip off their friends that haciendas were on sale at prices so low that they could possibly be paid for with one year's crop. Walker's judge advocate general, John H. Marshall, informed his father in August 1856 that he had just accepted the additional assignment of serving as "one of three commissioners to take possession of all the property in the state subject to confiscation," so that it could be sold for the benefit of Walker's treasury. Marshall explained that the value and size of the coveted property was so great, he would have to postpone for months a scheduled visit home.[35]

Walker and his boosters, with the moral (or, we might say, immoral) support of expansionist newspaper editors in the United States, for a while succeeded in convincing numbers of Americans that opportunities beckoned in his domain. As one New Orleans sheet put it, the sudden emergence of "stable government" in an area that not only boasted a delicious climate and fertile soil but also was bound to become the "highway of future commerce between Asia and the civilized world" provided ambitious Americans with a compelling motive for emigration. Along similar lines, a paper in San Fran-

cisco published a letter from one of Walker's officers on leave in the city asking persons to call on him for particulars if they were interested in helping the
filibusters develop Nicaragua's rich cotton, sugar, coffee and grain crops, as
well as its mineral wealth.[36]

All sorts of Americans took the bait. Sidney Breese, a former U.S. senator
from Illinois, noted in March 1856 that his son, a lawyer of "enterprising disposition," hoped to seek his fortune in Nicaragua, "where he and I think, a
fine field is open." Later that year, a graduate of the Eclectic Medical Institute
in Cincinnati solicited Walker's designated minister to the United States, Appleton Oaksmith, for a chance to treat tropical diseases in Granada, expressing the hope that his ministrations would contribute to the success of "liberal
principles" in Walker's republic. The New Orleans firm Livingston and Company announced its inauguration of an express delivery service to Nicaragua
for packages (25 cents each) and letters.[37]

Even African Americans might seek their fortune in Nicaragua. James
Thomas, a free black barber living in Walker's birthplace, Nashville, and his
nephew John H. Rapier Jr. traveled to Walker's headquarters in Granada in
early 1856, bearing a letter from Walker's father. Thomas and Rapier did not
stay, but in a reminiscence Thomas left an intriguing description of the famous filibuster. Thomas noted that Walker kept a picture of his sister Alice in
a concealed gold case that dangled from his neck, and that he maintained an
ample supply of cigars and liquor for the enjoyment of callers, though he apparently neither smoked nor drank. More to the point, Thomas rationalized
his trip in response to those of his acquaintances who questioned its logic:
contemporary newspapers had been regularly referencing the "grand opportunities" that awaited emigrants to Walker's domain. Presumably, Thomas
had been reading press accounts of American hotels, commercial firms, and
other businesses popping up in Walker's republic.[38]

Alone among the filibusters, moreover, Walker bridged the gender gap. Although it is tempting to label filibustering as an exclusively male enterprise,
a few women turn up here and there in documents about the expeditions. A
lieutenant in one of the Mexican invasions, for instance, praised the contributions of the spouse of a fellow officer, who had "handled a rifle and a pistol
on several occasions so manfully, that she was looked upon as about as good a
man as any one of the party." Henry L. Kinney's newspaper at Greytown employed a female associate editor.[39] But only Walker's Nicaraguan intervention
involved a number of females. His ability to attract them testifies to the quasi-
stability, and potential domesticity, of his regime.

Some of Walker's officers, for example, brought their wives and other fe-

Playbill for theatrical production in New York City celebrating William Walker's conquests in Nicaragua. (Courtesy Tennessee Historical Society, War Memorial Building, Nashville)

male relations into the country. E. J. C. Kewen informed a San Francisco paper in February 1856 that the former U.S. army officer Philip R. Thompson, who was to serve as Walker's adjutant general, had just arrived in the country along with his "accomplished lady." Kewen apparently saw nothing overly risky about Thompson's decision, because he brought his own wife to the filibuster republic for a time the following spring. In January 1857 Walker presided over an Episcopalian service at which one of his brigadiers, Edward J. Saunders, married Elizabeth Swingle, the daughter of Alfred Swingle, a colonel in his army. By that time, General Birkett D. Fry's "beautiful and intelligent wife" had already passed one stint on filibustering terrain and soon would be planning another, contingent on her husband's completing a recruiting mission for Walker in California.[40]

But officers' wives were not the only American women gravitating to Walker's republic. Sarah Pellet, a graduate of Oberlin College and a prominent temperance lecturer in California, visited the country in February 1856, possibly to win new converts to her cause. According to one press report, the "fair" Miss Pellet was received with "extraordinary civility" by Walker's "gallant" troops. That July, the former Jane McManus Storm, now Jane Cazneau, turned up in Granada with her husband William, recently U.S. commissioner in the Dominican Republic, to attend Walker's inauguration as Nicaraguan president. Apparently the woman who coined the term "manifest destiny" and her spouse ventured to Nicaragua for speculative purposes, though they also endorsed Walker's cause as a means of promoting the territorial and commercial expansion of the United States. While there, William invested in mines and signed a contract to send Walker 1,000 male colonists from the United States. After their visit, Jane agitated for recognition of Walker's régime by the United States, and she urged attorney general Jeremiah Black to persuade President Buchanan to intervene militarily against Walker's enemies as a means of guaranteeing the survival of his government.[41]

A registry kept by Walker's agency in New Orleans lists families emigrating to the country, such as that of one Benjamin F. Turner, who left for Nicaragua with his wife and two children, taking along eight trunks, two boxes, and three carpet bags. Along similar lines, a correspondent aboard a steamer bound from San Francisco to San Juan del Sur reported ten emigrants for Nicaragua among the vessel's passengers, "only half of them Walker recruits, the rest migrating on their own hook." The "most interesting" of the latter, he explained, were a Mr. and Mrs. York. They had migrated from Illinois to California with their three sons back in 1846, then tried their hands at mining mercury as well as farming, and now were drawn to Walker's domain by "that peculiar instinct of frontier life—the impulse to 'move on.'" Similarly, a correspondent in Virgin Bay informed his paper that he had just encountered "several ladies" who had traveled to Nicaragua "as settlers or visitors" on the most recent steamer from New York City.[42]

Most such émigrés seem to have been influenced by publicity about Walker's land decrees. Elleanore Callaghan, who along with her sister and brother-in-law and their child had left Council Bluffs, Iowa, for Walker's domain, later recalled that their goal, along with that of the six other families who boarded ship with them in New Orleans, had been to take advantage of the Rivas government's "inducements" to "colonize" the area. Clearly she meant Rivas's land decree of November 1855. But not all incoming families intended to work the land. In 1857, a correspondent for the *New-York Times* recounted the saga of Christopher Lilly, who had circulated among the "fancy" in San Francisco for a while, but run afoul of the Vigilance Committee and fled with his spouse to Granada. There he set up a gambling establishment and cheated many of Walker's officers out of their cash and land warrants, before buying a ship to profiteer in the coastal coffee trade.[43]

Normality was more mirage than reality even in Walker's Nicaragua, however. As Edward Kewen inadvertently revealed at the height of the invaders' success, high mortality rates in the filibuster army belied propaganda that the invaders were luxuriating in a tropical paradise. In August 1856, trying to discredit a newspaper report that only fourteen of Walker's fifty-six "Immortals" were still alive, Kewen proved that the number of survivors was in fact thirty-nine, by listing each surviving filibuster along with his present military rank or other circumstances ("discharged, now in New Orleans"; "discharged, now farming in Nicaragua"), as well as listing each man deceased along with the cause of death ("killed in the second battle at Rivas"). Kewen's attempt to whitewash the filibuster experience actually tarnished it, by exposing how more than 30 percent of the filibusters had died in little more than a year of action.[44]

A daring but by no means brilliant commander, and almost always outnumbered, Walker suffered heavy losses in battle. "We are continually fiting [*sic*] with the natives," one of Walker's men wrote home in one letter, before noting that in the most recent engagement ten members of his company "was killed and nine wounded" and that he was very lucky to "come clear" since there were five enemy soldiers for every two filibusters. In a surprise attack with some 550 men on Costa Rican troops who had just seized Rivas in April 1856, Walker took 58 fatalities in addition to 62 men wounded. In late November and early December 1856, Charles Henningsen's command of 419 filibusters, under siege at Granada, suffered 110 casualties before reinforcements arrived and they escaped the trap. The filibusters' casualty rate of more than 20 percent in such episodes exceeded that of many of the American Civil War's most notoriously bloody battles. Union forces, for instance, took total losses of 10.9 percent in their horrible defeat at Fredericksburg in 1862.[45]

Others in Walker's army died of complications from their wounds after returning to the United States. Marsh Taylor, who returned to Lafayette, Indiana, wracked with malaria and carrying a ball in his body, survived his debilities and lived until 1879. But a surgeon in Key West, Florida, remarked in a letter in June 1856 that one of the two wounded Walker veterans in his hospital had died; and the *New York Tribune* in July 1857 reported that an Ohioan had passed away at Bellevue Hospital from wounds received while in Walker's service.[46] Unfortunately, no figures exist as to exactly how many of Walker's followers came to similar ends.

There were other fatalities unrelated to battle. One filibuster, for instance, died at Granada when he removed his coat and a pistol in one of his pockets discharged accidentally, firing a ball into his head. Kewen's listing of dead Immortals in August 1856 indicates that five of the deceased filibusters had died from causes other than enemy fire: one in a private dispute, one from execution after being convicted by court-martial, and three from natural causes. A harsh disciplinarian, Walker had a number of men executed for desertion and other reasons.[47]

As in the Mexican and Civil wars, moreover, American soldiers suffered more from diseases than they did from battle wounds, with malaria, cholera, and yellow fever taking the greatest toll. Walker's men often contracted fevers soon after arriving in the country. So, for instance, John Marshall informed his father in August 1856, after being in the country only two months, "I like the climate although I have had two attacks of fever since I came down." He never returned to the United States, dying aboard ship on his way back that November having again, as one of Walker's officers put it, "taken sick with the fever peculiar to the climate." A month earlier, Walker consoled the wife of one of his officers about the loss of her husband, who had been "attacked by the fever" just after arriving in the country, and then contracted "an acute inflammation of the stomach and bowels" during his recovery. Tellingly, one filibuster later recalled that his very first sight upon arriving in Nicaragua was that of a Walker recruit with yellow skin in the "last stage of fever."

Cholera raged through Walker's ranks. In July 1856 John Brenizer, now on detached duty as an apothecary in Walker's service, slipped into an otherwise upbeat report home that the filibuster army had "considerable cholera here lately and good many died," and that he was "getting as used to this disease as the common head-ache." During the siege of Granada, Henningsen lost 125 men to the disease, more than his total casualties.[48]

Walker undoubtedly would have reduced his losses had he provided his soldiers with sanitary quarters and decent hospital care. This was generally not the case, though Brigadier General C. C. Hornsby of his army asserted in one public letter that Walker had a "Board of Surgeons" that weeded out unqualified doctors, and another of Walker's officers claimed that Walker visited his hospital daily and that his sick received "the best attention from experienced physicians."[49]

Such claims seem far-fetched, given considerable evidence to the contrary. James Thomas recalled of his visit to Granada that after a while he began to notice that "when a man was taken sick and sent to the hospital you might expect to hear the dead march next." A similarly negative assessment came from one of Walker's disillusioned veterans, who charged in a piece for *Harper's Weekly* in January 1857 that Walker's soldiers were housed in quarters so damp and littered that they were unfit for hogs, and that they were not even provided with blankets. The filibuster's doctors were drunken "quacks," and his hospital's rawhide beds lacked mattresses. No one cleaned the beds, not even for new patients. Elleanore Callaghan later recalled that the filibusters ran so short of medical supplies during the siege of Granada that they were ripping up women's underskirts and making them into bandages.[50]

For all their suffering, moreover, Walker's enlisted men apparently never collected their promised wages. David Deaderick recalled that Walker's practice was "to discharge his solders' wages with scrip of no cash value whatever, or so little that many neglected to draw it when due them." His charge is substantiated by other sources. As one of Walker's embittered veterans put it cynically, the typical recruit discovered, far too late, that his wages amounted to "nothing a month, and six feet of earth."[51]

Sadly, some of Walker's unpaid recruits were not even serving of their own volition. During the latter stages of his tenure in Nicaragua, Walker resorted to impressment in a desperate attempt to maintain his ranks. That is, males who emigrated from the United States to Nicaragua to claim the free land that he was offering were compelled into his army immediately upon their arrival in the country. If they tried to buy a return ticket from the Transit Company, or sought assistance from the U.S. minister, they were informed that Walker required a passport issued by him for anyone leaving the country, and that nothing could be done. Walker even posted sentries at the gangplanks of departing steamers, to cut off the possibility of escape.[52]

Henry Foster, one near-victim, later gave a graphic description of how the system operated:

In Broadway, New York, I saw a flag, and on the flag were the words "Free farms, free emigration, by steam to Nicaragua." I went into the office, and the clerk asked me if I wished to go to Nicaragua? I said yes. On the 24th of January 1857, I went to the office and took my ticket to go in the steamer "Tennessee." I embarked . . . for Nicaragua, and all things went on smoothly until the arrival of that vessel at Greytown, and I was turned over to the steamer Texas on the morning of the 8th of February. The morning of the 9th the uniform of General Walker was served out, which I refused, be-

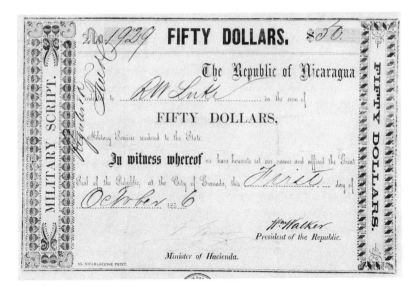

Example of military scrip that William Walker dispensed to his recruits in lieu of wages. (Courtesy Tennessee Historical Society, War Memorial Building, Nashville)

cause nothing had been said in New York about bearing arms. Nothing new was said until . . . morning, when the river steam boat came alongside the "Texas" and took on arms and ammunition. . . . One of Walker's Captains who had charge of the volunteers for him came to me and ordered me into the boat, and I told him I would not go. He then drew a revolver . . . and said if I did not go into the boat, he would shoot me.

At this tense moment, a British naval officer at the scene intervened and rescued Foster from involuntary service. But other deluded emigrants were far less fortunate. When one victim appeared at Walker's headquarters and complained about being deceived by Walker's agency in New Orleans, Walker retorted that the offending agent was not an authorized representative of his government, and that the complainant would have to serve his requisite twelve months.[53]

Desertion to the enemy, in such cases, provided the only hope of escape. But new agonies awaited the hundreds of impressed and disaffected soldiers who safely reached Costa Rican lines. Although Costa Rican officers initially treated deserters well, providing them with rations and spending money, conditions declined once so many deserters turned up in camp that they seemed to present a security threat. At that point Costa Rican officers had them removed from the war zone to Costa Rica, where they were kept briefly at the

Pacific port of Puntarenas on the Gulf of Nicoya, before being taken to San José in the interior, fifty miles away. An American who happened to be traveling through Puntarenas at the same time the deserters were there judged the "Billy busters" as "destitute of all the comforts of life." While at San José, the deserters were quartered in a vermin-infested building that had been a prison. Three of them died at the Costa Rican capital.

In mid-July 1857 Costa Rican authorities finally sent a large party of deserters off on a difficult journey to Greytown, so that they could get ship passage out of Central America. At least two of them, and possibly more, died while traveling. One of the survivors claimed that six stragglers dropped out of his party on the way and "were never heard from again." After languishing for two weeks at Greytown, the deserters, as well as some filibusters who had been taken prisoner of war by Costa Rica, embarked on August 10 for New York City. Other deserters, meanwhile, remained stranded in Costa Rica. A U.S. diplomatic agent encountered a group of them more than a month later and described the unfortunates as "nearly naked," "sore covered," and "without shelter day or night." Under banishment by a Costa Rican decree and unable to get jobs, they lacked the funds to leave, slept in the open, and risked being thrown into prison or put on a chain gang at any moment.[54]

Not only did Walker force innocent emigrants into service, but he also denied discharges to soldiers whose terms of enlistment had expired. Walker's General Order Book indicates that he discharged some men on schedule, and that he also dispensed releases to soldiers who procured certificates of disability from his medical staff. Yet as early as June 1856, one of his recruits informed his family in the United States that he doubted he would get out of the service when his six months' commitment ended, since other men in Walker's ranks who had been soldiering for over a year could not procure their own releases. The next month, another filibuster, insecure for the same reason, asked U.S. Secretary of War Jefferson Davis to intervene with Walker on his behalf and secure his release so that he could return to the United States and care for his elderly father. About a year later, one Henry Bartow turned up at the office of the *New-York Daily Tribune* and explained to its staff how he had enlisted in Walker's army for six months but been refused his discharge at the end of that period. Walker had then promised as a man of honor that he would be released after a year. Yet Bartow had been "peremptorily refused, and ordered back to his company" when the stipulated additional period was over.[55]

In mid-1856, after the U.S. government recognized the filibuster government, Secretary of State William Marcy, under pressure from Senator James

A. Bayard of Delaware, was able to pressure Walker to release three Americans serving against their will. But in February 1857, after the United States broke relations with Walker's régime, Marcy had to reluctantly inform the distressed mother of one of Walker's recruits that he could do nothing to facilitate the return of her son since the United States no longer had a minister in Nicaragua.[56]

A healthy skepticism about glowing reports of life in Nicaragua's filibuster régime would seem to be in order. Major Weir wrote of Nicaragua to the editor of the *San Joaquin Republican* (Stockton, Calif.), "I wish you could come down and see it; if you would . . . I know you would at least encourage emigration . . . if you did not locate yourself." Likewise, another filibuster entreated a San Francisco paper, "The boys are in fine health and spirits, and if any of your readers desire a few months pleasant 'prospecting,' they cannot do better than to pay us a visit." Behind the celebratory language, one senses the hope of seducing unwary American youths into likely self-destruction. Life insurance companies apparently saw through such posturing. According to a New Year's Day report in 1857, not one of them would assume coverage for a "Nicaraguan emigrant."[57]

IN RETROSPECT, it is less remarkable that so many filibusters died than that a large number of them survived. Diplomatic pressure from Washington, as we shall see, helped to procure the release of many filibusters who might well have perished during their internments in foreign prisons. But acts of mercy by U.S. and British naval officers, as well as by British colonial officials, preserved additional filibuster lives. Repeatedly, U.S. naval officers rescued distressed filibusters, which in addition to saving their lives allowed, as one lieutenant objected, the "pirates" to regroup and filibuster again. During William Walker's invasion of Lower California, for example, Commander Thomas Dornin of the USS *Portsmouth* arrived off Walker's encampment at Ensenada, as part of a federal effort to interdict filibuster reinforcements from California. After Walker evacuated Ensenada, Dornin took pity on sick and wounded men whom Walker had left behind without medicine or decent food, and without any guards to protect them from the "tender mercies" (as Dornin put it) of angry nearby rancheros. With the stranded filibusters begging him "to take them off," Dornin ordered them carried aboard a rented commercial vessel attached to his command, from which they were transferred for conveyance to San Francisco by a private steamer.[58]

In 1857, the U.S. naval commander Charles H. Davis and other American

USS *St. Mary's*. (U.S. Naval Historical Center photograph)

officers, with assistance from their British counterparts, extricated hundreds of filibusters from life-threatening situations during the collapse of Walker's Nicaraguan regime. Davis, commanding the sloop-of-war *St. Mary's*, a vessel in Commodore William Mervine's Pacific Squadron, arrived on February 6, 1857, at San Juan del Sur under orders to protect American persons and property from harm by the contending forces in the filibuster war. By the time of Davis's appearance, Walker had already lost control of the San Juan River, as well as river and lake transit steamers, to Costa Rican forces. Cut off from contact with Greytown, Walker could no longer receive reinforcements from U.S. Gulf and Atlantic ports; hundreds of fresh recruits under the command of Colonel Samuel A. Lockridge wound up stranded at Greytown, after attempting unsuccessfully to reach the filibuster army at Rivas. Further, the filibusters had taken high losses in recent forays against allied Central American forces holding the villages of Obraje and San Jorge.[59]

In the weeks after Davis's arrival, Walker's prospects worsened. Bottled up in Rivas, the filibusters ran short of food and were reduced to eating horses and mules. Suffering horribly, a number of Walker's men fled to enemy lines, taking up an offer that President Juan Rafael Mora of Costa Rica had made in December 1856 of free transportation to Greytown and then New York City for deserters. By late March the Costa Rican general (and brother of President Mora) José Joaquín Mora, who had assumed command of allied Central American forces around Rivas, was bombarding the town with intermittent cannon fire.[60]

Certain that Walker's position was hopeless, Davis in late April persuaded General Mora to allow an officer from the *St. Mary's* to evacuate children and women who were trapped in Rivas with Walker's troops. This accomplished, Davis offered his services as a mediator between Walker and Mora, in order to prevent, as he explained to Commodore Mervine, further unnecessary bloodshed.

On April 30, joined by his ship's surgeon and two other men, Davis set out for Mora's camp. After an interview with Mora, Davis exchanged notes with Walker and met on three occasions with his representatives General Henningsen and Colonel John P. Waters, convincing them that it was futile to wait for Lockridge's reinforcements. Davis also put the filibusters on notice that should they try to break through enemy lines and escape aboard their only war vessel, the schooner *Granada*, at San Juan del Sur, he would prevent them from leaving the harbor. Finally Walker caved in, signing an agreement with Davis on May 1: Walker and sixteen members of his staff, keeping their arms and horses, would proceed from Rivas to San Juan del Sur and there board the *St. Mary's* for Panama; the balance of Walker's officers, as well as his noncommissioned officers, governmental employees, privates, and civilian supporters in Rivas would proceed with naval escort to Panama. On May 2 Davis compelled Walker to order Callender Fayssoux, captain of the *Granada*, to surrender the vessel to the U.S. Navy, by having the *St. Mary's* broadside trained on the filibuster ship.[61]

Though Walker and his staff rode on horseback to a hotel in San Juan and subsequently made an expeditious return to the United States,[62] the evacuation of the rest of his force proceeded less smoothly. For one thing, the U.S. naval lieutenant David McCorkle, who received the assignment of getting the filibusters to Panama, had to leave Walker's sick and wounded at Rivas. In addition, Davis stipulated that McCorkle had to use whatever routes and means to get to Panama that General Mora indicated, since Mora had promised to pay the operation's costs. Rather than permit McCorkle's large group of more than 300 men to make the short march to San Juan del Sur for their conveyance to Panama, Mora insisted that they travel all the way to Puntarenas, where they would be provided with ship passage to the Panamanian isthmus. During their subsequent journey, made initially by lake steamer from Virgin Bay to the southern shore of Lake Nicaragua, then on foot and by overcrowded river bungos (flatboats), the filibusters endured lengthy delays, spoiled food and brackish water, harassment by Costa Rican civilians, and other indignities.

By the time a Costa Rican barque turned over the men, many of them suffering from dysentery, ulcers, and other ailments, to Commodore Mervine at the Bay of Panama on June 18, Walker was already back in the United States. Mervine, feeling tremendous sympathy for the filibusters' plight, then made arrangements for sending the filibusters by rail across Panama to Aspinwall on the Caribbean side of the isthmus, pledging without authorization that the U.S. government would repay the railroad. At Aspinwall, the filibusters waited an additional week in the harbor aboard the three-decker U.S. steam frigate *Roanoke* and the war sloop *Cyane*. Although a U.S. naval lieutenant on the *Roanoke* objected to his vessel's being converted into a "ho[s]pital," the commander of the vessel, Captain John Montgomery, treated the filibusters humanely. He saw to it that they each got medical care, two sets of sailors' clothes, shampoos, and, in the case of sick and wounded, hammocks to sleep in. Finally, after the filibusters' health improved somewhat, the naval vessels conveyed the appreciative veterans to New York and Boston.[63]

Meanwhile, the British naval captain John Erskine, commanding the H.M.S. *Orion*, extricated the members of Lockridge's party from their predicament at Greytown, where he found them at the mercy of their Costa Rican enemies and "helpless & starving." According to a deal that Erskine negotiated involving Costa Rican authorities and the Morgan and Garrison transit interests, the British navy transported 375 members of Lockridge's force from Greytown to Aspinwall aboard two war vessels, with the understanding that the transit company would then convey the filibusters to an American port at Costa Rica's expense. Subsequently, when the agent of the United States Mail Steamship Company, whose firm serviced Aspinwall, refused to honor the transit company's draft, a British naval captain at the port carried some 200 of the filibusters on to New Orleans. One of Lockridge's men remarked later that the filibusters' "British cousins" had saved them from the wrath of their enemies and provided them with medical supplies, all the while damning them as pirates![64]

In June, Commodore Hiram Paulding, commanding the navy's Home Squadron off the Caribbean coast of Central America, transported 138 men, women, and children connected with Walker's republic from Aspinwall to New York aboard his flagship, the *Wabash*. Paulding felt compassion for these people, all of them in "extreme destitution," who earlier in the month had been rescued at Greytown and been brought to Aspinwall by the U.S. naval sloop *Cyane*. A midshipman aboard the *Cyane* observed that many of these survivors were "covered" with wounds and "disgusting sores," and "at the point of death." Rather than await authorization from Washington to fund the filibusters' return to the United States, and risk having their condition worsen, Paulding tried to arrange their passage home by private conveyance. When the Mail Steamship Company's agent refused outright to receive sick or wounded passengers aboard company vessels, and demanded what Paulding considered an extortionate price merely to take them to New Orleans ($40 for adults, $20 for children), the commodore decided to convey the filibusters back to the United States himself. He chose New York rather than New Orleans as his destination partly because his surgeon felt that the incapacitated filibusters would do better in a northern climate. Before he left, Paulding instructed Commander Frederick Chatard to sail to Greytown with the war sloop *Saratoga* and there take aboard, clothe, and bring to Aspinwall any more of Walker's followers who happened to turn up.[65]

Despite these large-scale evacuations, U.S. naval officers in Central American waters were hardly finished with Walker's survivors. On August 4, the day the *Roanoke* arrived in New York, yet another U.S. vessel of war, the sloop *Decatur*, arrived from Puntarenas at the city of Panama, carrying twenty-six of the sick and wounded whom Walker had left behind at Rivas after his surrender. In November, Mervine asked his surgeons to determine whether sickly filibusters still on the *Decatur* had the fortitude to survive a voyage around Cape Horn to Norfolk, Virginia, aboard the naval vessel *John Adams*, and whether they posed a health threat to U.S. sailors. As late as May 1858 the commander of the *Decatur*, Henry K. Thatcher, was still providing medical care aboard ship to a filibuster who had surrendered at Rivas but would never regain use of his limbs. As an "act of humanity," John C. Long, the new commander of the Pacific Squadron, decided to send the veteran home aboard a naval store ship.[66]

Because of the U.S. and British navies, Walker and many of his followers remained alive. Only a handful of filibusters perished during the evacuation process. Yet Walker never acknowledged a debt to his rescuers, adamantly insisting that Davis had engaged in a conspiracy with the British navy to get him to surrender unnecessarily and against his will. Embittered by Walker's ingratitude, Davis in turn lambasted Walker as the world's worst pirate since Sir Henry Morgan in the seventeenth century. In March 1858 Davis claimed redemption after some U.S. Army officers called on him in California and rendered their opinion that he had rescued Walker and his cohorts from Henry Crabb's fate, and after a couple of Walker's subordinate officers contacted him and thanked him for his efforts.[67]

Not long after Davis's vindication, the U.S. naval commander Charles H. Kennedy may have saved Henry L. Kinney from a mob while commanding the warship *Jamestown* in Greytown harbor during one of filibustering's strangest incidents.. In April 1858 Kinney, who had given up on his Mosquito colony about a year earlier, suddenly reappeared at Greytown with a handful of associates. He not only reoccupied his former residence but took an ex-mayor captive and claimed governing authority in the town, supposedly in the name of Nicaragua's post-Walker regime. Just as a mob was about to enforce an order from the current mayor for Kinney's arrest, Kennedy, who had learned about the situation from the British consul, landed armed marines and informed the mayor that although he would allow Kinney's apprehension, he would forbid any bloodshed. The following day, when a mob forced Kinney to surrender, Kennedy again landed and this time persuaded Kinney to sign a pledge to board the *Jamestown* and give up his impractical scheme.[68]

Later that year, Superintendent Frederick Seymour of the British colony of Belize came to the assistance of filibusters participating in Walker's *Susan* expedition, which on December 16, 1858, grounded at Glover's reef in the Bay of Honduras, near the lighthouse that lit the channel to the town of Belize, the capital of the colony. The filibusters had hoped to reach Omoa on the Honduran coast, and then, after Walker arrived with reinforcements, make their way back to Nicaragua.

Seymour not only welcomed the captain of the *Susan*, Harry Maury, and the leader of the expedition, Colonel Frank Anderson, to his official residence when they turned up in town; he also immediately dispatched the war steamer *Basilisk* to pick up the rest of the stranded adventurers at Glover's reef and take the entire filibuster party immediately back to its starting point, Mobile, Alabama. Seymour supervised the evacuation himself, going to the cay where the filibusters were stranded, telling them that every English officer felt "friendly feelings" for Americans, and personally offering them passage home. As the *Basilisk* got under way on the morning of December 26, the appreciative filibusters, according to a correspondent for the *New York Herald*, gave "nine cheers and a 'tiger' for his Excellency Governor Seymour," blissfully unaware that the primary reason for Seymour's generosity was his apprehension that the filibusters might capture an ammunition shipment passing through the area and then resume their campaign against Omoa and hurt the trading interests of merchants in Belize.[69]

Finally, we should recall that even Norvell Salmon, the British naval commander who in 1860 accepted Walker's surrender and then turned him over to the Hondurans who later executed him, had no desire to see filibusters slaughtered and helped to preserve their lives. In the agreement of September 5 by which he transferred Walker and his men to Honduran custody at Tru-jillo, Salmon stipulated that the Honduran commanding general could do what he wanted with Walker and his second-in-command, A. F. Rudler, but that he would have to allow the other prisoners to return to the United States (provided that they swore never to filibuster again). Salmon also provided the captured men with extra rations, in case the Hondurans did not feed them ad-equately. Nine days later, upon hearing that the Hondurans had not fulfilled the agreement, Salmon rushed back to Trujillo. Discovering that the Hon-durans indeed had done nothing to send the filibusters home, Salmon took the responsibility upon himself and arranged for the British warship *Gladi-ator* to deliver the men to New Orleans.[70]

Profilibustering Americans were too Anglophobic to credit Salmon with preserving the lives of some seventy Americans. In Cairo, Illinois, the Sons of Malta resolved that Salmon's "outrage" violated the Monroe Doctrine. They would wear badges of mourning for five days in remembrance of the "igno-miniously slaughtered" General Walker. In Fayetteville, Arkansas, a newspa-per editor pronounced Salmon's "perfidious" decision as a "stain upon En-gland's navy." And in New Orleans, a gang of toughs got some misguided revenge by roughing up the very British naval officer who had brought Walker's lucky survivors home.[71]

THE FINAL degradation occurred when America's surviving filibusters ar-rived on American soil and found themselves charity cases. Sadly, there was nothing unique about the encounter of New York City's authorities and resi-dents in 1857 with pathetic filibustering returnees. For example, a number of "miserable-looking," "forlorn" "creatures" congregated in Mobile, Alabama, in the fall of 1849 after the collapse of Narciso López's first plot against Cuba. The next May, hundreds of "destitute" survivors of López's *Creole* expedi-tion lingered at Key West, Florida, after their vessel docked there. Just months later, forty-two men who had dropped out of the same expedition but been incarcerated as filibusters by the Spanish anyway turned up at Mobile after their release, broke and almost naked aboard a U.S. war sloop . In the spring of 1851, Jacksonville, Florida, hosted stranded members of the expedition that López had just aborted.[72]

Residents in Washington and New York City in 1852 encountered wretched filibusters after Spain's government released captives from López's last expe-dition. That March, the filibuster colonel William Scott Haynes, in a letter to the *Washington Daily Union*, summoned the public to render financial assistance to two "honest, good citizens" who had served in his regiment during the Cuba campaign but were now "needy." He also begged President Millard Fillmore and Secretary of State Daniel Webster to provide federal funds to assist his former comrades, noting that the bulk of the prisoners would soon land in New York, wearing their prison uniforms and covered in vermin and filth. When the administration refused to help out, Cuban refugees in New York came up with $500, which they put in the trust of the alderman William Marcy Tweed (later the "Boss" of Tammany Hall). Tweed promised that the funds would be applied to relieving the "necessities" of the "persecuted" filibusters.[73]

In later years, similar stories unfolded elsewhere. The U.S. sloop-of-war *Cyane* dumped fifty-three of Walker's filibusters, including four deserters, at Boston on July 31, 1857, many of them suffering from wounds, grotesque sores, and severed limbs. The next December, Commodore Hiram Paulding, after breaking up Walker's second expedition to Nicaragua, detached Commander Frederick Chatard to carry the filibuster's army to Norfolk, Virginia, aboard Chatard's warship, the *Saratoga*. Although the filibuster officer C. C. Hornsby subsequently accused Chatard of stowing him and his comrades in the ship's hold "like Coolies" and called for a congressional investigation into the Navy's treatment of captured filibusters, Chatard informed the secretary of the navy that he had found it "painful" to witness people so "very destitute of means and clothing." Much of what the filibusters were wearing on their arrival at Norfolk, he noted, had been given them by the ship's officers and crew.[74]

Municipal officials and residents in these ports, much like New Yorkers, found it difficult to ignore these human eyesores. Authorities in Mobile, for example, arrested stranded filibusters who had been sleeping in the building that housed the city market, though the mayor released them after they told him that they had come to the city looking for railroad work. In New Orleans, "vigilant" city officials beefed up the police force, closed barrooms where the filibusters gathered, and took other steps to mollify citizens who were uneasy about the potential for violence that the filibusters represented. A newspaper correspondent in Key West reported that the filibusters there had become "a heavy tax upon the citizens" but that the community had raised enough money to send off hundreds of the adventurers. In Norfolk, where Walker's men were reported to be "wandering about the city in a destitute condition, without money and poorly clad," a local newspaper announced that the authorities were considering arresting Chatard for foisting the filibusters on the community and fining him $20 for each one that was a pauper, unless he would remove them beyond the city's jurisdiction. Although many residents in these cities sympathized with the filibustering cause and felt compassion for the suffering adventurers, it does not seem that anyone wanted to keep filibusters around for very long.[75]

Nor were ports of arrival the only American communities to confront the welfare of filibustering, since charitable contributions in these communities often did little more than get the filibusters on their way. A Walker participant from Illinois who found his way to the nation's capital after leaving Norfolk begged his U.S. senator, Stephen A. Douglas, for assistance so that he could make it all the way home:

> Mr. Douglass I wish to explain my case to you and wish a favour of you. I went with Genl Walker last fall to Nicaragua and was landed in Norfolk off the Saratoga last month entirely out of money and amongst strangers along ways from my home. I have made out to get this far . . . and I now ask . . . you to loan me Ten dollars so as to enable me to get to the Ohio river if I get that far I can make out to get to Alton as my father lives near that place. I assure you sir I will send it back to you the minute I get home. I would call on you personally only my situation is such that I feel a delicacy in doing so, as I lost nearly all my clothes the day Genl Walker surrendered to Com Paulding.

Many other filibusters found themselves in similar embarrassments. Seventeen of the filibusters stranded at Key West in 1850 left in a fishing smack for Tampa Bay, from which they made a six-day foot journey to Pilatka, arriving, as a newspaper correspondent explained, with no money or clothing. Fortunately General David E. Twiggs, in command of Fort Brooke at Tampa Bay, dipped into army supplies, providing them with two days' worth of rations so that they could proceed on their way. In addition, the citizenry of Pilatka raised relief funds to send the men on by steamer to Savannah. One of a different party of *Creole* survivors later remembered having nothing to eat but raw pork and hard crackers for days after leaving Key West. Luckily many Floridians, including a grandson of Davy Crockett and a hotel proprietor in Tallahassee, gave him assistance during his homeward odyssey.[76]

APTLY RECYCLING a phrase that had been widely used to describe the agonies of military campaigning during the Mexican War, the reviewer of one of the many filibuster reminiscences that were published in the 1850s observed that

William Walker's "boys" had "certainly seen the Elephant." The surprising thing, given the horrors of most of these expeditions, is that so many of the adventurers filibustered more than once. One would think that all of filibustering's veterans would have reacted like the officer who told people on his return from López's last invasion of Cuba that he had already experienced "quite enough of expeditions to last him for the balance of his days."[77]

CHAPTER EIGHT

The State Department's Albatross

What! shall a blunder or two and a bluster
  Got up by governments for their own ends,
Or the fierce pranks of some shrewd
  fillibuster,
Turn into enemies kinsmen and friends?
—*The Liberator*, September 5, 1856

IT WAS A close call. When traveling to Mexico on assignment for the U.S. government around the time of the 1851 Carbajal expedition, Abner Doubleday, an army lieutenant and the reputed founder of baseball, learned the perils of being mistaken for a filibuster. After arriving at San Luis Potosí, Doubleday later recalled, one of the members of his party had too much to drink and "began boasting in a garrulus [*sic*] manner that he had been a filibuster in some expedition into Mexico." Taking these pronouncements seriously, local authorities assumed that Doubleday and his companions must be spying for "another invasion" and threatened them with imprisonment. Doubleday talked his way out of the tight situation by claiming that his foolish comrade had "already gained the reputation of manufacturing stories," and that the filibustering admission was "another of his Arabian Nights lucubrations." Luckily, the Mexicans were convinced, allowing the Americans to escape punishment.[1]

Had Doubleday been less persuasive and wound up in a Mexican jail, his companion's indiscreet remark might well have triggered a major diplomatic incident with Mexico. Arguably no other matter caused the State Department more grief than filibustering expeditions did. On one occasion, when Secretary of State Daniel Webster was dealing with expeditions to Cuba and Mexico as well as rumored attacks on Hawaii at the same time, he lamented to America's minister in Madrid that filibustering had been absorbing Washington's attention "week to week" and "day to day" for "many months." Since filibustering sometimes drew the government to the brink of war, the State Department dared not take it lightly.[2]

How could these ventures, we might wonder, cause so much diplomatic trouble, given that almost every one of them was an abysmal failure? What, moreover, were their long-range implications for U.S. relations with other countries and for America's territorial expansion? The filibusters generally attacked or threatened locales that U.S. policy makers hoped to add to the national domain: President Pierce tried to annex Hawaii, and both Pierce and President Buchanan attempted to buy Cuba from Spain as well as persuade Mexico to cede land to the United States. Yet the United States failed to acquire significant territory during this period, except for the relatively limited Gadsden Purchase from Mexico (negotiated in 1853 and ratified in 1854), which added approximately 45,000 square miles in the Southwest.[3] Perhaps filibustering explains the slowing of America's territorial growth.

It may also be asked whether the expeditions affected the course of American commercial expansionism. American entrepreneurs were deeply invested in many of the areas that the filibusters chose to invade. Did the expeditions retard or assist these investments and the progress of what some historians have dubbed America's "informal empire"—its commercial hegemony over foreign countries?

A MESSAGE THAT Peru's minister to the United States sent to the State Department in March 1858 is instructive. The message warned that citizens of the United States "well known for their filibustering propensities" had reached an understanding with exiles from his own country, and that the combined forces were planning an expedition against Peruvian territory. According to "knowledge" that had come his way, the adventurers were already collecting arms in New York and New Orleans for the enterprise. The minister suggested that Washington instruct its officials in the two cities to stop the scheme, lest the United States put at risk its "relations of amity" with Peru.[4]

The Peruvian minister may or may not have been on to something. Given his failure to identify the sources for his "knowledge," it is uncertain whether an invasion of his country was at hand. But his demands invite consideration not only because they highlight filibustering's potential for damaging U.S. relations with another state, but also because they were commonplace. During an age when American filibusters were attacking countries all over the hemisphere, foreign diplomats understandably became alarmed by the frequent rumors in American newspapers that new expeditions were in the making. Throughout the pre–Civil War years, therefore, secretaries of state had to devote an inordinate amount of time to parrying warnings from foreign governments that fresh expeditions were about to occur.

No one proved more adept at keeping the heat on Washington than Spain's veteran minister Angel Calderón de la Barca. Drawing his information from the American press as well as from a network of Spanish consuls and spies in port cities of the United States, Calderón kept State Department officials busy reacting to his laboriously detailed requests for intervention against real and phantom expeditions.

During Narciso López's last attack on Cuba, for instance, Calderón forwarded information from Spain's consul in New York City incriminating the author Ned Buntline. This charge, whether accurate or not, was by no means farfetched. Buntline not only had experience as a naval midshipman but had displayed a violent side as a leading agitator in the Astor Place Riots of 1849. Calderón was certain that Buntline had taken charge of the steamer *Monmouth* in Baltimore. Soon he would load arms that had been purchased in Philadelphia, and invade Cuba. In March 1852 Calderón insisted that three Cuban exiles, one of them nicknamed the Solitaire, were making their way to Savannah, where the filibuster recruiter José Delgado—who had stolen $20,000 from the Royal Treasury in Havana—was supposedly already operating.[5]

Occasionally, the State Department scoffed at this diplomatic rumor mill. Webster's predecessor as secretary of state, John M. Clayton, reassured Britain's minister that his "countrymen" would not attack British possessions in Central America, since they already had "elbow-room enough" (though he added the ominous phrase "for the present"). Franklin Pierce's secretary of state, William L. Marcy, declared that British reports of a filibuster to Ireland were patently absurd. But no secretary of state dared defend filibustering, which, as foreign governments repeatedly emphasized, violated U.S. and international law, as well as specific treaties. Rather, the State Department repeatedly maintained that American presidents sincerely wanted the invasions stopped, and they often pointed to preventive measures being taken by federal port and military authorities.[6]

Foreign leaders occasionally conceded Washington's good intentions. Pope Pius IX, upon greeting America's new minister to the Papal States in November 1858, praised President James Buchanan's proclamation against "filibusteri," which had appeared just that morning in a Roman newspaper. Nicaragua's government felt so relieved by the Navy's interception of Walker's second invasion of Central America that it offered Commodore Paulding a sword and a tract of land as a reward. But trust in Washington only went so far. Mexico's minister to the United States, Juan N. Almonte, approved Franklin Pierce's antifilibustering proclamation of January 1854 but attacked the "scandalous" federal officials who recently had failed to prevent filibusters from sailing out of San Francisco.[7]

Some foreign diplomats simply assumed that Washington secretly supported the filibusters, given the adventurers' success at evading U.S. law en-

John M. Clayton. (Courtesy
of the Historical Society of
Delaware, Wilmington)

forcement officers time after time. Surely America's chief executives, or perhaps disloyal cabinet officers, were sending instructions or hints that port and
border authorities should abdicate their responsibilities. Paraguay's secretary
of foreign relations confessed relief after an agent of the U.S. State Depart-
ment told him that filibusters were not running the American government.
Britain's minister to the United States, Lord Napier, confided to the Earl of
Clarendon, the British foreign secretary, that President James Buchanan and
Secretary of State Lewis Cass appeared to "sincerely deprecate" William
Walker's second foray against Nicaragua, but that he had less confidence in
Cass's colleagues in the cabinet.[8]

Foreign diplomats especially distrusted Washington's intentions during
Pierce's presidency. As early as November 1853, America's minister at Mexico City announced a prevailing "suspicion" in the capital that the administration "secretly favored these movements." In September of the next year, in
response to reports that the Pierce administration might try to buy a naval station from Monaco, Lord Clarendon predicted dramatically that soon "filibustering steamers" would be fitting out in the Mediterranean Sea.[9]

Nicaragua's minister to the United States, José de Marcoleta, became so
distraught before Henry L. Kinney's venture to the Mosquito Coast that he

attempted to stop the expedition by bypassing the president entirely and getting help from a former American secretary of state, John M. Clayton, now a
U.S. senator. Marcoleta implored pitifully, "I beg you, Sir, to do whatever you
may deem proper. . . . For God's sake, come to our help and believe that
Nicaragua will bless and revere your name and your fame." Even after federal
intervention delayed the expedition, and then caused Kinney to depart with a
seriously weakened force, foreign suspicions of Pierce persisted. Kinney,
Lord Clarendon authoritatively announced to Prime Minister Lord Palmerston, had been "of course acting under secret instruction" from Washington.[10]

Pierce's official recognition of William Walker's régime the following May
only served to confirm foreign suspicions of a holy alliance between the president and the filibusters. Even before the administration acted, Sardinia's
chargé d'affaires in Washington and Britain's minister consulted as to whether
it would do them any good to protest Pierce's failure to prevent reinforcements from reaching Walker, and concluded that such a remonstrance would
be a waste of their time. After the administration actually received Walker's
minister to the United States, Marcoleta unloaded his "bitter" resentment on
Clayton, as he damned the president's "rascallity."[11]

FROM THE standpoint of foreign governments, little distinguished America's
adventurers from the most audacious criminals in human history. If filibusters
had their way, Calderón explained, they would sack and burn cities, kill people, and commit every other crime that would "put them in the rank of buc-
caneers and pirates." Foreign diplomats summoned many epithets for filibusters. But their favorite was pirate.[12]

Given this assumption, foreign diplomats found it astonishing that American leaders did so little to prevent invasions from occurring, and that they so
rarely meted out punishment for them. Showing little patience with the American legal umbrella—including rules of evidence and the right to a jury trial
—that allowed notorious expeditionists to remain at large, foreign representatives implored American authorities to make the invaders accountable. In
July 1850, two months after filibusters landed at Cárdenas, Calderón complained to the State Department about the effrontery of Narciso López and
his associate Ambrosio Gonzales, who lodged at one of Washington's "principal hotels" and boasted "with impunity of their crime," when they should be
receiving "exemplary and severe punishment." American leaders, in response,
schooled foreign diplomats in American law and explained the difficulties of
enforcing the Neutrality Act.[13]

Paradoxically, filibustering also generated American grievances against foreign states, especially concerning the fate of adventurers taken prisoner abroad. Foreign authorities claimed the right to take whatever punitive steps against captured filibusters they deemed necessary to discourage future expeditions. International law recognized self-preservation as a fundamental right of all nations, and nothing more blatantly threatened the survival of nations than foreign invasions did. Being "pirates without country," filibusters, according to injured governments, forfeited the protection of their own country's flag. After being taken prisoner, they became liable for whatever penalty the invaded countries wished to mete out, including summary execution. As a Mexican officer rather graphically boasted in 1857 after the execution of Henry Crabb and his party, "I had the opportunity to cut Crabb's head off and I have got it in a preserve to remember the piraticle action of Crabbism."[14]

Theoretically, the U.S. government conceded that foreign states had the right to try and punish captured filibusters at will. As Secretary of State Lewis Cass explained to the Honduran and Costa Rican minister Luis Molina in 1860, the United States had "no concern" with the policy that Honduras adopted "towards such adventurers" after their capture. Presidential antifilibustering proclamations cautioned prospective expeditionists that they would automatically forfeit their government's protection. In Zachary Taylor's stern language, filibusters should not anticipate federal intervention "in any form on their behalf, no matter to what extremities they may be reduced in consequence of their conduct."[15]

Yet American leaders and diplomatic agents recoiled when foreign states treated filibusters as pirates, and they contested the characterization. Spain should beware, Secretary of State Clayton lectured Calderón on one occasion, of applying such a "confusion of ideas" in its "diplomatic intercourse" about filibustering. Even filibusters who committed murder and robbery did not do so on the high seas, and therefore did not technically commit piracy.[16] Besides, the American argument went, the typical filibustering recruit had more benign intentions than the high seas buccaneer. Very likely he had been "seduced" into enlisting under false pretenses. If so, he merited pity, if not clemency; having suffered terribly during his expedition, it was unlikely that he would filibuster again. The U.S. minister to France, William C. Rives, reacted to Spain's execution of William Crittenden's party in 1851 by arguing that Americans "who may have honestly believed" that they were aiding "an oppressed people" deserved better than being "considered pirates and robbers, and shot down in cold blood." Similarly, America's consul at Matamoros complained the next year that Mexican authorities should not have forced four members of one of the Carbajal expeditions to face a firing squad. Although "principles of violated law" justified the executions, "humanity" and the "utter inutility of the sacrifice" suggested that leniency would have been more appropriate.[17]

American diplomats found it particularly appalling that foreign states sometimes executed or incarcerated filibusters without providing them procedural safeguards that Americans took for granted, particularly the Sixth Amendment guarantee of trial by jury. In the wake of López's first invasion of Cuba, Secretary Clayton informed the American consul in Havana that President Taylor "demands that those who may be charged with guilt, shall have a fair trial." After hearing about Henry Crabb's fate, the U.S. Minister to Mexico, John Forsyth, complained that even humanity's "worst class of Criminals" deserved the same procedural guarantee.[18]

Further, American officials objected to precautions that foreign states took to discourage filibustering invasions. From the perspective of U.S. policy makers, foreign governments, in their anxiety to ward off attack, violated the safety, liberties, and legitimate business interests of innocent Americans abroad. Worse, some of these preventive measures put the national security of the United States at risk by contravening the Monroe Doctrine's injunction against further European colonization of the Americas.

TO GRASP filibustering's explosiveness in diplomacy, one need only examine the relations of the United States with Spain, Britain, and France over Cuba. Six consecutive years of Cuba expeditions and plots produced continual friction with Spain, and war crises with all three European powers. As early as the summer of 1849, at the time of Narciso López's Round Island plot, relations with Spain began deteriorating over filibustering. That August, President Taylor instructed the State Department to take "decided measures" to uphold American "honor" in response to reports that Spain's consul in New Orleans, Don Carlos España, had abducted Juan Garcia Rey—a Cuban exile with ties to the filibusters—and compelled his return to and imprisonment in Cuba. Spanish authorities, though claiming that Rey had left American territory under his own volition, relented to pressure from Washington and later in the month returned him to New Orleans. However, the affair occasioned angry anti-Spanish rhetoric in America's expansionist press and remained an irritant in relations between the countries until December, when a federal grand jury declined to indict the consul.[19]

By then, the filibusters were only months away from landing in Cuba. Suspecting "the connivance of all Americans in the expedition," as America's consul in Havana Robert Campbell put it, Spanish authorities unleashed a witch hunt against Americans residing in or visiting the island, further straining relations.[20] At the time of López's landing at Cárdenas in May 1850, Spanish authorities harassed and held in temporary custody American passengers on commercial vessels visiting Havana. Throughout western Cuba, authorities rounded up Americans whom they deemed suspicious, sometimes on circumstantial evidence. Spanish officials arrested Edward K. Lambdin, an American working as a cooper at an estate at Sagua la Grande, as well as his employer James H. West, an American from Bristol, Rhode Island, after discovering gunpowder at a building in the vicinity, and charged West with smuggling the gunpowder into Cuba. On the night of June 12, three officials burst into the hotel room at Cienfuegos of Pierre Antoine Giraud, a naturalized U.S. citizen from New Orleans on a business trip to purchase sugar, and threw him in prison because he reportedly had told a French resident of Cienfuegos that he favored the invasion.[21]

Giraud's case highlights the gap between Anglo-American and Spanish systems of jurisprudence that lay behind much of the diplomatic friction. When the U.S. consul at Trinidad, Samuel McLean, traveled to Cienfuegos to investigate Giraud's incarceration, he was informed by the local governor that Giraud was being held even though the charges against him had never been proved. A revealing exchange ensued: McLean complained about the "injustice of imprisoning a man against whom no proof of guilt was produced," evoking the governor's retort that "'Mr. Giraud had not proved his innocence.'" Spanish law, McLean discovered, rejected the American presumption that accused persons were innocent until proven guilty.[22]

Calderón justified Spain's conduct to the State Department, explaining that the captain general in Cuba had learned from informants that "a large number" of the American ship passengers at Havana were connected with the expedition. Some of them, the minister claimed, had even donned the same red shirts and oilskin caps that López's army adopted as its uniform. But Secretary of State Clayton instructed Campbell to investigate the persecution of innocent Americans in Cuba and do what he could to guarantee that they received a fair trial. That July, Clayton asked America's consul in Matanzas to check out reports that two Americans had been taken into custody in the middle of the night by Spanish authorities because one of them had accidentally caused a percussion cap to explode while he was preparing his gun for a hunting excursion.[23]

Once it became clear that López's expedition had been thoroughly repulsed, Spanish officials did release Lambdin, West, and Giraud. However, Spanish officials kept West's property sequestrated and compelled West and Lambdin to post bail to ensure that they would not leave the island. Further, Spanish authorities continued harassing Americans residing in and visiting their colony, for fear that they might assist López if he invaded it a second time. In January 1851 President Millard Fillmore's Secretary of State, Daniel Webster, complained to Calderón that Americans in Cuba were "constantly" being penalized because of groundless suspicions.[24]

Meanwhile, López's first expedition had produced the imbroglio of the Contoy prisoners. Just before leaving Contoy Island, off Yucatán's coast, in the final stage of his invasion of Cuba, López had allowed thirty-nine men to quit his army. A diplomatic crisis occurred when Spanish warships captured the group before it could get away from the island, along with López's vessels *Susan Loud* and *Georgiana* and crew members from both ships.

Even before the State Department intervened, a U.S. naval officer, assuming that Spain lacked authority under international law to seize American vessels and citizens beyond Cuba's territorial waters, came close to committing an act of war by trying to rescue them from Spanish custody. The secretary of the navy, William Ballard Preston, had dispatched several vessels to Cuba, instructing their officers that President Taylor wished them to protect peaceful Americans in Cuba as well as prevent any filibuster landings. On the morning of May 24, Commander Victor M. Randolph of the sloop-of-war *Albany*, accompanied by Consul Campbell, called on Spain's captain general at Havana and argued that Spain should turn over the captured vessels and men to the United States. After this request was refused, Randolph put to sea with two vessels, hoping to intercept the *Georgiana* and the *Susan Loud* (which Spanish authorities had to transfer from their points of capture to Cuban territory), even though he was aware that the vessels and prisoners might well be convoyed by Spanish warships.

Perhaps fortunately, a second U.S. naval officer proved to be more levelheaded. Captain Josiah Tatnall, commanding the steam warship *Saranac* and under orders to cooperate with Spanish authorities against filibusters, arrived on the scene and compelled Randolph to desist, allowing the captured vessels and prisoners to be brought into Havana harbor. Spanish authorities confined the Contoy prisoners on a seventy-four-gun warship in the harbor, where they were put in leg shackles, held incommunicado, and committed to secret trial before a marine court.[25]

Although the Taylor administration conceded Spain's right to punish filibusters captured in the act of invading Cuba,[26] it eventually did contest Spain's taking of the *Georgiana*, the *Susan Loud*, and the men at Contoy. Not only had neither the ships nor men been seized within Spain's jurisdiction, but the administration had cause to believe that the Contoy prisoners lacked criminal intent.

The administration reached its conclusion about the prisoners' innocence because of revelations by some of the filibusters who had returned to the United States after their failed attack on Cárdenas. After being repulsed, López and most of his surviving invaders, joined by seven slave stowaways, had reboarded the *Creole* and fled to Key West. Although federal officials allowed most of the expeditionists to disperse to other parts, they did initiate criminal actions against several officers in the court of William H. Marvin, federal judge for the Southern District of Florida. During these proceedings, the filibusters testified that their former associates remaining at Contoy had refused to invade Cuba. Judge Marvin alerted Robert Campbell in Havana to the testimony, and Campbell then tipped off Secretary of State Clayton, who in turn requested Marvin to supply him with copies of affidavits that he wrongly assumed Marvin had taken during the court proceedings. Marvin, who only had rough memoranda of the testimony, was unable to comply, but he did subsequently take and forward to Washington depositions maintaining the innocent intent of the Contoy prisoners, including one from the chief engineer of the *Creole*.[27]

Clayton then sent Commodore Charles Morris of the Navy to Cuba to demand that the captain general release the captives, and alerted Calderón on June 3 about allegations that the prisoners had never intended to invade Cuba. Clayton implored Spain's minister to intervene on the prisoners' behalf, lest innocent lives be jeopardized. Even if the prisoners originally expected to filibuster when they left American soil, Spain would err, under international law, if it punished them capitally for mere intent to commit wrongdoing. Furthermore, the United States did not concede Spain's right to capture American citizens on Mexican soil. Spain would be wise to put the captives under U.S. custody for possible prosecution under the Neutrality Act of 1818, rather than risk "difficulties."[28]

Was Clayton implying war? Two days earlier, the secretary had alerted Campbell of the president's resolve "that the Eagle must and shall protect" the Contoy captives, and told Campbell to inform Spain's captain general in Cuba that if he "unjustly sheds one drop of American blood . . . it may cost the two countries a sanguinary war." If we can trust Clayton's recollections (and there is no reason why we should not, since they were written after only six months had passed), these bellicose instructions were the product of

heated debate during a meeting of Taylor's cabinet, at which Clayton requested permission to make a peremptory demand for the prisoners' liberation. Although several cabinet members voiced reservations, the president
weighed in on the secretary's side, declaring "that if one of the prisoners
taken in the neutral Territory, or out of the Spanish jurisdiction was executed," the president would send a war message to Congress.[29]

Since Taylor died on July 9 and Spanish officials began making concessions
around the same time, we will never know whether the president would have
carried out his threat. As the president lay on his deathbed on the 8th, the
Count of Alcoy, captain general in Cuba, informed Calderón that investiga-
tions had indeed confirmed the refusal of the Contoy prisoners to filibuster,
and intimated that the case against them would be dismissed. The next day,
Spain's military judge at Havana announced the acquittal of forty-one of the
captives and the pardon of an additional prisoner who had confessed and
turned informant. As it was, however, news of the concessions did not travel
quickly enough to ward off a posthumous threat of war by Taylor's administration. On August 27 America's minister in Madrid, Daniel M. Barringer,
implemented State Department instructions dated July 1 and warned Spain's
foreign minister that Spain might commit a "fatal" mistake and jeopardize its
peace with the United States were it to continue holding the Contoy prisoners.

Although Spain's lenity dispelled the immediate prospect of what might
well have been America's first war against Spain, it did not entirely erase the
possibility of hostilities. For one thing, the authorities at Havana confiscated
the *Georgiana* and *Susan Loud* as prizes, despite claims by their American
owners that the vessels should be returned because they were the innocent
victims of a filibuster scam: the filibusters had chartered the ships for the ostensibly legitimate purpose of taking passengers for California from New Orleans to Chagres on the coast of Panama, and had commandeered the ships
after leaving port for their military scheme. Moreover, Spain's officials also
proceeded with trials of Captain Rufus Benson of the *Georgiana* and the
mates of both vessels, and held seven crew members in custody to compel
their testimony in court.[30]

Issues remained outstanding, therefore, when Commodore Morris arrived
at Havana on July 10 to carry out the State Department's prior orders relating
to its demand for the release of prisoners. During an interview with the captain general on the 15th, Morris demanded that the remaining captives be liberated. The captain general was unresponsive, however, and making matters
worse, Benson appeared to be suffering from acute mental distress because of
his confinement. During a visit to a mental hospital where the captain had

been transferred, Morris observed Benson hallucinating that López was present in his room. Subsequently, Spanish authorities sentenced Benson to ten years at hard labor, the mates of the *Georgiana* to eight years, and the mates of the *Susan Loud* to four years, and in September sent them to prison overseas.[31]

Finally, in October, the Queen of Spain pardoned the captain and mates, and for a brief time, relations with the United States seemed on the mend. Threats of war from Washington subsided, and Spain's foreign minister praised the subdued tone of communications from Millard Fillmore's secretary of state, Daniel Webster.[32] Then, in August 1851, López perished in his second attack on Cuba. Washington Irving, a onetime U.S. minister to Spain, reasonably assumed that the finality of Spain's victory over the invaders would spare the United States from further "trouble and perplexity" with foreign nations over filibustering. But instead López's last expedition again brought the United States and Spain to the brink of war. This time, moreover, the filibusters pulled Britain and France into the vortex.[33]

From Spain's perspective, U.S. authorities bore responsibility for these latest transgressions. Calderón submitted a manuscript to Orestes Brownson, a Catholic and editor of *Brownson's Quarterly Review*, charging that federal officials abetted the invaders by failing to punish participants in earlier plots. Calderón intended his manuscript to form the nucleus of an article by Brownson, which, as Calderón's wife indicated, might so expose the base motives of filibuster leaders as to dissuade additional "young Americans" from being misled again into the "path of perdition."[34]

Calderón also complained to the State Department that federal officials had made insufficient use of the information that he and Spain's consuls had provided them about López's plans, including the identity of the vessel that transported his invading force (the *Pampero*) and the filibusters' port of initial embarkation (New Orleans). In fact, Calderón all but accused the U.S. collector in New Orleans, William Freret, of purposely allowing the *Pampero* to escape: the vessel's purposes should have been obvious since it had never been cleared.[35] Spain, moreover, had additional grievances. Mobs had assaulted Spaniards residing on America's Gulf coast after news broke that the authorities in Havana on August 16 had executed captured filibusters. The most disturbing outbreaks occurred in New Orleans on August 21. After Roberdeau Wheat and other filibustering cronies stirred up a meeting at Lafayette Square, the crowd demolished the presses of the antifilibustering Spanish-language newspaper *La Union*, attacked the fruit stands, cigar stores, and coffee establishments of Spanish proprietors, and even violated the Spanish consulate—defacing a painting of the Spanish queen, shredding the Spanish flag, and causing Consul Juan Y. Laborde to flee. In Mobile, mobs threatened shipwrecked Spanish sailors, forcing Spain's vice consul to charter a schooner to extricate them quickly to Cuba. At Key West, ruffians destroyed several Spanish properties.[36]

News of these outrages caused a furor in Spain. Several Spanish newspapers, U.S. minister Barringer reported, wanted their government to declare war. In October Calderón officially protested the riots to the State Department and demanded an indemnity. Ominously, Calderón warned that Spain "could do no less, than to sustain, at all hazards, the honor of the Castilian flag." The next month, Calderón threatened that Spain would break relations unless America's government rendered a public salute to the Spanish flag.[37]

Spain had leverage that it could apply to its demands. Although the authorities in Havana executed some of the filibusters who fell into their hands that August, they also took 173 men prisoner, eventually shipping most of them to quarantine at Vigo on Spain's Atlantic coast, before their planned distribution as convict laborers to Ceuta in Spanish Morocco and other penal colonies. Given the position of the United States that foreign countries could punish filibusters captured within their own jurisdiction, the State Department and Barringer could only ask but not demand mercy for these unfortunates: on October 29, Webster instructed Barringer to present to Spain's queen a petition from citizens of Alabama asking pardons for all the American captives. Spanish leaders, for their part, linked clemency to American restitution for the Gulf coast riots.[38]

Yet even as López's second invasion of Cuba led Spain to make diplomatic demands on the United States, it also caused American leaders to consider going to war with Spain. For López's assault rekindled one of the issues that had sparked U.S. hostilities in 1812—the right of foreign ships to search American vessels on the high seas. On August 16 the commander of a Spanish war steamer intercepted the United States Mail Steamship Company's merchant vessel *Falcon* some forty miles from Havana, and by firing several shots across the bow forced the commander, Lieutenant Henry Rodgers,[39] to submit to an unfruitful search for filibusters and war matériel. After the incident Rodgers complained about the boarding to the new U.S consul in Havana, Allen F. Owen, claiming that he would have returned fire had he not feared jeopardizing the safety of his passengers and the security of a large gold shipment that he was carrying. Owen reported the incident to Washington, despite receiving an apology from the captain general. The next month the acting U.S. secretary of state, William S. Derrick, lodged a formal complaint with Calderón suggesting, somewhat disingenuously, that Spain's insult to the

American flag might have been the underlying cause of the recent New Orleans riots.[40]

President Fillmore refused to concede Spain's right to intercept any American ship on the high seas, even the most obvious filibuster vessel, and worried that further such incidents might occur. After landing in Cuba, López had sent the *Pampero* back to Florida for reinforcements. What if the Spanish should create "a very delicate and embarrassing question" by attacking the *Pampero* before the ship next arrived in Cuban waters?[41]

Relations with Spain became so tense that the president, feeling a need to remain in Washington where he could "act promptly," postponed a trip to Boston. Believing his acting secretary of state too "feeble" for such a serious crisis, Fillmore asked Attorney General John J. Crittenden, an influential former governor of Kentucky and U.S. senator as well as the uncle of the filibuster officer William Crittenden (recently executed by Spain), to assume Derrick's sensitive responsibilities.[42] By the time Crittenden assumed his new duties in late September, however, the administration had more serious concerns than the navy of Spain, one of Europe's weaker military powers. All month long, rumors circulated in U.S. diplomatic circles abroad and in the American press that France had committed a squadron to shield Cuba against further filibuster assaults, and that the French were pressuring Great Britain to do so as well. On September 27 the British minister John F. Crampton informed Crittenden that Britain's warships on the West India Station had indeed been issued orders to use force against any filibuster descent on Cuba. On October 8 France's minister followed suit. Finally in November, America's minister in England sent the State Department an extract from a speech by President Louis Napoleon of France confirming that the British and French navies were coordinating their operations.[43]

The Anglo-French policy caused an angry backlash in Washington. Fillmore told Webster on October 2 that if the British were really serious about stopping filibustering, they would have to search the entire American merchant marine in Cuban waters, which would surely disrupt friendly relations between the two nations. Webster agreed, arguing that such attempts "could never be submitted to." Crittenden subsequently informed Crampton that Britain's exercise of "police" over American ships and citizens in nearby waters would likely initiate dangerous "abuses and collisions" with the United States, and conveyed the same admonitions respecting France's navy to her minister. Fillmore's annual message to Congress on December 2 reaffirmed that the administration would never permit any American ship "to be visited or searched for the purpose of ascertaining the character of individuals on board."[44]

By then, however, the crisis was already waning. Over the course of the fall, Spanish officials gave a number of signs that they might be willing to back down on the prisoner issue. For instance, in response to an appeal from a lieutenant on a U.S. revenue cutter, they released the filibuster captain Robert H. Ellis, who because of a hand wound had been hospitalized in Havana rather than sent overseas for imprisonment. In a sensitive missive to Calderón in mid-November, Webster paid flowery homage to Spain's flag ("that Castilian Ensign, which, in times past, has been reared so high, and waived so often, over fields of acknowledged and distinguished valor"). He promised that Consul Laborde would be given a formal salute if he would return to his post in New Orleans. Further, the administration would ask Congress to indemnify Laborde for his losses. The Queen of Spain responded in December by pardoning all U.S. citizens remaining in Spanish custody who had participated in the expedition.[45]

In early 1852, moreover, Her Majesty made yet another goodwill gesture by liberating John Sidney Thrasher, a suspected filibuster accomplice whom Spanish authorities had taken into custody on October 16 in the wake of the second invasion. Thrasher, a native of Portland, Maine, had been living in Havana since the early 1830s (apart from a few months in the United States). There he had passed several years as a clerk and subsequently as a partner in the mercantile establishment of Charles Tyng and Company, before becoming editor of *El Faro Industrial de la Habana* in 1850. After López's failed second invasion, Thrasher befriended the filibusters imprisoned in Havana, raising money to ease their discomforts in prison and, so far as the Spanish were concerned, confirming suspicions that he had been one of their on-site collaborators. Spanish authorities arrested Thrasher for treason and confined him to the dungeon of Punta Castle. The next month a Spanish military court pronounced him guilty and sentenced him to eight years of hard labor, in chains, at Ceuta.

Although Thrasher's case became something of a cause célèbre in the United States, generating press commentary as well as a petition to Congress and U.S. Senate and House resolutions, the State Department had hesitated to demand his release once Calderón established that Thrasher had previously taken out a domiciliatory letter—an official step toward Spanish citizenship that gave him occupational privileges in return for a profession of Catholicism and a renunciation of his claims to U.S. protection. In an opinion by Chief Justice John Marshall, the U.S. Supreme Court ruled in 1804 that U.S. citizens automatically forfeited their right to American interposition once they became subjects of another country. Nevertheless, Barringer did persuade Spain's government to release the prisoner.[46]

The queen's generosity prompted another round of conciliatory gestures from the United States. Initially, the Fillmore administration had ruled out reparations for the rioters' damages to the property of ordinary Spaniards living in the United States, using the argument that the victims' proper remedy lay within the American court system. But in 1852 it reversed policy and in August secured a congressional appropriation of $25,000 to cover damages to Spanish property in Key West and New Orleans in addition to the consul's losses. Furthermore, the governor of New York, upon Calderón's petition, granted clemency to a Spaniard facing the death penalty for murder.[47]

Had not the Lone Star and Quitman plots arisen from the ashes of López's conspiracies, Cuban filibustering might have faded away as a diplomatic problem. The new conspiracies, however, caused Spain to alert Washington of its resolve to search suspected filibuster vessels at sea. Moreover, Britain and France continued to assign naval forces to Cuban waters. In April 1852 their governments pressured American leaders to accede to a "tripartite" pact, by which the three nations would mutually and permanently disavow any intention to annex Cuba (an agreement that presumably would discourage American expansionists from supporting filibusters to the island), and also repress efforts to take Cuba by any "individual." Crampton suggested, in a note promoting the scheme, that Spanish tariffs against U.S. goods shipped to Havana would likely be reduced if Spain did not have to expend inordinate sums defending the island against filibuster attacks.

Although the proposed three-power alliance would surely have ended the filibustering threat against Cuba, Fillmore and his secretaries of state Webster and (after Webster's death) Edward Everett resisted the pressure. None were strident territorial expansionists. All three realized, however, that they would damage their Whig Party as well as their own reputations by ruling out the annexation of Cuba, which had been a diplomatic goal of the United States since Jefferson's presidency.

Rather than acquiesce, therefore, the administration promised to help Spain defend Cuba against filibustering, while simultaneously restating America's long-standing "no-transfer policy," by which the United States resolutely opposed Spain's conveying the island to any other European nation (meaning Britain or France—stronger powers with the ability to keep Cuba forever). Everett's answer to France's minister even claimed that the filibusters would be more apt to attack Cuba should the tripartite agreement go through, because they would want to preempt its implementation. Disappointed, the British foreign secretary, Lord John Russell, informed Everett that it was pitiful that the "Chief of a great state" had to confess his inability to stop mere filibustering bands. Russell cautioned that America's position left Britain and France free to take whatever steps regarding Cuba would best serve their own interests.[48]

Given America's rejection of the tripartite pact, it is not surprising that additional incidents occurred in Cuban waters. In September 1852 Spain's new captain general, Valentín Cañedo, provoked yet another dispute when he prevented the United States Mail Steamship Company's vessel *Crescent City* from discharging passengers and mail at Havana. Acting on reports that its purser William Smith had previously written anti-Spanish revolutionary propaganda and distributed it in Cuba, Cañedo forced the vessel to put out to sea again in a gale.[49]

The *Crescent City* affair set off a new anti-Spanish backlash in the United States. The New York diarist George Templeton Strong professed disgust with "the filthy imbecility of the worn-out Spanish breed" and reflected that he was "rapidly being demoralized into a filibuster." In New Orleans, William Tecumseh Sherman learned that Smith was being thrown a public dinner in the city, and predicted to his wife that Cuba would be America's "next war egg." Certainly the mood had turned militant in the Gulf South. Francis Mace, an adventurer who would later become involved in William Walker's Nicaraguan movement, informed John Quitman that a brigade of volunteers was mobilizing in New Orleans to fight in Cuba as soon as war broke out. Governor Henry Foote of Mississippi even asked his state's legislature to pledge support for any retaliatory measures taken by the U.S. government.[50]

Rather than immediately call upon Congress for a declaration of war, however, President Fillmore dispatched a U.S. naval officer to Havana to investigate the affair, and he angrily rejected an offer by the Steamship Company's trustees that they have the vessel open fire in the harbor should Spanish authorities deny it admittance a second time. Fillmore rightly accused the trustees of attempting to usurp Congress's war-making powers. Still, the president did direct Barringer to suggest to Spain's government that such incidents, by arousing the American public against Spain, might make it harder for federal authorities to enforce the Neutrality Act against the next set of filibusters. This crisis evaporated when Cañedo lifted his ban on Smith, who had sworn to an affidavit that he had not been involved in anti-Spanish propaganda efforts.[51]

A more serious difficulty occurred during the final weeks of Quitman's conspiracy in 1855, after Captain General José de la Concha declared Cuba to be in a state of siege and proclaimed a blockade to defend its coasts. On March 6 the commander of a Spanish corvette fired a warning shot that halted the

U.S. mail steamship *El Dorado* about eight miles from Cape San Antonio on Cuba's far western tip. Then he examined the *El Dorado* before allowing the vessel to continue. The Spanish government justified the search, arguing that it had occurred within Cuban waters at a time when "a piratical expedition" from the United States had been expected momentarily. Franklin Pierce's administration, however, contested Spain's definition of territorial waters (the United States claimed waters only three miles out) and argued that the incident occurred beyond Spanish jurisdiction. Secretary of State William L. Marcy warned Spain's minister that the United States would resist Spanish searches of American commercial vessels on the high seas "at every hazard," and reminded him that the U.S. government had opposed British attempts to board American vessels suspected of violating treaties against the African slave trade. The secretary of the navy, James C. Dobbin, sent vessels from the Home Squadron to Havana to back up Marcy's threat and temporarily detached a vessel from the navy's African Squadron to assist in the show of force.

Again the possibility of war with Spain loomed, so much so that Augustus C. Dodge, America's newly appointed minister to Spain, despaired of ever being able to commence his duties. Fortunately, Quitman's plot collapsed, giving Concha a face-saving way out of the confrontation. Without conceding the points at issue, he declared the blockade at an end in May. The U.S. government then removed warships from Cuban waters.[52]

For the last time before the Civil War, relations between the United States and Spain survived a filibustering crisis, though they were irritated by claims issues arising from the expeditions, and Spanish leaders remained apprehensive about new invasions. After learning in 1856 that Cuban exiles and former López operatives in the United States had contracted with William Walker in the hope of using Nicaragua as a base from which to invade Cuba, Spain's new minister Alfonso de Escalante lodged fresh complaints with the State Department. When Marcy responded that such an expedition was "extremely improbable," Escalante retorted, reasonably, that given "the history of the last five years," such presumptions were naïve.[53]

OBVIOUSLY, López, Quitman, and company seriously compromised relations with England, France, and Spain. But to a lesser degree, filibustering also concerned other Europeans, as the adventure-seeking American Walter Gibson discovered when he sailed his schooner to the Netherlands East Indies, apparently in search of trading opportunities. Soon after arriving at Bangka island in January 1852, he was accosted by a Dutch official who displayed a newspaper account of López's recent invasion of Cuba and implied that Gibson intended similar mischief. And the expeditions fostered a bitter anti-American backlash in Central America and Mexico. One Mexican officer lectured a U.S. Army doctor in reference to Crabb's invasion, "stay always at home, never come to forren country, we do not like Yankees no more on account of their bad action."[54]

Anecdotal evidence suggests that the governments and peoples of Central America and Mexico sporadically took out their frustrations over being invaded upon innocent American citizens residing in or passing through their countries. Mexican authorities on the Rio Grande, for instance, retaliated with new passport fees and temporary bans on American civilians traveling within their jurisdiction. During the Carbajal campaign in 1851, a correspondent reported from the border that Mexican authorities had arrested and sentenced to execution an American hide dealer whom they discovered at Camargo in violation of a ban, before releasing him after a protest by a U.S. Army captain. More typically, Mexican officials vented their irritation by engaging in petty harassment, as the U.S. Treasury agent and popular author J. Ross Browne discovered in 1854. Traveling via Mexico on his way to Oregon and California during William Walker's invasion of Sonora, Browne was searched at Vera Cruz and had his baggage detained for so many hours that he missed connections and was stranded for days. This occurred even though he carried a passport from the State Department and a visa and cover letter from Mexico's consul at New Orleans. While passing time in the city, Browne discovered that local authorities had routinely been breaking the seals on letters addressed to Americans and been reading their contents. He also learned that Mexican officials had recently imprisoned the captain of a wrecked American vessel.[55]

Similar harrying of innocent Americans occurred in Central America. The future Civil War nurse Amy Morris Bradley, who went to Costa Rica to better her health and was teaching school in San José at the time of Walker's wars, discovered that the authorities there feared she might be "una Filibustera" and were reading her mail.[56]

Unfortunately, foreign officials not only harassed Americans because of filibustering but were less than fully committed to shielding American citizens from unprovoked mob attacks. At the time of Kinney's expedition to the Mosquito Coast, Nicaragua's minister informed Secretary Marcy that his government would protect Americans if the U.S. government would dispatch a warship to dispute Kinney's landing, implying that Nicaragua might be less scrupulous should the United States be uncooperative. On occasion, Mexican and Central American officials incited paranoia about Yankees. In 1858 local officials in Guaymas, Sonora, according to one correspondent, had been stirring up anti-Americanism by "promenading the streets" and proclaiming that filibusters were on their way to "devastate" the region.[57]

As a result of such attitudes, many Americans living and working in Mexico and Central America feared for their safety. The U.S. consul at La Paz in Baja California reported to Washington during one panic that it "would have required but little" to induce a mob attack against him and other foreign residents, and that his life had been threatened repeatedly. In 1855 the American minister to Guatemala expected that "malicious persons" might "direct popular fury" against foreigners because of filibustering. The next year, *Frank Leslie's Illustrated Newspaper* reported that Americans laborers were fleeing Honduran mines because of anti-Americanism stirred up by William Walker's presence in neighboring Nicaragua. When Walker invaded Central America in 1860, Americans flooded into the U.S. consulate at San Juan del Sur, Nicaragua, seeking protection.[58]

Certainly local authorities did little to protect Americans during the Panama riot of 1856, an event that erupted in part because of simmering resentment of Walker's occupation of Nicaragua and had serious diplomatic consequences. On the evening of April 15, 1856, in the city of Panama, the Pacific coast terminus of the Panama Railroad Company (the American-owned concern that managed a line across the state of Panama in what was then New Granada), natives went on a rampage, physically assaulting Americans and pillaging foreign-owned property, including hotels and the railroad station. Rather than protect American travelers in the city, local police joined in the melee. By the time the disturbance ended, at least fourteen Americans had been killed and many others wounded. After news of the affair reached California, a speaker at a mass meeting in San Francisco called for volunteers to organize companies that would rush to the isthmus on the next steamer for the purpose of "blowing Panama to h-ll"![59]

Although historians generally attribute the riot to economic dislocations resulting from the completion of the railroad in the previous year, as well as long-standing tension between unruly Americans crossing the isthmus and local inhabitants, evidence exists that filibustering lurked behind the disturbance. Soon afterward, New Granada's leaders had protested American recognition of Walker's régime. Just before the riot, an agent of Commodore Vanderbilt had diverted a ship filled with Californian recruits for Walker from putting in at San Juan del Sur, causing them to debark at Panama city. The

British chargé d'affaires, Philip Griffith, reported from New Granada that the riot was provoked by rumors of a takeover by disembarked filibusters of the state of Panama. In fact, according to Griffith, native peoples believed that Walker's intervention in Nicaragua signaled "the commencement of a plan" that was "to end eventually in the annexation of the whole of Central America" to the United States. When New Granada's negotiators later met with American commissioners concerning U.S. grievances about the affair, they attacked the United States for breeding filibusters and excused the riots by noting the prior arrival of this "gang."[60]

After the incident, a U.S. naval officer on the scene and the acting governor of Panama exchanged acrimonious letters, and the State Department sent agents to investigate "barbarous cruelties" against American lives and property. To discourage further attacks, President Pierce deployed war vessels on both ends of the crossing. But relations with New Granada worsened further after negotiations in Bogotá broke down in February 1857, when New Granada's commissioners rejected U.S. terms that included reparations as well as the cession of islands in the bay of Panama city for an American naval station. In separate dispatches in May and June to James B. Bowlin, U.S. minister in New Granada, Secretary Marcy cautioned that New Granada might expect "serious consequences" should it not respond to the grievances and demands of the United States. Marcy warned that Washington might be compelled to intervene militarily to protect Americans crossing the isthmus.[61]

Heightening the tension, in May 1857 Commodore William Mervine of the U.S. Navy's Pacific Squadron, without the permission of Panamanian authorities, deployed a twelve-man marine guard to protect William Walker and his staff from mob attacks as they crossed Panama by rail during their return to the United States from Nicaragua after the overthrow of the filibuster régime. Mervine's decision prompted the governor of Panama to protest what he considered an infringement of the territorial sovereignty of his country (that is, New Granada). Mervine justified the military escort by noting that there was anti-American sentiment on the isthmus, and that the marines were returning to the United States anyway and did not conduct military maneuvers while sitting in Walker's railroad car.[62]

Finally, in September, New Granada's minister in Washington, Pedro A. Herran, admitted his country's liability for damages from the riot. In a convention with Secretary of State Cass, Herran agreed that a joint commission would review American claims, and he conceded to the United States the right to purchase or lease one hundred acres of land for a coal depot on an island in the bay of Panama. Although New Granadian leaders deleted the provision for a coal depot before ratifying the agreement in 1858, the U.S. Senate accepted the amended convention the next year and the accord went into effect in November 1860. Yet another diplomatic crisis that had been spawned at least indirectly by filibustering passed without leading to war, though the claims were not fully settled until 1874.[63]

In the case of the Zerman captives in Mexico, the State Department championed imprisoned Americans who, like the Contoy prisoners at Havana, might have been miscast as filibusters by a foreign government. Jean Napoleon Zerman, an elderly native Venetian and onetime French officer in the Napoleonic wars, had settled in San Francisco. In 1855 he accepted a commission as an admiral in Mexico's navy from agents of Juan Álvarez, leader of the liberal Ayutla Revolution against the dictator Santa Anna. Zerman agreed to deliver to Acapulco the barque *Archibald Gracie* with munitions, supplies, and funds for the Liberal cause. The ship, manned by a mixed crew of mostly Americans and Frenchmen, left San Francisco on October 11 under the U.S. flag, supposedly on a trading voyage to Mazatlán. Three days after sailing, Zerman took over the vessel from Captain Samuel Dennison and proclaimed himself commander of the Mexican Pacific Squadron, renamed his ship the *Restoradora* and raised the Mexican flag, meeting no resistance from his crew.

During a stop for fresh water and wood at Cape San Lucas, Zerman learned that Santa Anna had already abdicated power. Rather than proceed directly to Acapulco, Zerman decided to help the Liberals repress any remaining pockets of resistance in the region, and to assist in the mission he chartered the whaling ship *Rebecca Adams*, which the *Archibald Gracie* fell in with shortly after leaving the cape. When he debarked with a small party at La Paz for consultations with the authorities there, however, Baja California's governor José María Blancarte put him and his companions under arrest as suspected filibusters. Subsequently, Blancarte opened fire on Zerman's ships in the bay, killing one man and forcing the party's surrender; the combined crews were taken captive.[64]

At first, Mexican officials treated Zerman and his followers shabbily. The prisoners were robbed while at La Paz, and for a while they were denied anything to eat. However, conditions improved after the captives were sent to Guadalajara and then confined at Mexico City (though crew members had to march in chains to get there). Eventually, they were released on parole in the capital. Still, many were reduced to begging because they only received fifty cents a day from the Mexican government for food and had difficulty finding gainful employment while their case made its painful progress through a series of Mexican courts. Long before a decision of the Mexican Supreme

Court on November 25, 1857, cleared them of filibustering, almost all the captives other than Zerman had violated their parole and returned to the United States, often with the blessing of the U.S. minister John Forsyth.[65]

Forsyth, his predecessor James Gadsden, and Secretary of State Marcy all championed the prisoners' cause. Forsyth complained to Mexico's foreign minister about Blancarte's "brutality" and argued that Mexico had no right to confiscate the *Rebecca Adams*, since the captain had presumed that the vessel had been chartered by Zerman with the approval of Mexican authorities. Marcy alerted the Mexican government to evidence that the crew of the *Archibald Gracie* had not intended to filibuster and to reports that the prisoners had been mistreated. In response, Mexico's minister to the United States, Manuel Robles Pezuela, conceded that American citizens in Mexico were harassed more than other foreign residents in his country. Still, he justified the discrimination on the basis of earlier filibuster invasions of Mexico by the United States, as well as Mexican nervousness about Walker's and Kinney's expeditions to Central America, in progress at the very time that Zerman was incarcerated.

Eventually the U.S. government filed claims on behalf of 108 of the Zerman captives. Finally in 1874, an umpire operating under the auspices of the United States and Mexican Claims Commission rejected Zerman's case. However, he awarded payments to the captains and owners of the *Archibald Gracie* and the *Rebecca Adams*, as well as the latter's first mate and one of its passengers.[66]

CLEARLY, filibustering had immediate diplomatic ramifications. But it had important long-range ones as well. Walker's and Kinney's invasions of Central America, for instance, influenced the outcome of a decadelong effort by American leaders to augment their influence on the isthmus by pressuring Great Britain into giving up its colonial holdings in the area. By 1850 British settlements on the Bay of Honduras, established in the seventeenth century for control over the region's logwood (a source of dyes for textiles), had evolved into the de facto colony of British Honduras, or Belize.[67] In 1839 agents of Belize's superintendent seized Roatán to the south, the largest of an island group off the coast of Honduras, to control mahogany cuttings in the area. Further, the British claimed a protectorate over the Miskito (or Mosquito) Indians living on the coast of today's Nicaragua and Honduras.[68]

Despite strictures against further European colonization of the Western Hemisphere created by the Monroe Doctrine (1823), American leaders refrained from interposing against Britain before the Mexican War. But the acquisition of Oregon and California, and the discovery in 1848 of California's gold deposits, suddenly made the status of Central American transit routes, whether by road, river, rail, or canal, a vital concern for American policy makers. As we have seen, American entrepreneurs by the early 1850s had established transit operations in both Nicaragua and Panama. As a result, Washington and its diplomatic agents began challenging the English in the region.

Tensions mounted, especially after British forces in 1848 expelled Nicaraguan officials from San Juan del Norte, the likely eastern terminus of a Nicaraguan canal, and renamed the port Greytown in honor of their governor in Jamaica, Sir Charles Grey; they increased further after Britain's navy in 1849 seized Honduras's Tigre Island, off the Pacific end of a likely canal route, which Honduras had just granted to the United States in a yet unratified treaty. The Anglo-American Clayton-Bulwer Treaty of 1850, which, in addition to provisions respecting the prospective construction of a Central American canal stipulated that neither country would occupy, fortify, or colonize any part of Central America, papered over rather than resolved the dispute. The United States claimed that the agreement necessitated Britain's surrendering the Bay Islands and the Mosquito Coast protectorate. Britain argued that the agreement merely ruled out future colonies. Meanwhile in 1852, as what one scholar labels the most "prolonged" dispute over a treaty in American history raged on, Britain formally proclaimed Roatán and five neighboring islands the Colony of the Bay Islands.[69]

American filibusters who invaded Central America therefore intruded upon a global trouble spot. Kinney set up his colony at Greytown, the most important port within the Mosquito Protectorate. Walker likewise threatened the British, since, by taking over Nicaragua's government, he inherited Nicaragua's prior claim to the Mosquito Coast, a claim that the U.S. government had supported during its negotiations with Britain over the Clayton-Bulwer Treaty. In fact, rather than appoint a consul to British Greytown, the United States maintained a lower-ranking commercial agent, commissioned to the state of Nicaragua, at the port.[70]

Not surprisingly, Britain contested both filibusters. Although the British naval officer on station at Greytown did not interfere with Kinney's landing, Britain denied Kinney and Walker diplomatic recognition. Furthermore, British leaders dispatched additional war vessels to Nicaraguan waters and promised to arm Costa Rican forces warring against Walker. British naval officers implemented their government's policy of watchful hostility by renouncing Kinney's intrusion, preparing to repulse any attack that Walker made on Greytown, pressuring American naval commanders to intervene against the filibusters, and themselves interfering with reinforcements attempting to reach Walker's army.

When a British naval captain in the spring of 1856 boarded the U.S. commercial steamer *Orizaba* in Greytown's harbor and scrutinized its passenger list to determine if any of Walker's recruits were aboard, the stage was set for yet another crisis over the issue of search. The Pierce administration rushed warships to Greytown, even detaching a vessel from a Mediterranean cruise, with instructions that no foreign search could be "tolerated or submitted to." The U.S. minister to Britain, George M. Dallas, warned the British foreign secretary Lord Clarendon that the incident was "extremely serious and delicate"; the interference was unjustified even if every passenger on board was en route to Walker's service.[71]

This incident was soon resolved amicably: the U.S. government dropped its complaint once information reached Washington that the contested visitation had been invited by the owner of the *Orizaba*.[72] But a potentially more explosive confrontation occurred in 1858. That October, after word arrived in London of Walker's planned third attempt to conquer Nicaragua, the Earl of Malmesbury, Britain's foreign secretary, requested the Admiralty to protect Britain's Mosquito Protectorate by posting two ships at Greytown. Malmesbury recommended that these vessels be instructed to respond positively when asked to intervene against the filibusters by either Nicaragua or Costa Rica. In addition, Malmesbury solicited a warship for Nicaragua's Pacific coast, asked France to send one or two warships to Greytown, and had Britain's minister at Washington, Lord Napier, officially inform the U.S. State Department of the policy.[73]

Malmesbury's stand raised the diplomatic stakes one more time. Secretary of State Cass told Napier that the policy seriously jeopardized U.S. relations with Great Britain. Learning that France had assented to the British proposal, Cass warned its minister that French naval intervention would "excite much feeling" in the United States. He also instructed the American ministers in Britain and France to file protests and asked America's minister to Nicaragua and Costa Rica to dissuade both states from requesting European intervention. Cass argued that Britain was violating the Clayton-Bulwer Treaty, which prohibited both parties from occupying, fortifying, or colonizing Central America—a contention that Malmesbury denied on the logic than neither Britain nor France sought actual control over any Nicaraguan or Costa Rican territory.[74]

Rapidly, the dispute escalated. In late November James M. McIntosh, commanding vessels of America's Home Squadron off San Juan del Norte, learned that the British naval captain W. C. Aldham had boarded the U.S. mail steamer *Washington* at San Juan to search for filibusters and that another British naval officer had boarded the steamer *Catharine Maria* in the nearby Colorado River on a similar quest. McIntosh, who considered it an insult to his own country that the Central American republics looked to Britain for protection, protested to Aldham that he had no right to upstage the U.S. Navy, which had strict orders to prevent Walker's landing. McIntosh promised the Navy Department that he would "protect the honor" of the flag if British officers persisted in examining U.S. merchant vessels for filibusters, even if "the most serious consequences" resulted. In January, moreover, the commander of America's Pacific Squadron sent a warship to the Gulf of Fonseca to "resist" British attempts to search vessels for filibusters off Central America's western shores.

Fortunately, Walker's expedition soon wrecked, McIntosh and Aldham negotiated an understanding, and Britain's government, placated by conciliatory comments about the "amicable" state of Anglo-American relations in President Buchanan's annual message of December 6, decided not to send any more vessels to the waters around Greytown. The crisis dissolved. But the Anglo-American dispute over Central America remained unsettled.[75]

WE MAY NEVER know for certain whether the United States before the Civil War would have acquired more land than it did had there been no filibusters. But one suspects that the adventurers harmed American expansionism by fostering acute distrust of the United States in other countries, including some that were never invaded by the filibusters. Luis Molina pointedly informed the State Department that all "hispano-american countries" suffered from fear of "filibusterism." Even in distant Santiago, Chile, the U.S. minister John Bigler detected this reaction. He reported to Washington on one occasion that Chileans made a habit of complaining about William Walker, and that they truly seemed to believe "that the Yankee nation are but waiting for an opportunity to devour them."[76]

Naturally, anti-Americanism took its most extreme course in countries immediately threatened by filibustering. Soon after arriving in Nicaragua after William Walker's second invasion, America's new minister, Mirabeau Buonaparte Lamar, sensed a pervasive "deep seated terror, that, when the Americans are admitted into it, the natives will be thrust aside—their nationality lost—their religion destroyed—and the common classes be converted into hewers and drawers of water." Amy Morris Bradley reflected in her journal after Costa Rica declared war on Walker that she now resided "in the midst of a Country fighting for what it considers its Liberty."[77]

According to the historian E. Bradford Burns, Walker's invasions did more to foster Nicaraguan nationalism than any other single event. Before Walker's advent, Nicaraguans had been so divided that they lacked a legitimate national identity. But virtually all Nicaraguans, including Indians, eventually joined the struggle to expel the invaders, creating a framework for a shared national consciousness. In fact, governments throughout Central American came to regard resistance to the filibusters as a kind of holy crusade for survival. Such desperation helps to explain the "Rivas Manifesto," a secret polemic signed by the presidents of Nicaragua and Costa Rica on May 1, 1858. It not only accused the United States of intending to use the filibusters' next invasion as a means of conquering Central America, but also requested that England, France, and Sardinia—the powers that had supported Turkey's independence against Russia in the Crimean War—play the same role in Central America against U.S. intruders.[78]

In addition to seeking European protection against filibusters, Latin American leaders organized an antifilibustering alliance as a defensive strategy. In 1856 plenipotentiaries representing Chile, Ecuador, and Peru signed a Treaty of Union at Santiago that among other things defined filibustering as piracy, pledged mutual aid against invasions, and invited all other Latin states to join the alliance. The governments of Costa Rica, Guatemala, El Salvador, and Nicaragua indicated their intention to affiliate. However, the alliance was scuttled by its sponsors in September 1857, partly because by then Walker had been ejected from Central America.[79]

Mexico's case is particularly instructive. During his negotiations with Mexican leaders in 1853, the U.S. minister, James Gadsden, concluded that William Walker's invasion of Baja California had hardened Mexican resistance to land cessions. For damage control, Gadsden requested U.S. naval officers on the Pacific coast to intercept additional expeditionists reported sailing for Mexico, and he also included an antifilibustering provision in his draft treaty. When Mexico's foreign secretary complained about filibustering, Gadsden promised that President Pierce would use all the means at his disposal to prevent further incursions, and also predicted Walker's failure since federal officials in San Francisco had compelled the filibusters to leave port before they were ready. Still, Gadsden conceded the constraints that filibustering imposed on the "progress of Anglo Saxon muscle" in Mexico. Had it not been for Walker, the minister decided, he might have fulfilled the State Department's instructions to include Baja California within his "Purchase."[80]

Gadsden's successor reached almost identical conclusions. John Forsyth traveled to Mexico in October 1856, only to discover that filibustering had already caused so much distrust of Americans in Mexico's northern reaches as to preclude people living in the states of Sonora and Chihuahua from seeking annexation to the United States, even though they realized that the United States could provide them with far better protection against Indian attacks than their own government did. Now, Mexican newspapers carried rumors of Henry Crabb's pending invasion of Sonora. "The expeditionists have certainly chosen an unfortunate time for their movements," Forsyth lamented. Forsyth became so convinced of Mexican hostility to territorial proposals that he reacted unenthusiastically to the State Department's instructions of July 17, 1857, which among other things called on him to negotiate the purchase of Baja California, Sonora, and part of Chihuahua. In fact, one historian suggests that he sabotaged his own negotiations because of his pessimism.[81]

For a brief moment during Hawaii's extended filibuster scare, which lasted from 1851 to 1855, the U.S. commissioner, David L. Gregg, thought that the islands' leaders might seek annexation to the United States for protection against the dreaded adventurers. In January 1854 Gregg informed Washington that news of William Walker's "recent operations in Lower California" seemed to have unsettled Prince Alexander Liholiho, the expected heir to the Hawaiian throne and previously a staunch opponent of annexation. Gregg predicted, as a result, that the prince would now acquiesce in an American takeover. But this was not to be. Later that same year, Gregg conceded that incessant rumors of expeditions from California had engendered considerable prejudice against Americans, lessening the likelihood of annexation.[82]

Instead of selling Cuba to avoid its forfeiture to filibusters, Spanish leaders held the U.S. government responsible for the expeditions, and utilized filibustering as a rationale for declining the sale. Horatio J. Perry, secretary of the American legation in Madrid, informed Secretary of State Marcy in September 1854 that Spain might sell Cuba to the United States but that "Genl Quitman and the Cuban Junta" threatened to "ruin" the possibility. Marcy agreed, writing the next spring to the U.S. minister in Madrid that the collapse of Quitman's plot might well improve Spanish relations with the United States to the point where Spain would consider a "voluntary cession."[83]

In addition to impeding territorial expansion by the United States, filibustering interrupted American commercial penetration of the invaded regions. Spain, for example, retaliated for Narciso López's first invasion of Cuba by raising tariffs on U.S. goods entering the island. In 1852 Mexico's Congress rejected a treaty with the United States that would have recognized the claim of New Orleans businessmen to a large land grant for the purpose of constructing a railroad across Mexico's isthmus of Tehuantepec. William M. Burwell, a special agent with the State Department who had been in Mexico to assist in the negotiations, attributed the treaty's failure in part to "prejudices" against Americans that had been "greatly increased by the Lopez Expedition and the [Carbajal] invasion of the Rio Grande."

Even in countries spared from filibustering, reports of the expeditions did their damage. In 1854 a Spanish agent in the Dominican Republic helped to defeat efforts by the American commissioner William Leslie Cazneau to negotiate a lease on Samaná Bay for a U.S. coaling station, by playing off fears that the harbor would become a filibuster "den" that might threaten Cuba and Puerto Rico. Two years later, the naval oceanographer Matthew Fontaine Maury, in the final stages of his ultimately successful campaign to persuade Brazil to open the Amazon River to international commerce, complained that Brazilian opponents had been stigmatizing him as a filibuster in an effort to sabotage the project. Not long afterward, news about William Walker's aggressions in Nicaragua helped to derail negotiations in Bolivia by the American chargé d'affaires John Dana for a trade agreement.[84]

Most obviously, Walker's wars caused the once lucrative American-operated Nicaraguan transit route to close down in March 1857. That November, Antonio José de Irisarri, a Guatemalan representing Nicaragua's post-Walker government,[85] signed a treaty with Secretary of State Cass that if implemented would have enhanced the influence of the United States on the isthmus: the agreement, which Nicaragua's legislative assembly did ratify, authorized the U.S. government to intervene militarily in Nicaragua for the protection of transit routes as well as American lives and property. However, President Tomás Martínez of Nicaragua opposed the Cass-Irisarri Treaty and made certain that it was not ratified within the requisite nine months.

The U.S. minister to Nicaragua, Mirabeau Buonaparte Lamar, arrived at a substitute agreement with Nicaragua's minister of foreign affairs Pedro Zeledón on March 16, 1859, which was a virtual replica of Cass's treaty except for a Nicaraguan provision (article 16) mandating that the United States would "use all legal means and reasonable vigilance to prevent the formation within their Territories of hostile expeditions destined for those of the Republic of Nicaragua." The Buchanan administration, however, bridled at the implication that the United States was not fulfilling its international obligations. Cass informed Nicaragua's new minister to the United States, Máximo Jerez, that the clause insultingly authorized a foreign power to instruct Americans on what laws they should pass and how they should be implemented. After the U.S. Senate struck the provision, Nicaragua's president refused to call his country's legislative assembly into a special session to ratify the revised treaty, citing the emergency conditions caused by Walker's occupation of Truxillo, Honduras, during his final expedition. Nicaragua had only until December 27, 1860, to exchange ratifications with the United States. Since the assembly was not scheduled to meet until January 1861, the Lamar-Zeledón Treaty, like its predecessor, fell by the wayside.[86]

Nicaraguan authorities apparently preferred to leave the route closed rather than risk its becoming a conduit for future filibusters. Before negotiating his treaty with Cass, Irisarri in June 1857 had contracted with President H. G. Stebbins and Joseph L. White of the Atlantic and Pacific Ship Canal Company to reopen the transit. However, Nicaragua subsequently revoked the grant on the grounds that the company had failed to begin service within the time stipulated by the contract, and in November 1858 the Nicaraguan government prevented passengers arriving at Greytown on a company vessel from crossing through Nicaragua to the Pacific coast. In December 1859 Alexander Dimitry, Lamar's successor as minister, reported to the State Department that Nicaragua's acting president had informed an agent of U.S. transit concerns that it was "not to the interest of the Republic" that the transit be reopened, since "all are convinced that its active operations must infallibly result in the sweeping of their country by hordes of filibusters." In July 1861, after Walker's death, Nicaragua granted a new transit charter to the Stebbins group. But the crossing remained closed until October 1862, primarily because the filibuster wars had damaged vessels, carriages, buildings, and other facilities on the route, and the revival proved to be brief. In April 1868, the once-lucrative Nicaraguan transit shut down for good.[87]

The impact of filibustering on U.S. expansionism, however, was double-edged in at least one way. The incessant expeditions may have influenced Britain's decision to conciliate the United States in the heated dispute over the Clayton-Bulwer Treaty and withdraw from most of its Central American holdings. Britain's pullback, in turn, facilitated the long-range growth of American military and commercial influence in the region.

Even before Kinney or Walker invaded Central America, British leaders attempted to negotiate with the United States a pullout from the Mosquito Protectorate. In late 1856, at the height of Walker's wars, the foreign secretary, Lord Clarendon, determined that Britain could also afford to give up the Bay Islands. In the Dallas-Clarendon Convention, signed on October 17, the foreign minister and America's minister to Britain agreed to the abolition of the Mosquito Protectorate and a cession of the Bay Islands to Honduras, subject to stipulations protecting both the Miskito Indians and British subjects in the islands. Greytown would become a self-governing free port within Nicaragua's jurisdiction.

The convention failed of ratification in 1857, over the U.S. Senate's striking of the qualifications about the Bay Islands. But Britain still wanted to end the impasse, and it sent out William Gore Ouseley, a career diplomat married to an American, to achieve a British pullback by means of bilateral settlements with the Central American states involved. When Ouseley faltered, he was assisted and ultimately superseded by Charles Lennox Wyke, the British chargé d'affaires in Guatemala. In separate treaties with Honduras (November 1859) and Nicaragua (January 1860), Wyke acknowledged the claims of both countries to the Mosquito Coast, while protecting its Indian inhabitants. Wyke also surrendered the Bay Islands to Honduras in the first agreement, and in a pact with Guatemala (April 1859) agreed to a southern boundary for Belize that was less inclusive than Britain's former claims.[88]

British leaders might have been more tenacious had it not been for the filibusters. During the spring of 1856 British policy makers became dismayed over seeming evidence, including President Pierce's recognition of Walker's régime, that the U.S. government was using the filibusters as surrogates in the Anglo-American rivalry in Central America. Britain's minister in Washington reported that Pierce's decision reflected popular outrage in the United States at Britain's military support for Walker's Costa Rican enemies. Moreover, not only did news of the *Orizaba* affair anger Americans, but Walker released to the U.S. government captured correspondence that documented British promises to provide muskets to the Costa Ricans. Walker also personally alerted the expansionist senators Stephen Douglas and John B. Weller to Britain's intervention, and they had given addresses championing the filibusters.[89]

Rather than allow the confrontation with the United States in Central America to escalate, British leaders backed down. Lord Clarendon believed that hostilities with the United States over filibustering would prove unacceptable to influential British textile interests dependent on Southern cotton, noting that the government would command "no backing at home" if Britain "frightened the Cotton Lords on account of Nicaragua." By releasing Central American colonies, Britain could avoid a military conflict on the immediate heels of the Crimean War (which ended with the Treaty of Paris in March 1856) that might jeopardize its hold on Canada. Surely such a capitulation would influence U.S. leaders to take more energetic preemptive action against filibustering than in the past, creating more stable conditions in Central America for British commercial interests.[90]

Lord Palmerston, British prime minister during the policy shift, illumi-

nated the impact of filibustering on his thinking in a remarkable message to
Lord Clarendon. Palmerston instructed him to sound out the U.S. government as to its wishes regarding the Clayton-Bulwer Treaty, even its outright
abrogation, since the "Yankees" were such "ingenious Rogues" that they
would get their way regardless in Central America "by the indirect agency of
such men as Walker & his followers." The filibusters, Palmerston assumed,
would establish "independent North American States" in the region, "in alliance with the United States if not in Union with them, in short Texas all
over again." Similarly, William Gore Ouseley reported to the foreign office
from Washington during his mission that the Clayton-Bulwer Treaty put
Britain at a disadvantage, since it allowed the United States to expand by
means of filibustering, even as it put a damper on Britain's formerly expansionist course.[91]

Yet paradoxically, filibustering almost reversed the very British withdrawal
from the Bay Islands that it helped to initiate. As early as 1856, during the
preliminary phase of Britain's planned disengagement, Charles Lennox Wyke
reported that Guatemalan leaders opposed having Honduras gain possession
of the colony, lest filibusters take advantage of Honduran military weakness
and establish a "fresh nest there."[92] William Walker's expedition in 1860
caused British leaders, by this very logic, to delay implementation of their cession treaty.

It was no coincidence that shortly after Britain ceded the Bay Islands to
Honduras, Walker chose Roatán as the advance base for his final escapade. In
February 1860 Arthur Callaghan, three years earlier a surgeon in William
Walker's Nicaraguan army, informed Walker's agents in New Orleans from
Roatán that some of the white residents of the Bay Islands were so upset
about their pending transfer from British to Honduran sovereignty that they
had been considering "inviting Walker to come and invade Honduras" from
Roatán. Walker subsequently sent Charles Allen, a lieutenant in his *Susan* expedition in 1858, with nine accomplices, as advance agents to work out the
scheme. Allen and the island's dissidents agreed that Walker should send to
Roatán fifty to seventy-five men to be dispersed to the residences of affiliated
landed proprietors throughout the islands, where they would remain incon-
spicuously until after the British formally turned the colony over to the Honduran authorities. At that point, unless the Hondurans made concessions to
the islanders, the dissidents would declare independence and ask the military
assistance of the filibusters. In return, Walker could use Roatán as a "rendezvous for any expedition" that he might "wish to fit out directed to the main
land." Walker himself arrived at Roatán in June, before invading the Honduran coast.[93]

Unfortunately for the filibusters, British authorities in the Bay Islands got wind of the plot by late February. As a result, they were able to foil Walker's plans by sending extra soldiers, a rocket battery, and a warship to the Bay Islands, prohibiting military drilling on Roatán, threatening arrests, and, most important, postponing indefinitely the transfer of the colony to Honduran sovereignty. Since Walker's plans were based upon a revolution that was to break out after the transfer, Britain's delay mystified the filibusters, disrupting the whole operation. On May 8 Allen informed Walker, still in New Orleans, that no one on Roatán knew whether the treaty had even been ratified. Walker was a bit more discerning. Less than a week after his own arrival at Roatán, he predicted that the transfer would not occur "so long as" his "people were there." Rather than risk having his men and supplies seized, Walker evacuated his force on June 21.[94]

Even after Walker's subsequent capture and execution, filibustering cast a shadow over Britain's retreat from Central American colonialism. Honduran leaders, disbelieving that the expeditions were truly over, sought Great Britain's continuing intervention in the region. Days before British officials on January 1 allowed Nicaragua's flag to be raised in Greytown signaling the end to the Mosquito Protectorate, the Honduran minister in London submitted a formal proposal that Britain provide a protectorate over both the Bay Islands and the Mosquito Coast. But British leaders rejected the initiative. Asked by the British foreign minister, Lord John Russell, for advice on Honduras's protectorate proposal, Charles Wyke warned that such a step "would be certain to reawaken the jealousy of the United States Government and Press," since Americans would consider it a violation of the still extant Clayton-Bulwer pact. Russell in May ruled against the deployment of British forces against filibusters on the Central American mainland. Finally on June 24, 1861, a full year after Walker left Roatán, Britain, to Honduras's disappointment, turned over the Bay Islands.[95]

ALTHOUGH HISTORIANS generally treat antebellum filibustering expeditions as a chapter in the history of American expansionism, the phenomenon did more to impede the nation's territorial growth than speed it along. Nothing makes this point more subtly than a remarkable letter that a California newspaper received from an American who arrived at the city of Panama in January 1853. After describing the place as filled with ruins and "hordes of naked urchins," the traveler laments the lack of piers in the harbor and wonders how long such an unprogressive "state of things" would continue "if the stars and stripes were floating in the Plaza?" Yet after beginning what seems to be a call in the rhetoric of manifest destiny for a U.S. takeover, the correspondent suddenly pulls his punches, noting that he should not answer his own question, since "it is not deemed 'proper' to talk about such things in these filibustering times."[96] The filibusters, even before William Walker invaded Nicaragua, have so discredited the process of territorial growth that, in today's parlance, they have made calls for American expansion politically incorrect.

CHAPTER NINE

Judge Campbell's Nightmare

Says, it is no more than justice
To sustain the fillibusters
In the slave regeneration
Of the Nicaraguan nation!
—"Get Out of the Way, Old Buchanan"
(quoted in Thomas Drew, comp., *The Campaign of 1856*)

EVEN BEFORE a single state seceded, Justice John Archibald Campbell of the U.S. Supreme Court damned the filibusters for the calamity befalling his country. Six days after Abraham Lincoln's election as president in November 1860, Campbell, an Alabamian, linked William Walker's invasions of Nicaragua to what he believed to be the precise moment when southern fire-eaters had hatched their secession plot. "I have long been persuaded," he reflected, "that the programe of disunion was settled in Montgomery in 1858. . . . The Southern league, African slave trade, and the conquest of Nicaragua [were] made part of it."

Nothing that occurred over the subsequent weeks disabused Campbell of his notion that disunion was connected with filibustering, though in a letter to former president Franklin Pierce on December 29 he predated this partnership back to 1850. "Their societies were concerned in the plan of Genl Quitman," he now recalled, "to take Cuba & then of Genl Walker to take Nicaragua." Given these presumptions, one can almost anticipate Campbell's prediction in January 1861, after Alabama had seceded, that filibusters would now be running things. After all, he reasoned, only filibusters and slave traders had cause to crave their freedom from U.S. law.[1]

Was Campbell merely venting a grudge? Ever since 1854, when he had compelled John Quitman to post bond so that he would not invade Cuba, the filibusters and their boosters had been vilifying him for enforcing the Neutrality Law. Quitman, before posting bond, had submitted a written protest to the clerk of Campbell's court, renouncing Campbell's ruling as illegal and unconstitutional. He later issued a circular, distributed through the press, attacking Campbell for misrepresenting grand jury proceedings and findings. In Vicksburg, Mississippi, a "Cuba sympathy" public meeting had passed resolutions denouncing Campbell. Profilibustering southern newspapers accused Campbell of employing "monstrous" and "latitudinarian" doctrines that threatened to extinguish freedom of expression in America. Luckily, Campbell could only guess the terrible things that the filibusters and their friends such as the former secretary of the treasury Robert J. Walker were saying about him in their private circles.[2]

Campbell smarted from these calumnies for years. In December 1858, almost half a year after Quitman's death, Campbell complained bitterly to Attorney General Jeremiah Black about the recently deceased filibuster chief: "I rec'd a day or two ago a portion of Quitman's circular reviewing all the plans & calculations of the Cuban expedition. This was extracted in consequence of his lying letter to me of 1854. Hero, as some call him, he was in my judgement a very base man." Still troubled a year later by the continuing refusal of Quitman's supporters to bury their animosity toward him, Campbell again lamented Quitman's "dishonorable" handling of the matter. Believing himself misunderstood, Campbell insisted to Black not only that had he been well within the law in demanding bond of Quitman, but that Quitman had been treated courteously and patiently in his court.[3]

By secession's winter, moreover, Campbell had also crossed swords with William Walker's crew. In the summer of 1858, Walker had issued a public letter accusing the judge of deviously distorting the wording of the Neutrality Act in his charge to the jury during Walker's recent trial in New Orleans. Arriving at Mobile, Alabama, in November 1858 just before the *Susan* expedition, Campbell encountered instant hostility from local filibusters and their supporters, who feared that his U.S. Circuit Court might interrupt their plans: "I reached here Saturday morning in the stage. That morning there had appeared a threatening article in the Mobile *Register*, directed particularly against me & my purpose in convening the court, & menacing some consequences if I charged the [grand] jury as I had done in New Orleans." Campbell proceeded to charge the jurors anyway, assuming that his enemies would refrain from assaulting him physically, but anticipating that he would become the butt of insults in the days ahead. Once Walker's band circumvented Campbell's court and left port, a Mobile sheet fulfilled his prophecy in mocking verse that celebrated how the filibusters had successfully defied "*Impartial* Judges."[4]

Yet if Campbell in 1860 held grudges against the filibusters, he also had reason to associate them with disunionism, the slave trade, a "Southern league," and events that had occurred two years earlier in Montgomery, Alabama. In May 1858 William Walker had appeared there, at the very time that the most significant conclave of southern disunionists since 1850, the Montgomery

Commercial Convention, was in session. Leading fire-eaters, including Robert Barnwell Rhett of South Carolina, William L. Yancey of Alabama, and Edmund Ruffin of Virginia, attended this gathering, as did lesser lights such as Leonidas W. Spratt, the editor from Charleston who was gaining notoriety for his crusade to reopen the African slave trade.

The delegates did debate reviving the slave trade throughout the five-day gathering, and also passed a resolution endorsing Walker's movement. Meanwhile, during a party at Yancey's home, Walker conversed with Ruffin. Before returning to Virginia from the conference, Ruffin won Yancey's agreement to cooperate in a "League of United Southerners," a projected alliance of local committees of safety that might ultimately spearhead the South's secession. Two months later, Walker and Yancey appeared jointly at Bethel Church in Montgomery, where each gave a speech and radical enthusiasts adopted a constitution for an organization, the Leaguers of the South, that had as its goal an independent southern republic.[5]

Still, to concede Campbell's rationality by no means concedes his perspicacity, even if other southern Unionists expressed almost identical opinions. The slaveholding congressman John H. Reagan of Texas, future postmaster general of the Confederacy, made antifilibustering diatribes a staple in his re-election campaign of 1858–59, telling his constituents in a public circular, "I do not attribute to all who advocate the doctrines of filibustering and the reopening of the slave trade revolutionary purposes. . . . But I do charge that the purposes and objects of the leaders of these movements are revolutionary." Likewise, in a letter that he wanted kept private, Reagan attacked a profilibustering editor from Texas for falling into the trap of that "new & peculiarly Southern School of politicians," who intended by advocating filibustering and the slave trade to bring about the denationalization of the Democratic Party and the dissolution of the Union.[6] Campbell, Reagan, and others like them surveyed the filibustering movement as outsiders, however. If we want to understand the place of filibustering in Civil War causation, we must listen to other voices.

ATHOUGH CAMPBELL suggested to former president Pierce that the nexus between filibustering and disunion began in 1850, many Americans at the turn of the decade did not even consider filibustering a southern phenomenon, much less a disunionist one. After learning that his city had been maligned as López's base of operations in northern newspapers, a journalist in Savannah rejoined, with good cause, that in New York persons brazenly strutted along the streets with "bands and music, openly proclaiming their participation in the Cuban movement." How hypocritical for the northern press to cast stones, he believed, when López's "treason" had been "hatched and nurtured" in New York.[7]

As we have seen, Northerners were in fact deeply implicated in López's plot, so much so that one recent scholar chides historians for reducing the invaders to pawns of the slavocracy. Tom Chaffin's book-length study of López's expeditions not only highlights Yankees who were involved in filibustering but also identifies Southerners, most notably Louisiana sugar planters, who disparaged it: had filibustering eventuated in U.S. annexation of Cuba, American tariff barriers against imported Cuban sugar would have automatically dropped. Furthermore, white Southerners had reason to question the advisability of championing the right of outsiders (Americans) to impose their values upon other peoples (Cubans and Spaniards). Might not that very reasoning justify eventual interference by the U.S. government with slavery?[8]

A similar logic applies to later filibuster operations. Quitman, Kinney, and Walker all recruited Northerners and depended considerably upon financiers and merchants in such non-Southern cities as New York and San Francisco. Had Sam Houston carried out his threatened invasion of Mexico, he could have commanded a sectionally integrated army: Northerners, on hearing rumors of his intentions, volunteered their services.[9]

Still, it would be misleading to assume that the expeditions were somehow removed from the slavery question that was tearing the Union apart. Even before the Mexican War, Southerners occasionally filibustered to alleviate alleged threats to slavery. Adventurers invading Spanish East Florida during James Madison's presidency hoped to preempt a rebellion by Georgia's slaves, which they feared might occur because of Spain's decision to deploy runaway American slaves and other blacks as soldiers in East Florida. John Quitman filibustered during the Texas revolution of 1836 partly because of rumors that Mexican authorities would encourage slaves in Louisiana, where Quitman owned a plantation, to run away.[10]

The transformation of filibustering from a national phenomenon to a primarily southern crusade began behind the scenes of López's expeditions. Publicly, López's agents projected an inclusive image, hoping to attract backing from all parts of the United States. Thus in May 1850, Laurent Sigur's *Daily Delta* summoned youths "from every valley and mountain in the country" to reinforce the expeditionists, who had just landed on Cuba's coast.[11] Privately, however, López's cronies utilized flagrantly sectional appeals when soliciting the support of influential Southerners, dwelling on the likelihood that slavery would end in Cuba unless the filibusters intervened to prevent it.

Ever since Great Britain's abolition of the slave trade in 1807, and especially after Parliament in 1833 passed legislation to free slaves throughout the Empire, Britain had been exerting antislavery pressures on Cuba. In 1817 and 1835 Britain secured Spain's agreement to measures curtailing the traffic in African slaves to Cuba, and in 1840 Britain assigned an outspoken abolitionist as consul in Havana. Spanish officials neither enforced the treaties with Britain nor their own regulations against the slave trade with any consistency. However, several slave insurrection scares occurred in Cuba between 1842 and 1844, greatly alarming the island's slaveowning *criollos*. Furthermore, in 1849 Spanish authorities took under consideration and leaked to the press a proposal to free and arm all the slaves should the Creoles rebel for independence. Instead of intimidating Cuba's slaveowners, this policy only added to their uneasiness. Making matters worse, France liberated its West Indian slaves in 1848, and seemed to have joined Britain's antislavery crusade.[12]

When approaching prominent Southerners, López and his collaborators insisted that filibustering would avert a disastrous setback to slavery that was about to occur not all that far from their plantations. Alluding to the former French West Indies colony of Saint Domingue, where rebellious slaves half a century earlier had massacred many thousands of whites and created the world's first black republic, Haiti, John L. O'Sullivan implored John C. Calhoun, "You are aware of the standing threat of the Spanish Gov't, to make a San Domingo of Cuba if necessary to keep it. The South ought . . . to flock down there in 'open boats', the moment they hear the tocsin." Similarly, O'Sullivan urged that John Quitman command an auxiliary force during López's invasion, "to aid in preserving the social tranquility of the country (I refer to the blacks)," lest Cuba's slaves take advantage of the confusion caused by the filibusters' arrival and revolt for their freedom.[13]

Additionally, López and his associates manipulated the concerns of Southerners monitoring political developments in Washington. The congressional measures known collectively as the Compromise of 1850 admitted California to the Union as a free state without providing for an offsetting slave state. Many Southerners believed that if this pattern continued, northern antislavery leaders might eventually gain the political clout to enact a law or constitutional amendment ending slavery. After all, each new free state would have two senators and at least one representative in Congress. Historians still debate whether López would have annexed Cuba to the United States had his army successfully overrun the island. But he apparently was not above giving Southerners the impression that Cuba, once liberated with its slave system intact, might join the Union. When López and Gonzales visited Quitman in March 1850 and attempted to enlist him in the cause as "general-in-chief," they indicated that he could produce Cuba's "ultimate annexation" to the American Union.[14]

Some Southerners joined, considered joining, or supported López primarily because they viewed his expeditions as benefiting the slave states. John Henderson made this point somewhat abstractly when he urged Quitman to increase his financial aid to López, presenting the matter as "a Southern question" whose "magnitude" could hardly be exaggerated. Other boosters more precisely linked Cuban filibustering to the current sectional disputes. As the press paraphrased the comments of a speaker at a pro-López rally in Jackson, Mississippi, though Northerners had "gained a large preponderancy" in Congress through their dominance of western territories, Cuba would save the South by "restoring the equipoise of the Confederacy." Similarly, a prospective recruit believed that once Cuba applied for admission to the Union as a slave state, Southerners could learn from the reaction of northern congressmen whether there was any hope left for their institution in the United States. If Northerners refused to admit a slave state, Southerners could only expect things to get worse, since the North's "abolition population" would achieve a "graphic increase" in the future.[15]

Southern sectionalism, merely an undercurrent in the López expeditions, played a more causative role in Cuban filibustering after John Quitman contracted with the Cuban Junta in 1853 to command the next liberating army. Cuba's Africanization scare neared its climax that year, as Spanish authorities proclaimed that Africans previously imported illegally ("emancipados") were henceforth to be free. Spain's new captain general and ruler of the island as of December 1853, Juan de la Pezuela, subsequently promulgated decrees that sought to implement this policy, notably by registering Cuba's plantation slaves to determine which laborers had been acquired from slave traders and ought to be liberated (masters presumably would have written documents in the case of slaves legally purchased from other Cubans). Since the emancipados represented a sizable proportion of Cuba's slave population, many persons on and off the island naturally concluded that Pezuela's measures foreshadowed slavery's doom, especially given the arrival in Cuba of thousands of Chinese contract laborers and other signs that slavery was eroding. Pezuela recruited free blacks and mulattos for Spain's army in Cuba. He also initiated policies enabling slaves to hire themselves out and accumulate funds toward the purchase of their own freedom; and he announced an apprenticeship program, by which free Africans would be brought to the island to supplement Cuba's labor force.[16]

Although Pezuela initiated the apprenticeship program to relieve Cuba's labor shortage and apparently did not intend general emancipation, many Southerners jumped to the assumption that Cuban slavery was in its death throes, at grave risk to their own region's labor system. Thus the *Mississippian* complained that Spain, at the bidding of the former British foreign secretary Lord Palmerston, would create "another St. Domingo at our very doors"—"a blow at the institutions peculiar to the Southern Members of the Confederacy." In the U.S. Senate, Stephen R. Mallory of Florida asked that the Committee on Foreign Relations consider a resolution condemning Spain's "settled design to throw Cuba ultimately into the hands of its negro population, and to revive there, within a few hours' sail of our shores, the scenes of San Domingo's revolution." Southerners believed that there would be no way to insulate their own slaves from the transformation in Cuba. News of Spain's policy, as the *Richmond Enquirer* explained, would inspire their own slaves to run away to Cuba or rebel for their freedom.[17]

Sensitive to southern concerns, Secretary of State Marcy, a New Yorker, was eager to investigate Spanish intentions, and to this end he sought the assistance of the American consul at Havana, Alexander M. Clayton, his successor and acting consul William H. Robertson, the minister to Spain, Pierre Soulé, and the minister to Great Britain, James Buchanan. He even dispatched to Cuba a secret agent, Charles Augustus Davis, to discern whether emancipation was truly being effected. Marcy believed that should Spain turn Cuba into "an African Colony given over to barbarism," it would so destabilize the South as to threaten "the repose of the Union." What he learned, however, was not reassuring. Robertson reported that Spain's policies of freeing emancipados and importing apprentices, including white, Chinese, and Indian laborers, indeed would lead to a breakdown of discipline on Cuba's plantations and the ultimate takeover of the island by its "colored population." Davis concluded that Pezuela intended general emancipation, and predicted that his policies would provoke race war and compel U.S. intervention. Soulé warned that "the dream of Lord Palmerston" would "become a reality" as soon as Spain implemented its policy of freeing and enfranchising the emancipados.[18]

Quitman's filibustering plot of 1853–55 was fueled by southern panic about Cuba's Africanization, though a few of his followers, such as the "young man with mustache" who boasted to a fellow passenger aboard a Mississippi River steamer in October 1854 that he was going downriver to join Quitman and gain a sugar plantation, might have hoped to establish themselves as Cuban slaveowners if the expedition succeeded. Quitman informed Benjamin F. Dill, editor of the *Memphis Appeal*, in a letter intended for publication, that "Spain under advice of England has determined to Africanize Cuba," that it was arming Cuban blacks, and that southern "self-preservation" depended on his filibustering to the island. John Henderson likewise publicly charged Spain with endangering the interests of "Southern citizens" and promised that Quitman's filibuster would salvage "the security of the South." After his state's legislature adopted resolutions denouncing Spain's intentions, Senator John Slidell of Louisiana presented them for congressional consideration along with his own proposal that the federal government suspend enforcement of the neutrality laws.[19]

Men volunteered for Quitman's contingent, or offered Quitman material assistance, because they believed themselves to be the saviors of southern slavery against the infection of Cuba's Africanization. Thus the overseer of one of Quitman's plantations announced that he would raise a company of filibusters before Spain's program transformed Cuba into a "howling desert." A judge on the Arkansas Supreme Court, upset with the "English and French policy of Africanization," endorsed the application of an acquaintance wanting to join the invading party. Felix Huston, Quitman's cohort in Texan filibustering two decades earlier and now a Louisiana planter, offered to raise 3,000 men for the expedition and sell bonds on its behalf, because once "the Cortes [Spain's legislature] meets . . . the abolition of slavery in Cuba will be agitated, and there is no time to be lost." Alexander H. Stephens, the future Confederate vice president, predicted that the expeditionists would be on their way to Cuba before Pezuela could ever carry out his planned registration of slaves.[20]

Given the danger of Africanization, Quitman and his collaborators envisioned a three-step process that would stymie Pezuela's scheme as well as enhance southern power in the U.S. government. First, because of their secret preparations, they would catch the Spanish in Cuba off guard with a filibustering strike, and seize the island preemptively before Pezuela carried out his emancipation program. Second, as Quitman explained to a reporter, the filibusters would proclaim Cuba an independent republic and ensure that the new country's constitution guaranteed the perpetual existence of slavery. During this interim stage, Cuba's Creole planters would revoke all prior Spanish legislation tending toward emancipation, purifying the island for American annexation. Eventually, following Texas's precedent of a decade earlier, Cuba would enter the Union as one or more slave states, thwarting the intentions of antislavery Yankees to control Congress. The Kansas-Nebraska Act of 1854, which opened to slavery areas in today's Midwest that had been closed to it by prior congressional legislation (the "Missouri Compromise" of 1820), was at that very time provoking the rise of a new northern political movement, which eventually became the Republican Party, dedicated to preventing any expansion of slavery. Hoping to counter this threat, Quitman's supporters, as the Texas Ranger John S. Ford put it, envisioned Cuban filibustering as a guarantee "for the future extension of slave territory."[21]

Some of the southern filibusters expected, moreover, that commercial advantages would accrue to their region, should they conquer Cuba and eliminate Spain's tariffs and other restrictions that impaired American trade with the island. The Louisiana sugar planter Samuel R. Walker, one of Quitman's most important collaborators, argued that an annexed Cuba would open "commercial eminence" to the slave states: "What wealth will float upon our waters! What a bright gem will she, 'the Queen of the Antilles,' be in the coronet of the South, and how proudly she will wear it."[22]

Quitman and his agents emphasized the enlistment of Southerners, sought financial backing from slaveowners, put their recruits up on a Louisiana plantation before their expected departure, and conceptualized their project in sectional terms. Thus Samuel Walker told Quitman that the "whole South" was "ripe" for his filibuster, and Quitman referred privately to the project as a "great Southern movement." When the Pierce administration enforced the Neutrality Law against the expedition, Quitman and company interpreted its policy as an attack on the South. Pierce, Quitman believed, had fallen under the control of an antislavery faction in his cabinet. Even though his administration had been cognizant for over a year that Spain intended the creation of a "mongrel empire" on America's borders, the president would jeopardize the security of the South and the perpetuity of the Union rather than allow the filibusters to preserve the South's $1.5 billion investment in slavery. Southerners, Quitman believed, should discard their fantasy that northern moderates like Pierce had the will to protect slavery.[23]

Nevertheless, Quitman recruited Northerners for his invading force and drew upon Northerners for monetary and political support. Quitman endorsed the outside of a letter from an Indiana editor, who had previously consulted with him during a visit to Natchez: "communicated to him general outlines—He will write to me whether he will join & with how many men." When visiting New York City in the summer of 1853, Quitman solicited George Bolivar Hall, an acquaintance from the Mexican War, to join the cause. Hall not only agreed to serve but tried to persuade other former New York volunteers who had served in Quitman's division in the Mexican War to do the same. And the expansionist New York shipping magnate George Law provided Quitman with guns.[24]

Quitman, like López, depended heavily upon the services of the Northerner John L. O'Sullivan, who served as an important go-between with Creole revolutionaries in Cuba and Cuban exiles in the United States. O'Sullivan informed Quitman in August 1853, for instance, that he had been getting information in cipher from Havana, and that although Cuban revolutionaries had little money to invest in Quitman's expedition, they hoped to persuade a Spanish officer on the island to declare for Quitman at the time of the filibusters' landing. Presumably this Spanish turncoat would carry with him a large part of Spain's occupation forces. Quitman also drew upon Mike Walsh, a congressman from New York, and the prominent Philadelphia lawyer John Cadwalader, who was elected to Congress in 1854. Walsh raised funds and recruits, sought out transports, and served as one of Quitman's intermediaries with the Pierce administration and politicos such as Senator Stephen Douglas. Cadwalader, on one occasion, referred the Cuban Junta treasurer Domingo de Goicouria to his brother George, a former Mexican War general, along with "the list of what Genl. J. A. Quitman desires" from him.[25]

But Northerners like Law, O'Sullivan, Walsh, and Cadwalader hardly represented a cross-section of the population of the free states. Generally Democratic in their politics, Quitman's northern associates tolerated and even condoned slavery, sometimes expressing views strikingly similar to those of proslavery Southerners. O'Sullivan identified himself on one occasion as a "New York Free Soiler," but he had close ties to slaveowning Cubans because of his sister's marriage to Cristóbal Madan, a wealthy Creole planter, merchant, and member of the Havana Club. O'Sullivan maintained that blacks were inferior to whites, and he opposed giving the suffrage to free blacks in the North. The Irish-born labor advocate Mike Walsh, as Sean Wilentz notes, "regarded political interference with slavery as a violation of democratic rights by Yankee entrepreneurs and as a diversion from the war on capital." Walsh bragged of his services in causing New York Democrats to disassociate themselves from party members "tainted in any way with abolitionism," and cultivated Quitman by arguing that slavery was the "mildest and most rational" form of labor available to govern relations between employers and employees. Walsh wanted Cuba in the Union as a slave state or states. Cadwalader felt that the United States should, if necessary, send troops to Cuba unless Spain disavowed any intentions of abolishing slavery. Even Law, who joined the Republican Party in 1856, maintained privately that immediate emancipation would be a disaster for both whites and blacks, and that if it ever occurred, it should come about gradually as the result of having southern state legislators change local laws.[26]

Furthermore, Northerners as a whole simply had less interest in Cuban filibustering by the mid-1850s than Southerners did. Frederick Law Olm-

sted, writing for the *New-York Times* during a trip to New Orleans in the middle of Quitman's scheme, registered shock at how Southerners had succumbed to the filibustering spirit. He claimed that for every "true gentleman"
whom he met in the South, he encountered two men who were consumed with
"filibustering schemes" and other "sensual and exciting projects."[27]

Quitman's Cuban plot originated in southern apprehensions about slavery,
and it dissolved in 1855 once southern concerns about Cuba's Africanization
were relieved. To be sure, Quitman was induced to cancel the expedition because of interference from the executive and judicial branches of the U.S.
government, as well as intelligence that Spain was prepared to meet any invasion with formidable military resistance. But it is no coincidence that this
Mississippi slaveowner aborted the scheme once it became evident in the
United States that Spain did not really intend to free Cuba's blacks. As early
as May 1854, Captain General Pezuela had announced that his reforms did
not herald a general emancipation. Later that year, José de la Concha replaced
Pezuela and immediately repealed Pezuela's most controversial decrees. In
fact, Concha informed Senator Hamilton Fish of New York during Fish's
stay in Cuba in March 1855 that he would instantly resign his office should
the Spanish government order him to abolish slavery.[28]

From the filibusters' perspective, the very threat of invasion had at least
momentarily saved their white "brothers of the Island of Cuba," as John S.
Thrasher put it privately, "from social death, under the iniquitous plottings of
black European philanthropy." Whatever urgency Cuban filibustering held
dissipated considerably by mid-1855, though Quitman would call for annexation of the island, and caution that Britain's disavowals of its Africanization
plan could not be trusted, from the seat in Congress to which he was elected
later that year.[29]

WHEN SOUTHERNERS, particularly Texans, joined parties invading Mexico
during the antebellum period, they likewise filibustered to render slavery more
secure, though they were not always as open as the Cuban conspirators about
the bearing that their expeditions had on the peculiar institution. Ever since
the Texas Revolution, Mexico, which abolished slavery in 1829, had provided
a haven for Texan fugitive slaves, a number of whom had escaped during the
confusion of the Texan rebellion. In 1850 northern Mexico's runaway black
population grew noticeably with the arrival of Wild Cat, a Seminole Indian
Chief from America's Indian Territory (now Oklahoma). On his initial trip
into Mexico and after a recruiting trip back to the United States that same

year, Wild Cat brought with him hundreds of Seminoles and Southern Kick-apoos, over 200 maroons (quasi-free black American runaways and their de-scendants who had been integrated into Seminole society before the Semi-noles' earlier removal from Florida), and slaves who had absconded from Creek and Cherokee owners in the Indian Territory. In 1855 John Ford esti-mated that approximately 4,000 former slaves in all, worth over $3,200,000, had made their way to Mexico.

In the late 1840s Texan politicians began demanding that the State De-partment negotiate an extradition agreement with Mexico that would allow their constituents to recover their human property. Sam Houston, who him-self had lost two slaves to Mexico's freedom, brought the matter before Con-gress in 1850, and the Texas legislature subsequently passed a joint resolution endorsing extradition. Texan delegates, moreover, introduced the question at the Southern Commercial Convention in New Orleans in 1855. But though the Polk, Taylor, Pierce, and Buchanan administrations all attempted diplo-macy to close the sanctuary, Mexican leaders refused to sign an accord.[30]

Texans would never have rallied so enthusiastically to Carbajal's expedi-tions of the early 1850s had he not promised them a free hand in capturing es-caped slaves. During Carbajal's expedition in the fall of 1851, a notorious slave catcher, Warren Adams, led a simultaneous but unsuccessful Texan attack, endorsed beforehand by the governor of Texas, Peter H. Bell, against the Seminole maroon colony at Monclava in Coahuila and seized a black family before recrossing the Rio Grande.[31]

It is also unlikely that James H. Callahan would have conducted his inva-sion of Mexico in October 1855 without the lure of recapturing runaways. Be-fore the expedition, Texan slaveholders held public meetings at San Antonio, Bastrop, and other communities offering rewards ranging from $200 to $500 to persons returning fugitives to their owners. In July, Rip Ford, who had been deeply involved with Carbajal and John Quitman and hoped to fashion a proslavery, republican government in Mexico, complained to Quitman that the runaway problem had reached its crisis stage, that the epidemic threat-ened slavery far beyond Texas's borders, and that the solution was to conquer Mexico and then use Tampico or some other Mexican port as a base for Quit-man to finally launch his Cuban filibuster. That way, the Mexican and Cuban problems could be simultaneously resolved: "Something must be done for the protection of slave property in this State. Negroes are running off daily. Dur-ing the past week seven slaves left this portion of the country. Let the frontier of slavery begin to recede and when or where the wave of recession may be ar-rested God only knows."

Ford, Callahan, and associated Texans feared that more Texan blacks would abscond to Mexico once they learned of the proximity across the border of Wild Cat's maroons, on lands provided by Mexican authorities. Hoping that the north Mexican cacique Santiago Vidaurri, who had led the insurgency in Coahuila and Nuevo León that helped to overthrow Santa Anna in August 1855, would cut a deal with them respecting the recovery of slaves, Texan slave interests initiated discussions with Colonel Emil Langberg, Vidaurri's intermediary.

Callahan's expedition occurred after these negotiations broke down, though he claimed in what might be called an after-action report to Governor Elisha M. Pease of Texas that one of the Texan agents had procured preliminary authorization from "revolutionary authorities" across the border for his crossing and "the recovery of runaway negroes." During the intrusion, Captain William R. Henry, commanding part of the invading force, attempted unsuccessfully to seize black women and children at the Seminole colony of Nacimiento de los Negros in Coahuila. Not surprisingly, Seminole maroons played a major role in driving off both Henry and Callahan.[32]

Even after Callahan's failure, Texans continued to plan filibusters into Mexico in order to regain former slaves. In February 1856 Ford recommended to a fellow Ranger that they solicit planters on the Brazos River for funds to underwrite a new foray to capture the runaways. Three years later, Henry alerted Governor Hardin Runnels that he had decided to conduct "an Expedition across the Rio Grande near the villages of San Fernando and Santa Rosa, with a view of recovering the runaway negroes belonging to this State." Henry expressed confidence such an expedition would stabilize slavery on the frontier, and that enough slaves could be "rescued" to bring a profit to the expedition's participants.[33]

One filibustering conspiracy deserves remembrance as the most stridently proslavery of all the plots against Mexico, though it never carried out its threatened crossing of the Rio Grande in 1860. The Knights of the Golden Circle, dominated by Texans and led by a Virginian, George Bickley, were named in honor of a proposed slave empire, roughly circular in shape, that would radiate out from Cuba and include not only Mexico and the South but also parts of Central America, South America, and Kansas. Bickley, in a public letter issued from Richmond in July 1860, called on all Southerners to contribute to the Knights one dollar for each slave they owned (and identified agents throughout the region to whom they could forward their donations), so that his adventurers could carry forth their mission of getting Mexico "Americanized and *Southernized.*" Once slavery had been extended into Mexico, Bickley claimed, the South would equal the North in population, have nearly as much territory, and be able to hold its own against the abolitionists.[34]

Those Americans who filibustered into Mexico from California do not seem, at first glance, to have been motivated by the same kind of proslavery intent that drove the invaders based in Texas. True, William Walker had been born and raised in Nashville in the slave state of Tennessee, but his family had been "nonconformist" regarding slavery, if not openly opposed to it, and his father paid wages to blacks who worked as servants in the household. During his prefilibustering stints in California journalism, Walker did work in San Francisco as an editor of the stridently pro-southern *Herald* in 1850–51, but after his Mexican expedition of 1853–54 Walker became identified with the antislavery wing of the California Democratic Party, led by David C. Broderick, and he served briefly on the staff of the *Democratic State Journal* a paper allied with Broderick and published in Sacramento. Still, Walker's decision to apply Louisiana's unique Civil Code of 1825 in his Lower Californian and Sonoran "republics" spread the impression in some circles that Mexican filibustering served the slavocracy, since slavery was allowed by Louisiana law.[35]

Furthermore, Walker's fellow native Tennessean Henry Crabb played a conspicuously proslavery hand in California politics before his thrust into Sonora in 1857, and he may have had thoughts of extending the institution into Mexico. Five years before his invasion, Crabb steered through California's state assembly a fugitive slave law to protect the human property rights of slaveowners then holding persons to labor under loopholes in the constitutional ban on slavery enacted by the state in 1849. Although little is known about Crabb's filibustering companions, one Californian at the time remarked in his diary that they were "said to be all Southern men" and that they intended to "erect another slave state from a portion of Sonora." A letter from Crabb's "surgeon general" written shortly before the expedition suggests that the party indeed attracted proslavery types. The former California legislator Thomas J. Oxley, who died with Crabb, sent his regards in June 1856 to the "black ones" back home in Missouri, and complained that "Blue Blood Yankees" and their "Black Republican" party were seizing control in California.[36]

JUST WEEKS AFTER Oxley registered his complaints about California's antislavery Republicans, perhaps the most prominent among them, the presidential nominee and recent U.S. senator John C. Frémont, turned up at the docks of New York to join a crowd of onlookers seeing off over 400 passengers for William Walker's Nicaragua. Frémont, who had conferred with Walker in San

Francisco before the beginning of the Nicaraguan filibuster and encouraged the project, likely saw in Walker a kindred spirit: a decade earlier, Frémont himself had commanded exploring expeditions by the U.S. Army into Mexican territory in the Southwest that verged on filibustering. Just as importantly, Frémont lacked cause, as Walker reflected in his autobiography, to suspect that Walker intended to promote slave labor in Central America.[37]

Frémont was by no means the only antislavery politician to fall into the trap of condoning Walker during the early stages of the Nicaraguan filibuster. After all, as James R. Doolittle of Wisconsin later explained to the U.S. Senate, Walker took with him to Nicaragua something of a reputation as a "free-State man" who had opposed slavery's legalization in California. Doolittle's comments help explain why the fiery antislavery Kentuckian and Republican presidential aspirant Cassius Clay in June 1856 could uphold the legality of Walker's presence in Nicaragua. Clay even told the former secretary of state John M. Clayton that the United States should aid Walker, so long as he allowed free elections and refrained from war with neighboring states.[38]

Walker's initial restraint about slavery also eased the task of supporting filibustering for manifest destiny's northern Democrats, including Senator Stephen Douglas of Illinois, whose Kansas-Nebraska Act had come under attack throughout the North for facilitating slavery's expansion. Douglas, under heavy private pressure from Walker and his agents, spoke out in the Senate in early 1856 for recognition by the United States of the filibusters' régime, and Douglas also sent Walker a letter of recommendation on behalf of the son of a former U.S. senator, Sidney Breese. Many other northern Democrats felt similarly. At their national convention in June 1856, northern and southern Democrats combined, by a vote of 221 to 38, to pass a party platform plank that announced their sympathy with Walker's efforts to "regenerate" Nicaragua.[39]

Naturally, some Southerners hoped from the outset that Walker would expand their institution to Nicaragua. But during his first year in Nicaragua, Walker had not accommodated their wishes. As a newspaper in Austin lamented in February 1856, the "only drawback" to Walker's régime thus far seemed to be its "want of slaves."[40]

Everything changed once Walker issued a decree on September 22, 1856, legalizing slavery in Nicaragua and began promoting his cause as a means by which Southerners could protect and spread their way of life. As a follower put it in a private letter from Nicaragua that was released in the American press, Walker offered Southerners a "magnificent country" where they could now take their slaves to cultivate crops of cotton, indigo, coffee, and sugar in a frost-free environment. Walker's recruiter Edward J. C. Kewen, during a visit to the

Gulf states that November, predicted that Central America would "bloom and blossom as the rose" once Walker conquered all its states and American Southerners committed several thousand of their slaves to the region.[41]

Although an officer in the filibuster army later claimed confidential knowledge that Walker had intended to revive slavery in Nicaragua from the beginning, it seems likely that he made his decision shortly before issuing the decree, and that he did so because of his régime's desperate plight. For one thing, the U.S. government was stalling on recognizing his takeover of the Nicaraguan presidency; moreover Costa Rica, to the south, had been at war with him since March, and he had been unable to consolidate his hold over large areas of Nicaragua. In July Nicaragua's northern neighbors, Guatemala, Honduras, and El Salvador, formed a military alliance against him. On September 18, just four days before the slavery decree, an enemy army of about 1,800 men initiated the campaign that half a year later would overthrow him. Furthermore, Britain supported the cause of Walker's opponents. Walker seems to have issued his decree in the hope of salvaging his cause with an infusion of southern assistance.[42]

Possibly Walker got this idea from Pierre Soulé of Louisiana, a proslavery former U.S. senator and former U.S. minister to Spain who traveled to Nicaragua that August to finalize arrangements for marketing the filibuster's bonds in the United States. Before visiting, Soulé had been instrumental in drafting the national Democratic Party's plank in 1856 endorsing Walker's efforts to "regenerate" Nicaragua. More revealingly, Soulé argued in a public address, "If, by any chance, Nicaragua should become a part of this republic, the preponderance of the North is gone. . . ." It is not difficult to imagine Soulé pressuring Walker to legalize slavery as a means of boosting Walker's popularity in the South, which of course could only assist those like him who were hawking Nicaraguan bonds in the Gulf states. Nor is it difficult to imagine Walker, given his precarious situation, deciding that he had little to lose by making an all-out bid for southern support.[43]

Whether Walker embraced human bondage for expediency or because he had always been a closet proslavery enthusiast is immaterial, given the stateside reaction to his decree. The gamble generated fresh enthusiasm for his cause among Southerners. John Wheeler of North Carolina, the U.S. minister to Nicaragua, rejoiced, explaining to the State Department that anyone living in Nicaragua for the shortest time would immediately realize that only slaves could cultivate rice, cotton, indigo, cacao, sugar, and other crops there. The Southern Commercial Convention, meeting in Savannah in December 1856, passed a resolution endorsing slavery's expansion into Central America.

Around the same time Felix Huston, a perennial filibuster, alerted an acquaintance that he was thinking of recovering his health in Nicaragua, and,
after judging whether "the reestablishment of slavery is the making of that
country," might well make some investments there.[44]

After his expulsion from Central America in May 1857, Walker further
cultivated his image as southern crusader, hoping to rally support in the slave
states for his later efforts to reconquer Nicaragua. In the speech that he gave
upon arriving in New Orleans, Walker blamed his overthrow on the northern
abolitionists who had turned the United States and British governments
against him in order to prevent slavery from spreading. How unfortunate for
his cause, he remarked sarcastically, that he had been born in a southern state
and could not "consider slavery a moral or political wrong."

Walker kept hammering away at sectional themes until the end of his life.
In an address at Alabama's state capitol in January 1858, he maintained, somewhat misleadingly, that the U.S. government had been friendly to his régime
before his slavery decree. At a banquet in his honor in Richmond that same
month, he couched his return to Nicaragua as a matter "of great importance
to the South." That March, he recommended a former Nicaraguan filibuster
for an Arizona territorial office to Alexander H. Stephens, noting the applicant's "devotion to Southern interests." In July, a paper in Vicksburg, Mississippi, reported Walker as traveling through the eastern part of the state, "trying
to excite sympathy on the 'nigger' question." That October, Walker entreated
a contact in his native state to support the cause, since Tennesseans and other
citizens in the "border slave States" were "sleeping on a volcano" that a new
expedition might help avert.[45]

Walker pushed his proslavery argument the furthest in chapter 8 of his autobiographical account *The War in Nicaragua* (1860). Arguing that only in recent years had "the really beneficial and conservative character" of slavery
gained appreciation in the United States, Walker suggested that the institution permitted society "to push boldly forward in the pursuit of new forms of
civilization" because it put the relations of labor and capital upon a solid
foundation. In Nicaragua, where vast tracts of land had been going to waste,
"the white man . . . [with] the negro-slave as his companion" would displace
a useless "mixed race" and deploy the "supply of constant and reliable labor
requisite for the cultivation of tropical products." While blacks discovered
their "natural climate" in Nicaragua and continued to benefit from an institution that provided them "the ineffable blessings of a true religion," whites
would fashion a "firm and harmonious civilization."[46]

Walker dwelled on why Southerners should help him reconquer Nicaragua. His decree positioned the filibusters as "champions of the Southern States of the Union in the conflict truly styled 'irrepressible' between free and slave labor." By 1856, Walker maintained, it had become evident from developments in Kansas that all future American territory would be reserved for the North's free labor system: immigrants in the North found it easier than Southerners to migrate to western territories; the North's labor surplus guaranteed that persons would be available to move to them. True, President Buchanan and some of his northern Democratic friends had supported the "abstract right" of Southerners to take slaves into the Kansas Territory, but their efforts on behalf of Kansas's proslavery Lecompton Constitution only gave the South a hollow triumph, since antislavery Republicans would never permit Kansas to be admitted under that constitution to the Union. Slavery's field of battle lay in the tropics. The only way to "strengthen slavery," the only way to reverse the Republican Party's attempt to confine slavery and thus gradually destroy it by the miner's "sap," was for Southerners to force their institutions into Central America, creating a buffer zone so that southern slavery would not be entirely surrounded by hostile people devoted to free labor. Those filibusters who had already died from cholera, typhus, and wounds in Nicaragua had "yielded up their lives for the interests of the South." The time had come for southern whites to redeem their sacrifice by implanting slavery "in the natural seat of its empire."[47]

Walker's strategy paid off in endorsements from slavery expansionists. "Gen. Wm Walker made a fine speech at the Capitol this evening," noted Randal McGavock of Nashville, a believer in the "regeneration of Central America by our race," when Walker was lionized by his hometown in July 1857. "We are Walker, Nicaragua, pro-slavery men," proclaimed a Memphis paper in January 1858. Henry Hughes joined eight other slavery expansionists from Claiborne County, Mississippi, in a public letter to Walker a year later, endorsing his "bold and indomitable effort to organize in Central America, a republic founded on the supremacy of a superior race, and on the industrial subordination of an inferior race." Undoubtedly Walker's proslavery stance inspired some of his subsequent southern recruits. A North Carolinian expressed interest in signing up as "a Southern Man, strictly of southern feelings," citing the "duty" the slave states now had to support the filibusters.[48]

Walker's southern boosters, moreover, reacted passionately when his expedition in late 1857 was broken up by Commodore Paulding. Proclaiming filibustering the "moral necessity" of "all progressive races," South Carolina's prolific author William Gilmore Simms denounced Paulding's decision as "brutally insolent." The Navy's intervention, one Georgian congressman complained, constituted "a great wrong done to the South." Alexander H. Stephens, also representing Georgia in the House, maintained privately that the Buchanan administration opposed Walker "because if successful he would introduce African slavery there." A number of Walker's southern supporters tried unsuccessfully to get Congress to suspend or repeal the Neutrality Law in order to facilitate future invasions, and also without success attempted to get Congress on record as opposing Paulding's intervention. Noting that his own state legislature had taken up resolutions condemning Paulding, Edmund Ruffin observed that "the dissatisfaction of Southern men" with the government in Washington had deepened considerably.[49]

After Walker's evacuation of Trujillo, Honduras, during his last expedition, British officials discovered among the papers he left behind a printed preamble for a projected constitution of a "Supreme Grand Lodge of the League of the Red Star, of the United States." In this document, the "friends of the South & her institutions" agreed to join a league pledged to "guard, perpetuate & extend the Institution of 'Negro Slavery,' as the basis of the most solid, durable & beneficial social & industrial system which exists in the world." Walker, to the last moments of his life, had played out on the world stage his understudy role as slavery's expansionist.[50]

GIVEN HOW ENTWINED slavery and filibustering became, it is not surprising that many Americans habitually came to associate the two, assuming that any expedition must have a proslavery design. The *New York Herald* in December 1854, for instance, predicted that because whites would never be able to labor successfully in the Mosquito Coast's sickly climate, Henry L. Kinney would introduce "African servitude" into Central America, perhaps in the process siphoning off the North's unwanted free black population.[51] More significantly, slavery and filibustering became so conflated that Americans projected the expeditions upon facets of the growing rift between North and South over slavery that at least superficially had little to do with invasions of foreign countries. Southern and northern moderates, for instance, cautioned filibustering enthusiasts with some justification that the expeditions provided fodder for northern resistance to the Fugitive Slave Act of 1850 and for John Brown's attack on Harpers Ferry. Antislavery Northerners indeed rationalized their disobedience to the fugitive slave legislation by citing the filibusters' disregard of the Neutrality Law. Further, they accused Southerners of filibustering into Kansas in order to impose slavery upon the contested territory.[52]

Admittedly, filibustering retained some hold on the northern imagination

THE LATE GENERAL WALKER, THE FILIBUSTER.

Harper's Weekly (October 13, 1860) announces the death of America's most famous filibuster.

to the end of the decade, especially in its northern emporium, New York City. In December 1856, months after Walker reinstituted slavery in Nicaragua, William Marcy Tweed served as one of many vice presidents of a rally that raised donations of money, rifles, and food for Walker's faltering cause. *Harper's Weekly*, the next month, hailed him as "this most enterprising of the Northmen," who might still conquer the "cowardly" Central Americans and transform their backward society. "We have again and again called Walker a hero. We shall not take it back," the journal insisted. A year later, after Commodore Paulding's apprehension of Walker, *Frank Leslie's Illustrated Newspaper* in a lead article denounced the Navy for doing the bidding of the British and committing an "anti-American" act.[53] Moreover New York's citizenry, as we have seen, treated Walker as a national hero when he visited.

Nevertheless, slavery so tainted the image of filibustering by the late 1850s that many expansionist Northerners found the expeditions less appealing, and certainly less politically palatable, than they had in earlier years. In a revealing House vote in 1859 brought about by the Paulding affair, twenty-five northern Democrats voted in favor of a resolution endorsing the commodore's intervention, while only twelve northern Democrats opposed his seiz-

ing Walker. Even Stephen Douglas, though he assumed an anti-Paulding position in congressional debates and never denounced Walker's position on
slavery, backed off a bit from the movement, describing himself as "no fillibuster" in one public address and conceding that filibustering had done more
harm than good for U.S. expansion in a Senate speech. It is revealing, moreover, that President Buchanan gloated about picking up political support in
the North at Douglas's expense, because his administration had taken a firm
stance against Walker.[54] And if northern Democrats, members of the most
expansionist and least antislavery Yankee political organization, felt uneasy
about supporting filibustering by the late 1850s, the unease was all the greater
with antislavery citizens and politicians, particularly members of the Republican Party.

Long before Walker's decree of September 1856, abolitionists and freesoilers, detecting the proslavery undertones of filibustering, had instinctively recoiled from the movement. As early as 1849 Lewis Tappan complained to an
English abolitionist on the stationery of the American & Foreign Anti-Slavery Society that the adventurers then gathering on the U.S. coast to invade
Cuba were connected to the hopes of southern slaveholders to annex the island with its slavery system intact. Several years later, the antislavery poet
John Greenleaf Whittier, in a rather remarkable verse, carried the thought
further, suggesting that filibusters serving cotton's interests were as drugged
as Asians under the influence of hashish:

> The man of peace, about whose dreams
>   The sweet millennial angels cluster,
> Tastes the mad weed, and plots and schemes,
>   A raving Cuban filibuster![55]

Narciso López attracted fewer recruits and less backing in New England,
where antislavery feeling was relatively strong, than in the mid-Atlantic states
or the Midwest. Reporting to the State Department at the time of López's last
expedition, a U.S. district attorney in Massachusetts discovered that there
was "no disposition in this part of the country to engage in the unhappy expedition." The relative passivity of New England might be attributed to the
region's distance from Cuba, but antislavery feeling played its part. A paper in
Springfield, Massachusetts, contended that López filibustered to "subserve
the ends of Slavery" and condemned the affair as "one of the foulest, the most
rotten-hearted and detestable" schemes that the American people had ever
originated.[56]

John Quitman's plot of 1853–55 served to confirm the entanglement of filibustering with slavery expansion. Quitman and his followers were so adamant

in their public remarks and writings about the need to prevent Cuba's Africanization and expand southern slavery that antislavery Northerners found it impossible to overlook their priorities. James Redpath, a Scottish-born antislavery reporter for the *New York Tribune*, endorsed Cuba's admission as a slave state in 1854, on the logic that it would at least open up the island to abolitionist agents, whereas the Spaniards had prohibited the Cuban people from being exposed to "Garrisonian goods." Then Redpath traveled south, and encountered such fanatic proslavery militancy among Quitman's followers that he entirely reversed positions: "In one of my letters," he confessed in March 1855, "I said that I would vote for the admission of Cuba even with the Institution of Slavery. . . . I retract that statement. I would not vote for the admission of another slave State on any terms. I have met the Fillibusters here!"[57]

By 1856 most antislavery Americans had simply grown suspicious of all filibustering leaders, and as evidence of their despicability they hardly needed Walker's ruling on slavery. Frederick Douglass, for instance, gave a speech to the State Convention of the Colored People of the State of New York in September 1855, before Walker even seized political power in Nicaragua, in which he accused Walker's band of being the agents of slavery expansionists. Similarly, the *National Era* (Washington) in May 1856 announced its hostility to Walker on the basis of what it assumed were his plans to expand slavery.[58] Walker's decree merely sealed the animosity toward filibustering that had been mounting anyway among antislavery Northerners. John Frémont's campaign songs of 1856 expose the hardening of northern antislavery attitudes around the time of Walker's decree. One of the tunes predicted that "nor'westers" on John Frémont's train would clear the track of filibusters. Another denounced the Democratic candidate James Buchanan, presuming that he would surely support Walker's cause if elected, given his prior tolerance of slavery's expansion.[59]

Naturally, the more Walker embellished his proslavery credentials in the United States after his expulsion from Central America, the more he repulsed antislavery Northerners. Antislavery Yankees by no means opposed filibustering solely for its agency in slavery's extension. Many Northerners genuinely believed filibustering to be a stain on the nation's honor, or opposed territorial expansion in principle. Henry David Thoreau on one occasion condemned America's expansion to the Pacific as a "heathenish" case of what he termed "filibustering." Still, Walker's proslavery position rendered irrevocable the alienation of antislavery Northerners, and especially the New England region, from filibustering.[60]

During the late 1850s antislavery Northerners almost invariably lined up against the filibusters. Senator Charles Sumner of Massachusetts, who became a living martyr for the antislavery cause after his caning in May 1856 by Representative Preston Brooks of South Carolina, applauded Paulding's seizure of Walker in a letter to one of his British contacts in 1858 as the "most creditable" act of Buchanan's presidency. That same year, Governor William A. Newell of New Jersey, a Republican, in his annual message to the state legislature accused Walker's apologists and advocates of wanting to use his expedition for the "extension of slavery." House Republicans voted unanimously in 1859 to endorse Commodore Paulding's intervention.[61]

Throughout the period, moreover, William Lloyd Garrison's *Liberator* issued invective denouncing the "great scoundrel" Walker and his southern supporters. The paper suggested that Walker's opening Nicaragua to slavery meant that the American Union was not worth retaining, and it censured Senator Robert Toombs of Georgia, one of Walker's congressional proponents, for speaking on behalf of "the perfidious, lawless, and filibustering South."

Meanwhile, at their conventions and other gatherings, abolitionists scorned the invaders for extending "the empire of the lash." Franklin B. Sanborn's prologue, performed before the staging of two plays at an antislavery festival in Concord, Massachusetts, presented the character Manifest Destiny attempting to defend Walker as a "Gideon chosen of the Lord" and telling a despondent Slavery to forget his recent loss in Kansas and join in the crusade for Cuba and Nicaragua. Both are then run off stage by the "Genius of America." After William Walker's execution in 1860, the *Chicago Tribune*, a Republican paper, chastised the New Orleans press for lamenting the passing of a pirate whose aim had been the "extension and perpetuation of Slavery."[62]

Antislavery speakers, newspapers, and politicians argued repeatedly that filibusters had exposed themselves as the mere tools of ruthless slaveholding southern aristocrats, often collectively designated the "slave power" or "slave oligarchy," who would stop at nothing to force their way of life upon others. Worse, these southern fanatics had conspired successfully to get northern politicians, notably Presidents Pierce and Buchanan, to support their filibustering lackeys' efforts to spread slavery. Nothing else could explain their success in launching expeditions. Thus the spirited antislavery orator the Rev. Theodore Parker proclaimed that President Pierce and his cabinet had "encouraged" the filibusters, and the black abolitionist Sarah P. Remond told an audience at Warrington, England, in 1859 that the expeditions provided clear proof of "the mass of corruptions that underlaid the whole system of American government." Decades after the Civil War, Frederick Douglass would still be denouncing the filibustering excesses of the slave power.[63]

Most importantly, some antislavery Northerners took this logic one step further, warning that the filibustering conspiracy might well eventuate in the creation of a southern slave empire outside the Union. "Their ultimate object is of course Cuba and if necessary a *Southern* republic," asserted a northern army officer stationed in the Kansas Territory in January 1858 about the Walker expeditionists, claiming that he had inside information about this from a soldier in his regiment with "well known" connections to John Quitman and Pierre Soulé. The filibusters' plans, the Republican congressman Francis P. Blair Jr. told the U.S. House of Representatives that same month, entailed the creation of a "southern slave-holding Republic" should the acquisition of neighboring states fail to allow the slaveholders to dominate the U.S. government. Three years later, while the Confederacy was in its formative stages, the prominent New York lawyer David Dudley Field anticipated that the new country would "enter upon a new career of conquest." After all, he exaggerated, each of the expeditions that had previously "disgraced" the country had sailed from the ports of the Confederate states.[64]

FIELD'S PREDICTION brings us full circle back to Judge Campbell's statement blaming the filibusters for southern disunionism. It should be obvious that many of the expeditions revolved around the issue of slavery's security and expansion, and that Campbell's impressions were shared by antislavery commentators. But is there any evidence for Campbell's charges beyond Walker's hobnobbing with the South's leading fire-eaters at Montgomery and the announced program of the Knights of the Golden Circle that the filibusters intended for their expeditions to destroy the Union?

Certainly many secessionists, notably John Quitman, played a prominent role in filibustering. In 1835, as the temporary governor of Mississippi, Quitman had informed the state legislature that secession might prove the only remedy to northern abolitionism. In 1850–51, while Mississippi's elected governor, Quitman had actually attempted to act upon that threat, calling on the legislature to convene a secession convention. Historians today generally recognize that this "representative man of the filibuster cause," as one reporter identified Quitman, was also one of the Old South's half-dozen or so most prominent disunionists.[65]

Naturally Quitman attracted into filibustering persons who shared his radical proclivities, such as the Georgia probate judge who identified himself as a "fire eater" when inquiring about a slot in Quitman's planned expedition. Judge Cotesworth Pinckney Smith of Mississippi's High Court of Errors and Appeals (and its chief justice from 1851 to 1863), indicted in 1850 along with

Quitman as one of Narciso López's organizers, had joined Quitman in a States' Rights Party supporting South Carolina's nullification of the federal tariff as early as the 1830s, and he was one of Quitman's associates in 1851 in the Adams County Southern Rights Association. Felix Huston, every bit as fanatic in his southern extremism as Quitman, issued a public letter in February 1849 announcing his "utmost confidence in the military strength of the Southern States" and their capacity for forming a "powerful confederacy." The next year he privately urged Quitman, then governor, "Let Georgia or Mississippi take the lead and secede." Quitman's Texas cohort "Rip" Ford would later play a leading role during the winter of 1860–61 in calling Texas's secession convention over Governor Sam Houston's resistance, and he helped to draft Texas's ordinance of secession while serving as a delegate to the convention. One could go on and on in this vein.[66]

Not only did secessionists filibuster, but some filibusters turned up in "Bleeding Kansas" during the mid-1850s, participating in the disruptive territorial events that contributed so powerfully to the ultimate breakup of the Union. W. M. Weaver applied to be an aide-de-camp to John Quitman in the canceled Cuban expedition of 1855, before joining the notorious band of proslavery Kansas colonists led by the Alabamian Jefferson Buford and participating in the "sack" of Lawrence, one of the antislavery communities in the contested territory. One of Weaver's companions in the destruction of Lawrence's Free State Hotel and printing presses, Henry Theodore Titus, had served as a lieutenant in Narciso López's Kentucky Regiment during the Cárdenas expedition of 1850, commanded the Jacksonville, Florida, battalion as a colonel in López's aborted expedition in the spring of 1851, and tried unsuccessfully to serve as a colonel in an expedition to reinforce López during his last landing in Cuba. After participating in the attack on Lawrence, Titus recruited some of his "Border Ruffians" for Nicaraguan service, later that year, defying the warning of one of the territory's newspapers that any exodus of proslavery types to Central America might drain away the very manpower required to impose slavery upon Kansas. Henry Miles Moore, a territorial politician, noted in his diary on December 5 that Titus had that day left for Nicaragua, taking along "about 125 of the Bohoys." The adventurers arrived in early February 1857, and participated in some of Walker's fighting.[67]

Likewise, southern filibusters, as Campbell and others suspected, joined radical Southerners in efforts to legalize and revive the African slave trade. C. A. L. Lamar, a Savannah entrepreneur who was enough connected with the Quitman filibuster to buy and sell Cuban bonds as well as recommend a suitable starting point for the expedition, a few years afterward was indicted by federal authorities for possessing illegally imported slaves as one of the owners of the yacht *Wanderer*—the most infamous American slaving vessel of the 1850s. J. Egbert Farnham, a captain in Walker's Nicaraguan army, suffered arrest as supercargo aboard the *Wanderer*. Appleton Oaksmith, appointed William Walker's minister to the United States in 1856, was arrested and imprisoned in 1861 after trying to board a barque that he owned and had converted into an African slaver. Filibusters and their proponents, including Quitman, the Alabama fire-eater Yancey, and the secessionist Mississippian Henry Hughes of the Cuban Lone Star order, promoted the slave trade in their writings and speeches. William Walker's former second-in-command Charles Frederick Henningsen justified the trade in a private letter, published in a Savannah newspaper in December 1859, almost exactly one year before he came out in a public letter urging secession.[68]

But evidence that secessionists filibustered and that filibustering was linked to other southern radical causes by no means proves that the expeditionists designed their invasions to destroy the Union. In 1856 Walker did insist to his appointee as minister to Great Britain, Domingo de Goicouria, that rather than effect Nicaragua's annexation to the United States, he would create a militarily powerful "compact Southern Federation" that might serve Britain's interest as a barrier to U.S. expansionism. This admission might imply, at first glance, an intent to make Nicaragua part of a post-secession southern empire. But Walker's instructions do not necessarily express his true purposes: they were drafted as propaganda, intended to persuade Britain's cabinet to support his régime as an anti-American measure. After all, before filibustering Walker had not advocated disunion. Although he never sought Nicaragua's annexation to the United States after his rise to power there, this does not prove that his expeditions served a secession conspiracy.[69]

Rather, evidence suggests that southern filibusters hoped to improve the security of slavery by means of the expeditions, so as to render secession unnecessary. Quitman made exactly this point in August 1854 in a letter to Thomas Reed, a lawyer from Fayette, Mississippi, when he argued that once the European powers succeeded in Africanizing Cuba, they would exacerbate North-South disputes over slavery and "very probably eventually crown their scheme by bringing about a dissolution of the Union." Likewise James Longstreet, a native South Carolinian and U.S. Army major, considered organizing and commanding a filibuster into Chihuahua while stationed at Albuquerque in 1860, because "she can very readily be brought in as a slave state."[70]

This generalization holds true also for William Walker's southern supporters, many of whom either were unaware of or discounted Walker's disclaimers of intent to annex Nicaragua to the United States. B. D. Palmer, a student at the University of Missouri who wrote to a friend in March 1857 of his interest in going to Walker's Nicaragua, predicted that as long as northern freesoilers did not get their way, the United States would regenerate, "take possession of Central America," and ultimately fulfill Nature's plan that the "vast continent" should become one nation. Thomas Claiborne, a U.S. army officer from Tennessee, called on an acquaintance to help "Bill Walker," whose success would "ensure the integrity of the whole south." Should Walker fall to defeat, a replacement would have to effect "this necessary acquisition." Certainly the profilibustering Unionist Alexander H. Stephens would never have supported Walker's cause had he suspected that the expeditionary leaders intended secession.[71]

One searches in vain for the "smoking gun," the document or documents proving that the filibusters invaded foreign territory as part of a secessionist plot, and that they consciously intended the disruption of the Union by their activities. Admittedly, many Southerners hoped that these expeditions would expand slave labor. As a Georgia newspaper put it in 1860, "Anglo-Americans" needed to control Mexico, and it would be best if Sam Houston's rumored invasion would push its Indians "into the sea, enslave the negroes and mixed breeds, and let our people try their hand at developing the country." Undoubtedly, too, many of filibustering's southern activists and proponents believed that such conquests would strengthen a southern confederacy should secession occur. But this does not mean that they favored the invasions as a means of expediting disunion. As a self-defined "adherent of southern rights" told Quitman, Cuba's acquisition by filibuster was necessary "for the safety of the South" if the Union remained intact, and would be a vital acquisition if the slave states gained their independence. Likewise, a commentator in a southern periodical rallied support for William Walker's filibusters with the logic that Nicaragua represented "a new State soon to be added to the South, in or out of the Union."[72]

Certainly Walker's discussions with leading fire-eaters at Montgomery in 1858 mean little, without evidence that a conspiracy was truly in the works. For if William Yancey had already enlisted Walker in plans to disrupt the Union, he never clued in his fellow radical, Edmund Ruffin. Ruffin noted twice in his diary during the Montgomery Commercial Convention that he was trying to avoid Walker, whom he considered unsophisticated and vulgar. On one occasion, Ruffin even walked out during one of Walker's addresses on Nicaraguan matters, rather than give others the misleading impression that he was a party to filibustering. Ruffin confessed that he talked to Walker over the

course of the Montgomery convention only because he was the last person introduced to Walker at Yancey's party, and there was simply no way to avoid
conversation without being rude.[73]

IN THE MIDDLE of the national debate in 1858 over Commodore Paulding's
apprehension of William Walker, William Gilmore Simms predicted that
some "final issue," perhaps Mormonism but "possibly filibustierism," would
inevitably produce the desired objective of southern independence. Simms,
more than Judge Campbell, understood the true relationship between filibustering and disunion. Filibustering leaders did not invade foreign domains to
destroy the Union; but the *issue* of filibustering helped to produce secession.
That is, the expeditionists' constant setbacks contributed to the gradual alienation of many Southerners from the Union during the mid- and late 1850s.
Conversely, southern secession might never have occurred had the expeditionists achieved their objectives. As an Arkansas journalist lamented just before Lincoln's election, if Walker had conquered Nicaragua permanently,
"slavery would . . . now present a totally different feature to what it shows,
and the storm now lowering over us, been averted."[74]

This is not to imply that the filibusters commanded majority support in the
South. Had there been public opinion polls in the 1850s, they would probably
have revealed that a solid majority of voters and politicians in the northern-
most slave states were opposed to filibustering, and possibly that a majority
opposed filibustering even in the Gulf South, where the movement was stron-
gest. Although representatives of slave states in Congress voted 52–20 to cen-
sure Commodore Paulding for interfering with Walker's expedition, state legislatures in Virginia, Alabama, and Texas either rejected or tabled similar
motions. Furthermore, in what may have been a Deep South referendum of
a sort on filibustering, John H. Reagan won reelection to his seat in the U.S.
House of Representatives in 1859 by a margin of 7–1 despite making repeated
denunciations of the expeditions during his campaign.[75]

Rather, the point is that southerners might have been more willing to preserve the Union in 1860–61 had the filibusters succeeded in opening permanently new outlets for the expansion of slavery. The filibuster John T. Pickett
urged John Quitman in 1854 to effect the annexation of Cuba and Mexico, so
that Southerners could achieve immunity from "fanatical Northern dema-
gogues" (meaning abolitionists) and thus no longer be dependent for help
upon their "compromising vacillating brethren" (meaning northern Democratic politicians who were not hostile to slavery). But Quitman and others

had not conquered Cuba or Mexico, nor had Walker been able to hold on in Nicaragua.[76]

In attributing blame for their failure, the filibusters and their backers sometimes generically condemned all Northerners for not grasping the necessity and justice of slavery's expansion. The *Louisiana Courier*, for example, editorialized during the Fillmore administration's attempt to repress the López expeditions, "It does not require any thing more than ordinary discernment, to perceive what is the real source of all this opposition, in the North, to aiding Cuba. . . . It is the fear that its independence acquired through private aid from this country could be speedily followed by an application for annexation, which if granted, would add another slave State to the Union." When a mass meeting in Mobile demanded in 1858 that the secretary of the navy put Commodore Paulding on trial for preventing Walker's conquest of Nicaragua, its "prosecutors" specified that at least half of any jury must consist of Southerners. Northern jurors could hardly be expected to dispense justice "without prejudice to this section." But profilibustering Southerners especially fastened on antislavery northern Republicans for their flagrant hostility to the expeditions, and on northern Democratic presidents for enforcing the Neutrality Law in a display of gross insensitivity to the needs of the slave states. Thus Jefferson Davis blamed "black republicanism at the North" for the flow of arms and gold to the Costa Ricans fighting Walker, and Quitman indicted the Pierce administration for caring more about Canadian fisheries than about Spain's threat to Africanize Cuba. When John J. McRae of Mississippi ran for Congress in 1858, he blamed the Buchanan administration for neglecting the National Democratic Party's platform plank of 1856 endorsing Walker's cause, and warned that soon William Seward and his Republican cronies would have so much power in Washington as to prevent the South's ever annexing Mexico, Central America, and Cuba.[77]

Federal crackdowns on filibustering made few, if any, Unionists of Southerners who would otherwise have been secessionists; but they contributed to the radicalization of those who might otherwise have felt more secure about preserving the nation. In January 1858 Ethelbert Barksdale, editor of the *Mississippian*, told Jefferson Davis of his fervent hope as one of the "friends of the Administration" that President Buchanan would "stamp with emphatic disapproval" Commodore Paulding's recent "high handed" termination of Walker's invasion of Nicaragua. During the disunion crisis in 1860, Barksdale promoted secession as a member of the Jackson Minute Men, a radical pressure group in his state's capital. Presumably Buchanan's unwillingness to champion Walker over Paulding had something to do with Barksdale's alienation from his national political party and government between 1858 and 1860, as well as the distancing of other like-minded Southerners from their former national affiliations.[78]

The *issue* of filibustering, moreover, influenced the decisions of President-elect Abraham Lincoln and other Republicans, around the time of South Carolina's secession in 1860, to reject a last-ditch sectional agreement that might have saved the Union. After Lincoln's victory in November, the influential Republican editor Thurlow Weed of the *Albany Evening Journal* proposed that in order to ward off secession, his party soften its ironclad opposition to expanding slavery by permitting the restoration of the old Missouri Compromise line, thus allowing slavery in all U.S. territory below the parallel of 36°30'. The proposal elicited bitter denunciations from Weed's fellow Republicans, but attracted considerable attention throughout the country and helped to germinate the most promising compromise designed by an American political leader on the eve of the Civil War. John J. Crittenden of Kentucky, chairman of a U.S. Senate select committee of thirteen members, on December 18 presented a comprehensive package of proposed resolutions and constitutional amendments, the most significant of which was an amendment stipulating that African slavery would be prohibited "in all the territory of the United States now held, or hereafter acquired, situate north of latitude 36°30'" while "recognized" and "protected" below that line.[79]

Crittenden's proposal aroused considerable enthusiasm among moderates in both the North and the South. But President-elect Lincoln, while willing to reassure Southerners that he would enforce the Fugitive Slave Act and not interfere with slavery where it already existed, informed Republicans in and out of Congress that he would not tolerate any compromising of his party's traditional policy of preventing slavery's expansion. Subsequently, Republicans unanimously opposed the proposal in committee and in a later Senate vote.[80]

Why did Republicans, especially Lincoln, react so negatively to Crittenden's proposal? Republicans found much of Crittenden's intended legislation objectionable, but particularly recoiled from his territorial stipulations. The senator's phrasing about territories "hereafter acquired," they assumed, would not only encourage southern efforts to acquire new slave territory in the tropics through diplomacy or war, but would also initiate a new epidemic of filibustering expeditions. Previously, filibusters had not been certain that Congress would permit slavery in their conquests or incorporate their domains into the Union as new slave states. But Crittenden would guarantee slavery in conquered regions.

Lincoln was most explicit on this point. Instinctively opposed to filibustering, Lincoln had told a political club in Springfield, Illinois, back in 1852 that Spanish authorities in Cuba had been justified in executing López's American followers, since the invaders had implicitly renounced their U.S. citizenship. Not surprisingly, given these attitudes as well as his long-standing commitment to slavery's containment, Lincoln found Crittenden's proposal intolerable. He exhorted Representative Elihu B. Washburne of Illinois on December 13 to prevent any of their "friends" from agreeing to "compromise of any sort" on the territorial matter, because if the proposal passed, "immediately filibustering and extending slavery recommences." Just four days later he informed Thurlow Weed, then considering the possibility of calling a conference of governors to deal with the crisis, that should the Missouri Compromise line be extended, "filibustering for all South of us, and making slave states of it, would follow." The very next day, he used exactly the same language in a letter to yet another correspondent. However, most Republicans needed little prompting on this matter. As a correspondent of Senator Lyman Trumbull of Illinois put it, once the "hereafter" clause became law, "the democracy in company with the disunionists will commence their filibustering for the acquisition of Cuba, Mexico, South America &c."[81]

Filibustering, to be sure, hardly caused the Civil War. But during the late antebellum period, some Southerners became increasingly discouraged about slavery's future in the Union because of the filibusters' constant setbacks; and on the eve of war, northern memories of filibustering helped to stymie a compromise that might have averted the conflict. Had Americans never filibustered, the Union might have weathered the storm.

"COLONEL JACK ALLEN, the filibuster, was in the city yesterday, arranging for a regiment or two to aid the Southern Confederacy," a newspaper in Louisville announced in March 1861, before noting that Allen, a Kentuckian who had already compiled quite a military record, would be an "acquisition" for any army. He had "fought at San Jacinto; was in the Mexican war, and under Lopez in Cuba. He served under Walker in Nicaragua—and ever with gallantry and conceded ability."[1]

Such a résumé should not surprise, given what we have already learned about filibustering careerists. In fact, had the author known more about Jack Allen's past, he might have added that Allen had been indicted for participation in the Carbajal filibusters against Mexico and been involved in the Quitman plot against Cuba.[2] Still, this news item provokes some final reflections about filibustering in American history.

Well before the Civil War, some observers in the United States had believed that filibustering was a spent force. After William Walker's first expulsion from Nicaragua, for instance, the *New York Herald* in 1857 had predicted that "filibustering in behalf of 'manifest destiny' is used up."[3] Such prognostications, as we have seen, were premature. But the coverage of Allen's doings by the Louisville paper makes one ponder the impact of the Civil War on the filibustering movement. Did other adventurers, like Allen, forsake their filibustering ways for Civil War soldiering? If so, was there a filibustering revival after Appomattox? And perhaps most important, what legacy, if any, did manifest destiny's filibusters bequeath to later generations, both in this country and elsewhere?

BY THE TIME OF Abraham Lincoln's election, which occurred after William Walker's death, most of the men who had participated in filibustering had given up all intent of doing so again. Only George Bickley's Knights of the Golden Circle kept the flame alive through the fall of 1860; and around the time of Lincoln's election, most Knights units transformed themselves into paramilitary forces conducting torchlight parades and other activities to intimidate Texans into supporting secession from the Union. After the Texas secession convention's "Committee of Public Safety" appointed Ben McCul-

loch colonel of cavalry, members of the Texas Knights' "castles" joined Mc-
Culloch's march on San Antonio in February 1861. McCulloch's force caused
the U.S. Army's departmental commander in Texas, David E. Twiggs, to surrender all federal forts and other public property in the state to the government of Texas. Knights members elsewhere likewise gave up their intentions
of invading Mexico, folding their organizations into the Confederate cause.
Thus a businessman in Camden, Arkansas, recorded in his diary on April 29,
1861, that the local Knights commander intended to take his company of
some eighty men "into the war."[4]

Gradually, the Knights dissolved as a separate entity in the South, while
reemerging in parts of the North as a much feared but vastly overrated "Cop-
perhead" organization, reportedly conducting subversive activities on behalf
of the Confederate cause. In November 1861 federal authorities arrested
Parker H. French, William Walker's onetime "minister" to the United States,
after he turned up in Branford, Connecticut, with a copy of the constitution
and by-laws of the Knights in his possession. During 1863 people throughout
the lower Midwest panicked over rumors of Knights conspiracies—most of
them spread by calculating Republicans who stood to gain politically from
such reports, since the Knights had links to Democrats favoring a negotiated
peace with the Confederacy. Later, some Union authorities tried unsuccessfully to link the Knights to Lincoln's assassination. Generally forgotten in all
this was the organization's initial filibustering raison d'être.[5]

Meanwhile, other former filibusters took up Civil War soldiering, some of
them as officers in the Union army. William H. Young, editor of Henry L.
Kinney's filibuster newspaper and "attorney general" of his Mosquito colony
government, commanded a Union cavalry regiment in the first year of the
war. Congressman-elect James Kerrigan, who had taken a group of adventurers to Walker's Nicaragua in 1856, also joined the Yanks despite proslavery
tendencies, recruiting the 25th New York Volunteers. After winning election
as its colonel, Kerrigan served in the army until February 1862, when he was
discharged after his arrest and court-martial for being drunk on duty.
Notwithstanding this disgrace, he assumed his congressional seat, becoming
a thorn in the side of the Lincoln administration. Marsh B. Taylor of Lafayette, Indiana, another member of Walker's Nicaraguan force, raised a company for the Union's 10th Indiana Volunteer Infantry Regiment at the start of
the war and rose to the rank of lieutenant colonel. Taylor assumed regimental
command during the battle of Chickamauga after its colonel became mortally
wounded. Some former filibusters served the Union in other ways. A wartime
resident of Galveston, Texas, recalled how a notorious desperado known as

"'Nicaragua' Smith" served as a pilot for Union naval forces arriving at the island in 1862.[6]

Naturally, given the increasingly southern character of the expeditions of the late 1850s, filibusters turned up far more frequently in Rebel ranks. A newspaper correspondent observed early in the war that the "*filibusteros* who filled the world with so much angry declamation a few years ago are figuring prominently in the Southern armies at the present time," and went on to name a number of filibusters who had accepted commissions in the Confederate forces. After the war Charles W. Doubleday, who fought for the Union, recalled that every one of his "old associates of Nicaragua" had been "on the 'other side.'"[7]

During the formative moments of the Confederacy, many onetime filibusters apparently streamed into Montgomery, Alabama (the initial capital of the new government), seeking commissions on the basis of their military experience. Others solicited positions by mail, claiming precedence on the basis of their filibustering credentials. Mary Chesnut recorded in her famous diary on March 4, 1861, "Henningsen the filibuster is here," adding that William Walker's former brigadier seemed to be slipping mentally since he could not remember her husband, a Confederate provisional congressman, ten minutes after they were introduced. On May 5 William Howard Russell, a corespondent for the *Times* of London, observed "many filibusterers" among the guests at his hotel and heard repeated mentions of the Knights of the Golden Circle. Perhaps one of them was that Texas publicist for the Carbajal, Quitman, and Walker causes, Hugh McLeod. Circumstantial evidence suggests that McLeod had earlier joined the Knights. At any rate, he did travel to Montgomery in April, hoping for a commission. Although McLeod did not have immediate success, he received a major's appointment in August and achieved a colonelcy before dying of pneumonia in January 1862.[8]

Elsewhere, former expeditionists organized or joined Southern state forces, sometimes boasting of their filibustering records. A Texan recalled after the war that so many "veterans from Nicaragua sprung up as if by magic" in his brigade's ranks that he suspected many of them of being "parlor" knights who had never really seen service abroad.[9] However, there is ample evidence that many filibustering claims were real enough. In Alabama, for instance, Theodore O'Hara assembled the Mobile Light Dragoons, a unit that in January 1861 played a role in seizing Fort Barrancas, a U.S. Army post at Pensacola harbor. A. F. Rudler no sooner gained a pardon from Honduran authorities in March 1861 for his recent role as second-in-command of Walker's final expedition than he returned to his former hometown, Augusta,

Georgia, and began raising a company for the Southern cause. Around the same time, the habitual filibuster Chatham Roberdeau Wheat came from even further away to fight, hurrying back to North America from Italy. Wheat assembled in New Orleans what became known as the 1st Special Battalion, Louisiana Infantry (which included the Walker Guards, a company consisting of former filibusters), gained election as its major, and then proceeded with his soldiers to join the fighting in Virginia—where on June 27, 1862, he died after taking a wound in the battle of Gaines's Mill. Way out west, Brigadier General Henry Hopkins Sibley appointed Samuel "Nicaragua" Lockridge as major of the 5th Texas Mounted Volunteers, part of the brigade that he assumed would soon conquer New Mexico for the Stars and Bars and eventually take possession of California and northern Mexico.[10]

Several former filibustering activists, including the Cuba plotters Allison Nelson and Gustavus W. Smith, William Walker's expeditionist Birkett D. Fry, and Elkanah Greer of the Knights of the Golden Circle, achieved general rank in the Confederate service. Ambrosio José Gonzales, who had married the daughter of a South Carolina planter in 1856, joined General P. G. T. Beauregard as a volunteer aide-de-camp during the Confederate assault on Fort Sumter, played a key role in organizing southern defenses on the South Atlantic coast in the early stages of the war, and on June 8, 1862, received a colonelcy from the Confederate war department. Also reaching that rank was Harry Maury, the perpetual filibustering ship commander, who finally got the land action he had thought of seeking in Mexico at Dixie battle sites like Murfreesboro and Chickamauga. Other filibustering veterans served the Confederacy in civilian capacities. John Pickett became the Confederate State Department's commissioner to Mexico. John L. O'Sullivan applied for Confederate citizenship and traveled to London, where he published pro-Rebel propaganda. John Thrasher was affiliated with the Southern Associated Press, a Confederate newspaper organization.[11]

However, former filibusters compiled a mixed record at best as Confederate officers, and their short-lived nation paid a diplomatic price for whatever military advantage it gained from having these adventurers in its army ranks. By the time of the Civil War, many foreign observers had come to see filibustering as more of a southern phenomenon than an American one, and such perceptions disadvantaged Confederate efforts to muster support from other countries during the war. The Guatemalan minister Antonio José de Irisarri, for instance, informed Secretary of State William Seward in October 1861 that there was "no foreign Nation which can have less cause for sympathy with the enemies of the American Union, than the Republics of Central

America, because from the Southern States were set on foot those filibustering expeditions."[12]

Naturally, Union diplomats tried to capitalize on such memories. In northern Mexico, the Union consul C. B. H. Blood at Monterrey cautioned Santiago Vidaurri, the pro-Confederate governor of Nuevo León and Coahuila, that by cooperating with Texans he was dealing with "rebels and filibusters" of a lower order than "uncivilized Indians." The North's chargé d'affaires at Madrid, Horatio Perry, similarly emphasized in his dealings with the Spanish "the connexion of the principal actors in the present rebellion with former filibustering schemes against Cuba." Vidaurri, who had allowed Confederates to evade the Union blockade by exporting cotton through ports under his control and even approached Southern authorities about amalgamating his domain into the Confederacy, brushed off Blood's caveat. Perry, moreover, had only limited success with such tactics in Spain, where a Confederate diplomatic counteroffensive convinced Spanish authorities that Southerners no longer coveted Cuba. Although Spain never granted recognition to the Confederacy, it did allow Confederate blockade-runners, and sometimes privateers, to utilize Puerto Rican and Cuban ports.[13] Still filibustering's legacy did imperil Confederate relations with Mexico, as well as with the governments of Central American states.

The Confederates' choice of a former filibuster as commissioner to President Benito Juárez's central Mexican government was especially disastrous. On one occasion following his arrival at Mexico City in July 1861, Pickett hot-headedly threatened Mexico's foreign minister that "30,000 Confederate diplomats" might cross the Rio Grande. Pickett was upset at the time over unofficial reports that Mexico had agreed to allow Union forces to traverse Mexican territory in an effort to secure Arizona against Confederate occupation. But it was stupid to provide Mexican officials with a veiled reminder of Southern filibustering. Before the year was out, for this and other reasons, Pickett suffered arrest and then expulsion from the country.[14]

None of the Central American states recognized Confederate independence; and some of them adopted anti-Confederate policies. For example, Guatemala banned the export of supplies to Confederate ports, and Honduras issued a decree banning Confederate privateers from its ports. The late antebellum South's dominance of filibustering may not have been the sole explanation for these policies, but it certainly was a contributing factor.[15]

THE CIVIL WAR, therefore, swallowed up many of America's filibustering veterans. Yet the fighting only temporarily interrupted America's filibustering habit. The war had barely ended when "Fenians" began leaving U.S. soil for attacks on the Canadas and Britain's other North American provinces.[16] Back in March 1858, at a timberyard in Dublin, Irish nationalists had founded the Irish Revolutionary Brotherhood to promote the cause of freedom from British rule. That fall, the agitator James Stephens crossed the Atlantic to found a U.S. branch of the movement, at Tammany Hall in New York, called the Irish Revolutionary Brotherhood in America, a name changed the next year to the Fenian Brotherhood (after the leader of a militia group in pre-Norman Ireland). Fenian membership grew to about 10,000 by the end of the Civil War, about which time Stephens and his associates began recruiting volunteers—many of them naturalized Irish immigrants who had served in the Union army—for filibustering expeditions. As with prewar filibusters, many recruits joined up more for adventure and gain than for the larger cause at stake. "And we'll go and capture Canada," explained a line in the Fenians' marching song, "for we've nothing else to do."

The Fenian organizers hoped to conquer British North America as a base for privateering ventures that might pressure Britain into conceding Irish independence, or, if that failed, to provoke an Anglo-American war that might play into the Irish nationalists' hands. So in 1866 Fenian leaders, including the onetime Nicaraguan filibuster and ex-congressman James Kerrigan, launched several attacks on Canadian territory.

That spring, several hundred Fenians plotted to capture Campo Bello, a coastal island in the "Maritime Provinces" near New Brunswick's border with Maine, and a small party of expeditionists temporarily occupied nearby Indian Island. But they lost their nerve after U.S. customs officials intervened and temporarily impounded their arms, and eventually they vacated the border area. A more serious intrusion occurred beginning the night of May 31, when some 1,000 Fenians crossed the Niagara River by canal boats. They remained on Canadian soil until June 3. Once a U.S. gunboat cut off reinforcements, the invaders tried to retreat to U.S. territory, only to be stopped midriver by U.S. authorities, who took them prisoner. Days later, General George Meade and other federal authorities broke up yet another Fenian invasion, this one directed at Montreal. The few filibusters who evaded arrest and crossed the border encountered an unfriendly reception from British regulars and Canadian volunteers, and they were forced to flee back to U.S. territory.

Several years later, the Fenians launched another series of assaults. In 1870 the U.S. government broke up a crossing near Franklin, Vermont. Then in

October 1871 the defrocked priest "General" William B. O'Donoghue and the longtime Fenian officer John O'Neill led forty-one men armed with breech-loading rifles out of St. Paul on an invasion of Manitoba. They occupied the Hudson's Bay Company's trading post at Pembina, but U.S. regulars from nearby Fort Pembina crossed the border in pursuit and broke up the invasion, confiscating arms and ammunition and taking thirteen of the filibusters into custody.[17]

The Fenian expeditions did not achieve their purpose, as the adventurers neither conquered Canada nor liberated Ireland. Irish independence would be deferred until 1937. However, the Fenians triggered new neutrality proclamations (as well as renewed charges of presidential complicity in filibustering), and they proved an irritant in Anglo-American relations for several years.[18]

By the time Fenianism petered out, filibusters were on the move southward again. Motivated by the outbreak in 1868 of renewed revolution in Cuba against Spanish rule, Cuban émigrés for the next several years sent munitions and men from U.S. ports to assist the revolutionary cause. One of the Americans involved in these filibusters was Thomas Jordan, a graduate of West Point and Mexican War and Confederate veteran who rose to the rank of chief of staff to the nominal president of the Cuban insurgents, Carlos Manuel de Céspedes. Even after the "Ten Years War" ended with Spanish rule intact, the Cuban exile community in the United States continued planning filibusters, and supported several expeditions in the early 1880s. Filibustering activity revived one more time when Cuba again erupted in insurrection in 1895. These invasions helped to sustain the cause until 1898, when the United States intervened to end Cuba's colonial status in the Spanish-American War.[19]

Filibusters in the late nineteenth century and the early twentieth also looked toward Mexico, Honduras, and Nicaragua. In 1888 the Order of the Golden Field, an organization based in Los Angeles with branches in Arizona and Texas, intended to conquer Lower California and declare it a republic. Although this scheme fell through because of press coverage, the Order renewed its plotting with the backing of an English syndicate that owned millions of acres in the peninsula. Press exposure and surveillance by U.S. and Mexican agents ultimately caused the cancellation of an operation scheduled to begin on August 1, 1890. In 1911 several filibustering parties, with support from the Industrial Workers of the World, crossed the border into Baja California in an effort to help Mexican revolutionaries overthrow the régime of the longtime dictator Porfirio Díaz. After one of the groups captured Tijuana, then a small village, the filibuster leader Caryl Ap Rhys Pryce, a native Welsh-man, tried to make money off the occupation by charging admission fees to American tourists and taxing the profits of gamblers from southern Califor-nia who had begun operations during the occupation. After Díaz's fall from power on May 24, 1911, Mexican military forces chased those filibusters still remaining in the country back across the U.S. border.[20]

Customs officials at New Orleans in March 1899 stopped more than one hundred adventurers from beginning an expedition against Honduras via Guatemala, by temporarily withholding clearances to two steamships and re-moving suspicious passengers from the vessels before their departure. After the turn of the century, many U.S. adventurers took part in Central America's internecine wars, especially in Nicaragua and Honduras. Although most of these men traveled singly to the region as mercenaries, some left U.S. ports as members of armed filibustering parties. The former Honduran president Don Manuel Bonilla and the Mississippi adventurer Lee Christmas, for in-stance, loaded twenty men aboard the onetime U.S. naval vessel *Hornet* in 1910 at New Orleans, fooled U.S. surveillant agents by hanging out at a local bordello, and then rushed by yacht to Ship Island. There the plotters boarded the *Hornet*, took cases of rifles, ammunition, and a machine gun on board, and set out for Honduras as part of an ultimately successful campaign to restore Bonilla to power. In February 1911 a federal grand jury in New Orleans in-dicted Bonilla, Christmas, and others for violating the Neutrality Act.[21]

Not surprisingly given the frequency of such expeditions, filibustering re-mained within the American vernacular even as the term incurred its modern legislative meaning. In October 1869 the *New York Herald* printed a story with the headline "Great Filibustering Expedition Off for the Coast," describ-ing how a steamer crammed with Cuba-bound adventurers had left port, run a gauntlet of federal forts and revenue cutters, and escaped to the coast of Florida, where she would link up with other filibustering vessels headed for the island. Similarly, Lydia Maria Child railed against President Ulysses S. Grant's plan to annex the Dominican Republic as a "filibustering project."[22]

Filibustering also maintained enough of a foothold in popular culture for a Boston publisher to bring out a young-adult novel (based in part on Walker's Nicaraguan campaigns) with "filibusters" in its subtitle. In 1904 M. Witmark & Sons published "The Filibuster: A Comedy-Opera," a 146-page score for a three-act performance. Its twenty-seven numbers included "The Filibuster," with lyrics explaining that there was something in the blood that made certain men filibuster, and that they loved "liberty and equal rights for all—No matter what pedantic laws may say about it." Around the same time,

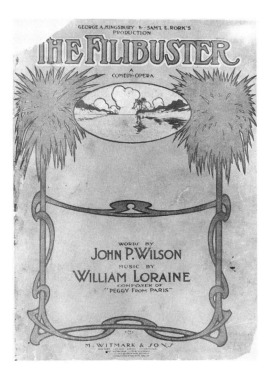

Cover page of score for
"The Filibuster: A Com-
edy-Opera." (Courtesy of
the Harris Collection of
American Poetry and Plays,
Brown University Library)

filibustering's Lost Cause merged into the Confederate Lost Cause. James C.
Jamison, a onetime captain in William Walker's "First Battalion of Light Infantry" as well as a former Confederate soldier, published a piece about
Nicaraguan filibustering in the magazine *Confederate Veteran*, the most important organ of Dixie's surviving soldiers.[23]

As before the Civil War, several authors of adult fiction became involved
with filibusters at either the experiential or the literary level. During Reconstruction, the Freedmen's Bureau agent John W. De Forest featured a hard-
drinking, mustached, native Virginian and confessed former filibuster Colonel
John Carter in *Miss Ravenel's Conversion from Secession to Loyalty*, a novel
about the Civil War largely based on the author's experience in the Union
army. De Forest probably picked up a lot of gossip about filibustering while
serving as a captain in the 12th Connecticut Infantry during General Benjamin Butler's occupation of New Orleans, for the book is loaded with asides
that only a filibuster insider or an unusually avid reader of prewar newspapers
would know, even though it misleadingly alludes to William Walker as fighting
in Cuba. One senses the López, Quitman, Walker, and Reneau conspiracies

virtually coursing through De Forest's passages about a character whom he
appropriately labels a "Dugald Dalgetty." De Forest relates, for instance, that
many antebellum filibusters were ignorant of their intended destinations, that
organizers of expeditions attracted West Point graduates and U.S. Army regulars with their commissions, and that prewar filibusters tried to "bully" the
White House's "venerable public functionary" (President Buchanan) into ap-
proving their doings. While aboard ship en route to New Orleans, Carter even
drops the names of some of the movement's actual collaborators in a moment
of nostalgia that also evokes filibustering's outrageous romanticism and im-
perialistic excess:

> Three years ago I expected to take a regiment or so across this gulf on a
> very different errand. I was, by (this and that) a filibuster and pro-slavery
> champion in those days; at least by intention. I was closeted with the
> Lamars and the Soulés—the Governor of South Carolina and the Gover-
> nor of Mississippi and the Governor of Louisiana—the gentlemen who
> proposed to carry the auction-block of freedom into Yucatan, Cuba, the is-
> land of Atlantis, and the moon. I expected to be a second Cortez. . . .
> I might have been monarch of all I surveyed by this time, if the world had
> turned as we expected.

De Forest informs us, just as an authentic Knight of the Golden Circle might
have confided to a comrade during the war, that the "arch conspirators" of the
scheme had aborted the invasion once it became apparent that Abraham Lincoln would win the presidency, and that they would be needed for the cause of
Southern independence.[24]

Certainly some of the most prominent novelists of the following decades
addressed filibustering in their writings. Mark Twain recollected adventurers
whom he had known in his autobiography, including a onetime major under
Walker who taught dueling to a neophyte in Virginia City, Nevada Territory,
during the Civil War. The novelists Stephen Crane and Richard Harding
Davis boarded separate filibustering vessels bound for Cuba in the winter of
1896–97, in order to report the Cuban revolution for newspapers in the United
States. Crane's piece in *Scribner's Magazine* in 1897, "The Open Boat," drew
upon his unsuccessful voyage, which ended with his vessel sinking off the
Florida coast and Crane escaping to shore in a dinghy. That same year, Crane
published "Flanagan and His Short Filibustering Adventure" in *McClure's
Magazine*. Davis's writings give filibusters plenty of attention. The narrator
of the fictitious *Captain Macklin: His Memoirs* (1909), who joins a force of insurrectionary Liberals in Honduras as a soldier of fortune, has to overcome

his cousin Beatrice's complaint that he is turning into a filibuster. On his voyage to Central America, Royal Macklin fantasizes that he is on a filibustering ship trying to escape from a U.S. man-of-war; and Macklin discovers upon arriving at the Liberal encampment in Honduras that a major in the rebel army had served under William Walker when only a boy. Davis's *Real Soldiers of Fortune* (1911) includes an entire chapter about Walker, as well as a justification of filibustering methods. Around the same time that the book appeared, newspapers in the United States published false reports that the novelist Jack London was trying to join filibuster forces then in Mexico, and that he had been taken into custody by Mexican authorities.

ON JULY 28, 1986, almost exactly 130 years after William Walker's inauguration as "president" of Nicaragua, U.S. authorities arrested a band of fourteen people in Louisiana, including a wheelchair-bound forty-five-year-old woman, for plotting an airborne invasion to aid dissidents in overthrowing the leftist government of Suriname in South America. According to newspaper reports the reputed leader of the plot, Tommy Lynn Denley, claimed that he had been hired by the government of the Netherlands and encouraged in his enterprise by several unnamed U.S. senators, and that some onetime Navy Seals were also involved. Agents from the FBI and the Customs Service broke up the conspiracy with the help of wiretaps, arresting thirteen of the plotters while they were on their way to a small airport at Hammond, Louisiana (north of New Orleans), where a chartered D-3 aircraft was waiting with guns and ammunition already on board.

Although federal officials initially charged the suspects with violating the Neutrality Act, they eventually allowed all but four of the accused to plead guilty to lesser charges. As had been their practice before the Civil War, federal authorities were far more interested in going after ringleaders rather than their recruits. By September 18 all the defendants had entered guilty pleas. On November 5 a federal judge sentenced Denley to two thirty-month prison terms (to run concurrently) and three defendants to lesser terms in federal prison, while he agreed to suspend the sentences of nine others, stipulating that they be placed on three years' probation.[25]

These arrests suggest the survival of filibustering into recent decades, as well as its shifting targets. Indeed, the Suriname plot was hardly the only U.S. filibuster of the Cold War. Five years previously a group of ten American adventurers—a majority reputedly with Ku Klux Klan and neo-Nazi connections—had gathered arms, ammunition, maps, mosquito repellent, and other equipment for an invasion of Dominica, a tiny banana-exporting island in the Caribbean. In that instance, the FBI broke up the plot after being tipped off by a ship captain who the adventurers hoped would take them on the expedition.[26]

Back in 1967, federal customs agents, assisted by local officials, had seized seventy-six persons at Coco Plum Beach in the Florida Keys. These adventurers, seized in the act of loading munitions onto a tiny vessel, planned to overthrow Haiti's infamous dictator "Papa Doc" François Duvalier, with the idea of afterward using Haiti as a base for operations across the Windward Passage against the communist regime of Fidel Castro in Cuba. Their commander Rolando Masferrer Rojas, a Cuban exile and onetime strongman for Cuba's former dictator Fulgencio Batista, bitterly complained after his surrender that the arrests were absurd. Why should the U.S. government oppose his attempt to fight communists ninety miles from Florida, when it was doing that very thing ten thousand miles distant in Vietnam? That November, a federal jury took but two hours and fifteen minutes to convict six of the conspirators, only one of them an American, for conspiring to violate the neutrality laws.[27]

But if filibustering remains a part of America's evolving story, its history has slipped from public memory. As late as 1948, when reporting on the activities of a group of adventurers known as the "Caribbean Legion" that was trying to overthrow dictatorships in the Caribbean basin, *Time* magazine reported that the U.S. State Department intended to oppose "filibustering" in the area. But one sifts in vain through press coverage of the Suriname and Dominica plots for the term "filibuster," or even background stories about America's filibustering tradition or the origins of the Neutrality Act. By the late twentieth century, Americans had come to regard such occurrences as bizarre and idiosyncratic, forgetting their former frequency and importance. Thus, the federal judge who presided over the case of the Suriname plotters reportedly exclaimed at their sentencing, "I've been on the bench 20 years and this is about as far out a case as I've ever heard." Just about every American filibustering expedition, a historian might retort, has been "far out."[28]

In 1911 Richard Harding Davis lamented in *Real Soldiers of Fortune* that "to members of the younger generation the name of William Walker conveys absolutely nothing." Already, America's antebellum filibusters were slipping from public memory, and few efforts were being made to preserve their story or relics for later generations. Some years later, fittingly, the *Mobile Register* related how an electric lighting company worker in the city doing repair work had stumbled upon a rusting sword lying in the street. Its gold mounted scabbard bore the inscription "Col. Louis Lay to Captain Harry Maury, Nicara-

guan navy." While one would not want to draw too much significance from
the discarding of a single item of filibustering's material culture, the incident
nonetheless speaks as a metaphor to Davis's complaint.[29]

Since the early twentieth century, Americans have developed a collective
public amnesia about America's pre–Civil War adventurers, despite the efforts
of historians to reconstruct their story. Most of the filibusters, such as Henry
Crabb, Henry Kinney, and John Quitman, are entirely unknown names to the
American public, even its most educated elements. William Walker's story received a bit more play in the twentieth century, but nothing commensurate
with his historical significance.[30] Ignored by television and film, rarely recalled at historical sites and museums, filibusters have virtually disappeared.
Forgotten is the cumulative effect that these adventurers had on American
politics, law, diplomacy, and popular culture in the years before the Civil War.

Manifest destiny's filibusters, it would seem, have had a far more profound
impact on historical memory in the countries they invaded than in the nation
that produced them. On April 6 every year, Caborca in the Mexican state of
Sonora puts on a fiesta to celebrate the anniversary of the defeat there in 1857
of Henry Crabb's invaders. Tourists visiting Caborca take in the mission La
Purísima Concepción de Nuestra Señora, whose exterior still bears holes
from the filibusters' bullets. An obelisk on Cuba's northern coast erected in
1951 by cadets of the Cuban naval academy identifies the spot where López
landed during his fatal expedition one hundred years earlier. Certainly the
United States lacks filibustering icons comparable to the Republic of Cuba's
national flag: ever since gaining independence in 1902, Cubans have flown
that designed for López's plot of 1850. Ironically, given Cuba's hostile relations with the United States throughout much recent history, its one white
star on a red background—itself imposed over a background of blue and
white stripes—harkens to the lone star of the Texas Republic and Texas's
eventual incorporation into the United States.[31]

Bitter memories of filibusters especially persist in Central America.
Walker's invasions significantly affected Central American political culture,
especially in the decades immediately following the expeditions, but also into
modern times. Since the filibusters had initially been invited to Nicaragua by
the country's Liberal Party, the net effect of Walker's aggressions was to discredit liberal political movements throughout the isthmus. Before the expeditions, many Central American liberals had shared a faith in the beneficence of
Anglo-American ideologies and institutions. But Walker, as Lowell Gudmundson puts it, disabused liberals "once and for all" of such notions, while
conversely strengthening conservative ideologies and institutions within Cen-

The Mission La Purísima Concepción de Nuestra Señora. (Photograph by Donald L. Parman, Purdue University Department of History, 2001)

tral American states. Guatemala and Costa Rica, for instance, maintained much larger military establishments after Walker's expulsion than they had before his arrival. In Nicaragua, the Conservatives maintained a hold on political power until 1893.[32]

Over the long haul, Walker's expeditions fostered Central American nationalism and anti-Americanism. Despite living in different countries, Central Americans came to refer to the united military effort they mustered against the filibusters in 1856–57 as their "National War." Modern Costa Ricans, moreover, celebrate Juan Santamaría as their national martyr for his bravery in April 1856 while fighting the Americans at Rivas, Nicaragua. Given orders to set a building on fire that was occupied by filibusters, Santamaría, despite taking a bullet in his right arm, carried out his instructions. Eventually he suffered a mortal wound in the effort.

Today, one visits Costa Rica's central valley by flying into the Juan Santamaría International Airport, and perhaps one later views the exhibits at the

Juan Santamaría Museum in the nearby town of Alajuela. In the capital of San José, in the middle of the largest park in the city, stands Costa's Rica's national monument, depicting how the united republics of Central America drove away the filibusters. Across a street from the park is a statue of Juan Santamaría, holding the torch that set the filibuster position ablaze.[33]

Walker's legacy, as one might expect, holds special meaning in Nicaragua, where schoolbooks give considerable play to how Central American resistance reversed his conquest of the country. President Violeta Barrios de Chamorro, in her autobiography, published in 1996, recalled that her parents visited her in boarding school to celebrate "the *Fiestas Patrias*, the holiday in which we commemorate our independence and the defeat of the American invader William Walker." No wonder, given such memories, that Nicaraguans reacted so strongly in February 1988 when the surrealistic Universal Pictures release "Walker," starring Ed Harris as the filibuster, opened in Managua. The film had flopped at box offices in the United States. But people in Managua turned out in droves to see it, incredibly paying in many cases more money for their admission than they earned for an entire day's labor.[34]

Throughout the twentieth century, in fact, Nicaraguan revolutionaries and leftists used Walker's filibusters as a frame of reference for revolutionary and often anti-American activities. Augusto César Sandino, who from 1927 to 1933 led insurgent forces against U.S. Marines occupying Nicaragua, constantly found inspiration for his resistance in Walker's story. As one scholar puts it, for Sandino Nicaragua's enemies "included not only the Wall Street bankers and the U.S. government, but also the American people, personified by Gen. William Walker." Sandino regularly referred to American "pirates" and "freebooters," and considered the marines an "avalanche of Walker's descendants" upholding the cause of U.S. imperialism. In one of his battle accounts, Sandino reported how his men inflicted "thirty-two casualties upon the filibusters" during a two-hour skirmish.[35]

Similarly, when Nicaragua's ruling leftist Sandinistas in the 1980s confronted the Reagan administration's efforts to topple their régime, they drew lessons and inspiration from earlier resistance to Walker. The Sandinista leader Daniel Ortega, addressing the United Nations General Assembly in 1983, recalled how "William Walker and his mercenaries" had invaded Central America in 1855. Ortega claimed that the Sandinistas' ascent to power was the result of a "long struggle against U.S. domination, which began in 1855 against Walker." Another Sandinista leader reminded a Peruvian journalist how the Nicaraguan people had "risen up" to defeat Walker, and explained they would do so again if the Reagan administration intervened militarily in their country. One Sandinista partisan commented in a later autobiographical account that he was following in the footsteps of his great-grandfather, who had "fought in the famous battle of San Jacinto, against the filibusterers of William Walker."[36]

IN DECEMBER 1855, at the height of America's filibustering epidemic, *Frank Leslie's Illustrated Newspaper* imagined the day when Henry Kinney's "name will be ornamented . . . in the founding of a future empire." But neither Kinney nor any of his filibustering peers conquered anything for very long, and they left a quite different legacy. As we have seen, these criminals from manifest destiny's underworld instead stalled America's territorial and commercial expansion, contributed to their own country's near-destruction in the Civil War, and tarnished the reputation of the United States throughout much of the Western world for a long time afterward. Modern Americans may find it convenient to overlook this ugly chapter in the nation's past. But the descendants of filibustering's victims, it would seem, remember. In at least some parts of Latin America, one could still say, as a British author did in the first words of a historical romance published in 1862, "Who has not heard of the filibusters?"[37]

Abbreviations

ACdlB	Angel Calderón de la Barca
AO	Appleton Oaksmith
BRBM	Beinecke Rare Book and Manuscript Library, Yale University, New Haven
Con Print	Kenneth Bourne and D. Cameron Watt, eds., *British Documents on Foreign Affairs: Reports and Papers from the Foreign Office Confidential Print*
DAB	*Dictionary of American Biography*, 10 vols. (1927–36; reprint, New York, 1964)
DAC	*Daily Alta California* (San Francisco)
Dipl Corr	William R. Manning, comp., *Diplomatic Correspondence of the United States: Inter-American Affairs, 1831–1860*, 12 vols. (Washington, 1932–39)
DJ	Department of Justice
DS	Department of State
DU	William R. Perkins Library, Duke University, Durham, N.C.
DW	Daniel Webster
FLIN	*Frank Leslie's Illustrated Newspaper*
FO	Foreign Office, Great Britain
H. Ex. Doc.	*House Executive Documents*
HML	Hagley Museum and Library, Wilmington, Del.
HSP	Historical Society of Pennsylvania
HU	Houghton Library, Harvard University, Cambridge, Mass.
JAQ	John Anthony Quitman
JB	James Buchanan
JMC	John Middleton Clayton
LC	Library of Congress, Washington
MDAH	Mississippi Department of Archives and History, Jackson
M&P	James D. Richardson comp., *A Compilation of the Messages and Papers of the Presidents*, 20 vols. (New York, 1897–1911)
ML	Miscellaneous Letters
NA	National Archives
NODP	*New Orleans Daily Picayune*
P&C	James J. Barnes and Patience P. Barnes, eds., *Private and Confidential: Letters from British Ministers in Washington to the Foreign Secretaries in London, 1844–67* (Selinsgrove, Pa., 1993)

PDW   Kenneth E. Shewmaker and Kenneth R. Stevens, eds., *Papers of*
               Daniel Webster: Diplomatic Papers, 2 vols. (Hanover, N.H., 1983,
               1987)
PRO   Public Record Office, Great Britain
RG   Record Group
S. Ex. Doc. *Senate Executive Documents*
SFDH   *San Francisco Daily Herald*
SHC   Southern Historical Collection, University of North Carolina,
               Chapel Hill
SHQ   Southwestern Historical Quarterly
SquadL   Letters Received by the Secretary of the Navy from Commanding
               Officers of Squadrons, Record Group 45 (Department of the Navy),
               M89, National Archives
TSLA   Tennessee State Library and Archives, Archives and Manuscripts
               Section, Nashville
UT   Center for American History, University of Texas, Austin
WDNI   *Washington Daily National Intelligencer*
WLM   William L. Marcy
WWP   Callender I. Fayssoux Collection of William Walker Papers, Latin
               American Collection, Howard Tilton Memorial Library, Tulane
               University, New Orleans

Chapter One

1. "Hampden" to JMC, Aug. 28, 1849, JMC Papers, LC; Washington correspondent of the *Journal of Commerce*, quoted in *Springfield* (Mass.) *Daily Republican*, Aug. 27, 1849. "Aaron Burr scheme" alluded to former vice president Burr's descent down the Mississippi River with a small party of men in the winter of 1806–7. Burr's intentions remain in doubt, but may have included a filibustering attack on Spanish territory in the Southwest. Before he could carry out his plans, he was arrested by U.S. authorities. Subsequently he was tried for treason and acquitted.

2. Charles H. Brown, *Agents of Manifest Destiny: The Lives and Times of the Filibusters* (Chapel Hill, 1980), 62–66, 77–88; J. Wilson to DW, Oct. 27, 1851, *PDW* 2:392.

3. George Templeton Strong Diary, July 29, Aug. 24, 28 (quotation), Sept. 4, 5, 12, 1851, *The Diary of George Templeton Strong*, ed. Allan Nevins and Milton Halsey Thomas, 4 vols. (New York, 1952), 2:59, 63–65; Sam Houston to Henderson Yoakum, Sept. 1, 1851, *The Writings of Sam Houston, 1813–1863*, ed. Amelia W. Williams and Eugene C. Barker, 8 vols. (1938–43; reprint, Austin, 1970), 5:306; Thomas Butler King Jr. to his mother, Sept. 30, 1851, Thomas Butler King Papers, Thomas Claiborne to Captain T. Claiborne, June 14, 1850, Thomas Claiborne Papers, Francis L. Barton to John M. Berrien, Sept. 10, 1851, John Macpherson Berrien Papers, SHC; James Brown Clay to Henry Clay, June 18, 1850, quotation from Clay's speech of May 21, 1850, Clay to William N. Mercer, Aug. 1, 1851, *The Papers of Henry Clay*, ed. James F. Hopkins, Mary W. M. Hargreaves, Robert Seager II, et al., 11 vols. (Lexing-

ton, Ky., 1959–92), 10:752, 730, 907–9; John Park Diary, May 23, 1850, Boston Public Library; Edward Fales to Charles J. E. Fales, Oct. 3, 1851, Edward Fales Papers, BRBM.

4. Ralph Waldo Emerson Journal, 1851 [no exact date], *The Journals and Miscellaneous Notebooks of Ralph Waldo Emerson*, ed. William H. Gilman, 16 vols. (Cambridge, Mass., 1960–82), 11:374; *M&P* 5:113–39. Fillmore devoted paragraphs 2–17, roughly one quarter of his entire remarks, to the expeditions and their diplomatic complications.

5. [J. C. Davis], *The History of the Late Expedition to Cuba, by O. D. D. O., One of the Participants* . . . (New Orleans, 1850), 26, 39, 43; C. T. Onions, ed., *The Oxford Dictionary of English Etymology* (Oxford, 1966), 355; *The Oxford English Dictionary*, 20 vols. (1933; 2d edn., Oxford, 1989), 5:906; Mitford M. Mathews, *A Dictionary of Americanisms on Historical Principles*, 2 vols. (Chicago, 1951), 1:604; George Templeton Strong Diary, Sept. 5, 1851, *Diary of George Templeton Strong* 2:65; *NODP*, Dec. 24, 1851; *New Orleans Delta*, June 23, 1850, quoted in Tom Chaffin, *Fatal Glory: Narciso López and the First Clandestine U.S. War against Cuba* (Charlottesville, 1996), 1; John Henderson testimony in *Washington Daily Union*, Jan. 28, 1851. Throughout this study, I have followed the modern scholarly practice of spelling filibustering with one "l." However, pre–Civil War Americans frequently used a double-"l" spelling.

6. Boston *Christian Watchman & Reflector*, Sept. 11, 1851; *WDNI*, Aug. 29, 1851; *The Destiny of Nicaragua: Central America As It Was, Is, and May Be* (Boston, 1856), 15; William Frank Stewart, *Last of the Fillibusters; or, Recollections of the Siege of Rivas* (Sacramento, 1857), introductory page; *Harper's New Monthly Magazine* 6 (Jan. 1853): 266; *National Magazine* 6 (Jan. 1855): 90.

7. Frank Lawrence Owsley Jr. and Gene A. Smith, *Filibusters and Expansionists: Jeffersonian Manifest Destiny, 1800–1821* (Tuscaloosa, 1997); Stanley Elkins and Eric McKitrick, *The Age of Federalism: The Early American Republic, 1788–1800* (New York, 1993), 349–50; Arthur Preston Whitaker, *The Spanish-American Frontier: 1783–1795: The Westward Movement and the Spanish Retreat in the Mississippi Valley* (1927; reprint, Gloucester, Mass., 1962), 107–15; Buckner F. Melton Jr., *The First Impeachment: The Constitution's Framers and the Case of Senator William Blount* (Macon, Ga., 1998), 90–125, 156–57, 232.

8. Louisiana was retroceded by Spain to France in the second Treaty of San Ildefonso of 1800; but the transfer of sovereignty was not actually effected until November 30, 1803—twenty days before France's delivery of the region to the United States under the provisions of the Louisiana Purchase.

9. Harris Gaylord Warren, *The Sword Was Their Passport: A History of American Filibustering in the Mexican Revolution* (Baton Rouge, 1943); Richard W. Gronet, "The United States and the Division of Texas, 1810–1814," *Americas* 25 (Jan. 1969): 281–306; Rembert W. Patrick, *Florida Fiasco: Rampant Rebels on the Georgia-Florida Border, 1810–1815* (Athens, Ga., 1954); Julius W. Pratt, *Expansionists of 1812* (New York, 1925); Isaac Joslin Cox, *The West Florida Controversy, 1798–1813: A Study in American Diplomacy* (Baltimore, 1918), 124, 457–86; Rufus Kay Wyllys, "The Filibusters of Amelia Island," *Georgia Historical Quarterly* 12 (Dec. 1928): 297–325;

William Spence Robertson, *The Life of Miranda*, 2 vols. (Chapel Hill, 1929), 1:293–300; J. Kevin Graffagnio, "'Twenty Thousand Muskets!!!': Ira Allen and the Olive Branch Affair, 1796–1800," *William and Mary Quarterly* 48 (July 1991): 409–31.

10. Alexander DeConde, *This Affair of Louisiana* (Baton Rouge, 1976), 44–62, 199; Samuel C. Hyde Jr., *Pistols and Politics: The Dilemma of Democracy in Louisiana's Florida Parishes, 1810–1899* (Baton Rouge, 1996), 18–21; Owsley and Smith, *Filibusters and Expansionists*, 61, 64–65, 119–20, 179; David J. Weber, *The Spanish Frontier in North America* (New Haven, 1992), 275–81; Wyllys, "Filibusters of Amelia Island," 299; Pratt, *Expansionists of 1812*, 66, 67, 103–4; Patrick, *Florida Fiasco*, 53–54; Harris Gaylord Warren, "Southern Filibusters in the War of 1812," *Louisiana Historical Quarterly* 25 (Apr. 1942): 292.

11. Harry McCorry Henderson, "The Magee-Gutierrez Expedition," *SHQ* 55 (July 1951): 43–44; DeConde, *Affair of Louisiana*, 43; Warren, *Sword Was Their Passport*, 4–5, 143, 146–48; Dwight F. Henderson, *Congress, Courts, and Criminals: The Development of a Federal Criminal Law, 1801–1829* (Westport, Conn., 1985), 124, 130–32, 175; Wyllys, "Filibusters of Amelia Island," 302, 309–10, 322, 323; Harold A. Bierck Jr., "Dr. John Hamilton Robinson," *Louisiana Historical Quarterly* 25 (July 1942): 656, 659.

12. Warren, *Sword Was Their Passport*, 74–76, 92, 233–36; Wyllys, "Filibusters of Amelia Island," 297–98.

13. Pratt, *Expansionists of 1812*, 73–79, 86–88, 96–100, 104–7; Patrick, *Florida Fiasco*, 4–15, 53–57, 83–84, 100–101; Owsley and Smith, *Filibusters and Expansionists*, 64–70.

14. Robertson, *Life of Miranda* 1:299; Warren, *Sword Was Their Passport*, 76, 96, 98, 144–45, 237, 256–57; Patrick, *Florida Fiasco*, 44–46, 65; Arthur P. Whitaker, *The United States and the Independence of Latin America, 1800–1830* (1941; reprint, New York, 1964), 236–37; Wyllys, "Filibusters of Amelia Island," 300–302.

15. Ian Brownlie, *International Law and the Use of Force by States* (Oxford, 1963), 13; Henry Wheaton, *Elements of International Law*, ed. George Grafton Wilson (1836; reprint of 1866 edn., New York, 1984), 23–24; Daniel George Lang, *Foreign Policy in the Early Republic: The Law of Nations and the Balance of Power* (Baton Rouge, 1985), 10–11, 15, 22; Robert W. Tucker and David C. Hendrickson, *Empire of Liberty: The Statecraft of Thomas Jefferson* (New York, 1990), 48; Gregg L. Lint, "The Law of Nations and the American Revolution," in Lawrence S. Kaplan, ed., *The American Revolution and "A Candid World"* (Kent, Ohio, 1977), 111–12; Roy Emerson Curtis, "The Law of Hostile Military Expeditions as Applied by the United States," *American Journal of International Law* 8 (Jan. 1914): 1–3; Charles G. Fenwick, *The Neutrality Laws of the United States* (Washington, 1913), 40, 40n; Henderson, *Congress, Courts, and Criminals*, 10–11; Henry Bartholomew Cox, *War, Foreign Affairs, and Constitutional Power: 1829–1901* (Cambridge, Mass., 1984), 20–21.

16. "An Act in addition to the 'Act for the punishment of certain crimes against the United States,' and to repeal the acts therein mentioned," Apr. 20, 1818, *Annals of Congress*, 15th Cong., 1st Sess., 2:2567–70. The 1838 legislation, a measure supplementary to the 1818 act, expired, according to one of its provisions, after two years. Cox, *War, Foreign Affairs, and Constitutional Power*, 20–21.

17. Robert W. Coakley, *The Role of Federal Military Forces in Domestic Disorders, 1798–1878* (Washington, 1988), 25–28; Fenwick, *Neutrality Laws,* 33; Henderson, *Congress, Courts, and Criminals,* 56–66, 124, 131; Frederick S. Calhoun, *The Lawmen: United States Marshals and Their Deputies, 1789–1989* (Washington, 1989), 25–26, 64; James Ripley Jacobs, *The Beginnings of the U.S. Army, 1783–1812* (Princeton, 1947), 194–95; Warren, *Sword Was Their Passport,* 17, 30–32, 37, 65, 204, 245, 250; Owsley and Smith, *Filibusters and Expansionists,* 59–60, 130–31, 169–71, 178–79; James E. Lewis Jr., *The American Union and the Problem of Neighborhood: The United States and the Collapse of the Spanish Empire, 1783–1829* (Chapel Hill, 1998), 81–83; Henderson, "Magee-Gutierrez Expedition," 45; Bierck, "Dr. John Hamilton Robinson," 657–61.

18. Pratt, *Expansionists of 1812,* 78–115, 217–30; Patrick, *Florida Fiasco,* 41, 66–84, 92–113, 121–39, 159–63, 193–94, 258–65; Owsley and Smith, *Filibusters and Expansionists,* 67–81. Mathews died in Georgia on September 1, 1812, when on the way to Washington, apparently to protest the Madison administration's disavowal of his mission.

19. Wyllys, "Filibusters," 314–22; Weber, *Spanish Frontier,* 298; Harris Gaylord Warren, "Southern Filibusters," 292; Ed Bradley, "Fighting for Texas: Filibuster James Long, the Adams-Onís Treaty, and the Monroe Administration," *SHQ* 102 (Jan. 1999): 329, 333–38. Aury's deployment of black troops from Haiti disturbed Florida's population and Georgia slaveholders, contributing to the U.S. government's decision to oust the filibusters. Owsley and Smith, *Filibusters and Expansionists,* 136–40.

20. Alwyn Barr, *Texans in Revolt: The Battle for San Antonio, 1835* (Austin, 1990), 1–4, 8, 17–18, 35, 37–38; Paul D. Lack, *The Texas Revolutionary Experience: A Political and Social History, 1835–1836* (College Station, Tex., 1992), 114–34; Joseph Milton Nance, *After San Jacinto: The Texas-Mexican Frontier, 1836–1841* (Austin, 1963), 14–16; Kimberly Ann Lamp, "Empire for Slavery: Economic and Territorial Expansion in the American Gulf South, 1835–1860" (Ph.D. diss., Harvard University, 1991), 71–72, 77–84; Robert E. May, *John A. Quitman: Old South Crusader* (Baton Rouge, 1985), 76–89; JAQ Diary, Apr. 12, 1836, quoted in J. F. H. Claiborne, *Life and Correspondence of John A. Quitman,* 2 vols. (New York, 1860), 1:147.

21. Robert V. Remini, *Andrew Jackson and the Course of American Democracy, 1835–1845* (New York, 1984), 357; *M&P* 4:1370; JAQ Diary, Apr. 8, 1836, quoted in Claiborne, *Quitman* 1:144–45; J. W. Lesesne to JAQ, June 8, 1854, JAQ Papers, HU; James E. Winston, "Mississippi and the Independence of Texas," *SHQ* 21 (July 1917): 44. Some of the filibusters in Texas later became involved in the filibustering of the 1850s. Lamp, "Empire for Slavery," 146, 172, 188n, 191–93; *Central American* (San Juan del Norte), Oct. 27, 1855 (about James McNabb).

22. Stuart D. Scott, "The Patriot Game: New Yorkers and the Canadian Rebellion of 1837–1838," *New York History* 68 (July 1987): 283–84; Kenneth R. Stevens, *Border Diplomacy: The Caroline and McLeod Affairs in Anglo-American-Canadian Relations, 1837–1842* (Tuscaloosa, 1989), 7–11; Albert B. Corey, *The Crisis of 1830–1842 in Canadian-American Relations* (New Haven, 1941), 34–35, 78; Lillian F. Gates, *After the Rebellion: The Later Years of William Lyon Mackenzie* (Toronto, 1988), 12–22.

23. Stevens, *Border Diplomacy,* 12–19; Corey, *Crisis of 1830–1842,* 48–50, 62–64;

Howard Jones, *To the Webster-Ashburton Treaty: A Study in Anglo-American Relations, 1783–1843* (Chapel Hill, 1977), 23–26; Francis Deák and Philip C. Jessup, eds., *A Collection of Neutrality Laws, Regulations and Treaties of Various Countries*, 2 vols. (Washington, 1939), 2:1177–79; Timothy D. Johnson, *Winfield Scott: The Quest for Military Glory* (Lawrence, Kans., 1998), 12–130. Van Buren turned against the filibusters after some waffling: he undermined his own November 1837 neutrality proclamation by professing sympathy for the Canadian freedom struggle, and he delayed sending troops to the border for several weeks. Corey, *Crisis of 1830–1842*, 46–47.

24. Corey, *Crisis of 1830–1842*, 38–40, 65; Irving King, *The Coast Guard under Sail: The U.S. Revenue Cutter Service, 1789–1865* (Annapolis, 1989), 98; Johnson, *Winfield Scott*, 131–32; Gates, *After the Rebellion*, 17–19, 25–26.

25. Corey, *Crisis of 1838–1842*, 40–42; Harwood Perry Hinton, "The Military Career of John Ellis Wool, 1812–1863" (Ph.D. diss., University of Wisconsin, 1960), 136–40, 153–54; King, *Coast Guard*, 98; Michael Mann, *A Particular Duty: The Canadian Rebellions, 1837–1839* (Salisbury, Eng., 1986), 78–79.

26. Stevens, *Border Diplomacy*, 36–41; Scott, "Patriot Game," 285; Oscar A. Kinchen, *The Rise and Fall of the Patriot Hunters* (New York, 1956), 25–27; Corey, *Crisis of 1830–1842*, 70–78; Jones, *Webster-Ashburton Treaty*, 25–27; Reginald C. Stuart, *United States Expansionism and British North America, 1775–1871* (Chapel Hill, 1988), 135–38. Estimates of membership in the Hunters' Lodges range from 20,000 to 160,000. Stevens, *Border Diplomacy*, 36; Kinchen, *Patriot Hunters*, 37, 44.

27. Kinchen, *Patriot Hunters*, 65, 72–73, 81–85, 94–111; Corey, *Crisis of 1830–1842*, 79–81; Jones, *Webster-Ashburton Treaty*, passim; Mary Beacock Fryer, *Volunteers and Redcoats, Rebels and Raiders: A Military History of the Rebellions in Upper Canada* (Toronto, 1987), 66, 116–19. For the generally antifilibustering attitudes and policies of U.S. army officers on the border during the crisis, see Samuel Watson, "United States Army Officers Fight the 'Patriot War': Responses to Filibustering on the Canadian Border, 1837–1839," *Journal of the Early Republic* 18 (Fall 1998): 485–519. Watson argues that army officers overcame profilibustering attitudes of U.S. civil officials in the area.

28. Sam W. Haynes, *Soldiers of Misfortune: The Somervell and Mier Expeditions* (Austin, 1990), 61–76; David M. Pletcher, *The Diplomacy of Annexation: Texas, Oregon, and the Mexican War* (Columbia, Mo., 1973), 151; *Jackson* (Miss.) *Southron*, Dec. 30, 1841. The Mier expedition did not originate as a filibuster, since its participants crossed the Rio Grande as part of a larger force whose invasion was authorized by the Texas republic's government. It evolved into one when over 300 of the troops refused to obey the decision of Alexander Somervell, their commander, to recross the river into Texas. Haynes, *Soldiers of Misfortune*, 61–62.

29. Antonio Rafael de la Cova, "Ambrosio Jose Gonzales: A Cuban Confederate Colonel" (Ph.D. diss., West Virginia University, 1994), 27; Chaffin, *Fatal Glory*, 12–13.

30. Nelson Reed, *The Caste War of Yucatan* (Stanford, 1964), 3–74; Jacob Oswandel Journal, May 27, 1848, in Oswandel, *Notes of the Mexican War, 1846–47–48* (Philadelphia, 1885), 560; *Daily American Star* (Mexico City), May 27, 1848. The proposal for a U.S. protectorate was extended by a Yucatecan agent who arrived in Wash-

ington late in the war. President James K. Polk did submit the matter to Congress, but a Senate bill for U.S. intervention, after heated debate, was allowed to die without a vote. Frederick Merk, *Manifest Destiny and Mission in American History: A Reinterpretation* (New York, 1963), 202–7; Reginald Horsman, *Race and Manifest Destiny: The Origins of American Racial Anglo-Saxonism* (Cambridge, Mass., 1981), 246–47.

31. JB to Romulus M. Saunders, June 17, 1848 (quoting Campbell's dispatch of May 18), in *The Works of James Buchanan, Comprising His Speeches, State Papers, and Private Correspondence*, ed. John Bassett Moore, 12 vols. (Philadelphia, 1908–11), 8:90–102; Basil Rauch, *American Interest in Cuba, 1848–1855* (New York, 1948), 75–76; José Sanchez Iznaga to José Aniceto Iznaga, May 25, 1848, quoted in Herminio Portell Vilá, *Narciso López y su época*, 3 vols. (Havana, 1930–58), 1:221–22; Rauch, *American Interest*, 75–76; de la Cova, "Gonzales," 28.

32. Robert B. Campbell to Matthew C. Perry, July 7, 1848, SquadL, M89, R89, NA.

33. Ambrosio José Gonzales, *Manifesto on Cuban Affairs Addressed to the People of the United States, Sept. 1st, 1852* (New Orleans, 1853), 6; Henry Jackson Hunt to James Duncan, June 2, 1848, James Duncan Papers, U.S. Military Academy Library, West Point, N.Y.

34. James K. Polk Diary, May 10, 30, June 1, 3, 6, 9, 17, 1848, in Milo Milton Quaife, ed., *The Diary of James K. Polk during His Presidency, 1845 to 1849* (1910; reprint, New York, 1970), 3:446–93; *WDNI*, June 23, 1848; JB to Romulus M. Saunders, June 17, 1848, *Works of Buchanan* 8:90–102; Sheldon Howard Harris, "The Public Career of John Louis O'Sullivan" (Ph.D. diss., Columbia University, 1948), 275–76.

35. Helen Chapman to her mother, June 13, 1848, in Caleb Coker, ed., *The News from Brownsville: Helen Chapman's Letters from the Texas Military Frontier, 1848–1852* (Austin, 1992), 49–50; *WDNI*, Aug. 18, 28, 1848; James K. Polk Diary, Aug. 29, 1848, in Quaife, ed., *Diary of James K. Polk* 4:104–5. The concept of a Republic of the Sierra Madre, or Rio Grande, began in the 1830s as a reaction of Mexican Federalists to the centralized Mexican government that had been established by Santa Anna. While Texas was a republic, many of its citizens became involved in the scheme, some even attending a convention called to create a Republic of the Rio Grande that would have included part of Texas. Nance, *After San Jacinto*, 142–377.

36. JB to Robert Rantoul, June 23, 1848, JB to the Venezuelan Minister for Foreign Affairs, Aug. 7, 1848, *Works of Buchanan* 8:105, 159–60; Viscount Palmerston to George Bancroft, Aug. 21, 1848, and enclosed memorandum of Thomas Redington, Dublin Castle, Aug. 15, 1848, *Con Print*, pt. I, series C, ed. Kenneth Bourne (Frederick, Md., 1986), 3:1–3; Robert B. Campbell, to JB, Sept. 25, 1848, *Dipl Corr* 11:451.

37. *WDNI*, Nov. 10, 1848; JB to Nathan Clifford, Oct. 10, 1848, *Dipl Corr* 9:5–6. A transplanted New Yorker, Besançon had a long editorial and political career in Mississippi and Louisiana before the Mexican War. *Natchez* (Miss.) *Courier*, Jan. 25, 1853; (Natchez) *Mississippi Free Trader*, Sept. 1, 1849; William B. Hamilton and Ruth K. Nuermberger, "An Appraisal of J. F. H. Claiborne, with His Annotated 'Memoranda' [1829–1840]," *Journal of Mississippi History* 7 (July 1945): 152n; *Jackson Mississippian*, Jan. 6, 1843.

38. *Niles' National Register* 74 (Aug. 23, 1848): 127; *NODP*, Oct. 29, 1848, Mar. 14, 24, Apr. 18, May 20, June 2, 1849; *Charleston Courier*, Nov. 28, 1848; Ebenezer Farrand to Matthew C. Perry, Dec. 28, 1848 (extract), enclosed in J. Wilkinson to John Y. Mason, Jan. 30, 1849, SquadL, roll 90; *WDNI*, Dec. 11, 1848, Mar. 24, 1849; L. A. Besançon to George W. White, Apr. 2, 1849, David Dixon Porter Papers, LC.

39. *New Orleans Delta*, quoted in *WDNI*, May 21, 1849.

Chapter Two

1. Harry Maury to G. W. Smith, Mar. 23, 1855, JAQ Papers, MDAH; Erwin Craighead, *From Mobile's Past: Sketches of Memorable People and Events* (Mobile, 1925), 155-56.

2. Powhatan Jordan to JAQ, Jan. 3, Mike Walsh to JAQ, Jan. 25, 1855, JAQ Papers, MDAH; *NODP*, Feb. 25, 1855. Walsh apparently persuaded Kinney to allow him to acquire a ship for Quitman's project in Kinney's name. Henry L. Kinney to Mike Walsh, Feb. 23, 1855, Mike Walsh Papers, New-York Historical Society.

3. E. B. Boutwell to William Mervine, May 21, 1855 (copy), SquadL, roll 37; WLM to Philo White, July 11, 1855, RG 59, DS, Diplomatic Instructions, M77, R52, NA; Mark J. Van Aken, *King of the Night: Juan José Flores and Ecuador, 1824-1864* (Berkeley, 1989), 246-47. Guano, sea bird excrement, was highly sought after in the 1850s as a commercial fertilizer.

4. William H. Emory to James A. Pearce, Jan. 17, 1855, James A. Pearce Papers, Maryland Historical Society, Baltimore; William H. Goetzmann, *Army Exploration in the American West, 1803-1863* (New Haven, 1959), 195-97; George S. Denison to his mother, July 1, 1855, in James A. Padgett, ed., "Some Letters of George Stanton Denison, 1854-1866: Observations of a Yankee on Conditions in Louisiana and Texas," *Louisiana Historical Quarterly* 23 (Oct. 1940): 1157; Thomas Tyree Smith, *Fort Inge: Sharps, Spurs, and Sabers on the Texas Frontier, 1849-1869* (Austin, 1993), 80-81.

5. *Harrisburg* (Pa.) *Weekly Telegraph*, Nov. 20, 1856 (quotation); *Cincinnati Enquirer*, June 24, 1854, May 4, 1856; *Tuskegee* (Ala.) *Republican*, Jan. 28, 1858; T. Robinson Warren, *Dust and Foam; or, Three Oceans and Two Continents* (New York, 1859), 212-13; C. W. Doubleday, *Reminiscences of the "Filibuster" War in Nicaragua* (New York 1986), 104-5; *Richmond Whig*, Jan. 16, 1858; Charles H. Brown, *Agents of Manifest Destiny: The Lives and Times of the Filibusters* (Chapel Hill, 1980), 174-218, 267-70.

6. David L. Gregg to WLM, Mar. 22, 1855, RG 59, DS, Despatches from United States Ministers in Hawaii, T30, roll 6, NA; John F. T. Crampton to Lord Clarendon, Sept. 4, 1855, *P&C*, 134; WLM to JB, Nov. 12, 1855, *Dipl Corr* 7:123-24.

7. Charles Mackay, *Life and Liberty in America; or, Sketches of a Tour in the United States and Canada, in 1857-8* (2 vols., 1859; reprint in one vol., New York, 1971), bk. 2:77.

8. Brown, *Agents of Manifest Destiny*, 42; Antonio Rafael de la Cova, "Ambrosio Jose Gonzales: A Cuban Confederate Colonel" (Ph.D. diss., West Virginia University, 1994), 18-20, 33-40; Tom Chaffin, *Fatal Glory: Narciso López and the First Clandestine U.S. War against Cuba* (Charlottesville, 1996), 37, 44-46.

9. John L. O'Sullivan to Thomas J. Rusk, Sept. 13, 1849, Thomas J. Rusk Papers, UT; Ambrosio José Gonzales, *Manifesto on Cuban Affairs Addressed to the People of the United States, September 1st, 1852* (New Orleans, 1853), 7. On September 1, a U.S. naval officer reported 450 recruits on Round Island. One of them claimed in an affidavit on September 19 that "about 460" men had left for the rendezvous. On the other hand, the U.S. collector in New Orleans learned from an agent who had infiltrated the filibuster encampment in mid-August that the force included "about 550 men, their number . . . daily increasing." U.S. Army general David E. Twiggs claimed that 600 filibusters had assembled on the island. V. M. Randolph to William B. Preston, Sept. 1, 1849, Affidavit of Edwin B. Scott, Sept. 19, 1849, enclosed in Randolph to Preston, Sept. 20, 1849, Samuel J. Peters to William M. Meredith, Aug. 21, 1849, all in *S. Ex. Doc.* 57, 31st Cong., 1st Sess., 87−89, 101, 118−19; Twiggs's estimate mentioned in William Ballard Preston to F. A. Parker, Aug. 9, 1849, K. Jack Bauer, ed., *The New American State Papers: Naval Affairs*, 10 vols. (Wilmington, Del., 1981), 2:125.

10. *New-York Daily Tribune*, Aug. 25, 29, 30, Sept. 1, 1849; *WDNI*, Aug. 27, 1849; *Springfield* (Mass.) *Daily Republican*, Aug. 27, 28, 31, 1849.

11. *WDNI*, Sept. 10, 1849 (quoting the *Philadelphia Public Ledger*), Jan. 16, 1850 (quoting the *Louisville Chronicle*). That September, the U.S. district attorney in New York arrested the Philadelphian Lewis Carr as one of the conspirators. J. Prescott Hall to JMC, Sept. 7, 1850 (telegraph), JMC Papers, LC. For Carr's recruiting activities, see *WDNI*, Aug. 23, 1849. For Gaither's prior military record, see *Historical Register and Dictionary of the United States Army, from its Organization, September 29, 1789, to March 2, 1903*, comp. Francis B. Heitman, 2 vols. (Washington, 1903; reprint, Urbana, 1965), 1:442.

12. Rose Greenhow to John C. Calhoun, Aug. 29, John L. O'Sullivan to Calhoun, Aug. 24, 1849, in J. Franklin Jameson, ed., "Correspondence of John C. Calhoun," *Annual Report of the American Historical Association for the Year 1899*, 2 vols. (Washington, 1900), 1203−4, 1202−3. Calhoun had met with López earlier in the year when López was in Washington, and, according to later accounts by J. F. H. Claiborne (who had connections with several of López's collaborators), and Gonzales, expressed himself in favor of the Cubans' cause. However, the North Carolina congressman Abraham W. Venable asserted in 1853 that two days before Calhoun's death (which occurred on March 31, 1850), the senator had requested Venable to dispel rumors that he supported filibustering. Ambrosio José Gonzales to editors of the *Charleston Mercury*, Aug. 24, 1851, in *Jackson Mississippian*, Sept. 12, 1851; J. F. H. Claiborne, *Life and Correspondence of John A. Quitman*, 2 vols. (New York, 1860), 2:55; Frederick Merk, *The Monroe Doctrine and American Expansionism, 1843−1849* (New York, 1966), 270n.

13. Victor M. Randolph to William Preston Ballard, Aug. 25, 1849, Randolph, "To The Persons Encamped on Round Island Near Pascagoula," Aug. 28, 1849, Randolph to Preston, Sept. 5, 1849, J. Prescott Hall to JMC, Sept. 8, 1849, *S. Ex. Doc.* 57, 33d Cong., 1st Sess., 74−75, 78−79, 90−91, 15−16; Antonio Rafael de la Cova, "The Taylor Administration versus Mississippi Sovereignty: The Round Island Expedition of 1849," *Journal of Mississippi History* 62 (Winter 2000): 306−22.

14. "Translation of the address of the Council in January 1850," JAQ Papers, MDAH; de la Cova, "Gonzales," 64−65, 73−77; Basil Rauch, *American Interest in*

Cuba, 1848–1855 (New York, 1948), 121–22; Cristóbal Madan to George Cadwalader, Jan. 30, Mar. 6, 1850, George Cadwalader Papers, HSP.

15. Cristóbal Madan to George Cadwalader, Mar. 6, 1850, George Cadwalader Papers, HSP.

16. *Washington Republic*, Dec. 10, 1849.

17. Lewis Pinckney Jones, "Carolinians and Cubans: The Elliotts and Gonzales, Their Work and Their Writings" (Ph.D. diss., University of North Carolina, 1952), pt. 1:83; de la Cova, "Gonzales," 28, 39; Raphael P. Thian, comp., *Notes Illustrating the Military Geography of the United States, 1813–1880* (Austin, 1979), 46–49; J. T. Sprague [to W. Watts Sherman], May 22, 1849, W. Watts Sherman Papers, Newport Historical Society, Newport, R.I. In 1851 Worth's son-in-law, who as a U.S. Army officer had traveled with Worth to his new assignment in Texas, issued a statement conceding that Worth had negotiated with the Cubans, but denying that Worth had ever agreed to filibuster. J. T. Sprague to the editors of the *NODP*, Oct. 10, quoted in *WDNI*, Oct. 31, 1851.

18. De la Cova, "Taylor Administration," 297–98, 298n–99n; de la Cova, "Gonzales," 64; John L. O'Sullivan to Thomas J. Rusk, Sept. 13, 1849, Rusk Papers, UT.

19. De la Cova, "Gonzales," 74, 78; Robert E. May, *John A. Quitman: Old South Crusader* (Baton Rouge, 1985), 147–206, 237–38.

20. Cristóbal Madan to George Cadwalader, Jan. 30, 1850, George Cadwalader Papers, HSP; [Cristóbal Madan?] to JAQ, Feb. 24, 1850, in Claiborne, *Quitman* 2:283–84; de la Cova, "Gonzales," 79–82. Cadwalader's close relations with Quitman are reflected in Quitman's request in 1849 that Cadwalader serve as a mentor to his son, then attending Princeton. JAQ to George Cadwalader, Jan. 21, 1849, JAQ Papers, HSP.

21. JAQ to Mansfield Lovell, Mar. 15, 1850, Mansfield Lovell Papers, Huntington Library, San Marino, Calif.; Louisa Quitman to Eliza Quitman, July 5, 1850, Quitman Family Papers, SHC.

22. JAQ to Narciso López and Ambrosio Gonzales, Mar. 18, 1850, in Claiborne, *Quitman* 2:385; Thomas R. Wolfe to John Thomas Wheat, May 9, 1850, John Thomas Wheat Papers, SHC; Gonzales to JAQ, Apr. 5, 1850, John Henderson to JAQ, May 16, 18, 1850, John L. O'Sullivan to JAQ, June 26, 1850 (2 letters, same date), Laurent J. Sigur to JAQ, Nov. 7, 1850, Mar. 25, 1851, JAQ Papers, MDAH.

23. Henry J. Hartstene to JAQ, May 26, 1850, JAQ Papers, MDAH; *Jackson Mississippian*, June 7, 1850; *Vicksburg* (Miss.) *Weekly Whig*, May 21, 1851; John Henderson to JAQ, May 16, 18, George Marcy to JAQ, May 24, A. B. Bannon to JAQ, May 25, 1850, JAQ Papers, MDAH. In November 1850 Henderson asked Quitman to provide "further pecuniary assistance" so that López could negotiate the acquisition of a steamship for his next expedition. John Henderson to JAQ, Nov. 6, 1850, Claiborne, *Quitman* 2:69–71.

24. Foreign immigrants seem to have made up slightly more than one third of López's force. But only four Cubans, out of some six hundred Cuban exiles then in the United States, accompanied López's departure from U.S. territory. Chaffin, *Fatal Glory*, 239n; de la Cova, "Gonzales," 103–4.

25. The Count of Alcoy to ACdlB, May 22, 1850 (copy) in *S. Ex. Doc.* 41, 31st Cong., 2d Sess., 45; Chaffin, *Fatal Glory*, 104–28; Brown, *Agents of Manifest Destiny*, 57–67. The thirteen men who deserted at Mujeres managed to procure passage back to the United States. The thirty-nine men left at Contoy were taken into custody by Spanish naval forces. Their fate is discussed in chapter 8.

26. De la Cova, "Gonzales," 111–20; Robert G. Caldwell, *The López Expeditions to Cuba, 1848–1851* (Princeton, N.J., 1915), 66–74; Chaffin, *Fatal Glory*, 130–38.

27. *New-York Daily Times*, Mar. 17, 1852; Duncan Smith [Dr. Henry Burtnett], "Narrative of Events Connected with the Late Intended Invasion of Cuba," quoted in L. M. Perez, ed., "López's Expeditions to Cuba, 1850–51: Betrayal of the *Cleopatra*, 1851," *Publications of the Southern History Association* 10 (Nov. 1906): 349–50, 355–56.

28. A. J. Gonzales to Mirabeau Buonaparte Lamar, Mar. 14, 1851, in *The Papers of Mirabeau Buonaparte Lamar*, ed. Charles Adams Gulick, 6 vols. (1921–27; reprint, 1973), 4, pt. 1:282–84; Peter Hamilton to Foxhall A. Parker, Apr. 18, 1851, SquadL, M89, roll 92. Lamar declined investing in the April 1851 plot, though he made it clear that he sympathized with the filibusters. Mirabeau B. Lamar to Ambrosio José Gonzales, Apr. 12, 1851 (calendar summary), in *Papers of Mirabeau Buonaparte Lamar* 4, pt. 1:284; de la Cova, "Gonzales," 135–36.

29. *Newark* (N.J.) *Daily Advertiser* and *New York Mirror* quoted in *WDNI*, Apr. 30, 28, 1851; *New-York Daily Tribune*, Apr. 29, 1851; Louis Schlesinger to John L. O'Sullivan in *New-York Daily Times*, Mar. 20, 1852.

30. J. Reneas to Millard Fillmore, Apr. 10, enclosed in William S. Derrick to ACdlB, Apr. 16, 1851, *Dipl Corr* 11:103n; Jacksonville correspondent's letter, Apr. 25, 1851, in *Newark* (N.J.) *Daily Advertiser*, May 1, 1851, quoted in *New-York Daily Tribune*, May 2, 1851; *Jacksonville Republican* and *Savannah Republican*, quoted in *WDNI*, May 9, 10, 1851; *Savannah Morning News*, May 3, 1851; Antonio Rafael de la Cova, "Cuban Filibustering in Jacksonville in 1851," *Northeast Florida History* 3 (1996): 19–23; *Griffin* (Ga.) *American Union*, May 22, 1851, quoted in *WDNI*, May 27, 1851. Britain's minister to the United States reported to the U.S. Department of State that López had recruited "about a thousand young men" in Georgia, South Carolina, and Alabama. A Spanish spy, temporarily detained by some of the expeditionists, claimed that the filibusters expected to join 1,500 Georgians for the invasion. Henry Lytton Bulwer to DW, Mar. 10, 1851, *Dipl Corr* 7:432; *Savannah Morning News*, May 1, 1851.

31. Cornelius Cook to Ike Cook, July 31, enclosed with Edward H. Cook to DW, Sept. 12, 1851, *PDW* 2:381–82; "Personal Narrative of Louis Schlesinger of Adventures in Cuba and Ceuta," *Democratic Review* 31 (Sept. 1852, Oct. 1852, Nov.–Dec. 1852): 212–13, 217–18; *WDNI*, Aug. 23, 1851; Brown, *Agents of Manifest Destiny*, 74–77; de la Cova, "Gonzales," 193–203; Chaffin, *Fatal Glory*, 196–202. After the return of the López filibusters to Key West from Cárdenas, Mallory had allowed Gonzales to recover from his wounds at his Key West residence. Jones, "Carolinians and Cubans," pt. 1:93.

32. "Personal Narrative," 352–57, 566n; Chaffin, *Fatal Glory*, 202–16; Brown, *Agents of Manifest Destiny*, 79–88.

33. John V. Wren letter, Sept. 1, 1852, to the editors of the *New York Sachem*,

reprinted in (Natchez) *Mississippi Free Trader*, Dec. 29, 1852; *WDNI*, Oct. 6, 1851; *NODP*, Nov. 6, 1851.

34. *New Orleans Daily Delta*, Dec. 27, 1851; *WDNI*, Aug. 26, 1852; Henry Hughes Diary, Oct. 24, Nov. 28, 1852 (typewritten copy), MDAH; Announcement of meetings of the "Lone Star Division No. 3" and report of large numbers of Lone Stars participating in a memorial procession for Narciso López in *NODP*, July 25, Sept. 2, 1852. Claims that the Order had up to 20,000 members probably exaggerate its manpower. See Rauch, *American Interest*, 228; Philip S. Foner, *A History of Cuba and Its Relations with the United States*, 2 vols. (New York, 1962–63), 2:66. For Hughes's proslavery treatises, see Douglas Ambrose, *Henry Hughes and Proslavery Thought in the Old South* (Baton Rouge, 1996), 70–180.

35. ACdlB to William Hunter, May 14, ACdlB to Charles M. Conrad, Sept. 30, 1852, *Dipl Corr* 11:661–62, 664–65; George Parr to Daniel M. Barringer, Aug. 17, 1852, Daniel M. Barringer Papers, SHC; *WDNI*, Oct. 21, 1852; Rauch, *American Interest*, 229–30; "The Order of the Lone Star," *Democratic Review*, new series, 1 (Jan. 1853): 80–85. Rauch asserts that an expedition was scheduled to sail in June 1852 in coordination with an uprising being planned in Cuba by López's brother-in-law, but that it was postponed or canceled and that the conspiracy in Cuba collapsed in August.

36. *WDNI*, Oct. 15, 22, 1852; "The Cuban Junta," *Our Times* 1 (Oct. 1852): 187–88.

37. May, *John A. Quitman*, 271–75; "Articles Entered Into between the Cuban Junta and General Quitman, and Signed by Them Respectively," in Claiborne, *Quitman* 2:389–90.

38. Henry Gillespey to JAQ, Feb. 9, 1855, Pierre Sauvé to JAQ, Dec. 24, 1857, JAQ Papers, HU; John Cadwalader to Peter G. Washington, Aug. 27, 1853, Maupin-Washington Papers, College of William and Mary, Williamsburg, Va.; *New Orleans Daily Delta*, Dec. 27, 1851; (Austin) *Texas State Gazette*, Apr. 8, 1854; C. A. L. Lamar to John S. Thrasher, Feb. 25, 1855, in "A Slave-Trader's Letter Book," *North American Review* 143 (1886): 448; C. Stanley Urban, "The Idea of Progress and Southern Imperialism: New Orleans and the Caribbean, 1845–1861" (Ph.D. diss., Northwestern University, 1943), 613n.

39. JAQ to Juan Manuel Macias, Dec. 28, 1853 (draft), JAQ to C. A. L. Lamar, Jan. 5, 1855, W. A. Lacy to JAQ, Feb. 19, 1855, JAQ Papers, HU; JAQ to the Cuban Junta, Apr. 16, 1854, in Claiborne, *Quitman* 2:391. A Washington correspondent of the *Mobile Tribune* in December 1854 claimed to have seen a letter in which Quitman reported having gathered an army of 5,000 men. *Tribune* correspondent quoted in *NODP*, Dec. 20, 1854, supplement.

40. W. A. Lacy to JAQ, Feb. 19, 1855, JAQ Papers, HU; May, *John A. Quitman*, 279–80; W. D. Ron to JAQ, June 7, Reuben Davis to JAQ, Mar. 6, 1854, JAQ Papers, MDAH; *Louisville Democrat* quoted in *Galveston Weekly News*, Nov. 7, 1854. A. L. Saunders, one of Quitman's closest collaborators, confirmed privately Allen's success at mustering 1,000 men. Saunders to JAQ, Feb. 4, 1855, JAQ Papers, HU. For examples of letters listing recruits, see William Estelle to JAQ, Dec. 19, 1854, William H. Woods to JAQ, Feb. 1, 1855, JAQ Papers, HU.

41. C. H. Mott to JAQ, Jan. 29, 1855, JAQ Papers, HU; J. W. Lesesne to JAQ, June

6, Robert W. Shufeldt to JAQ, June 7, Samuel Walker to JAQ, July 7, 1854, JAQ Papers, MDAH; Edward W. Callahan, comp., *List of Officers of the Navy of the United States and of the Marine Corps from 1775 to 1900* (New York, 1901), 496; Frederick C. Drake, *The Empire of the Seas: A Biography of Rear Admiral Robert Wilson Shufeldt, USN* (Honolulu, 1984), 1, 11, and passim.

42. May, *John A. Quitman*, 292–95; Rauch, *American Interest*, 298–99; de la Cova, "Gonzales," 243.

43. *Galveston Weekly News*, July 3, 1855; R. W. Downs to WLM, Dec. 23, 1853, DS, M179, roll 138, NA; *New-York Daily Times*, Mar. 16, 1855. For Rynders, see Richard B. Stott, *Workers in the Metropolis: Class, Ethnicity, and Youth in Antebellum New York City* (Ithaca, 1990), 236–37; Anthony Gronowicz, *Race and Class Politics in New York City before the Civil War* (Boston, 1998), 119.

44. (Corpus Christi) *Nueces Valley Weekly*, Sept. 22, 1851, quoted in *Galveston Weekly News*, Oct. 7, 1851.

45. Arnoldo De León uses the term Tejano to characterize all Mexican residents of Texas, whether born in the United States, the Republic of Texas, or Mexico. Carbajal was born while Spain still ruled Mexico at San Fernando de Béxar, later San Antonio. Arnoldo De León, *They Called Them Greasers: Anglo Attitudes toward Mexicans in Texas, 1821–1900* (Austin, 1983), xiii; "Carbajal, José María Jesús," in Roy R. Barkley, ed., *The New Handbook of Texas*, 6 vols. (Austin, 1996), 1:971.

46. Summation of reports from Galveston newspapers in *WDNI*, Sept. 25, 1851; John Moretta, "Jose Maria Jesus Carvajal, United States Foreign Policy and the Filibustering Spirit in Texas," *East Texas Historical Journal* 33 (Fall 1995): 3–10; Earnest C. Shearer, "The Carvajal Disturbances," *SHQ* 15 (Oct. 1951): 201–9; [Teresa Griffin Vielé], *"Following the Drum": A Glimpse of Frontier Life* (New York, 1858), 146–48; Moretta, "Carvajal," 3. U.S. borderlands merchants had other grievances against Mexican officials besides their enforcement of tariff restrictions. See J. Fred Rippy, *The United States and Mexico* (New York, 1931), 42–43, 88–89.

47. "Carbajal, José María Jesús," Barkley, ed., *New Handbook of Texas* 1:971; Moretta, "Carvajal," 3–4; Edmund Kirby Smith to his mother, Mar. 16, 1853, Edmund Kirby Smith Papers, SHC.

48. John Salmon Ford, *Rip Ford's Texas*, ed. Stephen B. Oates (Austin, 1963), xviii–xxvii, 142; W. J. Hughes, *Rebellious Ranger: Rip Ford and the Old Southwest* (1964; reprint with foreword by Walter L. Buenger, Norman, 1990), 74–98, 101. Ford's Ranger company, initially mustered into federal service on August 23, 1849, to repress Indian raids and bandits in the borderlands, was finishing its fourth term of federal service. There was a one-month gap between the company's second and third terms, and not all members of the company reenlisted each time.

49. Clarence C. Clendenen, *Blood on the Border: The United States Army and the Mexican Irregulars* (New York, 1969), 18–19; Moretta, "Carvajal," 8–9; Hughes, *Rebellious Ranger*, 101–2; *New Orleans Crescent*, Oct. 31, quoted in *New-York Daily Tribune*, Nov. 10, 1851.

50. Roger Jones to the Secretary of War, Dec. 5, 1851, RG 107, Letters Received by the Secretary of War: Registered Series, M221, roll 160, NA; J. F. Waddell to DW, Oct.

1, 7, Nov. [no exact date] 1851, Despatches from United States Consuls in Matamoros, M281, roll 2, NA; letter from Brownsville correspondent, Oct. 29, in *NODP*, Nov. 4, quoted in *WDNI*, Nov. 12, 1851; *Brownsville American Flag*, Dec. 10, 1851, quoted in *Washington Daily Union*, Jan. 6, 1852; Ford, *Rip Ford's Texas*, 200–202.

51. Letters from Brownsville correspondent, Oct. 29, 1851, Mar. 29, 30, 1853, in *NODP*, Nov. 4, 1851, Apr. 5, 1853; *Brownsville [American] Flag*, Feb. 28, 1852, Jack R. Everett letter from Rio Grande City, Feb. 24, 1852, in *New Orleans Delta*, quoted in *WDNI*, Mar. 15, 17, 1852; J. F. Waddell to DW, June 16, 1852, Despatches from United States Consuls in Matamoros, M281, roll 2, NA; Rippy, *United States and Mexico*, 90; Ernest C. Shearer, "The Carvajal Disturbances," *SHQ* 55 (Oct. 1951): 226; Hughes, *Rebellious Ranger*, 105; Moretta, "Carvajal," 15, 17.

52. Antonio Rafael de la Cova, "Ambrosio Jose Gonzales: A Cuban Confederate Colonel" (Ph.D. diss., West Virginia University, 1994), 41–45; Rippy, *United States and Mexico*, 87–90.

53. Horace Bell, *Reminiscences of a Ranger; or, Early Times in Southern California* (1881; reprint, Santa Barbara, 1927), 205–7; Charles S. McCauley to William A. Graham, Apr. 24, May 28, 1852, SquadL, roll 35; Van Aken, *King of the Night*, 32–207, 241–45; Alexander Bell letter, Aug. 2, in *San Joaquin Republican* (Stockton, Calif.), quoted in *DAC*, Aug. 25, 1852; Brown, *Agents of Manifest Destiny*, 164–67. Many secondary works suggest that Bell organized the expedition in 1850 or 1851, and give the impression that the Americans actually left California and merged with Flores's forces in 1851. See Edward S. Wallace, *Destiny and Glory* (New York, 1967), 101; Andrew F. Rolle, *California: A History* (New York, 1969), 257; Brown, *Agents of Manifest Destiny*, 166–67; William O. Scroggs, *Filibusters and Financiers: The Story of William Walker and His Associates* (New York, 1916). Van Aken, however, makes it clear that they arrived in 1852. Van Aken, *King of the Night*, 245. I suspect that Bell's party did not even leave California until April 1852. The *Daily Alta California* (San Francisco) on August 25, 1852, mentioned that Bell's group had sailed to South America on the steamship *Quickstep*. Advertisements in that paper earlier in the year show that before April, the *Quickstep* had been plying the Pacific coast between San Francisco and Portland, Oregon Territory. However, in March and April agents for the vessel, which had changed hands, suddenly advertised that its next runs would be to Callao, Peru. *DAC*, Mar. 13, 24, Apr. 4, 1852.

54. William Walker, *The War in Nicaragua* (1860; reprint, Tucson, 1985), 19; Alejandro Bolaños-Geyer, *William Walker: The Gray-Eyed Man of Destiny*, vol. 2: *The Californias* (Lake St. Louis, Mo., 1989), 260–61, and San Francisco correspondent's letter, Oct. 1, in *Herald*, Oct. 28, 1853, quoted on p. 206; Robert G. Cleland, "Bandini's Account of William Walker's Invasion of Lower California," *Huntington Library Quarterly* 7 (Feb. 1944): 153–66; *DAC*, Jan. 27, 1854; William Walker, "Address of President Walker, to the People of the United States," and *DAC*, Feb. 5, 1854, both quoted in Arthur Woodward, ed., *The Republic of Lower California, 1853–1854* (Los Angeles, 1966), 31–33, 36–37; "The Ensenada: Colonel Walker's Expedition to Sonora," *National Magazine* 4 (June 1854): 502–5; Lawrence Greene, *The Filibuster: The Career of William Walker* (Indianapolis, 1937), 30–46; Brown, *Agents of Manifest Destiny*,

194–209; Stout, *The Liberators*, 81–101; Rufus Kay Wyllys, "William Walker's Invasion of Sonora, 1854," *Arizona Historical Review* 6 (Oct. 1935): 61–67.

55. Kevin Mulroy, *Freedom on the Border: The Seminole Maroons in Florida, the Indian Territory, Coahuila, and Texas* (Lubbock, 1993), 76–80; J. H. Callahan to E. M. Pease, Oct. 4, 1855, Elisha Marshall Pease Papers, Austin History Center, Austin Public Library; Ronnie C. Tyler, "The Callahan Expedition of 1855: Indians or Negroes?" *SHQ* 70 (Apr. 1967): 574–85. For more on Henry's involvement with Callahan, see Smith, *Fort Inge*, 80–81.

56. (Vicksburg) *Weekly Whig*, July 15, Aug. 1, 1844; (Vicksburg) *Tri-Weekly Whig*, Apr. 5, July 3, Nov. 20, 1849; Ethan Allen Hitchcock Diary, Oct. 9, 1853, in *Fifty Years in Camp and Field: Diary of Major-General Ethan Allen Hitchcock, U.S.A.*, ed. W. A. Croffut (New York, 1909), 402; *DAC*, Oct. 11, 18, 1854; Robert H. Forbes, *Crabb's Filibustering Expedition into Sonora, 1857* (Tucson, 1952); Rufus Kay Wyllys, "Henry A. Crabb: A Tragedy of the Sonora Frontier," *Pacific Historical Review* 9 (June 1940): 183–93; Stout, *The Liberators*, 143–68; "Crabb, Henry Alexander," in Dan L. Thrapp, *Encyclopedia of Frontier Biography*, 3 vols. (Glendale, Calif., 1988), 1:333–34.

57. William R. Henry [to Hardin Richard Runnels], Feb. 3, 1859, Special Orders, no. 12, Head Quarters, Department of Texas, Mar. 3, 1859 (copy), both in Governors' Papers, Hardin Richard Runnels, Texas State Library, Archives Division, Austin; Houston speech, July 9, 1859, Houston to John B. Floyd, Feb. 13, 15 (quotation), in *The Writings of Sam Houston, 1813–1863*, ed. Amelia W. Williams and Eugene C. Barker, 8 vols. (1938–43; reprint, New York, 1970), 7:362, 441–42, 474, 478–79. For the Cortina disturbances, see De León, *They Called Them Greasers*, 53–54, 83; Robert J. Rosenbaum, *Mexicano Resistance in the Southwest: "The Sacred Right of Self-Preservation"* (Austin, 1981), 42–45. Texas Rangers cooperated with U.S. Army forces in a crossing of the border that routed Cortina. Clendenen, *Blood on the Border*, 37.

58. George Bickley to Lewis Cass, Apr. 13, 1860, RG 59, DS, ML, NA; *Montgomery Daily Confederation*, Feb. 25, 1860; *Greenville* (Ala.) *Southern Messenger*, Apr. 4, 1860; Daniel W. Crofts, *Old Southampton: Politics and Society in a Virginia County, 1834–1869* (Charlottesville, 1992), 173; James Pike, *Scout and Ranger, Being the Personal Adventures of James Pike of the Texas Rangers in 1859–60* (1865; reprint, Princeton, 1932), 124–26; (Philadelphia) *Saturday Evening Post*, Oct. 13, 1860; Edward L. Hartz to Samuel Hartz, May 2, 1859 [1860], Edward L. Hartz Papers, LC; Frank L. Klement, "Bickley, George Washington Lafayette," in John T. Kneebone, J. Jefferson Looney, Brent Tarter, and Sandra Gioia Treadway, eds., *Dictionary of Virginia Biography* (Richmond, 1998–), 1:481–83. The Knights' leader in Texas, Elkanah Greer, solicited Houston in February to take over the Knights' thousand-man regiment of mounted volunteers then assembled east of the Trinity River. Houston, however, never made a formal commitment. Pike, *Scout and Ranger*, 124; I. W. Barrett to Sam Houston, Feb. 20, 1860, enclosing Greer to Houston, Feb. 20, 1860, Greer to Houston, Mar. 22, 1860, Governors' Letters, Sam Houston, Texas State Library. See also C. A. Bridges "The Knights of the Golden Circle: A Filibustering Fantasy," *SHQ* 44 (Jan. 1941): 287–302; Olliger Crenshaw, "The Knights of the Golden Circle," *American Historical Review* 47 (Oct. 1941): 23–50; Jimmie Hicks, ed., "Some Letters Concern-

ing the Knights of the Golden Circle in Texas, 1860–1861," *SHQ* 65 (July 1961): 80–86.

59. Samuel P. Heintzelman Journal, Apr. 13, July 28, 1860, in Jerry Thompson, ed., *Fifty Miles and a Fight: Major Samuel Peter Heintzelman's Journal of Texas and the Cortina War* (Austin, 1998), 231, 268, 268n.

60. *New York Evening Post*, Mar. 22 (description of Kinney), July 18, 1855; *Writings of Sam Houston* 7:442n–44n; Nicaraguan Land and Mining Company, *A Home in Nicaragua! The Kinney Expedition: Its Character and Purposes . . .* (New York, 1855); Robert E. May, "Kinney, Henry L.," *Encyclopedia of Latin American History*, ed. Barbara A. Tenenbaum, 5 vols. (New York, 1996), 3:350; James T. Wall, *Manifest Destiny Denied: America's First Intervention in Nicaragua* (Washington, 1981), 49–52; Craig L. Dozier, *Nicaragua's Mosquito Shore: The Years of British and American Presence* (University, Ala., 1985), 3–4, 33, 48–49, 55–57, 94–95; W. B. Phillips to Joseph P. Shillen, Dec. 30, 1854, enclosed in WLM to Henry L. Kinney, Feb. 21, 1855, in *New York Evening Post*, May 3, 1855; (Tampa) *Florida Peninsular*, Mar. 3, June 30, 1855. Kinney's complicated dealings with Daniel Webster are dispersed through rolls 10, 11, 12, 17, 21, and 22 of the microfilm edition of the Daniel Webster Papers. For Kinney's prefilibustering financial difficulties, see Kinney to Samuel C. Reid Jr., Feb. 17, 1854, Samuel Chester Reid Family Papers, LC; Paul N. Spellman, *Forgotten Texas Leader: Hugh McLeod and the Texan Santa Fe Expedition* (College Station, Tex., 1999), 148–51.

61. *New York Evening Post*, Aug. 28, Sept. 8, 1855; Wall, *Manifest Destiny Denied*, 56–57, 61, 65–66, 68, 69; *DAC*, May 30, 1858. Walker never recognized the legitimacy of Kinney's régime. In February 1856 he issued a decree annexing all of the Mosquito coast, including Kinney's domain, to Nicaragua. Wall, *Manifest Destiny Denied*, 66.

62. List of filibusters in letter from E. J. C. Kewen to the editor, *SFDH*, Aug. 10, 1856; Brown, *Agents of Manifest Destiny*, 216–18.

63. Brown, *Agents of Manifest Destiny*, 273–76.

64. Walker, *War in Nicaragua*, 42–141; Brown, *Agents of Manifest Destiny*, 273–307, 343–46; Karl Bermann, *Under the Big Stick: Nicaragua and the United States since 1848* (Boston, 1986), 57.

65. Walker's relations with Vanderbilt and the details of his surrender are spelled out in depth in chapters 6 and 7.

66. *New-York Daily Times*, June 2, Aug. 19, 1857; Muster Roll: 1855–1856, General Orders, no. 170, Sept. 25, 1856, list of 314 passengers on steamer *Texas*, register book, New Orleans Agency of Nicaraguan Emigration Company, all in WWP; *New Orleans Daily Creole*, Oct. 10, 1856; *DAC*, Oct. 20, Aug. 7, 1856; *SFDH*, Dec. 18, 1855; (Stockton, Calif.) *San Joaquin Republican*, Jan. 23, Apr. 24, 1857; Charles Edward Rand to his father and mother, Feb. 20, 1857, Charles Edward Rand Papers, BRBM; Scroggs, *Filibusters*, 230–32; Brown, *Agents of Manifest Destiny*, 365–67. John P. Heiss (soon to be Walker's chargé d'affaires in the United States) wrote privately in March 1856, from Granada, that there were then fifteen hundred Americans in the country. Apparently he included civilians in his figure. John P. Heiss to Stephen Douglas, Mar. 14, 1856, Stephen A. Douglas Papers, University of Chicago.

67. (Austin) *Texas State Gazette*, June 13, 1857; William Walker to A. Dudley Mann, July 16, 1857, William Walker Papers, LC; William Walker to Lewis Cass, Sept. 29, 1857, *H. Ex. Doc.* 24, 35th Cong., 1st Sess., 6.

68. William Walker to Mrs. Tom Smith, Mar. 3, 1858, William Walker ML, TSLA.

69. *Mobile Daily Register*, Nov. 15, 1857, Jan. 3, 1858; Joshua R. Sands to Hiram Paulding, Dec. 28, 1857, *S. Ex. Doc.* 63, 35th Cong., 1st Sess., 5; B. Squire Cotrell to Lewis Cass, Nov. 30, 1857, *H. Ex. Doc.* 24, 35th Cong., 1st Sess., 27; C. I. Fayssoux Journal, Nov. 11, 1857, WWP. After the expedition was broken up, the captain of Walker's vessel told a correspondent that he had carried 186 filibusters and "some eight or ten 'outsiders'" (presumably passengers with no connection to Walker) from Mobile to Central America. *New-York Times*, Dec. 15, 1857. The figure 186 correlates precisely with the number of filibusters who surrendered and later returned to the United States aboard two U.S. Navy naval vessels. See *New-York Times*, Dec. 28, 1857; *New York Herald*, Feb. 1, 1858. On the other hand, a U.S. customs inspector who boarded the *Fashion* just before her departure discovered approximately 270 passengers on board. Melancthon Smith to T. Sanford, Nov. 14, 1857, *H. Ex. Doc.* 24, 35th Cong., 1st Sess., 41.

70. *New-York Times*, Jan. 7, 1858; William Walker to JAQ, Jan. 19, 1858, JAQ Papers, HU; Walker to Callender Irvine Fayssoux, Jan. 9, 1858, WWP; *New York Herald*, Jan. 13, 11, 1859. U.S. revenue cutter officers claimed that there had been over 220 men on the *Susan* before the ship's departure. Log of the *Robert McClelland*, Dec. 6, 1858, Department of Transportation: Records of the United States Coast Guard, and Francis H. Hatch to Howell Cobb, Dec. 14, 1858, Records of the Department of the Treasury, both in RG 26, NA. Further confusing the picture, the British superintendent at Belize reported that 108 filibusters had been stranded in the colony. Frederick Seymour to E. B. Lytton, Dec. 26, 1858, Great Britain, PRO, Consular Despatches from Honduras, FO 39/7.

71. William Walker to Callender Fayssoux, Jan. 15, Apr. 19 (quotation), 4, James T. Van Slycke to Fayssoux, Feb. 7, Charles J. Macdonald to Fayssoux, Feb. 26, 1859, WWP; *New York Herald*, Feb. 11, 1859, *DAC*, Apr. 19, 1859; Henry Miller to Jeremiah S. Black, Sept. 28, Oct. 8, 20, 25, 1859, Joseph M. Kennedy to Black, Oct. 8, 1859, DJ, Attorney General's Papers, Letters Received, Louisiana, NA; *New-York Times*, Oct. 5, 6, 14, 24, 26, 1859.

72. William Walker to Callender Fayssoux, Nov. 8, 23, 1859, Feb. 29, Mar. 12, 14, 26, Apr. 28, June 5, 22, July 14, 1860, A. Callaghan to William Norvell, Feb. 7, 1860, Charles Allen to Walker, May 1, 5, 8, 21, 1860, J. S. West to Fayssoux, May 20, 1860, Francis Morris to Walker, May 29 [1860], [H. G. Humphries?] to Fayssoux, Aug. 21, 1860, WWP. Walker apparently was alerted to unrest on the islands by some landowners there who traveled to New Orleans, hunted him down, and invited his intervention. See Frederick Seymour to C. Fortescue, Sept. 18, 1860, PRO, FO 39/10. Roatán is spelled, alternatively, Ruatán.

73. William Walker to Callender Fayssoux, June 22, July 14, Aug. 6 1860, WWP; Brown, *Agents of Manifest Destiny*, 449–55; T. Price to E. Hall, July 18, 1860, Norvell Salmon to William Melhado, Sept. 5, 1860 (copy), Salmon to the Senior Officer, Ja-

maica (copy), Sept. 17, 1860, PRO, Consular Despatches from Honduras, 39/10, Unsigned draft, July 31, 1860, FO 39/9.

74. Norvell Salmon to Samuel Morrish, Sept. 11, 1860, PRO, Consular Despatches from Honduras, FO 39/10; "Men and Stores sent to Caribbean Sea 1860," J. S. West to William Walker, June 12, 1860, WWP.

75. John Griffin to Matthew Quay, Dec. 12, 1852, "Your Coz Sue" to Quay, Feb. 9, 1853, Matthew Stanley Quay Papers, LC; "Matthew S. Quay Papers," *Library of Congress Acquisitions, Manuscript Division, 1988* (Washington, 1990), 9–11.

76. *Philadelphia Public Ledger*, May 22, 1855; *New York Evening Post*, Nov. 24, 1855; Charles Boarman Letterbooks, May 30, 1855, LC; Robert E. May, "The Slave Power Conspiracy Revisited: United States Presidents and Filibustering, 1848–1861," in *Union and Emancipation: Essays on Politics and Race in the Civil War Era*, ed. David W. Blight and Brooks D. Simpson (Kent, Ohio, 1997), 20; *New-York Daily Times*, Feb. 25, 1857.

77. F. H. Hatch to Lewis Cass, Nov. 28, 1857, B. Squire Cotrell to Cass, Nov. 30, 1857, *H. Ex. Doc.* 24, 35th Cong., 1st Sess., 27; [William Kingsford], *Impressions of the West and South, during a Six Weeks' Holiday* (Toronto, 1858), 61; *Galveston News*, Nov. 26, 1857, quoted in *Pittsburg Post*, Dec. 14, 1857; *New-York Times*, Dec. 15, 1857; (Tampa) *Florida Peninsular*, Jan. 16, 1858; William H. Clowes to "Dear General," Jan. 1, in *New York Herald*, Jan. 8, 1858; R. Raub to JAQ, Jan. 18, 1858, JAQ Papers, HU; Edmund Ruffin Diary, May 14, 1858, LC.

78. Stout, *The Liberators*, 43; Henry E. McCulloch to Mrs. F. F. McCulloch, Oct. 11, 1855, McCulloch Family Papers, UT; Henry E. McCulloch to Elisha M. Pease, Oct. 17, 1855, Elisha M. Pease Papers, Austin History Center; Harold J. Weiss, Jr., "McCulloch, Henry Eustace," Barkley, ed., *New Handbook of Texas* 4:385–86; John A. Jaques to AO, Oct. 2, 1856, AO Papers, DU; William Frank Stewart, *Last of the Filibusters; or, Recollections of the Siege of Rivas* (Sacramento, 1857), 8; *DAC*, Mar. 20, May 16, 1857; *San Joaquin Republican* (Stockton, Calif.), May 8, 1857; James McEwen to "Dear Wife," Feb. 5, 1854, James McEwen Jr. Papers, Missouri Historical Society, St. Louis.

79. *WDNI*, Nov. 4, 1851.

80. *Galveston* (Tex.) *Tri-Weekly News*, Jan. 27, 1857; Jones, "Carolinians and Cubans," 97–98; "Personal Narrative," 217–18.

81. M. W. Mearis to JMC, [Oct.] 17, 1849, DS, Special Agents, M37, roll 9, NA; E. Peshine Smith to Henry C. Carey, July 25, 1858, Henry C. Carey Papers, HSP; *Columbus* (Ohio) *Gazette* quoted in *Lafayette* (Ind.) *Daily Argus*, July 21, 1859; *By-Laws of Knickerbocker Lodge, No. 76, I.O.S.M.* (Albany, 1859); *Cincinnati Enquirer*, Oct. 19, 1860. According to one source, the Sons of Malta parodied the era's proliferation of secret societies with elaborate initiation ceremonies, but usually became dormant rather quickly. Albert C. Stevens, comp. and ed., *The Cyclopedia of Fraternities* . . . (New York, 1907), 284.

82. Robert E. May, *The Southern Dream of a Caribbean Empire, 1854–1861* (Baton Rouge, 1973), 68–69, 72, 163–69. For a fuller treatment of Buchanan's expansionism, see Frederick Moore Binder, *James Buchanan and the American Empire* (Selinsgrove, Pa. 1994).

83. N. S. Reneau to JB, Jan. 6, 1859, with copy of Reneau to José de la Concha, Oct. 25, 1859, JB Papers, HSP; Reneau to JB and Jacob Thompson, Oct. 25, 1859, James Fox Potter Papers, State Historical Society of Wisconsin, Madison; Muster Roll, Co. G, 1st Tennessee Mounted Infantry, Compiled Military Service Records, United States Volunteers, Mexican War, RG 94, NA. In January 1859 a Havana correspondent of a South Carolina paper alluded to reports of Reneau's making an offer to Concha. Reneau also contacted Buchanan in May and June 1859, claiming that the Cuban rebels were requesting the president to give Reneau permission to represent them, and repeating his request for the use of five U.S. warships. *Charleston Courier*, Jan. 15, 1859; Reneau to JB, May 30, June 13, 1859, JB Papers, HSP. During the Civil War, Buchanan would deny receiving Reneau's October 25 letter, and suggest that it might have been purposely withheld from him because of its lack of worth. JB to John B. Blake, Jan. 7, 1863, JB Papers, HSP. Previously, Reneau apparently operated a dry-goods store in Granada, Mississippi. Mississippi correspondent's report, Jan. 15, 1859, in *New York Herald*, Feb. 6, 1859.

84. *New York Herald*, Feb. 6, 1859; *Natchez Courier*, May 12, 1859; *Memphis Daily Appeal*, Oct. 21, 1859, Dec. 29, 1858; *DAC*, Jan. 24, 1859; JB to John B. Blake, Jan. 7, 1863, JB Papers, HSP.

85. Van Aken, *King of the Night*, 241–47; "Fores, Juan José," in *Biographical Dictionary of Latin American and Caribbean Leaders* (Westport, Conn., 1988), 159–60; Wallace, *Destiny and Glory*, 101–7; Gustave A. Nuermberger, "The Continental Treaties of 1856: An American Union 'Exclusive of the United States,'" *Hispanic American Historical Review* 20 (Feb. 1940): 44n–45n; Manuel Ortiz de Zevallos to John Randolph Clay, Nov. 26, 1857, Thomas de Vivero to Ortiz, Oct. 1, 1857, Juan Ygnacio de Osma to Lewis Cass, Mar. 15, 1858, *Dipl Corr* 10: 793–94 (quotation), 793n, 799–800; "Mack-Kaui" letter from Lima, in *DAC*, Apr. 10, 1858.

86. Stephen B. Oates, *To Purge This Land with Blood: A Biography of John Brown* (New York, 1970), 130.

87. Donald S. Spencer, *Louis Kossuth and Young America: A Study of Sectionalism and Foreign Policy, 1848–1852* (Columbia, Mo., 1977), 167; Charles Callan Tansill, *The United States and Santo Domingo, 1798–1873* (Baltimore, 1938), 119, 124, 137–68; Theodore O'Hara to John T. Pickett, Dec. 8, 1851, Pickett to C. F. Henningsen, Sept. [no exact date] 1852 (draft), John T. Pickett Papers, LC; *M&P* 5:122; *Our Times* 1 (Oct. 1852): 115.

88. Luther Severance to DW, Nov. 14, 15, Dec. 8, 1851, Mar. 8, 16, May 3, June 30, 1852, DS, Despatches from United States Ministers in Hawaii, NA; *Honolulu Polynesian*, Nov. 22, 1851, Mar. 13, 1852; Andrew F. Rolle, "California Filibustering and the Hawaiian Kingdom," *Pacific Historical Review* 19 (Aug. 1950): 251–63.

89. *The Federal Cases, Comprising Cases Argued and Determined in the Circuit and District Courts of the United States*, 30 vols. (St. Paul, 1894–97), 26:1013–20.

90. "Detention of the Sch 'Susan,'" *Extraordinary Operations & Legislation, 1790–1870*, 259–62, in RG 26, Coast Guard, NA (account by Captain J. J. Morrison of the cutter *McClelland*); William Walker to Callender I. Fayssoux, June 25, July 12, 1859, Harry Maury to Fayssoux, July 3, 1859, H. G. Humphries to Fayssoux, Oct. 1, 1860, WWP; *New-York Times*, Oct. 14, 24, 1859; Joseph M. Kennedy to Jeremiah

Black, Oct. 8, 1859 (telegram), RG 60, DJ, Attorney General's Papers, Letters Received: Louisiana, NA.

Chapter Three

1. *St. Paul Daily Pioneer and Democrat*, Oct. 9, 1856.

2. Luis Molina to WLM, Dec. 20, 1855 (first quotation), Antonio José de Irisarri to Lewis Cass, Oct. 8, 1857, Molina to WLM, Dec. 6, 20, 1855, James B. Bowlin to Cass, Dec. 29, 1858, *Dipl Corr* 4:498, 4:609–10, 4:492, 10:188; *WDNI*, June 29, 1850 (second quotation); John S. Lumley to Lord Clarendon, Dec. 7, 1856 (third quotation), *P&C*, 169; Charles Mackay, *Life and Liberty in America; or, Sketches of a Tour in the United States and Canada, in 1857–8* (1859; reprint, New York, 1971), bk. 2:76–77; Martin Crawford, *The Anglo-American Crisis of the Mid-Nineteenth Century: "The Times" and America, 1850–1862* (Athens, Ga., 1987), 50, 76; [John David Borthwick], "Nicaragua and the Filibusters," *Blackwood's Edinburgh Magazine* 79 (Mar. 1856): 314.

3. *DAC*, Mar. 24, Oct. 19, 1854, Jan. 14, 1857; *Fayette* (Miss.) *Watch Tower*, Sept. 4, 1857.

4. *St. Paul Daily Pioneer and Democrat*, Oct. 9, 1856; George R. Harrington Reminiscence, George R. Harrington Papers, Missouri Historical Society, St. Louis. See also the attack by the *New-York Times* (May 31, 1860) on Britain's "fair-weather political moralists" who hypocritically attacked U.S. filibustering.

5. DW to Millard Fillmore, Oct. 4, 1851, *PDW* 2:385; William C. Rives to DW, Oct. 31, 1851, RG 59, DS, Despatches from United States Ministers to France, M34, roll 36, NA. The U.S. government pioneered the concept of neutrality legislation. Green Haywood Hackworth, *Digest of International Law* (Washington, 1943), 7:345; Roy Emerson Curtis, "The Law of Hostile Military Expeditions as Applied by the United States," *American Journal of International Law* 8 (Jan.–Apr. 1914): 3, 238–39; *Report of the Neutrality Laws Commissioners; Together with an Appendix Containing Reports from Foreign States and Other Documents* (London, 1868), 38.

6. *New-York Evening Post*, July 9, 1855 (quotation); *House Reports* 74, 35th Cong., 1st Sess., 8; George Templeton Strong Diary, Sept. 4, 1851, *The Diary of George Templeton Strong*, ed. Allan Nevins and Milton Halsey Thomas, 4 vols. (New York, 1952), 2:63; William Dowe, "A Word about Mexico: Its History, Resources, and Destiny," *Graham's Magazine* 45 (Oct. 1854): 323; *New-York Daily Times*, Apr. 10, 1857, July 16, 1858; *WDNI*, Apr. 2, 1858.

7. *DAC*, Mar. 27, 1854 (quotation), Mar. 23, 1857; (Tampa) *Florida Peninsular*, July 18, 1857; (Boston) *Flag of Our Union*, July 3, Aug. 7, 1858; *New-York Daily Times*, Jan. 30, 1855, May 19, 1857; George Mifflin Dallas to Lewis Cass, Aug. 3, 1860, George Mifflin Dallas, *A Series of Letters from London Written during the Years 1856, '57, '58, '59 and '60*, ed. Julia Dallas, 2 vols. (Philadelphia, 1869), 2:259; Lewis Cass to Luis Molina, Nov. 26, 1850, *Dipl Corr* 4:178.

8. Hugh Blair Grigsby to Henry Stephens Randall, Aug. 1, 1857, in *The Correspondence between Henry Stephens Randall and Hugh Blair Grigsby, 1856–1861*, ed. Frank J. Klingberg and Frank W. Klingberg (New York, 1972), 100; Thomas B. Macaulay to

Henry Stephens Randall, May 23, 1857, in *The Letters of Thomas Babington Macaulay*, ed. Thomas Pinney, 6 vols. (Cambridge, Eng., 1974–81), 6:94–96; *New-York Daily Times*, Apr. 10, 1857; *Philadelphia Public Ledger*, Nov. 29, 1855; *Congressional Globe*, 34th Cong., 3d Sess., appendix, 176; Thomas Claiborne to Tom Claiborne, June 14, 1850, Thomas Claiborne Papers, Philo White to John W. Ellis, John W. Ellis Papers, SHC; George Mifflin Dallas to Lewis Cass, Sept. 28, 1857, *Series of Letters* 1:209; *New York Evening Post*, July 9, 1855; Charles H. Davis to William Mervine, RG 45, Lists of Logs and Journals of Vessels of the United States Navy, William Mervine, Letters Received Letterbook, vol. 4, NA.

9. *Philadelphia Public Ledger*, Nov. 29, 1855; WLM to George M. Dallas, June 16, 1856, *Dipl Corr* 7:138–41; *St. Paul Daily Pioneer and Democrat*, June 20, 1856; *New York Herald*, Jan. 8, 1858; *Baltimore Sun*, June 12, 1856.

10. Janice E. Thomson, *Mercenaries, Pirates, and Sovereigns: State-Building and Extraterritorial Violence in Early Modern Europe* (Princeton, 1994), 188; Curtis, "Law of Hostile Military Expeditions," 2; William Javier Nelson, *Almost a Territory: America's Attempt to Annex the Dominican Republic* (Newark, Del., 1990), 42.

11. Geoffrey Moorhouse, *India Britannica* (London, 1983), 28, 40, 44–46, 57, 86, 126, 128; James S. Olson, ed., *Historical Dictionary of European Imperialism* (Westport, Conn., 1991), 133, 300–302.

12. Samuel Eliot Morison, *Admiral of the Ocean Sea: A Life of Christopher Columbus* (Boston, 1942), 86, 104–5. Likewise the Spanish conquistadores of the 1500s conquered in the name of monarchy, and anticipated titles, powers, and land from the crown as their rewards. David J. Weber, *The Spanish Frontier in North America* (New Haven, 1992), 22–24, 35–36, 45–46, 50, 64–65; Edward J. Goodman, *The Explorers of South America* (New York, 1972), 45. Columbus's full title was "Admiral of the Ocean Sea, Viceroy and Governor of the said islands and mainland," in reference to the lands that he was expected to discover and claim.

13. Robert Pringle, *Rajahs and Rebels: The Ibans of Sarawak under Brooke Rule, 1841–1941* (Ithaca, 1970), 3–4, 73–96; Steven Runciman, *The White Rajahs: A History of Sarawak from 1841 to 1946* (Cambridge, 1960), 45–156. Ultimately, in 1946, Britain took over Sarawak as a colony. In 1963 it became part of the Federation of Malaysia.

14. Rudyard Kipling, "The Man Who Would Be King," in *The Best Short Stories of Rudyard Kipling*, ed. Randall Jarrell (Garden City, N.Y., 1961), 129–54; Laurence Oliphant to Mrs. J. J. Pringle, Mar. 6, 1857, R. F. W. Allston Papers, South Carolina Historical Society, Columbia; Laurence Oliphant, *Episodes in a Life of Adventure; or, Moss from a Rolling Stone* (Edinburgh, 1887), 112–19. Kipling's story relates the tale of two men who want to "Sar-a-whack" somewhere and become kings, and their plans to take over a province in eastern Afghanistan. Oliphant (1829–88) was born in Capetown, South Africa. Later in his life he served in Britain's Parliament and became a well-known author. Tom Winnifrith, "Oliphant, Laurence," in *Victorian Novelists After 1885*, ed. Ira B. Nadel and William E. Fredeman (Detroit, 1983), 231–34.

15. See, for example, Sandra Caruthers Thomson, "Filibustering to Formosa: General Charles LeGendre and the Japanese," *Pacific Historical Review* 40 (Nov. 1971):

442–56; "Hungary's Filibustering Episode," *Current History* 15 (Nov. 1921): 342–43; Charles D. Ameringer, *The Caribbean Legion: Patriots, Politicians, Soldiers of Fortune, 1946–1950* (University Park, Pa., 1996), 27–35.

16. Nancy Nichols Barker, *The French Experience in Mexico, 1821–1861* (Chapel Hill, 1979), 137–40, 145–46; Joe A. Stout, *The Liberators: Filibustering Expeditions into Mexico, 1848–1862, and the Last Thrust of Manifest Destiny* (Los Angeles, 1973), 59–79, 103–21; *Mobile Daily Register*, Apr. 15, 17, 1859; *DAC*, May 5, June 1, 1859; Robert Benson Leard, "Bonds of Destiny: The United States and Cuba, 1848–1861" (Ph.D. diss., University of California, 1953), 142n. Raousset's first expedition was based on his contract with Jecker, Torre, and Company (a French and Mexican banking house) to colonize and develop Sonoran gold and silver mining regions near the U.S. border. This contract had the support of Mexico's government. Since the venture became transformed into a hostile military enterprise only after the adventurers encountered interference from Sonoran state authorities after their arrival at Guaymas, Sonora, it arguably was not truly a filibuster. His second expedition had a more obvious filibustering character, though it too proceeded under colonizing pretenses. Stout, *The Liberators*, 61, 63, 103–7; Barker, *French Experience*, 134–36, 144.

17. Barbara Jelavich, *History of the Balkans*, 2 vols. (Cambridge, 1983), 209–11. For an earlier instance of possible Russian filibustering, consult Terence Armstrong's analysis of Russian penetration of Siberia in the late 1500s in Armstrong, ed. and trans., *Yermak's Campaign in Siberia* (London, 1975), 1–9.

18. Mark J. Van Aken, *King of the Night: Juan José Flores and Ecuador, 1824–1864* (Berkeley, 1989), 42, 91, 119, 193, 206–7, 209–47; Lawrence A. Clayton, "Steps of Considerable Delicacy: Early Relations with Peru," in T. Ray Shurbutt, ed., *United States–Latin American Relations, 1800–1850: The Formative Generations* (Tuscaloosa, 1991), 81–82. Scholars have identified the Bolivian general and onetime protector of the Peruvian-Bolivian Confederation Andrés de Santa Cruz as another South American filibuster, on the basis of expeditions to Chile and Peru that he organized, and sometimes led, in the late 1830s and early 1840s. Van Aken, *King of the Night*, 151–53; T. Ray Shurbutt, "Personal Diplomacy: The United States and Chile, 1812–1850," in Shurbutt, ed., *United States–Latin American Relations*, 245. However, Santa Cruz's expeditions against Peru left Ecuador with the blessing of Juan Flores—then Ecuador's president.

19. Jasper Ridley, *Garibaldi* (New York, 1974), 401–21, 435–44, 474–79, 530–44, 580–90; Charles L. Dufour, *Gentle Tiger: The Gallant Life of Roberdeau Wheat* (Baton Rouge, 1957), 62–65, 80–99, 112; King of the Belgians to Queen Victoria, Nov. 2, 1860, in *The Letters of Queen Victoria: A Selection from Her Majesty's Correspondence between the Years 1857 and 1861*, ed. Arthur Christopher Benson and Viscount Esher, 3 vols. (London, 1907), 3:521–22; W. G. Clark, "Naples and Garibaldi," in *Vacation Tourists and Notes of Travel in 1860*, ed. Francis Galton (Cambridge, Eng., 1861), 31.

20. Robin W. Winks, *The Historian as Detective* (New York, 1968), 317–18; Theodore C. Caldwell, ed., *The Anglo-Boer War: Why Was It Fought? Who Was Responsible?* (Boston, 1965), x, 26–31; Olson, ed., *Historical Dictionary*, 327–28; "Ōsaka Incident," *Japan: An Illustrated Encyclopedia* (Tokyo, 1993), 1163; Mikiso Hane,

Reflections on the Way to the Gallows: Rebel Women in Prewar Japan (Berkeley, 1988), 16. Some historians maintain that the British colonial secretary Joseph Chamberlain was complicit in Jameson's raid.

21. *Hartford Daily Courant*, Aug. 14, 1851; *Harper's Weekly*, Jan. 10, 1857, p. 24; John S. Lumley to Lord Clarendon, Dec. 7, 1856, *P&C*, 134; Tredwell Moore to his mother, Apr. 15, 1854, Tredwell Moore Papers, State Historical Society of Wisconsin, Madison; P. Drayton to John A. Dahlgren, Feb. 27 [1855], John A. Dahlgren Papers, George Arents Research Library, Syracuse University, Syracuse, N.Y. That the index for the *Historical Dictionary of European Imperialism* has no entries for filibuster, filibustero, or flibustier is revealing.

22. *WDNI*, Aug. 25, 1851; *Richmond* (Ind.) *Palladium*, Sept. 3, 1851. Tom Chaffin emphasizes that the press's focus on filibustering reflected the need of penny newspapers to build circulation by sensationalizing news. Tom Chaffin, *Fatal Glory: Narciso López and the First Clandestine U.S. War against Cuba* (Charlottesville, 1996), 145–56. Even radical, German-language newspapers covered López's expedition. See Steven Rowan, ed. and trans., *Memoirs of a Nobody: The Missouri Years of an Austrian Radical, 1849–1866* (St. Louis, 1997), 140n.

23. Millard Fillmore to DW (no date given), in *Millard Fillmore Papers*, ed. Frank H. Severance, 2 vols. (1907; reprint, New York, 1970), 1:350–52.

24. *Pittsburg Daily Morning Post*, Aug. 28, 1851; *New-York Daily Tribune*, Aug. 23, 27, 28, 29, 30, 1851; *NODP*, Aug. 29, 1851; J. R. Ingersoll to Francis Markoe, Aug. 20, 1851, Galloway-Maxcy-Markoe Papers, LC; *WDNI*, Aug. 28, 1851 (quotation on New York conditions); (Harrisburg) *Pennsylvania Telegraph*, Sept. 3, 1851.

25. *Newport* (R.I.) *Mercury*, Dec. 19, 1857; *FLIN*, Jan. 9, 1858; (Boston and Portland) *Zion's Herald and Wesleyan Journal*, Dec. 16, 30, 1857, Jan. 6, 13, 20, 1858; *Harper's Weekly*, Jan. 9, 16, 1858; *New-York Christian Inquirer*, Jan. 16, 1858; Josiah Gorgas Diary, June 7, 1857, Feb. 9, 1858, in *The Journals of Josiah Gorgas*, ed. Sarah Woolfolk Wiggins (Tuscaloosa, 1995), 11, 14–15.

26. *Louisville Daily Courier*, Jan. 15, 1858; *Journal of the House of Delegates of the State of Virginia for the Session of 1857–58* (Richmond, 1857 [1858?]), 121–22; *Richmond Daily Dispatch*, Jan. 5, 12, 15, 1858; Patsy McDonald Spaw, ed., *The Texas Senate*, vol. 1: *Republic to Civil War, 1836–1861* (College Station, Tex., 1990), 297; *WDNI*, Feb. 11, 1858; letter dated Jan. 10, 1858, in [Hiram Fuller], *Belle Brittan on a Tour at Newport, and Here and There* (New York, 1858), 26–27; *New-York Christian Inquirer*, Jan. 16, 1858.

27. *SFDH*, Dec. 8, 14, 1853; Glasgow & Bro., St. Louis, to Webb & Kingsbury, Santa Fe, June 17, 1854, Webb Collection, Missouri Historical Society, St. Louis.

28. *Harper's Weekly*, May 23, 1857; (Stockton, Calif.) *San Joaquin Republican*, June 10, 1857; *Springfield* (Mass.) *Daily Republican*, Jan. 4, 10, 15, Feb. 15, 29, Apr. 18, May 15, 19, 1856; *Columbus* (Ohio) *Gazette*, Aug. 16, 1856; *Fayette* (Miss.) *Watch Tower*, Aug. 2, 1856; *FLIN*, Mar. 15, 1856; (Boston) *Flag of Our Union*, Dec. 20, 1856, July 4, 1857; (Philadelphia) *Saturday Evening Post*, Nov. 15, 1856. Amy Greenberg argues that the media's fascination with Walker derived especially from socioeconomic change. At a time when character was increasingly being evaluated in terms of mone-

tarily driven criteria, pro- and antifilibustering commentators alike projected their anxieties about changing values on Walker and his men, doing so within a discourse about the filibusters' manliness. Amy S. Greenberg, "A Gray-Eyed Man: Character, Appearance, and Filibustering," *Journal of the Early Republic* 20 (Winter 2000): 673–99.

29. *New Orleans Daily Creole*, Aug. 30, Dec. 12, 1856; *NODP*, Aug. 27, 1856; Norvell Salmon to Samuel Morrish, Sept. 11, 1860, PRO, Consular Despatches from Honduras, FO 39/10; *New York Evening Post*, July 18, 20, Aug. 6, 7, 28, Sept. 8, Oct. 1, 2, 1855; William Cullen Bryant to Frances F. Bryant, Sept. 30, 1855, in *The Letters of William Cullen Bryant*, ed. William Cullen Bryant II and Thomas G. Voss, 6 vols. (New York, 1975–92), 3:372, 373n; *Baltimore Sun*, Sept. 11, 1856; *DAC*, Jan. 10, 1854; (Austin) *Texas State Gazette*, May 17, 1856; *Clarksville* (Tex.) *Standard*, Mar. 11, 1854; *New York Herald*, Jan. 13, 1859; *Mobile Daily Register*, Jan. 3, 1858; *San Francisco Daily Placer Times and Transcript*, Jan. 13, 30, Feb. 6, 20, Mar. 22, 1854; *SFDH*, Dec. 9, 1853, Dec. 6, 7, 18, 19, 25, 1855, Jan. 20, Feb. 20, Mar. 10, Apr. 11, June 2, 17, Aug. 10, Dec. 14, 1856; (Stockton, Calif.) *San Joaquin Republican*, Feb. 12, Apr. 1, 1857. The *Fayette* (Miss.) *Watch Tower*, Apr. 25, 1856, identified the *Picayune*'s correspondent as Charles Callahan, who served the Walker régime as a customs collector. Walker, *War in Nicaragua*, 286.

30. (Austin) *Texas State Gazette*, Jan. 6, 1855; (Austin) *Texas Southern Intelligencer*, Jan. 6, 1858; *WDNI*, Jan. 6, 1858, June 3, 1857 (quoting the *Louisville Journal*); (Philadelphia) *Saturday Evening Post*, Apr. 12, 1856; *Columbus* (Miss.) *Democrat*, June 6, 1857; *DAC*, July 6, 1856; *Democratic Review*, new series, 3 (Dec. 1854): 492–94; (Boston) *Liberator*, Feb. 19, 1858.

31. *DAC*, Oct. 16, 1855; *Cincinnati Enquirer*, June 3, 4, 5, 1856; *New York Evening Post*, May 10, 1855; *Vicksburg Daily Whig*, Mar. 4, 1856; *New Orleans Daily Creole*, July 22, Dec. 16, 1856; *Newport* (R.I.) *Mercury*, May 10, 1856; *Columbus* (Ohio) *Gazette*, Aug. 29, 1856; *New York Albion*, Jan. 10, 1857; *Fayette* (Miss.) *Watch Tower*, Sept. 4, 1857; *Santa Cruz* (Calif.) *Pacific Sentinel*, May 2, 1857; (Stockton, Calif.) *San Joaquin Republican*, Apr. 11, 1857; *WDNI*, Aug. 30, 1851; Jeffrey A. Zemler, "The Texas Press and the Filibusters of the 1850s: Lopez, Carvajal, and Walker" (M.A. thesis, North Texas State University, 1983), 151.

32. *WDNI*, July 2, 1850; *Cincinnati Enquirer*, Aug. 3, 1851; *DAC*, Feb. 22, 1854; (Tampa) *Florida Peninsular*, Nov. 15, 1856; *New-York Daily Times*, May 12, 1857. See also Attorney William A. Bickle's notice comparing collecting debts to Cuba filibusters. *Richmond Palladium*, Sept. 10, 1851.

33. Antonio Rafael de la Cova, "Ambrosio Jose Gonzales: A Cuban Confederate Colonel" (Ph.D. diss., West Virginia University, 1994), 134; *NODP*, June 14, 1854, Dec. 26, 1858, Jan. 1, 1859; Florence M. Jumonville, comp., *Bibliography of New Orleans Imprints, 1764–1864* (New Orleans, 1989), 497; playbill for "Nicaragua; or, Gen. Walker's Victories," in John P. Heiss Scrapbook, TSLA; *SFDH*, Sept. 13, 1856; George B. Bryan, "[Purdy's] National Theatre Company," in Weldon B. Durham, ed., *American Theatre Companies, 1749–1887* (Westport, 1986), 376–77; Frederic Rosengarten Jr., *Freebooters Must Die! The Life and Death of William Walker, the Most No-*

torious Filibuster of the Nineteenth Century (Wayne, Pa., 1976), 145; *DAC*, Dec. 23, 1857. For Bingham, see *Harper's Weekly*, Feb. 7, 1857; Rosengarten, *Freebooters Must Die!* 160–62.

34. *NODP*, Sept. 4, 1851; *New-York Daily Times*, June 18, 22, 1857. See also the telegraphic dispatch from New Orleans about the announcement at the St. Charles Theatre of Paulding's interception of Walker, in the *Memphis Daily Appeal*, Dec. 30, 1857.

35. Sophia Hawthorne to her mother, Aug. 1, 1850, in Rose Hawthorne Lathrop, *Memories of Hawthorne* (Boston, 1897), 131–34; Nathaniel Hawthorne to Horatio Bridge Washington, June 6, Hawthorne to William D. Ticknor, June 6, 1856, in *Nathaniel Hawthorne: The Letters, 1853–1856*, ed. Thomas Woodson, James A. Rubino, L. Neal Smith, and Norman Holmes Pearson (Columbus, Ohio, 1987), 496–97, 499; *New York Mirror* quoted in *Cincinnati Enquirer*, Sept. 7, 1851; (Springfield) *Illinois Daily Journal*, Dec. 10, 1851; Ned Buntline, *The Mysteries and Miseries of New Orleans* (New York, 1851); Edd Winfield Parks, "Webber, Charles Wilkins," *DAB* 10, pt. 1:580–81; Henry Nash Smith, *Virgin Land: The American West as Symbol and Myth* (Cambridge, Mass., 1950), 72–77, 114–15; "Mr. Seedy," *Harper's New Monthly Magazine* 15 (Sept. 1857): 529–33. Lucy Petaway Holcombe, a southern belle who later married Francis Pickens (who became governor of South Carolina), also wrote a novel about the López filibusters—this one possibly semi-autobiographical since it concerned a relationship of a young woman with an expeditionist. Henrietta M. Hardimann [pseud.], *The Free Flag of Cuba; or, The Martyrdom of Lopez: A Tale of the Liberating Expedition of 1851* . . . (New York, 1855); Cynthia Myers, "Queen of the Confederacy," in *The Women's War in the South: Recollections and Reflections of the American Civil War*, ed. Charles G. Waugh and Martin H. Greenberg (Nashville, 1999), 293–94.

36. *New-York Daily Tribune*, Sept. 8, 1851; *DAC*, Nov. 16, 1854, May 22, 1860; *Philadelphia Public Ledger*, Feb. 4, 1856; *Washington* (D.C) *Constitution*, Mar. 30, 1860; *New-Orleans Delta* quoted in *New-York Times*, Jan. 5, 1860; *Sacramento Phoenix*, Dec. 13, 1857. See also the prospectus for *The Cuban Liberator* in *Washington Southern Press*, Oct. 1, 1851, the advertisement for William Wells's book on William Walker in the *New York Daily Times*, June 4, 1856, and the publisher's notice in the *Florida Peninsular*, May 28, 1859, for Peter F. Stout's *Nicaragua: Past, Present and Future* (Philadelphia, 1859), which promoted sales by noting that the volume included "a history of the Filibusters."

37. *New-York Daily Times*, June 17, 1857; *The Filibuster Polka* (Baltimore, 1852), microfilm copy in Performing Arts Reading Room, LC; "Nicarauga [*sic*] National Song," Rose Music Collection, TSLA; "John Fremont's Coming" and "Get out of the way, old Buchanan," in *The Campaign of 1856: Fremont Songs for the People, Original and Selected*, comp. Thomas Drew (Boston, 1856), 16–17, 56–58. See also the announcement for "The Flag of Cuba" and mention of "The Lopez Dead March" in *NODP*, Oct. 25, 1851, Sept. 2, 1852; and the advertisement of Smith, Bangs & Co. for "A Life-Like Portrait of General Lopez" in *New-York Daily Tribune*, Aug. 30, 1851.

38. *DAC*, Apr. 7, 8, 1858, Apr. 9, 1860; Basil Rauch, *American Interest in Cuba,*

1848–1855 (New York, 1948), 230; (Austin) *Texas State Gazette*, Sept. 16, 1854; *NODP*, Sept. 1, 1852.

39. *DAC*, Jan. 15, 1860, July 21, 1856; (Austin) *Texas State Gazette*, Sept. 16, 1854; *Pittsburg Daily Morning Post*, May 31, 1851; *New-York Daily Times*, Dec. 22, 1856; "A Visit to General Walker and Suite," in *FLIN*, June 27, 1857; *Mobile Daily Register*, Jan. 23, 1858; *New York Herald*, Aug. 20, 1858; Announcement of the "Fancy Dress Ball" of the Order of the Lone Star in *New Orleans Daily Delta*, Dec. 27, 1851; *New-York Daily Times*, June 17, 1857; *NODP*, Sept. 4, 1851; *Clarksville* (Tenn.) *Jeffersonian*, Aug. 2, 1854. Transparencies were images painted onto large fabrics, and illuminated from behind by candles.

40. John Letcher to James O. Davidson, Jan. 2, 1858, James O. Davidson Papers, State Historical Society of Wisconsin, Madison; (Stockton, Calif.) *San Joaquin Republican* quoted in *San Francisco Daily Placer Times and Transcript*, Jan. 13, 1854.

41. [Richardson Hardy], *The History and Adventures of the Cuban Expedition, from the First Movements Down to the Dispersion of the Army at Key West, and the Arrest of General Lopez . . .* (Cincinnati, 1850), 16; *Fayette* (Miss.) *Watch Tower*, Apr. 25, 1856; *New-York Times*, Oct. 6, 1859; *New York Herald*, Jan. 13, 1859; *Philadelphia Public Ledger*, Jan. 11, 1856; *New Orleans Daily Creole*, Oct. 28, 1856; *New-York Daily Times*, Dec. 25, 1856.

42. *New York Evening Post*, Apr. 28, June 8, 1855; *DAC*, Oct. 14, 1854; *New York Daily Tribune*, May 27, 1850; *Savannah Daily Morning News*, May 27, 1850; *Philadelphia Public Ledger*, Apr. 30, 1855; *Springfield* (Mass.) *Daily Republican*, May 28, 1850; *New-York Times*, Oct. 24, 1859; *SFDH*, Oct. 3, 1854.

43. John Washington Graham Senior Oration, Aug. 16, 1856, Minutes, Dialectic Society, Aug. 28, 1857, Oct. 16, 1860, Addresses/Debates, Dialectic Society Records, Minutes, Philanthropic Society, Sept. 5, 1851, Oct. 12, 1860, Philanthropic Society Records, all at University of North Carolina Archives, SHC; Minutes, June 18, 1851, United Brothers Society Papers, Brown University Archives, John Hay Library, Providence; Minutes, Philozenian Society, May 28, 1856, Case Western Reserve University Archives, Cleveland; Record of Questions Debated (no dates provided), Calliopean Society, Yale University Archives, Sterling Memorial Library, New Haven; Herbert C. Bradshaw, *History of Hampden-Sydney College: From the Beginnings to the Year 1856* (Privately printed, 1976), 349. See also R. H. Bennett's address at Bethany College, Feb. 22, 1853, cadet William W. McCreery's Independence Day oration at West Point in 1859, and plebe Henry A. Du Pont's comment on an 1856 address at West Point. R. H. Bennett, "Fillmore's Administration and Cuba," in *Columbus* (Miss.) *Standard*, May 7, 1853; "An Address Delivered by Cadet W. W. McCreery of the First Class, to the Corps of Cadets of the U.S. Military Academy, West Point, N.Y., on 4th July 1859," U.S. Military Academy Library, West Point, N.Y.; Henry A. Du Pont to his father, July 7, 1856, Henry A. Du Pont Papers, HML.

44. Henry Wadsworth Longfellow Journal, Jan. 2, 1853, in *Life of Henry Wadsworth Longfellow, with Extracts from his Journals and Correspondence*, ed. Samuel Longfellow (Boston, 1886), 2:231; B. D. Palmer to "Friend Reeves," Mar. 13, 1857, Missouri University Papers, Missouri Historical Society, St. Louis.

45. Asbury Harpending, *The Great Diamond Hoax and Other Stirring Incidents in the*

Life of Asbury Harpending, ed. James H. Wilkins (1915[?]; reprint, Norman, 1958), 5; Charles C. Jones Jr. to Rev. and Mrs. C. C. Jones, Sept. 9, 1851, in *A Georgian at Princeton*, ed. Robert Manson Myers (New Haven, 1972), 226; John T. McMurran Jr. to L. P. Conner, Sept. 10, 1851, Lemuel Conner Papers, Department of Archives and Manuscripts, Louisiana State University, Baton Rouge; A. J. McNeil to JAQ, June 10, 1854, JAQ Papers, MDAH; William Mason to JAQ, July 15, 1854, JAQ Papers, HU. See also Major Horace Bell, *Reminiscences of a Ranger; or, Early Times in Southern California* (Santa Barbara, 1927), 232.

46. *New-York Evangelist*, Aug. 21, 1856; *Springfield* (Mass.) *Daily Republican*, May 21, 1856; *New-York Daily Tribune*, July 18, 1857; Jay Monaghan, *Civil War on the Western Border, 1854–1865* (Boston, 1955), 55–57, 76–77, 93; *Washington National Era*, Nov. 27, 1856; James A. Rawley, *Race and Politics: "Bleeding Kansas" and the Coming of the Civil War* (Philadelphia, 1969), 129–30. *Brownson's Quarterly Review* connected filibustering to Kansas by arguing that Stephen Douglas's squatter sovereignty "involves the error of filibusterism." See the *Review* 17 (July 1860): 106.

47. *Harrisburg* (Pa.) *Morning Herald*, Sept. 10, 11, 14, 15, 20, 21, 22, 24, 25, 28, Oct. 9, 1855; Ben McCulloch to his nephew, Jan. 31, 1858, McCulloch Family Papers, UT; Bellows letter, Jan. 6, 1857, in (Boston) *Liberator*, Feb. 6, 1857; *New-York Times*, Apr. 26, 1860. Catherine Fisk and Erwin Chemerinsky identify an 1853 comment by U.S. congressman Albert Gallatin Brown as the first instance when the term was used to designate legislative obstructionism, and link the two meanings of the term by saying that the "obstruction of Congress" and private expeditions both represent "adventurism" to "thwart a government." Fisk and Chemerinsky, "The Filibuster," *Stanford Law Review* 49 (Jan. 1997): 192–93. See also "Fillibustering at the Lagoon," *DAC*, Feb. 25, 1854, which interjected the term into a local controversy respecting street construction.

48. DW to Millard Fillmore, July 30, 1852, *PDW* 2:704; (Boston) *Flag of Our Union*, Feb. 2, 1856; *Galveston Weekly News*, Jan. 31, 1854; *DAC*, Mar. 10, 1858.

49. John F. Crampton to Lord Clarendon, Sept. 25, 1853, *P&C*, 84; William Craft, *Running a Thousand Miles for Freedom; or, The Escape of William and Ellen Craft from Slavery* (1860; reprint, Miami, 1969), 31; "Diary of J. Alexander Fulton, Esq., Kept on a Trip West and South October 1, 1854 to January 3, 1855" (microfilm copy: partly typed, partly handwritten), Delaware State Archives, Hall of Records, Dover.

50. Henry Miles Moore Journal, Sept. 25 (quotation), 29, 1860, BRBM; (Little Rock) *Arkansas Whig*, Aug. 28, 31, 1851; Frederick Douglass speech, Dec. 3, 1860, quoted in *The Negro's Civil War: How American Negroes Felt and Acted during the War for the Union*, ed. James M. McPherson (1965; reprint, Urbana, 1982), 12–13.

51. *New-York Times*, Oct. 5, 1859.

Chapter Four

1. John H. Goddard to Alexander H. H. Stuart, June 15, 17, 1850, Logan Hunton to DW, Oct. 2, 1850 (copy), RG 48, Department of the Interior, Records Concerning the Cuban Expedition of 1850–51, NA.

2. *New-York Daily Tribune*, Aug. 21, 1849.

3. *New York Express*, Aug. 21, 1849, quoted in *WDNI*, Aug. 23, 1849; "Slocum, John S.," in *Historical Register and Dictionary of the United States Army, from Its Organization, September 29, 1789, to March 2, 1903*, comp. Francis B. Heitman, 2 vols. (1903; reprint, Urbana, 1965), 1:892; John S. Slocum to Albert Tracy, June 27, 1849, Albert Tracy Papers, New York Public Library; *New Orleans Delta* list of López's officers in *New-York Daily Tribune*, June 1, 1850; *List of Officers of the Army of the United States from 1779 to 1900 . . .*, comp. William H. Powell (New York, 1900), 5; Charles L. Dufour, *Gentle Tiger: The Gallant Life of Roberdeau Wheat* (Baton Rouge, 1957), 25-31; R. Jones to Winfield Scott, Aug. 27, 1847, RG 94, Adjutant General, Letters Sent, NA; Anderson C. Quisenberry, *López's Expeditions to Cuba, 1850-1851* (Louisville, 1906), 45; Allison Nelson to JAQ, June 4, 1854, JAQ Papers, MDAH; "Nelson, Allison," in Ezra J. Warner, *Generals in Gray: Lives of the Confederate Commanders* (Baton Rouge, 1959), 223.

4. Joe A. Stout, *The Liberators: Filibustering Expeditions into Mexico, 1848-1862, and the Last Thrust of Manifest Destiny* (Los Angeles, 1973), 38-39; Robert E. May, *John A. Quitman: Old South Crusader* (Baton Rouge, 1985), 147-215; Cadmus M. Wilcox, *History of the Mexican War* (Washington, 1892), 690; "Army Register, N.A.," Feb. 26th 1857," WWP; *FLIN*, Feb. 9, 1856; War Department Adjutant General's Office, General Orders, no. 42, July 28, 1848, in "U.S. Army: Rank and Brevets 1847-1848," bound volume in Albert Tracy Papers, New York Public Library; *Baltimore Sun*, Oct. 4, 1856; R. A. Brock, "General Birkett Davenport Fry," *Southern Historical Society Papers* 18 (1890): 286-88; *New-York Daily Times*, Dec. 22, 25 (quotation), 1856; Feb. 3, 1857; *Pittsburg Post*, Nov. 26, 1857.

5. [F. C. M. Boggess], *A Veteran of Four Wars: The Autobiography of F. C. M. Boggess* (Arcadia, Fla., 1900), 8; *Historical Register and Dictionary* 1:968; John S. Slocum to Albert Tracy, June 27, 1849, Albert H. Tracy to Albert Tracy, Aug. 13, 1849, Albert Tracy Papers, New York Public Library; *New York Express*, Aug. 21, 1849, quoted in *WDNI*, Aug. 23, 1849. Tracy claimed to have studied art under the inventor of the telegraph, Samuel F. B. Morse. Martha A. Sandweiss, Rick Stewart, and Ben W. Huseman, *Eyewitness to War: Prints and Daguerreotypes of the Mexican War, 1846-1848* (Fort Worth, 1989), 9.

6. [J. C. Davis], *The History of the Late Expedition to Cuba, by O. D. D. O., One of the Participants . . .* (New Orleans, 1850), 26; George Bolivar Hall to JAQ, Aug. 2, 1853, JAQ Papers, HU.

7. JAQ to Mansfield Lovell, Mar. 15, 1850, Mansfield Lovell Papers, Huntington Library, San Marino, Calif.; A. B. Bannon to JAQ, May 25, 1850, JAQ Papers, MDAH.

8. *American Star* (Mexico City), Sept. 20, Oct. 15, 1847; Mansfield Lovell Diary, May 4, 1848, Mansfield Lovell Papers, Huntington Library, San Marino, Calif.; C. C. Danley to JAQ, Sept. 14, 1847, June 27, 1854, A. W. Hobson to JAQ, June 20, 1854, Henry Gillespey to JAQ, Feb. 9, 1855, Cadmus M. Wilcox to JAQ, May 8, 1854, JAQ Papers, MDAH; Robert Farquarson to JAQ, Feb. 7, 1855, George Bolivar Hall to JAQ, Aug. 2, 1853, JAQ Papers, HU; Leonne M. Hudson, *The Odyssey of a Southerner: The Life and Times of Gustavus Woodson Smith* (Macon, Ga., 1998), 10; *List of Officers of the Army*, 594-95; *Historical Register and Dictionary* 1:644, 898.

9. Antonio Rafael de la Cova, "Filibusters and Freemasons: The Sworn Obligation," *Journal of the Early Republic* 17 (Spring 1997), 95–120; *Richmond Palladium*, Sept. 10, 1851; Luis Martínez-Fernández, *Torn between Empires: Economy, Society, and Patterns of Political Thought in the Hispanic Caribbean, 1840–1878* (Athens, Ga., 1994), 129–30.

10. May, *John A. Quitman*, 31, 112, 373; Thomas Jones Pope to JAQ, May 5, C. G. F. Bell to JAQ, Oct. 27, 1851, JAQ Papers, MDAH.

11. [Teresa Griffin Vielé], *"Following the Drum": A Glimpse of Frontier Life* (New York, 1858), 192; Paul N. Spellman, *Forgotten Texas Leader: Hugh McLeod and the Texan Santa Fe Expedition* (College Station, Tex., 1999), 25, 44–45, 148–49, 154, 166; William Walker, *The War in Nicaragua* (1860; reprint, Tucson, 1985), 105; George R. Canton to "Dear Friend," Dec. 14, 1855, in *DAC*, Jan. 6, 1856.

12. Persifor F. Smith to R. Jones, July 18, 1852, *S. Ex. Doc.* 1, 32d Cong., 2d Sess., 15–16.

13. Barbara A. Tenenbaum, *The Politics of Penury: Debts and Taxes in Mexico, 1821–1856* (Albuquerque, 1986), 18–20, 29, 37, 40–43, 52, 91, 127–28, 182; Michael C. Meyer and William L. Sherman, *The Course of Mexican History* (3d edn., New York, 1987), 294–331; Donathon C. Olliff, *Reforma Mexico and the United States: A Search for Alternatives to Annexation, 1854–1861* (University, Ala., 1981); Ray F. Broussard, "Comonfort: Misunderstood Reformer," *West Georgia College Studies in the Social Sciences* 6 (June 1967): 81–92.

14. E. Bradford Burns, *Patriarch and Folk: The Emergence of Nicaragua, 1798–1858* (Cambridge, Mass., 1991), 35–42, 53, 56–57 148–52 (quotation on p. 39). After breaking from Spanish rule in 1821, Central America briefly fell under the orbit of Iturbide's Mexican Empire. From 1823 to 1838 Nicaragua was part of the United Provinces of Central America, though it did not organize as a state within this federation until 1826. In 1838 Nicaragua withdrew from the Central American union.

15. Franklin W. Knight, *Slave Society in Cuba during the Nineteenth Century* (Madison, 1970), 88–90, 102; Martínez-Fernández, *Torn between Empires*, 59–65, 121–24; Anton L. Allahar, "Sugar, Slaves, and the Politics of Annexationism: Cuba, 1840–1855," *Colonial Latin American Historical Review* 57 (Dec. 1994): 281–304; Philip Foner, *A History of Cuba and Its Relations with the United States*, 2 vols. (New York, 1962–63), 1:53–55, 139–40, 179; Hugh Thomas, *Cuba, or the Pursuit of Freedom* (London, 1971), 207–8; Christopher Schmidt-Nowara, *Empire and Antislavery: Spain, Cuba, and Puerto Rico, 1833–1874* (Pittsburgh, 1999), 14–32.

16. David J. Weber, *The Mexican Frontier, 1821–1846: The American Southwest under Mexico* (Albuquerque, 1982), 22, 26, 32–34, 247–50; Joseph Milton Nance, *After San Jacinto: The Texas-Mexican Frontier, 1836–1841* (Austin, 1963), 142–377; Justin Harvey Smith, "La República De Río Grande," *American Historical Review* 25 (July 1920): 660–75; Tenenbaum, *Politics of Penury*, 22–23. Conservatives sought support from the European Catholic powers of France and Spain, and drew strength from Mexico's privileged clergy, aristocracy, and army. Mexican liberals had ties to their country's professionals, and especially promoted progress through public education, lower tariffs (or free trade), the distribution of clergy-held lands, the develop-

ment of a transportation infrastructure, and the application of science and technology to Mexico's problems. Many Mexican liberals had spent time in the United States. Olliff, *Reforma Mexico*, 13–24; Weber, *Mexican Frontier*, 31, 34; Walter V. Scholes, *Mexican Politics during the Juárez Regime, 1855–1872* (Columbia, Mo., 1957), 1–3.

17. Walker's statement reprinted in Alejandro Bolaños-Geyer, *William Walker: The Gray-Eyed Man of Destiny*, vol. 2: *The Californias* (Lake St. Louis, Mo., 1989), 369–71.

18. William O. Scroggs, *Filibusters and Financiers: The Story of William Walker and His Associates* (New York, 1916), 34, 34n; Stout, *The Liberators*, 84; Charles H. Brown, *Agents of Manifest Destiny: The Lives and Times of the Filibusters* (Chapel Hill, 1980), 191; Weber, *Mexican Frontier*, 37, 86–87, 89, 109–10; James E. Officer, *Hispanic Arizona, 1536–1856* (Tucson, 1987), 300–302; J. Fred Rippy, *The United States and Mexico* (New York, 1931), 77–80; William A. Depalo Jr., *The Mexican National Army, 1822–1852* (College Station, Tex., 1997), 149, 154–55. Many Apache attacks originated in land acquired by the United States in the Treaty of Guadalupe-Hidalgo ending the Mexican War. The treaty's Article 11 obligated the United States to prevent such attacks. Donald S. Frazier, ed., *The United States and Mexico at War: Nineteenth-Century Expansionism and Conflict* (New York, 1998), 516; Rippy, *United States and Mexico*, 77–78.

19. (Tubac) *Weekly Arizonian*, Mar. 10, 1859; (Stockton, Calif.) *San Joaquin Republican*, Feb. 10, 1857; Stuart V. Voss, *On the Periphery of Nineteenth-Century Mexico: Sonora and Sinaloa, 1810–1877* (Tucson, 1982), 136–40; Officer, *Hispanic Arizona*, 300–302; Stout, *The Liberators*, 19–21, 144–48; William Allen Wallace Diary, Mar. 11, 1857, BRBM; Henry A. Crabb to Don José Maria Redondo, Mar. 26, 1857, *H. Ex. Doc.* 68, 35th Cong., 1st Sess., 31. Pesqueira's feud with Gandara bore upon Mexico's Federalist-Centralist split. Voss, *On the Periphery*, 137; Officer, *Hispanic Arizona*, 302.

20. Brown, *Agents of Manifest Destiny*, 217–18; Burns, *Patriarch and Folk*, 192–94; Frederic Rosengarten Jr., *Freebooters Must Die! The Life and Death of William Walker, the Most Notorious Filibuster of the Nineteenth Century* (Wayne, Pa., 1976), 71–80. Walker earlier that year had edited the *San Francisco Commercial-Advertiser*, a paper owned for part of Walker's editorship by Cole. Brown, *Agents of Manifest Destiny*, 216–17.

21. John L. O'Sullivan to Samuel J. Tilden, May 17, 1850, quoted in Sheldon Howard Harris, "The Public Career of John Louis O'Sullivan" (Ph.D. diss., Columbia University, 1958), 299; Antonio Rafael de la Cova, "Cuban Filibustering in Jacksonville in 1851," *Northeast Florida History* 3 (1996): 21; Charles A. Downer et al. to Daniel M. Barringer, [Oct.?] 31, 1851, in *Dipl Corr* 11:639n; "Personal Narrative of Louis Schlesinger of Adventures in Cuba and Ceuta," *Democratic Review* 31 (Sept. 1852, Oct. 1852, Nov.– Dec. 1852): 566n; *Vicksburg Weekly Whig*, May 21, 1851. Tilden would be called as a defense witness in O'Sullivan's 1852 filibustering trial. *New-York Daily Times*, Mar. 30, 1852.

22. JAQ to C. A. L. Lamar, Jan. 5, 1855, JAQ Papers, HU; Basil Rauch, *American Interest in Cuba, 1848–1855* (New York, 1948), 154–58; May, *John A. Quitman*, 275, 282, 292; Foner, *History of Cuba* 2:92.

23. Abraham Lincoln, "Address before the Young Men's Lyceum of Springfield,

Illinois, Jan. 27, 1838," *The Collected Works of Abraham Lincoln*, ed. Roy P. Basler, 9 vols. (New Brunswick, N.J., 1953–55), 1:109; David Herbert Donald, *Lincoln* (New York, 1995), 80–83; M. W. Mearis to JMC, no date but marked "Recd 27.Sept.49" (quotation), RG 59, DS, M37, roll 9, NA; Robert H. Smith to Jeremiah S. Black, Dec. 21, 1858, DJ, Attorney General's Papers, Letters Received: Alabama, NA; Helen Chapman to her mother, Oct. 21, 1851, in *The News from Brownsville: Helen Chapman's Letters from the Texas Military Frontier, 1848–1852*, ed. Caleb Coker (Austin, 1992), 265; John S. Lumley to Lord Clarendon, Dec. 7, 1856, *P&C*, 167–69; *Chicago Tribune*, Oct. 28, 1859; *Connecticut Courant*, July 19, 1851, quoted in *WDNI*, July 22, 1851.

24. George S. Denison to Jim, Aug. 23, 1855, in James A. Padgett, ed., "Some Letters of George Stanton Denison, 1854–1866: Observations of a Yankee on Conditions in Louisiana and Texas," *Louisiana Historical Quarterly* 23 (Oct. 1940): 1158–59; Richard Maxwell Brown, *Strain of Violence: Historical Studies of American Violence and Vigilantism* (New York, 1975), 97 (quotation), 134–43; Francis Edward Russwurm to his brother, Mar. 11, 1857, Russwurm Family Papers, TSLA; W. Eugene Hollon, *Frontier Violence: Another Look* (New York, 1974), 56–79. Horace Bell, a major in Walker's Nicaraguan army until he deserted, was a former member of a Los Angeles area vigilante group rather than one of the vigilantes' targets. "Army Register, N.A. Feb 26th 1857," WWP; "Bell, Horace," in *Encyclopedia of Frontier Biography*, 3 vols. (Glendale, Calif., 1988), 1:90.

25. *Vicksburg Tri-Weekly Whig*, Sept. 26, 1848; J. H. Sims to JAQ, Feb. 19, 1851, Thomas C. Hindman to J. S. Thrasher, June 12, 1854, T. C. Hindman to JAQ, Jan. 31, 1855, JAQ Papers, MDAH; *Galveston Weekly News*, Jan. 10, 1854; J. McDonald to JAQ, Mar. 26, 1854, JAQ Papers, HU; Dunbar Rowland, ed., *The Official and Statistical Register of the State of Mississippi* (Madison, 1917), 238. Crabb's case was brought before a grand jury in Warren County, Mississippi, which failed to find a true bill against him. Hindman was eventually cleared of the charges against him. *Vicksburg Tri-Weekly Whig*, Apr. 19, 1849; Diane Neal and Thomas W. Kremm, *Lion of the South: General Thomas C. Hindman* (Macon, Ga., 1993), 24–27.

26. Mrs. C. S. Tarpley to JAQ (no date), JAQ Papers, HU; William A. Wallace Diary, Sept. 12, 1856; Lacy K. Ford Jr., *Origins of Southern Radicalism: The South Carolina Upcountry, 1800–1860* (New York, 1988), 293–94. Walker eventually executed Estelle for killing another second lieutenant in the filibuster army. Tillman was convicted of manslaughter after his return to the United States and served a two-year jail sentence. General Orders, no. 167, Sept. 18, 1856, General Order Book, WWP; Ford, *Origins*, 294. One group of deserters from Walker's army characterized his officer corps (and agents) as illiterate murderers, thieves, "brothel-house bullies," prize fighters, U.S. army rejects, and other disreputable types. "The Deserters Manifesto," Aug. 16, 1857, *New-York Daily Times*, Aug. 19, 1857.

27. William Miles, *Journal of the Sufferings and Hardships of Capt. Parker H. French's Overland Expedition to California, Which Left New York City, May 13th, 1850* (1851; reprint, New York, 1916), 5, 12, 16; M. Baldridge, *A Reminiscence of the Parker H. French Expedition through Texas and Mexico to California in the Spring of 1850* (Los Angeles, 1959), introd. (unpaged), passim; Gershom Flagg to Willard Flagg, Apr. 5,

1852, in *The Flagg Correspondence: Selected Letters, 1816–1854*, ed. Barbara Lawrence and Nedra Branz (Carbondale, Ill., 1986), 184; *WDNI*, Jan. 4, 1858.

28. James Madison Miller to JAQ, Sept. 17, 1854, JAQ Papers, HU; Rosengarten, *Freebooters Must Die!* 2–3; John H. Gerould, "O'Hara, Theodore," *DAB* 7, pt. 2:5; Nathaniel Cheairs Hughes Jr. and Thomas Clayton Ware, *Theodore O'Hara: Poet-Soldier of the Old South* (Knoxville, 1998), 8–12; first verse of "The Bivouac of the Dead," poem reproduced in full in *Confederate Veteran* 7 (May 1899): 202; John E. Kleber, ed., *The Kentucky Encyclopedia* (Lexington, 1992), 689.

29. (Stockton, Calif.) *San Joaquin Republican*, Aug. 9, 1851; Dan L. Thrapp, *Encyclopedia of Frontier Biography*, 3 vols. (Glendale, Calif., 1988), 1:333–34; May, *John A. Quitman*, 29–129, 200–235.

30. May, *John A. Quitman*, 270–95; James Pinckney Henderson to JAQ, Oct. 6, 1854, JAQ Papers, HU; W. J. Hughes, *Rebellious Ranger: Rip Ford and the Old Southwest* (Norman, 1964), 104; W. M. Estelle to JAQ, May 25, 1854, JAQ Papers, MDAH; receipt for shares of stock, Dec. 1854, in Thomas Jefferson Rusk Papers, UT; "Cooper, James," in *Biographical Directory of the American Congress, 1774–1996* (Alexandria, Va., 1997), 861; J. G. Howard, "Edward J. C. Kewen," in *Representative and Leading Men of the Pacific . . .*, ed. J. G. Howard (San Francisco, 1870), 341–46; John C. Reid, *Reid's Tramp; or, A Journal of the Incidents of Ten Months Travel through Texas, New Mexico, Arizona, Sonora, and California . . .* (1858; reprint, Austin, 1935), 201–19; Cornelius C. Smith Jr., *William Sanders Oury: History-Maker of the Old Southwest* (Tucson, 1967), 86, 93–96.

31. William R. Henry to the people of Texas, Sept. 22, 1857, in *Galveston News*, reprinted in *New-York Times*, Oct. 19, 1857; Henry to the editors, Oct. 3, 1857, in (Corpus Christi) *Nueces Valley Weekly*, Oct. 10, 1857; Manuel Guerra, "Henry, William R.," in Roy R. Barkley, ed., *The New Handbook of Texas*, 6 vols. (Austin, 1996), 3:564.

32. Stout, *The Liberators*, 38; *Cincinnati Enquirer*, Aug. 30, 1851; "Memoirs of John Salmon Ford," 7 vols., typescript, 4:640, at Texas State Library, Archives Division, Austin; *WDNI*, Aug. 6, 1853; "Bigger, Samuel," "Morehead, James Turner," in *Biographical Directory of the Governors of the United States*, ed. Robert Sobel and John Raimo, 4 vols. (Westport, Conn., 1978), 400, 515–16; "Marshall, Thomas Francis," in *Biographical Directory of the United States Congress*, 1448.

33. The old soldier of 1814 to Charles M. Conrad, undated but endorsed in December 1852, RG 107, Secretary of War, Letters Received: Registered Series, M221, roll 162, NA.

34. Stephen Thernstrom and Peter R. Knights, "Men in Motion: Some Data and Speculations about Urban Population Mobility in Nineteenth-Century America," in *Anonymous Americans: Explorations in Nineteenth-Century Social History* (Englewood Cliffs, N.J., 1971), 149 (quotation); Charles N. Glaab and A. Theodore Brown, *A History of Urban America* (New York, 1967), 26; Richard B. Stott, *Workers in the Metropolis: Class, Ethnicity, and Youth in Antebellum New York City* (Ithaca, N.Y., 1990), 71; Stanley Nadel, *Little Germany: Ethnicity, Religion, and Class in New York City, 1845–80* (Urbana, 1990), 1, 16–18; Dennis C. Rousey, *Policing the Southern City: New Or-*

leans, 1805−1889 (Baton Rouge, 1996), 38. More immigrants arrived in the United States in 1845−54 than in the previous seven decades put together. Tyler Anbinder, *Nativism and Slavery: The Northern Know Nothings and the Politics of the 1850s* (New York, 1992), 3.

35. Charles A. Downer et al. to Daniel M. Barringer, [Oct.?] 1851, *Dipl Corr* 11:639n; *Harper's Weekly*, Apr. 18, 1857; John A. Campbell to Jeremiah Black, Nov. 22, 1858, Jeremiah S. Black Papers, LC; William E. Prince to Don Jose Maria J. [?] Carvajal, Oct. 6, 1851 (copy), William E. Prince Papers, BRBM; *New York Evening Post*, July 18, 1855; Foxhall A. Parker to William A. Graham, Sept. 25, 1851, SquadL, roll 92.

36. Edward H. Cook to DW, Sept. 12, 1851 (with enclosed extract copied from Cornelius Cook to Ike Cook, Aug. 5, 1851), *PDW* 2:381−82; Henry S. Lee to DW, Sept. 11, 1851, O. B. Brown to DW, Sept. 30, 1851, Frances Patterson to DW, Nov. 7, 1851, DS, ML, M179, rolls 127, 128, NA; John Marshall to Dear Father, Aug. 3, 1856, Marshall Family Papers, Filson Club Historical Society, Louisville; J. T. Van Slycke to Callender I. Fayssoux, Feb. 7, 1859, WWP; Sophia Du Pont to Clema, Jan. 20, Sophia Du Pont to Henry A. Du Pont, Jan. 24, Sophia Du Pont to Samuel Francis Du Pont, Feb. 12, 1856, Mrs. Samuel Francis Du Pont Papers, HML; *WDNI*, Sept. 11, 29, 1851.

37. F. L. Claiborne to JAQ, June 15, 1854, JAQ Papers, MDAH; J. C. Pickett to Messrs. Gales & Seaton, Sept. 1, 1849, in *WDNI*, Sept. 3, 1849; *Cincinnati Enquirer*, Apr. 6, 1850.

38. J. A. W. Brenan to his father, Dec. 19, 1855, J. A. W. Brenan Miscellaneous Manuscript, Department of Archives and Manuscripts, Louisiana State University, Baton Rouge; *New York Express*, Aug. 23, 1849, quoted in *WDNI*, Aug. 23, 1849; Stott, *Workers in the Metropolis*, 74. Theodore O'Hara asserted that López's 1850 expedition consisted of tattered wretches recruited from the levees and pavilions of U.S. cities. Theodore O'Hara to William Nelson, Mar. 18, 1854, JAQ Papers, MDAH.

39. Malcolm W. Mearis to JMC, Aug. 10, 1849, RG 59, DS, Special Agents, NA; Lawrence Greene, *The Filibuster: The Career of William Walker* (Indianapolis, 1937), 34; John A. Jacques to AO, Oct. 1, 10 (quotation), 1856, P. F. Moncosos to AO, Oct. 8, 13, 1856, AO Papers, DU; *New-York Daily Times*, Feb. 2, 13, 1857; William Clark Griggs, *The Elusive Eden: Frank McMullan's Confederate Colony in Brazil* (Austin, 1987), 7; William Walker to Callender I. Fayssoux, Sept. 14, 1859, WWP.

40. Edward M. Coffman, *The Old Army: A Portrait of the American Army in Peacetime, 1784−1898* (New York, 1986), 152, 154, 50. The pay of second lieutenants varied depending on branch of service.

41. Auguston Mizell commission, Apr. 8, Narciso López promissory note to Mizell, Apr. 10, 1850, Auguston Mizell Papers, MDAH; P. Hamilton to JMC, Aug. 4, 1849, Statements of Edwin B. Scott and others, enclosed with V. M. Randolph to William Ballard Preston, Sept. 20, 1849 (copy), *S. Ex. Doc.* 57, 31st Cong., 1st Sess., 4, 101−4; *WDNI*, Sept. 1, 1849, Apr. 23, 1851; *New-York Daily Tribune.* Sept. 1, 1849, Sept. 23, 1851; John H. Goddard to Thomas Ewing, June 17, 1850, Records Concerning the Cuban Expedition 1850−51, RG 48, Department of the Interior, NA; statement of Henry Stephens and others enclosed with P. Hamilton to DW, Aug. 7, 1850, *H. Ex. Doc.* 83, 32d Cong., 1st Sess., 110−12, 116.

42. *San Francisco Daily Placer Times and Transcript*, Jan. 13, 1854; *DAC*, Jan. 6, 1856; Decree of the "Supreme Government of the Republic of Nicaragua," Nov. 23, 1855, Register Book: New Orleans Agency of Nicaraguan Emigration Company, WWP; "An Address to Those Who Still Continue to Cling to the Filibuster Walker," Feb. 24, 1857, in SquadL, roll 38; T. B. Childress to Lewis Cass, Oct. 30, 1857, sworn statement of Douglas B. DeSaussure, Dec. 3, 1857, enclosed with James Conner to Lewis Cass, Dec. 7, 1857, *H. Ex. Doc.* 24, 35th Cong., 1st Sess., 9–10, 31; (Greensboro) *Alabama Beacon*, Oct. 23, 1857; (Tampa) *Florida Peninsular*, Sept. 12, 1857; district court testimony of Phillip Thomson in *New York Herald*, Feb. 1, 1858.

43. *SFDH*, Jan. 28, 1856; *Scout and Ranger, Being the Personal Adventures of James Pike of the Texas Rangers in 1859–60* (1865; reprinted with introd. and notes by Carl L. Cannon, Princeton, 1932), 124.

44. *San Francisco Daily Placer Times and Transcript*, Jan. 13, 1854; *New-York Daily Times*, Mar. 20, 1852; John S. Brenizer to his brother-in-law and sister, Oct. 17, 1855, John S. Brenizer Papers, TSLA.

45. "Prisoners brought to Habana from the late Cuban Expedition under the Command of Narciso Lopez, and the final disposition of them as far as known," SquadL, roll 92; Walker's Army Register and "Emigrants to Central America Sept 16th 1860 Dew Drop W. S. Terry," in ledger entitled "Men and stores sent to Caribbean Sea 1860 No 2," WWP; William Sydney Thayer to A. O. P. Nicholson, Oct. 8 [1855], Alfred Osborne Pope Nicholson Papers, Manuscript Department, New-York Historical Society; *DAC*, Feb. 22, 1854.

46. *Philadelphia Public Ledger*, Dec. 5, 1856; William O. Scroggs, "William Walker's Designs on Cuba," *Mississippi Valley Historical Review* 1 (Sept. 1914): 198–211; Brown, *Agents of Manifest Destiny*, 326–27, 332, 355–58; *DAC*, Jan. 5, 1856; Richard Dillon, *Fool's Gold: The Decline and Fall of Captain John Sutter of California* (New York, 1967), 326, 335–36; *FLIN*, Feb. 9, 1856.

47. Peter N. Stearns, *1848: The Revolutionary Tide in Europe* (New York, 1974), 1–2; E. J. Hobsbawm, *The Age of Capital, 1848–1875* (1975; reprint, New York, 1984), 4–5; Brown, *Agents of Manifest Destiny*, 61; *New-York Daily Times*, Mar. 24, 1852, Aug. 19, 1857; General Orders, no. 53, General Order Book, WWP; Kossuth bonds in John T. Pickett Papers, Anna J. Sanders Journal, Aug. 7, 1855, George N. Sanders Papers, LC; *FLIN*, Mar. 26, 1859; Sean Wilentz, *Chants Democratic: New York City and the Rise of the American Working Class, 1788–1850* (New York, 1984), 327–28; *Fatal Glory: Narciso López and the First Clandestine U.S. War against Cuba* (Charlottesville, 1996), 103n.

48. Francis C. Kajencki, "Charles Radziminski: Soldier of the American Southwest," *New Mexico Historical Review* 66 (Oct. 1991): 382.

49. *Baltimore Sun*, Sept. 11, 1856; Walker, *War in Nicaragua*, 180–87, 281.

50. *New-York Daily Tribune*, May 26, 1851; Havana *Faro Industrial* list in *WDNI*, Sept. 5, 1851; "Personal Narrative of Louis Schlesinger of Adventures in Cuba and Ceuta," *Democratic Review* 31 (Sept. 1852, Oct. 1852, Nov.–Dec. 1852): 210–24, 352–68, 553–92; Louis Schlesinger to JAQ, May 18, 1853, JAQ Papers, HU; Schlesinger to JAQ, July 12, Sept. 3, 1853, Sept. 9, 1854, JAQ Papers, MDAH; *Pittsburg Post*, May 13, 1856; *New-York Times*, Oct. 26, 1857; Quisenberry, *Lopez's Expeditions*, 75–76.

51. *New-York Daily Tribune*, Apr. 28, 1851; *St. Paul Daily Pioneer and Democrat*, Jan. 3, 1857.

52. Mike Walsh to JAQ, Jan. 25, 1855, JAQ Papers, MDAH; James Cooper to Mr. Hopkins, May 30, 1855, enclosed in José de Marcoleta to WLM, June 2, 1855, *Dipl Corr* 4:465n; Brown, *Agents of Manifest Destiny*, 258; W. S. T. letter in *New York Evening Post*, July 18, 1855; *Savannah Georgian* quoted in *WDNI*, June 15, 1850.

53. W. J. Rorabaugh, *The Craft Apprentice: From Franklin to the Machine Age in America* (New York, 1986), 32; Amy Bridges, *A City in the Republic: Antebellum New York and the Origins of Machine Politics* (Cambridge, England, 1984), 49–51, 53; Michael Kimmel, *Manhood in America: A Cultural History* (New York, 1996), 30–33.

54. Elliott J. Gorn, *The Manly Art: Bare-Knuckle Prize Fighting in America* (Ithaca, N.Y., 1986), 46, 74–75, 131–32, 137, 140–43; Timothy J. Gilfoyle, *City of Eros: New York City, Prostitution, and the Commercialization of Sex, 1790–1920* (New York, 1992), 92–116; Kimmel, *Manhood in America*, 30–39, 56, 61–71; Joseph F. Kett, *Rites of Passage: Adolescence in America, 1790 to the Present* (New York, 1977), 94; Amy S. Greenberg, *Cause for Alarm: The Volunteer Fire Department in the Nineteenth-Century City* (Princeton, 1998), 9, 43, 52, 54, 59–65; *New-York Daily Tribune*, Aug. 30, 1851; Amy Gilman Srebnick, *The Mysterious Death of Mary Rogers: Sex and Culture in Nineteenth-Century New York* (New York, 1995), 48. It might also be hypothesized that middle-class males who found their way into filibustering through the intermediate stage of membership in fraternal lodges likewise were subconsciously addressing perceived threats to their masculinity. Mark Carnes argues that Victorian-era American males joined lodges partly in reaction against the growing feminization of the church and the "moral authority" that this status gave women within the home. Mark C. Carnes, *Secret Ritual and Manhood in Victorian America* (New Haven, 1989), 72–123.

55. *DAC*, Jan. 26, Feb. 19, 1854; Charles Edward Rand to his father and mother, May 16, 1854, Charles Edward Rand Papers, BRBM. I find no evidence in the former U.S. diplomat Ephraim George Squier's published writings about Nicaragua for Albert Z. Carr's theory that sexually deprived California males were drawn to filibustering by the descriptions of nude and semi-nude native females in Squier's work. Albert Z. Carr, *The World and William Walker* (New York, 1963), 115–16.

56. Charles Edward Rand to his father and mother, Feb. 20, 1857, Rand Papers, BRBM; [David Deaderick III], "The Experiences of Samuel Absalom, Filibuster," *Atlantic Monthly* 4 (Dec. 1859): 653; *DAC*, Jan. 26, Feb. 19, 1854; Stout, *The Liberators*, 42.

57. Anna Paschall Hannum, ed., *A Quaker Forty-Niner: The Adventures of Charles Edward Pancoast on the American Frontier* (Philadelphia, 1930), 1–3, 171, 286–88, 328, 334–35, 372–73 (quotations).

58. Henry Forno to JAQ, Jan. 23, 1855, JAQ Papers, HU; John H. Goddard to Thomas Ewing, June 17, 1850, RG 48, Department of the Interior, Records Concerning the Cuban Expedition 1850–51; *Lafayette* (Ind.) *Daily Courier*, July 6, 7, 1857; *Cincinnati Enquirer*, Apr. 6, 1850.

59. George D. Bayard to Jane Dashiell Bayard, Apr. 20, 1856, George D. Bayard Papers, U.S. Military Academy Library, West Point, N.Y.

60. T. Harry Williams, *P. G. T. Beauregard: Napoleon in Gray* (Baton Rouge, 1955), 42, 42n; Johnson Kelly Duncan to George McClellan, July 23, 1857, quoted in Stephen W. Sears, *George B. McClellan: The Young Napoleon* (New York, 1988), 52–53; John S. Thrasher to JAQ, Feb. 19, 1858, JAQ Papers, C. M. Wilcox to JAQ, May 8, 1854, J. F. H. Claiborne Papers, MDAH; Joseph G. Dawson III, *Doniphan's Epic March: The 1st Missouri Volunteers in the Mexican War* (Lawrence, Kan., 1999), 226. Duncan had resigned his army lieutenancy in January 1855.

61. *NODP*, Sept. 2, 1852; *DAC*, Jan. 5, 1856; James Grant Wilson and John Fiske, eds., *Appleton's Cyclopaedia of American Biography*, 6 vols. (New York, 1886–89), 3:40; clipping, undated, about George B. Hall in JAQ Papers, MDAH; "Hall, George," in Kenneth T. Jackson, ed., *The Encyclopedia of New York City* (New Haven, 1995), 517; George Bolivar Hall to JAQ, Aug. 2, 1853, JAQ Papers, HU; Register of William Walker's Nicaraguan Army, Aug. 1, 1856, Elijah D. Taft to Hall, Feb. 12, 1856 (quotation), AO Papers, DU. Hall's father, George Hall, was elected mayor in 1855. Walker's officer Birkett D. Fry had just previously been captain of a California volunteer rifle company. *SFDH*, Sept. 11, 1855.

62. William Bland, *The Awful Doom of the Traitor; or, The Terrible Fate of the Deluded and Guilty . . .* (Cincinnati, 1852), 6–7; Samuel G. Jones to Lewis Neale Whittle, Jan. 20, 1858, Lewis Neale Whittle Papers, SHC; William O. Eaton, "The Deserter. A Sketch From Life in Nicaragua," (Boston) *Flag of Our Union*, Jan. 10, 1857; M. C. Taylor Diary, Apr. 20, 1850, in [A. C. Quisenberry, ed.], "Col. M. C. Taylor's Diary in Lopez['s] Cardenas Expedition, 1850," *Register of the Kentucky State Historical Society* 19 ([Sept.] 1921): 81; Edward M. Taylor and Leo Black to JAQ, Apr. 15, 1855, JAQ Papers, HU; *Congressional Globe*, 35th Cong., 2d Sess., 1059; Rosengarten, *Freebooters Must Die!* 9; Carr, *The World and William Walker* (New York, 1963), 36–38, 74; William Walker to Mrs. Tom Smith, Mar. 3, 1858, Miscellaneous Collections, TSLA; Theodore O'Hara to John T. Pickett, Dec. 8, 1851, John T. Pickett Papers, LC; May, *John A. Quitman*, 109–10; Erwin Craighead, *From Mobile's Past: Sketches of Memorable People and Events* (Mobile, 1925), 159–60, 182; account by Edward Hendiboe in *FLIN*, June 21, 1856.

63. *New York Herald*, Jan. 8, 18, 1858; Benjamin Hayes Diary, Sept. 25, 1857, in Marjorie Tisdale Wolcott, ed., *Pioneer Notes from the Diaries of Judge Benjamin Hayes, 1849–1875* (Los Angeles, 1929), 170–71. See Ebenezer Larkin Childs to Thomas Oliver Larkin, Jan. 19, 1856, in *The Larkin Papers*, ed. George P. Hammond, 10 vols. (Berkeley, 1951–68), 10:234, respecting an alcoholic physician who apparently left his wife with the intention of going to Walker's Nicaragua.

64. John Allen public letter in *Louisville Democrat*, printed in *Galveston Weekly News*, Nov. 7, 1854; Henry E. McCulloch to Elisha M. Pease, Oct. 17, 1855, Elisha M. Pease Papers, Austin History Center, Austin Public Library; *Scout and Ranger*, 126; "Departure of Recruits for Col. Walker," *DAC*, Oct. 21, 1855; T. Butler King Jr. to his mother, Sept. 30, 1851, Thomas Butler King Papers, SHC.

65. John S. Thrasher to Hugh McLeod, Jan. 24, 1855, Hugh McLeod Papers, Texas State Library; Vernon L. Parrington, *The Romantic Revolution in America* (New York, 1927), vii–xiv; Merle Curti, *The Growth of American Thought* (2d edn., New

York, 1951), 238−42; William H. Goetzmann, *When the Eagle Screamed: The Romantic Horizon in American Diplomacy, 1800−1860* (New York, 1966), xiii−xvii, 92−94.

66. Robert W. Johannsen, *To the Halls of the Montezumas: The Mexican War in the American Imagination* (New York, 1985), 68−72, 144−70; Marcus Cunliffe, *Soldiers and Civilians: The Martial Spirit in America, 1775−1865* (Boston, 1968), 402−4; Albert H. Tracy to Albert Tracy, Aug. 13, 1849, Albert Tracy Papers, New York Public Library; *WDNI*, Jan. 16, 1850; [Davis], *History of the Late Expedition*, 1; William Walker, "Address to the Army," in Rufus Kay Wyllys, "William Walker's Invasion of Sonora, 1854," *Arizona Historical Review* 6 (Oct. 1935): 63; William Frank Stewart, *Last of the Fillibusters; or, Recollections of the Siege of Rivas* (Sacramento, 1857), 33; *An Authentic Exposition of the K.G.C. by a Member of the Order* (Indianapolis, 1861), 12; C. W. Doubleday, *Reminiscences of the "Filibuster" War in Nicaragua* (New York 1986), 176; Guy M. Bryan to Laura Jack, Apr. 3, 1858, Guy M. Bryan Papers, UT; *New Orleans Daily Creole*, Oct. 10, 1856. Scott's Dalgetty can be found in *A Legend of Montrose*. One disillusioned filibuster explicitly cited Scott for romanticizing war and misleading youthful Americans into the expeditions: [Deaderick], "Experience of Samuel Absalom," 50.

67. John W. Fleener to JAQ, Aug. 17, 1854, JAQ Papers, MDAH; Robert Farquharson to JAQ, Feb. 7, 1855, JAQ Papers, HU; *Journal of the Executive Proceedings of the Senate of the United States of America, from December 6, 1852, to March 3, 1855, Inclusive* (Washington, 1887), 9:84, 100; B. D. Palmer to "Friend Reeves," Mar. 13, 1857, Missouri University Papers, Missouri Historical Society, St. Louis; Griggs, *Elusive Eden*, 6−7; *Scout and Ranger*, 124−26; Lawrence Oliphant, *Patriots and Filibusters; or, Incidents of Political and Exploratory Travel* (Edinburgh, 1860), 175; John S. Ford to Hugh McLeod, Jan. 14, 1855, Hugh McLeod Papers, Texas State Library.

68. Tom Bryan Memoir, TSLA, 1, 7−12; A. C. Allen Diary, "The Walker Expedition" (photocopy), Jan. 3, 1857, UT; AO to James Neal, June 14, 1856, J. H. Williamson to AO, Sept. 28, 1856, AO Papers, DU; Stewart, *Last of the Fillibusters*, 7; M. C. Taylor Diary, May 4, 1850, in [Quisenberry, ed.], "Colonel M. C. Taylor's Diary," 82; F.[?] B. Flournoy to JAQ, Feb. 24, 1855, JAQ Papers, MDAH; Dufour, *Gentle Tiger*, 32−33; Edward H. Cook to DW, Sept. 12, 1851, *PDW* 2:381; O. B. Brown to DW, Sept. 30, 1851, DS, ML, M179, roll 127, NA; Asbury Harpending, *The Great Diamond Hoax*, ed. James H. Wilkins (2d edn., Norman, 1958), 5; William O. Eaton, "The Deserter. A Sketch from Life in Nicaragua," in (Boston) *Flag of Our Union*, Jan. 10, 1857; John S. Slocum to Albert Tracy, June 27, 1849, Albert Tracy Papers, New York Public Library; Marcellus French, "Expedition of the Alamo Rangers," ed. Franklina Gray Bartlett, *Overland Monthly*, 2d series, 221 (May 1893): 520; Caleb Carr, *The Devil Soldier: The Story of Frederick Townsend Ward* (New York, 1992), 6, 58−59.

69. [Richardson Hardy], *The History and Adventures of the Cuban Expedition, from the First Movements Down to the Dispersion of the Army at Key West, and the Arrest of General Lopez . . .* (Cincinnati, 1850), 3; E[dward] J. C. K[ewen] to the editor of the *San Francisco Herald*, Nov. 5, 1855, *SFDH*, Dec. 6, 1855.

70. "Men and Stores sent to Caribbean Sea 1860," WWP.

71. *SFDH*, Aug. 10, 1856; William V. Wells, *Walker's Expedition to Nicaragua: A*

History of the Central American War (New York, 1856), 97; *New York Herald*, Aug. 5, 1857, Jan. 13, 1859; *New-York Daily Tribune*, Aug. 19, 1857; List of 39 men and 6 officers enclosed with Hiram Paulding to Isaac Toucey, Jan. 2, 1858, M89, roll 97, NA; "Prisoners on board the United States sloop 'Saratoga,'" *H. Ex. Doc.* 24, 35th Cong., 1st Sess., 79; *NODP*, Aug. 27, 1856, Oct. 9, 1859; [Davis], *History of the Late Expedition*, 15–19. Colonel A. Francis Rudler, Walker's second-in-command in 1860, moreover, had been lieutenant of the First Infantry in Walker's Nicaraguan army in early 1857. "Army Register N.A. Feb. 26th 1857," WWP; Brown, *Agents of Manifest Destiny*, 454.

72. *Pittsburg Daily Morning Post*, June 13, 1850; *SFDH*, Nov. 3, 1853.

73. William Walker to Callender I. Fayssoux, Jan. 9, 1858, James T. Van Slycke to Fayssoux, Aug. 12, 1859, WWP.

74. Arthur Woodward, ed., *The Republic of Lower California 1853–1854* (Los Angeles, 1966), 27, 27n; *SFDH*, Aug. 10, 1856; Walker, *War in Nicaragua*, 42–52; Bolaños-Geyer, *William Walker* 2:267–68, 281; *DAC*, Jan. 6, Mar. 23, 1856; Brown, *Agents of Manifest Destiny*, 414; New Orleans correspondent of the *San Francisco Bulletin*, quoted in (Stockton, Calif.) *San Joaquin Republican*, Nov. 17, 1858; [Calender I. Fayssoux?] to William Walker, Sept. 9, 1860, WWP; *NODP*, Nov. 22, 1858; register of Walker's army, Aug. 1, 1856, AO Papers, DU. W. O. Scroggs claimed that 30 of 270 members of Walker's second Nicaraguan expedition had been involved in his first intervention there. Scroggs, *Filibusters and Financiers*, 323–24.

75. A. L. Saunders to JAQ, Feb. 4, 1855, R. Harris to JAQ, Jan. 3, 1855, JAQ Papers, HU; Allison Nelson to JAQ, June 4, 1854, J. C. Bates to JAQ, Jan. 3, 1855, W. C. Capers, to JAQ, Jan. 11, 1855, JAQ Papers, MDAH; [Davis], *History of the Late Expedition*, 24.

76. Laurence Oliphant, *Episodes in a Life of Adventure; or, Moss from a Rolling Stone* (Edinburgh, 1887), 115; John S. Ford to Hugh McLeod, Jan. 14, 1855, Hugh McLeod Papers, Texas State Library.

77. Ernest C. Shearer, "The Carvajal Disturbances," *SHQ* 55 (Oct. 1851): 209, 217; Chatham R. Wheat to JAQ, June 15, Oct. 29, 1854, JAQ Papers, MDAH; John S. Ford to JAQ, July 2, 1855, JAQ Papers, University of Virginia, Charlottesville; John Salmon Ford, *Rip Ford's Texas*, ed. Stephen B. Oates (Austin, 1963), 197n.

78. Powhatan Jordan to JAQ, Dec. 2, 1854, Jan. 3, 1855, JAQ Papers, MDAH.

79. *Mobile Daily Advertiser*, July 19, 1855.

80. L. Norvell Walker to JAQ, Aug. 19, 1854, JAQ to Walker, Aug. 24, 1854, Hugh McLeod to JAQ, May 31, 1854, JAQ Papers, MDAH; Walker to JAQ, Mar. 20, 1855, William Mason to JAQ, July 15, 1854, JAQ Papers, HU; VMI Alumni Association, *The 1989 Register of Former Cadets of the Virginia Military Institute* (Lexington, Va., 1989), 60; *WDNI*, Aug. 6, 1853; *Galveston Weekly News*, Nov. 7, 1854; *Baltimore Sun*, May 23, 1856; *New York Daily Tribune*, Mar. 30, 1861; Spellman, *Forgotten Texas Leader*, 44–45, 163–65; John S. Thrasher to Hugh McLeod, Jan. 24, John S. Ford to McLeod, Jan. 14, 1855, Hugh McLeod Papers, Texas State Library. George Bolivar Hall, who had been involved with Quitman, joined the Walker movement in November 1855. See affidavit of Robert Hoggins, Jan. 11, 1856, in RG 60, DJ, Attorney General's Papers, Letters Received: New York, NA.

81. William Walker to Callender I. Fayssoux, Dec. 11, 23, 29, 1858, Lewis Snapp to Parker H. French, Apr. 19, 1856, WWP; Chaffin, *Fatal Glory*, 130, 203; Brown, *Agents of Manifest Destiny*, 348, 367, 417. See also the obituary for Michael J. Morgan, *NODP*, Mar. 7, 1856.

82. *New York Herald*, Jan. 28, 1858; Samuel A. Lockridge to Samuel Peter Heintzelman, Apr. 12, 1860, quoted in Jerry Thompson, ed., *Fifty Miles and a Fight: Major Samuel Peter Heintzelman's Journal of Texas and the Cortina War* (Austin, 1998), 237n.

83. E. Anthony Rotundo, *American Manhood: Transformations in Masculinity from the Revolution to the Modern Era* (New York, 1993), 3–4, 76–86; Donald Yacovone, "Abolitionists and the 'Language of Fraternal Love,'" in *Meanings for Manhood: Constructions of Masculinity in Victorian America*, ed. Mark C. Carnes and Clyde Griffen (Chicago, 1990), 85–86; "A Ranger's Life in Nicaragua," *Harper's Weekly*, Apr. 18, 1857, 248.

84. Chatham R. Wheat to JAQ, Nov. 9, 1853, JAQ Papers, MDAH; Harry Maury to Callender I. Fayssoux, July 3, 1859, WWP; *SFDH*, Dec. 7 (E. J. C. Kewen letter), 19, 1855; "I. H. S." letter, Aug. 11, 1856, in *New Orleans Daily Creole*, Aug. 30, 1856; Doubleday, *Reminiscences*, 176; Tunis C. Tarrant letter, Dec. 23, 1852 [1853], in *Daily Placer Times and Transcript* (San Francisco), Jan. 13, 1854; B. G. W. letter, Mar. 14, 1857, in (Stockton, Calif.) *San Joaquin Republican*, Apr. 1, 1857; John H. Goddard to Alexander H. H. Stuart, Nov. 23, 1850, RG 48, Department of the Interior, Records Concerning the Cuban Expedition 1850–51, NA; anonymous letter from the *Iowa Hill News* in *DAC*, Nov. 28, 1855; [Quisenberry, ed.], "Col. M. C. Taylor's Diary," Apr. 13, 19, 20, 1850, pp. 80, 81; Walker filibuster diary, Sept. 2, 1855, quoted in *The Destiny of Nicaragua: Central America As It Was, Is, and May Be* (Boston, 1856), 60; Stewart, *Last of the Fillibusters*, 33. In many cases, the term "brother" was literal. Brothers and other relations frequently congregated together in filibuster ranks.

85. Oliphant, *Patriots and Filibusters*, 170; *New-York Daily Times*, Apr. 4, May 30, June 2, June 24, 1857; *NODP*, May 20, 1852.

86. John Hope Franklin, *The Militant South* (Cambridge, Mass., 1956), 96–128 (quotations on p. 99).

87. Samuel A. Lockridge card in *New Orleans Delta*, quoted in *Galveston Weekly News*, Sept. 5, 1857.

88. Abijah Beckwith Diary, Mar. 1, 1853, Olin Library, Cornell University, Ithaca, N.Y.; *Richmond Palladium*, Aug. 27, 1851; William R. Henry to the editors, Oct. 3, 1857, in (Corpus Christi) *Nueces Valley Weekly*, Oct. 10, 1857; Allan Nevins, *Ordeal of the Union*, vol. 1: *Fruits of Manifest Destiny, 1847–1852* (New York, 1947), 43, 45–46.

89. Edward L. Widmer, *Young America: The Flowering of Democracy in New York City* (New York, 1999), 3–26, 53–63, 185–201; Merle E. Curti, "Young America," *American Historical Review* 32 (Oct. 1926): 34–55; David B. Danbom, "The Young America Movement," *Journal of the Illinois State Historical Society* 67 (June 1974): 294–306; Frederick Merk, *Manifest Destiny and Mission in American History: A Reinterpretation* (New York, 1963), 53–55, 195–200; Rauch, *American Interest*, 192–94; Robert Benson Leard, "Bonds of Destiny: The United States and Cuba, 1848–1861" (Ph.D. diss., University of California, 1953), 149, 151–54; Anna J. Sanders Journal, Nov. 4, Dec. 30, 1852, Jan. 14, 1853, George N. Sanders Papers, LC.

90. Theodore O'Hara to John T. Pickett, Dec. 8, 1851, John T. Pickett Papers, LC; correspondent's letter dated Mar. 10, 1856 in *FLIN*, Apr. 12, 1856; AO to James Neal, June 14, 1856, AO Papers, DU; William Walker to Callender I. Fayssoux, Feb. 17, 1860, WWP; Scroggs, *Filibusters and Financiers*, 144–45; Sean Wilentz, *Chants Democratic*, 328. It would be a mistake, however, to leap to the assumption that filibusters were necessarily Democrats. Many prominent filibusters, including E. J. C. Kewen, Chatham Roberdeau Wheat, and Henry Crabb, had Whig backgrounds. William Walker's conspirator Edmund Randolph claimed that Henry Crabb's expeditionists were "mainly from the Whig party." "Edward J. C. Kewen," 343; *DAC*, Sept. 5, 1854; Chatham R. Wheat to his grandfather, July 30, 1852, John Thomas Wheat Papers, SHC; "Crabb, Henry Alexander," in Thrapp, *Encyclopedia of Frontier Biography*, 334; *Speech of Mr. Edmund Randolph Delivered at Musical Hall, San Francisco, August 5th, 1859* (San Francisco, 1859), 10; Jack R. Everett letter, Feb. 24, 1852, in *WDNI*, Mar. 17, 1852; John S. Ford to Hugh McLeod, Jan. 14, 1855, Hugh McLeod Papers, Texas State Library. Of ninety-nine pro-López Cuban annexation committeemen in New Orleans, thirty were Whigs and sixty-nine were Democrats. Richard Tansey, "Southern Expansionism: Urban Interests in the Cuban Filibusters," *Plantation Society in the Americas* 1 (June 1979): 238. George Bickley, founder of Knights of the Golden Circle, had associated with the Know Nothing party in the mid-1850s. However, that party's national platform in 1855 rejected filibustering. Frank L. Klement, "Bickley, George Washington Lafayette," in John T. Kneebone, J. Jefferson Looney, Brent Tarter, and Sandra Gioia Treadway, eds., *Dictionary of Virginia Biography* (Richmond, 1998–), 481; Anbinter, *Nativism and Slavery*, 170.

91. Though attributing the term to O'Sullivan, historians have remarked that it appeared in unsigned articles in O'Sullivan's journals before he used it in signed pieces, and have traced variants of the phrase to prior expansionists. In an exciting new work, Linda S. Hudson uses textual analysis to make a convincing case that Storm originated the term. Merk, *Manifest Destiny*, 27, 31–32; Albert K. Weinberg, *Manifest Destiny: A Study of Nationalist Expansionism in American History* (Baltimore, 1935), 111–12; Julius W. Pratt, "The Origins of Manifest Destiny," *American Historical Review* 32 (July 1927): 795–98; Hudson, *Mistress of Manifest Destiny: A Biography of Jane McManus Storm Cazneau, 1807–1878* (Austin, 2001), 45–68.

92. Reginald Horsman, *Race and Manifest Destiny: The Origins of American Racial Anglo-Saxonism* (Cambridge, Mass., 1981), 1, 116–86, 219 (quotations), 229–36, 243–44, 279–82, 289–91; Thomas R. Hietala, *Manifest Design: Anxious Aggrandizement in Late Jacksonian America* (Ithaca, N.Y., 1985), 132–72; Richard Slotkin, *The Fatal Environment: The Myth of the Frontier in the Age of Industrialization* (New York, 1985), 248. Actually, there never was a true Anglo-Saxon people in England that was transplanted in North America. The myth derived from European romantic racialist and nationalist ideas as well as the fad of scientific racism gaining popularity in the mid-nineteenth-century United States. Horsman, *Race and Manifest Destiny*, 4, 116–86.

93. *New Orleans Daily Creole*, Oct. 28, Dec. 12, 1856; *SFDH*, Nov. 29, 1853.

94. E[dward] J. C. K[ewen] to the editor, Feb. 19, 1856, *SFDH*, Mar. 10, 1856; Wells, *Walker's Expedition*, 13; William R. Henry letter, Sept. 22, 1857, in *Galveston*

Weekly News, reprinted in *New-York Times*, Oct. 19, 1857; Guerra, "Henry," 3:564; AO to JAQ, July 6, 1855, JAQ Papers, MDAH; James D. B. De Bow, "The Late Cuba Expedition," *De Bow's Review* 9 (Aug. 1850): 167. Walker's organ during his rule in Nicaragua, *El Nicaragüense*, first connected the term to the filibuster in December 1855. Scroggs, *Filibusters and Financiers*, 128–29.

95. P. G. T. Beauregard to Persifor F. Smith, Jan. 24, 1856 (1857), Persifor Frazer Smith Papers, HSP; [Vielé], "*Following the Drum*," 205; William R. Henry to the editors, Oct. 3, 1857, (Corpus Christi) *Nueces Valley Weekly*, Oct. 10, 1857; Cornelius Cook to Ike Cook, July 31, enclosed with Edward H. Cook to DW, Sept. 12, 1851, *PDW* 2:381–82; Jack Everett to "Dear C.," Nov. 29, 1851, in *NODP*, Dec. 24, 1851; G. Bolivar Hall to JAQ, Aug. 2, 1853, James Madison Miller to JAQ, Sept. 17, 1854, T. S. Anderson to JAQ, Apr. 24, 1854, Samuel Mitchell to JAQ, Feb. 6, 1855, Edward M. Taylor and Leo Black to JAQ, Apr. 15, 1855, JAQ Papers, HU; A. J. McNeil to JAQ, June 10, 1854, W. C. Capers to JAQ, Jan. 11, 1855, C. H. Mott to JAQ, Jan. 29, 1855, AO to JAQ, July 5, 1855, JAQ Papers, MDAH; E. B. Gaither letter reprinted from *Louisville Chronicle* in *WDNI*, Jan. 16, 1850; A. C. Allen Diary, Jan. 1, 1857.

96. Letter from member of the Crabb expedition, Mar. 2, in *DAC*, Mar. 20, 1857; letter of a filibuster to his mother quoted in [Davis], *History of the Late Expedition*, 9; [Quisenberry, ed.], "Col. M. C. Taylor Diary," May 18, 1850, p. 85; *Vicksburg Sentinel*, July 11, 1850; *Savannah Morning News*, May 19, 1851.

97. Henry letter in *New-York Times*, Oct. 19, 1857; John S. Ford to Edward Burleson Jr., Feb. 15, 1856, Edward Burleson Papers, UT; *DAC*, May 21 (Kinney letter to John L. Stephens, Apr. 20, 1855), Sept. 29 (French card), 1855; Kinney to the *WDNI*, Jan. 8, reprinted in *NODP*, Jan. 17, 1855; William Walker's inaugural in *Dipl Corr* 4:544–45; Walker address, Nov. 30, 1855, in Woodward, ed., *Republic of Lower California*, 32–33; *New-York Times*, July 23, 1860. See also Hannum, ed., *A Quaker Forty-Niner*, 373; John P. Heiss to Stephen A. Douglas, Mar. 14, 1856, Stephen A. Douglas Papers, University of Chicago; Henry L. Kinney "card" in *New York Evening Post*, June 18, 1855; AO to James Neal, June 14, 1856, AO. Filibuster leaders were less likely to use racialist justifications for expeditions against Cuba. Felix Huston even claimed that the "Creole Cubans" were "a full-blooded white race, and not mongrels, like the Mexicans." *Jackson Mississippian and State Gazette*, Sept. 27, 1854.

98. Lawrence Berry Washington to Henry Bedinger III, July 28, 1851, Bedinger-Dandridge Family Papers, DU; W. Grayson Mann to William Trousdale, June 15, 1857, William Trousdale Papers, TSLA; B. D. Palmer to "Friend Reeves," Mar. 13, 1857, Missouri University Papers, Missouri Historical Society, St. Louis.

99. Eaton, "The Deserter"; unsigned letter dated Nov. 7, 1853, in *SFDH*, Dec. 9, 1853; I. H. S. letter Aug. 11, 1856, in *New Orleans Daily Creole*, Aug. 30, 1856; B. G. W. to the editor, Mar. 14, (Stockton, Calif.) *San Joaquin Republican*, Apr. 1, 1857; Stewart, *Last of the Fillibusters*, 27, 29, 34; *New-York Daily Times*, July 31, 1857; Felix Huston letter in *Jackson Mississippian and State Gazette*, Sept. 27, 1854; Jack R. Everett letter, Feb. 24, 1852, in *WDNI*, Mar. 17, 1852.

Chapter Five

1. William Pitt Ballinger to DW, Jan. 24, 1852, Samuel D. Hay to Jefferson Davis, Mar. 28, 1854, RG 59, DS, ML, M179, rolls 129, 139, NA; Minutes, District Court of the United States, Southern District of Texas, Brownsville Division, NA—Southwest Region, Fort Worth (7RA-241 [microfilm publication of NA—Southwest Region], roll 2); *Journal of the Executive Proceedings of the Senate of the United States of America, from December 6, 1852, to March 3, 1855, Inclusive* (Washington, 1887), 9:108; John Moretta, "Jose Maria Jesus Carvajal, United States Foreign Policy and the Filibustering Spirit in Texas," *East Texas Historical Journal* 33 (Fall 1995): 15–16; *Galveston Weekly News*, Jan. 10, 1854. By act of Congress (Mar. 3, 1851), the district judge for Texas was compelled to hold annual court sessions at Brownsville, Austin, and Tyler. *Statutes at Large*, 31st Cong., 2d Sess., ch. 32, p. 618.

2. William Pitt Ballinger to DW, Jan. 24, 1854, RG 59, DS, ML, M179, roll 129, William Hunter to Ballinger, Mar. 22, 1852, RG 59, Domestic Letters, M17, roll 38, NA. Before the creation of the Department of Justice in 1870, U.S. district attorneys operated independently of the attorney general in Washington, whose main responsibility was to provide legal advice to the president (and through the president to his cabinet). Nancy V. Baker, *Conflicting Loyalties: Law and Politics in the Attorney General's Office, 1789–1990* (Lawrence, Kan., 1992), 46, 49, 71–75.

3. Minutes, District Court of the United States, Southern District of Texas, Brownsville Division, NA—Southwest Region, roll 2; William Pitt Ballinger to DW, Jan. 24, 1854, RG 59, DS, ML, M179, roll 129, NA; letter from "E.," dated Edinburg, Mar. 28, in *NODP*, Apr. 5, 1853. The grand jury for the June 1853 session had also found bills against thirty-one men for additional filibustering acts, including Carbajal and several others who had been indicted in 1852. Hay did not prosecute these cases, since those arrested were either already under indictment or were recruits rather than leaders of the expeditions. Samuel Hay to Jefferson Davis, RG 59, DS, ML, M179, roll 139, NA; *Brownsville [American] Flag*, July 6, 13, 1853, quoted in *WDNI*, Aug. 6, 1853.

4. Samuel D. Hay to Sam Houston, Jan. 29, 1854, Houston (Andrew Jackson) Collection, Texas State Archives, Library Division, Austin; Hay to WLM, Feb. 17, 1854, Hay to Jefferson Davis, Mar. 28, 1854, RG 59, DS, ML, M179, roll 139, NA; Davis to Hay, Apr. 15, 1854 (letterbook copy), Records of the Office of the Secretary of War, Letters Sent, Military Affairs, M6, roll 35, NA.

5. *New-York Daily Times*, Mar. 18, 1852, Oct. 18, 1859; "Mr. Buchanan's Administration," *Atlantic Monthly* 1 (Apr. 1858): 749; Andrew F. Rolle, *California: A History* (New York, 1969), 256–57; Thomas Palmer to John Dowling, May 21, 1851, John Dowling Papers, Indiana State Historical Society, Indianapolis; "Ion" to the *Baltimore Sun*, quoted in *NODP*, Sept. 4, 1851; *Buffalo Express*, June 26, 1854, quoted in *New York Herald*, July 4, 1854; *FLIN*, Feb. 21, 1857; *New York Albion*, Dec. 19, 1857, 35:607; Philip S. Foner, *A History of Cuba and Its Relations with the United States*, 2 vols. (New York, 1962–63), 2:46; Harold M. Hyman and William M. Wiecek, *Equal Justice under Law: Constitutional Development, 1835–1875* (New York, 1982), 171; Karl Bermann, *Under the Big Stick: Nicaragua and the United States since 1848*

(Boston, 1986), 54, 89; John A. Crow, *The Epic of Latin America* (4th edn., Berkeley, 1992), 679.

6. George Parr to Daniel M. Barringer, Aug. 17, 1852, Daniel M. Barringer Papers, SHC; Laurence Oliphant Journal, May 26, 1852, in Oliphant, *Episodes in a Life of Adventure; or, Moss from a Rolling Stone* (Edinburgh, 1887), 47; Richard Elward to J. F. H. Claiborne, Nov. 14, 1852, J. F. H. Claiborne Papers, MDAH; *WDNI*, Oct. 9, 1852; David Potter, *The Impending Crisis, 1848–1861* (New York, 1976), 181–82; Basil Rauch, *American Interest in Cuba, 1848–1855* (New York, 1948), 227–28; Robert W. Johannsen, *Stephen A. Douglas* (New York, 1973), 370; *Jackson Flag of the Union*, Dec. 31, 1852; *Jackson Mississippian*, Jan. 16, 1852; Theodore Poesche and Charles Goepp, *The New Rome; or, The United States of the World* (New York, 1853), dedication and pp. 12–13.

7. Pierce inaugural, Mar. 4, 1853, *M&P* 5:198–99; "O'Sullivan, John Louis," in John E. Finding, *Dictionary of American Diplomatic History* (Westport, Conn., 1980), 366; Merle Curti, "George N. Sanders: American Patriot of the Fifties," *South Atlantic Quarterly* 27 (Jan. 1928): 84; Sheldon Howard Harris, "The Public Career of John Louis O'Sullivan" (Ph.D. diss., Columbia University, 1958), 307–8; "The Neutrality Law: What Does It Mean, What Prohibit and What Permit," *Democratic Review* 30 (June 1852): 497–512; Rauch, *American Interest*, 227–28; *Journal of the Executive Proceedings of the Senate* 9:212, 232; *Jackson Mississippian*, Jan. 16, June 18, 1852; Ambrosio Gonzales to Caleb Cushing, June 20, 1854, Caleb Cushing Papers, LC; *WDNI*, Sept. 17, 1853; John Belohlavek, "Race, Progress, and Destiny: Caleb Cushing and the Quest for American Empire," in *Manifest Destiny and Empire: American Antebellum Expansionism*, ed. Sam W. Haynes and Christopher Morris (College Station, Tex., 1997), 21–47. Sanders's nomination was rejected by the Senate on Feb. 16, 1854. *Journal of the Executive Proceedings of the Senate* 9:242.

8. Mike Walsh to JAQ, May 25, J. W. Lesesne to JAQ, June 8, 1854, JAQ Papers, HU. J. F. H. Claiborne, Quitman's acquaintance and first biographer, asserted that Quitman first learned that Pierce would tolerate his scheme during a trip east in the summer of 1853. J. F. H. Claiborne, *Life and Correspondence of John A. Quitman*, 2 vols. (New York, 1860), 2:195.

9. Pierce's message of Feb. 10, 1854, *M&P* 5:229–30; *Journal of the Executive Proceedings of the Senate* 9:260, 262, 263, 289–93; Robert L. Jenkins, "The Gadsden Treaty and Sectionalism: A Nation Reacts" (Ph.D. diss., Mississippi State University, 1978), 149–52; *Washington Daily Union*, Dec. 8, 1854, Aug. 24, Oct. 10, 1849, Sept. 4, 1850; Felipe Molina to WLM, Dec. 13, 1854, José de Marcoleta to WLM, Mar. 14, 1855, *Dipl Corr* 4:431–32, 446–50; James T. Wall, *Manifest Destiny Denied: America's First Intervention in Nicaragua* (Washington, 1981), 54; Anna J. Sanders Journal, Jan. 4, 1857, George N. Sanders Papers, LC; Caleb Cushing to John McKeon, Feb. 7, 1857, in Benjamin F. Hall, C. C. Andrews, J. H. Ashton, et al., comps., *Official Opinions of the Attorneys General of the United States, Advising the President and Heads of Departments . . .*, 25 vols. (Washington, 1852–1906), 8:375–76; *New-York Daily Times*, Feb. 9, 25, 1857; William O. Scroggs, *Filibusters and Financiers: The Story of William Walker and His Associates* (New York, 1916), 172. Pierce was willing to keep that part

of the antifilibustering article calling merely for U.S.-Mexican cooperation against the expeditions. The Senate, however, responding to a motion by the profilibustering Californian William Gwin, deleted the entire antifilibustering provision.

10. F. Jones to JAQ, June 10, 1854, JAQ Papers, Albert G. Brown to J. F. H. Claiborne, June 29, 1854, J. F. H. Claiborne Papers, MDAH; John Slidell to JB, June 17, 1854, JB Papers, HSP; Robert E. May, *John A. Quitman: Old South Crusader* (Baton Rouge, 1985), 285–95; C. A. L. Lamar to John S. Thrasher, Feb. 25, 1855, in "A Slave-Trader's Letter Book," *North American Review* 143 (Nov. 1886): 448. Pierce's organ in July 1854 defended the Neutrality Act and denied that Pierce had a "secret understanding" with the filibusters. *Washington Daily Union*, July 4, 6, 22, 1854.

11. Nancy V. Baker, *Conflicting Loyalties: Law and Politics in the Attorney General's Office, 1789–1990* (Lawrence, Kan., 1992), 75–76; Sidney Webster, "Mr. Marcy, the Cuban Question and the Ostend Manifesto," *Political Science Quarterly* 8 (Mar. 1893): 15; *Washington States*, Apr. 29, 1857; Jefferson Davis speeches, Nov. 4, Oct. 2, 1857, in *The Papers of Jefferson Davis*, ed. Haskell M. Monroe Jr., James T. McIntosh, and Lynda Lasswell Crist, 10 vols. (Baton Rouge, 1971–), 6:158, 139–46; May, *John A. Quitman*, 170–71, 172, 209, 257, 258, 282, 284, 436n. Davis rationalized his support for Walker by categorizing the latter as an emigrant to Nicaragua rather than a filibuster.

12. Randall O. Hudson, "The Filibuster Minister: The Career of John Hill Wheeler as United States Minister to Nicaragua, 1854–1856," *North Carolina Historical Review* 49 (Summer 1972): 288–89; Caleb Cushing circular to U.S. district attorneys, Dec. 8, Cushing to S. W. Inge, Dec. 14, Cushing to John McKeon, Dec. 26, 1855, *S. Ex. Doc.* 68, 34th Cong., 1st Sess., 10, 11, 13–14.

13. Caleb Cushing to the editors of the *Boston Daily Advertiser*, in *New-York Times*, Oct. 23, 1857; Robert W. Tucker and David C. Hendrickson, *Empire of Liberty: The Statecraft of Thomas Jefferson* (New York, 1990), 49–50; Richard Crallé to John A. Bryan, Oct. 30, 1844, quoted in Lawrence A. Clayton, "Steps of Considerable Delicacy: Early Relations with Peru," in T. Ray Shurbutt, ed., *United States–Latin American Relations, 1800–1850: The Formative Generations* (Tuscaloosa, 1991), 71–72; H. Lauterpacht, *Recognition in International Law* (Cambridge, England, 1947), 98–103, 124–25. Pierce's temporary recognition of Walker was also a matter of political and diplomatic expediency. Pierce hoped it might assist his renomination chances at the upcoming Democratic national nominating convention and give him leverage in diplomatic disputes with Great Britain over Central America (discussed in chapter 7). Robert E. May, *The Southern Dream of a Caribbean Empire, 1854–1861* (Baton Rouge, 1973), 96–98, 102–4; Larry Gara, *The Presidency of Franklin Pierce* (Lawrence, Kan., 1991), 144; Roy Franklin Nichols, *The Disruption of American Democracy* (New York, 1948), 26–27.

14. *New-York Daily Times*, Feb. 5, 6, 7, 9, 10, 12, 25, 28, 1857; Caleb Cushing to John McKeon, Feb. 7, 1857, Hall, Andrews, Ashton, et al., comps., *Official Opinions* 8:375–76; William Sidney Thayer to A. O. P. Nicholson, Oct. 8 [1855], Alfred Osborne Pope Nicholson Papers, New-York Historical Society.

15. Correspondent's letter, Apr. 30, in *New York Evening Post*, May 1, 1855.

16. *M&P* 5:230.

17. JMC to Zachary Taylor, June 9, 1850, JMC Papers, LC; Millard Fillmore to DW, Oct. 10, 1851, *Millard Fillmore Papers*, ed. Frank H. Severance, 2 vols. (Buffalo, 1907), 1:356–57; correspondent's letter dated Jan. 7, in *New York Herald*, Jan. 9, 1858; Francis Deák and Philip C. Jessup, eds., *A Collection of Neutrality Laws, Regulations, and Treatises of Various Countries*, 2 vols. (Washington, 1939), 2:1172–1207. The breakdown for the four presidents was Taylor, one proclamation, Fillmore two, Pierce three, and Buchanan one. Such proclamations also helped to fulfill a requirement under international law that states give "substantial evidence" to other states of their good intent to abide by their obligations. Roy Emerson Curtis, "The Law of Hostile Military Expeditions as Applied by the United States," *American Journal of International Law* 8 (Apr. 1914): 224–25.

18. Franklin Pierce proclamations of May 31, 1854, Dec. 8, 1856, Millard Fillmore proclamations of Apr. 21, Oct. 22, 1851, *M&P* 5:272–73, 388–89, 111–12.

19. Millard Fillmore Annual Message, Dec. 2, 1850, JB Annual Message, Dec. 8, 1857, *M&P* 5:78, 448.

20. Malcolm W. Mearis to JMC (n.d. but marked "Recd 27. Sept. 49"), RG 59, DS, Despatches from Special Agents, M37, roll 9, NA; Zachary Taylor Proclamation of Aug. 11, 1849, *M&P* 5:7–8; J. W. Lesesne to JAQ, June 8, Samuel Walker to JAQ, July 31, 1854, JAQ Papers, HU.

21. Zachary Taylor to JMC, Aug. 11, 1849, Preston Family Papers, Virginia Historical Society, Richmond; James K. Polk Diary, Aug. 29, 1848, *The Diary of James K. Polk*, ed. Milo Milton Quaife, 4 vols. (1910; reprint, New York, 1970), 2:104–5; J. W. Lesesne to JAQ, June 8, 1854, JAQ Papers, HU.

22. Jeremiah S. Black to Isaiah Rynders, Oct. 4, 1859 (letterbook copy of telegraph), DJ, Letters Sent: General and Miscellaneous, NA; William Ballard Preston to Foxhall A. Parker, Aug. 9, 1849, in K. Jack Bauer, ed., *The New American State Papers: Naval Affairs*, 10 vols. (Wilmington, Del., 1981), 2:125–26; JMC to Logan Hunton, June 9, 1850, Millard Fillmore executive order, Sept. 2, 1851, in *Dipl Corr* 11:83, 111n; DS Circular, Sept. 18, 1857, Lewis Cass to Thomas J. Semmes, Dec. 16, 1857, *H. Ex. Doc.* 24, 35th Cong., 1st Sess., 4–5, 35.

23. WLM to E. Warren Moise (marked "Same to Solomon W. Downs"), Dec. 16, 1853, June 5, 1854, WLM to Samuel W. Inge, June 13, 1854 (letterbook copies), DS, M40, roll 40, NA; James C. Dobbin to Bladen Dulany, Jan. 3, 1854, in *New American State Papers* 2:160; Caleb Cushing to B. F. Hallett and Hugh Q. Jewitt, Dec. 8, 1855, in Hall, Andrews, Ashton, et al., comps., *Official Opinions* 8:472–73.

24. JMC to Logan Hunton, June 10, 1850, DS, Domestic Letters, M17, roll 36, Hunton to DW, Dec. 26, O'Sullivan to DW, Nov. 20, 1851, DS, ML, M179, roll 128, Jeremiah S. Black to Robert H. Smith, Nov. 12, 1858, RG 60, DJ, Letters Sent: General and Miscellaneous, M699, roll 5, John McKeon to Caleb Cushing, Jan. 22, 1856, Attorney General's Papers, Letters Received: New York, NA; *New Orleans Bee*, June 13, 18, 1850; DW to J. Prescott Hall, Sept. 7, 1850, *Dipl Corr* 11:96n. For Hoffman's distinguished reputation, see *WDNI*, Sept. 30, Oct. 4, 1852; *FLIN*, May 17, 1856; Charles Lanman, *Biographical Annals of the Civil Government of the United States* (2d. edn., New York, 1887), 240.

25. James C. Dobbin to Levi D. Slamm (telegram, n.d.), *New American State Papers*

2:159; Lewis Cass to Franklin H. Clack, Nov. 13, 1857, *H. Ex. Doc.* 24, 35th Cong. 1st Sess., 22; WLM to Juan N. Almonte, Jan. 8, 1855, *Dipl Corr* 9:175; Howell Cobb to JB, Oct. 7, 1859, in "The Correspondence of Robert Toombs, Alexander H. Stephens, and Howell Cobb," ed. Ulrich Bonnell Phillips, in American Historical Association, *Annual Report*, 1911, 2 vols. (Washington, 1913), 2:447.

26. Letter from correspondent "P.," San Diego, Feb. 14, in *DAC*, Feb. 19, 1854; John A. Dahlgren to Patty, July 15, Nov. 16, 1858, John Adolphus Bernard Dahlgren Papers, Newberry Library, Chicago. Pierce's secretary of the navy was troubled by press reports of the fraternization at Ensenada. James C. Dobbin to Thomas A. Dornin, Mar. 31, 1854, *New American State Papers* 2:162.

27. Hiram Paulding [to James C. Dobbin?], Jan. 19, 1856, Hiram Paulding Papers, LC; Paulding to Dobbin, Jan. 22, 1856, RG 45, SquadL, roll 96.

28. Charles H. Davis to William Mervine, Mar. 4, 1857 (copy), RG 45, Lists of Logs and Journals of Vessels of the United States Navy, William Mervine, Letters Received Letterbook, vol. 4, NA. Davis, however, reversed himself on Walker within months. Davis to Samuel Francis Du Pont, May 20, 1857, Samuel Francis Du Pont Papers, HML.

29. Ambrose P. Hill to his father, Feb. 4, 1852, Ambrose P. Hill Papers, Virginia Historical Society, Richmond; William Tecumseh Sherman to his brother, May 6, 1851, William T. Sherman Papers, Ohio Historical Society, Columbus; Robert E. May, "Young American Males and Filibustering in the Age of Manifest Destiny: The United States Army as a Cultural Mirror," *Journal of American History* 78 (Dec. 1991): 882–85; T. Harry Williams, *P. G. T. Beauregard: Napoleon in Gray* (Baton Rouge, 1955), 42.

30. *Saturday Evening Post* (Philadelphia), May 17, 1856; *New-York Daily Times*, Dec. 22, 1856.

31. Henry Wilson to Jeremiah S. Black, Dec. 4, A. J. Requier to Black, Dec. 9, Robert H. Smith to Black, Dec. 21, 1858, RG 60, DJ, Attorney General's Papers, Letters Received: Alabama, NA.

32. William B. Skelton, *An American Profession of Arms: The Army Officer Corps, 1784–1861* (Lawrence, Kan., 1992), 109–347; Edward M. Coffman, *The Old Army: A Portrait of the American Army in Peacetime, 1784–1898* (New York, 1986), 96–99; Samuel Watson, "United States Army Officers Fight the 'Patriot War': Responses to Filibustering on the Canadian Border, 1837–1839," *Journal of the Early Republic* 18 (Fall 1998): 485–519 (quotation on p. 487).

33. James B. McPherson to his brother, Nov. 8, 1853, James B. McPherson Papers, LC; James L. Morrison Jr., *"The Best School in the World": West Point, the Pre–Civil War Years, 1833–1866* (Kent, Ohio, 1986), 92; John C. Pemberton to Israel Pemberton, June 1, 1850, Pemberton Family Papers, HSP; P. V. Hagner to Alex Hagner, Jan. 24, 1854, Peter Hagner Papers, Edmund Kirby Smith to his mother, Mar. 16, 1853, Edmund Kirby Smith Papers, SHC; Edward L. Hartz to Samuel Hartz, May 1, 1859 [1860], Edward L. Hartz Papers, LC; Ambrose P. Hill to his father, Feb. 4, 1852, Ambrose P. Hill Papers, Virginia Historical Society, Richmond; "History of Filibustering," part of January 1855 entry, in *The California Diary of General E. D. Townsend*, ed.

Malcolm Edwards ([Los Angeles], 1970), 95; William Tecumseh Sherman to John Sherman, Dec. 9, 1860, Sherman to Ellen Ewing Sherman, Jan. 5, 1861, in *Sherman's Civil War: Selected Correspondence of William T. Sherman, 1860–1865*, ed. Brooks D. Simpson and Jean V. Berlin (Chapel Hill, 1999), 16, 30–31; George W. Cullum, comp., *Biographical Register of the Officers and Graduates of the U.S. Military Academy at West Point, N.Y., from Its Establishment, March 16, 1802 to the Army Re-Organization of 1866–67*, 2 vols. (New York, 1868), 1:535–36, 507, 595, 2:410. The academy also had profilibustering enthusiasts. May, "Young American Males," 876–77.

34. John E. Wool to J. A. Hardie, May 4, June 17, 1857, James A. Hardie Papers, LC; J. R. Hagner to Peter V. Hagner, Aug. 20, 1855, Hagner Papers, SHC. Even non-West Pointers gaining commissions in the antebellum army had to "demonstrate proficiency" in international law during their appearances before examining boards. Morrison, *"Best School,"* 16.

35. Ethan Allen Hitchcock Diary, Oct. 4, 1851, in *Fifty Years in Camp and Field: Diary of Major-General Ethan Allen Hitchcock, U.S.A.*, ed. W. A. Croffut (New York, 1909), 389; Skelton, *American Profession of Arms*, 336; Joseph H. La Motte to Ellen La Motte, Dec. 22, 1851, La Motte-Coppinger Papers, Missouri Historical Society, St. Louis; Persifor F. Smith to R. Jones, July 18, 1852, *S. Ex. Doc.* 1, 32d Cong., 2d Sess., 18; Smith to Samuel Cooper, Sept. 8, 1855, DS, ML, M179, roll 147, NA; Robert E. Lee to Annie (Anne Carter Lee), Feb. 22, 1860 (copy), Lee Family Papers, Virginia Historical Society, Richmond; John E. Wool to Jefferson Davis, Apr. 14, 1854, *H. Ex. Doc.* 88, 33d Cong., 1st Sess., 53. Lee commanded the Department of Texas at the time. Emory M. Thomas, *Robert E. Lee* (New York, 1995), 183–84.

36. Victor M. Randolph to William Ballard Preston, Aug. 28, 1849, *S. Ex. Doc.* 57, 31st Cong., 1st Sess., 77; J. Bates to Millard Fillmore, Sept. 20, 1851, DS, ML, M179, roll 127, NA; Seth Phelps to Elisha Whittlesey, May 16, 1856, Dec. 2, 1857, quoted in Jay Slagle, *Ironclad Captain: Seth Ledyard Phelps and the U.S. Navy, 1841–1864* (Kent, Ohio, 1996), 84–86, 92–94; Samuel Francis Du Pont to Sophie Du Pont, Dec. 5, 1854, Mar. 24, 1858 (quotation), Thomas Turner to Samuel Francis Du Pont, Apr. 9, 1855, Franklin Buchanan to Samuel Francis Du Pont, Mar. 11, 1858, Samuel Francis Du Pont Papers, HML; letter from naval officer, Feb. 12, 1855, quoted in *New Era and Weekly Argus* (Honolulu), Mar. 16, 1854. Phelps's use of the term "strikers" was more derogatory than it seems. At the time, the term frequently connoted persons who, for a price paid by corrupt politicians, delivered large numbers of compliant voters. Mark W. Summers, *The Plundering Generation: Corruption and the Crisis of the Union, 1849–1861* (New York, 1987), 57.

37. P. Sherward Johnson to JMC, June 17, 1850, James Louis Petigru to DW, Mar. 13, 1852, *Dipl Corr* 11:86n, 132n; Caleb Cushing to Samuel W. Inge, Jan. 16, Inge to Cushing, Mar. 16, 1854, *S. Ex. Doc.* 68, 34th Cong., 1st Sess., 7–8; F. H. Hatch to Lewis Cass, Oct. 1, 1857, *H. Ex. Doc.* 24, 35th Cong., 1st Sess., 7.

38. DW to the U.S. Collector of Customs at New Orleans, Jan. 21, 1851, in Manning, *Dipl Corr* 11:98n; Jeremiah S. Black to Robert H. Smith, Dec. 14, 1858 (letter-book copy), DJ, Letters Sent: General and Miscellaneous, M699, roll 5, NA; Lewis Cass to Thomas J. Semmes, Dec. 16, 1857, *H. Ex. Doc.* 24, 35th Cong., 1st Sess., 35;

WLM to James Guthrie, Feb. 27, 1854 (letterbook copy), DS, Domestic Letters, M40, roll 40, NA.

39. Ethan Allen Hitchcock Diary, Oct. 9, 1853, in *Fifty Years in Camp*, 400–401; *California Diary*, 92–94. Inge's sympathies remain unclear. He later celebrated the convictions of two of Walker's associates. S. W. Inge to Jefferson Davis, June 1, 1854, *Jefferson Davis, Constitutionalist: His Letters, Papers and Speeches*, ed. Dunbar Rowland, 10 vols. (Jackson, 1923), 2:361–62.

40. ACdlB to William S. Derrick, with enclosure, Aug. 25, 1851, Millard Fillmore to DW, Sept. 2, 1851, *PDW* 2:369–72; *NODP*, Sept. 9, 1851; Senate Executive Journal, Dec. 9, 1857, in *Journal of the Executive Proceedings of the Senate, of the United States of America, from December 3, 1855, to June 16, 1858, Inclusive* (Washington, 1887), 10:261; JB Annual Message, Dec. 8, 1857, *M&P* 5:448; Bradford Ripley Alden to Ethan Allen Hitchcock, Jan. 17, 1854, Ethan Allen Hitchcock Papers, LC.

41. Theophilus F. Rodenbough, *From Everglade to Cañon with the Second Dragoons . . .* (New York, 1875), 168.

42. William E. Prince Diary, Nov. 25, 26, Dec. 1, 1851, Feb. 28, 1852 (including copy of Prince's Feb. 28 letter to T. J. Wood), BRBM; A. P. Hill to his father, Feb. 4, 1852, Ambrose P. Hill Papers, Virginia Historical Society, Richmond. The Fillmore administration implicitly recognized the anti-Carbajal efforts as a campaign, by recommending to the Senate for a "brevet," or honorary promotion, one of the army officers most active in patrolling the Rio Grande, Captain John S. Phelps, commander of the 4th Artillery at Fort Brown opposite Matamoros. *Journal of the Executive Proceedings of the Senate of the United States of America, from December 6, 1852, to March 3, 1855, Inclusive* (Washington, 1887), 9:30; *WDNI*, Nov. 13, 1851.

43. P. Sherward Johnson to JMC, June 17, 1850, *Dipl Corr* 11:86n; James P. Delgado, *To California by Sea: A Maritime History of the California Gold Rush* (Columbia, S.C., 1990), 120.

44. *New-York Times*, Dec. 23, 1857; *New York Albion*, Dec. 26, 1857.

45. Isaiah D. Hart to Thomas Corwin, Sept. 13, Henry Williams to the Secretary of State, Sept. 4, J. M. Hanson to William S. Derrick, Sept. 9, 11, George Call to DW, Sept. 12, 1851, DS, ML, M179, roll 127, NA.; *WDNI*, Sept. 11, 1851.

46. George Call to William S. Derrick, Oct. 8, 1851, DS, ML, M179, roll 127, NA; *New-York Daily Tribune*, Oct. 21, 1851; *Jacksonville* (Fla.) *Republican*, Dec. 18, 1851, quoted in *WDNI*, Dec. 26, 1851; Copy of Decision, Dec. 1851, *United States v. Sr. "Pampero"*, filed in Case 2056, "*The United States v. William Walker, Frank P. Anderson, Dudley McMichael, John S. West and Flavel Belcher*," Eastern District of Louisiana, New Orleans, Circuit Court General Cases, NA—Southwest Region.

47. J. Prescott Hall to JMC, Sept. 7, 1849 (telegraph), JMC Papers, LC; Hall to JMC, Sept. 8, 15, 25, 1849, *S. Ex. Doc.* 57, 31st Cong., 1st Sess., 15–18; *New-York Daily Tribune*, Sept. 8, 1849, Apr. 25, 28, 1851; *New York Mirror* quoted in *WDNI*, Apr. 28, 1851; Frederick S. Calhoun, *The Lawmen: United States Marshals and Their Deputies, 1789–1989* (Washington, 1989), 68–69; Harris, "John Louis O'Sullivan," 306, 312–13; *New-York Daily Times*, Jan. 26, Mar. 9, 13, 14, 15, 20, 1855; Samuel R. Walker, "The Diary of a Louisiana Planter" (typescript copy), Dec. 19, 1859, Howard-

Tilton Memorial Library, Tulane University, New Orleans; May, *John A. Quitman*, 294–95. On June 1, 1855, moreover, the captain of a U.S. revenue cutter seized the barque *Magnolia*, reportedly also involved in the Quitman plot against Cuba, at St. Joseph Bay on northwest Florida's Gulf Coast, and brought her into Mobile where the district attorney brought proceedings in admiralty to have the vessel forfeited to the government. Douglass Ottinger to Thaddeus Sanford, June 4, 1855, RG 26, Department of Transportation: Records of the United States Coast Guard, "Weekly Reports from the Commander of Rev: Cutter Rt. McClelland," NA; *Mobile Daily Advertiser*, July 17–19, 21, 1855; "*The United States* v. *Barque Magnolia*," filed in Case 2956, "*The United States* v. *William Walker, Frank P. Anderson, Dudley McMichael, John S. West and Flavel Belcher*," RG 21, Eastern District of Louisiana, New Orleans, Circuit Court General Cases, NA—Southwest Region.

48. Franklin Pierce to Charles Boarman, May 25, 1855 (copy), Charles Boarman Letterbook, LC; *New York Evening Post*, June 4, 1852; *Mobile Daily Register*, Jan. 20, 1858; Jeremiah S. Black to Junius Hillyer, Jan. 30, 1858, RG 60, DJ, Letters Sent: General and Miscellaneous, M699, roll 2, NA; Thaddeus Sanford to Howell Cobb, Oct. 16, Nov. 9, Dec. 1, 4 (telegraph) 1858, Cobb to Sanford, Oct. 25, Nov. 13, Dec. 8, 1858, *H. Ex. Doc.* 25, 35th Cong., 2d Sess., 4–6, 10–15, 18–19, 21; *New-York Times*, Oct. 5, 26, 1859; "*United States* v. *Steamship Philadelphia*," U.S. District Court for the Eastern District of Louisiana, RG 21, NA—Southwest Region.

49. JMC to J. Prescott Hall, telegraph marked "Confidential," Sept. 7, 1849 (copy), DS, Despatches from Special Agents, M37, roll 9, NA; JMC to Hall, June 25, 1850, *Dipl Corr* 11:85n; Thomas Ewing to Logan Hunton, June 10, D. C. Goddard to Hunton, July 27, 1850, William A. Graham to Hall, Aug. 26, 1851, RG 60, DJ, Letters Sent Concerning Judiciary Expenses, M700, roll 1; Jeremiah S. Black to Henry C. Wilson, Nov. 24, 1858 (letterbook copy), DJ, Letters Sent: General and Miscellaneous, Thomas J. Semmes to Jeremiah Black, Feb. 3, 1858, DJ, Attorney General's Papers, Letters Received: Louisiana, both in RG 60, NA; John A. Campbell to Black, Nov. 22, 1858, Jeremiah S. Black Papers, LC; Samuel D. Hay to Jefferson Davis, Mar. 28, 1854, RG 59, DS, ML, M179, roll 139, NA.

50. William R. Hackley to J. C. Clark, May 22, 1850, JMC to Logan Hunton (marked "*Same mutatis mutandis*" to Peter Hamilton), May 27, 1850 (telegraph with mail copies), *S. Ex. Doc.* 57, 31st Cong., 1st Sess., 44, 47; JMC to Henry Williams, May 25, 1850 (telegraph), RG 59, DS, Despatches from Special Agents, M37, roll 9, JMC to Logan Hunton, May 27, 1850, DS, Domestic Letters, M17, roll 36, NA; *Pittsburg Daily Morning Post*, May 28, 1850; Case 6688, U.S. District Court, Eastern District of Louisiana, Circuit Court General Case Files (E 121), RG 21, NA—Southwest Region.

51. Case 6688, U.S. District Court, Eastern District of Louisiana, Circuit Court General Case Files (E 121), RG 21, NA—Southwest Region; Logan Hunton to JMC, June 22, 1850, JMC Papers, LC; May, *John A. Quitman*, 240–41, 248–51; John Ray Skates Jr., *A History of the Mississippi Supreme Court, 1817–1948* (Jackson 1973), 14, 31. McCaleb remitted the case to the Circuit Court because of the "difficult and important questions of law" involved in its resolution. He presided at the Circuit Court

session because another judge was absent. Minutes, District Court, June 26, 1850, Case 6688; Antonio Rafael de la Cova, "Ambrosio Jose Gonzales: A Cuban Confederate Colonel" (Ph.D. diss., West Virginia University, 1994), 142. Meanwhile, in New York, District Attorney J. Prescott Hall arrested the Cuban exile Miguel Teurbe Tolón, secretary of the Cuban Council, editor of the Spanish- and-English language sheet *La Verdad*, and designer of the filibusters' flag. Robert Benson Leard, "Bonds of Destiny: The United States and Cuba, 1848–1861" (Ph.D. diss., University of California, 1953), 79–80; de la Cova, "Gonzales," 33–34.

52. *New-York Daily Times*, Mar. 9, 10, Apr. 5, 1852; *New-York Daily Tribune*, Apr., 29, 1851.

53. (Austin) *Texas State Gazette*, July 9, 1854; Campbell's charge quoted in Ronald Sklut, "John Archibald Campbell: A Study in Divided Loyalties," *Alabama Lawyer* 20 (July 1959): 236; Claiborne, *John Quitman* 2:196–97; (New Orleans) *Louisiana Courier*, July 2, 1854; JAQ to F. Henry Quitman, July 1, 1854, JAQ Papers, HSP; JAQ Protest, July 3, 1854, copy in JAQ Papers, MDAH.

54. Henry L. Kinney to WLM, Jan. 28, Feb. 13, 24, 1855, WLM to Kinney, Feb. 4, 21 (with enclosure), 1855, all in *New York Evening Post*, May 3, 1855.

55. Caleb Cushing to John McKeon, Apr. 25, 1855, *S. Ex. Doc.* 68, 34th Cong., 1st Sess., 9; Joseph W. Fabens to Henry L. Kinney, Mar. 17, 1855, Slavery Manuscripts, New-York Historical Society; shares of stock in the Nicaraguan Land and Mining Company, William Sidney Thayer Papers, LC; WLM to Joseph W. Fabens, Apr. 25, 1855, in *New York Evening Post*, July 26, 1855; telegraph from New York in *Galveston Weekly News*, May 22, 1855.

56. Caleb Cushing to John McKeon, May 25, 1855, *S. Ex. Doc.* 68, 34th Cong., 1st Sess., 9; *New York Evening Post*, Apr. 28, May 4, May 8, 10 (advertisement for May 19 sailing of the *United States*), 25, 1855; John McKeon to Caleb Cushing, Apr. 27, 28, May 21, 1855, RG 60, DJ, Attorney General's Papers, Letters Received: New York, NA; telegraph from New York in *Galveston Weekly News*, May 22, 1855; entry for R. Squire Cottrell, in List of U.S. Consular Officers, M587, roll 17, NA; *Philadelphia Public Ledger*, May 3, 16, 1855. Fabens denied any formal connection with Kinney's company, claiming that he had a grant from the Republic of Nicaragua for mineral-rich lands in Nicaragua's Chontales district, and that Kinney had contracted to bring workingmen to Fabens's mines and superintend Fabens's concern for a year following the emigration. Fabens to WLM, Apr. 26, June 26, 1855, *New York Evening Post*, July 26, 1855.

57. Alejandro Bolaños-Geyer, *William Walker: The Gray-Eyed Man of Destiny*, vol. 2: *The Californias* (Lake St. Louis, Mo., 1989), 281; *DAC*, Mar. 2, 3, 1854; de la Cova, "Gonzales," 90.

58. *DAC*, Oct. 18, 1854; John E. Wool to Winfield Scott, May 15, 1854, *S. Ex. Doc.* 88, 35th Cong., 1st Sess., 62; *SFDH*, Aug. 1, 1854. Wool had sent McKinstry to negotiate Walker's surrender after being alerted to Walker's approaching the border by the army commander at Fort Yuma (after deserters from Walker's force reached that post). Burton commanded the actual army detachment stationed on the border. Arthur Woodward, ed., *The Republic of Lower California, 1853–1854* (Los Angeles,

1966), 27; Harwood Perry Hinton, "The Military Career of John Ellis Wool, 1812–1863" (Ph.D. diss., University of Wisconsin, 1960), 256–57; Bolaños-Geyer, *William Walker* 2:292–93. Ogier, U.S. judge for California's southern district, presided in the case in the absence of Judge Hoffman. *DAC*, June 27, 1854; Harold Chase et al., *Biographical Dictionary of the Federal Judiciary* (Detroit, 1976), 211.

59. *FLIN*, Jan. 5, 1855; *Philadelphia Public Ledger*, Dec. 27, 1855; John McKeon to Thomas Lord, Jan. 4, 1856, McKeon to Caleb Cushing, Jan. 16, Feb. 4, 1856, affidavit of Francis V. R. Mace, Jan. 9, 1856 (enclosed with P. J. Joachimssen to Cushing, Jan. 11, 1856), RG 60, DJ, Attorney General's Papers, Letters Received: New York, NA; *Springfield* (Mass.) *Daily Republican*, Jan. 11, 1856; Cornelius Vanderbilt to McKeon, Feb. 6, 1856, *S. Ex. Doc.* 68, 34th Cong., 1st Sess., 81; *New-York Daily Times*, Feb. 2, 1857. The indicted filibusters from the *Northern Light* affair included Parker H. French (Walker's unrecognized minister to the United States, then in New York making arrangements for filibusters to board the *Northern Light*); French's private secretary; the *Northern Light*'s captain Edward L. Tinklepaugh as well as the ship's chief engineer; the recruiter George B. Hall (who was to accompany the men to Nicaragua at the rank of colonel; Joseph R. Malé (editor of Walker's paper, *El Nicaragüense*); the former Cuba filibuster Louis Schlesinger; and men with commissions in Walker's military.

60. *United States v. William Walker & al.*, Case 2826, RG 21, Eastern District of Louisiana, Circuit Court General Cases, entry 121, NA—Southwest Region; Franklin H. Clack to Lewis Cass, Nov. 23, James Conner to Cass, Dec. 7 (with deposition of Douglas B. De Saussure, Dec. 3), 1857, *H. Ex. Doc.* 24, 35th Cong., 1st Sess., 26–27, 28–31.

61. *New-York Times*, Dec. 27, 1857; Washington correspondent report of Dec. 29, 1857, in *Charleston Mercury*, Jan. 1, 1858; Jeremiah S. Black to Thomas J. Semmes, Jan. 12, 1858 (letterbook copy), DJ, Letters Sent: General and Miscellaneous, M699, roll 2, NA; Elbert B. Smith, *The Presidency of James Buchanan* (Lawrence, Kan., 1975), 73.

62. Thomas J. Semmes to Jeremiah S. Black, Jan. 21, 23, 26, Feb. 1, 3, 1858, Attorney General's Papers, Letters Received: Louisiana, A. J. Requier [to Semmes] (copy), Jan. 25, 1858, Letters Received: Alabama, all in RG 60, DJ, NA; Hiram Paulding to Isaac Toucey, Jan. 25, 1858, SquadL, roll 97; *WDNI*, Jan. 5 (quoting *Mobile Daily Advertiser*), Feb. 3, 1858; *Mobile Daily Register*, Jan. 24, 1858; "*The United States v. William Walker & Others*," Case 2956, Eastern District of Louisiana, Circuit Court, RG 21, NA—Southwest Region. Anderson's command, detached from the main body of Walker's troops at the time of arrival on Nicaragua's coast, had been conveyed to Key West by Commodore Paulding, where Anderson and his soldiers had been arrested and brought before William Marvin, U.S. judge for the Southern District of Florida. Marvin remanded Anderson, his officers, and over thirty men, in the custody of a marshal, to the authorities in New Orleans (because the criminal act had originated in jurisdictions of the U.S. courts for New Orleans and Mobile). It was their arrival that made Semmes confident of finally mustering testimony to convince the New Orleans jurors that Walker had committed a criminal act. The grand jury found true

bills against two captains, Flavel Belcher and Dudley McMichael, and lieutenant John S. West, in addition to those against Walker and Anderson.

63. Minutes, U.S. District Court, Eastern District of Louisiana, vol. 613, pp. 226, RG 21, NA—Southwest Region; *NODP*, Nov. 22, 29, 1858, Oct. 9, 18, 20, 1859; Joseph M. Kennedy to Jeremiah S. Black, Nov. 25, 1858, RG 60, DJ, Attorney General's Papers, Letters Received: Louisiana, NA; John A. Campbell to Black, Nov. 22, 1858, Jeremiah S. Black Papers, LC; Black to Robert H. Smith, Oct. 5, 1859 (letterbook copy of telegraph), DJ, Letters Sent: General and Miscellaneous, M699, roll 5, NA; *New-York Times*, Oct. 14, 24, 1859.

64. *WDNI*, Sept. 19, 1851; "*United States* v. *Lumsden et al.*," Case 15,641, *The Federal Cases, Comprising Cases Argued and Determined in the Circuit and District Courts of the United States*, 30 vols. (St. Paul, 1894–97), 26:1013–20; *Philadelphia Public Ledger*, Feb. 11, 1856; Stout, *Liberators*, 111; (Stockton, Calif.) *San Joaquin Republican*, Jan. 10, 1855. See also Henry Wilson to DW, Oct. 23, 1851, DS, ML, M179, roll 127, NA; Judge John McLean's charge to the U.S. Circuit Court in Ohio in October 1851, quoted in *WDNI*, Nov. 4, 1851; *DAC*, Mar. 29, 1856.

65. Apr. 25, 1851 letter of correspondent of *Newark* (N.J.) *[Daily] Advertiser* in *New-York Daily Tribune*, May 2, 1851; J. M. Hanson to William S. Derrick, Sept. 11, 1851, DS, ML, M179, roll 127, Court-Martial Case File HH 168 (6W4/3/7/B/box 205), NA; Tom Chaffin, *Fatal Glory: Narciso López and the First Clandestine U.S. War against Cuba* (Charlottesville, 1996), 169.

66. Millard Fillmore to Persifor F. Smith, Sept. 22 (copy), Smith to William S. Harney, Oct. 21, 1851 (copy), Testimony of Thomas J. Wood, May 19, 1852, in Court-Martial Case File HH 168 (6W4/3/7/B/box 205), NA.

67. Correspondent's letter from Rio Grande City, Nov. 28, in *NODP*, Dec. 24, 1851; testimony of Thomas J. Wood, May 11, 19, Joseph H. La Motte, May 3, 20, Gabriel R. Paul, May 20, 1852, William S. Harney to William P. Ballinger, Nov. 27, 1851 (copy), Harney to La Motte, Jan. 31(copy), Egbert L. Viele to Paul, Feb. 1, 1852 (copy), Viele to La Motte, Jan. 31 (copy), Robert Selden Garnett to Viele, Feb. 2, 1852 (copy), all in *NODP*, Dec. 24, 1851; *WDNI*, Feb. 9, 1852.

68. Gabriel R. Paul's questions to the defense witnesses Joseph H. La Motte and Thomas J. Wood, May 3, 11, 1852, Robert Selden Garnett summation, Judah Benjamin to Garnett, May 4, 1852, trial verdicts of May 13, 21, 1852, all in *NODP*, Dec. 24, 1851.

69. Persifor F. Smith statements confirming the courts' decisions, June 10, 1852, Charles M. Conrad statement, Aug. 28, 1852, "Published to the Army by Command of Major General Scott," in *NODP*, Dec. 24, 1851. See also War Department orders that General Twiggs in New Orleans consider prior antifilibustering instructions as perpetually in force. Conrad to David E. Twiggs, Apr. 15, William A. Graham to Twiggs, Aug. 11, 1852, RG 107, Records of the Secretary of War, NA.

70. Persifor F. Smith to the Assistant Adjutant General, June 10, 1852, Court-Martial Case File HH 168 (6W4/3/7/B/box 205), Smith to Samuel Cooper, Oct. 12, 1855 (copy), DS, ML, M179, roll 148, NA.

71. John E. Wool to Jefferson Davis, Mar. 1, May 30, 1854, Jan. [no exact date]

1855, Davis to Wool, Apr. 14, Aug. 18, Oct. 13, Dec. 13, 1854, *H. Ex. Doc.* 88, 35th Cong., 1st Sess., 10–11, 66–68, 111–14, 52, 98–100; *Washington Daily Union*, Nov. 1, 1854. Durwood Ball suggests that Davis's anger against Wool was politically motivated in part. See Durwood Ball, "Filibusters and Regular Troops in San Francisco, 1851–1855," *Military History of the West* 28 (Fall 1998): 178. California newspapers alluded to Watkins as both a colonel and a general in Walker's army. Arthur Woodward, ed., *The Republic of Lower California, 1853–1854* (Los Angeles, 1966), 27n.

72. Richard P. Hammond to Wool, Aug. 16, Wool to Hammond, Aug. 17, 1854, *H. Ex. Doc.* 88, 35th Cong., 1st Sess., 101, 102; William Walker letter of July 29, 1857, reprinted from the *WDNI* in *New York Herald*, Aug. 5, 1857; William Walker, *The War in Nicaragua* (1860; reprint, Tucson, 1985), 27–28.

73. Lida Mayo, "The Mexican War and After," in Maurice Matloff, ed., *American Military History* (Washington, 1969), 180–81; Russell F. Weigley, *History of the United States Army* (New York, 1967), 190; Winfield Scott to John B. Floyd, Nov. 13, 1858, RG 108, Letters Sent by the Headquarters of the Army (Main Series), M857, roll 5, NA. In 1857 the secretary of war reported that the army occupied sixty-eight permanent forts and seventy other posts. Francis Paul Prucha, *A Guide to the Military Posts of the United States, 1789–1895* (Madison, 1964), 20.

74. John Rogers to William Ballard Preston, May 21, 1850 (telegraph), *S. Ex. Doc.* 57, 31st Cong., 1st Sess., 65; William R. Hackley to Zachary Taylor, June 6, 1850, RG 48, Department of the Interior, Records Concerning the Cuban Expedition 1850–51, box 145, NA; Ambrose P. Hill to his father, May 5, 1850, Ambrose P. Hill Papers, Virginia Historical Society, Richmond; Arch Fredric Blakey, "Military Duty in Antebellum Florida: The Experiences of John Henry Winder," *Florida Historical Quarterly* 63 (Oct. 1984): 163; William Freret to the Commanding Officer, United States Navy, Pensacola, Aug. 30, Freret to W. W. S. Bliss, Aug. 16, 1851, in *Correspondence between the Treasury Department, &c., in Relation to the Cuba Expedition, and William Freret, Late Collector* (New Orleans, 1851), 27, 23; John E. Wool to Jefferson Davis, Jan. 10, Mar. 1 (quotation), May 30, Wool to Samuel Cooper, Jan. 14 (telegraph), 1854, *H. Ex. Doc.* 88, 35th Cong., 1st Sess., 5–6, 7, 10, 66. Wool's command at San Francisco, a small fraction of his total departmental force of about 1,300 men, was divided between Benicia (northeast of the city on the other side of the bay) and the Presidio. The number of soldiers at Benicia never exceeded 129 between 1851 and 1855. The Presidio's garrison grew from a mere 21 officers and men in 1851 to just 80 three years later. Ball, "Filibusters and Regular Troops in San Francisco," 164–65.

75. Correspondent's letter dated Nov. 28, 1851, in *NODP*, Dec. 24, 1851; William E. Prince to T. J. Wood, Feb. 28, 1852, copy in William E. Prince Diary; Helen Chapman to her mother, Oct. 21, 1851, in Caleb Coker, ed., *The News from Brownsville: Helen Chapman's Letters from the Texas Military Frontier, 1848–1852* (Austin, 1992), 265; Endorsement by David E. Twiggs, Aug. 9, 1858, on John H. King to John Withers, July 28, 1858, RG 94, Records of the Adjutant General, Letters Received, M567, roll 582, NA; Pat Kelley, *River of Lost Dreams: Navigation on the Rio Grande* (Lincoln, Neb., 1986), 2, 43.

76. J. F. Waddell to DW, Oct. 7, 1851, DS, Despatches from United States Consuls

in Matamoros, M281, roll 2, NA; Thomas T. Smith, "U.S. Army Combat Operations in the Indian Wars of Texas, 1849–1881," *SHQ* 99 (Apr. 1996): 504, 512; J. Fred Rippy, *The United States and Mexico* (New York, 1931), 74; Clarence C. Clendenen, *Blood on the Border: The United States Army and the Mexican Irregulars* (London, 1969), 11; Thomas Tyree Smith, *Fort Inge: Sharps, Spurs, and Sabers on the Texas Frontier, 1849–1869* (Austin, 1993), 11, 13; letter from correspondent in Brownsville in *NODP*, Apr. 5, 1853; William E. Prince to T. J. Wood, Feb. 28, 1852, copy in William E. Prince Diary. One army officer estimated that the Rio Grande was only 150 yards wide at Ringgold Barracks (Rio Grande City). Edmund Kirby Smith to his mother, Mar. 16, 1853, Edmund Kirby Smith Papers, SHC.

77. Irving H. King, *The Coast Guard under Sail: The U.S. Revenue Cutter Service, 1789–1865* (Annapolis, 1989), 112, 135–36; Stephen H. Evans, *The United States Coast Guard, 1790–1915: A Definitive History* (Annapolis, 1949), 64–66; John H. Schroeder, *Shaping a Maritime Empire: The Commercial and Diplomatic Role of the American Navy, 1829–1861* (Westport, Conn., 1985), 3–4; Millard Fillmore to DW, Apr. 16, 1815, in *Millard Fillmore Papers* 1:341.

78. V. M. Randolph to John Thomas Newton, Sept. 1, 5, 1849, *S. Ex. Doc.* 57, 31st Cong., 1st Sess., 89–90, 95; Henry Williams to the Secretary of State, Sept. 4, 1851, J. Prescott Hall to William A. Graham, Aug. 29, enclosed with Alexander H. H. Stuart to William S. Derrick, Sept. 2, 1851, DS, ML, M179, roll 127, Richard P. Hammond to Bladen Dulany, Sept. 30, 1853, Dulany to Thomas A. Dornin, Jan. 20, 1854 (copy), RG 45, SquadL, roll 36, Newton to the Secretary of the Navy, Mar. 16, 1853, Hiram Roberts to William L. Hodge, Apr. 16, 1851, William D. Lewis to Thomas Corwin, Sept. 3, 1851, RG 26, Department of the Treasury, U.S. Coast Guard, Revenue Cutter Service, Letters from Collectors, NA; John McKeon to Caleb Cushing, Jan. 16, 1856, RG 60, DJ, Attorney General's Papers, Letters Received: New York, NA.

79. Charles Boarman to James C. Dobbin, May 26, 27, Boarman to John de Camp, May 26, 1855 (copies), Charles Boarman Letterbook, LC; Boarman to Winfield Scott, May 30, 1855 (copy), Scott to Samuel Cooper, May 31, 1855, in RG 107, Records of the Office of the Secretary of War, Letters Received, M221, roll 175, NA; *Washington Sentinel* quoted in the *Eclaireur* 2 (Mar.–Apr. 1855): 122–23.

80. Letter from the Rio Grande, Nov. 28, 1851, in *WDNI*, Jan. 5, 1852; testimony of Daniel Huston Jr., Court-Martial Case File HH 168 (6W4/3/7/B/box 205), NA; *Philadelphia Public Ledger*, Dec. 25, 1855; *FLIN*, Jan. 5, 1856; Joseph M. Kennedy to Jeremiah S. Black, Oct. 8, 1859, RG 60, DJ, Attorney General's Papers, Letters Received: Louisiana, NA. For a filibuster officer threatening a U.S. marshal in New York City, see *Harper's Weekly*, Feb. 7, 1857.

81. Thaddeus Sanford to Howell Cobb, Dec. 5, 1858, *H. Ex. Doc.* 25, 35th Cong., 2d Sess., 19–20; Captain J. J. Morrison, "Detention of the Sch 'Susan,'" RG 26, Coast Guard, volume entitled "Extraordinary Operations and Legislation, 1790–1870," 259–62, A. J. Requier to Jeremiah S. Black, Dec. 9, 1858, RG 60, DJ, Attorney General's Papers, Letters Received: Alabama, NA. Similarly, William Walker defied county officials in California in getting off his first expedition to Nicaragua, by taking a deputy sheriff prisoner. *DAC*, May 5, 1855; Walker, *War in Nicaragua*, 29–32.

82. George P. Ihrie to Samuel Cooper, Sept. 30, 1857, RG 94, Records of the Adjutant General, Letters Received, M567, roll 581, NA; Edmund Ruffin Diary, May 14, 1858, LC.

83. John S. Thrasher to James Johnston Pettigrew, Jan. 2, 1854, Pettigrew Family Papers, SHC; report from *New York Express* and correspondent of the *Mobile Tribune* quoted in *WDNI*, Aug. 23, Sept. 26, 1849; Henry Williams to the Secretary of State, Sept. 4, 1851, DS, ML, M179, roll 127, NA; "*Facts Relative to the Expedition against the Island of Cuba*," H. Ex. Doc. 83, 32d Cong., 1st Sess., 116–18; *New Orleans Delta*, Oct. 8, 1859, quoted in *New-York Times*, Oct. 14, 1859. Tom Chaffin, however, notes that the filibusters never achieved secrecy comparable to covert republican plotting within absolutist European societies. The filibusters desired a certain amount of publicity to attract recruits. Chaffin, *Fatal Glory*, 75–77.

84. John L. O'Sullivan to JAQ, June 26, 1850, JAQ Papers, MDAH; William Walker to Callender I. Fayssoux, Oct. 19, 1858, Aug. 13, 1859, WWP; de la Cova, "Gonzales," 136, 137; Samuel R. Walker to JAQ, Dec. 21, 1854, JAQ Papers, HU.

85. Duncan Smith [alias for Henry Burtnett], "*Narrative of Events Connected with the Late Intended Invasion of Cuba*, in L. M. Perez, ed., 'Lopez's Expeditions to Cuba, 1850–51: Betrayal of the *Cleopatra*, 1851," *Publications of the Southern History Association* 10 (Nov. 1906): 350; William Walker to Callender I. Fayssoux, Aug. 9, Dec. 25, 1858, Apr. 19, Sept. 14, 1859, [no exact date] 1859, WWP; *New-York Times*, Sept. 23, 1858. Walker provided his code in a memorandum that has survived in box 2 of WWP. John Quitman apparently resorted to code during his mid-1850s Cuba plot. See James W. McDonald [Quitman's private secretary] to JAQ, Dec. 6, 1854, JAQ Papers, HU.

86. Testimony of P. F. Edey, Case 7479, "*United States* v. *Steamship Philadelphia*," U.S. District Court for the Eastern District of Louisiana, RG 21, NA—Southwest Region; William Freret to Thomas Corwin, Aug. 4, 13, 1851, *Correspondence between the Treasury Department . . . and William Freret*, 8, 10; *DAC*, Feb. 24, 1854, May 5, 1855; ACdlB to DW, Jan. 28, 1851, *Dipl Corr* 11:584.

87. E. Warren Moise to WLM, May 22, 1854, Henry Williams to DW, DS, ML, M179, rolls 140, 127, Thomas J. Semmes to Jeremiah S. Black, Dec. 21, 1858, RG 60, DJ, Attorney General's Papers, Letters Received: Louisiana, NA.

88. William Walker to John P. Heiss, July 25, 1857, John P. Heiss Papers, TSLA; Logan Hunton to JMC, May 14, 1850, *S. Ex. Doc.* 57, 31st Cong., 1st Sess., 26; Ambrosio Gonzales testimony in *Washington Daily Union*, Jan. 30, 1851; letter of Washington correspondent of the *Cleveland Herald*, Aug. 27, quoted in *New-York Daily Tribune*, Aug. 29, 1849.

89. James H. Kettner, *The Development of American Citizenship, 1608–1870* (Chapel Hill, 1978), 267–68, 269 (Jefferson quotation), 273–74; Jeremiah S. Black to JB, July 4, 1859, Hall, Andrews, Ashton, et al., comps., *Official Opinions* 9:357–58.

90. John L. O'Sullivan to John C. Calhoun, Aug. 24, 1849, in "Correspondence of John C. Calhoun," ed. J. Franklin Jameson, *Annual Report of the American Historical Association for the Year 1899*, 2 vols. (Washington, 1900), 2:1202–3; Joseph W. Fabens to Henry L. Kinney, Mar. 17, 1855, Slavery Papers, New-York Historical Society; *Central American* (San Juan del Norte), Sept. 15, 1855.

91. Kettner, *American Citizenship*, 275–76.

92. John Henderson letter, June 10, 1854, in *New York Herald*, July 4, 1854; Henry L. Kinney to the *New York Courier and Enquirer*, Apr. 29, 1857, quoted in *Natchez Courier*, May 10, 1855; William Walker to Lewis Cass, Sept. 29, 1857, in *H. Ex. Doc.* 24, 35th Cong., 1st Sess., 6; George Bickley to Cass, Apr. 13, 1860, DS, ML, NA; *New York Evening Post*, Mar. 22, 1855; David E. Twiggs to George W. Crawford, July 31, 1849, *S. Ex. Doc.* 57, 31st Cong., 1st Sess., 51–52; William Walker to Hiram Paulding, Nov. 30, 1857, SquadL, roll 97.

93. Since the early republic, the United States had claimed sovereignty over all waters within one marine league, or three statute miles, from its coasts. Philip C. Jessup, *The Law of Territorial Waters and Maritime Jurisdiction* (New York, 1927), 6, 53.

94. [J. C. Davis], *The History of the Late Expedition to Cuba, by O. D. D. O., One of the Participants* . . . (New Orleans, 1850), 3 (quotation), 16; L. Norvell Walker to JAQ, Aug. 19, JAQ to Walker, Aug. 24, 1854, JAQ Papers, MDAH; James Madison Miller to JAQ, and JAQ endorsement on envelope, Sept. 17, 1854, Henry Forno to JAQ, Feb. 6, 1855, JAQ Papers, HU; correspondent of the *Mobile Tribune*, Dec. 8, 1854, quoted in *NODP*, Dec. 20, 1854; deposition of Douglas B. De Saussure, Dec. 3, 1857, enclosed with James Conner to Lewis Cass, Dec. 7, 1857, *H. Ex. Doc.* 24, 35th Cong., 1st Sess., 28–31; testimony in U.S. district court, Key West, of Surgeon Henly, George Jackson, and Charles Brady, and Key West correspondent's letter, Jan. 25, 1858, in *New York Herald*, Feb. 1, 1858; T. Sanford to Howell Cobb, Oct. 16, 1858, *H. Ex. Doc.* 25, 35th Cong., 2d Sess., 4; James D. B. DeBow, "The Late Cuba Expedition," *De Bow's Southern and Western Review*, Aug. 9, 1850, 172; Samuel A. Lockridge card in the *Galveston News*, quoted in (Greensboro) *Alabama Beacon*, Apr. 2, 1858; testimony of D. F. Rezeau in *New-York Times*, Oct. 24, 1859.

95. "Personal Narrative of Louis Schlesinger," 221; Samuel J. Peters to William M. Meredith, Aug. 21, John J. Walker to Meredith, Aug. 22, 1849, *S. Ex. Doc.* 57, 31st Cong., 1st Sess., 119, 126; [Davis], *History of the Late Expedition to Cuba*, 26; Deposition of John C. Bates, July 6, 1850, enclosed with William Marvin to JMC, July 8, 1850, *H. Ex. Doc.* 83, 32d Cong., 1st Sess., 95–96; William Frank Stewart, *Last of the Fillibusters; or, Recollections of the Siege of Rivas* (Sacramento, 1857), 8; *NODP*, Sept. 4, 1849; Washington correspondent "s" letter Jan. 28, 1855, testimony of Robert Fuller, in *New-York Daily Times*, Jan. 30, 1855, Feb. 4, 1857. Many filibusters, however, made little effort to hide personal arms since legitimate travelers often carried weapons to protect themselves. Henry Kinney contended that his "colonists" were like armed "emigrants" to California or Kansas. Apparently recruits boarding the *Sierra Nevada* in October 1855 for Walker's Nicaragua mounted the gangway carrying their rifles, Colt revolvers, and knives. *New York Evening Post*, Apr. 28, 1855; *DAC*, Oct. 21, 1855.

96. Chaffin, *Fatal Glory*, 104; John H. Goddard to Thomas Ewing, RG 48, Department of the Interior, Records Concerning the Cuban Expedition 1850–1851, box 145, NA; *DAC*, Oct. 21, 1855; Affidavits of Francis R. Mace, William S. Kneass, Jan. 9, 1856 (enclosed with P. J. Joachimssen to Caleb Cushing, Jan. 11, 1856), RG 60, DJ, Attorney General's Papers, Letters Received: New York, NA; AO to George B. Hall, Mar. 5, 1856, AO Papers, DU; S. W. Inge to Caleb Cushing, Feb. 4, 1856, *S. Ex. Doc.*

68, 34th Cong., 1st Sess., 15–16; *Christian Inquirer* quoted in the *Liberator* (Boston), Feb. 27, 1857.

97. Persifor F. Smith to Samuel Cooper, Sept. 8, 1855, enclosed with Jefferson Davis to WLM, Sept. 29, 1855, RG 59, DS, ML, roll 147, NA; *Charleston Courier*, Sept. 21, 1848; Ben McCulloch to John R. [?] Garey [?], Oct. 22, 1854, RG 107, Records of the Secretary of War, Letters Received, M221, roll 172, J. Bates to Millard Fillmore, Sept. 20, 1851, DS, ML, M179, roll 127, NA; Fillmore to DW, Oct. 10, 1851, *Millard Fillmore Papers* 1:356–57; Moretta, "Carvajal," 15.

98. Samuel J. Peters to William M. Meredith, Aug. 21, 1849, Logan Hunton to JMC, May 14, 1850, *S. Ex. Doc.* 57, 31st Cong., 1st Sess., 119, 25; Peter Hamilton to DW, Sept. 9, 1851, DS, ML, M179, roll 127, John McKeon to Caleb Cushing, Feb. 4, 1856, Thomas J. Semmes to Jeremiah S. Black, Dec. 29, 1858, RG 60, DJ, Attorney General's Papers, Letters Received: New York and Louisiana, NA. On the other hand, an inspector of customs, sent to Round Island by the collector at Mobile, did report regular early morning drills. John J. Walker to William M. Meredith, Aug. 22, 1849, *S. Ex. Doc.* 57, 31st Cong., 1st Sess., 126. One expeditionist later stated that drilling had occurred until U.S. warships were spotted in the vicinity. Statement of John Holland, Sept. 19, 1849, enclosed with Victor M. Randolph to William Ballard Preston, Sept. 20, 1849, *S. Ex. Doc.* 57, 31st Cong., 1st Sess., 103.

99. Albert G. Brackett to John Withers, Apr. 12, 1858, RG 94, Adjutant General's Office, Letters Received, M567, roll 575, NA. Actually Henningsen had temporarily broken ties with Walker and decided to join the revolutionary campaigns of Santiago Vidaurri, the caudillo ruling the northeastern Mexican states of Nuevo León and Coahuila. Vidaurri, however, spurned Henningsen's services after receiving an inaccurate warning from Samuel A. Lockridge—another former officer in Walker's Nicaraguan service with his own hopes of joining Vidaurri—that Henningsen was Walker's agent and intended to conquer Mexico. William Walker to Callender I. Fayssoux, July 18, Aug. 5, 1858, WWP; (Greensboro) *Alabama Beacon*, Apr. 2, 1858; *Vicksburg Daily Whig*, May 12, Aug. 7, 1858; Ronnie C. Tyler, *Santiago Vidaurri and the Southern Confederacy* (Austin, 1973), 26–27, 30; *New York Herald*, Nov. 11, 1858.

100. John J. Walker to William M. Meredith, Aug. 22, 1849, *S. Ex. Doc.* 57, 31st Cong., 1st Sess., 127.

101. S. W. Inge to Caleb Cushing, Feb. 4, 1856, *S. Ex. Doc.* 68, 34th Cong., 1st Sess., 15–16; WLM to Luis Molina, Apr. 25, WLM to Henry L. Kinney, Feb. 4, 1855, Daniel M. Barringer to JMC, June 19, 1850, WLM to Alfonso de Escalante, May 8, 1856, *Dipl Corr* 4:81–83, 447n–48n, 11:501–2, 220–21; affidavit of Robert Hoggins, Jan. 9, 1856, attached to P. J. Joachimssen to Caleb Cushing, Jan. 11, 1856, RG 60, DJ, Attorney General's Papers, Letters Received: New York, NA; William L. Hodge to William Freret, Aug. 14, 1851, *Correspondence between the Treasury Department . . . and William Freret*, 11.

102. John McKeon to Caleb Cushing, Dec. 24, 1856, RG 60, DJ, Attorney Generals Papers, Letters Received: New York, NA; *New-York Daily Times*, Dec. 25, 1856.

103. Victor M. Randolph to William Ballard Preston, Sept. 14, 1849, *S. Ex. Doc.* 57, 31st Cong., 1st Sess., 99; Helen Chapman to her mother, Oct. 22, 1851, in Coker, ed.,

News from Brownsville, 266; William E. Prince Diary Jan. 3, 1852; *NODP*, Sept. 4, 1849; George H. Ritchie to Jenny Ritchie, Sept. 3, 1849, George H. Ritchie Letters, Ritchie-Harrison Papers, College of William and Mary, Williamsburg, Va.; Ambrose P. Hill to Lucy Russell Hill, Sept. 12, 1851, Ambrose P. Hill Papers, Virginia Historical Society, Richmond; Persifor F. Smith to the Assistant Adjutant General, Western Division, June 10, 1852, Court-Martial Case File HH (6W4/3/7/B/box 205); *New York Evening Post*, June 7, 1855; Proceedings of Mobile Public Meeting, Jan. 25, 1858, enclosed with William F. Cleveland to Isaac Toucey, Jan. 30, 1858, RG 45, Secretary of the Navy, Letters Received, M124, roll 336, NA; (Austin) *Texas State Gazette*, Jan. 3, 1854.

104. William Freret to W. W. S. Bliss, Aug. 30 (quotations), 16, 1851, Freret to Thomas Sands, Aug. 13, 1851, *Correspondence between the Treasury Department . . . and William Freret*, 24, 23, 32; *New York Evening Post*, June 4, 7, 1855. The New York mob was stirred up by a warning by Captain John Graham of the *United States* that the federal blockade would lead to layoffs on the New York docks. *New York Evening Post*, June 4, 1855.

105. Juan Y. Laborde to ACdlB, Aug. 6, 1851, *Dipl Corr* 11:601n; Thaddeus Sanford to Howell Cobb, Dec. 15, 1858, *H. Ex. Doc.* 25, 35th Cong., 2d Sess., 19–20; Persifor F. Smith to R. Jones, July 18, 1852, *S. Ex. Doc.* 1, 32d Cong., 2d Sess., 18; letter of Mobile correspondent, Dec. 30, 1857, quoted in *New York Herald*, Jan. 6, 1858; de la Cova, "Gonzales," 92; *WDNI*, June 10, 1853.

106. Robert H. Smith to Jeremiah S. Black, RG 60, DJ, Attorney General's Papers, Letters Received: Alabama, NA; Ethan Allen Hitchcock Diary, Oct. 9, 1853, in *Fifty Years in Camp and Field*, 400–402; Jefferson Davis to Thomas Smith, Mar. 10, 1854 (letterbook copy), Secretary of War, Letters Sent, Military Affairs, M6, roll 35, NA; Ball, "Filibusters and Regular Troops in San Francisco," 168–72. See also see *WDNI*, June 10, 1853; *Vicksburg Daily Whig*, June 11, 1858; de la Cova, "Gonzales," 92.

107. Henry Wheaton, *Elements of International Law*, ed. George Grafton Wilson (1836; reprint of 1866 edn., New York, 1984), 114; Opinion of Attorney General William Bradford, July 6, 1795, in Hall, Andrews, Ashton, et al., comps., *Official Opinions* 1:58; Foxhall A. Parker to William Ballard Preston, Sept. 9, 1849, Frederick Chatard to Hiram Paulding, Nov. 27, 1857, James McIntosh to Isaac Toucey, May 7, 1858, SquadL, rolls 91, 97, 98.

108. William A. Graham to Foxhall A. Parker, Apr. 12 (telegraph), May 2 (quotations), Graham to Charles S. McCauley, Nov. 17, 1851, James C. Dobbin to Bladen Dulany, Jan. 3, Dobbin to Thomas A. Dornin, Mar. 31, 1854, Isaac Toucey to Hiram Paulding, Dec. 18, 1857, in *New American State Papers* 2:134, 135, 149–50, 160, 161–62, 169; Frederick Chatard to Paulding, Nov. 27, 1857, SquadL, roll 97.

109. John C. Calhoun to Edward Everett, Sept. 25, 1844, in *A Digest of International Law*, comp. John Bassett Moore, 8 vols. (1906; reprint, Ann Arbor, 1965), 2, pt. 1:225; James McIntosh to Isaac Toucey, Mar. 19, 1858, RG 45, M89, roll 98, Luther Severance to DW, Nov. 14, 1851, Despatches from United States Ministers in Hawaii, T30, roll 4, NA; John J. Almy to Toucey, Oct. 7, 1847 [1857], *H. Ex. Doc.* 24, 35th Cong., 1st Sess., 51; Anonymous letter to the editor, Jan. 7, 1858, in *New York Herald*, Jan. 9, 1858.

110. Frederick Chatard to Hiram Paulding, Nov. 27, Dec. 1, 1857, RG 45, Hiram Paulding to Isaac Toucey, Dec. 11, 18, 1857 (with enclosures), SquadL, roll 97; untitled journal of Nov. 1857 Walker Expedition, WWP; report of correspondent "MUNROE" from Punta Arenas, Dec. 6, 1857, in *Mobile Daily Register*, Jan. 3, 1858; Hiram Paulding to Isaac Toucey, with Frank Anderson to Joshua R. Sands, Dec. 20, 1857 (enclosed), *S. Ex. Doc.* 63, 35th Cong., 1st Sess., 4–6.

111. JB message to the Senate, Jan. 7, 1858, *M&P* 5:466–69; Isaac Toucey to Hiram Paulding, Mar. 12, 1858, *S. Ex. Doc.* 63, 35th Cong., 1st Sess., 19; James Kellum to William Walker, Aug. 31, 1859, WWP; Isaac Toucey to James M. McIntosh, May 5, Nov. 17, Toucey to John C. Long, May 19, 1858, *New American State Papers* 2:170, 175, 174; Long to Toucey, Jan. 28, 1859, SquadL, roll 39, McIntosh to Toucey, May 7, Nov. 18, 1858, roll 98. Some contemporaries and later historians misinterpreted Buchanan's replacement of Paulding with McIntosh as a profilibustering punishment of Paulding, when actually it conformed with the Navy's two-year rotation policy. Robert E. May, "James Buchanan, the Neutrality Laws, and American Invasions of Nicaragua," in Michael J. Birkner, ed., *James Buchanan and the Political Crisis of the 1850s* (Selinsgrove, Pa., 1996), 127, 130, 136.

112. William Pitt Ballinger [to DW], Mar. 3, 1852, DS, ML, M179, roll 130, NA.

113. U.S. Department of Commerce, *Historical Statistics of the United States: Colonial Times to 1970*, 2 vols. (Washington, 1975), 164–65; Stanley Lebergott, *Manpower in Economic Growth: The American Record since 1800* (New York, 1964), 529, 177; Dennis C. Rousey, *Policing the Southern City: New Orleans, 1805–1889* (Baton Rouge, 1996), 96. Workers typically received extra pay in the form of food and lodging, but such amounts were insubstantial compared to $3,000 fines. In Louisiana in 1850, common laborers made only $0.73 a day even with board factored in. Lebergott, *Manpower*, 147, 541.

114. J. Prescott Hall to William A. Graham, Aug. 28, enclosed with Alexander H. H. Stuart to William S. Derrick, Sept. 2, 1851, DS, ML, M179, roll 127, NA; *Philadelphia Public Ledger*, Aug. 21, 1855; "*United States* v. *William Walker & al*," Case 2826, RG 21, Eastern District of Louisiana, Circuit Court General Cases, NA—Southwest Region; Henry C. Miller to Jeremiah S. Black, Oct. 8, 1859, Joseph M. Kennedy to Black, Oct. 8 (one telegram, one letter), RG 60, DJ, Attorney General's Papers, Letters Received: Louisiana, NA; *New-York Daily Times*, Apr. 7, 1852. Walker's surety, S. F. Slatter, appealed the forfeiture on a writ of error to the U.S. Supreme Court, which in December 1866 remanded the case to the Circuit Court. In 1892 the government settled with Slatter and his heirs, by reducing the forfeiture to $300. "*William Walker & S. F. Slatter Plffs. in Error* v. *The United States*," Case 3811, Supreme Court Appeals Case File, RG 267, NA.

115. Bolaños-Geyer, *William Walker* 2:281–82; Charles H. Brown, *Agents of Manifest Destiny: The Lives and Times of the Filibusters* (Chapel Hill, 1980), 212–13; *DAC*, Apr. 11, 18, 1854; Samuel W. Inge to Caleb Cushing, Apr. 1, 1856, RG 60, DJ, Attorney General's Papers, Letters Received: California, NA.

116. Index and Minutes, U.S. District Court for the Southern District of Texas, vol. A, 19–20 (7RA-241 [microfilm publication of NA—Southwest Region, roll 2]); *New*

Orleans Bee, Mar. 7, 1851; Logan Hunton to DW, Mar. 7, 1851, *PDW* 2:364; *New-York Daily Times*, Apr. 5, 1852; *DAC*, Oct. 20, 1854; *NODP*, June 3, 1858. See also *DAC*, June 30, 1858, for the acquittal of the alleged filibuster recruiter Thomas J. Mackey. In the 1856 U.S. Circuit Court case in Ohio about plots against Ireland, the judge threw out the charges, citing the 1852 O'Sullivan case in New York as a precedent. "*United States* v. *Lumsden et al.*," 1013–20.

117. *New York Evening Post*, May 4, June 6, 9, 18, 1855; Phyllis F. Field, "Van Buren, John," in *American National Biography*, 24 vols. (New York, 1999), 22:158–59; Frederick J. Blue, *The Free Soilers: Third Party Politics, 1848–54* (Urbana, 1973), 66; *New-York Daily Times*, Mar. 11, 30, 1852, Oct. 24, 1859; *New Orleans Bee*, June 8, 1850; *Philadelphia Public Ledger*, May 16, 22, 1855; *DAC*, Feb. 28, 1854; *Mobile Daily Register*, Nov. 14, 1857; John H. Goddard to Thomas Ewing, June 17, 1850, RG 48, Department of the Interior, Records Concerning the Cuban Expedition 1850–51, NA; *New-York Daily Tribune*, June 20, 1851; *FLIN*, Apr. 19, 1856; "Cutting, Francis Brockholst," in *Biographical Directory of the American Congress, 1774–1996* (Alexandria, Va., 1997), 898.

118. *Savannah Daily Morning News*, May 27, 1850; telegram from Savannah, May 26, 1850, in *Pittsburg Daily Morning Post*, May 28, 1850; report from Savannah in *New-York Daily Tribune*, May 31, 1850; [Davis], *History of the Late Expedition*, 61.

119. Hoffman quoted in Christian G. Fritz, *Federal Justice in California: The Court of Ogden Hoffman, 1851–1891* (Lincoln, Neb., 1991), 117–18.

120. *WDNI*, May 29, 1850; *DAC*, Oct. 20, 1854; (Austin) *Texas State Gazette*, July 9, 1854; *New-York Times*, Oct. 27, 1859; *The United States* v. *Lumsden et al.*, 1019. See also Judge John McLean's charge as reported in the *WDNI*, Nov. 4, 1851; District Judge Elisha Mills Huntington's charge to grand jury in case 18,266, *Federal Cases* 30:1021.

121. *Savannah Daily Morning News*, May 27, 1850; letter from New York correspondent, Apr. 28, 1855, in *Philadelphia Public Ledger*, Apr. 30, 1855; Thomas J. Semmes to Jeremiah S. Black, Jan. 26, 1858, RG 60, DJ, Attorney General's Papers, Letters Received: Louisiana, NA; *New Orleans Delta*, Oct. 18, quoted in *New-York Times*, Oct. 24, 1859; William Tecumseh Sherman to John Sherman, Dec. 9, 1860, in *Sherman's Civil War*, 16.

122. Report from Brownsville, Oct. 28, in *WDNI*, Nov. 15, 1851; Robert H. Smith to Jeremiah S. Black, Dec. 3, 1858, RG 60, DJ, Attorney General's Papers, Letters Received: Alabama, NA.

123. Samuel D. Hay to Jefferson Davis, RG 59, DS, ML, M179, roll 139, NA; J. Prescott Hall to DW, Aug. 8, 1852, Logan Hunton to DW, Feb. 14, Mar. 7, 1851, *PDW* 2:426–27, 363, 364; Hunton to Millard Fillmore, Mar. 26, 1852, DS, ML, M179, roll 130; Richard Elward letter from New Orleans, Feb. 13, in *Mississippi Free Trader* (Natchez), Feb. 19, 1851.

124. William Pitt Ballinger to William S. Harney, Jan. 25, 1852, Court-Martial Case File HH 168 (6W4/3/7/B/box 205), NA.

125. May, *Southern Dream*, 53, 66, 119; G. Chandler to JAQ, May 18 (quotation), Samuel Walker to JAQ, July 31, 1854, JAQ Papers, HU. John Henderson was dis-

turbed enough by Pierce's proclamation to issue an angry rebuttal: John Henderson letter, June 10, 1854, in *New York Herald*, July 4, 1854. Quitman, after his election to Congress in 1855, also fought for repeal of the Neutrality Law. May, *John A. Quitman*, 315–16, 325, 336–38.

126. WLM to Jefferson Davis, July 22, 1854 (letterbook copy), M40, roll 41, NA; Thomas W. Cutrer, *Ben McCulloch and the Frontier Military Tradition* (Chapel Hill, 1993), 129–30.

127. Caleb Cushing to WLM, Mar. 9, 1854, DS, ML, M179, roll 139. A faint endorsement on Cushing's letter seems to indicate that the Department of State eventually paid McQueen's account for $1200.

128. WLM to James M. Mason, July 30, 1856, New York State Library, Albany; Caleb Cushing to Robert McClelland, Aug. 24, 1855, in Hall, Andrews, Ashton, et al., comps., *Official Opinions* 7:358–59; Thomas L. Smith to Jefferson Davis, Mar. 6, Davis to Smith, Mar. 10, William Hunter to Davis, Aug. 30, Davis to McClelland, Oct. 13, 1854, summarized in the calendar in *Papers of Jefferson Davis* 5:317, 292; Elisha Whittlesey to McClelland, Sept. 2, McClelland to Jefferson Davis, Sept. 5, 1854, RG 92, Office of the Quartermaster General, Consolidated Correspondence File, Samuel Cooper to McClelland, June 2, 1855 (letterbook copy), Records of the Secretary of War, M6, roll 37, NA; "An Act Making Appropriations for the Civil and Diplomatic Expenses, of Government . . .," Mar. 3, 1855, 10 Stat. U.S. 664, 33d Cong., 2d Sess., ch. 175.

Chapter Six

1. "Smith, Francis Henney," in *Historical Register and Dictionary of the United States Army, from Its Organization, September 29, 1789, to March 2, 1903*, comp. Francis B. Heitman, 2 vols. (1903; reprint, Urbana, 1965), 1:897; John Hope Franklin, *The Militant South* (Cambridge, Mass., 1956), 149–50, 169 (first quotation); Marcus Cunliffe, *Soldiers and Civilians: The Martial Spirit in America, 1775–1865* (Boston, 1968), 261; Francis H. Smith to "My dear Sir" (the Secretary of the Navy?), Sept. 6, 1851, RG 45, Department of the Navy, Letters Received by the Secretary of the Navy, ML, M124, roll 265, NA.

2. "Articles entered into between the Cuban Junta and General Quitman, and signed by them respectively," Aug. 18, 1853, in J. F. H. Claiborne, *Life and Correspondence of John A. Quitman*, 2 vols. (New York, 1860), 2:147; Samuel Walker to JAQ, Sept. 21, 1854, Pierre Sauvé to JAQ, Jan. 2, 1855, JAQ Papers, HU; Samuel R. Walker, "The Diary of a Louisiana Planter" (typescript copy), Dec. 19, 1859, Howard-Tilton Memorial Library, Tulane University, New Orleans; estimate dated June 1854 in JAQ Papers, MDAH. Quitman's contract also provided that he (or his heirs) would get a million-dollar bonus if the venture succeeded. "Voluntary Proposition of the Cuban Junta to manifest their value of Quitman's influence to their cause," Aug. 18, 1853, in Claiborne, *Quitman* 2:147. Betancourt arrived in the United States in 1846 or 1847 and helped to found in New York City the Spanish- and English-language newspaper *La Verdad*, which favored annexation of Cuba by the United States. In August 1850

Spanish authorities banned him forever from Cuba for involvement in that year's López plot. In March 1854 Spain's queen granted amnesty to Betancourt and several affiliated exile conspirators; however, they renounced this decree in a public address. "The Cuban Junta," *Our Times* 1 (Oct. 1852): 187; Josef Opatrný, *US Expansionism and Cuban Annexationism in the 1850s* (Prague, 1990); Antonio Rafael de la Cova, "Ambrosio Jose Gonzales: A Cuban Confederate Colonel" (Ph.D. diss., West Virginia University, 1994), 139; (New Orleans) *Louisiana Courier*, May 14, 1854.

3. Samuel Walker to JAQ, July 31, 1854, John Marshall to JAQ, Sept. 18, 1854, JAQ to C. A. L. Lamar, Jan. 5, 1855, JAQ Papers, HU; [JAQ] to F. Henry Quitman, Feb. 3, 1855, JAQ Papers, HSP; Louis Schlesinger to JAQ, Sept. 9, 1854, JAQ Papers, MDAH; May, *John A. Quitman*, 289–95.

4. Correspondent's letter dated Apr. 25, 1851, in *Newark* (N.J.) *Daily Advertiser*, May 1, 1851, quoted in *New-York Daily Tribune*, May 2, 1851; "Personal Narrative of Louis Schlesinger of Adventures in Cuba and Ceuta," *Democratic Review* 31 (Sept. 1852, Oct. 1852, Nov.–Dec. 1852): 221; *New-York Daily Times*, Mar. 10, 24, 25, 1852; $600 bill for the engraving and printing of bonds for the Republic of Nicaragua in $500, $1,000, and $1,500 denominations, Benjamin F. Butler Papers, California Historical Society, San Francisco; receipt from Kittredge Folsom, Nov. 10, 1857, William Walker to Callender I. Fayssoux, Sept. 14, 1859, WWP; Henry G. Miller to Jeremiah S. Black, Sept. 28, 1859, RG 60, DJ, Attorney General's Papers, Letters Received: Louisiana, NA; Case 7479, "*United States* v. *Steamship 'Philadelphia,'*" United States District Court for the Eastern District of Louisiana, RG 21, NA—Southwest Region, Fort Worth.

5. Admiralty Case Files, Case File #7-372, RG 21, Records of District Courts of the United States, Records of the U.S. District Court for the Southern District of New York, NA, Regional Records Services Facility, New York City; General Case Files (E-121), Case #1965, Records of the U.S. District Court for the Eastern District of Louisiana, NA—Southwest Region, Fort Worth; *New-York Daily Times*, Mar. 16, 1852; J. W. Lesesne to JAQ, June 6, 1854, MDAH; Walker, "Diary of a Louisiana Planter," Dec. 19, 1859; *Philadelphia Public Ledger*, May 22, 1855; William Walker, *The War in Nicaragua* (1860; reprint, Tucson, 1985), 29–30.

6. J. W. Lesesne to JAQ, June 6, 1854, MDAH; Walker, "Diary of a Louisiana Planter," Dec. 19, 1859; *Philadelphia Public Ledger*, May 22, 1855; Walker, *War in Nicaragua*, 29–30; William Walker to Callender I. Fayssoux, June 22, July 14, 1860, WWP.

7. Ambrosio José Gonzales to JAQ, Apr. 5, 1850, JAQ Papers, MDAH; circular, Oct. 8, 1858, WWP.

8. *Philadelphia Public Ledger*, May 22, 1855; John A. Campbell to Jeremiah S. Black, Nov. 22, 24, 1858, Jeremiah S. Black Papers, LC; *WDNI*, Sept. 10, 1849; Henry Forno to JAQ, Jan. 23, 1855, JAQ Papers, HU; "Peterson" to Mansfield Lovell, Jan. 9, 1855, JAQ Papers, MDAH; Testimony of John Tzericz in *New-York Daily Times*, Mar. 25, 1852.

9. British consul in Savannah to Bulwer, Apr. 12, 1851, enclosed in Bulwer to DW, Apr. 22, 1851, *Dipl Corr* 7:433n; de la Cova, "Gonzales," 164, A. J. Gonzales to

Mirabeau Buonaparte Lamar, Mar. 14, 1851, in *The Papers of Mirabeau Buonaparte Lamar*, ed. Charles A. Gulick Jr., 6 vols. (1921–27; reprint, Austin, 1973), 4, pt. 1:283; Elisha M. Pease to James H. Callahan, July 5, 1855, in *The Indian Papers of Texas and the Southwest, 1825–1916*, ed. Dorman H. Winfrey and James M. Day, 5 vols. (1966; reprint, Austin, 1995), 3:220–21; Pease message to the Texas legislature, Nov. 5, 1855, in *Galveston Weekly News*, Nov. 13, 1855.

10. Commission of Auguston Mizell, Apr. 8, 1850, Auguston Mizell Papers, MDAH; John S. Thrasher to Hugh McLeod, Jan. 24, 1855, Hugh McLeod Papers, Texas State Archives and Library, Austin; JAQ endorsement on James Madison Miller to JAQ, Sept. 17, 1854, JAQ Papers, HU; *NODP*, Dec. 20, 1854, supplement; *Port Gibson* (Miss.) *Daily Southern Reveille*, Nov. 2, 1858; (Austin) *Texas State Gazette*, Feb. 21, 1857; *New-York Daily Tribune*, Sept. 1, 1849; W. H. Rainey [to Callender I. Fayssoux], June 28, 1860, WWP.

11. "Personal Narrative of Louis Schlesinger," 213; Ambrosio José Gonzales, *Manifesto on Cuban Affairs Addressed to the People of the United States* (New Orleans, 1853), 11; W. J. Hughes, *Rebellious Ranger: Rip Ford and the Old Southwest* (Norman, 1964), 101; de la Cova, "Gonzales," 57; Samuel Walker to JAQ, Sept. 21, 1854, JAQ Papers, HU; William O. Scroggs, *Filibusters and Financiers: The Story of William Walker and His Associates* (New York, 1916), 231; Charles H. Brown, *Agents of Manifest Destiny: The Lives and Times of the Filibusters* (Chapel Hill, 1980), 96–97, 366; John Haskell Kemble, *The Panama Route, 1848–1869* (Columbia, S.C., 1990), 75–76; Randolph G. Adams, "Law, George," *DAB* 6, pt. 1:39–40; Nathaniel Cheairs Hughes Jr. and Thomas Clayton Ware, *Theodore O'Hara: Poet-Soldier of the Old South* (Knoxville, 1998), 42.

12. David I. Folkman Jr., *The Nicaragua Route* (Salt Lake City, 1972), 18, 50–52, 57–58; Karl Bermann, *Under the Big Stick: Nicaragua and the United States since 1848* (Boston, 1986), 25–31; William O. Scroggs, "William Walker and the Steamship Corporation in Nicaragua," *American Historical Review* 10 (July 1905): 793; Scroggs, *Filibusters and Financiers*, 135; James P. Baughman, *Charles Morgan and the Development of Southern Transportation* (Nashville, 1968), 65–71.

13. *S. Ex. Doc.* 68, 34th Cong., 1st Sess., passim; Baughman, *Charles Morgan*, 71–81; Folkman, *Nicaragua Route*, 73–78; Scroggs, *Filibusters and Financiers*, 125, 133–38, 149–53; Brown, *Agents of Manifest Destiny*, 176–77, 181, 315–16, 320, Kemble, *Panama Route*, 74–75. Technically, the Rivas government transferred the concession to Edmund Randolph, Walker's close friend and former attorney in California (and grandson of George Washington's attorney general of the same name). Randolph arrived in Nicaragua in December 1855 and helped negotiate the deal. Randolph was a front for Morgan and Garrison, to whom he sold the transit privileges in August 1856.

14. Charles J. Macdonald to Amy Morris Bradley, June 27, 1857, Amy Morris Bradley Letterbooks, DU; William Walker to Callender I. Fayssoux, July 25, Aug. 5, 1858, Feb. 26, Apr. 19, July 8, 1859, WWP; Baughman, *Charles Morgan*, 71–79.

15. Callender I. Fayssoux to William Walker, Aug. 27, Sept. 9, 1860, Walker to Fayssoux, Apr. 19, Aug. 13, Nov. 8, 1859, Fayssoux [to H. G. Humphries?], June 30, 1860, C. J. Macdonald to Fayssoux, Feb. 26, 1859, WWP.

16. *Mobile Daily Register*, Nov. 15, 1857, Jan. 3, 1858; "*Manifest of all the goods, wares, merchandise, and specie, shipped by H. G. Humphries on board the steamer Fashion, . . .*" and *Report and Manifest of the cargo laden at the port of Mobile on board of the steamer Fashion . . .*, enclosed with T. Sanford to Howell Cobb, Nov. 12, 1858, *H. Ex. Doc.* 25, 35th Cong., 2d Sess., 6, 8; "An Act To incorporate the Mobile and Nicaragua Steamship Company," Feb. 8, 1858, *Acts of the Sixth Biennial Session of the General Assembly of Alabama, Held in the City of Montgomery, Commencing on the Second Monday in November, 1857* (Montgomery, 1858), 216–19; Jones M. Withers to JAQ, Dec. 11, 1854, JAQ Papers, MDAH; Kimberly Ann Lamp, "Empire for Slavery: Economic and Territorial Expansion in the American Gulf South, 1835–1860" (Ph.D. diss., Harvard University, 1991), 193–94. Hessee had been involved in financing the Quitman plot against Cuba in 1853–55. Julius Hessee to JAQ, Feb. 22, 1855, JAQ Papers, MDAH.

17. William Walker to Callender I. Fayssoux, July 11, 19, 25, Aug. 5, 9, 26, Sept. 9, Oct. 7, 1858, George H. Bowly to Walker, Aug. 6, 1858, WWP; H. G. Stebbins to Lewis Cass, Dec. 14, 1857, *H. Ex. Doc.* 24, 35th Cong., 1st Sess., 34; E. Bowly & Company to Mirabeau Buonaparte Lamar, Feb. 4, 1858, George H. Bowly to Lamar, Feb. 4, 1858, in *Papers of Mirabeau Buonaparte Lamar* 4, pt. 2:79–80; *New-York Times*, Nov. 8, 1858; Scroggs, *Filibusters and Financiers*, 354–56.

18. William Walker to Callender I. Fayssoux, Oct. 7, 19, 1858, H. G. Humphries to Walker, Aug. 6, 1860, Fayssoux to Walker, Aug. 27, 1860, Humphries to Fayssoux, Aug. 23, Sept. 13, 1860, WWP; *New-York Times*, Nov. 9, 10, 11, 1858.

19. Charles J. Macdonald to Callender I. Fayssoux, Feb. 26, 1859, William Walker to Fayssoux, May 17, Aug. 20, Nov. 8, 1859, WWP; *New-York Times*, Oct. 26, 1859; Case 7479, "*United States v. Steamship Philadelphia*," U.S. District Court for the Eastern District of Louisiana, RG 21, NA—Southwest Region; Kemble, *Panama Route*, 242. Possibly the United States Mail Steamship Company cooperated with Walker in response to its recently losing the U.S. mail contract for service from New York to Panama, after holding the concession for ten years. See Kemble, *Panama Route*, 12–17, 82–84.

20. López 1850 bond reprinted in *WDNI*, Sept. 30, 1851; *Washington Republic*, Dec. 10, 1849; Basil Rauch, *American Interest in Cuba, 1848–1855* (New York, 1948), 121; Chester Stanley Urban, "New Orleans and the Cuban Question during the López Expeditions of 1849–1851: A Local Study in 'Manifest Destiny,'" *Louisiana Historical Quarterly* 22 (Oct. 1939): 1122–23; Walker bond in *DAC*, reprinted in *WDNI*, Dec. 29, 1853; James T. Wall, *Manifest Destiny Denied: America's First Intervention in Nicaragua* (Washington, 1981), 52. López's 1850 bonds sought legitimization by including the signatures, as witnesses, of Ambrosio Gonzales and José Maria Sanchez Iznaga on behalf of López's junta as well as by Judge Cotesworth Pinckney Smith of Mississippi's supreme court.

21. Brown, *Agents of Manifest Destiny*, 282–83; *New Orleans Daily Creole*, Dec. 24, 1856; *Louisville Daily Courier*, July 15, 1858.

22. Gonzales, *Manifesto*, 10; Urban, "New Orleans and the Cuban Question," 1122; John Henderson to JAQ, Nov. 6, 1850, quoted in Claiborne, *Quitman* 2:70; list of

bonds entrusted to Juan M. Macías, signed by John S. Thrasher, May 19, Thomas Farrar to Thrasher, July 6, 1854, JAQ Papers, MDAH; JAQ to C. A. L. Lamar, Jan. 5, 1855, J. D. Rush McHenry to JAQ, Dec. 12, 1854, JAQ Papers, HU; William Walker to Callender I. Fayssoux, Feb. 17, 1860, and ledger entitled "Bonds Furnished," WWP. At the time, Henderson conducted a law practice in New Orleans while residing on an estate in Pass Christian, Mississippi. De la Cova, "Gonzales," 78.

23. J. D. Rush McHenry to JAQ, Dec. 12, 1854, Joseph W. Lesesne to JAQ, May 26, 1854, JAQ Papers, HU; C. A. L. Lamar to John M. Dow, Feb. 12, 1855, in "A Slave-Trader's Letter Book," *North American Review* 143 (Nov. 1886): 448; receipt for purchase of 5,000 shares in the "Central American Company," Thomas Jeffferson Rusk Papers, UT; L. M. Perez, ed., "Lopez's Expeditions to Cuba, 1850–51; Betrayal of the *Cleopatra*, 1851," *Publications of the Southern History Association* 10 (Nov. 1906): 350; Henry Forno to JAQ, Feb. 9, 1855, JAQ Papers, MDAH; J. Preston Moore, "Pierre Soulé: Southern Expansionist and Promoter," *Journal of Southern History* 21 (May 1955): 215; contract dated Oct. 22, 1856, and James B. Devoe to AO, Nov. 19, 1856, AO Papers, DU.

24. Ambrosio José Gonzales to Mirabeau Buonaparte Lamar, Mar. 14, 1851, in *Papers of Mirabeau Buonaparte Lamar* 4:282; Samuel R. Walker to JAQ, May 30, 1854, William Brantly to JAQ, Jan. 17, 1855, William H. Wood to JAQ, Feb. 1, W. A. Lacy to JAQ, Feb. 19, 1855, JAQ Papers, HU; William Walker to Callender I. Fayssoux, July 18, 1858, Harry Maury to Fayssoux, Mar. 29, 1859, WWP; JAQ to L. Norvell Walker, Aug. 24, 1854, Allison Nelson to JAQ, June 4, 1854, George B. Hall to JAQ, Jan. 14, Edward Latham to JAQ, Jan. 26, William M. Estelle to JAQ, Feb. 9, 1855, JAQ Papers, MDAH; John A. Jacques to AO, Oct. 2, 1856, AO Papers, DU.

25. W. A. Lacy to JAQ, Feb. 19, 1855, JAQ Papers, HU; Ambrosio José Gonzales to Mirabeau Buonaparte Lamar, Mar. 14, 1851, in *Papers of Mirabeau Buonaparte Lamar* 4:283; *San Joaquin* (Stockton, Calif.) *Republican*, Nov. 17, 1858; Savannah correspondent of the *Boston Courier*, quoted in *WDNI*, Apr. 21, 1851. A Spanish spy, however, claimed that López's bonds sold for up to forty cents on the dollar. Perez, ed., "Lopez's Expeditions to Cuba," 354.

26. William Walker to Callender I. Fayssoux, July 15, 1859, Apr. 28, 1860, Fayssoux to Walker, Aug. 27, Sept. 9, 1860, WWP.

27. William Allen Wallace Diary, Mar. 11, 1857, BRBM.

Chapter Seven

1. *New-York Daily Times*, June 30, 1857; *New-York Herald*, Aug. 19, 1857.

2. Hiram Paulding to Isaac Toucey, June 28, 1857, SquadL, roll 97; *New-York Daily Times*, June 30, Aug. 19, 1857; *New-York Herald*, Aug. 5, 1857; *New-York Daily Tribune*, Aug. 15, 1857; John Haskell Kemble, *The Panama Route, 1848–1869* (1943; reprint, Columbia, S.C., 1990), 248–49. Meanwhile the U.S. war sloop *Cyane* carried fifty-three of Walker's veterans to Boston. *Boston Evening Traveller*, July 29, 1857, reprinted in *New-York Daily Times*, July 31, 1857.

3. The *Times* observed that members of Walker's officer corps appeared to have better survived their ordeal than his rank-and-file. *New-York Daily Times*, June 30, 1857.

4. *New-York Daily Times*, June 30, 1857; *New-York Herald*, Aug. 5, 1857; *New-York Daily Tribune*, Aug. 19, 1857.

5. For New York's strained public charities, see Edward K. Spann, *The New Metropolis: New York City, 1840–1857* (New York, 1981), 73–75, 81–82.

6. *New-York Daily Times*, June 30, Aug. 19, 20, 21, 1857; *New-York Daily Tribune*, July 2, Aug. 19, 1857; *New York Albion*, Aug. 22, 1857.

7. *New-York Daily Times*, Aug. 19, 20, 21, 22, 1857; *New-York Daily Tribune*, July 6, Aug. 19, 1857.

8. (Boston and Portland) *Zion's Herald and Wesleyan Journal*, Aug. 19, 1857.

9. [Teresa Griffin Vielé], *"Following the Drum": A Glimpse of Frontier Life* (New York, 1858), 206–7.

10. New York correspondent's letter dated Jan. 9, 1856, in *Philadelphia Public Ledger*, Jan. 11, 1856; John Baylor's mother to John Baylor, Apr. 26, 1856 (copy), John R. Baylor Papers, UT.

11. William Crittenden to Lucien Hensley, Aug. 16, 1851, John Fisher to the editor of the *Louisville Courier*, Honore Tacite Vienne to his brothers and sisters, Aug. 16, 1851, Gilman A. Cook to Stanton & Co., Aug. 16, 1851, in *WDNI*, Sept. 11, 8, 1, 1851; William Crittenden to John J. Crittenden and the letters of Victor Ker, Thomas C. James, James Brandt, and R. C. Stanford, all dated Aug. 16, 1851, in Anderson C. Quisenberry, *Lopez's Expeditions to Cuba, 1850–1851* (Louisville, 1906), 90, 132–35.

12. [Richardson Hardy], *The History and Adventures of the Cuban Expedition, from the First Movements Down to the Dispersion of the Army at Key West, and the Arrest of General Lopez . . .* (Cincinnati, 1850), 6–11; John M. Wilcox letter, Sept. 1, 1851, *WDNI*, Sept. 8, 1851; M. C. Taylor Diary, Apr. 13, 1850, in [A. C. Quisenberry, ed.], "Col. M. C. Taylor's Diary in Lopez['s] Cardenas Expedition, 1850," *Register of the Kentucky State Historical Society* 19 ([Sept.] 1921): 80; Henry Wilson to Jeremiah S. Black, Nov. 24, 1818, Attorney General's Papers, Letters Received: Alabama, RG 60, NA.

13. *WDNI*, Sept. 10, 26 (quotation), 1849, May 27, Aug. 21, 1851; John A. Campbell to Jeremiah S. Black, Nov. 22, 1858, Jeremiah S. Black Papers, LC; Statements of Daniel Mulholland and James Bently, Sept. 19, 1849, enclosed with V. M. Randolph to William Ballard Preston, *S. Ex. Doc.* 57, 31st Cong., 1st Sess., 102, 103; M. C. Taylor Diary, Apr. 15–18, 19, 20, 1850, in [Quisenberry, ed.], "Colonel M. C. Taylor Diary," 80, 81; Antonio Rafael de la Cova, "The Taylor Administration versus Mississippi Sovereignty: The Round Island Expedition of 1849," *Journal of Mississippi History* 62 (Winter 2000): 303.

14. M. C. Taylor Diary, Apr. 20, 1850, in [Quisenberry, ed.], "Colonel M. C. Taylor's Diary," 80–81; [Hardy], *History and Adventures*, 19; John A. Jacques to AO, Oct. 2, 1856, AO Papers, DU; *DAC*, Mar. 20, 1857.

15. *SFDH*, Dec. 14, 1853; J. Egbert Farnham to George B. Hall, Feb. 1, 1856, AO Papers, DU; affidavit of Robert Hoggins, Jan. 9, 1856, RG 60, DJ, Attorney General's Papers, Letters Received: New York, NA; John T. TePaske, "Appleton Oaksmith: Filibustering Agent," *North Carolina Historical Review* 35 (Oct. 1958): 437; *New-York Daily Times*, Jan. 3, 1857.

16. [J. C. Davis], *The History of the Late Expedition to Cuba, by O. D. D. O., One of the Participants* . . . (New Orleans, 1850), 12; M. C. Taylor Diary, Apr. 26, 1850, in [Quisenberry, ed.], "Colonel M. C. Taylor's Diary," 81; Tunis C. Tarrant to "Messrs. Editors," Dec. 23, 1852 [1853], in *San Francisco Daily Placer Times and Transcript,* Jan. 13, 1854; *New York Evening Post,* July 18, 20, Aug. 6, 7, 1855; Harry Maury to the owners of the *Susan,* Dec. 21, 1858, in *New York Herald,* Jan. 11, 13, 1859; Charles H. Brown, *Agents of Manifest Destiny: The Lives and Times of the Filibusters* (Chapel Hill, 1980), 167.

17. Anonymous letter to "Friend D," Sept. 29, 1849, in *New-York Daily Tribune,* Oct. 8, 1849; "Personal Narrative of Louis Schlesinger," 213, 215; W. H. Burt to "General" [James Wilson Jr.], Oct. 16, 1855, James Wilson Jr. Papers, New Hampshire Historical Society, Concord; E. J. C. K. letter, Nov. 5, 1855, in *SFDH,* Dec. 6, 1855.

18. [Hardy], *History and Adventures,* 3; *New York Herald,* Jan. 13, 1859; A. C. Allen Diary, "The Walker Expedition" (photocopy), Jan. 4, 1857, UT; M. C. Taylor Diary, May 17, 18, 1850, in [Quisenberry, ed.], "Colonel M. C. Taylor Diary," 85.

19. Earnest C. Shearer, "The Carvajal Disturbances," *SHQ* 15 (Oct. 1951): 209; John Moretta, "Jose Maria Jesus Carvajal, United States Foreign Policy and the Filibustering Spirit in Texas," *East Texas Historical Journal* 33 (Fall 1995): 10; Jack Everitt [*sic*] to C., Nov. 29, 1851, in *NODP,* Dec. 24, 1851.

20. Brown, *Agents of Manifest Destiny,* 194–203; *New-York Daily Times,* Mar. 27, 1854; *DAC,* Jan. 10, Feb. 7, 19, 1854; *San Francisco Daily Placer Times and Transcript,* Jan. 30, Feb. 6, 8, Mar. 22, 1854 (quotations); *Clarksville* (Tex.) *Standard,* Mar. 11, 1854.

21. *New York Evening Post,* Aug. 6, 1855.

22. *New York Evening Post,* Aug. 28, Sept. 8 [Thayer letter of Aug. 29], 1855; *Central American* (San Juan del Norte), Sept. 15, 29, Oct. 13, 1855.

23. Moretta "Jose Maria Jesus Carvajal," 14; *DAC,* Jan. 10, 1854; James T. Wall, *Manifest Destiny Denied: America's First Intervention in Nicaragua* (Washington, 1981), 68.

24. Tom Chaffin, *Fatal Glory: Narciso López and the First Clandestine U.S. War against Cuba* (Charlottesville, 1996), 208–15; Brown, *Agents of Manifest Destiny,* 79–88; Edmund H. McDonald [to Anna A. McDonald], Sept. 5, 1851, Taylor-Cannon Family Papers, Filson Club Historical Society, Louisville; Luis Martínez-Fernández, *Fighting Slavery in the Caribbean: The Life and Times of a British Family in Nineteenth-Century Havana* (Armonk, N.Y., 1998), 17 (eyewitness quotation).

25. *DAC,* Apr. 28, Nov. 6, 1857; Henry A. Crabb to Don José Maria Redondo, Mar. 26, 1857, *H. Ex. Doc.* 64, 35th Cong., 1st Sess., 31; (Stockton, Calif.) *San Joaquin Republican,* Feb. 10, 1857. Crabb's party reached Sonoyta via the U.S. army post of Fort Yuma, on the west bank of the Colorado River opposite the present Yuma, Arizona, where it passed some time. Sylvester Mowry to Samuel Cooper, Mar. 3, 1857, *H. Ex. Doc.* 64, 35th Cong., 1st Sess., 32–33; *DAC,* Mar. 20, 1857; Robert B. Roberts, *Encyclopedia of Historic Forts: The Military, Pioneer, and Trading Posts of the United States* (New York, 1988), 100.

26. *DAC,* May 14, 16, Nov. 6, 1857, Nov. 5, 1858. The Crabb expeditionist spared by Mexican authorities was either fourteen or sixteen years old. *DAC,* Nov. 6, 1857; "Execution of Colonel Crabb and Associates," *H. Ex. Doc.* 64, 35th Cong., 1st Sess., 64–65.

27. John C. Reid, *Reid's Tramp: or, A Journal of the Incidents of Ten Months Travel through Texas, New Mexico, Arizona, Sonora, and California, Including Topography, Climate, Soil, Minerals, Metals, and Inhabitants* . . . (1858; reprint, Austin, 1935), 197–220.

28. *DAC*, May 6, Oct. 18, 1854; reports from San Diego and Los Angeles newspapers in *New-York Daily Tribune*, June 9, 1854; "The Ensenada. Colonel Walker's Expedition to Sonora," *National Magazine* 4 (June, 1854): 503–5; John E. Wool to Winfield Scott, May 15, 1854, *H. Ex. Doc.* 88, 35th Cong., 1st Sess., 62; Brown, *Agents of Manifest Destiny*, 202–9; Laurence Greene, *The Filibuster: The Career of William Walker* (Indianapolis, 1937), 45–46.

29. *SFDH*, Dec. 19, 1855; *Baltimore Sun*, Oct. 4, 1856; B. G. Weir to "*Editor Republican*," Jan. 25, in (Stockton, Calif.) *San Joaquin Republican*, Feb. 12, 1857.

30. John S. Brenizer to his brother-in-law and sister, Oct. 27, 1855, Brenizer to his brother-in-law, July 24, 1856, John S. Brenizer Papers, TSLA; correspondent's letter, Mar. 10, 1856, from Granada in *FLIN*, Apr. 12, 1856; Earl W. Fornell, "Texans and Filibusters in the 1850's," *SHQ* 59 (Apr. 1956): 414–15.

31. Anonymous letter to a friend (n.d.), published in *Iowa Hill News* and republished in *DAC*, Nov. 28, 1855; I. H. S. to unidentified recipient, Aug. 11, 1856, quoted in *New Orleans Daily Creole*, Aug. 30, 1856.

32. T. W. A. to "*Dear Express*," quoted in (Tampa) *Florida Peninsular*, Nov. 8, 1856; anonymous letter to a friend (n.d.), published in *Iowa Hill News*, and Jesse S. Hambleton to the *State Journal*, Oct. 29, both in *DAC*, Nov. 28, 1855; B. G. Weir to "*Editor Republican*," Jan. 25, 1857, in (Stockton, Calif.) *San Joaquin Republican*, Feb. 12, 1857; James T. Coleman to his father, May 21, 1856, in *Vicksburg Daily Whig*, July 3, 1856; "Texas" to "Eds. News," Dec. 30, 1856, in *Galveston Tri-Weekly News*, Jan. 22, 1857.

33. William Walker, *The War in Nicaragua* (1860; reprint, Tucson, 1985), 252–54; decree of Patricio Rivas, Nov. 23, 1855, in "Register Book: New Orleans Agency of Nicaraguan Emigration Company," WWP; Joseph W. Fabens to the editor of the *San Francisco [Daily] Herald*, Nov. 28, 1855, and "Decree of the Supreme Government of the Republic of Nicaragua," in *SFDH*, Dec. 19, 1855; Joseph W. Fabens to Henry L. Kinney, Mar. 17, 1855, Slavery Papers, New-York Historical Society; shares of stock signed by Fabens as secretary of the Nicaragua Land and Mining Company, William Sidney Thayer Papers, LC; William Walker to John Berrien Lindsley, Nov. 26, 1855, quoted in John Edwin Windrow, *John Berrien Lindsley: Educator, Physician, Social Philosopher* (Chapel Hill, 1938), 192. Walker's régime required persons seeking free land to first reside on their intended tracts for six months.

34. William O. Scroggs, *Filibusters and Financiers: The Story of William Walker and His Associates* (New York, 1916), 207–8.

35. James T. Coleman to his family, July 17, 1856, in *Vicksburg Daily Whig*, Aug. 13, 1856; register of Walker's Army, Aug. 1, 1856, AO Papers, DU; John Marshall to Thomas F. Marshall, Aug. 3, 1856, Marshall Family Papers, Filson Club Historical Society, Louisville.

36. *New Orleans Daily Creole*, Oct. 10, 1856; M. J. McCarthy to the editor, June 16, 1856, in *SFDH*, June 17, 1856.

37. Sidney Breese to Stephen A. Douglas, Mar. 29, 1856, Stephen A. Douglas Papers, University of Chicago; C. C. Schell to AO, Oct. 18, Thomas F. Fisher to AO, Aug. 13, 1856, AO Papers, DU; *New Orleans Daily Courier*, Oct. 1, 1856; William B. Mayson [?] to John Marshall, Sept. 19, 1856, Marshall Family Papers, Filson Club Historical Society, Louisville; Fornell, "Texans and Filibusters," 414–15; Corporal Pipeclay letter, May 23, 1856, *SFDH*, June 7, 1856.

38. Loren Schweniger, ed., *From Tennessee Slave to St. Louis Entrepreneur: The Autobiography of James Thomas* (Columbia, Mo., 1984), 2–5, 20, 134–40.

39. Tunis C. Tarrant letter, Dec. 23, 1852 [1853], in *San Francisco Daily Placer Times and Transcript*, Jan. 13, 1854; *Central American* (San Juan del Norte), Sept. 15, Oct. 27, 1855.

40. E. J. C. Kewen to the editor of the *San Francisco Herald*, Feb. 19, 1856, "J." letter of May 23, 1856, in *SFDH*, Mar. 10, June 7, 1856; "Army Register, N.A. Feb. 26th 1857," WWP; William A. Wallace Diary, Aug. 20, 1856, BRBM; *St. Paul Daily Pioneer and Democrat*, Mar. 26, 1857; register of Walker's army, Aug. 1, 1856, AO Papers, DU; letter from correspondent "JUNE," *DAC*, Feb. 11, 1857; "A Ranger's Life in Nicaragua," *Harper's Weekly*, Apr. 18, 1857, 248; *FLIN*, Apr. 12, 1856; George N. Perkins letter quoted in Carroll Storrs Alden, *George Hamilton Perkins, Commodore, U.S.N.: His Life and Letters* (Boston, 1914), 54; *New-York Daily Times*, June 30, 1857; *DAC*, Feb. 16, Mar. 23, 1857. Toward the end of Walker's rule, one of his recruiters discouraged volunteers from bringing their wives to Nicaragua. Testimony of Robert Fuller before a U.S. commissioner, Feb. 2, 1857, quoted in *New-York Daily Times*, Feb. 3, 1857.

41. *El Nicaragüense*, Feb. 16, 1856, quoted in *SFDH*, Mar. 8, 1856; William Downie, *Hunting for Gold* (1893; reprint, Palo Alto, Calif., 1971), 154–58; *DAC*, Sept. 23, 1854; Robert E. May, "Lobbyists for Commercial Empire: Jane Cazneau, William Cazneau, and U.S. Caribbean Policy, 1846–1878," *Pacific Historical Review* 48 (Aug. 1979): 386–404.

42. Register Book, WWP; "L." letter of Mar. 2, in *DAC*, Mar. 23, 1856; "J." letter, May 23, in *SFDH*, June 7, 1856. Some of the children ended up being orphaned in Nicaragua. The U.S. consul in San Juan del Sur informed the State Department in 1859 that he had helped to pay for their care out of his own pocket, and intended to send them to their acquaintances in Nashville. Ran Runnels to Lewis Cass, July 15, 1859, Despatches from United States Consuls in San Juan del Sur, T-152, roll 1, NA.

43. William O. Scroggs, ed., "With Walker in Nicaragua. The Reminiscences of Elleanore (Callaghan) Ratterman," *Tennessee Historical Magazine* 1 (Dec. 1915): 316–17; F. W. R. letter, Oct. 21, in *New-York Daily Times*, Feb. 25, 1857; *New-York [Daily] Times*, Nov. 5, 1857. Ratterman also recalled that the family took along a "little slave boy," a perplexing comment since Iowa was a free state and slavery was not legal in Nicaragua at the time.

44. E. J. C. Kewen to the editor of the *Herald*, in *SFDH*, Aug. 10, 1856.

45. Joseph Hall to his mother and uncle, Oct. 28, 1856, quoted in *New-York Daily Times*, Feb. 27, 1857; Brown, *Agents of Manifest Destiny*, 334–35, 370–77; Grady McWhiney and Perry D. Jamieson, *Attack and Die: Civil War Military Tactics and the Southern Heritage* (University, Ala., 1982), 8.

46. *Lafayette* (Ind.) *Daily Courier*, July 6, 7, 1857, July 28, 1879; William J. L'Engle to Edward L'Engle, June 18, 1856, Edward McCrady L'Engle Papers, SHC; *New-York Daily Tribune*, July 6, 1857.

47. "C." to the *SFDH*, Nov. 29, 1855, in *SFDH*, Dec. 19, 1855; General Orders, no. 167, Sept. 18, 1856, General Order Book, WWP; (Austin) *Texas State Gazette*, Nov. 18, 1856; "The Deserters Manifesto," Aug. 16, in *New-York Daily Times*, Aug. 19, 1857.

48. John Marshall to Thomas F. Marshall, Aug. 3, 1856, Jack Allen to Thomas F. Marshall, Feb. 24, 1857, Marshall Family Papers, Filson Club Historical Society, Louisville; William Walker to Mrs. William Hamilton Bowie, Oct. 1, 1856, William Walker Papers, California Historical Society, San Francisco; *SFDH*, Sept. 20, 1856; [David Deaderick III], "The Experiences of Samuel Absalom, Filibuster," *Atlantic Monthly* 4 (Dec. 1859): 654; John S. Brenizer to his brother-in-law, July 24, 1856, John S. Brenizer Papers, TSLA; Brown, *Agents of Manifest Destiny*, 377; K. Jack Bauer, *The Mexican War, 1846–1848* (New York, 1974), 397; James M. McPherson, *Battle Cry of Freedom: The Civil War Era* (New York, 1988), 485.

49. C. C. Hornsby to the editors, Dec. 24, 1856, *New Orleans Daily Creole*, Dec. 25, 1856; M. J. McCarthy to the editor, *SFDH*, June 17, 1856.

50. William Frank Stewart, *Last of the Fillibusters; or, Recollections of the Siege of Rivas* (Sacramento, 1857), 27n; *Harper's Weekly*, Feb. 7, 1857; Schweniger, ed., *Tennessee Slave to St. Louis Entrepreneur*, 136; "Trials of a Filibuster," *Harper's Weekly*, Jan. 10, 1857, p. 23; Scroggs, ed., "With Walker," 318.

51. [Deaderick], "Experiences of Samuel Absalom," 660; *Harper's Weekly*, Mar. 14, 1857; *New-York Daily Tribune*, July 2, 1857; Joseph Hall to his mother and uncle, Oct. 28, 1856, quoted in *New-York Daily Times*, Feb. 27, 1857.

52. *Philadelphia Saturday Evening Post*, July 12, 1856; *Harper's Weekly*, Mar. 14, 1857; [Deaderick], "Experiences of Samuel Absalom," 655; Callender I. Fayssoux to William Walker, Feb. 8, 1857, WWP.

53. Deposition of Henry Foster, Feb. 10, 1857, quoted in Craig L. Dozier, *Nicaragua's Mosquito Shore: The Years of British and American Presence* (University, Ala., 1985), 100; Robert Fulton to the editors of the *Times*, July 2, 1857, "The Deserters Manifesto," Aug. 16, 1857, quoted in *New-York Daily Times*, July 4, Aug. 19, 1857; Claim of Alex. Baumgaerten, *S. Ex. Doc.* 18, 35th Cong., 2d Sess., 93; "An Address to those Who Still Continue to Cling to the Filibuster Walker," Feb. 24, 1857, SquadL, roll 38; [Deaderick], "Experiences of Samuel Absalom," 659; extracts from statement of John Rivera, quoted in Kimberly Ann Lamp, "Empire for Slavery: Economic and Territorial Expansion in the American Gulf South, 1835–1860" (Ph.D. diss., Harvard University, 1991), 189; Benjamin Moran Diary, June 2, 1857, LC; *Harper's Weekly*, Mar. 14, 1857. According to one S. R. Weed, who arrived in San Francisco from Nicaragua in October 1856, Walker's government had issued a decree "impressing into active service every *white* male citizen resident within the State." *DAC*, Oct. 20, 1856.

54. Account of William Sterling in *New-York Daily Tribune*, Aug. 19, 1857; *New-York Daily Times*, Aug. 19, Sept. 4, 1857; Amy Morris Bradley Letterbook, May 3,

1857, Amy Morris Bradley Papers, DU; William Carey Jones to Lewis Cass, Sept. 14, 1857, Manning, *Dipl Corr* 4:601–2. Some of the deserters traveled the entire distance from San José by foot; others took advantage of the Serapiqui River for part of the journey, traveling down the waterway on rafts that they constructed themselves.

55. Special orders dated Feb. 25, 28, Mar. 3, 14, June 30, July 2, 3, 8, 9, 14, Aug. 10, Sept. 5, 1856, General Order Book, WWP; Eleuthera Du Pont Smith to Henry A. Du Pont, July 22 postscript to letter of July 20, 1856, Daughters of E. I. Du Pont Papers, HML; William E. Muir Jr. to Jefferson Davis, July 30, 1856, Jefferson Davis Papers, Special Collections, Transylvania University Library, Lexington, Ky.; *New-York Daily Tribune*, July 2, 1857.

56. John H. Wheeler to WLM, Aug. 10, 1856, RG 59, DS, Despatches from U.S. Ministers to Central America, M219, roll 10, NA; Joseph Hall to his mother and uncle, Oct. 28, 1856, WLM to Mrs. Thomas Casey, Feb. 19, 1857, in *New-York Daily Times*, Feb. 27, 1857.

57. B. G. Weir to "*Editor Republican*," Jan. 25, in *San Joaquin Republican* (Stockton, Calif.), Feb. 12, 1857; "C." to the *SFDH*, Nov. 29, in *SFDH*, Dec. 19, 1855; *New-York Daily Times*, Jan. 1, 1857.

58. Seth Ledyard Phelps to Elisha Whittlesey, Dec. 2, 1857, quoted in Jay Slagle, *Ironclad Captain: Seth Ledyard Phelps and the U.S. Navy, 1841–1864* (Kent, Ohio, 1996), 93–94; Thomas Dornin journal, Feb. 15, 19, 1854, RG 45, NA; *DAC*, Feb. 19, 1854; *New-York Daily Times*, Mar. 27, Apr. 10, 1854; James C. Dobbin to Dornin, Mar. 31, 1854, K. Jack Bauer, ed., *The New American State Papers: Naval Affairs*, 10 vols. (Wilmington, Del., 1981), 2: 161–62; Alejandro Bolaños-Geyer, *William Walker: The Gray-Eyed Man of Destiny*, vol. 2: *The Californias* (Lake St. Louis, Mo., 1989), 262–63, 267. Around the same time, the commander of a British corvette rescued from Mexican custody five men at sea—three of them Americans, the others English—who had been charged with participating in Walker's prior seizure of La Paz. After compelling the Mexicans to surrender the men, the British officer transferred them to an American revenue cutter for conveyance to San Francisco. James Gadsden to WLM, June 17, July 3, 1854, Manning, *Dipl Corr* 9:717–18, 719–21.

59. David F. Long, *Gold Braid and Foreign Relations: Diplomatic Activities of U.S. Naval Officers, 1798–1883* (Annapolis, 1988), 131; Brown, *Agents of Manifest Destiny*, 381–403; Scroggs, *Filibusters and Financiers*, 270–83. The Costa Rican campaign was hatched by Commodore Vanderbilt, who sent the English adventurer William Webster to work out a plan for seizing control of the transit route. The operations were conducted by the New Yorker Sylvanus M. Spencer, who sailed with Webster to Costa Rica and was given command of three hundred Costa Rican troops. Brown, *Agents of Manifest Destiny*, 378–81.

60. Brown, *Agents of Manifest Destiny*, 387, 393, 404; Scroggs, ed., "With Walker," 321–23.

61. Charles Henry Davis to William Mervine, Apr. 15, 28, Davis to Thomas T. Houston, Apr. 22, Davis to General José J. Mora, Apr. 25, Mora to Davis, Apr. 26 (translated summary), agreement, May 1, Davis to William Walker, Apr. 30 (2 notes), Walker to Davis, Apr. 30 (2 notes), Davis to David P. McCorkle, May 2, 1857, SquadL,

roll 38; C. J. Macdonald to Callender I. Fayssoux, Apr. 21, 1857, WWP; Mervine to
G. M. Totten, June 19, 1857 (copy), correspondence of William Mervine, letterbook,
RG 45, Secretary of the Navy, Letters Sent, NA; Walker, *War in Nicaragua*, 428. The
Granada, a former Costa Rican vessel called the *San José*, had been seized by Walker
in June 1856. Davis received a mild reprimand from the Navy Department for re-
turning the vessel to the Costa Ricans. Rosengarten, *Freebooters Must Die!* 147, 150;
Long, *Gold Braid*, 133; Francis X. Holbrook, "The Navy's Cross: William Walker,"
Military Affairs 39 (Dec. 1975): 199.

62. Apparently Walker was accompanied by thirty staff members, rather than the
sixteen stipulated in the surrender agreement. See William Mervine to Bartolome
Calvo, May 17, 1857, SquadL, roll 38.

63. Scroggs, ed., "With Walker," 324–25; David Porter McCorkle to Charles H.
Davis, May 30, William Mervine to Hiram Paulding, June 18, Mervine to G. M. Tot-
ten, June 19, Mervine to Isaac Toucey, July 3, 1857, Mervine letterbook; Mervine to
Toucey, June 19, 1857, SquadL, roll 38; John W. Dunnington to F. C. Dunnington,
July 19, 1857, Edward W. Carmack Papers, SHC (copy provided by TSLA); Stewart,
Last of the Filibusters, 46–56; *New-York Daily Times*, Aug. 5, Sept. 4, 1857. Mervine
persuaded the superintendent of the Panama Railroad Company at the city of Panama
to provide 299 of the filibusters with transportation to Aspinwall on credit in return
for Mervine's draft on the Department of the Navy for $7,475 ($25 a passenger),
counting on the department to honor the debt. At Aspinwall 257 members of the Mc-
Corkle party boarded the *Roanoke*. Shortly afterward, 29 of them were transferred to
the U.S. sloop-of-war *Cyane*, then also on station at Aspinwall. Eventually 205 filibusters sailed for New York on the *Roanoke*. In the interim, two men had died and others had gone ashore. Some of the filibusters who wanted to go elsewhere than New
York received financial assistance from the U.S. consul at Aspinwall. *New York Herald*,
Aug. 5, 1857; Stewart, *Last of the Fillibusters*, 57–58.

64. John Erskine to J. S. Bartlett, Apr. 6, Erskine to Lord Napier, Apr. 14, 1857, in
Dipl Corr 7:703n; Robert G. Robb to Hiram Paulding, May 13, 1857, document dated
Aug. 13 [Apr. 13] 1857 (copy), roll 97, Paulding to Toucey, June 28, 1857, SquadL, roll
98; A. C. Allen Diary, p. 4. Erskine procured Costa Rica's cooperation by getting the
transit company's agent Joseph Scott to promise that none of the company's property
at nearby Punta Arenas would be provided for the use of future filibustering operations. The agreement also stipulated that any of Lockridge's men with contagious diseases would be held at Aspinwall until being cured, and that Costa Rica and the company would share the expense.

65. Hiram Paulding to Isaac Toucey, June 16, 28, C. R. B. Horner to Paulding, June
17, Paulding to Frederick Chatard, June 17, 1857, SquadL, roll 97; George Hamilton
Perkins quoted in Alden, *George Hamilton Perkins*, 54.

66. *New-York Daily Times*, Sept. 4, 1857; William Mervine to Isaac Toucey, Oct. 20,
Mervine to T. M. Potter, John Ward, and T. G. Turner, Nov. 2, Potter, Ward, and
Turner to Mervine, Nov. 2, 1857, SquadL, roll 38, H. K. Thatcher to John C. Long,
May 8, Long to D. L. Edwards and others, May 8, Edwards and others to Long, May
11, Long to Toucey, May 17, June 2, 1858, SquadL, roll 39.

67. William Mervine to Isaac Toucey, July 18, 1857, RG 45, Records of the Office of the Secretary of the Navy, Correspondence of William Mervine, Letters Sent, NA; (Tampa) *Florida Peninsular*, June 13, 1857; George Hamilton Perkins quoted in Alden, *George Hamilton Perkins*, 54–55; Walker, *War in Nicaragua*, 414–29; Charles H. Davis, *Life of Charles Henry Davis, Rear Admiral, 1807–1877* (Boston, 1899), 103–4; Charles H. Davis to Samuel Francis Du Pont, May 20, 1857 (extract), Samuel Francis Du Pont Papers, HML.

68. *DAC*, May 30, 1858; Mirabeau B. Lamar to Lewis Cass, May 26, 1858, *Dipl Corr* 4:675–76; *Clarksville* (Tex.) *Standard*, July 17, 1858.

69. *New York Herald*, Feb. 5, 1859; *NODP*, Jan. 4, 1859; Frederick Seymour to E. B. Lytton, Dec. 26, 1858, PRO, Consular Despatches from Honduras, FO 39/7. Seymour granted the request of two filibusters to stay at Belize. Earlier in the decade W. Sidney Smith, a British diplomatic official in Cuba, rendered so much humanitarian assistance to filibusters imprisoned on the island that he was tendered all sorts of honors by filibusters and their supporters during his subsequent visit to the United States. See Elizabeth Bell to DW, Oct. 28, 1851, George W. Towns to DW, Oct. 1, 1851, DS, ML, M179, roll 127, NA; *NODP*, May 7, 19, June 10, 1852.

70. Norvell Salmon to Samuel Morrish, Sept. 11, agreement dated Sept. 5, Salmon to the Senior Officer, Jamaica, Sept. 17, 1860, PRO, Consular Despatches from Honduras, FO 39/10; *Liberator* (Boston), Oct. 5, 1860. Salmon noted in his September 17 letter that the Hondurans had sentenced Rudler to four years of imprisonment.

71. *Cincinnati Enquirer*, Oct. 19, 1860; *Fayetteville Arkansian*, Oct. 18, 1860; C. H. Darling to Commodore Dunlop, Oct. 22, Darling to Duke of Newcastle, Oct. 31, 1860, PRO, Consular Despatches from Honduras, FO 39/10; H. G. Humphries to Callender I. Fayssoux, Oct. 1, 1860, WWP.

72. *WDNI*, Oct. 10, 1849, June 10, 1850; [Hardy], *History and Adventures*, 49–50; P. Hamilton to DW, Aug. 7, 1850, *H. Ex. Doc.* 83, 32d Cong. 1st Sess., 110; "Monthly Abstract from the Journal of the U.S. Revenue Schr. 'Taney,' Thomas C. Rudolph, Esqr. Commander, Commencing May 1st 1851," May 14, 1851, entry, RG 26, U.S. Coast Guard, Revenue Cutter Service, NA.

73. William Scott Haynes to the editor, Mar. 2, *Washington Daily Union*, Mar. 3, 1852; Haynes to Millard Fillmore, Mar. 2, 1852, Haynes to DW, Mar. 5, 10, 1852, DS, ML, M679, roll 130, NA; *NODP*, Sept. 7, 14, 1851; *New-York Daily Times*, Mar. 19, 1852. In February 1852, Congress had appropriated $6,000 for the relief of American filibusters "lately imprisoned and pardoned by the Queen of Spain, and who are out of the limits of the United States." This act originated in a State Department request for reimbursement to a U.S. vice consul in Spain for purchasing clothing and other "indispensable necessaries" on the filibusters' behalf. The State Department turned Haynes down, arguing that Congress's act obviously intended to assist the filibusters only while they remained abroad. Later the administration worked out criteria for reimbursing filibusters for their expenses in getting to the United States, and got through Congress a supplemental act covering the expenses of the U.S. minister in Madrid and the U.S. consul in Gibraltar in aiding filibusters imprisoned and then pardoned by Spain who were not U.S. citizens. "*An Act for the Relief of American Citizens*

lately imprisoned and pardoned by the Queen of Spain," Feb. 10, 1852, *"An Act to Supply Deficiencies in the Appropriations for the Service of the Fiscal Year ending the thirtieth of June, one thousand eight hundred and fifty-three,"* U.S. Statutes at Large, 32d Cong., 1st Sess., 10:2, 183; Millard Fillmore message to the House of Representatives, Jan. 6, 1852, DW to Millard Fillmore, Jan. 5, 1852, Daniel M. Barringer to DW, Dec. 12, 1851, Emanuel Barcena to Barringer, Dec. 6, 1851, Barringer to Barcena, Dec. 11, 1851, *H. Ex. Doc.* 19, 32d Cong., 1st Sess., 1–4; DW to William Scott Haynes, Mar. 5, 1852, Elisha Whittlesey to William Hunter, Mar. 11, Whittlesey to DW, Mar. 11, 1852, DS, ML, M679, rolls 38, 130; Hunter to Whittlesey, Mar. 25, 1852, DS, Domestic Letters, M17, roll 38, NA.

74. *Boston Evening Traveller* quoted in *New-York Daily Times,* July 31, 1857; Hiram Paulding to Isaac Toucey, Dec. 11, 1857, SquadL, roll 97; C. C. Hornsby to Guy M. Bryan, Jan. 13, in *New-York Times,* Jan. 16, 1858; Frederick Chatard to Toucey, Jan. 1, 1858, *H. Ex. Doc.* 24, 35th Cong., 1st Sess., 77–78; *Richmond Daily Dispatch,* Jan. 11, 1858; *WDNI,* Jan. 4, 1858.

75. *WDNI,* Oct. 10, 1849, June 10, Aug. 17, 1850, June 6, 1858; *NODP,* Sept. 7, 14, 1851; *Liberator* (Boston), Jan. 15, 1858; [Hardy], *History and Adventures,* 51; *Richmond Daily Dispatch,* Jan. 9, 1858. The *Dispatch* on January 16 reported that Norfolk's mayor was in the process of billing the federal government for funds that city authorities had spent transporting the filibusters out of town.

76. A. W. Redding to Stephen A. Douglas, Feb. 6, 1858, Stephen A. Douglas Papers, University of Chicago; John H. Goddard to Thomas Ewing, June 15, 1850, Department of the Interior, RG 48, Records Concerning the Cuban Expedition 1850–51, NA; *WDNI,* June 15, 1850; [Hardy], *History and Adventures,* 51–54.

77. Robert W. Johannsen, *To the Halls of the Montezumas: The Mexican War in the American Imagination* (New York, 1985), 87; *Sacramento Phoenix,* Dec. 13, 1857; *NODP,* Oct. 21, 1851. See also William Bland, *The Awful Doom of the Traitor; or, The Terrible Fate of the Deluded and Guilty* (Cincinnati, 1852), 30.

Chapter Eight

1. Abner Doubleday MSS, vol. 2, ch. 4 (microfilm copy), New-York Historical Society.

2. DW to Daniel M. Barringer, Nov. 26, 1851, *Dipl Corr* 9:125.

3. Technically, the Gadsden Purchase was not the only U.S. territorial acquisition between the Mexican and Civil wars. In 1859 the State Department announced the acquisition of Navassa, an island near Haiti that was rich in guano (bird deposits that then served as an important fertilizer), under an 1856 act that allowed American citizens to claim guano islands. Roy F. Nichols, *Advance Agents of American Destiny* (Philadelphia, 1956), 183–85, 187–89.

4. Juan Ygnacio de Osma to Lewis Cass, Mar. 15, 1858, *Dipl Corr* 10:799–800.

5. ACdlB to William S. Derrick, Aug. 30, 1851, ACdlB to DW, Mar. 1, 1852, Juan Ygnacio de Osma to Lewis Cass, Mar. 15, 1858, *Dipl Corr* 11:603–4, 654–55, 10:799–800; Anthony Gronowicz, *Race and Class Politics in New York City before the*

Civil War (Boston, 1998), 124. Calderón, except for a brief interval, had been Spain's minister since 1835. Howard T. Fisher and Marion Hall Fisher, eds., *Life in Mexico: The Letters of Fanny Calderón de la Barca, with New Material from the Author's Private Journals* (1966; 2d edn., New York, 1970), xxv–xxix. For a report about Buntline's raising funds for a steamer to bring reinforcements to López in Cuba, see the *New York Mirror*, quoted in *Cincinnati Enquirer*, Sept. 7, 1851.

6. JMC to Sir Henry Bulwer, Apr. 24, 1850, in *Con Print*, series C, North America, pt. 1: *North America, 1837–1914*, ed. Kenneth Bourne, 15 vols. (Frederick, Md., 1986), 4:39; WLM to JB, Nov. 12, 1855, John J. Crittenden Memorandum of oral reply to John F. Crampton, Oct. 6, 1851, Crittenden to Count de Sartiges, Oct. 22, 1851, William S. Derrick to Robert P. Letcher, Sept. 24, 1851, James Gadsden to Miguel M. Arriaja, Nov. 16, 29, 1855, WLM to José de Marcoleta, May 15, 1855, *Dipl Corr* 7:123–24, 72; 6:461; 9:96–97, 795, 800–802; 4:68.

7. John P. Stockton to Lewis Cass, Dec. 10, 1858, in *United States Ministers to the Papal States: Instructions and Despatches, 1848–1868*, ed. Leo Stock (Washington, 1993), 125; Hiram Paulding to Isaac Toucey, Jan. 15, 1858, SquadL, roll 97; Maximo Gomez to Paulding, Mar. 31, 1858, *S. Ex. Doc.* 10, 35th Cong., 2d Sess., 2, 4–5; Luis Molina to Jeremiah S. Black, Jan. 3, 1860 [1861?], Robert P. Letcher to DW, Nov. 12, 1851, Juan N. Almonte to WLM, Jan. 20, 1854, *Dipl Corr* 4:963–64, 9:424, 696. Congress authorized Paulding to accept the sword, but not the land, in an amended joint resolution approved on Mar. 2, 1861. *Senate Journal*, 36th Cong., 2d Sess., 91, 325, 349–50; U.S. Statutes at Large, 36th Cong., 1st Sess., 252.

8. James B. Bowlin to Lewis Cass, Dec. 29, 1858, *Dipl Corr* 10:188; Lord Napier to Earl of Clarendon, Nov. 16, 1857, *Con Print*, series D, Latin America, pt. 1: *Latin America, 1845–1914*, ed. George Philip, 9 vols. (Bethesda, Md., 1991), 7:39.

9. James Gadsden to WLM, Nov. 19, 1853, *Dipl Corr* 9:666; Lord Clarendon quoted in Lars Schoultz, *Beneath the United States: A History of U.S. Policy toward Latin America* (Cambridge, Mass., 1998), 69.

10. José de Marcoleta to JMC, Jan. 6, 1855, JMC Papers, LC; Lord Clarendon to Lord Palmerston, Oct. 25, 1855, quoted in Kenneth Bourne, *Britain and the Balance of Power in North America, 1815–1908* (Berkeley, 1967), 187.

11. John F. Crampton to Earl of Clarendon, Mar. 3, 1856, *Con Print*, series C, pt. 1, vol. 4:384; José de Marcoleta to JMC, May 12, 1856, JMC Papers, LC; William Perry to Earl of Clarendon, June 7, 1856, Philip Griffith to Earl of Clarendon, July 6, 1856, PRO, General Correspondence: Columbia and New Granada, FO 55/124, 55/122.

12. ACdlB to JMC, June 7, 1850 (translation), *H. Ex. Doc.* 83, 32d Cong., 1st Sess., 53. See also Lord John Russell to John F. Crampton, Feb. 16, 1853, Mateo Mayorga to John H. Wheeler, Apr. 27, 1855, Juan de Zavala to Augustus C. Dodge, Aug. 16, 1855, *Dipl Corr* 7:492; 4:454; 11:881; José J. Mora to Charles Henry Davis, Apr. 26, 1857, SquadL, roll 38; William Gore Ouseley to Lord Clarendon, Jan. 9, 1858, *P&C*, 188; Earl of Malmesbury to Earl Cowley, Oct. 8, 1858, *Con Print*, series D, pt. 1, vol. 7:83; Charles Wyke to Lord John Russell, Jan. 17, 1861, Carlos Gutierrez to Russell, Aug. 14, 1861 (translation), PRO, Consular Despatches from Honduras, FO 39/12, 39/11.

13. Lucas Alamán to Alfred Conkling, May 3, 17 [16?], 1853, Conkling to Alamán,

May 5, 18, 1853, Manuel Diez de Bonilla to John S. Crimps, Jan. 30, 1854, Juan N. Almonte to WLM, Dec. 12, 1854, Oct. 18, 1855, ACdlB to DW, July 27, 1850, Luis de la
Rosa to John J. Crittenden, Oct. 23, 1851, Charles M. Conrad to ACdlB, Oct. 7, 1852,
WLM to José de Marcoleta, May 15, 1855, Antonio José de Irisarri to Lewis Cass,
Nov. 10, 1857, Jan. 11, 1858, Cass to Luis Molina, Nov. 26, 1860, *Dipl Corr* 9:576, 579,
415–17, 567–68, 570–71, 697–99, 89–90, 735–36; 11:526, 528–33, 136; 4:68, 636,
643–45, 176–84.

14. Robert B. Campbell to JMC, June 19, 1850 (reporting a conversation with
Cuba's Captain General), ACdlB to JMC, July 2, 1850, Lucas Alamán to Alfred Con-
kling, May 17 [16?], 1853, John H. Wheeler to WLM, Jan. 15, 1855 (quoting, second-
hand, a British naval officer), *Dipl Corr* 11:497–98, 516–17; 9:577, 4:436; Henry
Wheaton, *Elements of International Law*, ed. George Grafton Wilson (1866; reprint,
Oxford, 1936), 75; Jean Gottmann, *The Significance of Territory* (Charlottesville,
1973), 2–3; Ignacio Pesquiera Proclamation, Mar. 30, 1857, in *H. Ex. Doc.* 64, 35th
Cong., 1st Sess., 33; Earnest C. Shearer, "The Carvajal Disturbances," *SHQ* 15 (Oct.
1951): 224; J. C. Hernandez to George Hammond, Apr. 15, in (Stockton, Calif.) *San
Joaquin Republican*, May 30, 1857; Janice Thomson argues, however, that it is unclear
whether piracy is a crime under international law. International law deals solely with
sovereign states, but pirates operate outside of state authority. Janice E. Thomson,
*Mercenaries, Pirates, and Sovereigns: State-Building and Extraterritorial Violence in
Early Modern Europe* (Princeton, 1994), 108.

15. Lewis Cass to Luis Molina, Nov. 26, 1860, William S. Derrick to Allen F. Owen,
Sept. 1, 1851, *Dipl Corr* 4:184; 11:110; Zachary Taylor Proclamation, Aug. 11, 1849,
Millard Fillmore Proclamation, Apr. 25, 1851, Annual Message of Dec. 2, 1851,
Franklin Pierce Proclamation, Dec. 8, 1855, *M&P* 5:7, 111, 115, 388–89. Occasion-
ally American diplomats even equated filibustering with piracy. See James Gadsden to
Miguel M. Arrioja, Nov. 16, 1855, *Dipl Corr* 9:795; Ivor D. Spencer, *The Victor and the
Spoils: A Life of William L. Marcy* (Providence, 1959), 371.

16. JMC to ACdlB, June 25, 1850, *Dipl Corr* 11:84; Lord Palmerston to Lord
Clarendon, Jan. 6, 1858, quoted in Richard W. Van Alstyne, "American Filibustering
and the British Navy: A Caribbean Analogue of Mediterranean Piracy," *American
Journal of International Law* 32 (Jan. 1938): 141; Daniel M. Barringer to Pedro J.
Pidal, Sept. 19, 1850, *S. Ex. Doc.* 41, 31st Cong., 2d Sess., 24–29. Calderón responded
that the filibusters had committed "piratical" acts, even if they had not committed the
precise crimes defined as piracy in international law. ACdlB to JMC, July 2, 1850, *Dipl
Corr* 11, 516–17.

17. William C. Rives to DW, Sept. 10, 1851, DW to Daniel M. Barringer, Oct. 29,
Nov. 26, 1851, *Dipl Corr* 6:619; 11:117–18, 124–28; J. F. Waddell to DW, June 16,
1852, Despatches from United States Consuls in Matamoros, M182, roll 2, NA. Senator and former secretary of state Henry Clay deprecated the "cold-blooded massacre
of our Country-men at Cuba," even as he admitted their being "highly culpable." Clay
to Octavia Walton LeVert, Nov. 14, 1851, *The Papers of Henry Clay*, ed. James F. Hopkins, Mary W. M. Hargreaves, Robert Seagar II, et al., 11 vols. (Lexington, Ky.,
1959–92), 10:931.

18. JMC to Robert B. Campbell, May 31, 1850, William S. Derrick to Foxhall A. Parker, Aug. 23, 1851, John Forsyth to Juan Antonio de la Fuente, May 30, 1857, Forsyth to Lewis Cass, June 1, 1857, *Dipl Corr* 11:77–78, 106–7; 9:921–22, 924; J. F. Waddell to DW, June 16, 1852, Despatches from United States Consuls in Matamoros, M281, roll 2. The State Department approved Forsyth's protest. John Appleton to Forsyth, June 17, 1857, *H. Ex. Doc.* 64, 35th Cong., 1st Sess., 43–44. Later, President Buchanan denounced the execution of Crabb's party as a "massacre." JB Third Annual Message, Dec. 19, 1859, *M&P* 5:565.

19. JMC to Zachary Taylor, Aug. 18, 1849 (typewritten copy), ACdlB to JMC, Aug. 23, 1849, Taylor to JMC, Aug. 29, 1849, JMC Papers, LC; "Rey and Cuba," *Syracuse* (N.Y.) *Literary Union* 1 (Aug. 25, 1849): 329; *Saturday Evening Post* (Philadelphia), Sept. 1, 1849; Chester Stanley Urban, "New Orleans and the Cuban Question during the Lopez Expeditions of 1849–1851: A Local Study in 'Manifest Destiny,'" *Louisiana Historical Quarterly* 22 (Oct. 1939): 1106–14. Rey, a onetime turnkey at a prison in Havana, had fled to the United States with Cirilo Villaverde and another Cuban revolutionary after liberating them from jail. Villaverde participated in the December 1849 announcement founding Narciso López's junta. Basil Rauch, *American Interest in Cuba, 1848–1855* (New York, 1948), 116–17; Tom Chaffin, *Fatal Glory: Narciso López and the First Clandestine U.S. War against Cuba* (Charlottesville, 1996), 72–73; Antonio Rafael de la Cova, "Ambrosio Jose Gonzales: A Cuban Confederate Colonel" (Ph.D. diss., West Virginia University, 1994), 27.

20. Robert B. Campbell to JMC, May 19, 1850, *S. Ex. Doc.* 57, 31st Cong., 1st Sess., 34–36.

21. William Miles to the *Carlisle* (Pa.) *Volunteer*, May 20, 1850, in *Journal of the Sufferings and Hardships of Capt. Parker H. French's Overland Expedition to California, Which Left New York City, May 13th, 1850* . . . (1851; reprint, New York, 1916), 8–9; William A. Slack Diary, May 20, 1850, Dartmouth College Library, Hanover, N.H.; Pierre Antoine Giraud to Samuel McLean, June 21, 1850, McLean to JMC, July 2, 1850 (copy), John McKibbin and others to JMC, June 21, 1850, Despatches from United States Consuls in Trinidad, Cuba, T-699, roll 2, NA; *Pittsburg Daily Morning Post*, July 11, 1850. For the role of American residents in Cuba at the time, see Louis A. Pérez Jr., *Cuba and the United States: Ties of Singular Intimacy* (Athens, Ga., 1990), 18–22; Luis Martínez-Fernández, *Torn between Empires: Economy, Society, and Patterns of Political Thought in the Hispanic Caribbean, 1840–1878* (Athens, Ga., 1994), 85–86.

22. Samuel McLean to JMC, June 13, July 2, 1850, Despatches from United States Consuls in Trinidad, Cuba, T-699, NA, roll 2. McLean also reported that he had visited Giraud in jail, but that Spanish authorities had previously prohibited Giraud from communicating with anyone.

23. ACdlB to JMC, June 22, 1850, JMC to Robert B. Campbell, May 31, 1850, *Dipl Corr* 11:509–10; 77–78; JMC to Thomas M. Rodney, July 8, 1850 (copy), JMC Papers, Historical Society of Delaware, Wilmington.

24. Samuel McLean to JMC, July 2, Sept. 28, 1850, Despatches from United States Consuls in Trinidad, Cuba, T-699, roll 2, NA; Edward K. Lambdin to Emma L.

Lambdin, July 14, 1850, James H. West to Emma L. Lambdin, June 4, 1850, James W.
Chaplin to Emma C. Lambdin, Sept. [no exact date] 1850, all filed with Joseph R.
Chandler to C. M. Conrad, Oct. 4, 1850, Despatches from United States Consuls in
Trinidad, Cuba, T-699, roll 3; *S. Ex. Doc.* 18, 35th Cong., 2d Sess., 32; DW to ACdlB,
Jan. 19, 1851, Charles M. Conrad to ACdlB, Oct. 7, 1852, *Dipl Corr* 11:99, 136–37; J.
Wilson to DW, Oct. 27, 1851, *PDW* 2:390–91; Frederika Bremer, *The Homes of the
New World: Impressions of America*, trans. Mary Howitt, 2 vols. (New York, 1853),
2:257–58.

25. William Ballard Preston to Josiah Tattnall, May 15, 1850, Preston to Victor M.
Randolph, May 15, 1850, Preston to F. A. Parker, May 15, 1850, Preston to Charles
Lowndes, May 15, 1850, Preston to James H. Ward, May 15, 1850, Preston to Isaac
McKeever, May 17, 1850, *S. Ex. Doc.* 57, 31st Cong., 1st Sess., 54–62; *WDNI*, June 8,
1850; Robert B. Campbell to JMC, May 31, June 8, 1850, Charles Morris to JMC, July
23, 1850, *H. Ex. Doc.* 83, 32d Cong., 1st Sess., 120–21, 130–31, 103; *New-York Daily
Tribune*, June 24, 1850.

26. The State Department took no action regarding five filibusters accidentally left
behind during López's evacuation of Cárdenas, who were subsequently executed by
Spanish authorities. Chaffin, *Fatal Glory*, 139.

27. W. R. Hackley to J. C. Clark, May 22, Samuel J. Douglass to W. M. Meredith,
May 22, William H. Marvin to F. A. Browne, May 22, Marvin to Zachary Taylor, June
22, 1850, *S. Ex. Doc.* 57, 31st Cong., 1st Sess., 47, 130, 133, 131; *WDNI*, June 10,
1850; Robert B. Campbell to Count of Alcoy, May 29, Campbell to JMC, May 31,
1850, *H. Ex. Doc.* 83, 32d Cong., 1st Sess., 128–29, 120–21; JMC to Marvin, June 14,
JMC to Hackley, July 6, 1850, DS, Domestic Letters, M17, roll 36, NA; ACdlB to
JMC, May 27, 31, Marvin to JMC, July 8, 1850, *Dipl Corr* 11:484, 492n–493n. Judge
Marvin also traveled on Captain Tatnall's warship to Cuba in an attempt to converse
personally with the Contoy prisoners, but was rebuffed on May 30 by the captain general. Robert B. Campbell to JMC, May 31, 1850, *H. Ex. Doc.* 83, 32d Cong., 1st Sess.,
120–21. U.S. authorities in Key West turned the seven blacks over to Spain's vice consul at Key West so that they could be remanded to slavery in Cuba.

28. JMC to Charles Morris, June 29, 1850, *S. Ex. Doc.* 41, 31st Cong., 2d Sess., 4–5;
JMC to ACdlB, June 3, 1850, *Dipl Corr* 11:81. See also Clayton's June 4 warning to
Calderón against "inconsiderate acts" by the Cuban authorities, and U.S. minister to
Spain Daniel Barringer's protest against the taking of Americans and American ves-
sels in Mexican territory. JMC to ACdlB, June 4, 1850, *H. Ex. Doc.* 83, 32d Cong., 1st
Sess., 50; Barringer to Marquis of Pidal, Aug. 27, 1850, *S. Ex. Doc.* 41, 31st Cong., 2d
Sess., 14.

29. JMC to Robert B. Campbell, June 1, Daniel M. Barringer to Pedro J. Pidal, Aug.
27, 1850, *Dipl Corr* 11:78–79, 545–47; JMC to Thomas Hart Benton, Jan. 11, 1851
(copy), JMC Papers, Historical Society of Delaware, Wilmington. Clayton informed
Benton that he had threatened to resign if not allowed to send strong instructions to
Campbell. Meanwhile, Campbell suggested to Clayton that the only way to save the
prisoners was to demand their delivery to American authorities. Campbell to JMC,
June 8, 1850, *H. Ex. Doc.* 83, 32d Cong., 1st Sess., 130–31.

30. Count of Alcoy to ACdlB, July 8, enclosed in ACdlB to JMC, July 17, Robert B. Campbell to JMC, July 12, Daniel M. Barringer to Pedro J. Pidal, Aug. 27, 1850, *Dipl Corr* 11:523, 520, 545; *New-York Daily Tribune*, July 25, 1850; Charles Morris to JMC, July 23, Joseph Loud Jr. and James Tirrell to DW, June 3 (with enclosures), E. C. Knight and others to Zachary Taylor, June 12 (with enclosures), Samuel H. Jenks to DW, Aug. 26, 1850 (with enclosures), *H. Ex. Doc.* 83, 32d Cong., 1st Sess., 152–156, 159–65; JMC to Thomas Hart Benton, Jan. 11, 1851 (copy), JMC Papers, Historical Society of Delaware, Wilmington; JMC to Daniel Barringer, July 1, 1850, *S. Ex. Doc.* 41, 31st Cong., 2d Sess., 3. Charles Brown suggests that Spain's liberation of the captives was influenced by Narciso López's arrest in June by U.S. authorities. Charles H. Brown, *Agents of Manifest Destiny: The Lives and Times of the Filibusters* (Chapel Hill, 1980), 69.

31. Charles Morris to JMC, July 23, Robert B. Campbell to JMC, July 19, Pedro J. Pidal to ACdlB, Oct. 19 (translation), enclosed with ACdlB to DW, Nov. 16, Daniel M. Barringer to DW, Nov. 8, 1850, *H. Ex. Doc.* 83, 32d Cong., 1st Sess., 103–4, 152, 83–85, 35–36; Campbell to JMC, July 12, 1850, *Dipl Corr* 11:520–21; William S. Derrick to Sam Jenks, Nov. 7, 1850, DS, Domestic Letters, M17, roll 36, NA.

32. Daniel M. Barringer to DW, Oct. 9, 1850, *S. Ex. Doc.* 41, 31st Cong., 2d Sess., 30–33; Pedro J. Pidal to ACdlB, Oct. 19 (translation), enclosed with ACdlB to DW, Nov. 16, Barringer to DW, Nov. 8, 1850, *H. Ex. Doc.* 83, 32d Cong., 1st Sess., 83–85, 35–36. Spanish authorities returned Benson and the two mates to the United States in November aboard the British brig *Boundary*. The next year Spanish authorities released from a ten-year sentence the fireman of the *Creole*, William Wilcox, who claimed to have jumped overboard at Cárdenas harbor rather than participate in López's landing. Barringer to DW, Nov. 21, Dec. 12, 1850, *S. Ex. Doc.* 41, 31st Cong., 2d Sess., 36, 37–38; *NODP*, June 29, 1851.

33. Washington Irving to Charles A. Davy, Sept. 12, 1851, Washington Irving Papers, Alderman Library, University of Virginia, Charlottesville.

34. ACdlB to Orestes Brownson (n.d., trans. Fanny Calderón de la Barca), Sept. 4, 19, Nov. 6, 1851, Fanny Calderón to Brownson, Aug. 1, 1851, Orestes Brownson Papers, microfilm, roll 3. Brownson published the requested attack on filibustering. *Brownson's Quarterly Review*, new series, 6 (Jan. 1852): 66–95.

35. ACdlB to DW, July 16, Juan Y. Laborde to ACdlB, Aug. 6, ACdlB to William S. Derrick, Aug. 25, 1851, *Dipl Corr* 11:591–92, 601n, 600–602; William Freret to Thomas Corwin, Aug. 13, 1851, *Correspondence between the Treasury Department, &c., in Relation to the Cuba Expedition, and William Freret, Late Collector* (New-Orleans, 1851), 9–10.

36. Report from New Orleans dated Aug. 22, 1851 in (Harrisburg) *Pennsylvania Telegraph*, Sept. 3, 1851; Dennis C. Rousey, *Policing the Southern City: New Orleans, 1805–1889* (Baton Rouge, 1996), 64; Brown, *Agents of Manifest Destiny*, 89; Samuel R. Curtis Journal, Aug. 29, 1851, Missouri Historical Society, St. Louis; ACdlB to William S. Derrick, Sept. 13, 1851, *Dipl Corr* 11:609–610; Peter Hamilton to DW, Sept. 9, 1851, Ossian B. Hart to Thomas Brown, Dec. 26, 1851, DS, ML, M179, rolls 127, 129, NA. Even before the expedition, Calderón had complained to the State De-

partment about insults and threats of assassination against Spain's consul in New Orleans. ACdlB to DW, July 26, 1850, *Dipl Corr* 11:524. One scholar has argued that the riots in New Orleans had economic underpinnings relating to resentment of Spanish dominance of fruit sales, as well as Spanish cigar stores underselling American merchants by evading import duties on smuggled cigars and bribing policemen into allowing them to evade city taxes. Richard Tansey, "Southern Expansionism: Urban Interests in the Cuban Filibusters," *Plantation Society in the Americas* 1 (June 1979): 242-43.

37. Daniel M. Barringer to DW, Sept. 18 (quotation), 25, 1851, ACdlB to John J. Crittenden, Oct. 8, 14 (quotation), 1851, *Dipl Corr* 11:613-14, 615-16, 622-23, 623-25; ACdlB to DW, Nov. 4, 1851, DW Papers, microfilm edn. Privately, Calderón worried that Webster might deny Spain its due to cultivate the votes of chauvinistic Americans. Presumably, Calderón thought that Webster might run for president in 1852. ACdlB to Brownson, Nov. 6, 1851, Brownson Papers, roll 3.

38. Anderson C. Quisenberry, *Lopez's Expeditions to Cuba, 1850-1851* (Louisville, 1906), 111, 126-29; "*Prisoners brought to Havana late Cuban Expedition under the Command of Narciso Lopez, and the final disposition of them as far as known*," SquadL, roll 92; Brown, *Agents of Manifest Destiny*, 93; Chaffin, *Fatal Glory*, 217; Daniel M. Barringer to Alexander H. H. Stuart, Dec. 8, 1851, RG 48, Department of the Interior, Records Concerning the Cuban Expedition 1850-51, entry 142, box 145; William S. Derrick to ACdlB, Sept. 6, 8, DW to Barringer, Oct. 29, Marquis de Miraflores to Barringer, Dec. 3, 1851, *Dipl Corr* 11:111-13, 117-18, 644-45; Clyde N. Wilson, *Carolina Cavalier: The Life and Mind of James Johnston Pettigrew* (Athens, Ga., 1990), 56-58. Sources differ respecting the number of prisoners sent overseas by Spain. Numbers range from 135 to 162. The captain general released several prisoners before they were sent overseas, including Robert H. Breckenridge of Kentucky, a member of the expedition who had been picked up by the Spanish in international waters rather than on Cuban soil. *WDNI*, Oct. 10, Nov. 21, 1851; *NODP*, Nov. 21, 1851.

39. The company had been chartered by the New York State Legislature in 1848. In 1847 Congress had passed an act providing up to $290,000 for a company carrying the U.S. mail on a semimonthly basis from New York to New Orleans, as well as to Chagres on the Central American coast. Ships on the New York–New Orleans line were to stop en route at Charleston, Savannah, and Havana. The actual contract, for $230,000 annually, went to the merchant A. G. Sloo, who in a complex deal reassigned it to the group of men—George Law, Marshall O. Roberts, and Bowes R. McIlvaine—who became the trustees of the United States Mail Steamship Company. The *Falcon* operated on the route from New York to New Orleans and Chagres. Under its contract with the government, the company employed officers of the U.S. Navy (given leaves of absence) as commanders and watch officers on its vessels. The officers collected pay from both the Navy and the steamship company. John Haskell Kemble, *The Panama Route, 1848-1869* (Columbia, S.C., 1990), 12-13, 16-17, 32-34, 127, 225; James Findlay Schenck to Samuel Francis Du Pont, Feb. 28, 1861, E. W. Carpenter to Du Pont, Dec. 15, 1851, Samuel Francis Du Pont Papers, HML.

40. Allen F. Owen to DW, Aug. 17, 1851, William S. Derrick to ACdlB, Sept. 13,

1851, *Dipl Corr* 11:599–600; *New-York Daily Tribune*, Aug. 23, 1851; *WDNI*, Aug. 25, 1851. Webster was ill at the time.

41. Millard Fillmore to DW, Sept. 10, 1851, *Millard Fillmore Papers*, ed. Frank H. Severance, 2 vols. (1907; reprint, New York, 1970), 1:353.

42. Millard Fillmore to DW, Sept. 2, 1851, *PDW* 2:374; Fillmore to DW, Sept. 10, 1851, 353; Albert D. Kirwan, *John C. Crittenden: The Struggle for the Union* (Lexington, Ky., 1962), 270–71.

43. T. B. Livingston to the Secretary of the Navy, Sept. 3, 1851, ML Received by the Secretary of the Navy, M124, roll 265, NA; Samuel Francis Du Pont to Charles Henry Davis, Sept. 10, 1851, Samuel Francis Du Pont Papers, HML; William C. Rives to DW, Sept. 10, John J. Crittenden to Rives, Sept. 29, John Chandler B. Davis to DW, Sept. 19, 26, 1851, "*Memorandum of an interview between John F. Crampton, British Chargé d'Affaires ad interim at Washington, and John J. Crittenden, Acting Secretary of State of the United States,*" Sept. 27, 1851, Abbott Lawrence to DW, Nov. 7, 1851, *Dipl Corr* 6:619, 459–60, 7:439–40, 441, 441–42, 442–43.

44. Millard Fillmore to DW, Oct. 2, DW to Fillmore, Oct. 4, 1851, *PDW* 2:385; "*Memorandum of and oral reply of John J. Crittenden, Acting Secretary of State of the United States, to John F. Crampton, British Charge d'Affaires ad interim at Washington,*" Oct. 6, 1851, John J. Crittenden to Count de Sartiges, Oct. 22, 1851, *Dipl Corr* 7:443, 461, 6:460–64; *M&P* 5:117. In December 1851 Webster denied rumors that he had assured Crampton the United States had no objection to Britain's watching its coast. Webster told Fillmore that he had actually said publicly that any attempt by Britain to visit an American ship would "lead to immediate war." The British and French governments, meanwhile, reassured the U.S. government that their vessels would not interfere with legitimate U.S. commerce. Robert J. Walker to Millard Fillmore, Nov. 14, 1851 (marked "confidential"), Millard Fillmore Papers, Buffalo and Erie County Historical Society, microfilm, roll 32 (series 1); DW to Fillmore, Dec. 8, 1851, *PDW* 2:411–12; Lord Palmerston to John F. Crampton, enclosed in Crampton to DW, Nov. 12, 1851, DW to Count de Sartiges, Nov. 18, 1851, *Dipl Corr* 7:443n, 443, 6:464.

45. DW to ACdlB, Nov. 13 (quotation), 14, 15, Marquis de Miraflores to Daniel M. Barringer, Dec. 11, 1851, Barringer to DW, Dec. 12, 1851, *Dipl Corr* 11:118–22, 122–23, 123–24, 649–50, 651–52; *Washington National Era*, Oct. 16, 1851; John J. Crittenden to Edward H. Taylor, Oct. 5, 1851, Taylor-Cameron Family Papers, Filson Club Historical Society, Louisville; Fenton B. Hough to unidentified recipient in *NODP*, Dec. 27, 1851. Fillmore's removing Freret from his collectorship in September undoubtedly contributed to the softening of Spain's position. *NODP*, Sept. 9, 1851.

46. A. F. Owen to DW, Dec. 2, 1851 (2 letters), form of domiciliary letter (with oath), *H. Ex. Doc.* 14, 32d Cong., 1st Sess., 3, 6, 4, 5; *WDNI*, Oct. 25, Dec. 5, 1851, Feb. 16, 1852; correspondent of the *Charleston Courier* quoted in *New-York Daily Tribune*, Nov. 6, 1851; Millard Fillmore message with documents on the Thrasher case, *S. Ex. Doc.* 5, 32d Cong., 1st Sess.; petition of New Jersey citizens, *Congressional Globe*, 32d Cong., 1st Sess., 41, 96, 110–11, 197; Caleb Cushing to DW, Dec. 17, 1851, *PDW* 2:415–16; Mrs. F. P. Thrasher to the editor, Dec. 15, 1851, in *NODP*, Dec. 24, 1851; DW to Fillmore, Dec. 8, 13, 15, 31, 1851, Millard Fillmore Papers, Buffalo and Erie

County Historical Society, microfilm, series 1, roll 32; *Alexander Murray, Esq.* v. *The Schooner Charming Betsy*, quoted in James Brown Scott and Walter H. E. Jaeger, *Cases on International Law* (St. Paul, 1937), 163–64. According to Spanish law, foreigners resident in Cuba, if they wished to settle permanently, had to take out a domiciliatory letter within three months. Royal order of Oct. 21, 1817, *H. Ex. Doc.* 14, 32d Cong., 1st Sess., 4–5. Thrasher issued public statements proclaiming his innocence, but America's consul reported a pervasive belief among responsible persons in Havana that Thrasher had been "*deeply implicated.*" Tom Chaffin has identified Thrasher as the sole native American member of the pro-annexation Club de la Habana and noted that Thrasher had sent pro-annexation material to the *New Orleans Daily Picayune*, using the pseudonym "Peregrine." *WDNI*, Oct. 18, Dec. 5, 1851; Owen to DW, Dec. 2, 1851, *H. Ex. Doc.* 14, 32d Cong., 1st Sess., 6; Chaffin, *Fatal Glory*, 13.

47. ACdlB to Orestes A. Brownson, Jan. 31, 1852, Orestes Augustus Brownson Papers, microfilm, roll 3; *WDNI*, Feb. 19, 1852. Of the $25,000 appropriated, $12,682.05 went to Spain's consul in New Orleans. For details about how the claims were finally processed, as well as Laborde's return to the United States in early 1852, see ACdlB to WLM, May 18, 30, 1853, WLM to ACdlB, May 27, 1853, WLM to José María Magallón, Jan. 28, 1854, *Dipl Corr* 11:703–5, 707, 158, 168; Logan Hunton to DW, Feb. 14, 1852, DS, ML, M179, roll 129. Spain continued to hold eight Hungarian emigrants to the United States who had served with López. Later, Barringer negotiated their release. *WDNI*, June 16, 1853.

48. Franciso Lersundi to Daniel M. Barringer, July 9, 1853, Abbott Lawrence to DW, June 7, 1852, Lord Malmesbury to John F. Crampton, Apr. 18, 1852, Crampton to DW, Apr. 23, 1852, DW to Crampton, Apr. 29, 1852, *Dipl Corr* 11:722–23, 7:461, 459n–60n, 459–60, 75–76; H. U. Addington to the Secretary of the Admiralty, Apr. 10, 1852, *British Sessional Papers, 1852–1853* 102:286; John A. Logan Jr., *No Transfer: An American Security Principle* (New Haven, 1961), 227–28. The tripartite proposal revived a British proposal of 1825. Lester D. Langley, *The Cuban Policy of the United States: A Brief History* (New York, 1968), 13–14.

49. Rauch, *American Interest*, 231; Philip S. Foner, *A History of Cuba and Its Relations with the United States*, 2 vols. (New York, 1962–63), 2:68; John S. Chadbourne to Louisa Quitman, Oct. 11, 1852, Quitman Family Papers, SHC.

50. George Templeton Strong Diary, Oct. 20, 1852, *The Diary of George Templeton Strong*, ed. Allan Nevins and Milton Halsey Thomas, 4 vols. (New York, 1952), 2:106; William Tecumseh Sherman to Ellen Sherman, Nov. 10, 1852, William Tecumseh Sherman Family Papers, University of Notre Dame, microfilm, roll 2; Francis Mace to JAQ, Oct. 14, 1852, JAQ Papers, HU; affidavit of Francis R. Mace, Jan. 9, 1856, enclosed with P. J. Joachimssen to Caleb Cushing, Jan. 11, 1856, RG 60, DJ, Attorney General's Papers, Letters Received: New York, NA; *New Orleans Bee*, Oct. 15, 1852.

51. Charles M. Conrad to ACdlB, Oct. 7, 1852, Edward Everett to Daniel M. Barringer, Feb. 4, 1853, *Dipl Corr* 11:135–37, 150; Rauch, *American Interest*, 232–33; Foner, *History of Cuba* 2:68–69; *Vicksburg Weekly Whig*, Oct. 27, 1852; *Jackson Flag of the Union*, Oct. 23, 1852; John Thomas Newton to John P. Kennedy, Nov. 6, 1852, SquadL, roll 93; Millard Fillmore to Hugh Maxwell, Nov. 12, 1852, in *WDNI*, Nov.

27, 1852. Mississippi's legislature failed to act on Foote's recommendation. *Vicksburg Weekly Whig*, Nov. 3, 1852.

52. WLM to Chevalier L. A. de Cueto, Mar. 28, 1855, *S. Ex. Doc.* 1 , 35th Cong., Special Sess., 4−7; James C. Dobbin to Charles S. McCauley, Apr. 10, May 31, 1855, K. Jack Bauer, ed., *The New American State Papers: Naval Affairs*, 10 vols. (Wilmington, Del., 1981), 2:237−39, 123; Dobbin to Captain Thoms Crabbe, Apr. 3, 1855 (copy), Franklin Pierce Papers, New Hampshire Historical Society, Concord; McCauley to Dobbin, Apr. 20, May 17, 22, 24, 1855, SquadL, roll 95; Juan de Zavala to Augustus C. Dodge, Aug. 16, 1855, Dodge to Zavala, Aug. 22, Sept. 26, 1855, Dodge to Pedro J. Pidal, Nov. 24, 1856, *Dipl Corr* 11:880−82, 884−86, 892−93, 909; Robert Shufeldt to unidentified recipient (fragment), Apr. 4, 1855, Robert Shufeldt Papers, LC; Thomas Turner to Samuel Francis Du Pont, Apr. 9, 1855, Samuel Francis Du Pont Papers, HML. Pierce's hard line in the incident may have represented an attempt to appease expansionists in his party who were disappointed by his failure to support Quitman's expedition. Roy Franklin Nichols, *Franklin Pierce: Young Hickory of the Granite Hills* (rev. edn., Philadelphia, 1958), 394−95.

53. Alfonso de Escalante to WLM, Apr. 10, May 12, WLM to Escalante, May 8, 1856, *Dipl Corr* 11:901−2, 905, 220−21; Hiram Paulding to James C. Dobbin, Feb. 3, 1856, SquadL, roll 96; Gabriel García Tassara to the prime minister, Dec. 27, 1857 (extract), in Thomas Schoonover and Ebba Schoonover, eds. and trans., "Bleeding Kansas and Spanish Cuba in 1857: A Postscript," *Kansas History* 11 (Winter 1988−89): 241−42; James W. Cortada, *Spain and the American Civil War: Relations at Mid-Century, 1855−1868* (Philadelphia, 1980), 20. The claims of the owners and crew of the *Georgiana*, the master of the *Susan Loud*, forty-two Contoy prisoners, John Thrasher, the United States Mail Steamship Company (concerning the *Crescent City* affair), and James H. West remained unresolved at the very end of the Buchanan administration, after the U.S. Senate refused to ratify a U.S.-Spanish claims convention signed in March 1860. *S. Ex. Doc.* 18, 35th Cong., 2d Sess., 1−32; JB annual message, Dec. 3, 1860, *M&P* 5:641−42.

54. Walter M. Gibson, *The Prison of Weltevreden; and a Glance at the East Indian Archipelago* (New York, 1855), 71−77; J. C. Hernandez to George Hammond, May 30, in (Stockton, Calif.) *San Joaquin Republican*, May 30, 1857. Later, Dutch officials jailed Gibson for suspected treason. He escaped in April 1853 and subsequently filed a claim against the Dutch with the Department of State. Gibson, *Prison of Weltevreden*, 434−89; *The Diaries of Walter Murray Gibson*, ed. Jacob Adler and Gwynn Barrett (Honolulu, 1973), xi−xii.

55. Correspondent's letter from Rio Grande City, Nov. 30, in *NODP*, Dec. 24, 1851; *Galveston Weekly News*, July 17, 1855; J. Ross Browne to James Guthrie, Apr. 1854 (extract), enclosed with P. G. Washington to WLM, DS, ML, M179, roll 140, NA; Richard H. Dillon, "Browne, John Ross," in *American National Biography*, ed. John A. Garraty and Mark C. Carnes, 24 vols. (New York, 1999), 3:758−60.

56. Amy Morris Bradley Letterbook and Journal, Sept. 4, Oct. 6, 1856, DU; "Bradley, Amy Morris," in Edward T. James, ed., *Notable American Women 1607−1950: A Biographical Dictionary*, 3 vols. (Cambridge, Mass., 1971), 1:220−21.

57. José de Marcoleta to WLM, June 1, 1855, William Carey Jones to Lewis Cass, Jan. 1, 1858, Luis Molina to Cass, Oct. 2, 1860, *Dipl Corr* 4:463–64, 640–41, 933; *DAC*, Dec. 28, 1858; "Late From The Rio Grande," *NODP*, Dec. 24, 1851; *SFDH*, July 10, 1854; *New-York Times*, Jan. 29, 1858; James Thomas to Mirabeau Buonaparte Lamar, Feb. 5, 1858, in *Papers of Mirabeau Buonaparte Lamar* 4, pt. 2:88.

58. Thomas Sprague to Lewis Cass, June 4, 1857, Despatches from United States Consuls in La Paz, Mexico, M292, roll 1, NA; John L. Marling to WLM, Dec. 1, 1855, *Dipl Corr* 4:490; *FLIN*, Nov. 1, 1856; Ran Runnels to Cass, July 28, 1860, Despatches from United States Consuls in San Juan del Sur, 1847–1861, T-152, roll 2, NA. In April 1856 Costa Rican forces fighting Walker brutally executed some ten American civilian transit workers at Virgin Bay, Nicaragua, causing the U.S. government to lodge claims against Costa Rica in a serious dispute that persisted for years. Brown, *Agents of Manifest Destiny*, 333; JB annual messages of Dec. 6, 1858, Dec. 3, 1860, *M&P* 5:518, 644.

59. William Perry to Earl of Clarendon, Apr. 18, 1856, PRO, General Correspondence: Colombia and New Granada, FO 55/124; Don Francisco de Fabrega to Theodorus Bailey, Apr. 23, 1856, in *Panama Star Herald*, May 5, 1856; Kemble, *Panama Route*, 198–99; Stephen J. Randall, *Colombia and the United States: Hegemony and Interdependence* (Athens, Ga., 1992), 38–39; David F. Long, *Gold Braid and Foreign Relations: Diplomatic Activities of U.S. Naval Officers, 1798–1883* (Annapolis, 1988), 137; Larry Gara, *The Presidency of Franklin Pierce* (Lawrence, Kan., 1991), 145. According to the state of Panama's acting governor, the riot occurred after a railroad passenger refused to pay for fruit that he had purchased from a Panamanian, and fired his gun at the fruit vendor. Francisco de Fabrega to Theodorus Bailey, Apr. 12, 1856, in *Panama Star Herald*, May 5, 1856; *DAC*, May 8, 1856. Accounts differ regarding how many people died in the riot.

60. Randall, *Colombia and the United States*, 39; Kemble, *Panama Route*, 198–99; Long, *Gold Braid*, 136–37; Philip Griffith to Earl of Clarendon, July 10, 6, 1856, PRO, General Correspondence: Colombia and New Granada, FO 55/122; Lino de Pombo and Florentino González to Isaac E. Morse and James B. Bowlin, Feb. 23, 1857, *Dipl Corr* 5:853–55; Brown, *Agents of Manifest Destiny*, 331–32; Loren Schweniger, ed., *From Tennessee Slave to St. Louis Entrepreneur: The Autobiography of James Thomas* (Columbia, Mo., 1984), 140. For later Panamanian fears of U.S. filibusters, see Bartolome Calvo to John J. Almy (translated copy), Jan. 25, 1858, SquadL, roll 97.

61. Correspondence between Theodorus Bailey and Don. F. de Fabrega in *Panama Star Herald*, May 5, 1856; WLM to James B. Bowlin, May 3, June 4, 1856, DS, Diplomatic Instructions, M77, roll 44, NA; Schoultz, *Beneath the United States*, 66; Lino de Pombo and Florentino González to Isaac E. Morse and Bowlin, Feb. 23, 1857, *Dipl Corr* 5:849–58; Morse and Bowlin to New Granada's commissioners, Feb. 13, 1857 (copy), PRO, General Correspondence: Colombia and New Granada, FO 55/131.

62. William Mervine to Bartolome Calvo, May 17, 20, 1857, Calvo to Mervine, May 18, 19, 1857, Mervine to Isaac Toucey, June 2, 1857, SquadL, roll 38; William Frank Stewart, *Last of the Fillibusters; or, Recollections of the Siege of Rivas* (Sacramento, 1857), 40. Earlier, Mervine attributed anti-American "excitements" on the isthmus to

fears that Americans would enslave black Panamanians—an obvious reference to Walker's September 1856 decree, discussed in the next chapter, legalizing slavery in Nicaragua. Mervine to James C. Dobbin, Mar. 18, 1857, SquadL, roll 38.

63. Randall, *Colombia and the United States*, 39–42; Convention of Sept. 10, 1857, in Charles I. Bevans, comp., *Treaties and Other International Agreements of the United States of America, 1776–1949*, 12 vols. (Washington, 1968–74), 6:888–94.

64. Thomas Sprague to James Gadsden, Nov. 27, 1855 (copy), Sprague to José María Gomez, Dec. 7, 1855, Despatches from United States Consuls in La Paz, Mexico, M282, roll 1, NA; Eugene Keith Chamberlin, "Baja California after Walker: The Zerman Enterprise," *Hispanic American Historical Review* 34 (May 1954): 175, 177–84; Donathon C. Olliff, *Reforma Mexico and the United States: A Search for Alternatives to Annexation, 1854–1861* (University, Ala., 1981), 10, 30–32, 44, 53.

65. Thomas Sprague to James Gadsden, Nov. 27, 1855, Despatches from United States Consuls in La Paz, Mexico, M282, roll 1, NA; John Forsyth to WLM, Oct. 23, 1856, Jan. 30, 1857, *Dipl Corr* 9:850–53, 887; Chamberlin, "Baja California," 183, 185–87; *DAC*, Jan. 4, 1858.

66. WLM to Manuel Robles Pezuela, June 24, 1856, Robles to WLM, Feb. 12, 1857, John Forsyth to WLM, Oct. 23, 1856, Forsyth to Miguel Lerdo de Tejada, Dec. 2, 1856, memorandum of interview between Forsyth and Lerdo, Dec. 16, 1856, Ezequiel Montes to Forsyth, Jan. 21, 1857, Forsyth to Montes, Jan. 25, 1857, *Dipl Corr* 9:203–4, 893–96, 850–53, 866–72, 873, 879–83, 884; J. Fred Rippy, *The United States and Mexico* (New York, 1931), 191–92; *S. Ex. Doc.* 31, 44th Cong., 2d Sess., 28–32. The Claims Commission resolved a number of other filibustering-related claims. Thus a group of American businessmen were awarded $43,161.64 in Mexican gold for damages done by Mexicans to their trading post on the U.S.-Mexican border in 1857 in retaliation for the Crabb expedition, and the United States was assessed $50,000 so that Mexico's government could reimburse victims of the Callahan raid against Piedras Negras in 1855. Some filibustering-related claims were dismissed without award. *S. Ex. Doc.* 31, 44th Cong., 2d Sess., 5–7, 18–21, 24–27, 76–79.

67. The colony began as Belize, changed its name to British Honduras in 1840, and reverted to Belize with independence in 1973. Before the Civil War, Americans generally referred to it as Belize. A British superintendent governed Belize during these years, but it did not fully achieve colonial status until 1862.

68. Robert A. Naylor, *Penny Ante Imperialism: The Mosquito Shore and the Bay of Honduras, 1600–1914: A Case Study in British Informal Empire* (Rutherford, N.J., 1989), 92, 132–58; R. A. Humphreys, *The Diplomatic History of British Honduras, 1638–1901* (New York, 1961), 2, 45, 50; Wilbur Devereux Jones, *The American Problem in British Diplomacy, 1841–1861* (Athens, Ga., 1974), 66; Craig L. Dozier, *Nicaragua's Mosquito Shore: The Years of British and American Presence* (University, Ala., 1985), 47.

69. Paul A. Varg, *United States Foreign Relations, 1820–1860* ([East Lansing], 1979), 217–24 (quotation on p. 222); Charles L. Stansifer, "United States–Central American Relations, 1824–1850," in T. Ray Shurbutt, ed., *United States–Latin American Relations, 1800–1850* (Tuscaloosa, 1991), 27; Frederick Moore Binder, *James*

Buchanan and the American Empire (Selinsgrove, Pa., 1994), 142–46, 173–88; Elbert B. Smith, *The Presidencies of Zachary Taylor and Millard Fillmore* (Lawrence, Kan., 1988), 75–84; Dozier, *Mosquito Shore*, 55, 69–70, 83–86; Jones, *American Problem*, 65–98; Humphreys, *Diplomatic History*, 50, 53–55; William H. Goetzmann, *When the Eagle Screamed: The Romantic Horizon in American Diplomacy, 1800–1860* (New York, 1966), 78–82; Bevans, comp., *Treaties* 12:105–108. The treaty's negotiators issued a statement, which most Americans accepted, that the agreement did not apply to Britain's colony at Belize. However, the treaty outraged many Young America expansionists, who railed against it as an obstacle to America's eventual growth. Varg, *United States Foreign Relations*, 224–26; Henry A. Murray, *Lands of the Slave and the Free: or, Cuba, the United States, and Canada* (London, 1855), 339–40; James M. Woods, "Expansionism as Diplomacy: The Career of Solon Borland in Central America 1853–1854," *Americas* 40 (Jan. 1984): 399–415. For earlier U.S. interest in a Central American canal, see John M. Belohlavek, "A Philadelphian and The Canal: The Charles Biddle Mission to Panama, 1835–1836," *Pennsylvania Magazine of History and Biography* 104 (Oct. 1980): 450–61.

70. Dozier, *Mosquito Shore*, 56–57; Spencer, *Victor and the Spoils*, 355–58; Van Alstyne, "American Filibustering," 139–41; José de Marcoleta to WLM, Dec. 11, 1854, *Dipl Corr* 4:404–9; James C. Dobbin to Hiram Paulding, Nov. 16, 1855, *New American State Papers* 2:243; list of U.S. consular officers, M587, roll 17, NA.

71. Deposition of Edward L. Tinklepaugh, May 6, 1856, *S. Ex. Doc.* 68, 34th Cong., 1st Sess., 152–55; James Green to Lord Clarendon, July 16, enclosed with John F. Crampton to WLM, Sept. 1, 1855, George M. Dallas to WLM, May 23 (extract), 30, 1856, Manning, *Dipl Corr* 7:609n, 609–10, 645–47, 648–50; James C. Dobbin to Hiram Paulding, May 13, 1856, *New American State Papers* 2:247–48; Brown, *Agents of Manifest Destiny*, 287; Paulding to Dobbin, Jan. 2, 1856, SquadL, roll 96; William Perry to Thomas Sturchy [?], Mar. 25, 1856, PRO, General Correspondence: Colombia and New Granada, FO 55/124; Bourne, *Britain and the Balance of Power*, 197; Laurence Oliphant, *Episodes in a Life of Adventure; or, Moss from a Rolling Stone* (Edinburgh, 1887), 115–16. Britain did not intervene militarily against Kinney, because Greytown was in shambles after its bombardment by an American naval vessel in 1854, and its denizens welcomed Kinney in the hope that he would restore order. Dozier, *Mosquito Shore*, 95.

72. The spring 1856 incident was a byproduct of Cornelius Vanderbilt's falling out with Walker. After Walker canceled Nicaragua's contract with Vanderbilt's Accessory Transit Company, Vanderbilt sent an agent, Hosea Birdsall, on the *Orizaba*, to ensure that the company's property at Punta Arenas did not fall into Walker's hands. Vanderbilt authorized Birdsall to ask the British navy for help, unless U.S. naval assistance was available. Birdsall, fearing that some of the passengers on the *Orizaba* would seize the company's river boats to ascend the San Juan River and join Walker, asked the British naval captain John W. Tarleton, commanding the *Eurydice* outside Greytown, to board the ship and apprehend recruits for Walker's forces. Tarleton did not identify any filibusters aboard ship. Thomas Lord to Hosea Birdsall, Apr. 8, 1856 (copy), Hiram Paulding to John W. Tarleton, June 9, 1856, Tarleton to Paulding, June 9, 1856 (copy), Letters Received by the Secretary of the Navy from Commanding Officers of

Sqadrons, RG 45, M89, roll 96, NA; John Crampton to Lord Clarendon, May 12, 1856, *P&C*, 152.

73. E. Hammond to Secretary of the Admiralty, Oct. 11, 1858, Earl of Malmesbury to Earl Cowley, Oct. 8, 1858, *Con Print*, series D, pt. 1, vol. 7:84, 83-84; Lewis Cass to George M. Dallas, Nov. 26, 1858, *Dipl Corr* 7:202-3. Malmesbury directed that should Britain's navy apprehend filibusters, they be turned over to the U.S. consul or naval officer closest to the scene. Jones, *American Problem*, 168.

74. Memorandum of Lewis Cass's discussion with Lord Napier on Nov. 8, 1858, memorandum of Cass's discussion with M. de Sartiges, Nov. 21, 1858, Cass to Mirabeau B. Lamar, Dec. 1, 1858, Cass to George M. Dallas, Nov. 13, 26, 1858, Dallas to Cass, Nov. 26, 1858, "*Minute of a conversation between John Y. Mason, United States Minister to France, and Count Walewski, Minister of Foreign Affairs of France—begun on December 10, 1858, and continued on the 14th of the same month,*" *Dipl Corr* 4:133n, 134n-35n, 133-34, 7:202-3, 748-50, 6:695-97; Earl of Malmesbury to Lord Napier, Nov. 26, 1858, *Con Print*, series D, pt. 1, vol. 7:87-88.

75. James M. McIntosh to Isaac Toucey, Nov. 26, Dec. 3, 1858 (with enclosures), SquadL, roll 98; James McIntosh to Mirabeau B. Lamar, Nov. 27, 1858, *Dipl Corr* 4:727n; J. C. Long to Toucey, Jan. 28, 1859, ibid., roll 39; *Times* (London), Jan. 4, 1859; Jones, *American Problem*, 168-71; *M&P* 5:507.

76. Luis Molina to Jeremiah S. Black, Dec. 26, 1860 (translation), *Dipl Corr* 4:954; John Bigler to William Bigler, Nov. 15, 30, 1857, William Bigler Papers, HSP; John T. Reid, *Spanish-American Images of the United States, 1790-1960* (Gainesville, Fla., 1977), 70-71; Francisco Barquín Bilbao excerpt, 1856, in Gerald Michael Greenfield and John D. Buenker, eds., *Those United States: International Perspectives on American History* (Fort Worth, 2000), 195-96. See Luis Martínez-Fernández, "Caudillos, Annexationism, and the Rivalry between Empires in the Dominican Republic, 1844-1874," *Diplomatic History* 17 (Fall 1993): 585-86, for how one Latin American politician capitalized on this resentment.

77. Mirabeau Buonaparte Lamar to Lewis Cass, Feb. 26, 1858, Mirabeau B. Lamar Papers, Texas State Library, Archives Division, Austin; Amy Morris Bradley Journal, Mar. 24, 1856.

78. E. Bradford Burns, *Patriarch and Folk: The Emergence of Nicaragua, 1798-1858* (Cambridge, Mass., 1991), 210-13; Cass to Lamar, July 25, 1858, Beverly L. Clarke to Cass, Oct. 15, 1859, *Dipl Corr* 4:117-18, 784; Karl Bermann, *Under the Big Stick: Nicaragua and the United States since 1848* (Boston, 1986), 97; Brown, *Agents of Manifest Destiny*, 437-38; "Message of the President of New Granada on the Opening of Congress Bogota, Feb 1857" (translation), enclosed with Philip Griffith to Earl of Clarendon, PRO, General Correspondence: Colombia and New Granada, FO 55/131; Proclamation of Iginacio Pesquiera, Mar. 30, 1857, *H. Ex. Doc.* 64, 35th Cong., 1st Sess., 32-33. The Buchanan administration protested the Rivas Manifesto so vigorously, threatening to seek redress if necessary, that the presidents of Costa Rica and Nicaragua repudiated the document. Lewis Cass to Mirabeau Buonaparte Lamar, July 25, 1858, Cass to Máximo Jerez, Oct. 5, 1858, Lamar to Cass, Sept. 29, 1858, *Dipl Corr* 4:116-17, 128, 714-15.

79. William F. Sater, *Chile and the United States: Empires in Conflict* (Athens, Ga.,

1990), 22–23; Circular letter of Venezuela's Minister of Foreign Relations, Jacinto Gutiérrez, July 8, 1856, Treaty of Union, Sept. 15, 1856, *Documents on Inter-American Cooperation*, ed. Robert N. Burr and Roland D. Hussey, 2 vols. (Philadelphia, 1955), 1:128–29, 135–38; Gustave A. Nuermberger, "The Continental Treaties of 1856: An American Union 'Exclusive of the United States,'" *Hispanic American Historical Review* 20 (Feb. 1940): 32–55; Antonio José de Irisarri to Lewis Cass, Oct. 16, 1857, *Dipl Corr* 4:610–11; Philip Griffith to Lord John Russell, Sept. 5, 1859, PRO, General Correspondence: Colombia and New Granada, FO 55/145; Nancy Nichols Barker, *The French Experience in Mexico, 1821–1861: A History of Constant Misunderstanding* (Chapel Hill, 1979), 143–44; Ralph Lee Woodward Jr., *Rafael Carrera and the Emergence of the Republic of Guatemala, 1821–1871* (Athens, Ga., 1993), 305. On the other hand, in 1854 Ecuador sought a U.S. protectorate to ward off the filibuster Juan José Flores. A convention to this effect was signed in Washington, but the U.S. government never ratified it, partly because of protests from several Latin and European states. Mark J. Van Aken, *King of the Night: Juan José Flores and Ecuador, 1824–1864* (Berkeley, 1989), 247–48.

80. Manuel Diez de Bonilla to James Gadsden, Aug. 20, Nov. 15, 1853, Gadsden to Diez, Aug. 20, 1853, Gadsden to WLM, Nov. 19, 1853, Sept. 2, 1854, Nov. 5, 1855, "*Treaty between the United States and Mexico, signed at Mexico City, December 30, 1853*," Gadsden to Miguel M. Arrioja, Nov. 16, 29, 1855, *Dipl Corr* 9:601–2, 663–64, 602–3, 666–67, 728–30, 792–93, 795, 800, 691n–94n; Gadsden to the "Officer of the U.S. Navy Commdg any Squadron or vessel of war in the Pacific," Oct. 23, 1853 (copy), SquadL, roll 36, NA; Paul N. Garber, *The Gadsden Treaty* (Philadelphia, 1923), 97–98.

81. John Forsyth to Lewis Cass, Apr. 4 (quotation), 24, 1857, Forsyth to WLM, Oct. 23, 1856, *Dipl Corr* 9:902–9, 915–16, 850–53; Olliff, *Reforma Mexico*, 87–94.

82. David L. Gregg to WLM, Jan. 5, Nov. 14, 1854, Despatches from United States Ministers in Hawaii, T30, roll 5, NA; Robert E. May, "Manifest Destiny's Filibusters," in *Manifest Destiny and Empire: American Antebellum Expansionism*, ed. Sam W. Haynes and Christopher Morris (College Station, Tex., 1997), 146–48.

83. Cortada, *Spain and the American Civil War*, 17; Horatio J. Perry to WLM, Sept. 6, 1854, WLM to Augustus Dodge, May 12, 1855, WLM Papers, LC. See also Daniel M. Barringer to JMC, June 27, 1850 (draft), Daniel M. Barringer Papers, SHC.

84. Rauch, *American Interest*, 182; William M. Burwell to JMC, May 12, 1852, DS, Special Agents; Martínez-Fernández, *Torn between Empires*, 45–48; Robert E. May, "Lobbyists for Commercial Empire: Jane Cazneau, William Cazneau, and U.S. Caribbean Policy, 1846–1878," *Pacific Historical Review* 48 (Aug. 1979): 392–93; Matthew Fontaine Maury to Frank, Feb. 27, 1856, Matthew F. Maury Papers, LC; Kenneth D. Lehman, *Bolivia and the United States: A Limited Partnership* (Athens, Ga., 1999), 33–35; Kemble, *Panama Route*, 75–76; JB Message to Congress, Jan. 7, 1858, *M&P* 5:469. In 1853 Mexico did award Tehuantepec transit rights to A. G. Sloo's competing New Orleans concern, but the railroad project failed, partly because of legal disputes. Smith, *Presidencies of Zachary Taylor and Millard Fillmore*, 22–23.

85. Patricio Rivas, provisional president of Walker's régime beginning in October

1855, continued to claim Nicaragua's presidency after his split with the filibusters in June 1856. After Walker's expulsion in 1857, Nicaraguan conservative and liberal elements, in June, formed a provisional coalition government with two generals—the liberal Máximo Jerez and the conservative Tomás Martínez—serving temporarily as dual presidents. In November, Nicaragua's constituent assembly elected Martinez as president. Meanwhile, the State Department declined identifying a de facto government in Nicaragua, citing the instability in the country, until the fall of 1857 when it received Irisarri, who also represented Guatemala and El Salvador in Washington. Frederic Rosengarten Jr., *Freebooters Must Die! The Life and Death of William Walker, the Most Notorious Filibuster of the Nineteenth Century* (Wayne, Pa., 1976), 99, 138; Bermann, *Under the Big Stick*, 66–67, 95–96; WLM to AO, Sept. 13, 1856, WLM to John H. Wheeler, Sept. 27, 1856, WLM to Antonio José de Irisarri, Oct. 28, 1856, Lewis Cass to Irisarri, Oct. 15, 1857, *Dipl Corr* 4:86, 87–88, 88–89, 102–3.

86. Mirabeau Buonaparte Lamar to Lewis Cass, Mar. 27, Apr. 28, 1858, Mar. 20, 1859, Cass to Lamar, June 3, 1858, Mar. 4, 1859, Cass to Máximo Jerez, May 26, 1859, Pedro Zeledón to Lamar, May 9, 1859, Hermenegildo Zepeda to Alexander Dimitry, Sept. 11, 1860 (translation), Luis Molina to Cass, Oct. 1, 1860 (translation), *Dipl Corr* 4:663–64, 671–74, 740–41, 112–13, 135–36, 143, 746–49, 918–19, 928–29; *Journal of the Executive Proceedings of the Senate of the United States of America, from December 6, 1858, to August 6, 1861, Inclusive* (Washington, 1887), 11:160, 163–64; Mirabeau Buonaparte Lamar to David G. Burnet, Hugh McLeod, and W. Richardson, Oct. 2, 1859, quoted in *NODP*, Oct. 7, 1859; William O. Scroggs, *Filibusters and Financiers: The Story of William Walker and His Associates* (New York, 1916), 358. The French promoter Félix Belly, who arrived in Nicaragua in 1858 and misleadingly claimed to have his government's backing, influenced Martínez's policy. Belly contracted with the Costa Rican and Nicaraguan presidents for exclusive canal rights, but his project collapsed quickly for lack of funding. Meanwhile the scheme caused a temporary change in Walker's planning. Walker decided that given France's presumed military presence in Nicaragua, it would be best to conduct his next invasion "by indirection" (presumably overland) from Mexico's isthmus of Tehuantepec. Ran Runnels to Lewis Cass, June 8, 23, 1859, Despatches from United States Consuls in San Juan del Sur, Nic., T-152, roll 2, NA; Brown, *Agents of Manifest Destiny*, 435–38; William Walker to Callender I. Fayssoux, Apr. 19, 1859, WWP.

87. H. G. Stebbins to Lewis Cass, Dec. 14, 1857, *H. Ex. Doc.* 24, 35th Cong., 1st Sess., 34; *New-York Times*, Mar. 27, 1858; Alexander Dimitry to Lewis Cass, Dec. 7, 1859 (extract), *Dipl Corr* 4:819–22; Burns, *Patriarch and Folk*, 232; *DAC*, Jan. 21, 1858; Scroggs, *Filibusters and Financiers*, 355–57, 365–67. Pressure from Cornelius Vanderbilt's agents influenced Nicaragua's 1858 revocation of the Stebbins-White contract. In March 1858 Nicaraguan authorities transferred transit rights to Vanderbilt. However, Vanderbilt accepted a monthly payment from the rival Pacific Mail Company, which operated the transit across Panama, in return for keeping the Nicaraguan route shut down. Scroggs, *Filibusters and Financiers*, 357, 365. Nicaragua's 1861 contract was with the Central American Transit Company, really a renamed American Atlantic and Pacific Ship Canal Company. Eventually, Nicaragua's govern-

ment forced the company to forfeit its charter. David I. Folkman Jr., *The Nicaragua Route* (Salt Lake City, 1972), 107–22. Folkman emphasizes that fear of filibustering in Nicaragua had declined by mid-1863, and had less to do with the company's failure than did the desire of Nicaragua's government to squeeze as much revenue as possible from the company, even at the risk of driving it into bankruptcy.

88. Jones, *American Problem*, 91–92, 96–98, 104–7, 127, 131–32, 148, 153–60, 165–85; Dexter Perkins, *The Monroe Doctrine, 1826–1867* (Baltimore, 1933), 238; Humphreys, *Diplomatic History*, 58; Spencer, *Victor and the Spoils*, 379–80. The treaty with Honduras guaranteed the religious and property rights of the Miskito Indians, and granted them a Honduran subsidy for ten years. The treaty with Nicaragua set aside a Miskito reservation where the Indians would have limited self-government. By the late 1850s Britain would have accepted either arbitration or unilateral abrogation of the Clayton-Bulwer Treaty by the United States (something that American leaders threatened from time to time) as a basis for settlement. But American leaders balked at both approaches. The latter would have left Britain's colonial holdings intact. As a result, the Clayton-Bulwer Treaty remained technically in force until the Hay-Pauncefote Treaty of 1901. Perkins, *Monroe Doctrine*, 240; Binder, *James Buchanan*, 187; Jones, *American Problem*, 184–85, 165–66; Lord Napier to Earl of Malmesbury, Apr. 12, 1858, *Con Print*, series D, pt. 1, vol. 7:57.

89. John F. Crampton to Lord Clarendon, May 12, 1856, *P&C*, 152–53; WLM to George M. Dallas, June 16, 1856, *Dipl Corr* 7:138–41; William Walker to Stephen Douglas, Mar. 30, 1856, Stephen A. Douglas Papers, University of Chicago; Brown, *Agents of Manifest Destiny*, 339–43.

90. Lord Clarendon quoted in Bourne, *Britain and the Balance of Power*, 173–75, 191. Central Americans sometimes assumed that innocent British residents and businessmen were American filibusters, being unable to distinguish between the two nationalities owing to their racial and cultural commonalities. British property suffered in the Panama riot. In 1858 the chairman of the London-based Honduras Interoceanic Railway Company complained to Britain's foreign office that there had been interference with company surveyors in Honduras, because the Bishop of Guatemala had convinced the Bishop of Honduras that "our Company were filibusters." Then too, the filibusters themselves sometimes attacked British persons and property. See William Perry to Earl of Clarendon, Dec. 10, 1856, PRO, General Correspondence: Colombia and New Granada, FO 55/124, William Brown to Earl of Malmesbury, July 25, 1858, Consular Despatches from Honduras, FO 39/5; John Leefe to James Greene, Dec. 11, 1857, enclosed with R. Squire Cottrell to Hiram Paulding, Dec. 12, 1857, RG 45, SquadL, roll 97; Frederick Seymour to C. H. Darling, May 17, 1859 (copy), PRO, Consular Despatches from Honduras, FO 39, Consular Despatches, Honduras, 39/7. Britain's change of policy was also influenced by a recession in the mahogany market, new evidence throwing into question British title to the Bay Islands, and construction of the railroad across Panama (which lessened the strategic importance of the Nicaraguan crossing). See Jones, *American Problem*, 154; Binder, *James Buchanan*, 235; Schoultz, *Beneath the United States*, 69; Naylor, *Penny Ante Imperialism*, 191–92.

91. Lord Palmerston to Lord Clarendon, Dec. 31, 1857, quoted in Kenneth

Bourne, *The Foreign Policy of Victorian England, 1830–1902* (Oxford, 1970), 334–36; William G. Ouseley to Earl of Malmesbury, Mar. 20, 1858, *Con Print*, series D, pt. 1, vol. 7:50–52; Charles Wyke to Lord John Russell, Jan. 17, 1861, PRO, Consular Despatches from Honduras, FO 39/12; Crampton to Earl of Clarendon, Oct. 2, 1855, *P&C*, 138.

92. Charles Lennox Wyke to Earl of Clarendon, Nov. 30, 1856, *Con Print*, series D, pt. 1, vol. 7:6–7. Wyke reported similar reservations respecting British plans to turn over Greytown and the Mosquito Territory to Nicaragua. Wyke to Clarendon, Aug. 27, 1856, *Con Print*, series D, pt. 1, vol. 7:1–3.

93. A. Callaghan to William Norvell, Feb. 7, 1860, Nicaraguan Army Register, Feb. 26, 1857, Charles Allen to William Walker, May 1, 5, 1860, WWP; *New York Herald*, Jan. 13, 1859. Apparently one or more of the leading dissidents on Roatán visited New Orleans to solidify the plans. Alexander Moir to Governor Darling, May 5, Frederic Seymour to C. Fortesque, Sept. 18, 1860 (handwritten copy), PRO, Consular Despatches from Honduras, FO 39/9, 39/10.

94. Frederic Seymour to Governor Darling, Feb. 24, 1860 (handwritten copy), Frederic Rogers to Edmund Hammond, July 31, 1860, PRO, Consular Despatches from Honduras, FO 39/9, T. Price to E. Hall, July 18, 1860, Seymour to C. Fortescue, Sept. 18, 1860 (handwritten copy), PRO, Consular Despatches from Honduras, FO 39/10; Charles Allen to William Walker, May 8, 1860, Walker to C. I. Fayssoux, June 22, 1860, WWP.

95. James Green to Lord John Russell, Jan. 10, 1861, *Con Print*, series D, pt. 1, vol. 7:170–71; Carlos Gutierrez to Lord John Russell, Dec. 26, 1860, Frederic Rogers to Edmund Hammond, May 7, 1861, C. H. Darling to Duke of Newcastle, June 24, 1861, PRO, Consular Despatches from Honduras, FO 39/8, 39/12, 39/13. Ever since Walker first invaded Nicaragua, Central American states had been extending feelers to Britain for new protectorates. In 1857 the Foreign Office recommended instead that the Central Americans solve their problem by uniting against invaders. British policy prioritized the protection of British persons and property in the region rather than the sovereignty of the Central American republics. C. [Lord Clarendon?] to [Philip] Griffith, Sept. 12, 1857 (draft), PRO, General Correspondence: Colombia and New Granada, 55/130; Charles Lennox Wyke to Earl of Clarendon, Nov. 30, 1856, *Con Print*, series D, pt. 1, vol. 7:6–7; Bourne, *Britain and the Balance of Power*, 197–98.

96. Letter of "XXX," Jan. 28, 1852 [1853], in *DAC*, Feb. 22, 1853.

Chapter Nine

1. John A. Campbell to Daniel Chandler, Nov. 12, 1860, Jan. 21, 1861, *Southern Historical Society Papers* 42 (Oct. 1917): 18–19, 28; Campbell to Franklin Pierce, Dec. 29, 1860, Franklin Pierce Papers, LC, series 2, reel 2. Campbell owned slaves at various times and had served as a Southern rights delegate to the June 1850 Nashville Convention. However, Campbell expressed liberal attitudes about slavery, never endorsed secession, and played a role in attempts to reconcile North and South both in early 1861 and during the Civil War. Thelma Jennings, *The Nashville Convention: Southern*

Movement for Unity, 1848–1851 (Memphis, 1980), 124, 146; Robert Saunders Jr., *John Archibald Campbell, Southern Moderate, 1811–1889* (Tuscaloosa, 1997), 8, 15, 57–67, 82, 92, 103; James Murphy, "Justice John Archibald Campbell on Secession," *Alabama Review* 28 (Jan. 1975): 48–58.

2. JAQ protest, July 3, 1854, JAQ Papers, MDAH; *New Orleans Daily Delta,* Aug. 15, 1854; (Austin) *Texas State Gazette,* July 29, Sept. 9, 1854; (New Orleans) *Louisiana Courier,* June 14, 1854; *Vicksburg Weekly Whig,* June 28, 1854; (Little Rock) *Arkansas State Gazette and Democrat,* July 21, 1854; John Marshall to JAQ, June 14, July 18 (mentioning Robert J. Walker's opinion), Samuel R. Walker to JAQ, July 31, 1854, JAQ Papers, HU; JAQ to Thomas Reed, Aug. 24, 1854, JAQ to H. T. Ellet, in J. F. H. Claiborne, *Life and Correspondence of John A. Quitman,* 2 vols. (New York, 1860), 2:206–9.

3. John A. Campbell to Jeremiah S. Black, Dec. 1, 1858, Jeremiah S. Black Papers, LC.

4. William Walker letter, June 25, 1858, in *Mobile Mercury,* quoted in *New-York Times,* July 5, 1858; John A. Campbell to Jeremiah S. Black, Nov. 22, 1858, Black Papers; *NODP,* Nov. 29, 1858; *Mobile Mercury,* quoted in *Tuskegee* (Ala.) *Republican,* Dec. 30, 1858.

5. Edmund Ruffin Diary, May 14, 17, 1858, LC; Eric H. Walther, *The Fire-Eaters* (Baton Rouge, 1992), 69–71, 254–56; Vicki Vaughn Johnson, *The Men and the Vision of the Southern Commercial Conventions, 1845–1871* (Columbia, Mo., 1992), 146–53; *Montgomery Mail,* quoted in *New-York Times,* July 22, 1858.

6. "To The Voters of the First Congressional District," Apr. 12, 1859, in (Marshall) *Texas Republican,* Apr. 22, 1859; *Clarksville* (Tex.) *Standard,* Sept. 18, 1858; John H. Reagan to James W. Latimer (of the *Dallas Herald*), Oct. 7, 1858; John H. Reagan, *Memoirs: With Special Reference to Secession and the Civil War* (New York, 1906), 70–72; Dale Baum, *The Shattering of Texas Unionism: Politics in the Lone Star State during the Civil War Era* (Baton Rouge, 1998), 35–36. Reagan, who was reelected, later became a secessionist and served in the Texan secession convention. Philip J. Avillo Jr. emphasizes the conditional nature of Reagan's Unionism in "John H. Reagan: Unionist or Secessionist?" *East Texas Historical Review* 13 (Spring 1975): 23–33. For other Unionists who connected filibustering to Southern extremism, see William P. Craighill to Ben Allston, Apr. 18, 1859, R. F. W. Allston Papers, South Carolina Historical Society, Charleston; Paula Mitchell Marks, *Turn Your Eyes toward Texas: Pioneers Sam and Mary Maverick* (College Station, Tex., 1989), 208; Henry A. Wise to Stephen Douglas, Jan. 14, 1858, quoted in Craig M. Simpson, *A Good Southerner: The Life of Henry A. Wise of Virginia* (Chapel Hill, 1985); G. H. Calvert to John Pendleton Kennedy, Jan. 5, 1861, John Pendleton Kennedy Papers, Enoch Pratt Free Library, Baltimore.

7. *Savannah Daily Morning News,* June 3, 1850.

8. Tom Chaffin, *Fatal Glory: Narciso López and the First Clandestine U.S. War against Cuba* (Charlottesville, 1996), 4–8, 50–51, 82–98. See also Michael Morrison, *Slavery and the American West: The Eclipse of Manifest Destiny and the Coming of the Civil War* (Chapel Hill, 1997), 132–33; Antonio Rafael de la Cova, "The Taylor Ad-

ministration versus Mississippi Sovereignty: The Round Island Expedition of 1849," *Journal of Mississippi History* 62 (Winter 2000): 313. De la Cova notes that at the time of the Round Island affair, a former governor of Illinois headed up a profilibustering meeting at Belleville, Illinois, that tried to drum up recruits.

9. David Cahill to Sam Houston, Mar. 21, Governors' Letters, Texas State Archives, Library Division, Austin; Houston to John S. Bedwell, Mar. 31, 1860, *The Writings of Sam Houston, 1813–1863*, ed. Amelia W. Williams and Eugene C. Barker, 8 vols. (1938–43; reprint, Austin, 1970), 7:566.

10. Frank Lawrence Owsley Jr. and Gene A. Smith, *Filibusters and Expansionists: Jeffersonian Manifest Destiny, 1800–1821* (Tuscaloosa, 1997), 77–80; undated statement in Quitman's hand, filed 1837, JAQ Papers, SHC; *Vicksburg Daily Whig*, Feb. 10, 1843.

11. *New Orleans Daily Delta*, May 26, 1850.

12. Arthur F. Corwin, *Spain and the Abolition of Slavery in Cuba, 1817–1886* (Austin, 1967), 25, 28, 69–77, 96; Luis Martínez-Fernández, *Torn between Empires: Economy, Society, and Patterns of Political Thought in the Hispanic Caribbean, 1840–1878* (Athens, Ga., 1994), 12, 14–17, 26–27; Franklin W. Knight, *Slave Society in Cuba during the Nineteenth Century* (Madison, 1970), 23–29, 138–39; C. Stanley Urban, "The Africanization of Cuba Scare, 1853–1855," *Hispanic American Historical Review* 37 (Feb. 1957): 30–31. Britain's crusade reflected a mix of humanitarian and materialistic motives. Having abolished slavery in its own Caribbean holdings, Britain could enhance the relative competitive standing of its own sugar colonies by causing the price of labor to rise in Cuba.

13. John L. O'Sullivan to John C. Calhoun, Aug. 24, 1849, "Correspondence of John C. Calhoun," ed. J. Franklin Jameson, *Annual Report of the American Historical Association for the Year 1899*, 2 vols. (Washington, 1900), 2:1202–3; O'Sullivan to JAQ, June 26, 1850, JAQ Papers, MDAH; O'Sullivan to Thomas Ritchie, July 25, 1849, Ritchie-Harrison Papers, College of William and Mary, Williamsburg, Va.

14. Narciso López and Ambrosio José Gonzales to JAQ, Mar. 17 [?], to JAQ, Feb. 24, 1850, in Claiborne, *Quitman* 2:384, 380–83. For the debate regarding López's attitudes toward annexation, see Chaffin, *Fatal Glory*, xi, 12, 34, 39; Antonio Rafael de la Cova, "Ambrosio Jose Gonzales: A Cuban Confederate Colonel" (Ph.D. diss., West Virginia University, 1994), 5–7; Joseph Opatrný, *US Expansionism and Cuban Annexationism* (Prague, 1990), 7–26; Charles H. Brown, *Agents of Manifest Destiny: The Lives and Times of the Filibusters* (Chapel Hill, 1980), 140–41. Most scholars agree that a considerable faction of the Cuban Creoles underwriting the expeditions supported annexation. Gonzales, in 1858, insisted that López had intended annexation. Gonzales to the editor of the *New York Herald*, July 29, in *Herald*, Aug. 8, 1858.

15. John Henderson to JAQ, Nov. 6, 1850, in Claiborne, *Quitman* 2:70; Warren P. Anderson's remarks to a meeting at Jackson's city hall, paraphrased in *Jackson Mississippian*, Aug. 1, 1851; John Tyler Jr. to JAQ, July 31, 1851, JAQ Papers, HU; Leo Wheat, "Memoir of Gen. C. R. Wheat," *Southern Historical Society Papers* 17 (1889): 49; [J. C. Davis], *The History of the Late Expedition to Cuba, by O. D. D. O., One of the Participants . . .* (New Orleans, 1850), 3; James Robb to Zachary Taylor, May 6, 1850, William L. Hodge to Taylor, May 7, 1850, *S. Ex. Doc.* 57, 31st Cong., 1st Sess., 49–50,

50–51; Lawrence Berry Washington to Henry Bedinger III, July 28, 1851, Bedinger-Dandridge Family Papers, DU. Many Gulf Coast newspapers and politicians bitterly attacked the Navy's blockade on López's Round Island filibusters in 1849 as an infringement of Mississippi's state sovereignty, certainly an early sign of filibustering's linkage to sectional disputes. De la Cova, "Taylor Administration," 323–27.

16. Urban, "Africanization of Cuba Scare," 34–36, Robert Benson Leard, "Bonds of Destiny: The United States and Cuba, 1848–1861" (Ph.D. diss., University of California at Berkeley, 1953), 127–31; Luis Martínez-Fernández, *Fighting Slavery in the Caribbean: The Life and Times of a British Family in Nineteenth-Century Havana* (Armonk, N.Y., 1998), 8–10.

17. Leard, "Bonds of Destiny," 127; Henry A. Murray, *Lands of the Slave and the Free: or, Cuba, the United States, and Canada* (London, 1855), 297–303; *Jackson Mississippian and State Gazette*, Feb. 4, 1853, Mar. 24, 1854; (Little Rock) *Arkansas State Gazette and Democrat*, July 21, 1854; *Congressional Globe*, 33d Cong., 1st Sess., 1298, 1194; *Richmond Enquirer*, Sept. 6, 1853; *Augusta Daily Chronicle and Sentinel*, June 19, 1853.

18. WLM to Alexander M. Clayton, Oct. 26, Nov. 8, 1853, WLM to Charles Augustus Davis, Mar. 15, 1854, WLM to William H. Robertson, Apr. 8, 1854, WLM to Pierre Soulé, July 23, 1853, Davis to WLM, May 22, 1854, Robertson to WLM, Feb. 14, Mar. 10, Apr. 21, 1854, Soulé to WLM, Dec. 23, 1853, *Dipl Corr* 11:160–61 166–68, 170–73, 178–79, 733–34, 737, 748–49, 789–795, WLM to JB, July 2, 1853, *Dipl Corr* 7:93. Buchanan, a Pennsylvanian, argued that the attempted Africanization of Cuba would justify U.S. seizure of the island. See JB to WLM, Dec. 8, 1854, WLM Papers, LC.

19. "Diary of J. Alexander Fulton, Esq., Kept on a Trip West and South October 1, 1854 to January 3, 1855" (copy: part typed, part handwritten), microfilm, Delaware State Archives, Hall of Records, Dover; JAQ to B. F. Dill, June 18, 1854, JAQ Papers, HU; John Henderson letter, June 10, in *New York Herald*, July 4, 1854; *Vicksburg Weekly Whig*, June 28, 1854; *Congressional Globe*, 33d Cong., 1st Sess., 1021–24 (May 1, 1854). The Louisiana legislature took up the matter after Governor P. O. Hébert's annual message, which raised the specter of Africanization. During legislative debate, W. J. A. Roberts of New Orleans defended filibustering as a means of resolving the Cuban problem. See C. Stanley Urban, "The Idea of Progress and Southern Imperialism: New Orleans and the Caribbean, 1845–1861" (Ph.D. diss., Northwestern University, 1943), 501–16.

20. R. O. Love to JAQ, May 24, A. W. Hobson to JAQ, June 20, C. C. Danley to JAQ, June 27, F. R. Witter to JAQ, Oct. 17, 1854, JAQ Papers, MDAH; Felix Huston to JAQ, Sept. 13, 1854, JAQ Papers, HU; Felix Huston obituary, *American Almanac* 29 (1858): 355; Alexander H. Stephens to J. W. Duncan, May 26, 1854, "The Correspondence of Robert Toombs, Alexander H. Stephens, and Howell Cobb," ed. Ulrich Bonnell Phillips, *Annual Report of the American Historical Association, 1911*, 2 vols. (Washington, 1913), 2:345.

21. JAQ to B. F. Dill, June 18, 1854 (draft), A. G. Haley to JAQ, June 14, 1854, John Marshall to JAQ, July 18, 1854, Samuel Walker to JAQ, July 31, 1854, Alexander

Clayton to JAQ, Nov. 10, 1853, JAQ Papers, HU; Correspondent "Q. E. D." from Montgomery, in *New York Herald*, June 20, 1854; JAQ to Thomas Reed, Aug. 24, 1854, in Claiborne, *Quitman* 2:207; *New Orleans Daily Delta*, Aug. 25, 1854; John S. Thrasher, *Cuba and Louisiana: Letter to Samuel J. Peters, Esq.* (New Orleans, 1854), 4–8; Gaspar Betancourt, Esq., President of the Cuban Revolutionary Junta and J. S. Thrasher, Esq., *Addresses Delivered at the Celebration of the Third Anniversary in Honor of the Martyrs for Cuban Freedom at the Mechanics' Institute Hall, New Orleans, Sept. 1, 1854* (New Orleans, 1854), 5–8; John S. Ford to JAQ, July 2, 1855, JAQ Papers, University of Virginia, Charlottesville; A. J. McNeil to JAQ, June 10, 1854, JAQ Papers, MDAH. Quitman and his associates refused to endorse U.S. acquisition of Cuba by war or purchase: war would prompt Spain to rush Cuba's Africanization, making the island useless to Southerners; purchase would raise the same debates about slavery in Washington as during the California crisis, and U.S. courts might recognize Pezuela's antislavery decrees as legitimate. Robert E. May, *The Southern Dream of a Caribbean Empire, 1854–1861* (Baton Rouge, 1973), 43–44; JAQ to B. F. Dill (draft), J. W. Lesesne to JAQ, June 8, 1854, JAQ Papers, HU.

22. Samuel R. Walker, "Cuba and the South," *DeBow's Review* 17 (Nov. 1854): 519–25.

23. Samuel R. Walker to JAQ, July 31, 1854, JAQ to C. A. L. Lamar, Jan. 5, 1855, JAQ Papers, HU; JAQ to B. F. Dill, Feb. 9, 1855, H. Forno to JAQ, Feb. 9, 1855, JAQ Papers, MDAH; Alexander Walker to A. G. Haley, June 15, 1854, Jefferson Davis Papers, LC; John S. Thrasher to James Johnston Petigrew, Jan. 2, 1854, Pettigrew Family Papers, SHC.

24. John C. Walker to JAQ, Nov. 26 (with Quitman's endorsement), Dec. 13, 1854, George Bolivar Hall to JAQ, Aug. 2, 1853, James Madison Miller to JAQ, Sept. 14, 1854, JAQ Papers, HU; Hall to JAQ, Jan. 14, 1855, JAQ Papers, MDAH; "Hall, George," *Appleton's Cyclopedia of American Biography*, 6 vols. (1894–1900; rev. edn., New York, 1900), 3:40.

25. John L. O'Sullivan to JAQ, Aug. 29, Sept. 8, Mike Walsh to JAQ, Aug. 2, Oct. 3, 1853, JAQ Papers, HU; Mike Walsh to JAQ, Jan. 25, 1855, JAQ Papers, MDAH; JAQ to Mike Walsh, Mar. 14, 1854, Mike Walsh Papers, New-York Historical Society; John Cadwalader to George Cadwalader, Sept. 13, 1853, Domingo de Goicouria [to George Cadwalader], Sept. 17, 1853, George Cadwalader Papers, HSP; W. J. Rorabaugh, "Rising Democratic Spirits: Immigrants, Temperance, and Tammany Hall," *Civil War History* 22 (June 1976): 152–53; "Cadwalader, John," *Biographical Directory of the American Congress, 1774–1996* (Alexandria, Va., 1997), 763.

26. John L. O'Sullivan to John C. Calhoun, Aug. 24, 1849, Jameson, ed., "Correspondence of John C. Calhoun," 2:1202–3; Sheldon Howard Harris, "The Public Career of John Louis O'Sullivan" (Ph.D. diss., Columbia University, 1958), 53–54, 270, 275–76, 402–6; Sean Wilentz, *Chants Democratic: New York City and the Rise of the American Working Class, 1788–1850* (New York, 1984), 332–33; Anthony Gronowicz, *Race and Class Politics in New York City before the Civil War* (Boston, 1998), 119–20, 141–42; Mike Walsh to JAQ, Oct. 3, 1853, May 25, Sept. 6, 1854, JAQ Papers, HU; John Cadwalader to Peter G. Washington, Aug. 27, 1853, Maupin-Washington Papers,

College of William and Mary, Williamsburg, Va.; "Cadwalader, John," *National Cyclopaedia of American Biography* . . ., 64 vols.(New York, 1893–94), 15:305; George Law to Thomas Oliver Larkin, Oct. 6, 1856, *The Larkin Papers*, ed. George P. Hammond, 10 vols. (Berkeley, 1951–68), 10:312–13. O'Sullivan's sister, then a widow, had married Madan in 1845.

27. Frederick Law Olmsted, *The Cotton Kingdom: A Traveller's Observations on Cotton and Slavery in the American Slave States*, ed. Arthur M. Schlesinger (New York, 1953), 621.

28. Corwin, *Spain and the Abolition of Slavery*, 114, 120–21; Urban, "Africanization of Cuba Scare," 41–42; Martínez-Fernández, *Torn between Empires*, 50–51; William H. Robertson to WLM, Mar. 7, 1855, *Dipl Corr* 11:853–54. Once news about Quitman's resignation reached Cuba, Spanish authorities there took additional steps to stabilize Cuban slavery, including the disbanding of Pezuela's black military companies. Robertson to WLM, May 22, June 20, July 5, 1855, *Dipl Corr* 11:864, 869, 870.

29. John S. Thrasher to James Johnston Pettigrew, Dec. 7, 1855, Pettigrew Family Papers, SHC; *Congressional Globe*, 34th Cong., 1st Sess., 1061, appendix, 669–70. Quitman also called for Cuba's annexation during his campaign for Congress. (Natchez) *Mississippi Free Trader*, June 12, 1855.

30. Ronnie C. Tyler, "Fugitive Slaves in Mexico," *Journal of Negro History* 57 (Jan. 1972): 2–6; Patsy McDonald Spaw, ed., *The Texas Senate*, vol. 1: *Republic to Civil War, 1836–1861* (College Station, Tex., 1990), 236; Kevin Mulroy, *Freedom on the Border: The Seminole Maroons in Florida, the Indian Territory, Coahuila, and Texas* (Lubbock, 1993), 8–63; Ronnie C. Tyler, "The Callahan Expedition of 1855: Indians or Negroes?" *SHQ* 70 (Apr. 1967): 574–76; Kenneth W. Porter, *The Black Seminoles: History of a Freedom-Seeking People*, rev. and ed. Alcione M. Amos and Thomas P. Senter (Gainesville, Fla., 1996), 124–34.

31. John Salmon Ford, *Rip Ford's Texas*, ed. Stephen B. Oates (Austin, 1963), 196, 205; Tyler, "Fugitive Slaves," 6; Bob Cunningham and Harry P. Hewitt, "A 'lovely land full of roses and thorns': Emil Langberg and Mexico, 1835–1866," *SHQ* 98 (Jan. 1995): 402–3; Mulroy, *Freedom on the Border*, 70.

32. James H. Callahan to Elisha M. Pease, Oct. 13, 1855, Elisha M. Pease Papers, Austin History Center, Austin Public Library; Tyler, "Callahan Expedition," 576, 579–80; Mulroy, *Freedom on the Border*, 78–80; John S. Ford to JAQ, July 2, 1855, JAQ Papers, University of Virginia, Charlottesville; Cunningham and Hewitt, "Langberg," 408–11; Ford, *Rip Ford's Texas*, 214–15; Walter V. Scholes, *Mexican Politics during the Juárez Regime, 1855–1872* (Columbia, Mo., 1957), 3, 8.

33. Tyler, "Callahan Expedition," 585; William R. Henry [to Hardin Runnels], Feb. 3, 1859 (copy), Governors' Papers, Texas State Library, Archives Division, Austin.

34. C. A. Bridges, "The Knights of the Golden Circle: A Filibustering Fantasy," *SHQ* 44 (Jan. 1941): 297; George Bickley, "An Open Letter to the Knights of the Golden Circle," July 17, 1860, *Richmond Whig*, quoted in *New-York Times*, July 23, 1860; *Macon* (Ga.) *Daily Telegraph*, July 21, 1860; George Bickley to E. H. Cushing, Nov. 15, 1860, Jimmie Hicks, ed., "Some Letters Concerning the Knights of the Golden Circle in Texas, 1860–1861," *SHQ* 65 (July 1961): 84–85.

35. Albert Z. Carr, *The World and William Walker* (New York, 1963), 7, 91; Brown, *Agents of Manifest Destiny*, 178–79, 216; *Washington National Era*, Dec. 22, 1853; *New York Herald*, Oct. 28, 1853, quoted in Alejandro Bolaños-Geyer, *William Walker: The Gray-Eyed Man of Destiny*, vol. 2: *The Californias* (Lake St. Louis, Mo., 1989), 207; Laurence Greene, *The Filibuster: The Career of William Walker* (Indianapolis, 1937), 32–33; Frederic Rosengarten Jr., *Freebooters Must Die! The Life and Death of William Walker, the Most Notorious Filibuster of the Nineteenth Century* (Wayne, Pa., 1976), 47.

36. *Washington National Era*, Mar. 11, 1852, Apr. 14, 1853; Rudolph M. Lapp, *Blacks in Gold Rush California* (New Haven, 1977), 130–46; William Allen Wallace Diary, Jan. 25, 1857, BRBM; Thomas J. Oxley to his mother and brothers, June 18, 1856, J. Wing Oliver to James H. Oliver, Aug. 28, 1857, James Harvey Oliver Papers, Bancroft Library, University of California, Berkeley; Sylvester Mowry to Samuel Cooper, Mar. 3, 1857, *H. Ex. Doc.* 64, 35th Cong., 1st Sess., 32; Ernest S. Easter III, "Napoleonic Code," in *Encyclopedia of Southern Culture*, ed. Charles Reagan Wilson and William Ferris (Chapel Hill, 1989), 828. For an indication that slavery expansionist intentions also motivated Californians who filibustered with Juan José Flores in South America, see "ECUADOR" to the editor, *SFDH*, Nov. 3, 1853.

37. *FLIN*, July 5, 1856; William Walker, *The War in Nicaragua* (1860; reprint, Tucson, 1985), 29.

38. *Congressional Globe*, 35th Cong., 2d Sess., 967; Cassius M. Clay to JMC, June 10, 1856, JMC Papers, LC.

39. William Walker to Stephen A. Douglas, Mar. 30, Parker French to Douglas, Feb. 14, John P. Heiss to Douglas, Mar. 14, Sidney Breese to Douglas, Mar. 29, Aug. 7, 1856, Stephen A. Douglas Papers, University of Chicago; Robert W. Johannsen, *Stephen A. Douglas* (New York, 1973), 530–33; *Official Proceedings of the National Democratic Convention Held in Cincinnati, June 2–6, 1856* (Cincinnati, 1856), 27–31.

40. (Austin) *Texas State Gazette*, Feb. 23, 1856. See also the retrospective thoughts in the (Little Rock) *Arkansas State Gazette and Democrat*, Oct. 10, 1857.

41. Walker, *War in Nicaragua*, 254–56; Tuskegee (Ala.) *Republican*, Dec. 18, 1856; *New Orleans Daily Creole*, Nov. 27, 1856. Technically, Walker's decree repealed all acts and decrees of the United Provinces of Central America, to which Nicaragua had belonged from 1823 to 1838. Since the United Provinces had passed legislation banning slavery (which had never been a major institution in Nicaragua) Walker's measure allowed its reintroduction. E. Bradford Burns, *Patriarch and Folk: The Emergence of Nicaragua, 1798–1858* (Cambridge, Mass., 1991), 16, 32; Walker, *War in Nicaragua*, 255–56.

42. Charles W. Doubleday, *Reminiscences of the "Filibuster" War in Nicaragua* (New York, 1886), 167; May, *Southern Dream*, 103–5; Brown, *Agents of Manifest Destiny*, 325–50, 358–59; Rosengarten, *Freebooters Must Die!* 140; Ralph Lee Woodward Jr., *Rafael Carrera and the Emergence of the Republic of Guatemala, 1821–1871* (Athens, Ga., 1993), 287–89; Tuskegee (Ala.) *Republican*, Dec. 18, 1856; *New Orleans Daily Creole*, Nov. 27, 1856. In his autobiography, Walker admitted that the decree had been issued to facilitate his defense of Nicaragua against hostile Central American states. Walker, *War in Nicaragua*, 263.

43. *FLIN*, Aug. 30, 1856; *Baltimore Sun*, Oct. 4, 1856; *Mobile Daily Register*, June 3, 1856 (Soulé's speech); AO to William Walker, Aug. 9, 1856, AO Papers, DU; Walker, *War in Nicaragua*, 238–39; J. Preston Moore, "Pierre Soulé: Southern Expansionist and Promoter," *Journal of Southern History* 21 (May 1955): 207–8, 210–15. Soulé, a native Frenchman who had lived in Louisiana since 1825, had opposed the admission of California as a free state while serving in the Senate. David S. Heidler, *Pulling the Temple Down: The Fire-Eaters and the Destruction of the Union* (Mechanicsburg, Pa., 1994), 63.

44. John H. Wheeler to WLM, Sept. 30, 1856, *Dipl Corr* 6:574; *Cincinnati Enquirer*, Dec. 13, 1856; Felix Huston [to Richard T. Archer], Nov. 10, 1856, Archer Family Papers, UT; *Nashville Union and American*, Oct. 31, 1856.

45. (Austin) *Texas State Gazette*, June 13, 1857; *Tuskegee* (Ala.) *Republican*, Jan. 28, 1858; *New York Herald*, Jan. 18, 1858; William Walker to Alexander H. Stephens, Mar. 8, 1858, Alexander H. Stephens Papers, LC; *Vicksburg Daily Whig*, July 2, 1858; William Walker to William H. Ackland, Oct. 26, 1858, William H. Ackland Papers, SHC.

46. Walker, *War in Nicaragua*, 259–63, 271–72.

47. Walker, *War in Nicaragua*, 263–80.

48. Randal McGavock Journal, July 8, Dec. 19, 1857, in *Pen and Sword: The Life and Journals of Randal W. McGavock*, ed. Herschel Gower and Jack Allen (Knoxville, 1959), 422, 447; *Memphis Evening Ledger*, July 18, 1857; Henry Hughes and others to William Walker, July 27, 1858, in *Port Gibson* (Miss.) *Review*, Aug. 14, 1858; R. Raub [?] to JAQ, Jan. 18, 1858, JAQ Papers, HU; William DeForest Holly to C. J. Macdonald, Sept. 26, 1858, William Walker Papers, Bancroft Library, University of California, Berkeley; (Little Rock) *Arkansas State Gazette and Democrat*, Oct. 10, 1857. In July 1857 one of Walker's organizers predicted that all participants in the next invading army would hail from the "southern portion of the union." The following winter, a U.S. naval commander confirmed that the adventurers were, indeed, primarily southerners. C. J. Macdonald to Amy Morris Bradley, July 8, 1857, Amy Morris Bradley Papers, DU; Frederic Chatard to Isaac Toucey, Jan. 1, 1858, *H. Ex. Doc.* 24, 35th Cong., 1st Sess., 78.

49. William Gilmore Simms to William Porcher Miles, Jan. 25, 1858, in *The Letters of William Gilmore Simms*, ed. Mary C. Simms Oliphant, Alfred Taylor Odell, and T. C. Duncan Eaves, 5 vols. (1952–56), 4:11; Augustus Wright to Frank [?], Mar. 4, 1858, and undated, Augustus R. Wright Papers, LC; Alexander H. Stephens to his brother, Jan. 20, 1858, Alexander H. Stephens Papers, LC; May, *Southern Dream*, 114–33; Edmund Ruffin Diary, Jan. 5, 1858.

50. Copy in PRO, Consular Despatches from Honduras, FO 39/10.

51. *New York Herald*, Dec. 30, 1854. William Sidney Thayer the next August affirmed in a public letter that the colony's soil and climate invited slave labor, but added that any attempt by Kinney to introduce the institution would fail so long as "any portion" of the area's ten million mixed-blood peoples remained on the Mosquito Coast. *New York Evening Post*, Sept. 8, 1855.

52. For projections of filibustering onto the fugitive slave dispute, see *New-York Daily Tribune*, Oct. 18, 1850, May 2, 1851; *Pittsburg Daily Morning Post*, Sept. 8, 1851;

Brownson's Quarterly Review, new series, 6 (Jan. 1852): 95; J. D. Howland to George W. Hazzard, June 26, 1852, George Washington Hazzard Papers, U.S. Military Academy Library, West Point, N.Y.; John A. Campbell's charge to the jury, 1854, quoted in Ronald Sklut, "John Archibald Campbell: A Study in Divided Loyalties," *Alabama Lawyer* 20 (July 1959): 236; *Washington Constitution*, Oct. 8, 1859; William Tecumseh Sherman to John Sherman, Dec. 9, 1860, in *Sherman's Civil War: Selected Correspondence of William T. Sherman, 1860–1865*, ed. Brooks D. Simpson and Jean V. Berlin (Chapel Hill, 1999), 16. For the relationship to Brown's raid, see *Brownson's Quarterly Review* (July 1860), quoted in Henry F. Brownson, ed., *The Works of Orestes A. Brownson*, 20 vols. (1882–1907; reprint, New York, 1966), 17:116; Henry Raymond speech, Jan. 12, 1860, quoted in *New-York Times*, Jan. 17, 1860; Parmenas Taylor Turnley speech, Jan. 26, 1861, quoted in David Edward Cronin [pseud.], *Reminiscences of Parmenas Taylor Turnley from the Cradle to Three-Score and Ten by Himself, from Diaries Kept from Early Boyhood . . .* (Chicago, 1892), 303; Governor Samuel Kirkwood of Iowa, quoted in James M. McPherson, *Battle Cry of Freedom: The Civil War Era* (New York, 1988), 212. For the application of the term to Southern partisans in Kansas, see *Springfield* (Mass.) *Daily Republican*, May 21, 1856; *New Orleans Delta* quoted in *New-York Evangelist*, May 22, 1856; *New-York Daily Tribune*, July 18, 1857.

53. *New-York Daily Times*, Dec. 22, 1856; *Harper's Weekly*, Jan. 31, 1857; *FLIN*, Jan. 9, 1858; *New York Herald*, Jan. 3, 1858; *Democratic Review*, new series, 38 (Nov. 1856): 298–303; *New York Daily News*, Feb. 4, 1857.

54. "The Nicaraguan Question," *Democratic Review* 41 (Feb. 1858): 115–23; May, *Southern Dream*, 121–25; *Congressional Globe*, 35th Cong., 1st Sess., 223; *Pittsburg Morning Post*, Dec. 22, 1858; JB to Joseph B. Baker, Jan. 11, 1858, in *The Works of James Buchanan, Comprising His Speeches, State Papers, and Private Correspondence*, ed. John Bassett Moore (Philadelphia, 1908–11), 10:177.

55. Lewis Tappan to John Scoble, Sept. 19, 1849, in *A Side-Light on Anglo-American Relations, 1839–1858: Furnished by the Correspondence of Lewis Tappan and Others with the British and Foreign Anti-Slavery Society*, ed. Annie Heloise Abel and Frank J. Kingberg (Lancaster, Pa., 1927), 234–35; John Greenleaf Whittier, "The Haschish," in Whittier, *The Panorama, and Other Poems* (Boston, 1856), 113.

56. George Lunt to William S. Derrick, Sept. 6, 1851, R.G. 59, DS, ML, M179, roll 127, NA; *Springfield* (Mass.) *Daily Republican*, Aug. 29, 1851; *New-York Evangelist*, Sept. 11, 1851; *Washington National Era*, Sept. 20, 1849. The U.S. district attorney trying the López filibuster case in January 1851 in New Orleans tried to pack the jury with transplanted Northerners, apparently assuming that they had less enthusiasm for filibustering than Southerners did. A majority of the northern-born jurors in the Henderson trial did, in fact, vote for conviction. See de la Cova, "Gonzales," 143–144, 154.

57. John Ball Jr. [James Redpath] to the *New-York National Anti-Slavery Standard*, Dec. 2, 1854, Mar. 31, 1855, in *The Roving Editor; or, Talks with Slaves in the Southern States, by James Redpath*, ed. John R. McKivigan (University Park, Pa., 1996), 132, 170.

58. *Proceedings of the Black State Conventions, 1840–1865*, ed. Philip S. Foner and George E. Walker (Philadelphia, 1979), 1:94; *Washington National Era*, May 8, 1856.

59. "John Fremont's Coming" and "Get out of the way, old Buchanan," in *The*

Campaign of 1856: Fremont Songs for the People, Original and Selected (Boston, 1856), 16–17, 56–58.

60. Henry David Thoreau to Harrison Blake, Feb. 27, 1853, in *Familiar Letters of Henry David Thoreau*, ed. F. B. Sanborn (Boston, 1896), 252–53.

61. Charles Sumner to Dutchess of Argyll, Jan. 12, 1858, *The Selected Letters of Charles Sumner*, 2 vols. (Boston, 1990), 1:489–90; *New York Herald*, Jan. 16, 1858; May, *Southern Dream*, 125.

62. (Boston) *Liberator*, Feb. 27, Apr. 17 ("empire of the lash"), May 29, 1857, Oct. 24, 1856, Jan. 15 ("scoundrel"), Feb. 19 (Sanborn's prologue), 1858; *Chicago Press and Tribune*, Oct. 1, 1860. Henry W. Bellows described Southern editors as "intellectual pirates and moral fillibusters" for their defenses of slavery. (Boston) *Liberator*, Feb. 6, 1857.

63. (Boston) *Liberator*, July 3, Feb. 27, 1857, Oct. 24, 1856; *Washington National Era*, May 8, 1856; Sarah P. Remond speech, Jan. 24, 1859, in *The Black Abolitionist Papers*, ed. C. Peter Ripley, vol. 1: *The British Isles, 1830–1865* (Chapel Hill, 1985–92), 436; *Life and Times of Frederick Douglass, Written by Himself* (Boston, 1893), ed. Henry Louis Gates Jr. in *Frederick Douglass: Autobiographies* (New York, 1994), 734, 844–45; John Bigelow to William Cullen Bryant, Dec. 28, 1857 (copy), John Bigelow Papers, New York Public Library. See also Leonard L. Richards, *The Slave Power: The Free North and Southern Domination, 1780–1860* (Baton Rouge, 2000), 4, 8, 194.

64. George Washington Hazzard to J. D. Howland, Jan. 25, 1858, George Washington Hazzard Papers, U.S. Military Academy Library, West Point, N.Y.; *Congressional Globe*, 35th Cong., 1st Sess., 293; L. E. Chittenden, ed., *Debates and Proceedings in the Secret Sessions of the Conference Convention* (New York, 1864), 168.

65. Robert E. May, *John A. Quitman: Old South Crusader* (Baton Rouge, 1985), 70–71, 228–69; William L. Barney, *The Road to Secession: A New Perspective on the Old South* (New York, 1972), 86; Eric H. Walther, *The Fire-Eaters* (Baton Rouge, 1992), 83–111; James L. Abrahamson, *The Men of Secession and Civil War, 1859–1861* (Wilmington, Del., 2000), 44–45; Correspondent of the *Missouri Democrat* quoted in *New York Herald*, Jan. 18, 1858.

66. T. W. W. Sullivan to JAQ, Apr. 10, 1854, JAQ Papers, Felix Huston to JAQ, Sept. 19, 1850, J. F. H. Claiborne Papers, MDAH; John Ray Skates Jr., *A History of the Mississippi Supreme Court, 1817–1948* (Jackson, 1973), 31; Cleo Hearon, "Nullification in Mississippi," *Publications of the Mississippi Historical Society* 12 (University, Miss., 1912), 56n; (Natchez) *Mississippi Free Trader*, May 24, 28, 1851, Feb. 17, 1849; *Vicksburg Sentinel*, July 13, 1830; Ralph A. Wooster, *The Secession Conventions of the South* (Princeton, 1962), 123; Stephen B. Oates, "John S. 'Rip' Ford: Prudent Cavalryman, C.S.A.," in Ralph A. Wooster, ed., *Lone Star Blue and Gray: Essays on Texas in the Civil War* (Austin, 1995), 315–16.

67. W. M. Weaver to JAQ, Feb. 7, 1855, JAQ Papers, HU; Weaver to JAQ, June 12, 1856, JAQ Papers, MDAH; *New-York Daily Tribune*, June 1, 1850; Antonio Rafael de la Cova, "Cuban Filibustering in Jacksonville in 1851," *Northeast Florida History* 3 (1996): 18–19, 29–33; *WDNI*, Sept. 11, 1851; Jay Monaghan, *Civil War on the Western Border, 1854–1865* (Boston, 1955), 55–57, 77, 93; *Lecompton* (Kan.) *Union*, Nov.

6, 27, 1856; Henry Miles Moore Journal, Aug. 16, Dec. 5, 1856, BRBM; *Washington National Era*, Nov. 27, 1856; A. C. Allen Diary, "The Walker Expedition" (photocopy), p. 3, UT. See also the biographical sketch of William Clowes in the *New York Herald*, Jan. 12, 1858.

68. C. A. L. Lamar to John M. Dow, Feb. 12, 1855, Lamar to J. S. Thrasher, Feb. 25, 1855, in "A Slave Trader's Letter Book," *North American Review* 143 (Nov. 1886): 448; Ronald T. Takaki, *A Pro-Slavery Crusade: The Agitation to Reopen the African Slave Trade* (New York, 1971), 200–12; Register of Walker's Army, WWP; Warren S. Howard, *American Slavers and the Federal Law, 1837–1862* (Berkeley, 1963), 232; John J. TePaske, "Appleton Oaksmith: Filibustering Agent," *North Carolina Historical Review* 35 (Oct. 1958): 428, 430–31; *The Evolution of a Life Described in the Memoirs of Major Seth Eyland* (New York, 1884), 52–53; *Congressional Globe*, 34th Cong., 3d Sess., 123–26, appendix, 120; Eric H. Walther, *Fire-Eaters*, 69–70; Douglas Ambrose, *Henry Hughes and Proslavery Thought in the Old South* (Baton Rouge, 1996), 145–46, 149–50, 153–54, 157, 165; Charles Frederick Henningsen to Robert Farnham, Dec. 24, 1859, in *Savannah Express*, Dec. 30, 1859, reprinted in *New-York Times*, Jan. 5, 1860; *Macon* (Ga.) *Daily Telegraph*, Dec. 10, 1860.

69. William Walker to Domingo de Goicouria, Aug. 12, 1856, in *New-York Times*, Nov. 24, 1856. Walker's autobiography reiterated his disclaimer of ever desiring annexation to the United States. See Walker, *War in Nicaragua*, 266–70.

70. JAQ to Thomas Reed, Aug. 24, 1854, in Claiborne, *Quitman* 2:207; James Longstreet to William Porcher Miles, Feb. 27, 1860, William Porcher Miles Papers, UNC. Craig L. Symonds makes virtually the same point in his fine biography of Joseph E. Johnston, the Confederate general, who in the late 1850s had been involved in filibustering plots regarding Mexico. See Symonds, *Joseph E. Johnston: A Civil War Biography* (New York, 1992), 84–86.

71. B. D. Palmer to "Friend Reeves," Mar. 13, 1857, Missouri University Papers, Missouri Historical Society, St. Louis; Thomas Claiborne, undated fragment, filed with Annie Claiborne to her sister, Feb. 5, 1857, Thomas Claiborne Papers, UNC; Edmund Ruffin Diary, May 17, 1858; *Fayetteville Arkansian*, Oct. 18, 1860.

72. *Augusta* (Ga.) *Daily Chronicle and Sentinel*, Mar. 10 1860; F. R. Witter to JAQ, JAQ Papers, MDAH; *De Bow's Review* 21 (Jan. 1857): 108.

73. Edmund Ruffin Diary, May 10, 14, 15, 1858.

74. William Gilmore Simms to James Henry Hammond, Jan. 28, 1858, in *Letters of William Gilmore Simms* 4:16; *Fayetteville Arkansian*, Oct. 18, 1860.

75. *Congressional Globe*, 35th Cong., 2d Sess., 318; *Journal of the House of Delegates of the State of Virginia for the Session of 1857–58* (Richmond, 1857 [1858]), 121–22; *Richmond Daily Dispatch*, Jan. 5, 12, 15, 1858; Spaw, ed., *Texas Senate*, 1:297; Walter L. Buenger, "Texas and the Riddle of Secession," in Wooster, ed., *Lone Star Blue and Gray*, 5; Morrison, *Slavery and the American West*, 132–33. In the vote in the U.S. House of Representatives, members from the Upper South split 25–17 in favor of condemning Paulding.

76. John T. Pickett to JAQ, JAQ Papers, MDAH.

77. (New Orleans) *Louisiana Courier*, Aug. 13, 1851; Fred B. Shepard, Colin J.

McRae, and William F. Cleveland to Isaac Toucey, Jan. 30, 1858, RG 45, ML Received by the Secretary of the Navy, M124, roll 336; Jefferson Davis Speech, May 29, 1857, *The Papers of Jefferson Davis*, ed. Haskell M. Monroe Jr., James T. McIntosh, and Lynda Lasswell Crist, 10 vols. (Baton Rouge, 1971–), 6:122; JAQ to B. F. Dill, June 18, 1854 (draft), JAQ Papers, HU; (Natchez) *Mississippi Free Trader*, Sept. 23, 1858; Robert E. May, "The Slave Power Conspiracy Revisited: U.S. Presidents and Filibustering, 1848–1861," in *Union and Emancipation: Essays on Politics and Race in the Civil War Era*, ed. David W. Blight and Brooks D. Simpson (Kent, Ohio, 1997), 27–28; Edward P. Crapol, "John Tyler and the Pursuit of National Destiny," *Journal of the Early Republic* 17 (Fall 1997): 489–90; B. G. Weir to the editor, Mar. 14, 1857, (Stockton, Calif.) *San Joaquin Republican*, Apr. 1, 1857; F. R. Witter to JAQ, Oct. 17, 1854, JAQ Papers, MDAH; Christopher J. Olsen, *Political Culture and Secession in Mississippi: Masculinity, Honor, and the Antiparty Tradition, 1830–1860* (New York, 2000), 185–86. Quitman's reference to Canadian fisheries concerned the Marcy-Elgin Treaty with Great Britain, signed less than a week after Pierce issued his proclamation against Cuban filibustering, permitting Americans fishing rights in Canada's maritime provinces excluding Newfoundland.

78. Ethelbert Barksdale to Jefferson Davis, Jan. 8 1858, *Jefferson Davis, Constitutionalist: His Letters, Papers and Speeches*, ed. Dunbar Rowland, 10 vols. (Jackson, 1923), 3:134.

79. David M. Potter, *Lincoln and His Party in the Secession Crisis* (New Haven, 1942), 68–74, 101–10; May, *Southern Dream*, 226–32.

80. Abraham Lincoln to Lyman Trumbull, Dec. 10, Lincoln to William Kellogg, Dec. 11, Lincoln to Elihu B. Washburne, Dec. 13, Lincoln to Thurlow Weed, Dec. 17, Lincoln to John D. Defrees, Dec. 18, 1860, Lincoln to John T. Hale, Jan. 11, 1861, in *The Collected Works of Abraham Lincoln*, ed. Roy P. Basler, 8 vols. and index (New Brunswick, N.J., 1953), 4:149–50, 151–53, 154, 155, 172; May, *Southern Dream*, 213–16.

81. Abraham Lincoln speech to the Springfield Scott Club, Aug. 14, 26, 1852, in *New Letters and Papers of Lincoln*, comp. Paul M. Angle (Boston, 1930), 105–6; Abraham Lincoln to Elihu B. Washburne, Dec. 13, Lincoln to Thurlow Weed, Dec. 17, Lincoln to John D. Defrees, Dec. 18, 1860, in *Collected Works of Abraham Lincoln* 4:151, 154, 155; W. J. Gregg to Lyman Trumbull, Feb. 6, 1861, Lyman Trumbull Papers, LC; May, *Southern Dream*, 220–21.

Epilogue

1. *Louisville Courier* quoted in *New-York Daily Tribune*, Mar. 30, 1861. A captain in López's Kentucky Regiment in 1850, Allen six years later recruited some 160 Kentuckians for Walker's army in Nicaragua, and left Louisville with his troops on May 21, 1856. Commissioned a colonel in Walker's service on June 30, Allen returned to the United States that November after contracting a tropical fever. In October 1861 a Louisville paper reported that Allen had taken an oath of loyalty to the Union. Anderson C. Quisenberry, *Lopez's Expeditions to Cuba, 1850–1851* (Louisville, 1906),

121; *Baltimore Sun*, May 23, 1856; "Army Register, N.A., Feb. 26th 1857," WWP; William C. Smedes to unidentified recipient, Jan. 10, 1857, Jack Allen to Thomas Marshall, Feb. 24, 1857, Marshall Family Papers, Filson Club Historical Society, Louisville; *Louisville Democrat*, Oct. 19, quoted in *New York Herald*, Oct. 27, 1861.

2. *WDNI*, Aug. 6, 1853.

3. *New York Herald*, May 29, 1857, quoted in Charles H. Brown, *Agents of Manifest Destiny: The Lives and Times of the Filibusters* (Chapel Hill, 1980), 409; *DAC*, Feb. 2, 1859.

4. Roy Sylvan Dunn, "The KGC in Texas, 1860–1861," *SHQ* 70 (Apr. 1967): 557–61; Thomas W. Cutrer, *Ben McCulloch and the Frontier Military Tradition* (Chapel Hill, 1993), 176–85; Robert F. Kellam Diary, Apr. 29, 1861, quoted in Boyd W. Johnson, "Ouachita County and Secession," *Ouachita County Historical Quarterly* 8 (Mar. 1977): 6; Ollinger Crenshaw, "The Knights of the Golden Circle," *American Historical Review* 47 (Oct. 1941): 43–47. However, Thomas Schoonover notes that some Mexicans and North Americans under one "Moreno" raided Mexican territory from California in early 1861. Further, that April Bickley offered Confederate President Jefferson Davis 30,000 Knights to retaliate against Mexico should a rumored Mexican invasion of the Confederacy really occur. Thomas David Schoonover, *Dollars over Dominion: The Triumph of Liberalism in Mexican–United States Relations, 1861–1865* (Baton Rouge, 1978),15–16; William C. Davis, *"A Government of Our Own": The Making of the Confederacy* (Baton Rouge, 1994), 335.

5. *New York Herald*, Nov. 6, 11, 1861; Frank L. Klement, *The Copperheads in the Middle West* (Chicago, 1960), 134–52, 163, 176–82, 202–3, 244; James M. McPherson, *Ordeal by Fire: The Civil War and Reconstruction* (New York, 1982), 274. Earlier in the war, French, using the pseudonym Carlyle Murray and pretending to be "an unconditional Union man," had tried to interest Andrew Johnson and others in a scheme by which he would serve as a conduit for channeling funds to underwrite Unionist subversive activities in eastern Tennessee. Most likely, French intended either to pocket the money or divert it to Confederate authorities. Incarcerated at Fort Warren in Boston harbor until February 1862, French was freed upon his taking an oath of allegiance to the Union. Carlyle Murray to Andrew Johnson, July 12, 1861, and editors' comment, in *The Papers of Andrew Johnson*, ed. Leroy P. Graf, Ralph W. Haskins, and Paul H. Bergeron, 15 vols. (Knoxville, 1967–), 4:562–63, 563n.

6. *Central American* (San Juan del Norte), Sept. 12, 15, 1855; Edward K. Eckert and Nicholas J. Amato, eds., *Ten Years in the Saddle: The Memoir of William Woods Averell* (San Rafael, Calif., 1978), 335; *Philadelphia Public Ledger*, Jan. 11, 1856; Edward Longacre, "Kerrigan, James," and Robert J. Chandler, "Worthington, Henry Gaither," in *Biographical Directory of the Union: Northern Leaders of the Civil War*, ed. John T. Hubbell and James W. Geary (Westport, Conn., 1995), 285, 603–4; *Lafayette* (Ind.) *Daily Courier*, July 28, 1879; James Birney Shaw, *History of the Tenth Regiment Indiana Volunteer Infantry, Three Months and Three Years Organizations* (Lafayette, Ind., 1912), 320; Thomas North, *Five Years in Texas; or, What You Did Not Hear during the War* . . . (Cincinnati, 1871), 115–16.

7. *Baltimore Sun*, May 28 (quoting Richmond correspondent of the *Charleston*

Courier), 1861; Steven Z. Starr, *The Union Cavalry in the Civil War*, vol. 1: *From Fort Sumter to Gettysburg, 1861–1863* (Baton Rouge, 1979), 80; Charles W. Doubleday to A. Brady, Nov. 16, 1886, WWP; *New York Herald*, Aug. 3, 1861. Doubleday suffered a wound in Walker's very first battle on Nicaraguan soil. He also held a high command in the unsuccessful *Susan* expedition of 1858. William O. Scroggs, *Filibusters and Financiers: The Story of William Walker and His Associates* (New York, 1916), 109, 278; Charles W. Doubleday, *Reminiscences of the "Filibuster" War in Nicaragua* (New York, 1886).

8. Mary Chesnut Diary, Mar. 4, 1861, *The Private Mary Chesnut: The Unpublished Civil War Diaries*, ed. C. Vann Woodward and Elisabeth Muhlenfeld (New York, 1984), 22; William W. Boyce to Jefferson Davis, May 18, 1861, Letters Received by the Confederate Secretary of War, M437, reel 2 (typewritten copy, courtesy of Lynda Crist, ed., *The Papers of Jefferson Davis*); William Howard Russell Diary, May 5, 1861, in William Howard Russell, *My Diary North and South*, ed. Eugene H. Berwanger (1863; condensed edn., New York, 1988), 118; Paul N. Spellman, *Forgotten Texas Leader: Hugh McLeod and the Texan Santa Fe Expedition* (College Station, Tex., 1999), 166–67, 175–80; Birkett D. Fry to Jefferson Davis, Apr. 18, B. L. Jones to Davis, Sept. 2, 1861, calendar, *The Papers of Jefferson Davis*, ed. Haskell M. Monroe Jr., James T. McIntosh, and Lynda Lasswell Crist, 10 vols. (Baton Rouge, 1971–), 7:108, 319. Henningsen was commissioned a colonel in the 59th Virginia Regiment on August 1, 1861, and served the Confederacy, primarily in Wise's Legion, until he was relieved of command in November 1862. Stewart Sifkanis, *Who Was Who in the Civil War* (New York, 1988), 303.

9. Victor M. Rose, *Ross' Texas Brigade* (Louisville, 1881), 15; [Napier Bartlett], *A Soldier's Story of the War, Including the Marches and Battles of the Washington Artillery and of Other Louisiana Troops* (New Orleans, 1874), 71.

10. John H. Gerould, "O'Hara, Theodore," in *DAB* 7, pt. 2:5; *Augusta Dispatch* quoted in *Macon* (Ga.) *Daily Telegraph*, Sept. 26, 1860; *Baltimore Sun*, May 18, 1861; *New York Herald*, Aug. 13, 1861; Terry L. Jones, *Lee's Tigers: The Louisiana Infantry in the Army of Northern Virginia* (Baton Rouge, 1987), 1, 4–5; Leo Wheat, "Memoir of Gen. C. R. Wheat," *Southern Historical Society Papers* 17 (1889), 54–55; Mark Mayo Boatner, *The Civil War Dictionary* (New York, 1959), 909; Donald S. Frazier, *Blood and Treasure: Confederate Empire in the Southwest* (College Station, Tex., 1995), 75, 81–82, 133.

11. Sifkanis, *Who Was Who*, 469; Ellsworth Eliot Jr., *West Point in the Confederacy* (New York, 1941), 430–32; *The Writings of Sam Houston, 1813–1863*, ed. Amelia W. Williams and Eugene C. Barker, 8 vols. (1938–43; reprint, Austin, 1970), 7:495n–496n; R. A. Brock, "General Burkett Davenport Fry," *Southern Historical Society Papers* 18 (1890): 287–88; Antonio Rafael de la Cova, "Ambrosio Jose Gonzales: A Cuban Confederate Colonel" (Ph.D. diss., West Virginia University, 1994), 244–47, 267–84; Erwin Craighead, *From Mobile's Past: Sketches of Memorable People and Events* (Mobile, 1925), 156–57; Schoonover, *Dollars over Dominion*, 25–30; Sheldon Howard Harris, "The Public Career of John Louis O'Sullivan" (Ph.D. diss., Columbia University, 1948), 394–406; A. Curtis Wilgus, "Thrasher, John Sidney," *DAB* 9, pt. 2:510.

12. Antonio José de Irisarri to William Seward, Oct. 28, 1861 (translation), DS,

Notes from Central American Legations in the United States, T34, roll 6, NA; Carlos Gutierrez to Lord John Russell, Dec. 26, 1860 (translation), PRO, Consular Despatches from Honduras, FO 39, Consular Despatches, Honduras, 39/8; Gabriel García Tassara to the prime minister of Spain, Dec. 27, 1857, quoted in Thomas Schoonover and Ebba Schoonover, eds. and trans., "Bleeding Kansas and Spanish Cuba in 1857, A Postscript," *Kansas History* 11 (Winter 1988–89): 241–42.

13. Ronnie C. Tyler, *Santiago Vidaurri and the Southern Confederacy* (Austin, 1973), 45–56, 79–80, 97–99 (C. B. H. Blood quotation on p. 82); A. B. Dickinson to William Seward, Mar. 10, 1862, M219, roll 13, NA; Luis Martínez-Fernández, *Economy, Society, and Patterns of Thought in the Hispanic Caribbean, 1840–1878* (Athens, Ga., 1994), 156–57 (quotation), 159–64.

14. Schoonover, *Dollars over Dominion*, 8, 24, 31–32, 36–38, 40–45.

15. Ralph Lee Woodward Jr., *Rafael Carrera and the Emergence of the Republic of Guatemala, 1821–1871* (Athens, Ga., 1993), 306; Thomas D. Schoonover, *The United States in Central America, 1860–1911: Episodes of Social Imperialism and Imperial Rivalry in the World System* (Durham, N.C., 1991), 20, 22. Schoonover, however, notes that conservative rulers of Guatemala and Costa Rica found the Confederate cause more compatible ideologically than Lincoln's liberal régime in Washington, and that Nicaragua's rulers allowed Confederate privateers to use their ports under certain conditions. Schoonover, *United States in Central America*, 19–22.

16. Before the British North American Act of 1867, which created the Dominion of Canada, what today we call Canada was divided into many different British provinces and colonies, two of which used the name Canada. Further confusing matters, contemporaries variously referred to the colonies as Lower Canada and Upper Canada, Canada East and Canada West, and other terms including "the united Canadas." The Dominion of Canada at its creation, moreover, did not include all of present-day Canada. See Robin W. Winks, *Canada and the United States: The Civil War Years* (Baltimore, 1960), xv.

17. W. S. Neidhardt, *Fenianism in North America* (University Park, Pa., 1975), 2–15, 29, 33–34, 43–49, 55, 60–72, 77–80; Longacre, "Kerrigan," 285; Michael Gregory Walker, *The Fenian Movement* (Colorado Springs, 1969), 81–106, 183–91; marching song quoted in Winks, *Canada and the United States*, 323.

18. Sidney George Fisher Diary, June 6, 1866, in *A Philadelphia Perspective: The Diary of Sidney George Fisher Covering the Years 1834–1871*, ed. Nicholas B. Wainwright (Philadelphia, 1967), 517–18; Reginald C. Stuart, *United States Expansionism and British North America, 1775–1871* (Chapel Hill, 1988), 247–50; Charles Callan Tansill, *America and the Fight for Irish Freedom, 1866–1922* (New York, 1957), 34–38; Neidhardt, *Fenianism*, 24, 30, 43–44.

19. Gerald E. Poyo, *"With All, and for the Good of All": The Emergence of Popular Nationalism in the Cuban Communities of the United States, 1848–1898* (Durham, N.C., 1989), 33, 62–66, 113; Richard H. Bradford, *The Virginius Affair* (Boulder, Colo., 1980), 11; Charles Dudley Rhodes, "Jordan, Thomas," *DAB* 5, pt. 2:216; Hugh Thomas, *Cuba, or the Pursuit of Freedom* (London, 1971), 243–60; Samuel Proctor, "Filibustering Aboard the Three Friends," *Mid-America* 38 (Apr. 1956): 84–100; Stephen H. Halkiotis, "Guns for *Cuba Libre*: An 1895 Filibustering Expedition from

Wilmington, North Carolina," *North Carolina Historical Review* 55 (Jan. 1978): 60–75; Richard V. Rickenbach, "Filibustering with the *Dauntless*," *Florida Historical Quarterly* 28 (Apr. 1950): 231–53; Philip S. Foner, *The Spanish-Cuban-American War and the Birth of American Imperialism, 1895–1902*, 2 vols. (New York, 1972), 1:17–18, 177–78, 211.

20. Andrew F. Rolle, "Futile Filibustering in Baja California, 1888–1890," *Pacific Historical Review* 20 (May 1951): 159–66; Peter Gerhard, "The Socialist Invasion of Baja California, 1911," *Pacific Historical Review* 15 (Sept. 1946): 295–304; Oscar J. Martínez, *Troublesome Border* (Tucson, 1988), 47–50; Lowell L. Blaisdell, *The Desert Revolution: Baja California, 1911* (Madison, 1962), 99, 130, and passim. See also Joan M. Jensen, "The 'Hindu Conspiracy': A Reassessment," *Pacific Historical Review* 48 (Feb. 1979): 69–84, for federal prosecutions before and after U.S. entry into World War I of persons involved in a reputed plot of German agents and Indian ("Hindu") nationalists to use U.S. soil for expeditions to overthrow British rule in India. Jensen shows how U.S. authorities starting in 1912 employed a new tool, the federal conspiracy statute, to secure convictions of alleged filibusters.

21. John Bassett Moore, comp., *A Digest of International Law* 7 (1906; reprint, Ann Arbor, 1965), pt. 2:1025–26; Lester D. Langley and Thomas Schoonover, *The Banana Men: American Mercenaries and Entrepreneurs in Central America, 1880–1930* (Lexington, Ky., 1995), 31, 104, 115–40.

22. *New York Herald*, Oct. 2, 1869; Lydia Maria Child quoted in Edward P. Crapol, "Lydia Maria Child: Abolitionist Critic of American Foreign Policy," in Crapol, ed., *Women and American Foreign Policy: Lobbyists, Critics, and Insiders* (Westport, Conn., 1987), 12; Robert Shufeldt to Mary Shufeldt, Nov. 11, 1879, quoted in Kenneth J. Hagan, *American Gunboat Diplomacy and the Old Navy, 1877–1889* (Westport, Conn., 1973), 101.

23. Ashmore Russan and Frederick Boyle, *Through Forest and Plain: A Tale of Flowers and Filibusters* (Boston, 1895); "The Filibuster: A Comedy-Opera," words by John P. Wilson, music by William Loraine (New York, 1904); Register of William Walker's Nicaraguan Army, Aug. 1, 1856, AO Papers, DU; "Missouriana," *Missouri Historical Review* 37 (July 1943): 451; James C. Jamison, "Captain Fayssoux in Nicaraguan Expedition," *Confederate Veteran* 11 (Sept. 1903): 403–4.

24. John William De Forest, *Miss Ravenel's Conversion from Secession to Loyalty*, with introd. by Sharon L. Gravett (orig. pubd. 1867; reprint of 1939 edn, Lincoln, Neb., 1998), 18, 21, 24, 95–101, 166, 180 (all quotations from pp. 98–101).

25. *New Orleans Times-Picayune*, July 29, 30, 31, Aug. 2, Sept. 12, 18, Nov. 6, 1986; *New York Times*, July 29, Sept. 13, Nov. 6, 1986. Sentencing was postponed in one case because the defendant was too ill to attend court.

26. *New Orleans Times-Picayune / States-Item*, Apr. 29, May 1, 2, 7, 1981; *Jackson Clarion-Ledger*, Nov. 11, 1982. See Oscar Martínez, *Troublesome Border*, 50, for an explanation of why Baja California by the 1950s no longer presented an inviting target for filibustering.

27. *New York Times*, Jan. 3, 4, 5, 1967; *Chicago Tribune*, Jan. 3, 4, 1967; *Washington Post*, Jan. 5, 1967; *Indianapolis Star*, Nov. 17, 1967.

28. "Nicaragua: 'I'm the Champ,'" *Time* 52 (Nov. 15, 1948): 38-39; Judge Lansing Mitchell, quoted in *New Orleans Times-Picayune*, Nov. 6, 1986.

29. Richard Harding Davis, *Real Soldiers of Fortune* (New York, 1911), 147; *Mobile Register*, Mar. 4, 1917, quoted in Craighead, *From Mobile's Past*, 161.

30. Walker, for instance, occasionally gained a place in obscure twentieth-century novels. See Alfred Leland Crabb, *Dinner at Belmont: A Novel of Occupied Nashville* (Indianapolis, 1942); Robert Houston, *The Nation Thief* (New York, 1984).

31. "Festividades en el Estado de Sonora" <http://www.sonoraonline.com/cultura/festividades.asp> (Apr. 6, 2001); James S. Griffith, "Saints, Stories, and Sacred Places," in *The Pimería Alta: Missions and More*, ed. James E. Officer, Mardith Schuetz-Miller, and Bernard L. Fontana (Tucson, 1996), 102-4; Tom Chaffin, "A century before the Bay of Pigs, another failed *yanqui* invasion," *Miami Herald*, Nov. 10, 1996; Hugh Thomas, *Cuba, or the Pursuit of Freedom* (London, 1971), 217.

32. Lowell Gudmundson, "Society and Politics in Central America, 1821-1871," in Gudmundson and Héctor Lindo-Fuentes, *Central America, 1821-1871: Liberalism before Liberal Reform* (Tuscaloosa, 1995), 89, 109-10; Woodward, *Rafael Carrera*, 294, 298; Ralph Lee Woodward Jr., *Central America: A Nation Divided* (New York, 1976), 145-46; James Dunkerley, *Power in the Isthmus: A Political History of Modern Central America* (London, 1988), 18; Marc Edelman and Joanne Kenen, eds., *The Costa Rican Reader* (New York, 1989), 43. An exception was Honduras, where liberals reestablished themselves by 1859. Woodward, *Rafael Carrera*, 294.

33. Woodward, *Central America*, 144; Scroggs, *Filibusters and Financiers*, 188n; Richard Biesanz, Karen Zubris Biesanz, and Mavis Hiltunen Biesanz, *The Costa Ricans* (Englewood Cliffs, N.J., 1982), 20; Beatric Blake and Anne Becher, *The New Key to Costa Rica* (Berkeley, 1993), 124, 167.

34. Donald C. Hodges, *Intellectual Foundations of the Nicaraguan Revolution* (Austin 1986), 109-10; Violete Barrios de Chamorro with Sonia Cruz de Baltodano and Guido Fernández, *Dreams of the Heart: Autobiography of President Violeta Barrios de Chamorro of Nicaragua* (New York, 1996), 15, 34; *Los Angeles Times*, Mar. 5, 1988 (quotation).

35. Hodges, *Intellectual Foundations*, 107-12; Sergio Ramírez, comp. and ed., *Sandino: The Testimony of a Nicaraguan Patriot, 1921-1934*, ed. and trans. Robert Edgar Conrad (Princeton, 1990), 88-89, 290-92; Neil Macaulay, *The Sandino Affair* (Chicago, 1967).

36. Speeches by Daniel Ortega and Sergio Ramírez, and interviews with Tomás Borge, Sergio Ramírez, and Daniel Núñez, in *Nicaragua: The Sandinista People's Revolution: Speeches by Sandinista Leaders* (New York, 1985), 232, 332, 65, 223, 359; accounts of Reinaldo Antonio Téfel and Doris María Tijerino, in *Life Stories of the Nicaraguan Revolution*, ed. Denis Lynn Daly Heyck (New York 1990), 22, 57; Shirley Christian, *Nicaragua: Revolution in the Family* (New York, 1985), 295. The Sandinista government gave considerable material support to the filming of "Walker" in 1987, even providing army helicopters for the production. *New York Times*, Mar. 22, 1987.

37. *FLIN*, Dec. 22, 1855; Albany Fonblanque Jr., *The Filibuster: A Story of American Life, and Other Tales* (London, 1862), 1.